ESSAYS ON THE
LANGUAGE OF LITERATURE

ESSAYS

ON THE LANGUAGE

EDITED B

HOUGHTON MIFFLIN COMPAN

OF LITERATURE

EYMOUR CHATMAN
UNIVERSITY OF CALIFORNIA, BERKELEY

AMUEL R. LEVIN
HUNTER COLLEGE
OF THE CITY UNIVERSITY OF NEW YORK

OSTON NEW YORK ATLANTA GENEVA, ILL. DALLAS PALO ALTO

CONTENTS

Part Three • Grammar

Part Four • Literary Form and Meaning

Part Five • Style and Stylistics

PREFACE

For some time now we have been hearing of the need to reconcile linguistic and literary studies. "Reconciliation" would have rung strangely in the ears of nineteenth and early twentieth century scholars. To them, of course, linguistics and literary history were simply two peas in the philological pod. Questions of method and stance were not of great moment to men whose basic purpose was the elucidation of texts that had been obscured by history. In annotative occupations one moves easily and un-selfconsciously from grammatical explanation to historical commentary to critical pronouncement and back again.

But developments in the past forty or fifty years have brought about increasing specialization in literary as well as other academic studies and with it some breakdown of communication between emerging disciplines. The history of modern linguistics and the separation of modern literary criticism from literary history are too well known to be rehearsed here. What does need comment is the schism, particularly in America, between these fields. It is not quite clear why some linguists felt it necessary to be anti- (rather than merely *non-*) literary in establishing their laudable and famous rigor of method. At the same time, it is hard to see why some literary critics took so long to find any redeeming virtue in linguistics at all, let alone its possible utility in literary analysis — particularly since criticism itself was becoming so analytical, so concerned with verbal structures, as to be itself "linguistic," as witness the titles of some classics of criticism in the past three decades — *Seven Types of Ambiguity*, *The Structure of Complex Words*, *Articulate Energy: An Enquiry into the Syntax of English Poetry*, *The Verbal Icon*, *English Poetry and the English Language*, *Words and Poetry*, *The Language of Poetry* — to name a few outstanding examples.

But the causes of the rift are less important than its repair. It is clear from a glance at the annual bibliographies that reconciliation is in the air, and we wish to offer this volume as a contribution to it. We ask the principals and their students — linguists and literary critics alike — to see how much they have in common, both technically and substantively. The articles which we have collected do not demonstrate a need to continue the fray; on the contrary, they suggest surprising harmonies, and exemplify how much is to be won by friendly relations, indeed, where possible, by collaboration itself.

Seymour Chatman

Samuel R. Levin

ESSAYS ON THE LANGUAGE OF LITERATURE

Part One

SOUND TEXTURE

By "sound texture" we mean the effect imparted by the functioning in literary patterns of individual sounds, like /p/, /t/, and /k/, a function beyond their normal linguistic roles. The ordinary user of language pays little attention to the possibilities of additional organizations of discourse in terms of speech sounds. But poets characteristically assume phonological constraints — like meter, alliteration and so forth — as if the achievement were finer, more complex, more interesting if it were charged with an additional linguistic burden. The extra handicap whets the professional's appetite.

The study of sound texture is a field both vaguer and more susceptible to flights of fancy than the study of meter. But the subject is not unworthy of the interest it has been afforded.

One can think of three principal questions that face the theorist of sound texture: 1) What are the significant literary arrangements of individual sounds? 2) How are they best described? and 3) What is the relation of these sounds to meanings? Each article in this section considers these problems in a different way. The first by Masson, "Vowel and Consonant Patterns in Poetry," takes up the problem of sound-arrangement or "phonotactic" theory, finding widespread agreement among European poetic traditions in respect to principles like sequencing, bracketing, inverting, etc. The second part raises some important questions about "the evocative power" of sounds and sound combinations. The linguist will put most stock in naturalistic explanations, like recourse to lexicon, but he should not shrink from a consideration of other possibilities — listed by Masson as "acoustic" and "kinesthetic" — as well. The impressions of literary critics are part of "informant-response" in stylistics.

Ants Oras' comparison of the techniques of Spenser and Milton is also concerned with how to describe sound texture and its relation to meaning. Oras does not limit himself to the usual phonotactic features like assonance, alliteration, consonance and rhyme. He proposes as *stylistica* features not ordinarily investigated, for instance, consonant clustering habits — Spenser's preference for the "diminuendo" effect (clustering at the *beginning* of syllables) as opposed to Milton's crescendo (clustering at syllable-end). Semantic implications suggest themselves: for example, Spenser is so devoted to sound patterning that he sacrifices sense to it, as in the name-set Sansloy, Sansfoy, Sansjoy, worthies deprived by phonetic considerations of all but a token individuality.

Masson's second article, "Thematic Analysis of Sounds in Poetry," points up the complexities of sound texture, suggesting some uses and concepts: *bond-density, motif, series, progression, brackets,* etc. The second portion of the paper is devoted to discovering connections between sound-patterning and meaning in actual verse; it forms a model for sound-texture-analysis.

The article by Hymes, "Phonological Aspects of Style: Some English Sonnets," attempts to validate a hypothesis first formulated by James Lynch ("The Tonality of Lyric Poetry," *Word* IX [1953], 211–224), namely that there may exist in poems, particularly in sonnets, a kind of summation of sounds in some semantically crucial word, which often occurs in a final position in the poem. The statistical demonstration must be considered in light of the criticisms made by Fred Householder. (See *Style in Language* [New York, 1960], pp. 343–345). Portions of Jakobson's essay (below, pp. 316–319) also treat sound texture.

David J. Masson

VOWEL AND CONSONANT PATTERNS IN POETRY

I. Nature of the Patterns Themselves

Where lyrical feeling or sensuous description occurs in European poetry, there will usually be found patterns of vowels and consonants. (It is not proposed to consider in this article the *structural* or semistructural patterns of Germanic alliterative verse, of Welsh *cynghanedd,* or of the devices of the baroque age.) These patterns are seldom consciously worked out by the poet, and even more rarely are they consciously analyzed by the reader or listener. On the other hand, the poet with a good ear is aware that one version of a phrase or line sounds better than another, and the reader is aware to some extent of pleasure in the sound (though "pleasure," as will be shown, is not the most important effect of such patterns). The pattern seems to occur to the poet as a melody may to a composer. Certain poets, among them Mallarmé, Rilke, Valéry, G. M. Hopkins, must have worked consciously for certain of the patterns in their verse, at all events until they gained a mastery of their medium; but the poet is generally reticent on this subject, and neither Mallarmé, Rilke, nor Valéry descend to the discussion of technique. However, Hopkins' lecture notes on Rhetoric (in their section on "Lettering of syllables" [1]) make it clear that he understood very well what he was doing. His view of the function of repetitive patterns in verse is that "repetition . . . of the inscape must take place in order to detach it to the mind"; [2] — in fact, that the impression of the shape of words, neutralized by their use in everyday speech and writing, is re-activated by devices such as assonance and alliteration. The overriding importance that Hopkins gives to form is evident in his assertion that "Verse is . . . speech employed to carry the inscape of spoken sounds." [2]

Reprinted from *The Journal of Aesthetics and Art Criticism*, Vol. XII, No. 2, December, 1953, by permission of the author and of The American Society for Aesthetics.

[1] Gerard Manley Hopkins, *The Note-books and Papers*, ed. Humphry House (Oxford: O.U.P., 1937), pp. 242–8.
[2] *Ibid.*, p. 249.

In certain passages of prose a certain amount of pattern is also detectable, and has been remarked by such writers as Robert Louis Stevenson in English.

The effect upon the reader or listener, mainly unconscious, is one of *decoration* when the pattern reaches a certain degree of crudity or, conversely, a certain degree of refinement. Between these limits, however, the pattern tends to exert a species of magical or hypnotic effect, like that of a ritual *incantation.* The precise setting of these limits varies according to the taste of the age and of the individual reader or listener, and to his familiarity with the idiosyncracies of the poet himself. Decoration seems to have been regarded by Hopkins as the principal function of such patterns, since he states that rhythm's regular repetition "gives more tone, *candorem*, style, chasteness"; but that the intermittent repetition, e.g. 'ABCDABEFABGH,' of alliteration, rhyme, etc., gives "more brilliancy, starriness, quain, margaretting." [3] For W. B. Yeats, on the other hand, incantation is clearly all-important — "All sounds . . . call down among us certain disembodied powers, whose footsteps over our hearts we call emotions . . . the more various and numerous the elements that have flowed into [the] perfection [of a work of art], the more powerful will be the emotion, the power, the god it calls among us." [4] Similar views are suggested in Rilke's *Der Magier* and *Le Magicien.*

Patterns found in European poetry may be considered as variations and elaborations upon two polar types: (i) the pure *sequence;* in which certain sounds are repeated in the same order; e.g.,

(1) (La) Nature est un tem*pl*e où de vivants *pil*iers

Charles BAUDELAIRE, *Spleen et Idéal*, IV 1

(a pattern which, as the sounds are further apart in the second member, may be described as a *loosening* sequence of the elements P, L in two members); or

(2) *L*är*m*t *b*ei eure*n* *L*a*m*pe*n*

Karl WEITBRECHT, *Wenn ich Abschied nehme*, 7

(a crudely rhythmic *tightening* sequence of L, M, B/P, N); and (ii) the pure *chiasmus,*[5] in which the order is exactly reversed; e.g.,

(3) dans la *ru*elle,
Femme imp*ur*e!

Charles BAUDELAIRE, *Spleen et Idéal*, XXV 1–2

(a tight [6] chiasmus); or

(4) *forê*ts de *s*y*mbol*es
Qui *l'obser*v*e*nt

The same, IV 3–4

[3] *Ibid.*, p. 251.

[4] W. B. Yeats, in an early essay "The Symbolism of Poetry," *Essays* (London: Macmillan, 1924), pp. 192–3.

[5] This term is preferable to "inversion" which can be used for cases where a sequence or similar pattern occurs with reversal of order in certain of its elements only.

[6] A *rhyme* proper can be considered as a special case of a *tight sequence.*

In example (4), the *f—rê—s—bol* of the first member are exactly reversed (if we allow voiceless/voiced pairs such as F/V, S/Z-sounds to be single elements) in member no. 2: *lobserv;* but member 2 is *tight* (not dispersed among irrelevant sounds), and an extra instance of the O-element is intruded between F and R in member 1.

The sequence often appears in the guise of what we shall call a *bracket;* i.e., there are two perfect members, with one or more of their elements between them as a link. The bracket may be simple:

(5) *Sátiro de estr*ellas (bajas)
Federico Garcia LORCA, *Preciosa y el Aire*, 41

(where D suballiterates *in this position* with T); or it may be complex:

(6) W*enn* er *w*ie *d*ie Sommerso*nnenwend*e
Rainer Maria RILKE, *Eros*, 3

In (6) the perfect members are *wen . . . d*, *wend.* But the "intrusive" W of *wie* is really essential to the pattern, since an alternative view of this pattern is, that *WENN*, *W*IE *D*IE form two strands which are tied together in *WEND*E. A perhaps less satisfying case of intrusion is

(7) From the *dark dingles t*o the nigh*tingales*
Matthew ARNOLD, *The Scholar Gipsy*, 220

or the first O of no. (4) above. In (7) we have a 6-element sequence of two members, each with 7 temporal components (element T/D being repeated twice per member) except that what we may call an *allotype* (K) of element G intrudes in *dark.*

The sequence may be joined intimately with a bracket:

(8) *Sur* la plage *sonore* où la me*r* de *Sor*rente
Alphonse de LAMARTINE, *Le Premier Regret*, élégie, 1

Here we have a 3-member sequence S-R, members 2 and 3 also forming part of a bracket S-O-R with element 2 doubled in *sonore* and R as the link. There is also subassonance from the -EN- of *Sorrente.*

The chiasmus may appear as a *chiasmic bracket*, as in

(9) *Charm'd ma*gic casements . . .
John KEATS, *Ode to a Nightingale*, vii 10

Here the D suballiterates with CH, G, each of which, being an affricate, is to be regarded as a single sound rather than two. Or the chiasmus may appear with intrusions as in no. (4) above.

Very common is the *partial inversion*, often complicated by *intrusion:*

(10) Un*d wölbt* s*ich* n*icht* d*as überweltlich* Grosse
J. W. von GOETHE, *Trilogie der Leidenschaft:* Elogie, 35

Here the elements in true sequence order would be *welbtich.* Ö and E assonate (Goethe uses them as rhymes). The N's and S's can be ignored here, and the distant light E of *Grosse*. Despite the displaced second B, this pattern has a knotting-up effect similar to no. (6) above. Further examples may be similarly analysed on the principle that voiced/unvoiced homorganic consonants are equivalent: (11) "Piovean di fuoco dilatate falde" (DANTE, *Inferno*, XIV 29); (12) "L'homme y passe à travers de forêts de symboles / Qui l'observent avec de regards familiers" (Charles BAUDELAIRE, *Spleen et Idéal*, IV 3–4). No. (12), which has 12 elements, is an extension of no. (4).

Very common indeed are the more complex permutations such as the following:

(13) theôis men eksételna phroímion tóde
ta d'es to son phrónēma mémnēmai klýōn
kai phēmi . . .

AESCHYLUS, *Agamemnon*, 820–822[7]

Here only L and Y are irrelevant; aspirated P and T may be considered to alliterate with normal P and T; EI is equivalent to a lengthened E; "long" E and O are "broad" vowels which only subassonate with normal E and O. Thus the elements are P/PH, R, O, I, M, N, D/T/TH, E/EI, "long" E which subassonates with it, S, and the less relevant K, A. Similar permutations occur in

(14) De nos cœurs endurcis rompe l'assoupissement;
Dissipe l'ombre épaisse où les plonge le vice

Jean RACINE, *Le Mardi, à Laudes*, 14–15

Here the vowels which precede S-sounds, at least the "acute" vowels I, U, É, AI, may be considered as allotypes of one element. The other elements are D, S-sounds, P, L, nasal O, R, and "EN," with OU as a doubtful ninth.

Most frequently the pattern of a given passage is so complex that it can only be adequately expressed by analysis into separate *subpatterns*, which may be either independent, or interlocking on certain phonemes that they possess in common. In some cases these subpatterns can be readily distinguished by a sensitive ear.[8] For example

(15) *open*ing *on* the *fo*am
O*f perilous seas in fa*ery *l*and*s for*l*o*r*n*

John KEATS, *Ode to a Nightingale*, vii 10–11

can be felt to be composed of (A) a chiasmus 123321 in the elements "long" O (considered as a single phoneme-complex, though a diphthong), P/F (labials), N; (B) a bracket /1/123456,646,123456 in F/P, E/AE, R, I/EA/Y, L, S (the perfect member is /feril-s/); (C) a sequence in F, L, N with dissonance of vowels (a subject considered below); and perhaps (D) a tight chiasmus OPE*NI*NG, *IN*. Similar combinations of subpatterns can be felt in

[7] On Aeschylus' use of assonance, alliteration, rhyme, etc., see W. B. Stanford, *Aeschylus in His Style* (Dublin, 1942), pp. 80–85, esp. pp. 83–4.

[8] Including, perhaps, nos. (11) to (14) above.

(16) *Den Mandel*baum *zum zweiten Mal* im *Fl*ore
Stefan GEORGE, *Wir schreiten auf und ab im reichen Flitter*, 4 (Capitalization etc. normalized).

Here (A) we have an inverting pattern in D/T, N; (B) *ma . . . l, mal;* (C) *um zum zw mf*, with W/F as one element; (D) *w . . . l, fl*. More intricate and perhaps impossible of adequate analysis by a reader (though some of their subpatterns may be felt) are such passages as (17) "Te, Palinure petens, tibi somnia tristia portans / Insonti, puppique deus consedit in alta / Phorbanti similis" (VIRGIL, *Aeneid*, V 840–842) (where in effect every phoneme takes part in the pattern); (18) "*Doux comm*e un *chan*t *d'ois*eaux, / F*o*rt *comm*e un *choc d'arm*ures, / *Q*ua*n*d *la sourd*e *mêlé*e *étr*eint *les escadr*ons" (Victor HUGO, *Ce qu'on Entend sur la Montagne*, 15–17); (19) "Y *esto pasó en el reinado* de Hugo, / *Emperador de la barda florida*" (Rubén DARÍO, *Pórtico*, 151–2) (with suballiteration between F and B/P).

In the above instances no notice has (usually) been taken of suballiteration between stop consonant, fricative, nasal, trill, and/or lateral at one point of articulation; nor of subassonance between similar but differing vowels. These types of echoes have, indeed, their effect, particularly against a contrasting phonemic environment in the passage in which they occur. In a passage otherwise free from stop consonants (except perhaps in unstressed positions), two dissimilar stops may occupy the same place in two different members of a sequence, with an effect of likeness rather than of contrast (cf. no. [20] below). Thus a pattern of phonemes in modern European poetry may be considered as a delicate variation upon a crude substructure of broad phonetic types. In the most telling and magical passages, the intensity of their magical effect appears to be a function of the approximation of this crude substructure to a simple piece of primitive, or degenerated, spell-binding of the type of the Anglo-Saxon charm

ERIURIUTHDOL URIURITHOL WLAESTIPOTINOL.

(It is not suggested that such effects could be achieved by a poet working out his technique consciously on these lines; but analysis shows that this is what, in essence, they are.)

Thus the line

(20) No hungry generations tread thee down
John KEATS, *Ode to a Nightingale*, vii 2

can be considered as a civilized equivalent of the incantation

nəu ándri dsénə réisəns drédsi dáun

and its principal effect is seen to be due to the rising-and-sinking (or, taking into account the lowest formants of the vowels, more correctly *expanding-and-contracting*) pattern

nuá i é éi é i áun

and the syllables

ri rei re

together with the ruthless push [9] of the D-sounds.[10]

Similarly

(22) Voici la verte Écosse et la brune Italie
Alfred de MUSSET, *La Nuit de Mai*, 17

can be reduced to

và silavèr tekà selavrì nitalì

(where the contrasting K gives the necessary hardness and edge to the line, assisted by the modulation of V into B at BRUNE).[11] The line

(23) L'insecte net gratte la sécheresse
Paul VALÉRY, *Le Cimetière Marin*, xii 2

becomes

lasèk tə-nè krà tə-lasè sə-rè-s(ə)

while the lines

(24) Sie gleiten über ferne, wunderschwere,
Verschwiegne Flut, die nie ein Kiel geteilt
Hugo von HOFMANNSTHAL, *Der Tor und der Tod*, 31–2

become

si kláetn ívr vérne vúntr švére
vr švíkne vlút—ti ní aen kíl ke táelt.

But in such a pattern as

(25) Duerme, vuela, resposa:
Tambien se muere el mar!
Federico Garcia LORCA, *Llanto por Ignacio Sánchez Mejías*, last 2 lines of "Cuerpo Presente."

the sound is so nearly that of a primitive spell that it is hardly necessary to reduce it further to

doérme boéla resbósa
dambién-se moére-el már.

Similarly with (26) "(U, cyc)les, vibrements divers des mers virides" (Arthur RIMBAUD, *Voyelles*, 9). This suggests that, if 'music began with a savage beating a drum,' then poetry (or at all events lyric poetry) began with a savage muttering or shouting a spell.[12]

Dissonance and subtler vowel-variations (both are types of Hopkins' "vowel-

[9] The suggestive or illustrative powers of such sounds are considered in section II below.

[10] These sounds cannot be considered as either phonemic or phonetic in the strict sense so that the use of / / or [ ] to enclose them would be misleading.

[11] And the rounding of A into O and of I into U, immediately following these consonants, further improves upon the primitive substructure.

[12] Not necessarily inconsistent with Paul Valéry's "Le lyrisme est le développement d'une exclamation."

ling-off")[13] take a part in phonemic patterns. They may distinguish a short passage from its surroundings:

(27)
À la nue *accablan*te tu
*Bass*e de *basal*te et de *l*aves
Stéphane MALLARMÉ, "Shipwreck" Sonnet, 1–2

Here most of the sonnet is dominated by "acute" vowels U, É, Ê. Or these devices may be used in modulation to modify the monotony within a single pattern or pattern-complex, as in subpattern (C) of no. (15) above, or in

(28) *Since M*er*lin* pai*d* hi*s* *Demon* a*ll* the *monst*rou*s* *d*eb*t*
John KEATS, *The Eve of St. Agnes*, xix 9

Here, omitting the murmur-vowel, and allotting numbers in descending order of pitch for second formants,[14] the vowels are (1) 3 (1) 21 (1) 1—6—5—2 so that their pitch in the stressed syllables rises, falls deep, and rises again. This is contrapuntal to the italicized pattern.

Besides the influence upon it of the individual ear of the poet, of the general atmosphere of the poem or passage (see section II below), of the work of contemporaries or predecessors, and of the taste of the poet's age, the form of these patterns is greatly conditioned by the language in which the poem is written. Thus Spanish, with its 5 vowel phonemes, and Italian with its 7, afford no opportunity for the more delicate methods of "vowelling-off." On the other hand a poem in Spanish or Italian is necessarily bathed in a general atmosphere of assonance. The same is partly true of Greek and Latin, which, in addition, inevitably crowd into their poetry many alliterations and tight sequences composed of inflexional suffixes and prefixes. Germanic languages, particularly English, Icelandic, and German, afford abundant opportunity for tight or part-tight all-consonant subpatterns —

(29)
*Bl*ow, wi*ndes*, a*nd* *cr*ack you*r* *cheeks*! *rage*! *bl*ow!
You catara*cts* a*nd* *h*yrricano's, *sp*out
Till you ha*ve* *drench'd* our *st*eeple*s*, *drown'd* *th*e cocke*s*!
You su*lph'r*ous a*nd* *th*ought-executi*ng* *f*ires,
-*Vaunt*-*c*urri*ors* of oake-*cleavi*ng *thunderbolts*,
Si*ndge* *my* white head! A*nd* *th*ou, a*ll*-*sh*aki*ng* *th*u*nder*,
*Strike flat th*e thi*cke* *r*otu*nd*ity o'th' wo*rld*!
Crack Nature's moulds, a*ll* *germaines* *sp*ill at o*nce*
-*That makes* i*ngratef*ull *m*an! [14A]
William SHAKESPEARE, *King Lear*, III ii 1–9

[13] G. M. Hopkins, *The Note-books and Papers* (1937), p. 243, in "Lecture Notes: Rhetoric" — those on "rhythm and the other structural parts."

[14] Cf., e.g., Ralph K. Potter, G. A. Kopp, and H. C. Green, *Visible Speech* (New York: Van Nostrand, 1947), esp. pp. 55, 281.

[14A] Capitalization and punctuation (except plural in "o's"), and emendation "drown'd," are from Arden edition, revised by Kenneth Muir (London: Methuen, 1952). Spelling as in F 1, with U's for V's modernized.

whereas Romance languages, and particularly French, are more suitable for tight or part-tight consonant-vowel 2-element subpatterns, often with vowel modulation: (30) "*Vou*s *mourûtes* aux bor*ds* *où vous* *fûte*s lai*ssé*e!" (Jean RACINE, *Phèdre*, I iii 102). However, in Romance languages other than French, nasal/stop tight patterns are frequent, and in all, L/stop tight patterns are found. The possession of diphthongs (e.g., in English, Dutch, German) allows opportunities for part-tight all-vowel subpatterns: (16) "D*e*n M*a*nd*e*lb*au*m z*u*m zw*ei*ten M*a*l *i*m Fl*o*r*e*" [repeated from above] (with AU as A plus O, EI as A plus E, and I/E, U/O subassonating). The equivalent of the crackling violence of no. (29) in French would be something like pattern (18), or a passage using sibilants and *voyelles aigües* might, perhaps, have taken its place: greater economy of means are possible in such a language as French, or quite different devices may come into play. But this consideration really concerns section II, on the use of these patterns as "program music."

II. The Patterns as "Program Music"

On this somewhat controversial question, the poets themselves are rarely explicit. Yeats on "The Symbolism of Poetry" is suggestive:

> All sounds, all colours, all forms, either because of their pre-ordained energies or because of long association, evoke indefinable and yet precise emotions, or, as I prefer to think, call down among us certain disembodied powers, whose footsteps over our hearts we call emotions; and when sound, and colour, and form are in a musical relation, a beautiful relation to one another, they become as it were one sound, one colour, one form, and evoke an emotion that is made out of their distinct evocations and yet is one emotion. The same relation exists between all portions of every work of art, whether it be an epic or a song . . .[15]

For "pre-ordained energies" read 'correspondences with fundamental neural patterns' and for "long association" read 'conditioned reactions widely established by human culture patterns,' and we have a possible hypothesis for the psychology and physiology of aesthetics.

Mallarmé, who might be expected to reveal something of a universe of sound-symbolism, only throws off parenthetically the following hints: ". . . mon sens regrette que le discours défaille à exprimer les objets par des touches y répondant en coloris ou en allure, lesquelles existent dans l'instrument de la voix, parmi les langages et quelquefois chez un. À côté d'*ombre*, opaque, *ténèbres* se fonce peu; quelle déception devant la perversité conférant à *jour* comme à *nuit*, contradictoirement, des timbres obscur ici, là clair." [16]

This type of observation has been made sporadically from the days of Plato, if not before. That the sound of OMBRE seems darker than that of TÉNÈBRES, and that the sound of JOUR seems murky compared to that, relatively

[15] Partly quoted in section I above. From "Ideas of Good and Evil (1896–1903)," W. B. Yeats, *Essays* (London, 1924), pp. 192–3.

[16] Stéphane Mallarmé, "Crise de Vers," *Divagations* (Paris: Charpentier, 1935), p. 242.

bright or clear, of NUIT, will be admitted by a majority of persons, whatever the language they speak, for whom the sounds of speech have any evocative powers. But of what system are these the manifestations? It would seem to be a phonemic rather than a phonetic system, relative not absolute. Among general studies of this subject, the theories and findings of Maurice Grammont and M. M. Macdermott are useful as guides, and, though Macdermott only treats of vowels, and does not pretend to validity outside English verse, their respective findings are mutually supporting rather than otherwise, provided Macdermott's theories of formant boundaries for vowel-groups are not too rigidly adhered to (see below).[17] The present writer finds himself instinctively endorsing the majority of their claims for the effect of the various groups of sounds.

In this section an attempt is made to find means of establishing the limits and extent of suggestive power in the sounds of words in verse. Although there may be broad similarities between them, every reader's reactions to a specific passage vary both qualitatively and quantitatively. They may indeed exceed, fall short of, or sidetrack the intentions of the poet. But when all is said there remains the fact that certain sounds are acknowledged by a majority of sensitive readers to *be appropriate to* certain ideas and *inappropriate to* others. The poet with a good ear will tend to select (consciously or unconsciously) certain sounds appropriate to the mood or subject of the line or lines he is writing, and the sensitive reader will (consciously or unconsciously) accept for correct the colors with which the poet thus presents him.

There are three principal possible sources for the evocative power of the sounds of words, words either as they are used for the nonce in a given passage of poetry or prose, or as they reside in the general stock of a language. These sources may be called *acoustic*, *kinaesthetic*, and *lexical*. The two former categories correspond perhaps to Yeats' "pre-ordained energies": *lexical* origins are primarily those corresponding to his "long association." *Lexical* associations, which are proper to a given language (Mallarmé's "touches . . . lesquelles existent . . . parmi les langages *et quelquefois chez un*"), may be defined as those that arise from the occurrence, in the word, or in the poetical passage under consideration, of a morpheme which is the principal feature of a group of words that possess a striking common element of meaning or feeling (in the latter case the morpheme is called by some writers a phonaestheme); or, more frequently in poetry, that arise from the occurrence of a syllable or part-syllable which recalls that of other words in the language without possessing the objective status of a morpheme. Such associations may have arisen acoustically or kinaesthetically in the first place, but by the writer's definition here are distinguished from other associations by no longer possessing acoustic or kinaesthetic validity. Normal or potential lexical associations, for example, of NACHT in German are, perhaps,

[17] Maurice Grammont, *Traité de Phonétique*, 3rd ed. (Paris: Delagrave, 1946), pp. 377–416; *Petit Traité de Versification Française*, 3rd ed. (Paris, 1916), pp. 104–21. M. M. Macdermott, *Vowel Sounds in Poetry* (London: Kegan Paul, 1940).

(1) splendor (from PRACHT, STRAHL),

(2) violence, power, fear, awe, cruelty (from SCHLACHT, MACHT, ACHT, RACHE, GEFAHR, GRAM, AHNUNG, AHNDUNG),

(3) temporality (from SUCHT, NOCH, NACH),

(4) negation (from NICHT, NICHTS),

(5) damp (from NASS, FEUCHT).

In poetic passages or passages of poetic prose, an *ad hoc* lexical association may arise connecting one or more words, syllables or groups of syllables (A) with a specific word or words (B) in the same passage. This type of association may be distinguished by designating it *nonce-lexical* or *conditioned lexical.* Thus Rilke uses NACHT several times nonce-lexically with alliterating words such as ÜBERGEWICHT and GLEICH (for instance in *Duineser Elegien,* III 83–4) to suggest a *Bezug* or a *Polarität.*

To compare with NACHT its English and French equivalents, normal lexical associations for NIGHT are

(1) brilliance (from BRIGHT, WHITE, LIGHT, SIGHT, SHINE, FINE),

(2) the numinous, the spacious (from HEIGHT, MIGHT, RITE, RIGHT, FLIGHT, HIGH),

(3) alarms and excursions (from SMITE, FRIGHT, BITE, FIGHT, EXCITE, FLIGHT).

The French NUIT, on the other hand, is associated rather with

(1) glimmer, glow (from LUEUR, LUIR, LUSTRE, LUNE),

(2) scream or hoot (from CRI, AIGU, HUER, HUÉE), with, however, a strong *acoustic* element in this,

(3) ruin, danger (from NUIS, NUIRE, PUNI, FUI, FINI),

(4) intimacy (from NID, UNIS, BÉNIT, LUI, etc.).

Kinaesthetic associations arise from the proprioceptive sensations of the mouth, tongue, throat, glottis, etc., in pronouncing a given utterance. (Where static sensations are produced by simple vowels and continued fricatives, nasals, or laterals, '*topaesthetic*' or '*morphaesthetic*' would perhaps be more precise terms, but one hesitates to coin words unnecessarily.) They may be reproduced in the hearer or reader either by unconscious memory of his own utterance of similar sounds, or by unconscious pseudo-imitation like that of a man who rises on tiptoe when watching a high jump. (There is no difficulty in the first explanation, for all our sensory registrations of space and shape and direction are derived from unconscious memories.) In the reader who mouths the words half-consciously as he reads, kinaesthetic associations are clearly an important factor. In the majority of words they are dormant until activated by the proximity or by the lexical existence of other words containing the relevant morpheme or a more general phonemic similarity; or they may in a given passage be activated by phonemic contrast with their setting. The former type of activation resembles that referred to in Hopkins' precept, "repetition . . . of the inscape must take place in order to detach it to the mind." [18] The associations here of NACHT, NIGHT, and NUIT, though not striking, may come into play in such circumstances. On the analogy of Sir Richard Paget's theories of phonated gestures,[19] those of NACHT and NIGHT should be a simple curve or a lenticular shape, but that suggested by NIGHT should flatten or taper at the tail-end (the /i/ of /nait/), while that of NACHT suggests a rasping or gill-like obstruction towards that end (the /x/ of /naxt/). NUIT (with the unrounding from the semivowel U to the I) suggests a very short extrusive movement, or a shape like that of a minute spatula with a round handle (the U). Thus in a suitable poetic passage, NIGHT and NACHT could "illustrate" a leap or the arch of the sky, while NUIT cannot be used to illustrate anything so spacious.

The origin of language is unknown; but there can be little doubt that these associations are a potent factor continually operative at all stages in its evolution. They have probably encouraged the formation of morphemes such as the SP- of SPATE, SPATTER, SPEW, SPILL, SPIT, SPLASH, SPLATTER, SPOUT, SPRAY, SPRINKLE, SPROUT, SPURT, and in German the analogous SPATTELN, SPEICHEL, SPRIESSEN, SPRING, SPRITZE, SPRUDEL, SPRÜHEN, SPUCKE, groups of words which are therefore affected both *kinaesthetically* and *lexically*.

Acoustic associations arise "dans l'instrument de la voix" from the quality or structure of the sound *qua* physical sound. They include echoic associations of the "Ding-dong" type, such as link /i:/ with a scream and /ɑ:/ with a roar. But they may also account for whatever common substratum may exist in mood evocations, color synaesthesias, and the like. (The former may be due to the echoic principle that moods have a characteristic cry in children and animals, in origin perhaps a type of primitive 'phonated gesture.' If there is a common basis for many synaesthesias it may be that of the structure of formant spectra for vowels and vowel-like consonants.[20]) Like kinaesthetic associations, *acoustic* mechanisms are often dormant unless activated by the proximity or lexical existence of similar patterns. For NACHT, NIGHT, and NUIT these associations are once more not very striking, but may come into play in some contexts. The English and German words suggest tenor or baritone calls and warm colors, but NACHT evokes a deeper sound and a richer, purer, darker color, and its CH (/x/) rasps slightly. NUIT (described as of a timbre that is "clair" by Mallarmé) suggests a cold, livid, whitish (flash?), or a shrill squeak. Although some associations may be due to the pitch-structure of the sounds, M. M.

[18] Quoted in section I above. G. M. Hopkins, *Note-books and Papers*, pp. 242–8.

[19] Sir Richard A. S. Paget, *Human Speech* (London: Kegan Paul, 1930), esp. pp. 135, 137, 154–5.

[20] For these spectra see Potter, Kopp, and Green, *Visible Speech* (1947). Cf. the present writer's "Synesthesia and Sound Spectra," *Word*, VIII (1952), 39–41; Roman Jakobson, C. G. M. Fant, and M. Halle, *Preliminaries to Speech Analysis* (Massachusetts Institute of Technology, 1952), sec. 2.413 p. 28, sec. 2.4233 p. 32.

Macdermott's suggestion that *all* associations of vowels in English poetry are dependent on their formant spectra seems unlikely.[21]

Acoustic associations have also influenced the formation of morphemes, e.g., the vowel (and other elements) in CHEEP, SCREAM, SHRIEK, SQUEAK, SQUEAL, and similar words in other languages. Such groups of words are thus both lexically and acoustically bound together.

Acoustic and kinaesthetic mechanisms of association, though universal, are modified by the norms of the language in which the words are spoken and written, by the aesthetic conventions of the age in which they were composed or of that in which the passage is read, and by the immediate environment of the passage under consideration. The relative frequency of various types of sound in the language, and the position and timbre of its neutral vowel or 'position of rest,' probably affect both acoustic and kinaesthetic associations. For example, Grammont's *voyelles claires* (including *aigües*) correspond very well both in timbre and in associations with Macdermott's 'high-band' vowels.[22] But the frequency-boundaries given by Macdermott do not correspond to those for French *claires:* an adjustment, a series of shifts, is necessary in moving from English to French.[23] And though, for instance, NUIT sounds relatively shriller and more tense to an English ear than to a Frenchman, it is the French standpoint that must be considered.

Again, phonemes special to a given language produce associations which can only be matched in another language by the use of a different set of phonemic elements. Thus Grammont speaks of the nasal vowels in French as suitable evocators, when grouped, of "nonchalance," "mollesse," etc.[24] The diphthongs of English express swing and acceleration in suitable contexts; the English -NCE, -SH, -ST (with some lexical support in the storehouse of the language, e.g. from PRANCE, POUNCE, FLASH, RUSH, FAST, HASTE) express speed and hurry, which is expressed in French, according to Grammont, by the *voyelles claires* (among their other evocations).[25] Excess of a given phoneme in a language (e.g., through -S in Spanish, through D-, -S, -N in German, through TH- in English, and the sound /i/ in Modern Greek) may partly neutralize the evocative powers of that phoneme in the language. The same may be said for the commoner inflexions in Greek and Latin, and the commoner postpositions in Finnish.

A given set of purely lexical associations in one language may have analogues in related languages and in the past phases of the language. Nonce-lexical associations are by definition restricted to those passages of prose or poetry where their generating combinations of sound occur. A fifth group of evocative elements, however, is composed out of the residue of pattern in each particular

[21] Macdermott, *Vowel Sounds . . .*, pp. 68–9.

[22] Grammont, *Traité de Phonétique* (1946), pp. 405–6; Macdermott, *Vowel Sounds . . .*, pp. 89–90.

[23] As inferred by the present writer from the data in Paget's *Human Speech* (1930), pp. 90–93 (from Mlle. Coustenoble); for Macdermott, see note 21.

[24] Grammont, *T. de Phonétique* (1946), p. 407.

[25] *Ibid.*, p. 406.

poetic context, a residue which is acoustically, kinaesthetically, and lexically irrelevant, but which takes part in the incantatory or decorative pattern, and is not separated in the mind of the listener or reader from the total *Gestalt* of sound and mouth-movement: "and when sound, and colour, and form are in a musical relation, a beautiful relation to one another, they become as it were one sound, one colour, one form, and evoke an emotion that is made out of their distinct evocations and yet is one emotion." [26] Yeats was speaking, perhaps, of the impact of a whole poem or other work of art; but the principle is similar. This fifth group may be called *conditioned neutrals* or *impressed elements.* They, and some of the nonce-lexical associations, help not so much to illustrate the particular aspect depicted by the more fundamental association-mechanisms, as to emphasize the total *Gestalt* of the subject of the passage. The listener, reverting to a primitive type of reaction, unconsciously connects them with the situation in which they happen to be placed.

In the line

(23) L'in*s***e***cte* (n)**et** *g***ra***tte* la *s***éch***e***re***sse*
[Repeated from I above]

the letters in **bold type** are clearly those of sounds expressive of dryness and harshness (either singly or, as in the case of the CH, in combination with the others).[27] The association-mechanism is probably acoustic, *via* a primary connection with noises characteristic of dry, light, rustling, scratching objects. Such phonemes produce impressions the antithesis of those produced by /o/, /l/, /m/, or /w/, which suggest liquidity, softness, coolness, and a certain degree of density.[28]

The letters in *italics*, on the other hand, are those of sounds which, though far from being inappropriate to the atmosphere of the line, are connected to the ideas of dryness and harshness primarily by lexical associations: L'IN*SEC*TE has a "normal lexical" association with the word *sec;* and the italicized letters throughout are attached by nonce-lexical associations to the meaning and feeling-tones of GRATTE and SÉCHERESSE.

The remaining sounds, with the exception of the irrelevant and therefore bracketed N of NET, take part intimately in the total pattern of the line and are therefore "*impressed elements*"; pressed into service as supporting evocators of the total situation. With the exception of the "fluid" L-sounds, they are not totally inappropriate, but they are not *actively* suggestive of that situation.

[26] W. B. Yeats, *Essays* (London, 1924), p. 193.

[27] For a rather different interpretation of the atmosphere of this line see François Porché, *Paul Valéry et la Poésie Pure* (Paris: M. Lesage, 1926), p. 35; for his analysis of the sound pattern see pp. 46–7. M. Porché is principally concerned with the associations due to emotions and ideas which are attached to the words considered as *signs*, while this essay is restricted to the effects of words as *sounds*.

[28] Cf. M. M. Macdermott, *Vowel Sounds . . .*, p. 89, on "low-band" vowels; M. Grammont, *T. de Phonétique* (1946), p. 408, on nasals and L; Jakobson, Fant, and Halle, *Preliminaries to Speech Analysis* (1952), sec. 2.4233 p. 32, esp. on rounded vs. unrounded, and "grave" vs. "acute," which however would not include L.

Similarly in

(31) *Wenn er* w(ie) d(ie) **Somm***er***sonn***enwende*
(Frühlingliches Vorspiel) **unt***er*(bricht)
Rainer Maria RILKE, *Eros*, 3–4

(an extension of no. [6]), *WENN ER* is influenced nonce-lexically by the meaning of SOMM*ER*SO*NNENWEN*D*E*, and SOMMER-, -SONNEN-, have their normal associations of great light and heat, which bring in the S-sounds lexically with the rest, so that almost the whole line reinforces the meaning; but the real source of the phonemic suggestion of something brief, brusque, terrible, and of overwhelming significance crashing into something prolonged, timeless, delicate, idyllic, is the dark heavy *tight sequence* -OMME(R)/-ONNE(N), with its third member UN(T)E(R) in the next line, contrasted with the thin vowels, palatalized CH, and 'liquid' L-sounds of that line. This sequence creates images at once kinaesthetic (bulky shapes are outlined, bumping on the nasal consonants) and acoustic (the sound is thunderous and reverberating); the only normal lexical associations here effective are those of SOMMER, SONNE, referred to above, and the lexical-acoustic connection with D*ONNER*, B*OM*B*E*, of which the last is unlikely to have occurred to Rilke.

Conversely, the idyllic "prologue" of the pair before they are overtaken by passion, is expressed kinaesthetically, and perhaps acoustically, in

. . . . wie (d)ie . . . .
F**rühlinglich**es *V*(o)*rsp***iel** (unte)*rbr***ich**(t)

with nonce-lexical association to the meaning of *FR*ÜH*LI*NG*LI*CHES through labial/R sequence and I/L tight pattern and (through *V*O*RSP*IEL) by P/B alliteration.

Similarly, one may print

(32) A(nd) *c*ome where *l*ies a **co***ff***er** **bur**ly **all** *of* **blocks**
Buil(t) *of* . . .
Gerard Manley HOPKINS, *Epithalamion*, 36–7

(there is no stress accent on the word ALL) where the image evoked (chiefly kinaesthetically) is that of the hard dark heavy solid square rocks grouped about the bather's rock pool. *CO*FFER, BL*OCKS*, perhaps suggest R*OCKS*, the end-rhyme of the next line, by lexical and nonce-lexical association also.

In the lines

(33) **Lle***n*(o) de **len**g*u*as **cel***es***tes**
. . . .
Sátir(o) de *estr***ellas** (b)a(j)as
C(o)n *sus* **len**g*u*as **rel***u*cientes
Federico Garcia LORCA, *Preciosa y el Aire*, 22, 41–2

(an extension of no. [5]) the image evoked (principally by kinaesthetic mechanisms) is that of the lecherous licking tongues of the hot wind. Here the different categories are less easily sorted out. Nonce-lexical italicized elements in LLE*NO*, C*E*LE*STES*, *ESTR*ELLAS, derive their power chiefly from *RE*LUCI*ENTES*;[29] though *SÁTI*R*O* is also a source, irrelevant to the image of tongues but suggestive of lechery. One should forbear to italicize -AS, or -S as such, because -S is only too common in Spanish and the phoneme is therefore partly neutralized (see above).

Taking the image of the stormy sea, and not those of the sounds of lamentation of which it is a simile (and which extend over the three previous lines), one should, perhaps, print thus the following lines:

(34) Io venni in luogho *d*' ogni luce *m*uto
Ch*e m*uggh**i**a co*me* f**a mar** *pe***r** *tempest***a**,
*Se d***a** con*t***rar****i** ve*n*t*i* è co*mb***a***tt*u*t*o.

DANTE, *Inferno* V 28–30

Every sound takes part in the pattern, which, filling the previous three lines also, is extremely rich. *M*AR and *TEMPESTA* are the sources for the nonce-lexical associations shown, though it can be argued that ES, SE, VE, IV, IÈ carry acoustic echoes of tempest noises.

In the following passage there are two principal images: the (chiefly acoustic) one of Jove's voice

(35) **Pa***nd*(i)*t*u(r) (i)*nt*e(r)ea *d***om**u(s) **om**n(i)**po***t*e*nt*(is) **Olymp**(i),
conc(i)l(i)**umque uoca***t d*(i)**uom pa***t*e(r) **a***t***que** (h)**om**(i)**num** (r)ex

VIRGIL, *Aeneid*, X, 1–2

(assuming that the -M was pronounced in these lines); and that (kinaesthetic and lexical?) of the *stars* of his throne "**r**e**x**/**si***de***r***e*(a)m i(n) **s***ede*m, *t*e**rr**(a)**s** . . ." (The same, 2–3, (with elision at the end of the second word).[30]

A similar analysis might be attempted for Greek poetry and drama. W. Porzig distinguished and described in 1926 what are in effect nonce-lexical mechanisms, and acoustic or kinaesthetic mechanisms, in Aeschylus.[31] But examination of the passages he cites, on the lines of the first section of this essay, suggest that the specific word-rubrications which Porzig noted must have been largely smothered in the general richness of the sound-patterns, thus rather supporting than weakening the criticisms of Porzig made by Professor W. B. Stanford in 1942.[32]

These analyses, both of patterns and their connotations, have necessarily been highly compressed and must appear over-dogmatic. The crux of the matter is that there are such patterns, that they correspond to a quasi-musical faculty in the human make-up, both repetitive and contrast-making; and that they

[29] The pattern of (SUS) LENGUAS RELUCIENTES recalls, and gives added significance to, that of (LLENO DE) LENGUAS CELESTES.

[30] For a general account of Vergil's use of expressive sound with some reference to modern poetry, see W. F. Jackson Knight, *Roman Vergil* (London: Faber, 1944), pp. 242–253.

[31] W. Porzig, *Aischylos* (Leipzig: E. Wiegandt, 1926), pp. 73–81, 81–94.

[32] W. B. Stanford, *Aeschylus in His Style* (Dublin, 1942), pp. 82–3.

and their component sounds can be related to the poetic meaning in specific ways. By thinking in terms of the five categories — acoustic, kinaesthetic, normal lexical, and nonce-lexical associations, and impressed elements — and relating the first two to the general tone and structure of the language, it should be possible to steer a clear course between the Scylla of too-mechanical theories on the "meaning" of sounds and the Charybdis of mystical dilettantism. The subsequent voyage of discovery should be worth while.

Ants Oras

SPENSER AND MILTON: SOME PARALLELS AND CONTRASTS IN THE HANDLING OF SOUND

Spenser the mellifluous, Milton the "organ voice of England": these two clichés are well-established and, like many clichés, they contain an element of truth. The contrast between the smooth fluency of *The Faerie Queene* and the sonorous power of *Paradise Lost* is, on the whole, a very real one. Both poems belong to the same general tradition of the Renaissance epic. Milton learned much from Spenser, whom he regarded as "a better teacher than Scotus or Aquinas"; in his early poetry he was a Spenserian. Yet as we approach *Paradise Lost,* we should be hard put to it to discover two consecutive lines that could possibly be mistaken for Spenser's work. The use of language in all its complexity accounts for the difference, and scholars have devoted much time, labor, and insight to the study of each manner. What will be attempted at present is an examination of the two styles from one specific point of view, that of sound. Not the treatment of sound even in all its major aspects: sound is an infinitely intricate phenomenon, as all students of it know. I shall touch upon a few points only, starting with some of the simplest. Even so, it may prove possible to unravel a few tangles and make some contributions towards a more exact definition of the ways in which the two poets' individualities are manifested. It may appear that the "honeyed" flow of Spenser's verse contains more contrasts, even grittiness, and sometimes more impetuosity, than is usually assumed. It may perhaps also be demonstrated with somewhat greater technical precision than has so far been done that the "sudden blazes," the strength and majesty of Milton even at their most thunderous and overwhelming, in their phonetic aspect are largely the results of a consistent technique which is the very opposite of impetuous.

From *Sound and Poetry (English Institute)*, ed. by Northrop Frye, New York: Columbia University Press, pp. 109–133.

Let us begin with the most general features, vowels and consonants. Vowels, with their variations in pitch, length, and overtones, almost literally provide "music," whereas consonants, much more tangible and produced with a more clearly perceptible effort of articulation, supply what may be metaphorically called body, mass, and weight. Accumulated consonants — consonant clusters — create an effect of special massiveness and strength, although there are differences in this respect between voiced and unvoiced consonants, plosives and continuants, liquids and sibilants, to mention only a few of the possible distinctions.

One might expect two poets as different as Milton and Spenser to differ appreciably in the relative amounts of vowels and consonants they use. Surprisingly enough, such an expectation would be utterly wrong, if my examination of extreme consonantal and extreme vowel effects in a series of passages from *The Faerie Queene* and *Paradise Lost* affords any criterion. What I counted in 1,500 lines of each poem were stressed syllables beginning or ending with consonant clusters, and such syllables beginning or ending with vowels. I excluded cases in which there was some doubt as to the syllables to which some of the consonants belonged. Thus, *revenge, vengeful* were counted, but not *vengeance* or *avenger*. The results for both poems were almost precisely identical: 175 instances per hundred lines in *The Faerie Queene,* and 174 in *Paradise Lost* of syllables with clusters, and no difference at all — 91 cases per hundred lines for both poets — in the figures for syllables with initial or final vowels. These coincidences are so striking that one suspects that what they reflect is the structure of the language itself rather than the tastes and preferences of the two authors.

This, however, is where the resemblance begins and ends. A closer scrutiny of the exact positions within the syllables of massed consonants and of vowels unenclosed in a consonantal frame reveals two diametrically opposed tendencies. Spenser loves to place his consonant clusters at the beginning, as in *plain,* whereas Milton prefers them at the end, as in *first.*[1] The vowels in Milton, rather more often than in Spenser, are preceded only by single consonants or by no consonants at all. In Spenser, on the contrary, the tendency is to avoid anything heavier than a single consonant after the stressed vowel, which, of course, makes the vowel element more conspicuous. The contrast, reduced to its essentials, then, is: in Spenser, a vigorous initial consonantal effect followed by weakened consonantism or none — decrescendo; in Milton, an unobtrusive beginning followed by a strong consonantal finale — crescendo. The

[1] The passages examined are *The Faerie Queene,* I, i; I, ii; I, iii, st. 1–10; I, xi: *Paradise Lost,* I, 1–500; II, 1–500; VI, 1–500. Essential figures (counting only metrically stressed syllables) are: for initial clusters — Spenser 1,191, Milton 863; initial clusters at line end — Spenser 389, Milton 277; final clusters — Spenser 1,408, Milton 1,733; final clusters at line end — Spenser 371, Milton 601; syllables beginning with vowels — Spenser 666, Milton 859; such syllables at line end — Spenser 57, Milton 74; syllables ending with vowels — Spenser 694, Milton 501; such syllables at line end — Spenser 199, Milton 114; total number of clusters — Spenser 2,599, Milton 2,596; total number of stressed syllables beginning or ending with vowels — Spenser 1,360, Milton 1,360.

Miltonic formula is represented by such words as *earth, arms, Heav'ns, world, rowld, burnt;* that of Spenser by *prey, stray, bray, speed, steed, smoke, stroke.* Certain linguistic habits of Spenser's enhance this characteristic trend, especially his retention of vowels normally omitted in such forms as *framèd, crownèd, middèst,* which prevents the formation of clusters after the stressed vowel. The predilection of the mature Milton for syncopation and elision, on the other hand, enables him to crowd more and more consonants into the end of his syllables: *chos'n, grav'n, count'nance, breath'st, call'st.* Milton's growing dislike of syllabized *-ed* endings — special favorites of Spenser's — makes for similar results. Early lines like "In unreprovèd pleasures free" still have a quasi-Spenserian ring. In *Paradise Lost* such lines are scarce and become scarcer as the poem proceeds. The vowel barriers between the consonants are progressively removed.

I select a few passages in which the divergent patterns are represented somewhat more fully than usual. First some from Spenser:

> Upon a great adventure he was bond,
> That greatest Gloriana to him gave,
> That greatest glorious queene of Faery Lond . . . (I,i,3)
> A shadie grove. . . . .
> Whose loftie trees, yclad with sommers pride,
> Did spred so broad, that heavens light did hide . . . (I,i,7)
>
> He so disseized of his gryping grosse,
> The knight his thrillant speare againe assayd
> In his bras-plated body to embosse,
> And three mens strength unto the stroake he layd;
> Wherewith the stiffe beame quaked, as affrayd,
> And glauncing from his scaly necke, did glyde
> Close under his left wing, then broad displayd. (I,xi,20)

Alliteration or semi-alliteration (as in *trees, pride, spred, broad*) here helps to emphasize the initial clusters. Contrast between unvoiced sounds in the clusters and voiced final consonants or vowels without consonants at the end of the syllable increases the initial emphasis (*trees, spred, speare, three,* etc.). The disburdened vowels that follow the clusters ring out freely. In the last quotation the excessive massing of clusters blunts rather than strengthens their impact. Spenser's effort becomes too obvious. The effect of the topheavy syllables, at least for one reader, is somewhat contrived, yet primitive, even awkward.

Milton's favorite type of syllable is less conspicuous, partly because it is more common in English. It is only in extreme concentrations of it that we become fully aware of its presence, for example, in the much discussed line "Rocks, Caves, Lakes, Fens, Bogs, Dens, and shades of Death." Here all syllables, metrically stressed as well as unstressed, save only the last two, are of this kind. Usually the cumulative effect, though strong, does not advertize itself. What we feel is volume and weight without quite realizing the way this result is achieved:

He scarce had ceas't when the superiour Fiend
Was moving toward the shore; his ponderous shield
Ethereal temper, massy, large and round,
Behind him cast. . . . (I,283–86)

High on a Throne of Royal State, which far
Outshon the wealth of Ormus and of Ind,
Or where the gorgeous East with richest hand
Showrs on her Kings Barbaric Pearl & Gold . . . (II,1–4)

and the Orbes
Of his fierce Chariot rowld, as with the sound
Of torrent Floods, or of a numerous Host. (VI,828–30)

Spenser eagerly displays his technique, whereas that of Milton is far less ostentatious by its very nature. The former's delight in initial consonantal flourishes contrasts markedly with Milton's seemingly unemphatic reliance on gradually increasing consonantal strength.

The two methods are even more sharply contrasted in the line endings of the two poets, where the frequencies of Spenser's prevocalic and Milton's postvocalic clusters are more than doubled. Such an intensification of a dominant tendency does not come as a surprise in Spenser, since the rhymed endings are naturally treated with special care. It is more interesting to find the same trend in Milton's blank verse. It runs counter to the traditional notion that for him the individual line was a very subordinate unit intended to be submerged in the long flow of his paragraphs. Spenser's method, with its emphasis on the beginning of the syllable, may quite possibly be connected with the native alliterative tradition, to which, unlike his master Chaucer, he so patently belongs: a great number of his line endings alliterate with words within the line. In *The Pearl,* for example — a poem which perhaps influenced him — a similar combination of rhyme with even more pronounced alliteration yields closely parallel results. It would be tempting to regard Milton's approach as an outcome of his long apprenticeship in the use of rhyme, where the phonetic point of gravity should tend towards the end of the syllable. Unfortunately for the neatness of the contrast, such a theory seems untenable. His early verse is still fairly close to Spenser's practice: the features noted do not become prominent until after his Italian journey. This seems to support the view advanced by F. T. Prince [2] that he was influenced by the Italian ideal of *asprezza,* masculine strength, one of the main manifestations of which, according to Tasso, is "the sound, or, so to speak, the clamor of the double consonants, which strike the ear in the last syllable of the verse." Tasso's examples make it clear that

[2] *The Italian Element in Milton's Verse* (Oxford, 1954), Chapter 8.

he means postvocalic clusters. These he considers more than anything else to be conducive to "grandezza, e magnificenza nelle rime toscane."

There is more evidence than Mr. Prince has cited to confirm his theory. Tasso, like Milton, does not like to encumber the endings of his *versi sciolti* too often with prevocalic clusters. Moreover, the great majority of his final accumulations of consonants avoid extreme harshness by being voiced: *langue, rimbomba, mondo, eterno, Padre, interna, armi.* This is equally true of Milton, four-fifths of whose final clusters are voiced: *besides, deceiv'd, Peers, Arms, wilde, round, flames, comes.* In Spenser, about half of the final clusters contain unvoiced consonants, which every now and then are crowded at line end for brisk or grotesque effects: *betakes, witch, makes, pitch, unlich, stamp, switch, champ, ramp* (I,v,28); *came, lept, same, stept, kept, flasht, swept, washt, dasht* (II,vi,42). Such deliberate deviations from heroic grandeur savor less of Tasso than of Ariosto: *chioccia, croccia, roccia; cerchio, superchio, coperchio; braccia, slaccia, faccia.* This, we feel — and closer examination confirms our feeling — is the kind of thing that Milton's sense of decorum would very seldom permit him to do. Weight rather than excessive sharpness, gravity rather than harshness, strength combined with sonority characterize his heroic verse.

It seems very likely that Milton's thorough training in Latin versification inclined him to accept the Italian method of achieving phonetic magnificence. The quantitative strengthening of the body of his stressed syllables makes his verse often sound like classical hexameters: it adds to their Virgilian quality, so frequently felt yet so hard to define.

Spenser, as has just been seen in his treatment of consonant clusters, is far from disguising his art. He wants his effects to be duly noticed. This is true of him almost throughout. He likes to accumulate devices of the same kind, to show off his skill in playing with them, and to arrange them as clearly and geometrically as possible, which often leads to symmetry. His harmonious, or, to quote Arnold Stein, his "horizontal" style has often been contrasted with the jerky, uneven, "vertical" manner of other poets, above all Donne. This distinction, though valid, probably needs some qualification. Numerous contrasts, heavily underscored by repetition, are embedded in the stream of Spenser's verse. However, his vividly contrasting effects are distributed rather evenly, with few large-scale culminations. Our mind is not as a rule focused on any one point for any length of time — usually just for a moment or two; but the poet often takes great care to make the pictures and patterns presented as intense as possible while they last. This is seen as clearly in his handling of sound as in other respects.

In the two opening stanzas of the first canto of his poem Spenser portrays the Redcrosse Knight. One stanza describes the youthful dash and bravery of the "full jolly Knight," whereas the following stanza — almost depicting another person — emphatically turns to the more pensive, "too solemne sad" aspects of his character. The phonetic designs of these stanzas are sharply differentiated. Stanza 1 has a superabundance of "clear," high-pitched vowels, [i] and [ī].

Seven rhyme words have them: *shielde, fielde, wield, bitt, yield, sitt, fitt.* Consonance stresses the likeness of the vowels: "*sil*ver sh*iel*de," "Where*in* old *din*ts of *dee*pe woundes *di*d remaine," "*see*md . . . *si*tt," "*fie*rce . . . *fi*tt." [3] The second stanza switches over to equally strongly marked low-pitched vowels, [o], [ɔ], [ɔ̄]. Five rhyme words have one of these vowels: *bore, Lord, wore, ador'd, scor'd.* The r's of this series stand out against the l's of the previous one. The contrast, passing from one end of the vowel scale to the other, could hardly be missed by the most casual reader.

Similar dominant motifs in heavy accumulations, which may extend through more than one stanza, form part of Spenser's stock-in-trade. In many instances, the first and last rhymes of a stanza — a total of five endings out of nine — are the same. Stanza 42 of the opening canto has the endings *spake, vaine, awake, paine, againe, speake, braine, weake, break.* The next stanza has *wake, name, quake, blame, came.* Such large blocks of similar sound structure inevitably single out the passages involved.

Frequently abundant alliteration forcibly welds several lines into distinctive units. For instance:

> That when he heard, in *gr*eat perplexitie,
> His *g*all did *gr*ate for *gr*iefe and high disdaine;
> And knitting all his force, *g*ot one hand free,
> Wherewith he *gr*ypt her *g*orge with so *gr*eat paine. . . . (I,i,19)

Here assonance or complete identity of some of the linked syllables remarkably emphasizes the alliterations: *great, grate, great; gall, got, gorge; griefe, grypt.* Note the symmetrical play on the three vowels and the almost completely regular alternation of clusters with single consonants: *great, gall, grate, griefe, got, grypt, gorge, great.* The series begins and ends with the same word. This, it seems, is a craftsman's very deliberate demonstration of his superior skill in organization; yet the passion for copious repetition is there for anyone to see.

This passion often reaches a point at which nearly all conceivable figures of phonetic repetition may be compressed — one would sometimes like to say, squeezed — into seemingly inextricable tangles of similar sounds, which may even impede articulation unless they are read slowly, as Spenser in most cases probably wanted them to be read:

> The willow *worne* of *forlorne* para*mours* (I,i,9)
>
> Furthest from *end then, when* they neerest *weene* (I,i,10)
>
> Most *loth*som, *filth*ie, *foule,* and *full* of *vile* disdaine (I,i,14)
>
> Where *plain n*one might her *see,* nor *she see* any *plaine* (I,i,16)
>
> And ne*x*t her wrin*k*led *sk*in rough *sack-cl*oth wore (I,iii,14)

[3] It also makes us compare differences in the vowels, even such minute ones as that between [i] and [ī], as in *seemd, sitt.*

There is much art in most of these apparent tangles, however. A maximum of consonantal repetition with but vowel variation appears in a device used in the expressive, if not conventionally beautiful line "Most lothsome, filthie, foule, and full of vile disdaine." This verse seems clogged with reiterated consonants, but their arrangement is orderly. Three different vowels are placed in an identical consonantal frame, *f-l*. Gerard Manley Hopkins and Wilfred Owen systematically revived the use of this figure of sound.[4] It is capable of at least two formal functions: it strongly impresses on the mind the consonantal pattern, but it also brings out vividly the differences in the vowels, the only variables in the design in its pure form. Spenser often uses this device with much ingenuity in his line endings, interweaving two or more pairs of this type: *fyre, myre, respire, farre, marre, starre* (II,vi,44); *were, beare, feare, ward, unbar'd, far'd* (IV,ix,15). Correspondences within the lines may further complicate the pattern:

> On th' other *side,* in one con*sort,* there *sate*
> . . . .
> Disloyall Treason, and *hart*-burning *Hate;*
> But gnawing Gealosy, out of their *sight*
> *Sit*ting alone, his *bit*ter lips did *bight* . . . (II,vii,22)

Side. consort, sate, hart, Hate, sight, sitting, bitter, bight — nine close echoes exactly or approximately conforming to the type described: this seems abundance indeed. One wonders, however, whether this is not at least in part gratuitous abundance — a typically Elizabethan display of verbal dexterity, stimulating in its exuberance but not necessarily expressive of anything in particular. Only a few of the important words — *hart, Hate, bitter, bight* — are made to stand out in vivid relief.

By setting off one pattern, one dexterously woven arabesque against another, Spenser in any case achieves variety, and by spacing his varied designs carefully he attains unity of style and total atmosphere. But since he practices little economy to begin with, painting mainly in bright primary colors, so to speak, when he needs special vividness he is forced to heighten his coloring to the utmost. There are limits to this procedure of brightening, since the resources of language are not boundless. Milton, recognizing these limits of his medium, shows himself to be a master of strict economy in exploiting its possibilities to the best advantage. He subdues his phonetic background, thus needing but little intensification to affect us strongly. His intense effects are usually concentrated at the important focal points. With a slight stylistic effort he seems to be able to obtain the most momentous results.

Milton's rhetorical training must have been very like Spenser's, and he had studied the latter's practices with an accomplished expert's eye, so of course he

[4] See D. I. Masson's interesting paper "Wilfred Owen's Free Phonetic Patterns: Their Style and Function," *Journal of Aesthetics and Art Criticism,* XII (1955), 360–69. Masson calls the type in question "circumsyllabic."

knew all his technical tricks. He used most of them himself. It would be tedious to quote parallels. The important point is that he employed such devices more sparingly and that in general he toned them down.[5] The individual line in *Paradise Lost* is far less loaded with consonantal repetition than in *The Faerie Queene*. This applies above all to alliteration. Milton manages with not much more than half the amount of stressed alliterations within the same line that Spenser uses, keeping the alliterating syllables farther apart.[6] Identical initial consonant clusters — the most intense form of alliteration — are rare in his line. The repeated consonants more often than in Spenser appear not in the prominent opening syllable of a word but in the middle of longer words ("In*v*oke thy aid to my ad*v*entrous song," "Il*l*umine, what is *l*ow raise and support"). Assonance, more elusive than consonance, occurs almost as often as in Spenser but is less frequently supported by consonantal identity. Its effect is greater, however, since it need not compete with any end rhymes. The fairy-fury, foul-full, fierce-force type of uniformly framed vowels is mostly used to link different lines but with a controlled power of sound and of semantic suggestion that goes beyond Spenser:

> Of Mans *Fir*st Diso*bedien*ce, and the Fruit
> Of that *Forbidden* Tree. . . .

> And to the *fierce* contention brought along
> Innumerable *force* of Spirits arm'd. . . .

These are nearly all negative features which in themselves could hardly ensure any great poetic effectiveness. What they do, however, is to make even a slight relaxation of such restrictions immediately felt. Repetitions acquire a rarity value. Echoes become audible over a distance of several lines even when there is no correspondence in their metrical positions. Accumulated echoes attain a force of reverberation seldom achieved in *The Faerie Queene*. A comparison of two passages closely similar in some of their wording and imagery may help to realize the difference. Spenser is nearly at his most vigorous in describing the rage of the Dragon wounded by the Redcrosse Knight:

[5] In his treatment of Milton's style in *Paradise Lost and the Seventeenth Century Reader* (New York, 1948), B. Rajan points out consonantal accumulations in Milton's poem, quoting Book I, 44–47, where he finds thirteen instances of *m* and *n*, eleven of which, he says, occur in combination with an *i* or an *o*. As it happens, only seven of these instances appear in stressed syllables, the rest being half-concealed in unstressed positions. The vowels vary much more than Mr. Rajan suggests, for the *i* stands for several sounds, and the unstressed *o*'s are unlike the stressed ones. The critic confuses spelling with pronunciation. The technique here is typical of Milton: it is anything but obtrusive, but the cumulative effect is strong.

[6] Alliterations in stressed syllables (within the same line) in the same samples as above: Spenser 1,906 syllables; Milton 1,165 syllables. Assonance: Spenser 3,050 syllables; Milton 2,941 syllables. If linkages of long and short vowels and of different types of *o*-sounds are disregarded: Spenser 1,880 syllables; Milton 1,757 syllables. In my attempts to identify cases of alliteration and assonance I have been guided primarily by the researches of H. C. Wyld and H. Kökeritz on the pronunciation of sixteenth and seventeenth century English.

For griefe thereof, and divelish despight,
From his infernall fournace forth he threw
Huge flames, that dimmed all the heavens light,
Enrold in duskish smoke and brimstone blew . . . (I,xi,44)

Milton's Satan looks at hell for the first time after his fall into the abyss:

At once as far as Angels kenn he views
The dismal Situation waste and wilde:
A dungeon horrible, on all sides round
As one great Furnace flam'd, yet from those flames
No light, but rather darkness visible
Serv'd only to discover sights of woe . . . (I,59–64)

It would be difficult to decide which series of alliterations is more forcible in itself — Spenser's "*F*rom his in*fer*nall *four*nace *for*th he threw Huge *f*lames" or Milton's "As one great *F*urnace *fl*am'd, yet *f*rom those *f*lames." They are deceptively alike. Yet there is at least one cardinal difference. This is the first case in *Paradise Lost* of alliterative accumulation on such a scale with sounds of such intensity, whereas Spenser has already been prodigal in filling his lines with repeated consonants to suggest the fierceness of the struggle with the Dragon: "High *br*andishing his *br*ight dew-*b*urning *b*lade," "The *d*eadly *d*int his *d*ulled senses all *d*ismaid," "With *fowle* en*foul*dred smoke and *f*lashing *f*ire," and so forth. So, there is in Spenser hardly any heightening of intensity. He barely succeeds in maintaining a level already reached, which tends to be slightly lowered with every new use of the same stylistic moves. In the Miltonic passage, on the other hand, even such relatively distant correspondences as "A *D*ungeon horri*ble*" and "*d*arkness visi*ble*" contribute to the total impression of definite but finely graded design. What Milton has added, much as painters do by shading, is the dimension of depth. Indeed, his treatment of sound exactly corresponds to the scene he describes. In the deep gloom of hell nothing is clearly distinguishable except the flames, the source of light, however ghostlike. It is on the flames of hell that Milton concentrates the greatest phonetic energy. Both visually and aurally they are placed in the center of the picture.

I have paid only occasional attention so far to Spenser's and Milton's manner of arranging their line endings. Contrasts similar to those already observed, only frequently even more pronounced, will appear as we look more closely at this aspect of their treatment of sound.

Spenser's original contributions to rhyme arrangement, while not very numerous, are significant. They show above all a desire for firm, conspicuous design and balance, combined with at least some measure of climactic organization. The *Epithalamion* and *Prothalamion* stanzas, despite some variation, always fall into three relatively simply but differently constructed sections leading up to two final couplets, the conclusion of which is emphasized by lengthening the last line. In certain instances, notably at the beginning of the *Epithalamion,* rhyme links connect some of the separate sections. This linking technique is fully exploited in the Spenserian sonnet, apparently imitated from the Scots sonneteers but characteristic of Spenser's leanings. Here it results in uninterrupted continuity through three quatrains, up to the final couplet, which forms the point of culmination. The total impression is one of sinuosity, unbreakable unity, and transparency of construction. These features are intensified in *The Faerie Queene* stanza, the structure of which is exactly like that of the first nine lines of Spenser's sonnets, except for the greater length of the last line. The final couplet here is no longer isolated but is firmly built into the total design, which culminates emphatically in the final Alexandrine.

Milton's inventions in the field of rhyme arrangement are less obvious and transparent, but no less logically conceived. At their best they are much more subtle. He begins with comparatively simple structures, many of which characteristically use the Spenserian device of a climactic Alexandrine. Then, save for his sonnets, he almost entirely abandons set stanza forms, using more complex combinations, most of which show a sharply emphasized element of mounting gradation. The growing intricacy of these patterns, however, is always subjected to a firm control over their total structure, while the poet at the same time deftly and most economically contrives to conceal a basic regularity by using what I have called "structural blurs" at decisive points so as to produce an impression of effortless spontaneity. This method, the rudiments of which Milton may have learned from the Italian lyrists, is demonstrated most brilliantly in *Lycidas*. The essential contrasts with Spenser are in Milton's far greater complexity; in his endeavor generally to obscure rather than emphasize an underlying regularity without sacrificing it, while bringing it out with extreme clarity at certain crucial points; in the much wider range of his designs — 193 lines of constant variety combined with perfect unity in *Lycidas* — and in a greater capacity for gradual but powerful intensification working towards one all-important peak. Milton seems to be following the very principles that Poe two centuries later appeared to regard as his own personal innovation.

In *Paradise Lost* Milton does much the same in his blank verse that he had done in the rhymed verse of *Lycidas*. Having rejected formal rhyme, he by no means avoids subdued rhymelike effects. Quite on the contrary, he uses them systematically and organizes them carefully, pointing up the mood and matter of his poem both by the phonetic character and by the arrangement of his linked endings. Most of his line-end echoes amount to nothing more than assonance or consonance, but where the effect needs to be intensified, assonance and consonance are combined and may become rhyme. Even the varying frames of mind of the characters are reflected in his methods of patterning. Where mere emotion speaks, the echoes seem disorganized and tend to be heavily massed. Where cool deliberation has the upper hand, they fall into more regular designs, often verging on complete symmetry and extending through long paragraphs. Even so, absolute symmetry seems to be studiously avoided. Something is usually done slightly to upset the balance and thus to prevent an impression of mechanical arrangement. One pattern flows into another, connecting paragraph with paragraph and integrating them all into the infinitely complex larger patterns of the complete books. The variety, expressiveness and delicacy of shading in these patterns, which may include internal echoes and which are generally organized around some dominant central motif, exceed anything done along similar lines by Milton's predecessors in this technique, that is, most of the better writers of blank verse from Surrey onwards.

Spenser's use of a fixed stanza pattern obviously in itself makes such results difficult to achieve. True, phonetic motifs carried from stanza to stanza, as already hinted, provide a larger continuity and more comprehensive patterning for many parts of his poem.[7] Nevertheless, Spenser on the whole seems to do his best to mark the unity and distinctiveness of the individual stanza — for example, by strengthening his rhyme system by means of phonetic links placed more deeply in the line. Internal echoes tend to fall into the same metrical positions. Intense small-scale concentration is brought about in many stanzas by making their first and last rhymes sound alike. Such methods, while often astonishingly delicate in the manner they are applied, in general conspicuously strengthen the part rather than the whole. The microcosm of the stanza is elaborately shaped and consolidated, somewhat at the expense of the macrocosm of the episode or canto. This, by comparison with Milton's powerfully centralizing approach, must be called a method of decentralization — a term which, however, should in no way be taken to suggest lack of order or design.

The differences hitherto observed suggest another generalization. Milton's form, ornate and highly stylized as it often is in the established epic fashion of sustained magnificence, seems to me still essentially functional form, that is, within the limits of epic decorum the style — including the handling of sound — adapts itself to the varying matter. This may seem an oversimplified way of putting it, since the expression does not just reflect the matter but colors it and becomes a part of it. Nevertheless, in Milton the matter predominates to an extent that it does not in Spenser. Spenser's manner at times almost appears to be living a life of its own. Much of the matter is there for the sake of the manner: we often feel it to be essentially an item in a demonstration of style. The events, the scenery, the characters have allegorical meaning (when the author does not happen to forget about it) but a great deal in them seems interchangeable. Think of such triplets as Sansloy, Sansfoy, Sansjoy; Priamond, Diamond, Triamond; Despetto, Decetto, Defetto; of the knights Parlante, Jocante, Basciante, Bacchante, Noctante, and many more. The very names suggest that they have barely a token individuality, that often they are not even distinguishable types but exist for the sake of a geometrically conceived, highly abstract pattern — the pattern of a pageant that might go on almost indefinitely. It is the total arrangement of the pat-

[7] Linkages between different stanzas in Spenser are examined in considerable detail in the University of Florida dissertation by Paul Royce Smith, *Studies in Spenser's Rimes* (Gainesville, Florida, 1955).

tern, not any single figure, that counts. In such a formalized world of the imagination in which there is little that is real in the sense of having individual reality or much weight of its own, Spenser may frequently play with form without necessarily giving it more than a semblance of surface meaning and without subordinating it too strictly to any central motif so long as the unity of style is sufficiently maintained.

Milton, too, depicts a world the like of which has never been seen, but it stands for fundamental, often grim, realities, the importance of which he wishes to convey in every line and syllable of his poem. His epic has a beginning, a middle, and an end, and an extremely serious purpose to which every part is subservient. Hence, the form is always intended to convey as much meaning as it can possibly carry, with careful regard for the total context of the poem. However lovingly the expression may seem to be handled, its ultimate objective is never beauty alone: the element of artistic play scarcely ever becomes self-sufficient. Spenser is "sage and serious" in his basic intent, and his poem is obviously full of serious moments — often very long moments — but Milton, we cannot help feeling, is intensely serious throughout.

Let me try to illustrate this by briefly considering a few passages consisting primarily of proper names — an element of style capable of many functions and much favored by both poets. Both knew how to choose them for sound, but Spenser often comes close to using them for sound alone. In his catalogue of the Nereides towards the end of the wedding pageant of the Thames and the Medway he does not neglect scholarship: he keeps close to his classical sources, retaining most of the epithets, respecting the etymology of the names, and more or less following their original order. But what clearly interests him most is the opportunities that Mombritius' list affords for building a beautiful piece of *bel canto:*

White hand Eunica, proud Dynamene,
Joyous Thalia, goodly Amphitrite,
Lovely Pasithee, kinde Eulimene,
Light foote Cymothoe, and sweet Melite,
Fairest Pherusa, Phao lilly white,
Wondred Agave, Poris and Nesæa,
With Erato, that doth in love delite,
And Panopae, and wise Protomedæa,
And snowy neckd Doris, and milkewhite Galathæa,

Speedy Hippothoe, and chaste Actea,
Large Lisianassa, and Pronæa sage,
Evagore, and light Pontoporea,
And she that with her least word can aswage
The surging seas, when they do sorest rage,
Cymodoce, and stout Autonoe,

And Neso, and Eione well in age,
And seeming still to smile, Glauconome,
And she that hight of many heastes Polynome . . .

This is another one of Spenser's circular patterns: the beginning and conclusion of the passage as well as its middle parts rhyme with each other. The symmetry is almost mathematically perfect. Internal echoes abound. The degree of individualization in the adjectives — adopted by Spenser even though not invented by him — is mostly slight. Suggestions of charm and beauty, little differentiated in kind, are piled up. The arrangement is entrancing as verbal music. It has its purpose in the total design of the pageant as a final luminous patch of color, but this purpose is formal. This, as far as that is possible for anything expressed in words of some meaning, is autonomous form — intricate, rich, most skilfully shaped, but hardly reaching very far beyond itself.

Nothing of the sort occurs anywhere in Milton's numerous lists of names, not even in his earliest verse. The specific associations, the historical, geographical, and cultural context are scrupulously observed; indeed, they come first, even though the music hardly ever fails. The longest catalogue, that of the fallen angels in Book I of *Paradise Lost,* in effect constitutes a well-ordered compendium of heathen mythology; it has its larger purposes too, for example, that of definitely labeling all paganism as belonging to the devil's party. The second longest — that of the kingdoms of the future which Adam sees from the high hill in Book XI — systematically combines history with geography. Even when the subject on the face of it is the enchantment of pure romance, as in the simile in Book I comparing Satan's forces to the armies of heroic poetry, the order in time of the different epic cycles alluded to is carefully maintained: we are given a condensed piece of literary history. Nor is it likely to be due to mere chance that this orderly presentation so fully agrees with the orthodox military formation of the infernal battalions which Milton emphatically brings to our notice. These sound effects, never in the least distracting our attention from the logically arranged matter, are so discreet as almost to seem accidental:

And all who since, Baptiz'd or Infidel
Jousted in Aspramont or Montalban,
Damasco, or Marocco, or Trebisond. . . .

Damas*co,* Maroc*co,* Trebi*sond, Mont*alban, Aspra*mont:* parts of these names almost rhyme, but we need to strain our ear a little to notice the fact: this is deliberately muted music. It is muted to avoid any interference with a full realization of the meaning in all its implications.

Spenser is of course a man of the Renaissance, but in Continental terms we should, in defiance of chronology, feel inclined to call him a quattrocentist rather than a cinquecentist. He is still very close to the Middle Ages, no matter how much he may have learned from Tasso or Ariosto. His artistic approach, with his relative disregard of large-scale concentration and subordination, is pre–Neo-Aristotelian. Ariosto, at least in the way he treats his episodes and individual scenes, comes closer to Aristotle's standards: he draws his subjects more distinctly in the round. Spenser's formal skill, especially his handling of symmetry and balance, may owe much to the Italians of the High Renaissance, but he has not yet acquired, or does not care to apply, the art of perspective: we see foreground but little background, as in medieval romances and paintings. The care with which he elaborates the individual stanza or minor pattern almost defies belief. For parallels we should have to turn to such a poem as *The Pearl* or, to continue our excursions into another art, to the illustrations found in medieval illuminated manuscripts. His joy in the bright and the immediately perceptible leads us into the same chronological context. He loved Chaucer, but was much less able to resist the attraction of alliterative flashes woven into long series of sparkling designs. In this respect his art points to a more archaic stage of development than Chaucer's.

Milton, it goes without saying, as an artist had absorbed very nearly all that the Renaissance could teach him, and his art points beyond it. He understood Aristotle better than many of his most erudite contemporaries did, and knew the value of concentration and firm unity as well as of a style from which one could both descend and ascend, always keeping something in reserve. His avoidance of strict symmetry, of very obvious patterning, is post-High Renaissance. Here Tasso may in some measure have shown him the way, but Milton's gift for displays of mounting strength far exceeds that of Tasso. In this respect his only rival is Shakespeare, but Milton's method is more learned and elaborate: he fully utilizes all the lessons in intricate formal design that he has learned from the more academic poetry of the Renaissance both at home and abroad. His advantage compared with his models is in his superior genius for comprehensive organization and in his ability to kindle it with a new, purposeful energy. In the art of subduing in order to enhance effectively, the nearest parallel to him is found in the work of an exact contemporary of his about whom he probably knew nothing, Rembrandt van Rijn: the latter's concentration of light on only one point against a background of subtly patterned twilight is, in its manner as well as in its results, the precise pictorial equivalent of Milton's phonetic chiaroscuro with its centers of blazing intensity.

Dell H. Hymes

PHONOLOGICAL ASPECTS OF STYLE: SOME ENGLISH SONNETS

I

To speak of *style* implies a universe of discourse, a set and its stylistically differentiated components.[1] This universe may be of any magnitude, as broad as the set of civilizations [2] or as the set of all natural languages: Whorf successfully characterized the cognitive style of Hopi in contrast to some European members of that set, whatever we may think of his epistemology.[3]

Style may be investigated, both as deviations from a norm and as "a system of coherent ways or patterns of doing things." [4]

Linguists usually speak of style in reference to the universe of a single language, and emphasize deviation. Thus, from Bernard Bloch: "The style of a discourse is the message carried by the frequency distributions and transitional probabilities of its linguistic features, especially as they differ from those of the same features in the language as a whole." [5] But it should not be forgotten that

[1] By devising efficient methods for tabulating and checking data, and by helping in their use, my wife Virginia has been invaluable. I am indebted to Fellows of the Center for Advanced Study in the Behavioral Sciences (1957–1958) for discussion of sounds and sonnets, and especially to John Tukey and John Gilbert for statistical discussion. Mary Girschik valorously computed chi-squares for a coordinate study of these twenty sonnets; its results are omitted here to conserve space and unity. The account of procedures and results has been severely cut, and the original data and tabulations are also omitted, in this revision of the original work paper.

[2] A. L. Kroeber, *Style and Civilizations* (Ithaca, 1957).

[3] B. L. Whorf, *Language, Thought, and Reality*, J. B. Carroll, ed. (New York, 1956). See also H. Hatzfeld, *A Bibliography of the New Stylistics* (Chapel Hill, 1952), Chapter 10.

[4] Kroeber intends this as a pointer, not as a formal definition. He states: "A style is a strand in a culture or civilization: a coherent, self-consistent way of expressing certain behavior or performing certain kinds of acts. It is also a selective way: there must be alternative choices, though actually they may never be selected" (p. 150). The fit to natural languages is obvious.

[5] B. Bloch, "Linguistic Structure and Linguistic Analysis," in A. A. Hill, ed., *Report of the Fourth Annual Round Table Meeting on Linguistics and Language Teaching* (Washington, 1953), p. 42.

to some "sources," especially poets, style may be not deviation from but achievement of a norm. And if some stylistic universes are hierarchical, comprising a general norm and individual deviations, some are egalitarian, comprising a set of norms, such that it would be arbitrary to choose one norm as a standard from which the others depart. Hopi and English differ in cognitive style, but which is norm, which departure?

In literature, verbal art, both ways of regarding style are appropriate.

This paper analyses a universe of twenty English sonnets, ten by Wordsworth and ten by Keats. The analysis relates to the general question of the role of sound in poetry. A specific aim is to balance concern with style as norm and deviation, as what is common (to a language, author, genre), with concern for style as the accomplishment of the individual poem.[6]

II

It is a commonplace that the short poem or lyric depends heavily on the specific properties of language. Thus, from Suzanne Langer:

> The fullest exploitation of language sound and rhythm, assonance and sensuous associations, is made in lyric poetry . . . it is the literary form that depends most directly on pure verbal resources — the sound and evocative power of words, meter, alliteration, rhyme, and other rhythmic devices, associated images, repetitions, archaisms, and grammatical twists. It is the most obviously linguistic creation, and therefore the readiest instance of poesis . . . the lyric poet uses every quality of language because he has neither plot nor fictitious characters nor, usually, any intellectual argument to give his poem continuity. The lure of verbal preparation and fulfillment has to do almost everything.[7]

Such dicta can be taken as questions to be explored. In what sense can the exploitation of sounds in a poem, by participating in the lure of verbal preparation and fulfillment, be said to be appropriate to it? Or the use of some sounds in some poems? Put structurally, has a lyric, such as a sonnet, a structure of sounds which contributes with other structures to its lyric unity?

Two scholars who have recently tackled this problem in linguistic terms are Lawrence Jones and James Lynch. Jones has analyzed the distinctive features in successive lines of poetry. When applied to passages from Shakespeare's plays, his method has shown that utilization of distinctive features differs in different passages, and this in a way that seems appropriate to the tenor of the lines. Since Jones' work has not been published, I will not go into it further.

Lynch has analyzed the phoneme occurrences of whole poems. His goal is "first, to discover the total effect of the poem's euphony or tonality or musicality, or what Professor Wellek, following the Russian Formalists, calls

[6] I want especially to thank both Fred W. Householder, Jr., and Alfred Kroeber, who have made suggestive computations of their own from the tabulations of the original work paper.

[7] S. Langer, *Feeling and Form* (New York, 1953), pp. 258–259.

'orchestration,' and second, to relate its findings to 'meaning' in such a way that it can be seen how the poem's phonemic totality supports and contributes to its prose and poetic statement." [8] His key example is the Keats sonnet "On First Looking Into Chapman's Homer." After determining the dominant phonemes, and comparing them to "Silent," the word whose trochee begins the last line, he finds: "the word we found to occupy such an important position for numerous reasons, which in fact sums up the theme of the sonnet, also sums up its dominant sound structure. The poet's 'sixth sense,' whether operating consciously or unconsciously, led him to consummate his poem not only in terms appropriate to his meaning, but also in terms which climax the workings of the lyrical faculty on its most basic level, sound." [9]

Certainly this result fits Langer's phrase, "the lure of verbal preparation and fulfillment." It and its underlying approach, however, must be related to two general problems: the nexus between sound and meaning, and the statistical properties of language. How does such a result, fixing "silent" as summative in both meaning and sound, fit a definition of language as "arbitrary vocal symbols?" [10] How does it take account of "chance as the ever-present rival conjecture?" [11]

On the Nexus between Sound and Meaning

Many insist on its arbitrary nature. The minor role of onomatopoeia is stressed, its dependence on the pattern of particular languages noted, and classrooms encouraged to titter at "bow-wow" theories of language origin. This matter of origins, however, points to confusion back of a simple insistence on "arbitrary."

One confusion involves scope. Appropriateness of sound may be conceived as (A) universal, in fact or tendency, as (B) a fact of a given speech community, or as (C) pertaining to a given source. Another confusion involves level. In language, sound may be deemed (1) inherently appropriate to meaning or (2) contextually appropriate, in terms of (a) a phoneme, (b) a word, (c) a set of words, (d) a sequence of words, from a single line to a whole poem or text. (The context may be the immediate linear context or the substitution possibilities at a given point.) These distinctions, scope and level of reference, crosscut. Briefly, some putative examples are: (A1a) *m* is a sound of acceptance,[12] high vowels are smaller, low vowels are larger; [13] (B1a) schwa is a phonestheme in

[8] J. J. Lynch, "The Tonality of Lyric Poetry: An Experiment in Method," *Word*, IX (1953), 211–224.

[9] Lynch, p. 219.

[10] E. H. Sturtevant, *An Introduction to Linguistic Science* (New Haven, 1947), p. 2.

[11] G. Herdan, *Language As Choice and Chance* (Groningen, 1956), p. 5.

[12] K. Burke, *Attitudes to History* (New York, 1937), Vol. 2, p. 81, following Sir Richard Paget; but note Burke's view (in *The Philosophy of Literary Form* [Baton Rouge, 1941; New York, 1957], p. 13) that "Paget's theory should be presented as a contribution not to philology, but to poetics."

[13] E. Sapir, "A Study of Phonetic Symbolism," in *Selected Writings of Edward Sapir*, D. Mandelbaum, ed. (Berkeley, 1949), pp. 61–72.

English monosyllables; [14] (A1b) many or most languages have a term for a bird of the raven group with back stop and low central vowel; [15] (B1b) Zuni *z?ilili* expresses "be a hot day with the noise of insects"; [16] (B2b) of English words for headdress, because of rhyme associations, "cowl," not "toque" or "wimple," suggests something sinister or bad; [17] (B2c) in the history of English, "glare, gleam, glow, gloom, glimmer, flimmer, flare" and other blendings have accumulated and come together; [18] (B2d) Tennyson's "The murmuring of innumerable bees in immemorial elms."

Even the existence of universal sound symbolism cannot be dogmatically denied. There have been rash excesses, such as that of Johannesson, who explains supposed resemblances between Semitic and Indo-European by Paget's gesture-origin theory; [19] but the matter can be empirically investigated. Most recently, Brown and others have done so; their results show that it is rash to deny the existence of universal, or widespread, types of sound symbolism.[20]

As for sound symbolism within a language, speech community, or text, it simply misses the point to repeat that *cheval*, *pferd*, *misatim*, and *kiutan* all mean 'horse.' Consider the individual growing up in a particular speech community, ignorant of the ultimate origin of its linguistic forms but acquiring and exploiting them as indissoluble complexes of sound and meaning. It is his common error in thinking one language's particular set of complexes natural and universal that the linguist attacks with the slogan "arbitrary." But this "error" is just the point. From the standpoint of origins, it is truly an error, but from the standpoint of speech behavior, dismissing it is a form of genetic fallacy. If we are to understand a fair part of linguistic change, comprehend the use of language in speech and verbal art, take account of all the varied speech play in which a competent speaker may indulge, and to which he can respond, we must study his real and lively sense of appropriate connections between sound and meaning.

We can satirize the argument that high vowels are little, low vowels large, "as in *big* and *small*"; but such a pattern is the basis of much popular use and coinage, for example, "Poopsquawk — that's an elderly pipsqueak." [21] Tennyson's line certainly does not suggest bee sound if the meaning is slightly changed — even more slightly than John Crowe Ransom changed it, to "the murmuring

[14] F. W. Householder, "Accent, Juncture, and My Grandfather's Reader," *Word*, XIII (1957), 234–245.

[15] D. H. Hymes, "The Supposed Spanish Loanword in Hopi for 'Jaybird,'" *International Journal of American Linguistics*, XXIV (1958), 253–257.

[16] S. Newman, *Zuni Dictionary* (Bloomington, 1958), p. 48.

[17] D. L. Bolinger, "Rime, Assonance, and Morpheme Analysis," *Word*, VI (1950), 123.

[18] Sturtevant, pp. 111–112. Cf. Bolinger, p. 130: "It is generally recognized that English contains a pool of forms interrelated through rime and assonance. What is not appreciated is the vastness of the pool."

[19] A. Johannesson, *Origin of Language* (Reykyavik, 1949). Johannesson (p. 15) believes that many of the forms "must date from the first period of man's attempt to speak."

[20] R. W. Brown, A. Black, and A. Horowitz, "Phonetic Symbolism in Natural Languages," *Journal of Abnormal and Social Psychology*, L (1955), 388–393.

[21] Cited by Bolinger (p. 136, n. 44), after a popular radio program.

of *e*numerable bees"; but in the poem the particular nexus of sound *and* meaning seems appropriate and effective to English speakers. Bolinger has assembled many examples of the goings-on of association between sound and meaning in English and Louis Finkelstein has recently written on the great importance of the sound-meaning nexus in the Hebrew Bible.[22]

Insistence on the arbitrary nature of the connection between sound and meaning simply cuts off inquiry into a very real aspect of speech and language. For the relation of sound to meaning in poetry, two main points are to be made. First, any and all the various types of sound-meaning association may be utilized by a particular poet in a particular language and may be responded to by his audience. In a recent review [23] the statement is made:

> The second way in which Guiraud's slighting of the linguistic groundwork is unfortunate, is that it leaves him open to the seductive voices of Jespersen and Grammont in discussing sound symbolism. It is true that he begins with caution, but when he says . . . "*La Dormeuse,* full of shadow, languor, and of silence, is softened, veiled, and muffled by nasalization and labialization," he has left his caution behind him.

This cuts off inquiry into two important questions of fact: how prominent are nasalization and labialization in the particular poem, absolutely and in relation to other poems and French in general, and do speakers of French associate these sound qualities (by themselves or in a set of words bearing them) with the effects to which Guiraud alludes? Such facts can be established and are important to poetic style, whether or not there is any universal or original connection between nasalization, labialization, shadow, languor, and silence. In fact, Guiraud determines the percentage of sounds belonging to a variety of sound types for each of the three poems he analyzes in detail, and compares the results for each poem to the results for the other two and the mean for poetry of the period (1880–1920). Thus, "La Dormeuse" is said to be characterized by labialization, because 43.7% of its sounds are labials, compared to 21% and 24.5% for the other two poems and to 32.5% for the period mean.[24]

Second, if as a result of long-term speech experience the sound-meaning complexes of a language induce a sense of appropriateness in speakers, it is possible that the very short-term experience of sound-meaning complexes in a particular poem may also induce a sense of appropriateness. The first may have permanent effect: analogy, contamination, blending are familiar processes in the history of a language. Use can induce a sense of appropriateness that etymology does not justify, regarding the strands of similarity in sound and meaning running through a group of words. The second is a temporary effect. As I interpret Lynch's proposal, the use of words in a particular poem may bring certain meanings and sounds into prominence, so that it may then be sensed as appropriate for the two strands of prominence to come together. A word that

[22] L. Finkelstein, "The Hebrew Text of the Bible: A Study of its Cadence Symbols," in L. Bryson et al., eds., *Symbols and Society* (New York, 1955), pp. 409–426.

[23] A. A. Hill, Review in *Language*, XXI (1955), 251.

[24] P. Guiraud, *Langage et Versification d'après l'Oeuvre de Paul Valéry* (Paris, 1953), p. 89.

sums up the theme of a sonnet may be felt as also appropriate to the sonnet's particular aggregate of sound.

If this is the case, incidentally, it poses the possibility of inappropriate use of sound in the closing part of a sonnet. And I would suggest that an important part of the difference in value between Wordsworth's "Composed on Westminster Bridge" and his "At Dover" (sonnets 2 and 10 of this study) lies in the appropriate culmination of one and the inappropriate culmination of the other, regarding the two sonnets' dominant sounds.

In general, then, I argue that the mass of naive and linguistically unsophisticated reports about sound-meaning connections should not be dismissed (nor uncritically accepted), but should be taken as evidence of a very real linguistic phenomenon, the native speaker's sense of sound-meaning appropriateness; and this phenomenon should be investigated. Such study will be of value to the study of style in verbal art. One kind of induced appropriateness is implicit in the approach proposed by Lynch and is tested in Sections III, IV and V.

On Chance as the Rival Conjecture

Lynch does not place his results in a context of other information about the frequency or dominance of sounds, whether in other poems, in other works by the same author, or in the language generally. (He does indicate in a final footnote the difference in rank order for the sounds in the Keats sonnet from two computations for American English.)

This may be defended as adequate, as near the perspective represented by Leo Spitzer's procedure (as described by Hatzfeld): [25]

> Spitzer has no preestablished system, he even ignores the implications of the *langue* in his study of the *parole*. He simply starts reading, as he says, and is fascinated by something which strikes him. He jumps at once from description to an attempt at interpretation of the first discovered trait, i.e. of its possible psychological root. Only after having discovered this "radix" does he return to the collection of other traits eligible for the same interpretation. If all the traits investigated lead to the same conclusion, Spitzer declares, then he has found the informing principle of a literary work of art.

The response of the trained mind and congruity of pattern are important tools; and Kroeber states [26] that judgment, recognition of style is primary, its analysis and statistics secondary. Yet many will be troubled by another perspective, exemplified in a statement by Herdan: "What before were regarded as quite unique events, the products of willful creation, appear now when studied quantitatively as mere variants of typical expenditure of linguistic material, or as samples of one basic distribution of such material." [27]

[25] H. Hatzfeld, "Stylistic Criticism as Art-minded Philology," *Yale French Studies*, II (1949), 66.

[26] In *Style and Civilizations*.

[27] Herdan, p. 2.

Being so troubled, I have brought to bear on Lynch's approach some increment of additional information. It is by no means a question of complete and controlled analysis, which would require more than my resources permit. Indeed, beyond the sheer work, there are unresolved and fundamental questions of how to apply and interpret statistical methods for such a purpose as the stylistic investigation of a particular poem.

The additional information obtained here is simply the data yielded by the sounds of twenty sonnets, regarding their frequency, and the amount of weighting in stressed syllables, both in terms of absolute values and rank order. Essentially, the basis of interpretation has been broadened so that the significance of a sound and its use can be assessed relative not to just one sonnet but to twenty.

Chance, then, has not been statistically eliminated as a source of the particular frequencies taken as significant in the particular poems. I can state that the /ay/ of "silent" occurs more often in the Keats sonnet on Chapman's Homer than in any of the Wordsworth ten, more often than in all but two of the Keats ten. I can state that by the criteria used it has more weight in the sonnet on Chapman's Homer than it has in any other of all twenty. I can add that /ay/ achieves a relative rank order of weighting in this sonnet which is higher than any it achieves in the Wordsworth ten, as high as any in the Keats ten.

All this points toward importance for the sound as used in this sonnet. But it cannot demand conviction by statistical test. If, as one mathematician proposed, a good test for the importance of /ay/ in the Keats sonnet is to see how many /ay/'s can be put in a sonnet, it is disheartening that a dashed-off sonnet with 70 /ay/'s can be read and its trick go undetected by someone devoted to poetry. On the other hand, frequency and its associated statistical analysis is probably relatively insensitive, a vague mirror, when the focus is on the individual poem. It may well be that the sheer data, usefully arranged, is about as good a kind of statistics as we can get. The occurrences of the sounds do in fact differ from sonnet to sonnet, poet to poet, as the data state, and the stylistic critic can make of this what he can. Perhaps it is simply not worthwhile to attempt significance tests with regard to the importance of sounds in individual poems; perhaps a much more relevant test of significance is fit with other aspects of the poem, especially its structure of meaning.

Certainly the goal of stylistic analysis must be the comprehension of the individual work and its value; for otherwise, why pick on Keats instead of Robert Southey? But it is in the areas of broad comparison between whole bodies of work that statistical tools have the most to contribute. There they are in the forefront, but for a single sonnet they become background. When the focus is the individually valuable work, then no matter how intriguing the broader stylistic matters along the way, statistics is helpful but insufficient. We should push it as far as it will go but not expect it to go all the way. In this study, it is but one of three parameters in the interpretation of the individual sonnets.

The apparatus of charts, tables, and frequencies, then, should not mislead anyone into thinking that my concern is to test a statistical hypothesis about frequency of phonemes. I am *not* testing as a null hypothesis that the dominant phonemes of a sonnet are those that would be the most frequent in a same-size sample of English drawn at random. I am concerned with the stylistic achievement of particular sonnets. If it is useful to speak in such terms here, *the null hypothesis is threefold:* that in any same-size sample of English drawn at random (which meets the requirements of the sonnet form for meter, rhyme, and meaningfulness), some of or all the dominant sounds will (1) co-occur in (2) a word placed toward the end of the sample which (3) expresses a theme found in the whole. In point of fact, if this null hypothesis were found to be true, it would be a finding of the greatest interest. So far as twenty sonnets tell, it is not true; the satisfying of all three conditions is an aesthetic fact about particular sonnets, not about the sonnet form.

III

Space does not permit a detailed account of the procedure used. Brief comment must suffice.

The *transcription* derives from the Trager-Smith analysis of English, guided by my own speech, as subordinated to the "General American" norm. Like Lynch, I treat syllabic nuclei as units for the present purpose. The *weighting* follows fixed rules. I was not able to reduce to rules the weights Lynch assigns in his published example, but my assumptions are much the same as his. A sound is assumed to be given prominence by prose stress, metrical stress, and repetition. By "prose stress" is meant normal occurrence of primary or secondary stress. Metrical stress refers to the abstract metrical pattern of iambic pentameter, as interpreted for the four English stresses by Whitehall.[28] The two kinds of stress often coincide but need not. Repetition subsumes rhyme, alliteration, assonance, consonance, and a few other phenomena.

The domain of a stress level is a syllable, but syllable boundaries are not always clear-cut. Of consonants occurring between nuclei, a single consonant has been counted in the preceding syllable if its nucleus is a simple vowel, not if its nucleus is a diphthong. Of two or more consonants between nuclei, the last has been counted in the following syllable but not in the first.

In assigning metrical stress, I have been guided by the four principles for exceptions to regular iambic succession which John Crowe Ransom has stated.[29] I have not found the weighting of sounds so sensitive, or permissible metrical alternatives so common, that a different choice, where one has had to be made, would alter the dominant ranks in a given sonnet. For two sounds adjacent in rank and slightly different in total weight, an alternative choice might cause them to exchange places, but it does not seem able to make dominant a sound that otherwise was not, or to remove from among the dominant sounds

[28] H. Whitehall, "From Linguistics to Criticism," *Kenyon Review*, XVIII (1956), 418; "From Linguistics to Poetry," in N. Frye, ed., *Sound and Poetry* (New York, 1957), pp. 142–143.

[29] J. C. Ransom, "The Strange Music of English Verse," *Kenyon Review*, XVIII (1956), 471–472.

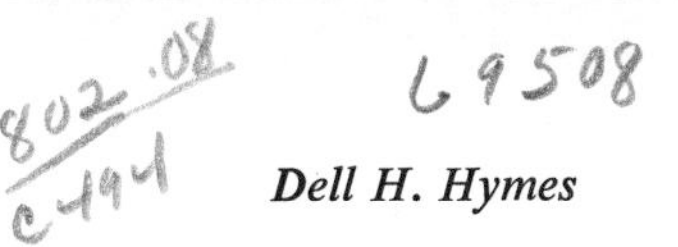

one that otherwise ranked high. Of course, the relation between weights is not arithmetic, and difference in weight for two sounds is an indication of their relative importance, not a measurement of it. (There is thus no automatic procedure for interpretation; we must look at all the high-ranking sounds and not be tempted to use the numerical indices as absolute differences.)

Given a decision as to stressed-syllable membership, a weight of 1 has been assigned for each of the following circumstances: (1) occurrence with primary or secondary "prose stress"; (2) occurrence with metrical stress; (3) recurrence in stressed syllables within a line, syntactic phrase, or rhyme scheme; (4) recurrence in a stressed syllable of a sound in the immediately preceding unstressed syllable. These weightings (1–4) are taken as independent and totaled as they occur. Some lesser types of repetition have been noted (5–7) but are counted as giving weight only when not duplicating the first four: (5) recurrence three times in a line in the same syllable position (nucleus, before nucleus, after nucleus) if the third occurrence is stressed; (6) exact repetition of a word or syllable in parallel syntactic circumstances; (7) recurrence of the same sound(s) before and after a given stressed nucleus. In principle, any kind of repetition and patterning of sound might contribute to dominance. In practice, as Householder has shown (see his formal discussion), only the major patterns are needed to approximate the results fairly well.

Consonants and nuclei are ranked separately, rather than in one order as Lynch ranks them. The phonetic and structural differences between the two classes justify this, and the almost two-to-one greater frequency of consonants would obscure the significance of the nuclei if both were combined in a single order. It should be noted that nuclei are more sensitive to variation between poems than the consonants.

For interpretation, two tables were prepared, one showing for each poem the rank order of sounds within it, the other showing for each sound the ranks it achieved in the various poems. The dominant sounds were listed, for the whole poem and for octet and sestet separately; separate lists were made of sounds whose weight was predominantly in the octet, predominantly in the sestet, and proportionately about even in both. Lists were made of those sounds whose rank in the given poem was the highest achieved in the ten by the particular author; of those whose rank in the poem was the second highest achieved; and of those whose rank was third highest achieved. The original sheets on which the frequency and weighting of the sounds had been recorded line by line were also examined to detect clustering and trends.

An interpretation of the theme of the poem was made, any contrast between octet and sestet being noted. The sonnet was examined for a word or words fulfilling three criteria: (1) on the level of sound, containing sounds dominant in the poem and/or much higher in rank than usual; (2) on the level of meaning, expressing the theme of the poem (or octet or sestet); (3) regarding position, placed so as to have a culminating effect. When all three criteria were met, the result has been termed a *summative* word. When only the first two criteria were met, the result has been termed a *key* word.

IV

There is a clear case for summative words in six of the twenty sonnets: (1) these, (2) still, (5) first blood, (12) silent, (15) unrest, still, (18) soul.

I would consider as key words: (7) forlorn, (14) never, (16) friendliness, (17) blind, name, (19) let, constrained. These occur in five of the sonnets.

Sometimes there is approximation to summative effects, instances that seem not clear-cut but still show something. Such are (3) inner shrine, (4) on herself, (6) great, away, (7) out of time (in the octet), (8) Sleep, joyous health, (9) voice, thee, (14) nothingness. These occur in seven of the sonnets.

In five cases I found no positive result at all: (9), (10), (11), (13), (20).

Some of the detailed analysis for each sonnet is summarized in the following paragraphs.

1. Wordsworth, "I Grieved for Buonaparte." The final word "these" has this strength: /iy/ is the dominant nucleus in octet, sestet, and the whole sonnet; /ð/ ranks eleventh among consonants, the highest it achieves in relation to other Wordsworth sonnets, in which its average rank is 17.1; /z/ ranks fourth among consonants here, the highest it achieves relative to the Wordsworth ten, in which its average rank is 12.7. This is the only sonnet of the twenty in which /z/ ranks in the top four consonants. It is steadily weighted through lines 4 to 14, having the most weight of any sound in the sestet. (Householder has noted that it is in excess in the sonnet, although we would expect its weighted rank to be lower than its frequency rank; see his formal discussion.) The word has syntactic prominence from the last three lines: "these are . . . , this is . . . , are these."

I sense an antithesis both in sound and meaning between "Buona*par*te" (line 1) and "true *Power*" (line 14). The contrast of masculine Buona*par*te and feminine Wisdom and the theme of courtship rather than of conquest give sexual import to "true Sway doth mount," "the stalk true Power doth grow on," and the suggestion of "rites" by "rights." To the extent that "these" sums up the proper "rights/rites" by anaphoric reference, the relative strength of its sounds makes it an appropriate final word, emphasized by repetition, syntactic parallel, and closure of the sonnet pattern.

2. Wordsworth, "Composed upon Westminster Bridge." The final word of the octet, "air," has its two dominant phonemes /e r/. In meaning, "smokeless air" may be seen as the basis of the whole scene and Wordsworth's delight in it; this is perhaps the only poem in which he responds to the city as a part of nature, with the kind of response he otherwise reserves for natural phenomena.

The final word of the sestet, "still," has the four dominant phonemes of the sestet, /l s t/ and /i/, and seems to sum up the essence of the sonnet; Wordsworth follows "still" with an exclamation mark. In the whole sonnet, /l s/ are the two top consonants, /t/ is the fourth consonant, and /i/ is the second nucleus. Although /e/ is the dominant nucleus, it does not occur after "very" of line 13; it is relatively evenly weighted in both octet and sestet, whereas /i/ rises in weight in the sestet (11 in the eight lines of the octet, 16 in the six lines of the sestet). (Indeed, as scored by Lynch, /l/ would be the dominant nucleus, for Lynch adds one point for each occurrence to the points for weighting; /i/'s 22 occurrences plus weight of 27 would give 49, and /e/'s 30 plus 12 would give 42.)

For the octet "air" and for the sestet and whole sonnet "still" may be seen as summative words.

3. Wordsworth, "It Is a Beauteous Evening, Calm and Free." (The strength of /i/, greatest in the poem and rising in the sestet, may lend some prominence to "with" in line 14.) The best approximation to a summative word or phrase for the whole sonnet is found in "inner shrine" (line 13); it has the two top consonants of sestet and sonnet, /r/ and /n/, and the top nucleus, /i/. The rank of /ay/ is fourth in the sonnet, second in the sestet, and it has here its second highest rank of the Wordsworth ten; it is well sustained through the poem, acquiring more weight in the sestet, and its first prominence is in "The holy time is quiet as a nun." As for /š/, this is its only occurrence in the sonnet; it may lend prominence, not by culmination but by contrast.

4. Wordsworth, "London, 1802." The words "on herself" have some cumulative force. The two stressed nuclei contain the dominant nucleus of the poem, /e/, and that of the sestet, /a/. (/a/ occurs only in the sestet.) The four dominant consonants of the sonnet are found in it (/r s l n/), whereas /h/ has in this sonnet its highest rank relative to the Wordsworth ten; /f/ has its second highest rank relative to the Wordsworth ten (7 compared to an average rank of 12.2). The word "duties" may have some prominence from contrast, this being the only weighted occurrence of /uw/ in the sonnet; this may set off the following words.

The theme of the poem may be taken as revolving about the opposition of "we are *selfish* men" (line 6) and the "lowliest duties *on herself* did lay." If so taken, "on herself" sums up the poem both in meaning and sound rather well.

5. Wordsworth, "It Is Not to Be Thought of." The words "[we are] sprung from earth's *first blood*" seem to culminate the poem both in sound and meaning. The words "first blood" contain the dominant five consonants of the sonnet, /d r s t l/, and the dominant nucleus of the sestet, /ë/. Were the sonnet transcribed by Lynch, identifying /ɨ/ and /ë/, the effect would be striking, making /ë/ the dominant nucleus of the whole poem. As it is, /ë/ has here its highest relative rank in Wordsworth's ten and the second rank in the poem. This is the only time /d/ ranks in the top four consonants in Wordsworth's ten, and here it is first.

The water imagery of the poem is caught up in "blood." This imagery starts with "flood" (line 1), whose sound is echoed in "blood"; indeed, the association of /l/ and /d/ is strong throughout the poem (flood, world's, flowed, old, hold, held, blood, manifold).

The dominant nucleus of the sonnet, /ɨy/, last appears in "we" (line 13), and this, plus the intentional setting off of the phrase by dashes, adds to the force of the whole. In imagery, theme, and sound, then, this phrase, especially "first blood," is summative.

6. Wordsworth, "On the Extinction of the Venetian Republic." The last word of the octet, "sea," contains its dominant consonant and vowel, /s iy/. Of the nuclei, /iy/ is dominant in the octet, /ey/ in the sestet, and this parallels the contrast between the octet's description of the glories of Venice, the sestet's comment on her fall. (Note, incidentally, "Venice" in the octet, "vanish" in the sestet.) Since /iy/ dominates seven of Wordsworth's ten, while /ey/ achieves second rank only in this, against an average rank of 7.1, I take it as the most significant nuclei. In this sonnet /w/ also achieves its highest rank relative to Wordsworth's ten, fifth against an average of 9.5, outranking /d/ and /n/. This relative prominence can be seen as giving force to the sonnet's final stressed syllable in "away." Its force is heightened by the fact that, after appearing in the octet's rhyme scheme, /ey/ completely takes over the rhyme scheme of the sestet.

Some effect is obtained by the recurrence of "once" in lines 1 and 14, but of its phonemes only /w/ and /s/ have strength in the sonnet. "Great" and "away" have some summative force, contributed chiefly by /ey/, backed by consonant strength either absolutely in this poem (/t r/) or relative to others by Wordsworth (/w g/), and abetted by alliteration ("grieve-great," "once-away").

7. Wordsworth, "The World Is Too Much With Us." In the octet "out of tune" is summative, having the two dominant nuclei /aw/ and /uw/ and the two dominant consonants /t/ and /n/. Note that the strength of the back diphthongs is confined entirely to the first eight and a half lines; after dominating these, and achieving their highest relative rank in Wordsworth, neither /aw/ nor /uw/ recurs in a weighted syllable.

In the sestet, /iy/, /ay/, and /ə/ come into prominence; /r l n/ dominate the sestet, and /r l n/ come to be dominant in the sonnet as a whole. No clear and strong instance of summative effect is found for the sestet or the poem. The final words, "wreathed horn," involve the dominant consonants (/r n/) and the dominant nucleus (/iy/) of the sonnet, but there is no connection with the theme of the poem in a summative way. The three dominant consonants of the sonnet and its sestet occur in the stressed syllable of "forlorn," together with the sestet's second-ranking nucleus.

In sum, there is a sharp contrast between the two parts of the poem in the use of nuclei. The octet has a summation in sound and meaning in "out of tune"; some key to the sestet is found in "forlorn," whose metrically stressed consonants (but not its nucleus) dominate the poem as a whole.

8. Wordsworth, "To Sleep." The dominant nucleus, reckoned for the whole sonnet, is /iy/, but its strength ends with the apostrophe to "Sleep!" in line 10. This is a summative effect within the sonnet.

In the sestet /e/ is dominant; all its sestet occurrences follow "Sleep" in line 10, and it emerges second-ranking nucleus in the poem. Of the consonants, /l/ is firm throughout the poem and is dominant. This gives some force to the final rhyme of the poem in "health." The most effect is achieved however, by contrast; neither /j/ nor /oy/ occurs in the poem until they occur together in the last line in "joyous health." What force the ending has, then, comes from a combination of contrast ("joyous") and culmination ("health").

9. Wordsworth, "Thought of a Briton on the Subjugation of Switzerland." Both sestet and octet end with "heard by Thee," although the sestet has also a following exclamation mark. In octet, sestet, and the poem as a whole, /iy/ is the dominant nucleus. Although /ð/ ranks only twelfth among the consonants of the poem, this is its second-highest rank relative to Wordsworth's ten, against an average rank of 17.1.

The other prominent word of the sonnet is "voice." Both /v/ and /oy/ have their highest ranks relative to Wordsworth's ten, seventh against an average rank of 12.7 for /v/, eighth against an average rank of 14.2 among vowels for /oy/. (/oy/ does not even occur in six of Wordsworth's ten.) The word, of course, is part of the subject of the poem, signaled by its repetition in lines 1 and 2.

Both "Thee" and "voice," then, have prominence by word repetition and phoneme rank relative to Wordsworth's other ten; "Thee" also has the dominant nucleus of the whole poem. The dominant consonants of the sonnet have no culminative force.

10. Wordsworth, "At Dover." In the sestet "cease" has its dominant nucleus and consonant, /s iy/, and "wonder" sums up and concludes the strength of /w/ and /ë/, both high in the octet and limited to it.

In the octet the final word "sin" has the two dominant consonants of the sonnet, but its nucleus, /i/, is only fourth in rank. The word "deaden" sums up a surge in the strength of /d/ in the sestet, and the whole sonnet strength of /e/, its second-ranking nucleus. I sense a rise in the poem with "speaks from out the sea" and "shrieks of crime." This probably is due, first, to the dominance of /s/ and /iy/ in the poem as a whole, and second, to the fact that /p k s ay/ have here their highest ranks relative to Wordsworth's ten, whereas /r/ is high throughout the sonnet.

Although these words may be prominent from the point of view of sound, none of them seems summative with regard to the meaning of the sonnet. In fact, there is a sharp disharmony between the theme, which is that of hush and peace, and the funneling of most of the sound into "speaks" and "shrieks of crime." (But René Wellek's interpretation of the sonnet would make "sin" summative — see his formal discussion.)

11. Keats, "Written in the Fields." The dominant nucleus of the sonnet, /e/, is spent in the octet, where it monopolizes the rhyme scheme. (It is the nucleus most often dominant in the ten Keats sonnets, having first rank six times.) Although it overwhelms other nuclei in the octet, it does not enter with the octet's dominant consonants, /t r n l/, into any summative word.

Several points can be made about the final words. Taken together, "clear ether silently" has the six dominant consonants of the sestet (including /k/) and the five dominant consonants of the sonnet; it has also the three dominant nuclei of the sestet, and /i iy/ do not contrast in their position in these words, (/ir/, /iy#/), so that their effect may seem pooled. (The dominant vowel of the poem, /e/, has been spent in the octet and is commonly dominant in Keats anyway.) All this points to considerable force for the sound of these words, but I am unable to generalize their meaning to the theme of the sonnet.

12. Keats, "On First Looking into Chapman's Homer." In the octet "bold" has two consonants and a nucleus whose weight is largely or wholly confined to the octet; /d/, third in rank for the sonnet, is first for the octet, but only in a four-way tie for eighth rank in the sestet. Both /b/ and /ow/ are weighted only in the octet.

By a slight margin /e/ is the sonnet's dominant nucleus, but it is dominant in neither octet nor sestet alone. This is another instance of Keats' preference for /e/. The octet is dominated by /iy/, the sestet by /ay/. Note that /ay/ is dominant at the moment it occurs in "silent" in line 14, for /e/ has a fair part of its total weight yet to come in "Darien."

Of the dominant sounds, the two chief consonants and two chief nuclei, /n l/ and /e ay/, have in this sonnet their highest rank relative to the Keats ten. My ranking for the consonants is in the order /n l d s t/; this differs from the ranking Lynch reports, /n d l t s/. Lynch, however, ranks the sum of added weights and number of occurrences, whereas I rank only the added weights. If the weights and number of occurrences I obtain are summed, and the sums ranked, the resulting order is the same as that of Lynch. This is encouraging, since it suggests that for this sonnet some differences in weighting and ranking do not obscure what may be considered true dominance.

In view of all this, it is fair to say that my procedure confirms Lynch, finding in "silent" a summative word, both in sound and meaning. It denotes the key emotional response to the poem's theme, as analyzed by Lynch in his paper (although, as Wimsatt has observed may happen, there is no simple English word for the theme itself).

13. Keats, "Happy Is England." None of the results show an integration of sound and meaning in the closing lines of the sonnet.

14. Keats, "When I Have Fears." We can read this sonnet and find "love," "fame," and "nothingness" key words: "love" pointing to the first four lines of the sestet, "fame" to the theme of the octet, and "nothingness" denoting not only the threat of annihilation to both but also the result of contemplating the threat. (The nucleus of "fame" also echoes the rhyme scheme of the octet.)

The word "never," repeated in lines 10 and 11, has the two dominant consonants of the sestet and sonnet /r n/, the dominant nucleus of the sestet and sonnet /e/, and a consonant /v/ which achieves in this poem its highest rank relative to the Keats ten. Since /n l/, the second- and third-ranking consonants of the sonnet, stay relatively strong throughout, and /ë/ emerges sharply in the sestet, "love" and the principally stressed syllable of "nothingness" are given strength, and "love" is repeated in the sestet, the first time occurring before an exclamation mark and a dash (line 12). The relative strength of sounds in "unreflecting" makes it also a suitable key word, contrasting "love" to the reflecting part. The only culminating force that I can clearly see is in the sustained strength of /n/, through the repetitions of "never" into "nothingness" in the final line. The sounds in "never" qualify it as a key word, but its position does not give it a summative role.

15. Keats, "Bright Star." The dominant nucleus of the octet is /a/, but it has only one weighted occurrence after that, whereas /e/ is the dominant nucleus both of the sestet and the whole sonnet. In the sestet /i/ rises sharply, acquiring second rank here and reaching third rank in the whole sonnet.

As to consonants, /s t l r/ dominate the sestet, but the order of dominance in the whole sonnet is /t s r l/. Omitting /a/ as confined mostly to the octet, these dominant sounds are found in the stressed syllable of "unrest" (line 13) and the succeeding words "still, still" (line 14).

The theme of the sonnet is a contrast between motionlessness and motion, between observing the moving waters and feeling a soft fall and swell. (The contrast between observing water and being in it runs through several Keats sonnets.) Between negatives ("not . . . no") the octet describes the unwanted state of motionlessness and apartness, and the sestet describes the wanted state of consummation. The stressed syllables, "rest" and "still," have the same meaning, motionlessness and apartness, yet here each is used with urgency regarding consummation. The words can be seen as expressing the tension between the octet and sestet states (for Keats was against his will in the situation of the "bright star"), or as "immersing," transforming the octet state.

Thus we can see "unrest" and "still, still" as summative both in sound and meaning.

16. Keats, "Keen, Fitful Gusts." In line 9 "friendliness" has the six consonants that are dominant in the sonnet, /r l s d f n/, and its dominant vowel /e/. It is a turning point between the immediate scene and the literary solace, a catalyst for the final lines and hence a clear key word. Of the interweaving of sounds and patterns in the sestet, none emerges as culminative.

17. Keats, "Written in the Cottage Where Burns Was Born." The dominant consonants of the sonnet are /n d m/; these and /b/ achieve here their highest rank relative to the Keats ten, and this is the only sonnet of the twenty in which /m/ achieves rank among the first four. The dominant nuclei of the sonnet are /æ ay ey/; these achieve here their highest rank relative to the Keats ten.

Despite its strength in the last two lines of the octet and the first five of the sestet, /æ/ has no concentrated force. The other dominant sounds are represented in the final words of lines 12 and 13, "blind" and "name." Both relate to the theme of the sonnet. Of course "name" involves the apostrophe "O Burns" in line 2, "pledging a great soul" in line 6, and the idea of "fame" in line 14. We can see "blind" in relation to Burns' infant state, "Happy and thoughtless of thy day of doom!" and to Keats' drunken state, "I cannot see" (line 7) from drink and from thought (line 12). Insofar as these words are taken as identifying two main aspects of the sonnet, they have some summative force, before the apostrophe of the final line, which rings out the poem's theme, identification with the famed poet.

18. Keats, "To Sleep." In the sestet the two dominant nuclei of the sonnet, /i ay/, are relatively weak and have no concentrated force; most of their weight

stems from use in the octet. The dominant nucleus of the sestet is /ow/, which ranks third in the whole sonnet, the highest rank it achieves relative to the Keats ten. The two dominant consonants of the sonnet are /s l/. These and /ow/ occur together in the sonnet's final word "soul."

Note that /z/ and /s/ achieve here their highest ranks relative to the Keats ten; /z/ is notable in the rhyme scheme of lines 6 to 13. This and the absolute dominance of /s/ may reflect phonesthematic associations of English speakers with these sibilants.

I see a connection between "soul" (possibly also "seal") and the theme of the sonnet. This is suggested by the religious terminology of "this thine hymn," "wait the Amen," "save me"; the association of "curious conscience" with the (Prince of?) darkness; the association of saviour Sleep with a key; and the implication of fate after death in the opening and closing lines: "O soft *embalmer* of the still midnight" and "And seal the hushed *casket* of my soul," as well as in "forgetfulness divine." All this indicates a carrying-out through the sonnet of a metaphoric treatment of Sleep as saviour of the soul.

19. Keats, "On the Sonnet." We note that the three dominant consonants of the poem are those in the word "sonnet," /t s n/. We see also that the six dominant consonants of the poem and of the octet (except /l/, the fifth) and the dominant nucleus of the octet /ey/ are found in the stressed syllable of "constrained" (line 4). (And /ey/ achieves in this sonnet its highest rank, third, relative to the Keats ten.) Both these words involve the poem's theme, that is, the constraints proper to an English sonnet.

Of words that occur in the sestet, "let" has the poem's dominant consonant and nucleus, and /l/ itself emerges as the dominant consonant of the sestet. The word itself recurs in lines 4, 7, 11, and 13, organizing much of the poem syntactically. Its appropriateness in this role is seconded by the fact that English has come to refer to two opposed meanings by this one phonemic sequence, permission and hindrance.

In both sound and meaning, then, "constrained" and "let" are appropriate key words.

20. Keats, "The House of Mourning." The dominant nuclei of the sonnet are /i a ey i/, all four of which achieve their highest rank relative to the Keats ten. The first three are dominant in that order in the octet as well, whereas /ay/ is dominant in the sestet but has no weighted occurrences outside it.

The dominant consonants of the sonnet are /r t d p n/; /p/ achieves its highest rank, fourth, relative to the Keats ten, and this is the only time in all twenty that it is among the top four. Of the consonants, /d/ acquires strength in the last three lines in "damned, Wordsworth's, Dover, Dover, *could*." The other dominant consonants occur in "write upon," together with the sestet's dominant nucleus /ay/ and /a/, whose strength has been noted.

Despite some summative force in sound, these words have little summative force in meaning, given the organization of the sonnet. Several of its disjunct items do concern writing, but there is no cumulation. Given the derogatory tone, it is amusing that the final word of the octet, "pot," has sounds which achieve such strength in this sonnet, and that the dominant vowel of the sonnet, /i/, last occurs weighted in "pit" (line 11). More significant is the way the prose stress seems to force metrical stresses into juxtaposition: "to a *friend's cot*," "a *curst lot*," "a *cold cof*fee pot," "a French *bon*net," "who *could write* upon it?" The piling up of ionic feet seems to underscore the display of a collection of vile curiosities.

V

In this section I shall evaluate the approach, relating it to other uses of sound in lyric poetry, in order to see its value and limitations.

As a preliminary, it is necessary to survey the other results obtained by the approach. In his article Lynch reports on analyses of poems by Wordsworth, Arnold, Spender, Collins, Marlowe, Raleigh, and Donne. I have experimented with the approach on a few pieces by William Carlos Williams and one of my own.

Perhaps the results obtained in some of the poems, yielding a summative word, depend on particular forms or conventions, such as lines of fixed length or rhyme. Suspecting that any short poem might exploit sound occurrences in this way, I analyzed several pieces by William Carlos Williams. Only the first resulted in a neat correspondence between dominant sounds and the theme in a summative word. The poem is "Flowers by the Sea":

> When over the flowery, sharp pasture's
> edge, unseen, the salt ocean
>
> lifts its form — chickory and daisies
> tied, released seem hardly flowers alone
>
> but color and the movement — or the shape
> perhaps — of restlessness, whereas
>
> the sea is circled and sways
> peacefully upon its plantlike stem.

It turns out that /s/ is by far the dominant consonant, /iy/ by far the dominant nucleus. Although the word itself occurs but once, these sounds of course form "sea." (And "restlessness" and "peacefully" are second in containing dominant sounds.)

In the other pieces by Williams, "To Waken An Old Lady," "A Sort of Song," and the final stanzas from "To A Dog Injured In The Streets" and "Choral: The Pink Church," the results direct attention to the unobtrusive skill and pattern by which Williams composes a "machine made of words" but do not point to summative or key words. In "A Sort of Song," the high rank of /k/ does direct attention to a series of words (snake, quick, strike, quiet, reconcile, compose, saxifrage, rocks). The dominance in "To Waken An Old Lady" of /s d n/ warns against the excesses to which such a method could lead, if guided by fertile imagination; for we might argue that this delicate waking song specifically avoids the word and thought "sudden," and that repressing the word has forced its consonants into prominence.

Analysis of a poem of my own [30] revealed an organization I had not suspected. The final word "ministry" summed up the dominant phonemes, and, as it turned out, provided a key to the poem's four stanzas, each of which could be seen as expressing a form of ministry.

In his analyses, Lynch has had complete success, although not uniform results. Out of six cases, he found three with summative words (the Keats sonnet, Wordsworth's "I Wandered Lonely as a Cloud," Spender's "Moving through the Silent Crowd"). In one poem difference within the poem matched other facts about it (Arnold's "Dover Beach"); in other poems differences between them matched differences in attitude (Marlowe, Raleigh, Donne); in one (Collins' "Ode Written in the Beginning of the Year 1746") the absence of a summative word was found to correspond appropriately to the poem's thought.

In a sample of twenty sonnets I found that a part clearly had summative words, a part had near-summative words, and a part did not have them at all. Some instances of key words were also found.

On the positive side, then, this can be said. Some short lyrics are so organized that the dominant sounds appear together in a word, appropriately placed, which sums up or gives expression to the subject or theme — there is a coming together both of sound and meaning. For most short lyrics this is probably not true, but charting and totaling the frequency and weighting of sounds directs attention to words and patterns that might be overlooked. It objectifies the occurrence and succession of phonemes and so provides materials the stylistic critic must take into account. If any appeal beyond personal taste is to be made, regarding the significance of sound in a poem, nothing short of a full account of the use of phonemes in the poem will do as a reference point.

It is the grave limitation of the purely intuitive approach (as exemplified by Spitzer) that it takes no such full, objective record into account. But it is equally the grave limitation of a purely statistical approach that it may forget it is dealing with an object, an aesthetic object.

I must reiterate here that this approach does not depend simply on the statistical frequency and weighting of sounds. There are three criteria for a putative summative word to meet; only their successful intersection in the same word is accepted. We may attribute entirely to chance the different dominant sounds among sonnets, although no poet will; it may be that each sonnet by chance will contain one or more words made up of several of its dominant sounds. That this word may also be placed at the end of the sonnet and also sum up the sonnet's theme — this clearly is not an artifact of the sonnet form and the English language; it happens only in about one-third of the twenty cases.

As his formal discussion shows, Fred Householder has subjected the data to

[30] D. H. Hymes, "I Do What I Can," *Accent*, XV (1955), 68.

a penetrating analysis. He points out that the summative or near-summative words almost always contain the consonants which are normally most frequent in English. But it must also be pointed out that the nuclei show much greater variation, among poems and between poets. Moreover, we must face the theoretical alternatives. A poet works with already structured material, language. But though he is not free to choose sounds at random, are we to believe that he can have no effect at all? One literary critic has said that the words considered summative by this approach are also those that his own response to the sonnets would pick out. Moreover, there are aesthetically two different ways to exploit sounds. The poet may work against the structure inherent in his language, so as to give prominence to sounds otherwise less important. Thus, Wordsworth makes /z/ the fourth most important sound in "I Grieved for Buonaparte," despite the fact, pointed out by Householder, that weighting would be expected normally to decrease its importance. The poet may also work with the structure inherent in his material, as the sculptor or carver may work with the structure inherent in his. If the dominant sounds of a poem must always include some or all of a small set of consonants, the poet may choose a word summative in theme which contains them and place it strategically so as to exploit the cumulative effect which his language unavoidably offers.

Finally, as Householder points out, the sounds below the dominant range may be ones to watch especially. Although not attaining dominance in a given poem, because English does not offer this possibility without a bizarre choice of words, such sounds may occur sufficiently in excess of their normal use to deserve notice. (Such are /v/ and /oy/ in Wordsworth's "Thought of a Briton on the Subjugation of Switzerland.")

In general, the comments on the use of words made in a recent review can be applied to the use of sounds:

> [certain words in Mallarmé] seem characteristic because of their absolute frequency in the text, which catches the eye, and not because of their relative frequency, which is not within the reach of linguistic consciousness. This consciousness will be sensitive to a hapax or a rare word but will become less and less discriminating as the words grow more common. That is, its absoluteness is enough to make a frequency visible and stylistically valid; if the frequency happens also to be relative, this interests the linguist but no longer the stylistician. In my opinion, this concept of *stylistic* consciousness as perception of the relation between a fact and a delimited context — not between a fact and the norm of language — makes the interpretation of frequencies more complicated than Guiraud realizes. . . .[31]

Some considerable limitations of the present approach must now be mentioned. Obviously no such approach can say much about long works. As to a poet's general style, the relative frequency and weighting of sounds are, of course, important: perhaps Eliot has a predilection for dental stops, Yeats and Williams a preference for labial stops, in alliterative patterns, perhaps not, but

[31] M. Riffaterre, Review in *Word*, XII (1956), 326.

this can be determined. Presumably, though, the longer the work or passage, the less any particular selection of sounds can escape being submerged by the normal frequencies of the language. The longest test and success are the twenty-four lines of Wordsworth's poem on the daffodils.

Related to this is the question of the domain of an effect. I have had recourse to more limited domains than that of the whole sonnet in analyzing these poems, for example, the culmination of /iy/ in "Sleep!" in the tenth line of Wordsworth's sonnet. One domain or delimited context is clearly the octet and next half-line in Wordsworth's "The World Is Too Much With Us."

A further important limitation is that this approach can take account of stylistic effects that depend on cumulation but not those that depend on contrast. I have given some notice to the effect of contrast, or noncumulation, in remarks on "rejoice" in Wordsworth's "To Sleep" and the initial consonant of "shrine" in Wordsworth's "It Is A Beauteous Evening, Calm and Free." But this approach provides no way to assess objectively the relative *non*cumulativeness, "surprise" value, of the sounds within or between poems, except for the rare sound used but once and then at the climax in a poem. It does not touch the giving of prominence to sounds in more limited domains by contrast with other sounds.

Another limitation which, as far as I know, all stylistic approaches share is the making of untested assumptions about the psychology of poet or audience. Many of these assumptions are reasonable and intuitively correct to the student or practitioner of verbal art. But we do not in fact know that the use of a sound in one part of a poem has any effect on a reader in a subsequent part; we have no "just noticeable differences" for the prominence of sounds by repetition in a sonnet. Rather, we analyze the poem, construct an interpretation, and postulate (or instruct) the reader's response.

The Lynch approach taps only one part of the use of sound in lyric poetry. The tonal organization may operate on levels both above and below that of the phoneme. We can study the use of distinctive features: of series, such as stops, continuants, vowels; of orders, such as labial, dental, velar; of classes, such as front vowels versus back vowels, low vowels versus high vowels. There is no reason to exclude from experimental study any dimension along which sounds can be grouped. Any may turn out to be utilized by one or more poets for particular effect in a particular poem or as a general stylistic trait. Of course, so-called suprasegmental features are important. Insofar as we wish to keep to the norm of the poem, rather than focus on a particular performance, the role of secondary and tertiary stresses in relation to the abstract metrical pattern is of the utmost significance.[32] This role inheres directly in the poem's structure in a way that can be ascertained fairly objectively, whereas voice qualifiers and the like seem much more susceptible to individual difference and momentary performance.

[32] S. Chatman, "Robert Frost's 'Mowing': an Inquiry into Prosodic Structure," *Kenyon Review*, XVIII (1956), 424–425.

The role of stresses in relation to metrical pattern, Chatman has observed, may involve "the close interplay of sound and meaning." [33] And this illustrates a kind of appropriate sound-meaning nexus more general than any Lynch's approach has led us to consider so far. The nexus may simply inhere in the sustained lyric effect of the whole poem, rather than be focused by culmination or contrast at a particular point. Regarding phonemes, the dominant sounds might show greater concentration in some lyrics than in prose; that is, they might account for a significantly greater proportion of occurrences. Or the poem might be a succession of brief domains and local effects, even using patterns of interplay more intricate than have been scored in this study, but none dominating the whole.

Finally, Lynch approaches the poem primarily as a quasi-simultaneous object. It would be equally possible to approach the use of the sounds primarily in terms of successiveness. Such an information theory type of approach would be very informative about the statistics of prominence by contrast and prominence by repetition.

What, then, of style in relation to value in the individual lyric? Wimsatt has argued "every good poem is a complex poem and may be demonstrated so by rhetorical analysis . . . and further it is only in virtue of its complexity that it has artistic unity." [34] Helmut Hatzfeld has argued that "A literary work is good, if the style elements fuse into a style compound as the discovered realization of the author's artistic intention; it is bad, if the style elements are contradictory in themselves, do not fuse into an entity, and do not translate the artistic intention of the author." [35] In a lyric either the complexity and unity of a "concrete universal" or a style compound presumably comprehends the use of sound along with its other components. In some sense, then, there must be appropriateness to the nexus of sound and meaning if the poem is to be regarded as good. It is noteworthy that the positive results obtained by Lynch's approach tend to be in the most highly regarded of the sonnets.

Still, the results of this approach are not themselves a criterion of value. They constitute neither a necessary nor a sufficient condition because they comprehend only a part of the use of sound in lyric poetry. I would say that a sonnet which showed no unity of sound and meaning was not a good one, but there are many ways in which unity can occur. So the absence of a summative word is not critical, and its presence does not guarantee the unity of the other dimensions in the use of sound.

I would say that the results of this approach are indications of value (positive in Wordsworth's "Westminster Bridge," negative in his "At Dover"), but that they are not decisive.

[33] Chatman, p. 437.

[34] W. K. Wimsatt, Jr., "The Structure of the 'Concrete Universal' in Literature," *Publications of the Modern Language Association of America*, LXII (1947), 275.

[35] Hatzfeld, "Stylistic Criticism as Art-minded Philology," p. 65. In *A Bibliography of the New Stylistics* he adds a second check: reference to parallels and literary theory.

David J. Masson

THEMATIC ANALYSIS OF SOUNDS IN POETRY

Most poetry, at least that of Western Europe and Europeanised America, exhibits complex patterning of sounds, over and above the set patterns which belong to the structure of the verse, such as rhymes, Germanic alliteration, formal assonances, or *cynghanedd.* This relatively free and informal patterning resembles that of oratory and advertisement, but is often much more subtle. Some kinds of poetry have a richer patterning, some poorer, of course, but few poems are free from it. It fulfils many functions, rhetorical, dialectical, depictive, imitative, 'musical,' hypnotic, and decorative. Only the most blatant forms are ever fully worked out by a poet, and though some poets have their theories about sounds few of them discuss technique. Indeed, it is not certain that 'technique' is the right pigeon-hole in which to place this phenomenon.

I have attempted to describe and classify types of sound-pattern elsewhere,[1] and more recently to distinguish the various functions.[2] Pattern-analysis demands either an expensive quasi-mathematical notation or a forest of new coinages, neither of which is particularly congenial to readers interested in literature. The original poetry is too easily buried under the weight of such apparatus. I shall take a short cut here, however, by forsaking pattern-analysis proper and listing the smaller and larger combinations of sound that connect words or subjects and that carry what may loosely be called expressive and magical effects. My examples of poetry, English, German and French, are all more or less well known.

When considering the sound-patterning of poetry, one useful concept is that

Reprinted, by permission of the Council, from Proceedings (Literary and Historical) of the Leeds Philosophical and Literary Society. Reprinted also with the permission of the author.

[1] 'Vowel and consonant patterns in poetry,' *Journal of Aesthetics and Art Criticism*, XII (1953), 213–27 [*Reprinted here pp. 3–18.*]; articles in *Modern Language Review*, XLVI (1951), 419–30; *ELH*, XX (1953), 136–60; *Neophilologus* (1954), 277–89; *JAAC*, XIII (1955), 360–69; chapter in *John Keats: a reassessment*, edited by Kenneth Muir, Liverpool, 1958, pp. 159–80.

[2] 'Sound in poetry,' in *Encyclopedia of Poetry and Poetics*, edited by Alex Preminger, Frank J. Warnke and O. B. Hardison, Jr. [Princeton U. Press, 1965, pp. 784–790.]

of *Bond Density*. This is an expression for the richness of phonetic echoes. (Of course, it could also be used for other kinds of echo, for instance those of overtones of meaning.) In the phrase 'Tit for tat' there are a number of bonds, or links, between like sounds. We may reckon these bonds as six, of which two are strengthened (or their score is weighted) by (1) occurrence of the connected sounds at equivalent positions relative to (*a*) syllable, (*b*) word, and (*c*) rhythm, while one bond is also strengthened by (2) the fact that it occurs between stressed sounds. Some weighting may also be given to the opposition between these similar sounds — [t] — and the mutually contrasting vowels which they surround — [ɪ] and [æ] — an opposition which throws their similarity into prominence. Some graded counter-weighting should no doubt be given in accord with their relative separation in time. The phrase would score a certain figure if it were weighted according to agreed rules, and if the figure obtained were divided by a number corresponding to the total length of the phrase (say in syllables) the result would be the index of its *bond density*. In practice, I doubt if a set of rules could be constructed upon which all persons would agree, but in principle the thing is possible and meaningful.

Again in principle, there is for any given language at any given phase in its history an average bond density obtaining in any particular use of words: conversation, working instructions, scientific treatises, political speeches, light verse, lampoons, lyrics, and so forth. Any score in excess of this average might be termed the *bond super-density*. A given poet will often have a characteristic bond density, or at least a characteristic structure of densities; and a given poem, a given passage, a given line, a given phrase will have its individual density. I cannot conceive of a method of scoring which would satisfy myself, even if the stupendous labour of reckoning were practicable; however, I am open to conviction. But it is easy to acknowledge or to demonstrate such characteristics as the extremely high density which is almost universal in a Gerard Manley Hopkins, the frequent but rather isolated passages of high density in a Shakespeare or an Alexander Pope, the single sonnets by Mallarmé which are densely bonded, the generally high density in Rilke, and so forth.

Another concept which is useful here is that of the *motif*. This is the recurrent combination of sounds. The motif in 'Tit for tat' is *t′-t*. (I use a broad phonetic notation but in italics instead of square brackets, and with accents conveniently for stresses.) No doubt some sub-motifs could be abstracted, *t′-* and *′-t*, but we may here ignore these. The phrase contains one motif and embodies one recurrence of it. In a given passage of poetry a number of motifs may intertwine, follow each other in succession or in irregular order, fuse, or return cyclically. In the 'The curfew tolls the knell of parting day, / The lowing herd winds slowly o'er the lea' we have motifs *′-l* (once recurring), *ó:l/ló:* (twice, unless 'slowly' is held to fuse two occurrences itself), *-d* (once), *li/li:* (once), a good assonance in *ɔ́:* (once), and a number of rather faint echoings. There are dormant motifs in these two lines which will come to life when the later lines are recited. The recurrence of a motif constitutes a motif-bond (as distinct from the elemental sound-bond which I have already described), and this type of bond has a reckonable density of its own in any given passage (so long as we can agree which are the motifs).

The patterning produced by a one-element motif may be called a *series* (or if there is only one recurrence, a *couple*). Any other easily recognisable motif usually occurs in *sequence*, that is, without change of order in its elements; *t'-t/t'-t* and *li/li:* are *sequence-pairs* or *straight pairs*. But in 'tolls . . . low' we have a *chiasmus*. More complex patterns can be recognised which undergo more complex permutations. Patterns resembling sequences, but irregular, I call *progressions*. Striking motif-patterns occur as pairs, but in poetry a number of members well above two may be found. I have elaborated elsewhere a descriptive nomenclature and notation for varieties of patterning, but do not propose to deploy these here.[3] The only other expression which will come in handy at present is *bracket:* a pair, somewhere between whose two members is a third, imperfect member: *tolls/knell/lowing* forms a chiasmic bracket from the point of view of the motif in *o:,l.*

As a first exercise of thematic analysis I am taking the first 26 lines of *Paradise Lost.* Here we shall go into more detail than in later examples. I am indebted to Professor Ants Oras of the University of Florida for pointing out to me the patterning of the opening lines. The analysis and interpretations that follow, however, are my own. The pronunciation is conceived to be one contemporary with Milton.

Of Mans First Disobedience, and the Fruit
Of that Forbidden Tree, whose mortal tast
Brought Death into the World, and all our woe,
With loss of *Eden*, till one greater Man
Restore us, and regain the blissful Seat,
Sing Heav'nly Muse, that on the secret top
Of *Oreb*, or of *Sinai*, didst inspire
That Shepherd, who first taught the chosen Seed,
In the Beginning how the Heav'ns and Earth
Rose out of *Chaos:* or if *Sion* Hill
Delight thee more, and *Siloa's* Brook that flow'd
Fast by the Oracle of God; I thence
Invoke thy aid to my adventrous Song,
That with no middle flight intends to soar
Above th' *Aonian* Mount, while it pursues
Things unattempted yet in Prose or Rhime.
And chiefly Thou, O Spirit, that dost prefer
Before all Temples th' upright heart and pure,
Instruct me, for Thou know'st; Thou from the first
Wast present, and with mighty wings outspread
Dove-like satst brooding on the vast Abyss
And mad'st it pregnant: What in me is dark
Illumine, what is low raise and support;
That to the highth of this great Argument

[3] footnote 1 above.

I may assert Eternal Providence,
And justifie the wayes of God to men.

Our first task is to see if some sort of connexion between the meaning and the sound-patterning can be found. There are certainly some general tie-ups between the theme of the words and their sound. What we have to look for are words related both by their subject (or function) and by their phonetic makeup. Where we cannot find such a parallel connexion, we may sometimes discover that the sounds themselves are expressive of the situation.

Let us consider the following sound-linkages, exemplified in the following sets of words, taken usually in order of each set's first member:

First; *Fruit*; *Forbidden Tree*; (*mortal tast*); (*Brought*); (*secret top . . . Oreb*); (*first taught*); (*Fast*). Here the Fall and its instruments are connected together by motifs in *f,r,t* and in *r,s,t*; while the Fall and its Redemption are connected by the motif in *r,s,t* and one in *ɔ:,r,t*. A later reverberation is heard over Horeb, and two more echoes further on, all apparently irrelevant. I shall later refer to these motifs together as theme *A*.

Disobedience; *Forbidden Tree, whose*; *Brought Death into*; *loss of Eden, till*; (*blissful Seat*); (*on the secret top*); (*didst inspire*); (*Seed, In the Beginning*); (*no middle*). Man's original disobedience is linked to its results in his expulsion and mortality, by motifs in *b,d,n*, in *i,d,n,t*, and in *i:,dən*. Some connexion with Moses might be thought established by similar motifs into which *s* or *z*, and/or *p* (as a variant of element *b*) enter. I am going to group these motifs as theme *B*.

World; *all our woe*; *With loss*; *till one* (*greater*). The motif in *w,*(*r*)*,l* cements the passage and again links Fall and Redemption. I call it theme *C*.

One greater Man; (*Restore*); *and regain*. Christ and His action as Saviour are linked by a motif in (*n*), *g*, *r*, *é:*, which shall be theme *D*.

(*Blissful*) *Seat*; (*Sing*); *secret* (*top*); *Sinai, didst inspire*; *Seed*; *Sion*; *and Siloa's*; *Song*; *Soar*; *pursues*. These words nearly all refer to numinous localities or to inspired speech or both. Eden (or the end of the passage upon the Fall) is again linked to Moses (or the next passage of the Book), by a motif in *s,í*(*:*)*,t/d*. Seats of divine inspiration or the Christian muse are connected by a related motif in *sə́i,*(*n*). Lastly an abbreviated version of these motifs, in which *s*'- with a deep vowel opens the final syllable of three successive lines, indicates the poet's break-through into an unheard-of enterprise. I group these motifs together as theme *E*.

That Shepherd; *taught the chosen*. Here Moses and his teaching share a motif in *ð,t,ʃ*, which we shall call theme *F*.

Chosen; *Rose*; *Siloa's*; *flow'd*; (*Fast by the Oracle*); (*Invoke*); (*Aonian*); *Prose*. The connexions here seem ancillary to those of theme *E*. The motifs are in *ó:z* (or *ó:,z* if *Siloa* was not a simple disyllable ['səɪlo:] — compare *Sinai* which may have been ['səɪne:]); in *lo:*; and perhaps in *f/v,l*, in *f/v,o:*, and even in *n,o:*. The motif in *ó:,z*, at least, we shall call theme *G*.

Sion Hill; *Delight*; *Siloa's*. Another ancillary link, restricted to the seats of the divine muse close to Jerusalem. Motif: in *ɔ́i,l.* Theme: *H.* Perhaps motif *lo:* should be placed with *H*, rather than with *G*.

Thence; *adventrous*; *intends*; *unattempted.* Milton's audacious project has the motif in (*ð/d,ɛ́,n,(t),(s/z)*, theme *I*.

My adventrous; *no middle flight*; *Aonian Mount*; *unattempted*; *Temples.* Motifs in *m,(d),n,t*, and in *tɛ́mp*, theme *J*, support theme *I* and its subject; but *tɛ́mp* is last heard in the subsequent passage, irrelevantly.

Pursues; *Prose*; *Spirit*; *dost prefer*; (*upright*); *pure*, *Instruct*; *Wast present*; *outspread*; *satst brooding*; (*Abyss*); *mad'st it pregnant*; *support*; *Providence.* Many of these words are among the key expressions of the last section of Milton's introduction; they describe the operations of the life-giving, and inspiring, spirit of God. The two first words, however, refer us to Milton's intentions, near the end of the previous section. Motifs are in *p,r,s*, in *s,p,r,t* (and *b*, a variation on *p*), and sometimes with *n*. *Present*, *outspread*, and *pregnant* share a richer motif in *prɛ́,(t/d)*, and refer to the original act of Creation. We shall group these motifs as *K*.

(*Spirit*); *dost*; *Instruct*; *know'st*; *first*; *Wast*; (*outspread*); *satst*; *vast* (*Abyss*); *mad'st*; *assert*; *justifie.* Some of these are second-person-singular verbs. Apart from this, the general effect of this motif *st* supports *K*, but we may perhaps detect a directly expressive function. The sounds, or their articulation, suggest effort, aspiration, upward movement, even exaltation. The theme index is *L*.

Prefer; *Before*; (*upright heart*); *pure*; *first*; *assert Eternal.* A set of minor echoes, some of which remind us of theme *A*. Motifs: *p/b,f,r*; *b/p,'-r*; *fə́r*;*ə́r,t.* Theme *M*, apparently supporting the invocation.

Wast present . . . with . . . wings outspread; *mad'st it pregnant: What.* Motif *w,s,t,prɛ́,(z)*; theme *N*; emphasises the image of the lines.

Dove-like satst broo/ding . . . vast Abyss. Motif *d,v,s,(t),st,b'-*; theme *O*; emphasises the image of this line.

Dove-like; *pregnant*; *dark*; *great*; *argument.* Motifs: *d'-,-k*; *r,(ɛ/e:),g,t*; *d/t,r,k/g*; *árk/árg.* Theme *P*, perhaps relates the creating to the inspiring faculty of the Holy Spirit.

And mad'st it; *in me is.* Motif *-nm'-i,s/z*, theme *Q*; supports subject?

Dove-like; *dark Illumine*; *is low*, *raise*; *this great.* Motifs: *d,l,k*; *r,il'-*; *iz/is,ré:.* Theme *R*, a set of minor echoes supporting the general subject and *P*.

Illumine; *Argument.* Further support. Motif *yu(:)m-n*, theme *S*.

So much for the relevance of the detailed sound-structure to aspects of the meaning. Very little of the sound-patterning seems redundant from this point of view. Naturally it cannot have been worked out in cold blood, but it would be strange if Milton were not to some extent aware of the rhetorical excellence of these lines, and had not to a great extent laboured to make them satisfactory. Or if he was totally unconscious of such effects, then his subconscious ear must have been a better artist than his conscious self.

Let us now, however, consider the general structure, and chiefly the coarse-structure, of the sound-patterning. In the first line are announced two main themes, *A* and *B*, something like *fr' st* and *bí(:)dən.* The whole line approximates to *ABA* (with garnishings) in its patterning. Line 2 continues this patterning by encapsulating *B* within an extended *A*, and bringing the long vowel [i:] of the *B*-theme up at the end of this group. An *A* pruned of *f* but partly reduplicated concludes the line. Line 3 begins with a greatly extended and attenuated *B* (incorporating elements from *A*) but introduces twice, in the second half, a new theme *C*, in *w′-l* or *′-l-w′-*. Line 4 repeats *C* twice (again switching the order of its elements as in line 3), first with the stress shunted over and then in a much compressed form; and these repetitions of *C* are found in alternation (firstly) with a strong echo of *B* and (secondly) with a fourth theme *D*, *ngré:*. Line 5 opens with a revised, stress-shunted, *f*-less version of *A*, in which the vowel [ɔ:] now seems to have established a claim; then repeats *D* with a difference; and ends on *E*, *sí:t*, of future importance, heralded by an inverted part-echo of itself fused with a motif echoing 'till' from line 4.

This brings us to the close of Milton's long initial phrase describing his whole subject. We may say that themes *A* and *B* form clearly at the outset and then disintegrate among new themes; or that they burst upon us and then subside. *C* and *D* are restricted in domain. The appearance of *E* presages its triumphant part in the next section, the invocation to Moses' inspiration and the first part of the invocation to the oracle at Jerusalem.

Line 6 produces mainly two versions of this simple theme, *sí* and *sí:-t*. Among occasional part-echoes from *A* and *B*, changed versions of *E* are heard in the next lines. Line 7 has *sə́i* twice, fused with a motif in *sə́i,n*. *E* (as *sí:d*) ends line 8, which begins with the restricted *F*, and the more widespread *G*. The next important statement is *G* again; this opens line 10, which ends in *E* in its line-7 form *sə́i(-)n*, fused with an extended form of *H*. The latter is twice heard in line 11, where as 'Siloa's' it incorporates most of the newer version of *E* and fuses onto *G* with a motif *lo:*, repeated once more at the end of the line. Two [ɒ] vowels, stressed, precede the first, incomplete, statement of theme *I* (which usually approximates to *tέns*). A chiasmus in *k,v* is heard in lines 12–13, faint echoes of *A* continue, a straight pair in *əi,-d* comes in line 13; *I* is heard in lines 13, 14 and 16. The *s′-* of *E* now has a contrasting vowel, at the end of each of lines 13–15. Lines 14–16 have *J* once each (*n,m,d/t*), and line 16 a last echo of *G*.

Thus in this passage we have theme *E* in three (or four) versions, mainly consecutive: *s′-(d/t)* with a shrill vowel; *sə́i* with or without *n*; and *s′-* with a dark or deep vowel. Other more restricted themes combine or contrast with *E*.

Towards the end of the passage are heard faint fore-echoes of *K*, which chiefly appears as *sprt* or *sbrd* in the last section of the introduction, the invocation to the creative spirit of God free from all localities. A partial version of *K* is *L*, worth distinguishing because it is often met alone and concentrated, and because it has an expressive function; this is *st*. *K* and *L* swell out in the earlier part of the section, and *K* is richest in lines 20 and 22. Then they subside (or disintegrate) during the last four lines. Meanwhile line 20 is also picked out by *N* in the form of a progression-bracket, the theme reappearing disorganised in line 22. Line 21 carries *O*, a progression-pair. *P* and *R* are two sets of motifs which slide into one another, whereas *Q* and *S* are single motifs clearly marked out.

The dominant themes of Milton's introduction, therefore, are, successively, *A* with *B*, *E* in three forms, and *K* with *L*; that is, approximately, *frst* with *bí(:)dən*, *sí(:)(t)/sə́i(n)/sO*, and *(s)pr(ɛ́n)t* with *st*. We can detect running throughout, then, an arch-motif or arch-theme *s,t/d*, most easily recognised in the *L*-form of stressed *st*. No quasi-lexical connecting-clue function can well be assigned to this, since at the beginning it is associated with the Fall, and only in later sections can a general connexion with the divine spirit be posited. However, I have already suggested that it may express aspiration or exaltation. The mechanism would be 'kinaesthetic,' on lines suggested by Sir Richard Paget in his search for the origins of speech.[4] Exalted aspiration is what we should expect to find in Milton beginning his great attempt.

To try these methods of analysis on a poet not usually thought rich in sound, let us take one of Donne's *Holy Sonnets*, no. VII. From now on we shall cut down discursive analysis and be more telegraphic.

At the round earths imagin'd corners, blow
Your trumpets, Angells, and arise, arise
From death, you numberlesse infinities
Of soules, and to your scattred bodies goe,
All whom the flood did, and fire shall o'erthrow,
All whom warre, dearth, age, agues, tyrannies,
Despaire, law, chance, hath slaine, and you whose eyes,
Shall behold God, and never taste deaths woe.
But let them sleepe, Lord, and mee mourne a space,
For, if above all these, my sinnes abound,
'Tis late to aske abundance of thy grace,
When wee are there; here on this lowly ground,
Teach mee how to repent; for that's as good
As if thou'hadst seal'd my pardon, with thy blood.

We begin our collections of sound-linkages with theme *A*: *At the round*; *imagin'd corners*; *Your trumpets*; *From death*; *numberlesse*. All one can claim here is that certain words in the opening lines carry motifs in *t,r,ə́,n,d,m,p/b* or some of these elements. (*Round* is [rə́ʊnd] approximately; *trumpets*, *numberlesse* have stressed [ə] in their first syllables.) Something of the glory of the image is brought out by the repetition of sounds.

B: *imagin'd*; *Angells*. A motif in *(i),'-dʒ,n* supports *A*.

C: *corners*; *trumpets*; *arise, arise*. Last-Trump image emphasised by motif in *r,ə,(ə́),(i),z/s*.

D: word-repetition 'arise, arise.'

E: *earths imagin'd*; *trumpets*; *numberlesse*; *infinities*; *scattred*; *bodies*; *did*. Motifs in *s,i,m*, and in *i,n,t/d,s/z*. A faint suggestion (kinaesthetic? acoustic?) of multiplicity and minuteness: myriads of entities dwarfed by the scale of the world.

[4] Sir R. A. S. Paget, *Human Speech*, 1930, pp. 132–75.

F: *soules*; *scattred . . . goe*; (*behold*; *woe*). A loosening straight pair in *s,ó:*, of doubtful relevance, and a simple assonance to the end-rhyme four lines further on.

G: *flood did, and fire shall.* Syntax supported by loosening straight pair in *f,l*, joined by series of *d*-sounds.

H: phrase-repetition of 'All whom.'

I: *dearth*, *age*, *agues*; *Despaire*; (*behold God, and*); *taste deaths.* Deaths linked by motifs using *d*,(*e:*),*έ:/ε,θ,r,n*.

J: *But let them sleepe, Lord*; (*late*; *lowly*). Prayer with the lips suggested kinaesthetically by this muttering *b-tl′-t-l′-pl-d*.

K: (*them sleepe*); *mee mourne a space*; *my sinnes.* The transition from one subject to the other is covered by a bridge-passage motif in *m,n,s*.

L: *if above*; *abound*; *abundance.* A near-pun supported by thrice-repeated *əbə́*.

M: *grace*; *ground*; *good.* Line-ends rhetorically emphasised by *gr′-*, *g′-d*, knotted together in the middle member.

N: *late*; *grace.* Assonant stressed couple, supports the sentence.

O: *here on this*; *ground*; *repent*; *pardon.* Remission of sins, words linked by *r,n,ð/d/t* with stress-shunting.

Observe that *E*, *J*, and possibly *F*, are expressive, though Donne is not usually considered this sort of poet.

General structure: The themes are shorter-lived than in the Milton quotation. There is less need to knit the sonnet together by such patterns of sound, since it is short, and already close-knit by rhymes and tradition. *D*, *H*, and *L* are echoes of sense-groups at least as much as of sound-groups, as one would expect from Donne. On the other hand it is less easy to assign a meaning to the other echoings. The whole is far less highly wrought, though bonded nearly as densely as is Milton's introduction; it is more haphazard. Some motifs have members very brief but stressed; others undergo so much scrambling and stress-shunting that they are difficult to grasp. The short-lived themes suggest tension, a mind jumping from one idea to another, living always at fever-pitch of thought and perhaps of feeling.

I now try analysis on an early German Romantic, Hölderlin (1770–1843). I will take the hackneyed *Hälfte des Lebens*, conveniently short. The poem should be thought of as composed in the poet's Swabian pronunciation, but for our present purposes modern standard Bühnensprache will do.

Mit gelben Birnen hänget
Und voll mit wilden Rosen
Das Land in den See,
Ihr holden Schwäne,
Und trunken von Küssen
Tunkt ihr das Haupt
Ins heilignüchterne Wasser.
Weh mir, wo nehm ich, wenn
Es Winter ist, die Blumen, und wo
Den Sonnenschein

Und Schatten der Erde?
Die Mauern stehn
Sprachlos und kalt, im Winde
Klirren die Fahnen.

Words linked: we begin with *A*: *Mit gelben Birnen.* Motif in *i,b,ə,n*; scrambling brings *i,b* under the stress. Rubrication of image.

B: *Mit . . . Birnen*; *mit . . . Rosen.* Parallel construction, supported by -*ən* plural and the stressed *r's* preceding, and by the disyllables.

C: *gelben*; *hänget.* Motif *έ'ə*, in support.

D: (*Mit gelben*); *voll mit wilden*; *Land in den*; *holden.* What we are concerned with here are various motifs using *t,l,ə,n,d,*(*i*),(*ɔ*). A suggestion of flowing curves, lush drooping languid beauty, in these liquid interchanges of sound.

E: *voll*; *wilden*; *holden.* An unknotting-and-knotting progression; motifs *f'-l/v'-l*; *ɔ́l*, and *'-ldən.* It is convenient to keep this separate from *D*. Adjectives of life and summer.

F: (*Rosen*); *den* *S̩ee*; *Schwäne.* Depending on the pronunciation, there may well be a motif in (*z*),*ə,n,é:*, again rubricating the images.

G: *Und trunken*; (*Küssen*); *Tunkt ihr.* The dominant motif is in *t,úŋk*, but *r,n*, and *u* by itself also come into play, also *k* by itself. General effect of a progression-bracket. Strikingly rubricates the image, and also functions as incantation.

H: *Küssen*; *-nüchterne.* Motif in *ý,ə,n*, connects polar opposites.

I: *Haupt*; *heilig-*. Here *háo/háe* (or *háu/hái*) add to the incantation.

J: *Küssen*; (*-nüchterne*); *Wasser.* Motif *'-sə*, with some assistance from *ər*. Supports *G–I*.

K: *Weh mir, wo nehm ich.* The phrase is rubricated by a motif in *v,é:,m,*(*i:/i*). To these words we add: *wenn*; *Winter ist*; *wo* (again). Now we have a common motif in *v,*(*i*),(*o:*),*n*. Altogether these motifs introduce the change of subject to winter. In the penultimate line *im Winde* re-echoes this theme.

L: *Sonnenschein*; *und Schatten*; *Mauern stehn.* A motif in *n,ə,ʃ,t* connects these words, of which the first two are linked by sense but the third is relatively disengaged. But *-schein*, *Schatten*, *Sprachlos*, (*kalt*), *Fahnen* are joined by a motif in *ʃá/ʃá:* and by simple stressed *a/a:*. *Den Sonnenschein*, *Schatten der Erde*, *im Winde*, and *Klirren die* share a motif in *d,n,s*, and, partly, motifs which include with these sounds *i*- and *e*-sounds. Perhaps we might group all these motifs under one theme of winter or of absence of summer.

M: *kalt*; *Klirren.* Here the *k,l* motif (tongue-cleaning, hence rejecting) suggests bleakness.

General structure and effect. Built into German is a frequently occurring sub-motif in *ən*, and there are several others which incorporate *d*, *s*, and/or *t*. Such echoes are partly neutralised by their very frequency in German, yet we cannot altogether disregard them. They interlace with almost all the themes of a poem. Taking the other elements, however, we find a special arrangement of themes in this poem: themes are comparatively restricted to particular sections in the first stanza, but are relatively overspread through the second stanza. Of particular interest in the first stanza is the 'musical' sound-patterning in its last three lines, a patterning that virtually coincides with the metrical and rhythmical beat-structure, while modulating phonetically between the themes:

G	HJ	
G	I	
I	H(J)	J

and between the stressed vowels approximating to:

u	i	
u	au	
ai	i	a

The whole is an incantation of great authority and a certain effect of mystery.

In the second stanza theme *K* exhibits a different kind of modulation, a quick, stress-shunting, scrambled pattern which goes with the poet's shuddering frantic search for comfort in the pitiless winter. The dark vowels [a], [a:], [ɔ] in stressed positions now seem to emphasise the blackness and waste of the scene. Theme *L* may, moreover, suggest steaming breath, theme *M* metallic chill. However, for a so-called Romantic poet Hölderlin seems rather sparing of expressive sound.

Now let us take a very different poem by the Swiss Conrad Ferdinand Meyer (1825–98): *Möwenflug.*

Möwen sah um einen Felsen kreisen
Ich in unermüdlich gleichen Gleisen,
  Auf gespannter Schwinge schweben bleibend,
  Eine schimmernd weisse Bahn beschreibend,
Und zugleich in grünem Meeresspiegel
  Sah ich um dieselben Felsenspitzen
Eine helle Jagd gestreckter Flügel
  Unermüdlich durch die Tiefe blitzen.
Und der Spiegel hatte solche Klarheit,
  Dass sich anders nicht die Flügel hoben
  Tief im Meer als hoch in Lüften oben,
Dass sich völlig glichen Trug und Wahrheit.
  Allgemach beschlich es mich wie Grauen,
  Schein und Wesen so verwandt zu schauen,
Und ich fragte mich, am Strand verharrend,
Ins gespenstische Geflatter starrend:
  Und du selber? Bist du echt beflügelt?
  Oder nur gemalt und abgespiegelt?
Gaukelst du im Kreis mit Fabeldingen?
Oder hast du Blut in deinen Schwingen?

It is to be noted that the rhymes, all 'feminine,' are arranged in a peculiar order: two couplets, one alternation ABAB, one cyclic group XYYX, then four couplets. We ought to consider the significance of this first. I — The opening two couplets describe the circling seagulls. II — The cross-rhymes describe their reflexion. III — The cyclic rhymes tell us of the absolute interchangeability of the two. IV — The remaining couplets speak of the poet's reactions, his self-questioning. It is clear that I is appropriate to an image of endless circling, the continuous passage of objects. The alternation in II suggests involuntary comparison, the discovery of the same thing in another place. III has the effect of confronting *object* with *image* (the two inner lines ending 'hoben' and 'oben') and surrounding both with the observer's first comment ('Spiegel . . . Klarheit/ . . . Trug und Wahrheit/'). The couplets of IV convey well the rather obsessive, repetitive, bound nature of the poet's thoughts.

Word-links: we begin with *A*: *Möwen*; *einen Felsen kreisen*; *gleichen Gleisen*; *schweben* (*bleibend*); (*schimmernd*); (*beschreibend*). This collection of -*ən* (and -*ənt* or -*ərnt*) at the start helps to link the words that make up the image, but it also goes with the evocation of perpetual motion in a circle, the continual passing of many small objects on one path, their continual return on the same path. Compare rhyme-group I above.

B: *einen*; *kreisen*; *gleichen Gleisen*; *bleiben*, *Eine*; *weisse*; *beschreibend*; *zugleich*; (-*spiegel*). Here we have motifs *áe'ə*(*n*), *láe'ən*, *ráe'ən*, *gláe*, *gl*/*g-l*; (word-repetitions) 'gleich-' and 'eine-'; and the rhyme-extensions in *b,áebənt.* The theme is concentrated in the motifs linking *gleichen* with *Gleisen*, and *gleichen* and *bleibend* severally with *beschreibend*, but has throughout the general property of suggesting monotony, continuity, repetitive dip-and-rise, gliding, smoothness, hypnotic rhythm (compare rhyme-group I and the general 'feminine' rhyme-system). The patterning is largely in unison with the rhythmic and metrical beats of these lines.

C: *Ich*; *unermüdlich.* Motif [ɪç] adds a grace-note in line 2 like the flicker of light on a feather. (Acoustic.)

D: *gespannter Schwinge schweben*; *schimmernd* (*weisse*); (-*spiegel*); (-*spitzen*); (*gestreckter*). Motifs in ʃ, [β], in ʃ*p*'-, and in ʃ,*t*. A suggestion of power, not carried by the meaning of the words so much as by the kinaesthesia; also a hint of 'swishing.'

E: *bleibend*; *Bahn beschreibend.* Motif in *b*,(*áe*/*a:*),*n*,(*t*). Emphasises the locus of the gulls' path, the continuous curve it describes, regarded rather as a fixed, permanent figure.

F: *dieselben Felsen-*; *helle*; (*gestreckter*). Main motif *ɛ́l*(')*ə*(*n*). May have the same function as *B*, and its existence in this position after *B* may also carry an implied suggestion of mirror-images (the subject of the context).

G: *Felsen-*; *Flügel.* (Lines 6–7.) Motif in *f*,*l*, no clear function.

H: *bleibend*; *dieselben*; *blitzen.* Motif *bl*/*lb*, no certain function. Much later with *gə-* (*selber*; *beflügelt*; *gemalt . . . abgespiegelt*; *Fabel-*; *Blut*) it focuses attention on the poet himself and the problem of his genuineness.

I: 'Flügel' repeated twice, again supports the notions of recurrence and reflexion. But see under *P* below.

J: *Flügel*; *unermüdlich*; (*blitzen*). Motif in *l*,*ý:*/*ɪ́*. Expressive of bright grace rather than lexically connective. But *Flügel* (line 10), *völlig* (line 12) may be linked by a straight bracket in *f*,*l*,*g*. Afterwards (lines 12–13) *völlig glichen*, *beschlich*, have motifs either in *liç* alone or in this and in *li,g*. These altered extensions of theme *J* are now implicated in what we may label the poet's 'equivalence assertion,' that object and image (cf. rhymes, III) are indistinguishable.

K: 'Tief-' repeated twice, emphasises the watery depths, and by implication the mysterious psychological regions at which the poet is hinting.

L: *Hoben*; *hoch . . . oben*. Aside from the rhyme, the motif is *h ó:*. It may suggest to some readers the poet instinctively raising his eyes quickly from the reflected movement to the original in the air (since the linked words mean 'raise,' 'high,' 'above') in order to compare them.

M: (*Wahrheit*); *Wesen*; *verwandt*; (*fragte*). Motifs in *v/f,a/a:,r,t*, and in *v'-,n*. Linking these words underlines the poet's confusion of fact and seeming.

N: (*Trug*); *Wahrheit*; (*Grauen*); (*verwandt*); *fragte*; *am Strand verharrend*; (*Geflatter*); *starrend*. Motifs in *a:/a,r,(g,u/u:),t,(fər)*; in *fər,á,nt*; and in *f,r,á/á:*. Meaning, attached to the situation rather than the words, seems to be that of the poet brought to a halt by the awful doubt reaching his consciousness.

O: 'Und' twice at the start of lines 15 and 17, stressed, supports *N*.

P: *Geflatter*; *beflügelt*. Motif in *əfl'-,g,t*, with extra *l*, seems to mark the notion of wings but lacks point. But this third repetition of '-flügel-' (theme *I*) now forces us to accept the poet's symbolic use of the 'wings' image to refer to his psyche, and perhaps to his inspiration.

Q: *beflügelt*; *Gaukelst*; *Fabeldingen*. Motifs in *f,l,ý:/ı́,t/d*, in (*b*),'-'*əlt/d*, and in *'-gəlt/'-kəlt*, connect 'winged' with illusion and jugglery and so support the expression of the poet's doubt.

R: *Gaukelst*; *Kreis*. Motif *k-s* supports *Q*.

S: *Gáukelst dù*; *hàst du Blút*. Motif in *l,st,u:*, and of course 'du' and *t* by itself, connect the polar opposites: the poet's moods as illusion, and as flesh-and-blood emotion.

T: (*Schauen*; *Strand*; *gespenstische*; *starrend*); *abgespiegelt*; *Schwingen*. Various motifs including *ʃ'-ə*, with a vaguely connective function.

The high proportion of *expressive* motifs may be noted.

General structure: The effect of the monotonous rhythm and the monotonous 'feminine' rhymes, especially when in couplets, is to some extent supported by the free sound-pattern themes, particularly by *B* and *I*, but it is in other respects countered by them, especially by *D*, *F*, *J*, and *M*. By comparison with Hölderlin's poem (and the Milton passage) many of the motifs here are short or, where long, unimpressive; *B* and *N* are exceptions. Indeed, though *B* and still more *N* dominate early and late sections respectively, there is a certain general effect of battering chaos and mess (bond density is very high but organisation in a formal sense, outside the structure itself, is low). Perhaps this confusion accords with the inner meaning of the poem, but to some extent it smothers the message and exhausts the reader, leaving him with an impression of some kind of neurotic fatigue. Much of this impression is kinaesthetic: anyone, for example, who tries to read to himself 'Ins gespenstische Geflatter starrend' will find he has stumbled on something of a tongue-twister.

Last of all, I take the closing stanzas of *Oceano Nox* by Hugo (1802–85). In uniform practice with the previous examples, motifs will be printed in a phonetic notation in italics, and *not* in French quasi-orthography. Thus *e* represents French 'é' and similar sounds, not French 'e' which is represented by *ə*; *u* stands for French 'ou,' but *y* for French 'u' etc.; *j* is a semivowel.

Et quand la tombe enfin a fermé leur paupière,
Rien ne sait plus vos noms, pas même une humble pierre
  Dans l'étroit cimetière où l'écho nous répond,
    Pas même un saule vert qui s'effeuille à l'automne,
    Pas même la chanson naïve et monotone
  Que chante un mendiant à l'angle d'un vieux pont!

Où sont-ils, les marins sombrés dans les nuits noires?
Ô flots, que vous avez de lugubres histoires!
  Flots profonds, redoutées des mères à genoux!
    Vous vous les racontez en montant les marées,
    Et c'est ce qui vous fait ces voix désespérées
  Que vous avez le soir quand vous venez vers nous!

The rhyme-scheme tells us that each stanza ought to begin with a statement, followed by a longer comment or answer which returns deviously to its original point. In fact, the argument is not so rigid and could not be, should not be over all the stanzas.

Word-links — *A*: *enfin a fermé*. A piece of rather slick rhetoric, motif *-f-* with stress-shunt.

B: rich-rhyme *paupière/pierre*; also these with *fermé*, *rien*, *cimetière*, *vert*. Motifs *pjɛr*; *jɛr*; *r,j,ɛ/ɛ̃*; *ɛr*; also the *p-* connecting this rich rhyme to the other in *répond*, *pont*. An elegiac effect in syllable [ɛ:ʀ].[5] And one might suspect that *pierre/cimetière* is a crude piece of 'programme-music' to suggest 'l'écho' that 'nous répond.' Compare *C*.

C: (*Quand*; *enfin*; *Dans*); *chante . . . mendiant . . . angle*. Motifs *ã* and *ãt*, a piece of barefaced onomatopoeia for the beggar's song.

D: *l'étroit*; *cimetière*; *l'écho*; *répond*. Line 3, motifs in *l,e,t,r* or some of them. More 'écho'?

E: rich-rhyme *automne/monotone*. The poem is supplied with more rich rhymes than ordinary rhymes, and this whole stanza is rich-rhymed.

F: repetitions of 'même' and 'Pas même.' Simple rhetoric.

G: (*tombe*; *noms*; *répond*; *chanson*; *pont*); *sont-ils*; *sombrés*; *profonds*; *montant*. Motif *õ*, tolling effect, also *sõ* and *p,õ*. We are now embarked on the last stanza.

H: *Où*; *vous avez* (lines 2 and 6); *redoutés*; *genoux*; *Vous vous* (line 4) and *vous* (line 5); *voix*; *vous venez vers nous*. Here are (i) word-repetition, the invocation to the waves; (ii) motif *u* suggesting ululation, but also ominous (grief,

[5] Pope uses [ẹ:] in graceful lament; *Elegy to the Memory of an Unfortunate Lady*, lines 43–44, 47–50 (*away*, *gaze*, *day*, *Shade*, *unpaid*, *complaint*, *pale*, *grac'd*). For the phonetic value at this date cf. Helge Kökeritz, *Mather Flint on Early Eighteenth Century Pronunciation*, Uppsala, Leipzig, 1944.

fear, storm-wind); (iii) motif *v*- (grief? wind?); [6] (iv) combinations culminating in *vuv-n-v-nu* at the close, a pure 'musical' incantation, though rather a forced one.

I: *marins*; (*sombrés*); *nuits noires*. Motifs *ar* and *n*-, combined. The first, in a French linguistic environment, suggests storm, violence.[7] The second is rhetorical emphasis. Both reintroduce the subject of men lost at sea.

J Ô flots; *Flots profond*; (*fait*). Word-repetition; and motifs in *o* and *f*, combined. Very similar in effect, though more restricted and slight, to the *u* and *v* of *H*.

K: *redoutés*; *racontés*; (*montant les marées*. Motif in *r*,(*a*),*t*,*e*; irrelevant?

L: *marins*; *mères à*; (*montant les*) *marées*. Motif in *m-r*,*a*. Probably unconscious infection: the mothers on their knees may have been partly suggested by the sound of the 'marins' and 'marées.' Also *m*- simple.

M: rich-rhyme *genoux*/*nous*.

N: rich-rhyme *marées*/*désespérées*.

O: *Et c'est ce*; *désespérées*. This motif, *esɛ̀s*/*ezɛ̀s* (line 5) (plus trimmings) is perhaps wind-music.

P: *Qui*; *que*; *quand*. Probably accidental and inevitable, like the echoes due to thick sprinkling of definite articles.

The proportion of expressive motifs (*B–D*, *H–J*, *O*), particularly with onomatopoeic and suggestive vowels, is very high. There are almost no pure meaning-links, but much verbal repetition, and some of the assonance and alliteration is rather coarse.

General structure. Ubiquitous in French are systems of motifs in [le], [lə], [la], [de], [də], [dy], [dez] and so on. They have to be largely ignored. Observe the piecemeal nature of many of the motifs, in contrast with the more frequently rich, multi-consonantal, and interestingly modulated patterns in English or German. (An exception to the general picture is *H* (iv) but this is severely restricted in time.) To some extent this difference is a reflexion of the syllabic structure of French; to some extent, of its relatively even accentuation but agility of articulation, where almost every sound is precisely placed.

In this particular poem, too, there is not such careful 'placing' of themes for effect as in Hölderlin's poem or even in Milton's lines, except for the setting of *C* and *H* (iv) at the ends of stanzas. Themes *B* and *D* are important in the penultimate stanza, themes *G*, *H* and *J* in the last one. Others are striking but restricted in extent. A point about such 'placing' is that both Milton's blank verse and Hölderlin's rhymeless odes of varying line-lengths, call for this kind of formal support from the otherwise free sound-patterning, whereas elaborate rhyme-schemes, 'feminine' rhymes, and rich rhymes, all tend to make such support unnecessary. All this is not to say that these stanzas lack high density of sound-bonding: the thirteen themes which are not mere rich rhymes represent a great wealth of motifs many of which are strongly reinforced by stress (for French) and position.

[6] Maurice Grammont, *Petit traité de versification française*, 13e éd., Paris, 1949, pp. 140–41.

[7] D. I. Masson, 'Vowel and consonant patterns . . . ,' *JAAC*, XII (1953), 219 referring to pattern 18 on p. 216. [*Reprinted here pp. 3–18.*]

I have analysed five selections of well-known poetry of considerable diversity. The analyses attempt to bring out contrasts in sound-patterning related to differences in the languages, in the form, the tone, the writer's personality and interests, and of course the literary climate of his time.

The methods of thematic analysis which I have thus explored might be selectively employed for any one or two of such purposes. A particular writer could be examined to see whether his work shows development in time, or whether his habits of sound-patterning are characteristic and uniform. Writers of a particular school or period might show similarities or contrasts in their sound-patterning. The comparison of different eras might disclose trends and fashions. Study of similar writers in different languages would perhaps reveal the essential differences of the potentialities in sound-patterning between one tongue and another. With care, the method may be extended to prose. Any demonstration, from a mathematically or scientifically minded reader, of some adequate statistical or mechanical way of attacking all these intricacies would be welcome; but if such weapons cannot penetrate the subtlest recesses of poetic craft and style, the variable and faulty but receptive human brain must do its best.

Part Two

METRICS

Among all literary topics, metrics has particularly attracted linguists. Clearly a subject in phonology and evidently systematic, it affords an opportunity for the kind of exact inquiry into particulars that is their usual stock in trade. Furthermore, it has been subject to such unclear treatment in the past, with such confusion of terms and misunderstandings about the nature of its linguistic elements, that linguists sympathetic to literary study feel it almost a duty to shed whatever light they can upon a needlessly darkened situation.

The necessity of re-examining and re-defining old terms was already clear to Jespersen in 1900. He recognized that the stress system of English was more complex than the metrical system, and asserted an essential principle — the relativity of ictus; that is, whether a syllable carries ictus is determined not intrinsically but by its environment. A comparatively light linguistic stress may be ictic because it occurs between still lighter stresses, while a comparatively heavy stress may be nonictic because it occurs between still heavier stresses. The principle is reaffirmed in different terms in each of the articles in this section. It is noteworthy that even the conservative statement of Wimsatt and Beardsley strongly espouses this principle (although with the implication that, as a consequence, the metrist need not concern himself further with linguistic details).

The further inference, again recognized in almost every article, is that one has to do with *two* systems in any performance of a poem, the metrical system (with its events and prominences), and the suprasegmental system of English (with its stresses, intonations and junctures, however they are analyzed). These co-existent systems are given different names: meter vs. performance, (traditional) meter vs. "rhythm" (potential or core), meter vs. its actualization, abstract frame vs. actual instance, schema or "normative fact" vs. particular, etc. Similarly, the relation between them is named variously: tension, interplay, counterpoint. But despite the variation in terminology, the principle is the same, and the solidarity of view inspires confidence in the validity of the distinction.

To what extent need the metrist be concerned with the linguistic specification of meter? Wimsatt and Beardsley think not at all, for the very reason that ictus-determination is a relative matter. But they acknowledge (and the linguist would assert) that there are "different estimates of significance." Wimsatt and Beardsley are content with the practical. The linguistic metrist is more likely to be theoretical: he wants to know as precisely as possible how and which elements of the language serve the metrical functions. The difference in attitude is not a matter of right or wrong, but simply of relative interest. One can hardly expect the literary critic to be as concerned with linguistic detail as are linguists; but, on the other hand, the relative disinterest of critics is surely no reason for linguists to limit *their* inquiry. It is not totally inconceivable, furthermore, that the linguists' greater concern with the linguistic surface may enable them to develop a neater analysis of the metrical system *per se*. This is perhaps what Hollander means when he speaks of the utility of phonology as a heuristic model for metrical analysis. (One should also note the considerable discussion of meter in Jakobson's essay, pp. 303–312.)

Otto Jespersen

NOTES ON METRE[1]

§ **1.** The iambic pentameter may without any exaggeration be termed the most important metre of all in the literatures of the North-European world. Since Chaucer used it in its rimed form (the heroic line) and especially since Marlowe made it popular in the drama in its unrimed form (blank verse), it has been employed by Shakespeare, Milton, Dryden, Pope, Thomson, Cowper, Wordsworth, Byron, Shelley, Tennyson, by Lessing, Goethe, and Schiller, as well as by numerous Scandinavian poets, in a great many of their most important works. I shall here try to analyse some peculiarities of this metre, but my remarks are directly applicable to other metres as well and indirectly should bear on the whole metrical science, which, if I am right in the theories advanced below, would seem to require a fundamental revision of its principles, system of notation, and nomenclature.

According to the traditional notation the metre mentioned above consists of five iambi with or without an eleventh weak syllable:

⏑ – | ⏑ – | ⏑ – | ⏑ – | ⏑ – | (⏑)

Her eyes, | her haire, | her cheeke, | her gate, | her voice. (1)
Give ev' | ry man | thine ear, | but few | thy voyce: | (2)
Take each | mans cen | sure, but | reserve | thy judg' | ment [2] (3)
Ein un | nütz Le | ben ist | ein früh | er Tod. (4)
Zufrie | den wär' | ich, wenn | mein Volk | mich rühm | te. (5)

[1] Read in Danish in the "Kgl. danske videnskabernes selskab" on the 16. Nov. 1900, printed as "Den psykologiske grund til nogle metriske fænomenet" in *Oversigt*, 1900, p. 487. Here translated with a few re-arrangements and many omissions, chiefly with regard to Danish and German examples and the refutation of the views of the Danish metrist E. V. D. Recke.

[2] The places from which quotations are taken will be indicated at the end of the paper. Quotations from Shakespeare are given in the spelling of the 1623 folio, except that sometimes an apostrophe is substituted for a mute *e*, and that the modern distinction of *u* and *v*, and of *i* and *j* is carried through.

§ **2.** But pretty often we find deviations from this scheme, a "trochee" being substituted for an "iambus." This phenomenon, which may be called briefly inversion, is especially frequent in the first foot, as in

– ⏑ ⏑ – ⏑ – ⏑ – ⏑ – ⏑
Told by | an id | iot, full | of sound | and fu | ry. (1)

Even two "trochees" may be found in the same line, as in

– ⏑ ⏑ – – ⏑ ⏑ – ⏑ – ⏑
Tyrants | themselves | wept when | it was | report | ed (2)
Ihn freu | et der | Besitz; | ihn krönt | der Sieg (*ihn* emphatic). (3)

Why, now, are such inversions allowed? How is it that the listener's sense of rhythm is not offended by the fact that once or even twice in the same line he hears the very opposite movement of the one he expected, a "trochee" instead of an "iambus"? He expects a certain pattern, a regular alternation in one particular way of ten syllables, and his disappointment at encountering one trochee can be mathematically expressed as affecting two tenths of the whole line; in the case of two trochees his disappointment is one of four tenths or two fifths; and yet he has nothing like the feeling of displeasure or disharmony which would seize him if in a so-called "hexameter" like

Strongly it bears us along in swelling and limitless billows

an "anapaest" were substituted for a "dactylus":

It is strong, bears us along in swelling and limitless billows;

or if in

Jack is a poor widow's heir, but he lives as a drone in a beehive

we substituted an "amphibrach":

Behold a poor widow's heir, but he lives as a drone in a beehive.

Naturally science cannot rest contented by calling deviations "poetical licences" or by saying that the whole thing depends on individual fancy or habit: as poets in many countries, however different their verse is in various other respects, follow very nearly the same rules, and to a great extent followed these before they were established by theorists, there must be some common basis for these rules, and it will be our task to find out what that basis is.

§ **3.** The permissibility of a trochee in an iambic metre is very often justified by the assertion that purely iambic lines following one another without intermission would be intolerably monotonous and that therefore a trochee here and there serves to introduce the pleasing effect of variety.[3] But there are several objections to this view. In the first place even a long series of perfectly regular lines are not disagreeably monotonous if written by a real poet. In

[3] "Their attractiveness may be due precisely to the fact that the accent of the first foot comes as a surprise to the reader," Sonnenschein, *Rhythm* 105.

one of Shakespeare's finest scenes we find in the first hundred lines not more than four inversions (*As you like it* II. 7); it can hardly be those four lines which make the whole scene so pleasing to the ear. In Valborg's speech in Øhlenschläger's *Axel og Valborg* III.69 we have 28 beautiful lines without a single deviation from the iambic scheme.

Secondly, if harmony were due to such irregularities, it would be natural to expect the same effect from similar deviations in trochaic and other metres. The reader of Longfellow's *Hiawatha* will no doubt feel its metre as much more monotonous than the five-foot iambus, yet here no deviations would be tolerated; an iambus in a trochaic metre is an unwelcome intruder, while a trochee in an iambic line is hailed as a friendly guest.

Thirdly, the theory gives no explanation of the fact that the use of trochees is subject to some limitations; if the only purpose were to relieve monotony, one would expect trochees to be equally welcome everywhere in iambic verses, but that is very far from being the case. True, the rare occurrence of trochees in the fifth foot is explained by saying that deviations from the ordinary pattern are always best tolerated in the beginning of the verse, because then there is still time to return to the regular movement. But if this were the only reason, we should expect trochees to tend to decrease as we approached the end of the line, the second foot presenting more instances than the third, and the third than the fourth; but this again does not tally with the actual facts, for the second foot has fewer inversions than any other foot except the fifth. König gives the following numbers for Shakespeare:

first foot more than	3000,
second foot only	34,
third foot more than	500,
fourth foot more than	400.

(*Der Vers in Shakespeares Dramen.* Strassburg 1888, Quellen und Forschungen 61, p. 79, cf. 77. Only "worttrochäen" are here numbered, not "satztrochäen.")

§ **4.** If we are to arrive at a real understanding of the metre in question and of modern metre in general, it will be necessary to revise many of the current ideas which may be traced back to ancient metrists, and to look at the facts as they present themselves to the unsophisticated ears of modern poets and modern readers. The chief fallacies that it is to my mind important to get rid of, are the following:

(1) *The fallacy of longs and shorts.* Modern verses are based primarily not on length (duration), but on stress (intensity). In analysing them we should therefore avoid such signs as – and ⏑, and further get rid of such terms as iambus (⏑ –), trochee (– ⏑), dactylus (– ⏑ ⏑), anapaest (⏑ ⏑ –), pyrrhic (⏑ ⏑), choriamb (– ⏑ ⏑ –), etc. To speak of an iambus and interpret the term as a foot consisting of one weak and one strong syllable is not quite so harmless a thing as to speak of consuls and mean something different from the old Roman con-

suls. It is not merely a question of nomenclature: the old names will tend to make us take over more than the terms of the old metrists. — There are other misleading terms: what some call "arsis" is by others termed "thesis," and inversely.

(2) *The fallacy of the foot*, i.e. the analysis of a line as consisting of parts divided off by means of perpendicular straight lines ⏑ – | ⏑ – | ⏑ – | etc. Such signs of separation can only delude the reader into "scanning" lines with artificial pauses between the feet — often in the middle of words and in other most unnatural places. On the other hand a natural pause, occasioned by a break in the meaning, may be found in the middle of a foot as well as between metrical feet. It is also often arbitrary where we put the division-mark: Are we to scan Tennyson's line

The de | light of | happy | laughter
or
The delight | of hap | py laugh | ter?

The line mentioned above (§ 1.1) is analysed by E. K. (now Sir Edmund) Chambers in his Warwick ed. of Macbeth as having "the stress inverted in every foot" and a dactylus in the first:

Told′ by an | i′diot, | full′ of | sound′ and | fu′ry.

Some metrists (Bayfield among them) even incline to treat such lines as § 1.3 as "trochaic" with an anacrusis:

Take | each mans | censure, | but re | serve thy | judg'ment.

In such cases it would almost seem as if the vertical stroke were used as the bar in music, to indicate where the strong note or stress begins, though most metrists would deny the legitimacy of that analogy.

We shall see below that the abolition of the fallacy of the foot will assist us in understanding the chief irregularities of blank verse.

(3) *The fallacy of two grades.* The ancients recognized only longs and shorts though there are really many gradations of length of syllables. In the same way most of the moderns, while recognizing that stress is the most important thing in modern metres, speak of two grades only, calling everything weak that is not strong. But in reality there are infinite gradations of stress, from the most penetrating scream to the faintest whisper; but in most instances it will be sufficient for our purposes to recognize four degrees which we may simply designate by the first four numbers:

4 strong
3 half-strong
2 half-weak
1 weak.

It is not always easy to apply these numbers to actually occurring syllables, and it is particularly difficult in many instances to distinguish between 3 and 2. Unfortunately we have no means of measuring stress objectively by instruments; we have nothing to go by except our ears; but then it is a kind of consolation that the poets themselves, whose lines we try to analyse, have been guided by nothing else but *their* ears — and after all, the human ear is a wonderfully delicate apparatus.

§ **5.** Verse rhythm is based on the same alternation between stronger and weaker syllables as that found in natural everyday speech. Even in the most prosaic speech, which is in no way dictated by artistic feeling, this alternation is not completely irregular: everywhere we observe a natural tendency towards making a weak syllable follow after a strong one and inversely. Rhythm very often makes itself felt in spite of what might be expected from the natural (logical or emotional) value of the words. Thus syllables which ought seemingly to be strong are weakened if occurring between strong syllables, and naturally weak syllables gain in strength if placed between weak syllables. *Uphill* is 24 in *to walk uphill*, but 42 in *an uphill walk*. *Good-natured* is 44, but becomes 43 or 42 in *a good-natured man*. The last syllable of *afternoon* is strong (4) in *this afternoon*, but weaker (2 or 3) in *afternoon tea*. *Back* is weaker in *he came back tired* than in *he came back with sore feet*, etc.

Illustrations of this principle are found in the following verse lines in which the middle one of the three italicized syllables is weakened, giving 434 (or 424) instead of 444:

But *poore old man*, thou prun'st a rotten tree. (1)
The course of *true love ne*ver did run smooth. (2)
Oh that this *too too sol*id flesh would melt. (3)
You are my ghests: do me no *foule play, friends.* (4)
The *still sad mus*ic of humanity. (5)
A *long street climbs* to *one tall-tow*er'd mill. (6)
Doch sein geschwungner *Arm traf ih*re Brust (*ihre* emphatic). (7)

§ **6.** Of two successive weak syllables that one is the relatively stronger which is the further removed from the strongly stressed syllable; consequently we have the formula 412 in *happily, gossiping, lexicon, apricot, Socrates*, etc., and the inverse 214 (or 314) in *condescend, supersede, disinter;* 2141 in *collocation, expectation, intermixture*, 21412 in *conversational, international, regularity*.

The effect of surroundings is seen clearly in the following line, where *when one* is 23 after the strong *know*, and 32 before the strong *lives:*

I know when one is dead, and when one lives. (1)

Other examples (*I, and, when* — now "weak," now "strong" without regard to meaning) are found in the passage analysed below in § 24. *It is* according to circumstances may be 12 or 21, and the same is true of *into* in Shakespeare and other poets. *Is* is "strong," i.e. 2 between two weak syllables (1) in

A thing of beauty is a joy for ever —

and any page of poetry affords examples of the same phenomenon.

§ **7.** Our ear does not really perceive stress relations with any degree of certainty except when the syllables concerned are contiguous. If two syllables are separated by a series of other syllables, it is extremely difficult even for the expert to tell which of them is the stronger, as one will feel when comparing the syllables of such a long word as *incomprehensibility: bil* is the strongest, *hen* is stronger than both *pre* and *si*, but what is the relation between *hen* and *com?* or between *in* and *ty?* Another similar word is *irresponsibility*, only here the first syllable is stronger than the second. What is decisive when words have to be used in verse is everywhere the surroundings: the metrical value of a syllable depends on what comes before and what follows after it.

Even more important is the fact that we have to do with *relative degrees of force only:* a sequence of syllables, a verse line may produce exactly the same metrical impression whether I pronounce it so softly that it can scarcely be heard at two feet's distance, or shout it so loudly that it can be distinctly perceived by everyone in a large theatre; but the strongest syllables in the former case may have been weaker than the very weakest ones in the latter case.

§ **8.** This leads us to another important principle: the effect of a *pause:* If I hear a syllable after a pause it is absolutely impossible for me to know whether it is meant by the speaker as a strong or as a weak syllable: I have nothing to compare it with till I hear what follows. And it is extremely difficult to say with any degree of certainty what is the reciprocal relation between two syllables separated by a not too short pause.

§ **9.** Let us now try to apply these principles to the "iambic pentameter." The pattern expected by the hearer is a sequence of ten syllables (which may be followed by an eleventh, weak syllable), arranged in such a way that the syllables occupying the even places are raised by their force above the surrounding syllables. It is not possible to say that the scheme is

14 14 14 14 14 (1),

for this is a rare and not particularly admired form, as in

Her eyes, her haire, her cheeke, her gate, her voice. (1)
Of hairs, or straws, or dirt, or grubs, or worms. (2)

Lines of that type were pretty numerous in the earliest days of blank verse, in Gorboduc and in Peele. But it was soon felt that it was much more satisfactory to make the difference in force between the strong and the weak elements of the line less than that between 1 and 4 and at the same time less uniform, for the only thing required by the ear is an upward and a downward movement, a rise and a fall, an ascent and a descent, at fixed places, whereas it is of no importance whatever how great is the ascent or the descent. It is therefore possible to arrange the scheme in this way, denoting the odd syllables by *a* and the even ones by *b:*

a╱b╲a╱b╲a╱b╲a╱b╲a╱b(╲a) —

or, if we denote relative strength by a capital,

aBaBaBaBaB(a).

§ **10.** It is the relative stress that counts. This is shown conclusively when we find that a syllable with stress-degree 2 counts as strong between two 1s, though it is in reality weaker than another with degree 3 which fills a weak place in the same line because it happens to stand between two 4s. This is, for instance, the case in

The course of true love never did run smooth (1):

did (2) occupies a strong place though no sensible reader would make it as strong as *love*, which counts as weak in the verse.

In consequence of this relativity it is possible on the one hand to find lines with many weak syllables, e.g.

It is a nipping and an eager ayre. (2)

Here *is* and *and* on account of the surroundings are made into 2s; the line contains not a single long consonant and only two long vowels.

On the other hand there are lines with many strong and long syllables, such as

And ten low words oft creep in one dull line. (3)
The long day wanes: the slow moon climbs: the deep
Moans round with many voices. (4)
Thoughts blacke, hands apt, drugges fit, and time agreeing. (5)
Day, night, houre, tide, time, worke, and play. (6)
Rocks, caves, lakes, fens, bogs, dens, and shades of death. (7)

In lines like the last two, however, the pauses make the regular alternation of 3 and 4 difficult or even impossible.

With inversion in the beginning we have Browning's dreadfully heavy

Spark-like mid unearthed slope-side figtree-roots (8)

A comparison of such extremes of light and heavy lines shows conclusively that *quantity as such has no essential importance in the building up of blank verse.*

The principle of relativity allows an abundance of variety; there are many possible harmonious and easy-flowing verses, with five, or four, or three really strong syllables (degree 4); and the variety can be further increased by means of pauses, which may be found between the lines or at almost any place in the lines themselves, whether between or in the middle of so-called feet.

So much for the normal "iambic pentameter."

§ **11.** Let us now analyse a line with inversion, e.g.

Peace, children, peace! the king doth love you well. (1)

The stress numbers for the first four syllables are 4314 (or possibly 4214, though 3 seems more likely than 2 for the second syllable). Here the ear is not disappointed in the first syllable: after the pause preceding the line one does not know what general level to expect: a syllable which objectively is pretty strong might turn out to be a relatively weak introduction to something still stronger. A mathematician might feel tempted to express this in the following way: the proportion between the 0 of the pause and the 4 of a strong syllable is the same as between 0 and the 1 of a weak syllable.

It is therefore not till this strong syllable is followed by one that is weaker instead of stronger that the ear experiences a disappointment and feels a deviation from the regular pattern. But the transition from the second to the third syllable is a descent in strict conformity with the pattern; and in the same way there is perfect regularity in the relation between the third and the (strong) fourth, and indeed in the whole of the rest of the line. The scheme accordingly is the following:

$$a\diagdown b\diagdown a\diagup b\diagdown a\diagup b\diagdown a\diagup b\diagdown a\diagup b,$$

which should be compared with the scheme given above, § 9, as normal.

This amounts to saying that while according to the traditional way of notation one would think that the departure from the norm concerned two-tenths (one-fifth) of the line if one heard a "trochee" instead of an "iambus," the ear is really disappointed at one only out of ten places. The deviation from the norm is thus reduced to one-tenth — or even less than that, because the descent is only a small one. The greater the descent, the greater will also be the dissatisfaction, but in the example analysed the descent was only from 4 to 3. A beginning 4114 is comparatively poor, but 4314 or 4214 does not sound badly, for from the second syllable (or from the transition to the third) one has the feeling that everything is all right and the movement is the usual one. In the case of two inversions in the same line we have in two places (not in four!) disappointments, each of them amounting to less than one-tenth, and so far separated from the other that they do not act jointly on the ear.

§ **12.** We shall now collect some classified examples which tend to show that poets have instinctively followed this hitherto never formulated principle.

A. First we have instances in which the three syllables concerned belong to the same word. Such words, of the stress-formula 431 or 421, are very frequent in Danish and German; I have therefore been able to find a great many lines like the following:

Sandhedens kilder i dets bund udstrømme. (1)
Staldbroder! hav tålmodighed med Axel. (2)
Granvoxne Valborg! — Elskelige svend! (3)
Kraftvolles mark war seiner söhn' und enkel. (4)
Unedel sind die waffen eines weibes. (5)
Hilfreiche götter vom Olympus rufen. (6)

In English, on the other hand, words of this type are comparatively rare, and in Elizabethan times there was a strong tendency to shift the stress rhythmically so as to have 412 instead of 431 or 421, thus in *torchbearer*, *quicksilver*, *bedfellow*, etc. (references in my *Modern Engl. Gr.* I 5.45). Cf. also the treatment of *berry* in *gooseberry*, *blackberry*, and of *kerchief* in *handkerchief*. But we have 431 in

Sleek-headed men, and such as sleepe a-nights. (7)
Grim-visag'd warre hath smooth'd his wrinkled front. (8)
All-seeing heaven, what a world is this? (9)

§ **13.** B. The first two syllables form one word.

Doomesday is neere, dye all, dye merrily. (1)
Welcome, Sir Walter Blunt, and would to God . . . (2)
England did never owe so sweet a hope. (3)
Something that hath a reference to my state. (4)
Nothing that I respect, my gracious lord. (5)
Ofspring of Heav'n and Earth, and all Earths Lord. (6)
Noontide repast, or Afternoons repose. (7)

This is frequent in Danish:

Valborg skal vorde Axel Thordsøns brud. (8)
Alting er muligt for et trofast hjerte. (9)

§ **14.** The first word is one syllable, the second two or more.

Urge neither charity nor shame to me. (1)
Dye neyther mother, wife, nor Englands queene! (2)
Peace, master marquesse, you are malapert. (3)
Peace, children, peace! the king doth love you well. (4)
First, madam, I intreate true peace of you. (5)

Danish and German examples:

Tak, høje fader, for din miskundhed! (6)
Spar dine ord! Jeg kender ikke frygt. (7)
Den bære kronen som er kronen voxen. (8)
Frei atmen macht das leben nicht allein. (9)
Sie rettet weder hoffnung, weder furcht. (10)

In cases like the following one may hesitate which of the first two syllables to make 4 and which 3:

Yong, valiant, wise, and (no doubt) right royal. (11)
Friends, Romans, countrymen, lend me your ears. (12)
Foule wrinkled witch, what mak'st thou in my sight? (13)
Ros, rygte, folkesnak i sold den ta'er. (14)
Rat, mässigung und weisheit und geduld. (15)

§ **15.** D. Two monosyllables.

Here there will naturally be a great many cases in which the correct distribution of stresses is not self-evident: one reader will stress the first and another the second word. I think however that in the following lines most readers will agree with me in stressing 4314 or 4214 (or 5314):

Long may'st thou live, to wayle thy childrens death. (1)
Greefe fils the roome up of my absent childe. (2)
God will revenge it. Come, lords, will you go. (3)
Their woes are parcell'd, mine is generall. (4)
Sweet are the uses of adversitie. (5)
Lye there what hidden womans feare there will. (6)
Cours'd one another downe his innocent nose. (7)
Knap var det sagt, så stod for dem den tykke. (8)
Klog mand foragter ej sin stærke fjende. (9)
Dank habt ihr stets. Doch nicht den reinen dank. (10)
Wohl dem, der seiner väter gern gedenkt. (11)

In the middle of a line:

As it is wonne with blood, *lost be it* so. (12)
Den nordiske natur. *Alt skal du* skue. (13)
So kehr zurück! *Thu, was dein* Herz dich heisst. (14)

§ **16.** While in the lines examined so far a natural reading will stress the second syllable more than the third, it must be admitted that there are many lines in which the words themselves do not demand this way of stressing. Nevertheless the possibility exists that the poet had it in his mind, and expert elocutionists will often unconsciously give a stronger stress to the second syllable just to minimize the deviation from the scheme and avoid the unpleasant effect of the sequence 4114. I think this is quite natural in cases like the following, in which a proper name or another important word calls for an emphatic enunciation which makes the second syllable stronger than it might have been in easy-going prose:

Clarence still breathes; *Edward* still lives and raignes. (1)
Never came poyson from so sweet a place. (2)
Never hung poyson on a fowler toade. (3)
Tyrants themselves wept when it was reported. (4)
Hakon er konge, Valborg er en mø. (5)
Himlen er ej så blå som disse blomster. (6)

Even in a line like:

Cowards dye many times before their deaths (7)

an actor may feel inclined to express his contempt and to point the contrast to the following words "The valiant never taste of death but once" by giving special stress (53 or 54) to *cowards* and by extra stress on *many* to weigh down *die* to something comparatively insignificant, which is all the more natural as the idea of death has been mentioned in the preceding lines, while *cowards* is a new idea: new ideas are well known to attract strong stress. It is worth noting how often the figure is used as a rhetorical device to emphasize a contrast, in exclamations and in personal apostrophe (cf. König, p. 78). It is particularly apt for this use because a forcible attack of the voice after a pause will immediately catch the attention, before the verse settles down in its usual even course.

§ **17.** In spite of all this there will remain some instances in which the second syllable cannot easily be made stronger than the third. Metrics is no exact science aiming at finding out natural laws that are valid everywhere. All we can say is that by arranging syllables in such and such a way the poet will produce a pleasing effect; but of course a poet is free to sacrifice euphony if other things appear more important to him — not to mention the possibility that he is momentarily unable to hit upon anything more felicitous.

§ **18.** In all the cases dealt with in the preceding paragraphs there was a pause immediately before the strong syllable which had taken the place of a weak. The pause is often, but of course not everywhere indicated by a full stop or other punctuation mark. A natural explanation of the varying frequency of inversion at different places in the line (see above § 3) is found in the fact that a pause is not equally natural at all places. In the vast majority of cases inversion is found at the very beginning of a line, because the end of the preceding line is more often than not marked by a break in the thought and, even where this is not the case, a reciter or actor will often make a pause between two lines. Not quite so frequently comes a pause and inversion in the middle of a line, after the second or third "foot." It is necessarily rarer after the first foot, because a division of the line into two such unequal parts (2 + 8 syllables) is not natural: the two syllables are awkwardly isolated and cut off from organic cohesion with the rest. This is even more true of a pause after the eighth syllable: a strong syllable here will not leave us time enough to regain the natural swing of the verse before the line is ended. In such a case as

It is his Highnesse pleasure, that the Queene
Appeare in person here in Court. Silence! (1)

it would not even be unnatural to shout out the two last syllables as 44 or 45.

§ **19.** In yet another way a pause may play an important role in the verse. If we analyse the following lines in the usual way we find that the syllables here italicized form trochees where we should expect iambs, and if we read them without stopping they are felt to be inharmonious:

Like to a step-*dame, or* a dowager. (1)
Lye at the proud *foote of* a conqueror. (2)

As wilde-*geese, that* the creeping fowler eye. (3)
And let the soule *forth that* adoreth thee. (4)
To bear the file's *tooth and* the hammer's tap. (5)
John of the Black *Bands with* the upright spear. (6)
A snow-*flake, and* a scanty couch of snow
Crusted the grass-*walk and* the garden-mould. (7)
Den, der er blind*født el*ler blind fra barndom. (8)
Nu, det var smukt *gjort, det* var vel gjort, godt gjort. (9)
Denn ihr allein *wisst, was* uns frommen kann. (10)

If, on the other hand, we read these lines with the pause required (or allowed) by the meaning, the ear will not be offended in the least. The line is in perfect order, because in the first place *dame* with its 3 is heard together with *step* (4) and thus shows a descent in the right place, and secondly *or* with its 2 is heard in close connexion with *a* (1), so that we have the required descent between these two syllables. Graphically:

Like to	a step-	dame, or	a dow	ager
. . . . . .	iamb	trochee	iamb	. . . .

. . . . . . 1 4 3 2 1 4 . . . . . .
. . . . . . a/b \a(\)b\ a/b . . . . . .

The descent marked in parenthesis between *dame* and *or* is not heard, and is thus non-existent. Similarly in the other examples: [4]

§ **20.** The phenomena dealt with here (in § 12 ff. and 19) are singularly fit to demonstrate the shortcomings of traditional metrics (cf. above, § 4). In the first case (inversion after a pause) we had a "trochee" whose second syllable acts in connexion with the first syllable of the following foot, as if the latter had been the second syllable of an iambus. In the second case (§ 19) we had a "trochee" whose first syllable as a matter of fact will be perceived in the verse as if it were the first part of an iambus, and whose second syllable is similarly playing the role of the latter part of an iambus, and yet it is impossible to call these two successive iambic syllables a real iambus. In both cases the ear thus protests against the paper idea of a "foot." In the former case the perpendicular line | is made to separate the two syllables whose mutual relation is really of great rhythmic importance and which accordingly ought to go together. In the latter case two similar straight lines join together syllables which are not to be heard together, and whose relation to one another is therefore of no consequence, while the syllables that have to be weighed against one another are by the same means separated as if they did not concern one another. Could anything be more absurd?

§ **21.** The irregularities in lines like

And they shall be one Flesh, one Heart, one Soule. (1)
The wretched annimall heav'd forth such groanes (2)

[4] A corresponding interpretation of the metre of Shakespeare's *Lucrece* 1611 and 1612 is found in A. P. van Dam, *W. Shakespeare, Prosody and Text*, Leyden, 1900, p. 206.

might be explained by means of a pause after *be* and *animal: shall be* is 12, and *one flesh* 34, and similarly *animal* is 412 and *heav'd forth* 34, but the irregular ascent between 2 and 3 is concealed by the pause: 1/2(/)3/4 or a/b(/)a/b.

This explanation does not, however, hold good for numerous groups of a similar structure, e.g.

In the sweet pangs of it remember me. (3)
And the free maides that weave their thred with bones. (4)
In the deepe bosome of the ocean buried. (5)
But the queenes kindred and night-walking heralds. (6)
Of the young prince your sonne: send straight for him. (7)
I will feede fat the ancient grudge I beare him. (8)
As his wise mother wrought in his behalfe. (9)
Of a strange nature is the sute you follow. (10)
Whose homes *are the dim caves* of human thought. (11)
The ploughman lost his sweat, *and the greene corne.* (12)
Did I deserve no more *then a fooles head?* (13)

This figure is frequent in English verse, but not in other languages. I incline to read it with 1234 and thus to say that the ascent is normal between the first and the second as well as between the third and the fourth syllable, so that there is only the one small anomaly of a slight ascent instead of a descent between the second and the third syllable. It is worth noting how frequently this figure contains an adjective (stressed 3) before a substantive (stressed 4); *fool's* before *head* is equivalent to an adjective.

Some metrists here speak of a double iambus (⏑ ⏑ – –). Robert Bridges (*Milton's Prosody*, 1894, p. 56) calls it "a foot of two unstressed short syllables preceding a foot composed of two heavy syllables" and says, "Whatever the account of it is, it is pleasant to the ear even in the smoothest verse, and is so, no doubt, by a kind of compensation in it."

§ **22.** The role of a pause which covers and hides away metrical irregularities is seen also in the case of extra-metrical syllables. In Shakespeare these are particularly frequent where a line is distributed between two speakers. The pause makes us forget how far we had come: one speaker's words are heard as the regular beginning, and the next speaker's as the regular ending of a verse, and we do not feel that we have been treated to too much, though this would not pass equally unnoticed if there had been no break. Examples may be found in any book on Shakespeare's verse; [5] one occurs in the passage of Henry IV analysed below (§ 24, line 33). An interesting use of an extra-metrical syllable is made in King Lear IV. 1. 72.

[5] But it is necessary to read these writers with a critical mind, for very often lines are given as containing such supernumerary syllables which are perfectly regular in Shakespeare's pronunciation, e.g.

I am more an antique Roman than a Dane (I am = I'm).
The light and careless livery that it wears (livery = livry).

(Let the superfluous . . . man . . . that will not see,)
Because he do's not feele, feele your power quickly:

the second *feel*, which is necessary for the meaning, is heard as a kind of echo of the first and therefore enters into its place in the line.

§ **23.** There is one phenomenon which is even more curious than those mentioned so far, namely that which Abbott has termed *amphibious section.* Recent metrists do not as a rule acknowledge it, but its reality seems indisputable. It will not be found in poets who write for the eye, but Shakespeare was thinking of the stage only and was not interested in the way his plays would look when they were printed. He could therefore indulge in sequences like the following:

He but usurpt his life. | Beare them from hence. | Our present businesse | is generall woe. | Friends of my soule, you twaine | Rule in this realme | and the gor'd state sustaine. (1)

This is a sequence of 6 + 4 + 6 + 4 + 6 + 4 + 6 syllables, and in all the places here marked | (except perhaps two) a pause is necessary; after *life* a new speaker begins. The audience will not be able to notice that anything is missing: they will hear the first 6 + 4 as a full line, but the same four syllables go together with the following six to form another full line, and so on. A modern editor is in a difficult dilemma, for whichever way he prints the passage one line is sure to be too short:

He but usurped his life. Bear them from hence.
Our present business is general woe.
Friends of my soul, you twain
Rule in this realm and the gored state sustain,

or

He but usurped his life.
Bear them from hence. Our present business
Is general, etc.

A second example is:

Utter your gravitie ore a gossips bowles,	
For here we need it not. | — You are too hot. |	6 + 4
Gods bread! it makes me mad. | (2)	6
or	
For here we need it not. —	6
You are too hot. Gods bread! it makes me mad.	4 + 6

And a third:

Who, I, my lord! We know each others faces,	
But for our hearts, | he knowes no more of mine |	4 + 6
Then I of yours; |	4
Nor I no more of his,[6] | then you of mine. |	6 + 4
Lord Hastings, you and he | are neere in love. | (3)	6 + 4

[6] Folio; Or I of his, my Lord.

Such passages are thus elaborate acoustic delusions which are not detected on account of the intervening pauses.

§ **24.** It may not be amiss here to give the analysis of a connected long passage according to the principles advocated in this paper. The passage (Henry IV A I. 3. 29 ff.) is metrically of unusual interest.

29 My liege, I did deny no prisoners.
30 But I remember when the fight was done,
When I was dry with rage and extreame toyle,
Breathlesse and faint, leaning upon my sword,
Came there a certain lord, neat and trimly drest,
34 Fresh as a bride-groome, and his chin new reapt
Shew'd like a stubble land at harvest-home.
He was perfumed like a milliner,
And 'twixt his finger and his thumbe he held
38 A pouncet-box, which ever and anon
He gave his nose, and took't away againe:
Who therewith angry, when it next came there,
Tooke it in snuffe: and still he smil'd and talk'd:
42 And as the souldiers bare dead bodies by,
He call'd them untaught knaves, unmannerly,
To bring a slovenly unhandsome coarse
45 Betwixt the wind and his nobility.

Line 29. *I* in weak position, but in 30 and 31 in strong position (2) on account of the surroundings, § 9. Similarly *when* strong (2) in line 30, but degree 1 in line 31.

Line 31. *Extreme* with rhythmic stress on *ex-* on account of its position before a strongly stressed word, see A. Schmidt, *Sh-Lex.* II, p. 1413, my *Mod. Engl. Gr.* I 5. 53 f., above, § 5. In the same way *untaught* line 43, but *unmannerly* and *unhandsome* with weak *un*.

Line 32. Two examples of inversion, § 13.

Line 33. Which of the two words *Came there* is the stronger, may be doubtful, § 15. — *Neat* an extra-metrical syllable, which is not felt as such on account of the pause, § 22.

Line 34. Beginning inversion according to § 15. — *groom* 3, *and* 2 with pause between them, § 19; *new* 3 between two 4's, § 5.

Line 35. *Showed like* inversion § 15.

Line 36. *Was* 2, stronger than *he* and *per-*. *Perfumed* 141. This is the ordinary stressing of the verb, also in our times; but in H4B III. 1. 12 we have rhythmic shifting 41 before 4: "Then in the perfum'd chambers of the great." — *Like* 2 as in preceding line.

Line 37. First *and* 1, second *and* 2 between weak syllables, § 6. The two following *and*'s also 2; this is likewise the case with *when* in line 40.

Line 41. Inversion § 17.

Line 42. *As* 2 § 6, but *dead* 3 or 2 between strong syllables, § 5.
Line 43. *Untaught* see above.
Line 44. *Slovenly* 412 or perhaps 413 before *un-*, § 6.
Line 45. *His* 2 or 3, probably not emphatic.

§ **25.** We have not yet offered an answer to the question raised in § 2: why is a trochee among iambs easier to tolerate than inversely an iamb among trochees? But the answer is not difficult on the principles we have followed throughout. Take some trochaic lines, e.g.

Tell me not, in mournful numbers,
Life is but an empty dream —

and substitute for the second line something like

A life's but an empty dream, — or
To live's but an empty dream.

The rhythm is completely spoilt. Or try instead of

Then the little Hiawatha
Learned of every bird its language —

to say:

The sweet little Hiawatha
Acquired every sound and language.
(*Every* of course in two syllables as in Longfellow.)

In such cases with 14 instead of 41 we have the disagreeable clash of two strong syllables, further, we have two disappointments per line. It is true that if we pronounced the first strong syllable weaker than the second, thus made the whole 1341, we should have only one disappointment: a╱b╱a╲b instead of the regular a╲b╱a╲b; but it will be extremely hard to find examples of the sequence 34 as regularly occurring in any of the cognate languages. We shall see in the next paragraph the reason why 34 is not found within one and the same word; and when a word of the formula 14 is placed before a strongly stressed word, it is not generally reduced to 13, as the ordinary tendency in such cases is rather to substitute for it 31 or 21, see many examples from English in my *Mod. Engl. Gr.* I 156 ff.: "The other *upon* Saturn's bended neck" (Keats), "Protracted *among* endless solitudes" (Wordsworth), "a spirit *without* spot" (Shelley), "in *forlorn* servitude" (Wordsworth). Danish examples see *Modersmålets fonetik* 139. The disinclination to "invert" in trochaic rhythms is thus seen to be deeply rooted in linguistic habits and in the phonetic structure of our languages.

§ **26.** What is the essential difference between a rising and a falling rhythm? (or, in the old terms, between an "iambic" or "anapaestic" rhythm on the one hand and a "trochaic" or "dactylic" rhythm on the other?) Some writers minimize this difference and say that they are virtually identical, as the "anacrusis" has no real importance; instead of the sequence 14 14 14 . . . (⏑ – | ⏑ – | ⏑ – | . . .) they would write 1 41 41 41 . . . , (⏑ | – ⏑ | – ⏑ | – . . .). According to them the initial weak syllable is just as unimportant as an up-beat (auftakt, mesure d'attaque) is in music.

But is such an up-beat (a note before the first bar begins) really unimportant in music? I have taken a number of music books at random and counted the pieces in which such an up-beat occurs; I found that it was less frequent in pieces with a slow movement (largo, grave, adagio, andante) than in those with a quick movement (allegro, allegretto, rondo, presto, prestissimo, vivace):

	Beethoven	Schubert	Schumann	Sum
Slow				
with up-beat	5	1	5	11
without up-beat	17	7	7	31
Quick				
with up-beat	31	14	12	57
without up-beat	19	11	10	40

This agrees with the general impression of verse rhythms: a sequence didúm didúm didúm . . . tends to move more rapidly than dúmda dúmda dúmda . . . I think this depends on a deeply rooted psychological tendency: there is a universal inclination to hurry up to a summit, but once the top is reached one may linger in the descent. This is shown linguistically within each syllable: consonants before the summit of sonority (which in most cases is a vowel) are nearly always short, while consonants after the summit are very often long; cp. thus the two *n*'s of *nun*, the two *t*'s of *tot*, the two *m*'s of *member*. Words of the type 43 with long second syllable are frequent: *football, folklore, cornfield, therefore*, while corresponding words with 34 are rare: they tend to become 24 or even 14: *throughout, therein, austere, naïve, Louise, forgive* — with more or less distinct shortening of the vowel.

In this connexion it is perhaps also worth calling attention to the following fact. As a stressed syllable tends, other things being equal, to be pronounced with higher pitch than weak syllables, a purely "iambic" line will tend towards a higher tone at the end, but according to general phonetic laws this is a sign that something more is to be expected. Consequently it is in iambic verses easy to knit line to line in natural continuation.[7] Inversely the typical pitch movement of a "trochaic" line is towards a descent, which in each line acts as an indication of finality, of finish. If a continuation is wanted, the poet is therefore often obliged to repeat something — a feature which is highly characteristic of such a poem as *Hiawatha*, where each page offers examples like the following:

Should you ask me, *whence* these stories?
Whence these *legends and traditions*,

[7] Two rimed lines in succession will, however, produce the impression of finish — a feature that is often found in the Elizabethan drama, more particularly when a scene or a speech ends with a sententious saying.

With the odours of the forest,
With the dew and damp of meadows,
With the curling smoke of wigwams,
With the rushing of great rivers,
With their frequent repetitions, (N.B.)
And their wild reverberations,
As of thunder in the mountains?
I should answer, I should tell you,
From the . . . etc. (*From the* 6 times.)
Should you ask where Nawadaha
Found these songs, so wild and wayward,
Found these *legends and traditions,*
I should answer, I should tell you
In the . . . (*In the* 4 times) . . .[8]

These, then, seem to be the distinctive features of the two types of metre: rapidity, ease of going on from line to line without a break on the one hand, — and on the other slowness, heaviness, a feeling of finality at the end of each line, hence sometimes fatiguing repetitions. Tennyson utilized this contrast in a masterly way in *The Lady of Shalott*, where the greater part of the poem is rising, but where a falling rhythm winds up the whole in the description of her sad swan-song:

Heard a carol, mournful, holy,
Chanted loudly, chanted lowly,
Till her blood was frozen slowly,
And her eyes were darkened wholly,
Turned to tower'd Camelot.

References for the lines quoted.

Sh = Shakespeare. The titles of plays indicated as in A. Schmidt's Shakespeare-Lexicon. Numbers of act, scene, and line as in the Globe edition.

PL = Milton's *Paradise Lost*, as in Beeching's reprint of the original edition of 1667.

Ø = Øhlenschläger, *Axel og Valborg*, number of page according to A. Boysen's edition of *Poetiske skrifter i udvalg*, III. 1896.

P–M = Paludan-Müller, *Adam Homo*. Anden deel. 1849.

H = Hertz, *Kong Renés datter*. 7de opl. 1893.

G = Goethe, *Iphigenie auf Tauris*. Number of act and line according to Sämtliche werke XI in Cotta's Bibl. d. weltlitt.

§ *1*. 1. Tro. I. 1. 54. — 2, 3. Hml. I. 3. 68, 69. — 4. G I. 115. — 5. G I. 226.

§ *2*. 1. Mcb. V. 5. 27. — 2. R3 I. 3. 185. — 3. G I. 27.

§ *5*. 1. As II. 3. 63. — 2. Mids. I. 1. 134. — 3. Hml. 1. 2. 129. — 4. Lr. III. 7. 31. — 5. Wordsw. Tint. Abb. — 6. Tennyson, En. Arden 5. — 7. G III. 317.

§ *6*. 1. Lr. V. 3. 260.

§ *9*. 1. Tro. I. 1. 54. — 2. Pope.

[8] These two things, a trochaic metre and constant repetition, are found together in Finnish popular poetry, which Longfellow imitated.

§ *10.* 1. Mids. I. 1. 134. — 2. Hml. I. 4. 2. — 3. Pope Ess. Crit. 347. — 4. Tennyson Ulysses. — 5. Pope. — 6. Rom. III. 5. 178. — 7. PL II. 621. — 8. The Ring and the Book I. 6.

§ *11.* 1. R3 II. 2. 17.

§ *12.* 1. P–M 21. — 2. Ø 8. — 3. Ø 23. — 4. G I. 329. — 5. G I. 483. — 6. G III. 242. — 7. Cæs. I. 2. 193. — 8. R3 I. 1. 9. — 9. ib. II. 1. 82.

§ *13.* 1. H4A IV. 1. 134. — 2. ib. IV. 3. 31. — 3. ib. V. 2. 68. — 4. As I. 3. 129. — 5. R3 I. 3. 295. — 6. PL IX. 273. — 7. ib. IX. 403. — 8. Ø 7. — 9. Ø 21.

§ *14.* 1. R3 I. 3. 274. — 2. ib. I. 3. 209. — 3. ib. I. 3. 255. — 4. ib. II. 2. 17. — 5. ib. II. 1. 62. — 6. Ø 17. — 7. H 95. — 8. Ø. Hakon Jarl. — 9. G I. 106. — 10. G III. 71. — 11. R3 I. 2. 245. — 12. Cæs. III. 2. 78. — 13. R3 I. 3. 164. — 14. P–M 40. — 15. G I. 332.

§ *15.* 1. R3 I. 3. 204. — 2. John III. 4. 93. — 3. R3 II. 1. 138. — 4. ib. II. 2. 81. — 5. As II. 1. 12. — 6. ib. I. 3. 121. — 7. ib. II. 1. 39. — 8. P–M 12. — 9. Ø 27. — 10. G I. 93. — 11. G I. 351. — 12. R3 I. 3. 272. — 13. Ø 8. — 14. G I. 463.

§ *16.* 1. R3 I. 1. 161. — 2. ib. I. 2. 148. — 3. ib. I. 2. 149. — 4. ib. I. 3. 185. — 5. Ø 15. — 6. Ø 8.

§ *18.* 1. Wint. III. 1. 10.

§ *19.* 1. Mids. I. 1. 5. — 2. John V. 7. 113. — 3. Mids. III. 2. 20. — 4. R3 I. 2. 177. — 5. The Ring and the Book I. 14. — 6. ib. I. 47. — 7. ib. I. 608–9.

§ *21.* 1. PL VIII. 499. — 2. As II. 1. 36. — 3. Tw. II. 4. 16. — 4. ib. II. 4. 46. — 5. R3 I. 1. 4. — 6. ib. I. 1. 72. — 7. ib. II. 2. 97. — 8. Merch. I. 3. 48. — 9. ib. I. 3. 73. — 10. ib. IV. 1. 177. — 11. Shelley Prom. I. 659. — 12. Mids. II. 1. 94. — 13. Merch. II. 9. 59.

§ *22.* Hml. V. 2. 352. — ib. IV. 7, 80.

§ *23.* 1. Lr. V. 3. 317. — 2. Rom. III. 5. 178. — 3. R3 III. 4. 11.

Postscript [1933]

During the more than thirty years since this paper was first written, I have read many books and papers on metre, but have found nothing to shake my belief in the essential truth of my views, though I have often had occasion to regret that I wrote my paper in Danish and buried it in a place where fellow metrists in other countries were not likely to discover it.

If E. A. Sonnenschein had been alive, I should probably have written some pages in refutation of much in his book "What Is Rhythm?" (Oxford 1925). Now I shall content myself with pointing out how his inclination to find classical metres in English and to attach decisive importance to quantity leads him to such unnatural scannings of perfectly regular lines as

The véry spirit of Plantágenèt
| ⏑ ⏑ ⏑ | ⌒ ⏑ ⏑ | ⌒ o | ⌒ – | ⏑ ⏑ |

The first foot is an iambus, but as such should contain a long syllable; now both *e* and *r* in *very* are known to Sonnenschein as short; he therefore takes *y* as part of a trisyllabic foot, but it must at the same time be the "fall" of the next foot (his mark for the "protraction" which makes this possible is ⌒); the second iambus again has as its "rise" the two short syllables *spirit*, of which the second again is protracted to form the "fall" of the third foot; but *of* "does not fill up the time of the rise completely, unless it receives a metrical ictus, which would be accompanied by lengthening" — this is marked o. In a similar way are treated

O pity, pity, géntle héaven, píty!
| – ⏑ ⏑ | ⌒ ⏑ ⏑ | ⌒ – | ⏑ ⏑ ⏑ | ⌒ ⏑ ⏑ | ⌒

and the shorter

Apollo's summer look
| ⏑ ⏑ ⏑ | ⏑ ⏑ ⏑ | ⌒ – | (Pp. 158–9).

We get rid of all such pieces of artificiality by simply admitting that short syllables like *ver-*, *spir-*, *pit-*, *-pol-*, *sum-* are just as susceptible of verse ictus as long ones.

Unfortunately experimental phonetics gives us very little help in these matters. Sonnenschein and others have used the kymograph for metric purposes, and "the kymograph cannot lie" (Sonn. 33): but neither can it tell us anything of what really matters, namely stress, however good it is for length of sounds. The experimentalist Panconcelli-Calzia even goes so far as to deny the reality of syllables, and Scripture finds in his instruments nothing corresponding to the five beats of a blank verse line. So I am afraid poets and metrists must go on depending on their ears only.

English prosodists are apt to forget that the number of syllables is often subject to reduction in cases like *general*, *murderous*, *separately*, *desperate*, compare the treatment of *garden* + *-er*, of *person* + *-al* and of *noble* + *-ly* as disyllabic *gardener*, *personal*, *nobly*, and the change of syllabic *i* before another vowel to nonsyllabic [j] as in *Bohemia*, *cordial*, *immediate*, *opinion*, etc., in which Shakespeare and others have sometimes a full vowel, sometimes syllable reduction, the former chiefly at the end of a line, where it is perfectly natural to slow down the speed of pronunciation. Compare the two lines (Ro. II. 2. 4 and 7) in which *envious* is first two and then three syllables:

Arise faire Sun and kill the envious Moone . . .
Be not her maid since she is envious.

Similarly *many a*, *many and*, *worthy a*, *merry as*, etc., occur in Shakespeare and later poets as two syllables in conformity with a natural everyday pronunciation (my *Mod. Engl. Gr.* I 278).

I must finally remark that the whole of my paper concerns one type of (modern) metre only, and that there are other types, based wholly or partially on other principles, thus classical Greek and Latin verse. On medieval and to some extent modern versification of a different type much light is shed in various papers by William Ellery Leonard (himself a poet as well as a metrist): "Beowulf and the Nibelungen Couplet"; "The Scansion of Middle English Alliterative Verse" (both in *University of Wisconsin Studies in Language and Literature*, 1918 and 1920), "The Recovery of the Metre of the Cid" (PMLA 1931) and "Four Footnotes to Papers on Germanic Metrics" (in *Studies in Honor of F. Klaeber*, 1929).

W. K. Wimsatt, Jr., Monroe C. Beardsley

THE CONCEPT OF METER: AN EXERCISE IN ABSTRACTION

Let us first of all confess that it is not as if we were writing under the persuasion that we have a novel view to proclaim. It is true that the view which we believe to be correct is often under attack today and is sometimes supposed to be outmoded by recent refinements. Its proponents too are often not sure enough of its actual character to defend it with accuracy. At the same time, a look into some of the most recent handbooks and critical essays reveals that there are some teachers and writers on our subject today who expound this view in a perfectly clear and accurate way. We have in mind, for instance, *A Glossary of Literary Terms* revised by Meyer Abrams for Rinehart in 1957 from the earlier work by Norton and Rushton, or the handbook by Laurence Perrine, *Sound and Sense: An Introduction to Poetry,* published in 1956 by Harcourt, Brace. In the lengthy *Kenyon Review* symposium on English verse, Summer 1956,[1] we admire the niceties of Mr. Arnold Stein's traditionally oriented discussion of Donne and Milton. There is also Mr. Stein's earlier *PMLA* article (lix [1944], 393–397) on "Donne's Prosody." In the *Kenyon* symposium there is, furthermore, Mr. Ransom. It would be difficult to frame a more politely telling, persuasive, accurate retort than his to the more extravagant claims of the linguists.

We are, therefore, in a position to do no more than take sides in a debate which is already well defined. Still this may be worth doing. Our aim is to state as precisely as we can just what the traditional English syllable-accent meter is or depends upon, to rehearse a few more reasons in its support, perhaps to disembarrass it of some of the burdens that are nowadays needlessly contrived for it.

Reprinted by permission of the Modern Language Association from *PMLA,* volume LXXIV (December 1959), 585–598.

1 Harold Whitehall, Seymour Chatman, Arnold Stein, John Crowe Ransom, "English Verse and What It Sounds Like," *The Kenyon Review,* XVIII, 411–477.

I

This essay is about the scanning of English verse. We want to consider two influential current schools of thought about scanning, and to examine critically a fundamental mistake which we believe is made by both of them, though in different ways. These two deviations from what the present writers see as good sense in metrics may be conveniently designated as on the one hand the linguistic and on the other the musical or temporal. The linguistic view, as it happens, has been authoritatively illustrated in the contributions to the *Kenyon* symposium of 1956 by Harold Whitehall and Seymour Chatman. The musical view has been very well represented in the more recent volume *Sound and Poetry, English Institute Essays 1956* (New York, 1957), and especially in its introductory essay "Lexis and Melos," by the editor, Northrop Frye — and no less in the same writer's larger book *Anatomy of Criticism,* published at Princeton in 1957.

Mr. Whitehall gives us an admirable summary of the linguistic system of George L. Trager and Henry Lee Smith, in part a reprint of his 1951 *Kenyon* review of their treatise, *An Outline of English Structure* (Norman, 1951). But his essay is more than a summary; it is a celebration. Indeed it makes a very large claim for what this system can contribute to the modern study of metrics:

> as no science can go beyond mathematics, no criticism can go beyond its linguistics. And the kind of linguistics needed by recent criticism for the solution of its pressing problems of metrics and stylistics, in fact, for all problems of the linguistic surface of letters, is not semantics, either epistemological or communicative, but down-to-the-surface linguistics, microlinguistics not metalinguistics. (*Kenyon,* XVIII, 415)

To Mr. Chatman falls the pioneer task of showing how these extraordinary claims are to be substantiated. He presents us with a careful and interesting analysis of eight tape-recorded readings of a short poem by Robert Frost, one of the readers being Frost himself. Mr. Chatman's essay is full of passages of good sense. Still we have some objections to urge against him: the gist of these is that through his desire to exhibit the stress-pitch-juncture elements in spoken English, he shows an insufficient concern for the normative fact of the poem's meter. It is true that he does not deny that the poem has an "abstract metrical pattern," and he acknowledges the "two-valued metrics of alternating stresses" (p. 422). But in his actual readings these seem to be of little interest.[2]

We are not quite sure we understand Mr. Chatman's idea of the relation between meter and Trager-Smith linguistics. One sub-heading of his essay,

[2] Mr. Chatman, in a paper subsequently prepared for a Conference on Style held at Indiana University in April 1958, has made it clear that his views on meter actually differ very little from those of the present writers. Our purpose here is only to use Mr. Chatman's text of 1956 as a point of departure for the exposition of an issue.

"Prosody and Meaning Resolution," probably ought to read "Intonation and Meaning Resolution." ("An 'intonation pattern,'" let us note well, "is an amalgam of features of stress, pitch, and juncture which occurs as part of a spoken phrase." — p. 422.) Mr. Chatman has learned from Frost's reading of his poem the correct intonation and meaning of the phrase "scared a bright green snake." Very well. Correct understanding *produces* correct intonation, and correct intonation *reveals* correct understanding. And one may choose or may not choose to indicate the intonation by Trager-Smith notation. And this intonation (whether indicated by Trager-Smith notation or not) may or may not affect the meter in the given instance. In this instance there is nothing to show that what Mr. Chatman learned about the intonation did change the meter. The same observations hold for Mr. Chatman's discovery of the meaning and intonation of the concluding phrase of the poem, "and left the hay to make." Through recorded readings of a poem Mr. Chatman learns something that another person might know through boyhood experience on a farm, or through a footnote. But again no need for Trager-Smith. And no change in meter. The point is brought out even more clearly in another recent article by Mr. Chatman, in *The Quarterly Journal of Speech.* He makes a shrewd observation about a passage in Spenser's *Faerie Queene* (I.ii.13. 4–5): "And like a Persian mitre on her head / She wore . . ." "We must," he says, "resist the temptation to read *And lîke a Per̂sian mítre.*" The obvious meaning is rather: "Like a Persian, she wore . . ." [3] Quite true. One stresses *Persian* a little more strongly, one pauses between *Persian* and *mitre.* But there is no change in meter, and no change in intonation that an old-fashioned comma will not provide for.

One of the good things about Mr. Chatman's *Kenyon* contribution is that, like Victor Erlich, whose *Russian Formalism* (The Hague, 1955) he aptly quotes (p. 438), Mr. Chatman prefers a "phonemic" analysis to the now somewhat old-fashioned total "acoustic" way of trying to study either language or metrics. (Phonemic differences, we can never remind ourselves too often, are those that make a real difference in the structure of a language, like the difference between *d* and *t* in English, rather than the difference between your pronunciation of *t* and mine.) Phonetic studies, observes Mr. Chatman, "before the discovery of the phonemic principle," were not really getting anywhere with the understanding of language. "It is unfortunately a truism that one cannot get more structure out of a machine than one puts in" (p. 422). We hold that for metrical study it is indeed necessary to remember the phonemic principle — in the broadest sense, the principle of linguistic significance in phonetic difference. But it is also necessary, while

[3] "Linguistics, Poetics, and Interpretation: The Phonemic Dimension," *QJS,* XLIII (Oct. 1957), 254. Cf. Ronald Sutherland, "Structural Linguistics and English Prosody," *College English,* XX (Oct. 1958), 12–17. Despite a generally superior attitude toward "conventional metrics," Mr. Sutherland reaches the correct conclusion "that much of the information accumulated by the new science is inconsequential to English prosody."

we work within that principle, to practice an even further degree of abstraction. Not just all or any phonemic features — not all or any intonational features — but a certain level of these is organized by the poet to make a metrical pattern.

Let us turn for a moment to our other authority and point of departure for the present argument, Northrop Frye. Mr. Frye's chief emphasis, both in his English Institute essay and in his *Anatomy,* is on the similarity or continuity between the pentameter line of Milton or Shakespeare and the older (and newer) English strong-stress meter, *Piers Plowman, Everyman, Christabel, The Cocktail Party.* "A four-stress line," he says, "seems to be inherent in the structure of the English language" (*Anatomy,* p. 251; cf. *Institute Essays,* pp. xvii, xx). It is true that Mr. Frye does not identify the four-stress pattern of the pentameter line with its meter; he clearly thinks of the "stress" pattern and the "meter" as two different things; for example, in a reading of Hamlet's soliloquy, "the old four-stress line stands out in clear relief against the metrical background" (*Anatomy,* p. 251). Nevertheless, it is also apparent from his neglect of any specific discussion of "meter" that he attaches little importance to it; he does not seem to believe that it has much to do with what he calls, in his special sense, the "music" of poetry. "To read poetry which is musical in our sense we need a principle of accentual scansion, a regular recurrence of beats with a variable number of syllables between the beats. This corresponds to the general rhythm of the music in the Western tradition, where there is a regular stress accent with a variable number of notes in each measure" (*Essays,* p. xvii). Rather than object more emphatically to Mr. Frye's views at this point, we allow our difference from him to emerge, as we go along, in later parts of our essay.

Let us round out our preliminary account of strong-stress rhythm by a return to Mr. Whitehall. Mr. Whitehall is much impressed by Kenneth L. Pike's principle (e.g., *The Intonation of American English* [Ann Arbor, 1945], p. 34) that in English "the time-lapse between any two primary stresses tends to be the same irrespective of the number of syllables and the junctures between them" (*Kenyon,* XVIII, 418). Mr. Whitehall distinguishes a type of "rhythm" which he calls the *isochronic:* it "depends on equal time-lapses between primary stresses" (p. 420). And he finds in a line of Gray's *Elegy* three "primary stresses" and hence three isochronic sequences of syllables. It is not wholly clear whether the term "rhythm," as Mr. Whitehall uses it, embraces, excludes, or nullifies the concept of "meter," for Mr. Whitehall eschews the latter term. But when we consider his other technical terms, we can assemble a view very much like that of Mr. Frye. He speaks of *syllabic* "rhythms" (p. 420) and among these the *isoaccentual,* and he says that in Pope's *Essay on Man* there is "undoubtedly isoaccentual counterpointed with isochronic rhythm," while "in much of Milton" there is "isochronic counterpointed with isoaccentual rhythm." The nature of Mr. Whitehall's "prosodic" observations might be made clearer if we were to substitute for one of his terms an apparent synonym: for "isoaccentual rhythm" read "meter," i.e., syllable-stress meter of the English pentameter tradition, Chaucer to Tennyson. In Pope and Milton there is both syllable-stress *meter* and an occasional pattern of strong stresses which can, if one wishes, be taken as a moment of the older strong-stress *meter*.

Again: when Mr. Whitehall speaks of "isoaccentual" rhythms, and when he speaks of "isosyntactic" rhythms, he is talking about ascertainable linguistic features, and hence about ascertainable and definable metric patterns. But when he adds that "the other type [of non-syllabic rhythm] is isochronic," he has slipped into another gear. This term is not on all fours with the others. Isochronism, observes Mr. Whitehall himself on an earlier page, is "not mentioned in the [Trager-Smith] *Outline";* it is "not directly a significant part of the English linguistic structure" (p. 418). It is something which may or may not occur in correct English speech.

At the same time, let us observe that if isochronism *were* a general principle, or even an approximate principle, of all English speech, it would clearly be a different thing from meter. It would not serve to distinguish the metrical from the non-metrical. Isochronism, according to the Pike theory, is not a special feat of language, managed by the poet, but a common feature of language. So long as a poet's lines had some strong stresses, and they always must have, the isochronism would take care of itself. In the actual English meters of the poets, even in the old strong-stress *Beowulf* and *Piers Plowman* meter, something quite determinate and special always *is* added: an approximately equal number of weaker syllables between the strong stresses, "configurational" heightening of the stresses, as by alliteration, and the syntactic entity of the lines and half-lines.

II

Some, though perhaps not all, of those who approach the sound of poetry from the two viewpoints we are here debating will want to reply to our argument by saying that we have lost sight of the primary poetic fact, which, they will say, is always this or that reading of a poem out loud — as by the bard with a harp, by the modern author for a tape-recording, or by actors on a stage. What our argument takes as the object of scansion will be referred to disrespectfully as a mere skeleton of the real poem. Mr. Chatman, for example, attempts to describe the verse line as it is actually 'performed'." And he likes the Trager-Smith system because it "demands a comparison between actual oral performances of poetry and traditional meters." "It incorporates both formula and performance" (p. 423). Let it be so. Let the difference between our view and that of the linguistic recorders be something of that sort.

There is, of course, a sense in which the reading of the poem is primary: this is what the poem is *for*. But there is another and equally important sense in which the poem is not to be identified with any particular performance of it, or any set of such performances. Each performance of the poem is an actualization of it, and no doubt in the end everything we say about the poem ought to be translatable into a statement about an actual or possible performance of it. But not everything which is true of some particular performance will be necessarily true of the poem. There are many performances of the same poem — differing among themselves in many ways. A performance is an event, but the poem itself, if there *is* any poem, must be some kind of enduring object. (No doubt we encounter here a difficult ontological question; we are not inclined to argue it. It seems necessary only to expose the fundamental assumption which we take to be inevitable for any discussion of "meter.") When we ask what the meter of a poem is, we are not asking how Robert Frost or Professor X reads the poem, with all the features peculiar to that performance. We are asking about the poem as a public linguistic object, something that can be examined by various persons, studied, disputed — univocally.

The meter, like the rest of the language, is something that can be read and studied with the help of grammars and dictionaries and other linguistic guides. In this objective study, Trager-Smith principles, for instance, may be largely helpful. At the same time they may be in excess of any strictly metrical need. For the meter is something which for the most part inheres in language precisely at that level of linguistic organization which grammars and dictionaries and elementary rhetoric can successfully cope with. So far as Trager-Smith is a refinement on traditional ways of indicating intonation patterns (by punctuation, by diacritical marks, by spelling and word separation), Trager-Smith may well be a help to saying something about meter. On the other hand, it may well become only a needless fussiness of symbols by which somebody tries to be scientific about the ever-present, the ever-different disparities and tensions between formal meter and the linguistic totality. Our argument is not specifically against Trager-Smith, but against certain ways of combining Trager-Smith with multiple readings. It is interesting to study the tape-recording of various performances of Frost's "Mowing." But we must not let this mass of data blind us to the possibility that some of our readers have failed to get the meter right.

In the same way we argue against the temporal theorists, the timers. In the broadest sense, we define their theory as one which says that meter either consists wholly in, or has as an essential feature, some principle of recurrence in equal, or approximately equal, times — analogous to musical pulse. And we respond, in brief, that meter must be a character of the poem, but that timing is a character of performance: what is done or can be done by a reader, a chanter, or a singer. Mr. John Hollander, in a recent article ("The Music of Poetry," *JAAC,* XV [1956], 232–244) has warned us against confusing a "descriptive" with a "performative" system of prosody. This is just what the timers have done since the beginning. Reciting poetry in equal times is a matter related to music, and there is no question that music can be imposed on verse — very readily on some verse — and that here and there in the history of poetic recitation music has been invoked to fill out what the meter did not do — where in effect the meter was insufficient. But the musician or the musicologist who comes in to perform these services or to point out their possibility ought to remember what he is doing.

Discussion of English meters seems to have been badly misled for a long time now by a prevalent supposition that the two main alternative, or complementary, principles of English meter are time and stress. Karl Shapiro's handy guide to modern English metrical theory (*A Bibliography of Modern Prosody,* Baltimore, 1948) reports that this is indeed the major split in the whole field of English metrical theory (of which the two great champions are Lanier for the timers and Saintsbury for the stressers), and Mr. Shapiro himself seems to welcome this alignment and to consider it more or less correct and inevitable. But the two main alternative principles of English meter, as we shall argue more in detail a little later, are actually two kinds of stress — strong stress (the Old English, the *Piers Plowman* tradition) and syllable stress (the Chaucer-Tennyson tradition). The difficulty of describing the difference between these kinds of stress meter and their occasional difficult relations with each other are causes that account in part for the experiments of the temporal theory.

The basic arguments against the temporal theories of English meter are now almost universally accepted so far as one main branch of these theories is concerned, namely, the "quantitative" — the theory of long and short *syllables,* on the classical analogy. The history of English prosody affords the futile instances of the Elizabethan "Areopagus" and in the eighteenth and nineteenth centuries the luxuriance of theories described in T. S. Omond's sympathetic *English Metrists* (Oxford, 1921). So far as the Greek and Latin patterns of long and short (dactylic hexameters, sapphics, hendecasyllabics or the like) have been *successfully* reillustrated in English, this has been done on strictly accentual (plus syllable-counting) principles:

> This is the forest primeval. The murmuring pines and the hemlocks . . .

> Needy Knife-grinder! whither are you going?
> Rough is the road, your wheel is out of order —
> Bleak blows the blast; — your hat has got a hole in't,
> So have your breeches.

> O you chorus of indolent reviewers,
> Irresponsible, indolent reviewers. . . .

Syllables, number of syllables, and stresses, primary, secondary, and weak, are linguistic features which you can find in the English dictionary. But long and short syllables are not found in the English dictionary. Some syllables are, of course, often, perhaps nearly always, spoken more rapidly than others. But the length of the syllable is not a part of correctness or incorrectness in speaking English. Quantity, so far as it appears in any determinate way, more or less rides along with stress. We can drag or clip the syllables of English words, and we may sound odd, affected, or funny, but still we shall not be *mis*pronouncing our words, or changing their meaning. Quantity is a dimension where you cannot make mistakes in pronouncing English. And where you cannot make mistakes, you cannot be right, as opposed to wrong. It follows that in such a dimension a writer in English cannot create a public pattern. The English language will not permit a quantitative meter.

It would seem, however, that some kind of quantitative assumption must inevitably reappear (or be added to the linguistic facts) whenever the other main kind of temporal theory, the "isochronic," is applied in an actual scansion of lines of English verse. Syllables which in themselves may be recognized as having no correct quantity, either long or short, now have quantity conferred on them by crowding or jamming ("accelerating and crushing together" — Mr. Whitehall's terms) or by stretching, to meet the demands of the isochronic assumption. This kind of processing or adjustment of syllables is taken as a justification for, and is symbolized by, the use of musical notation, and such notation is sometimes called "scansion."

Let us ask the question whether it is *actually the case* that readers of poetry always, or even generally, do perform their readings isochronically.[4] (That this *can* be done, by a sufficiently skilful, or a sufficiently musical, reader no one of course denies.) It may be that we have here to acknowledge a distinction between two rather different kinds of verse. Perhaps it *is* true that nursery rhymes and ballads, at least some ballads, are usually, and normally, and even *best,* read with an approximation to isochronism. (This may have something to do with their origin in close connection with music.) The most convincing examples of musical notation produced by the equal-timing prosodists are in this area: "Mary, Mary," — "O what is that sound that so thrills the ear?" — "But it's Din! Din! Din!" But then a Shakespeare sonnet or *Paradise Lost* or a lyric by A. E. Housman is a very different kind of thing.

When a poem is set to music, definite values have to be assigned to its

[4] The question is, of course, a psychological one, but the psychologists have not dealt much with it. A search of *Psychological Abstracts* for the last twenty years turns up (XXI [Sept. 1947], 387) one article (abstract 3211): Marguerite Durand, "Perception de durée dans les phrases rhythmées," *Journal de Psychologie Normale et Pathologique,* XXXIX (1946), 305–321. But Mlle. Durand apparently took isochronism for granted and had her passages (French and Czech) spoken to the beats of a metronome. Albert R. Chandler, *Beauty and Human Nature* (New York, 1934), pp. 244–256, gives a good account of some earlier investigations, of which the most interesting is that by J. E. W. Wallin. Wallin began with E. W. Scripture's concept of strong stresses, or "regions of strength," which Scripture called "centroids"; but in a careful investigation Wallin found no fixed length for intervals between centroids; "the longest observed was seven times the shortest when there was no intervening pause, and fourteen times the shortest when pauses occurred" (Chandler, p. 250). Ada L. F. Snell, "An Objective Study of Syllabic Quantity in English Verse," *PMLA,* XXXIII (1918), 396–408; XXXIV (1919), 416–435, presents experimental evidence against the assumption that readers of English verse observe any kind of "equal time intervals."

notes and rests, and consequently to its measures and phrases. And however this is done, we are introducing an extra-linguistic element, a precision of timing that does not belong to the linguistic elements, the words and syllables, just as such. Consider, for example, the opening of Ralph Vaughan Williams' setting of a Housman poem:

Thus we make "on" twice as long as "Wen-," or "Edge" three times as long as "wood's." For another good example, compare a normal *reading* of Edith Sitwell's poems in *Facade* with the way she recites them to the accompaniment of William Walton's music.

Both printed words and printed musical score are prescriptions, or directions, for performance. Our point is that they are different prescriptions — perhaps complementary and cooperating, but still different and independent. One, the musical score, is not an explication or explanation (like diacritical marks) of the other, the words, but an addition to it.[5]

Music — or at least music with bar-lines, which is all we are concerned with here — is precisely a time-measuring notation; it divides the time into equal intervals and prescribes a felt underlying "pulse."[6] It calls for the metronome or the tapping foot. If we ourselves wish to add to the poet's notation our own rhythmic pattern, say

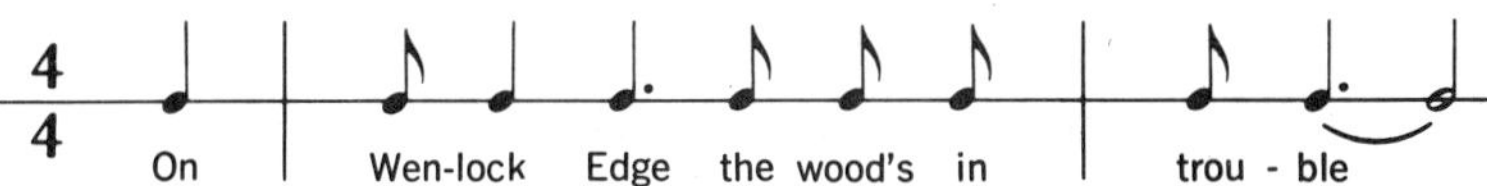

[5] A kind of middle or double service is performed by traditional marks of prosodic scansion — which in part, in large part, call attention to objective features of linguistic structure, but to some extent also are used for "promoting" or "suppressing" (or indicating the promotion or suppression of) such features in favor of a certain pattern. This double character of scansion marks has perhaps caused much of the difficulty in metrical theory.

[6] We take this term from Leonard B. Meyer's excellent discussion of musical rhythm in *Emotion and Meaning in Music* (Chicago, 1956), pp. 102–103. Pulse is the division of time into "regularly recurring, equally accented beats." What Meyer calls "meter" in music depends on pulse; but in this respect it is different from meter in verse. What he calls "rhythm" — e.g., the difference between an iambic and an anapestic or trochaic pattern — can occur without pulse and meter, he holds; as in plain chant or *recitativo secco*.

we are not scanning the verse, but either reporting on the way one reader performed it or else recommending that others perform it this way. Thus, Mr. Frye gives the following analysis of a line from Meredith's "Love in the Valley" (*Anatomy,* p. 254):

Couched with her
arms be-
hind her
gol-den
head

But another reader might, with equal plausibility, read it this way:

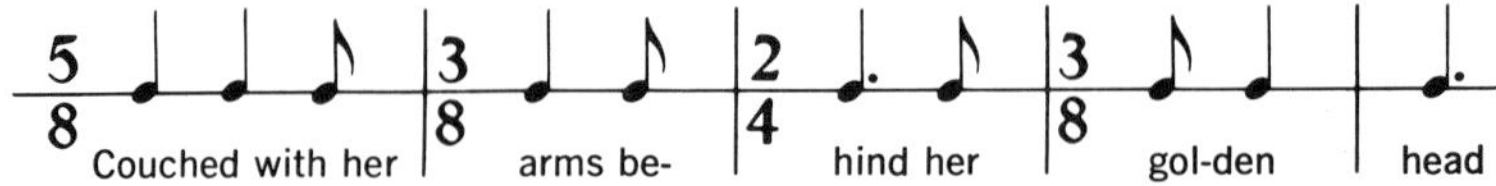
5
8
Couched with her
3
8
arms be-
2
4
hind her
3
8
gol-den
head

Meter involves measurement, no doubt, or it can hardly with much meaning be called "meter." But all measurement is not necessarily temporal measurement — even when the things measured occur in a temporal succession. If a person walks along the street hitting every third paling in a fence, he sets up a pattern, but he may or he may not do this in equal lengths of time. Better still, let every third paling be painted red, and we have a pattern which our person does not have to set up for himself but can observe objectively. He will observe or experience this pattern in time, but not necessarily in equal lengths of time. In either case, that of striking or that of simply seeing, we may further suppose the palings for some reason to be spaced along the fence at irregular intervals. Musical meter is a matching, or coordination, of two patterns, stress and time. But poetic meter is only one of these patterns. Why does one kind of measurement have to be matched with another kind? or translated into it? The measurement of verse is determined by some recurrent linguistic feature, peg, obstacle, jutting stress, or whatever. If we read this recurrence so as to give it equal times, this is something we do to it. Maybe we actually do, and maybe this is a part of our aesthetic satisfaction; still it is not a part of the linguistic fact which the poet has to recognize and on which he has to rely in order to write verses.

III

The meter inheres in the language of the poem, but in what way and at what level? We hold that it inheres in aspects of the language that can be abstracted with considerable precision, isolated, and even preserved in the appearance of an essence — mummified or dummified. An appropriate example is to hand and does not have to be invented. Back in the 1920's

I. A. Richards was much concerned, and properly, to show that the movement or rhythm of poetry was closely interdependent with its other kinds of meaning. The movement, he argued, could hardly be said to occur at all except as an aspect of some linguistic meaning. Or at least it had no poetic value except as an aspect of some meaning. It is not quite clear which point Richards was making. But for the sake of his argument he exhibited, in his *Practical Criticism,* a contrivance which he called a "double or dummy" — "with nonsense syllables" — "a purified dummy." The dummy showed several things, perhaps a good deal more than Richards had in mind. For it certainly was not a *pure* dummy. How could it be? It was a linguistic dummy. And so this dummy did have a meter — perhaps even a kind of rhythm. If it did not have a meter, how could it be adduced as showing that movement, or meter, apart from sense did not have poetic value? You can't illustrate the poetic nullity of a certain quality taken pure by annihilating that quality. You do it by purging or purifying, isolating, the quality. And if you can do that, you prove that the quality can be isolated — at least from *certain* other qualities, in this case, the *main lines* of the linguistic meaning. In order to get even this dummy of a meter, Richards had to leave in a good many linguistic features.[7]

J. Drootan-Sussting Benn
Mill-down Leduren N.
    Telamba-taras oderwainto weiring
Awersey zet bidreen
Ownd istellester sween. . . .

"If any reader," says Richards, "has any difficulty in scanning these verses, reference to Milton, *On the Morning of Christ's Nativity,* xv, will prove of assistance."[8] There are, indeed, several uncertainties in Richards' composition which correspond to greater certainties in Milton's full linguistic archetype. Still the Milton is not necessary. Let us list some of the things we know about this dummy. The "nonsense syllables" are divided into groups (words). As English readers we find little difficulty pronouncing them. Some of the groups are English words ("Mill," "down,"); others are English syllables, even morphemes ("ing," "ey," "een," "er"). The capital initials, the monosyllables, the hyphens, the rhymes, give us very strong indications, absolutely sure indications, where some of the stresses fall. And there are some syllables, notably some final syllables, which are surely unstressed. If we don't inquire too closely how much any given stressed syllable is stressed more than another (and who is to say that we should make that inquiry?), we will indicate the scansion of Richards' dummy somewhat as follows:

[7] The same can be said for the shorter nursery-rhyme type of dummy employed by George R. Stewart, Jr., *The Technique of English Verse* (New York, 1930), p. 3: "Fol-de-riddle, fol-de-riddle, hi-dee-doo."

[8] *Practical Criticism* (New York, 1935), p. 232.

J́. Dróotan-Śussting B́enn
Ḿill-d́own Lèdúren Ń.
  T̀elàmba-t́aras óderwáinto wéiring
Àwèrsey źet bidréen
Ównd istèllèster swéen . . . .

The main uncertainties will be with the groups "Leduren," "Telamba," "Awersey," "istellester," where there will be a choice or guess in placing the stress. But the choice in no one of the four cases is crucial to the meter. You can choose either way and not destroy the iambics. And Richards' readers who have read this dummy and admired the ingenuity of the argument have certainly all along been giving the dummy the benefit of some implicit scansion.

The dummy does two things for the present argument. It illustrates or strongly suggests the principle that meter may inhere at certain rudimentary levels of linguistic organization, and, more specifically, that the kind of English meter of which we are speaking, so far as it depends on syllabic stress, depends not on any kind of absolute, or very strong stress, but merely on a relative degree of stress — on a certain moreness of stress in certain positions. Of this latter we want to say something further before we finish. It is not a principle which is challenged by the linguists — though the exact sense in which they wish to apply it seems doubtful.

Let us now make some general prosodic observations. And first, that to have verses or lines, you have to have certain broader structural features, notably the endings. Milton's line is not only a visual or typographical fact on the page, but a fact of the language. If you try to cut up his pentameters into tetrameters, for example, you find yourself ending in the middle of words or on weak words like "on" or "the." Much English prose is iambic or nearly iambic, but it is only very irregular verse, because if you try to cut it regularly, you get the same awkward and weak result. Lines of verse are syntactic entities, though not necessarily similar or parallel entities. Depending on the degree of parallel, you get different kinds of tension between the fact of the lines and the fact of the overall syntax or movement.

Given the line then or the typographical semblance of a line (the possibility of a line) on the page, let us ask the question how we know we have a meter and know what meter it is. The line may indeed be only a syntactic entity and not metrical in any more precise way — as perhaps throughout Robert Bridges' *Testament of Beauty* [9] and in much so-called "free verse." With Mr. Whitehall we can call this a kind of "rhythm," *non-syllabic, isosyn-*

[9] Elizabeth Wright, *Metaphor, Sound and Meaning in Bridges' "The Testament of Beauty"* (Philadelphia, 1951), p. 26, says that Bridges' lines are to be timed equally, with the help of pauses at the ends of the lines.

tactic, so long as the syntactic entities, the phrases or clauses, are "in strictly parallel sequence," as in Hebrew verse and in *some* "free verse." But this is in fact a very narrow restriction. It rules out all mere cutting of ordinary prose into its phrases or clauses (as in much free verse, and perhaps in Bridges or in parts of Bridges). For again, like Pike's isochronism, phrases and clauses are inevitable, and if they by themselves make a "rhythm" (or a meter), it is impossible not to write in this "rhythm" or meter. To get a meter, some other kind of equality has to be added to the succession of syntactic entities. (Even strictly parallel syntactic entities will be improved metrically by the addition of some more precise kind of equality.) The meter in the sense that it is internal to a given line or that it is something that runs through the series of lines is some kind of more minute recurrence — some exact or approximate number of syllables, with probably some re-enforcement of certain syllables, some repeated weighting, what Mr. Whitehall calls a "configurational feature." Here if we take a wide enough look at the world's languages and literatures (at Chinese and classical Greek, as well as the Western vernaculars of our immediate experience), we can talk about pitch and quantity, as well as accent or stress. But for our discussion of English meters, stress is the thing. (Rhyme, assonance, alliteration too are auxiliary "configurational" and metric features — though Mr. Whitehall seems to count them out.)

The important principle of stress or accent in English verse is, however, a rather ambiguous thing, for there are in fact two main kinds of stress meter in English: the very old (and recently revived) meter of strong stress with indeterminate or relatively indeterminate number of syllables between the stresses, and the other meter, of the great English art tradition (Chaucer to Tennyson), which is a syllable-stress meter, that is, a meter of counted syllables and of both major and minor stresses.

There are certainly some lines of syllable-stress meter which taken alone could be read also as strong-stress meter (four beats instead of five). To use one of Mr. Frye's examples:

> To bé, or nót to be, thát is the quéstion:
> Whéther 'tis nóbler in the mínd to súffer
> The slíngs and árrows of outrágeous fórtune . . .

But the precise number of syllables in syllable-stress meter is always somewhat against the strong-stress interpretation. One stress out of five in a pentameter line will inevitably be the weakest; still, because of the numbering of the syllables, and the alternation of the stresses, this fifth too calls out for some recognition.

> To bé, or nót to bé, thát is the quéstion.
> With lóss of Éden, tíll one gréater mán . . .

And then we have the matter of the whole passage, the whole act and scene, the whole book, the whole long poem to consider. And Mr. Frye admits that the strong stresses vary in number from eight (the maximum apparently possible within the conditions of the pentameter — a virtuoso feat achieved by Milton) and the scarcely satisfactory three (eked out in musical terms, for a line of Keats by Mr. Frye's assumption of a preliminary "rest"). But the "pentameter" in a long poem by Shakespeare, Milton, Pope, Wordsworth, or Keats is not subject to such fluctuations. The pentameter is always there. It is *the* meter of the poem. The strong-stress lines of four, of three, of eight, and so on, come and go, playing along with the steady pentameter — and it it a good thing they do come and go, for if every line of *Hamlet* or *Paradise Lost* had the four strong beats which Mr. Frye finds in the opening four or five lines, Mr. Frye would begin to detect something marvelously monotonous; he wouldn't be so happy about his "inherent" and "common" four-stress rhythm. One principle of monotony is enough; it is *the* meter of the poem. In "pentameter" verse it is the iambic pentameter.

A few lines of Chaucer, Shakespeare, Spenser, Pope, Wordsworth, Tennyson, read consecutively, can hardly fail to establish the meter. What makes it possible for the lighter stresses to count in syllable-stress meter is the fact that it *is* a syllable meter. Following French and classical models, but in an English way, the poets count their syllables precisely or almost precisely, ten to a pentameter line, and this measuring out makes it possible to employ the minor accents along with the major ones in an alternating motion, up and down. The precise measurement tilts and juggles the little accents into place, establishes their occurrence as a regular part of all that is going on.

Likewise, the clutter of weaker syllables in a strong-stress meter is against an accurate syllable-stress reading, most often prevents it entirely. A few lines of *Piers Plowman* or of *Everyman* ought to suffice to show what is what.

In a somer seson, whan soft was the sonne,
I shope me in shroudes, as I a shepe were,
In habits like an heremite, unholy of workes,
Went wyde in this world, wondres to here.

Lorde, I wyll in the worlde go renne over all,
And cruelly out-serche bothe grete and small.
Every man wyll I beset that lyveth beestly
Out of Goddes lawes, and dredeth not foly.

This other kind of meter is older in English poetry and may be more natural to the English tongue, though again it may not be. Here only the major stresses of the major words count in the scanning. The gabble of weaker syllables, now more, now fewer, between the major stresses obscures all the minor stresses and relieves them of any structural duty. (Sometimes the major stresses are pointed up by alliteration; they are likely to fall into groups of two on each side of a caesura.) Thus we have *Beowulf, Piers Plowman,*

Everyman, Spenser's *February Ecologue,* Coleridge's *Christabel,* the poetry of G. M. Hopkins (who talks about "sprung rhythm" and "outrides"),[10] the poetry of T. S. Eliot, and many another in our day.

Let us now return and dwell more precisely for a moment on the principle of relative stress. This is a slight but very certain thing in English; it is the indispensable and quite adequate principle for recognizing and scanning verses composed precisely of a given number of English syllables — or more exactly, for seeing if they *will* scan (for not all sequences of equal numbers of syllables show a measured alternation of accents). This is the main point of our whole essay: simply to reassert the fact of English syllable-stress meter, to vindicate the principle of relative stress as the one principle of stress which in conjunction with syllable counting makes this kind of meter. Mr. Chatman has already quoted the landmark statement about relative stress made by Otto Jespersen in his "Notes on Metre," 1900 (*Linguistica* [Copenhagen, 1933], pp. 272–274), and we need not repeat this. In speaking of this principle let us explain firmly, however, that we do not find it necessary to follow either Jespersen or Trager-Smith in believing in any fixed or countable number of degrees of English stress. We wish in the main to avoid the cumbersome grammar of the new linguists. For all we know, there may be, not four, but five degrees of English stress, or eight.[11] How can one be sure? What one can nearly always be sure of is that a given syllable in a sequence is more or less stressed than the preceding or the following. Or, suppose that there are, as Jespersen and Trager-Smith seem to agree, just *four* degrees of English stress. The discriminations are not needed for discerning the meter — but only the degrees of more and less, even though in a given sequence of stresses we have to recognize more, more, and even more. How *much* more is always irrelevant.

The main thing to observe about the principles of relative stress and counted syllables is that by means of these you can explain the necessary things about English syllable-stress verse. For one thing, quite starkly, you can tell an iambic line from one that is not iambic.

Preserved in Milton's or Shakespeare's name.

When a student misquotes this Popean line in a paper, it is not our perfect memory of the poem but our sense of the meter (and our belief in meter) which tells us he has left out a word. The four-beat theory of the pentameter could not make this discovery.

[10] Yvor Winters, *The Function of Criticism* (Denver, 1957), pp. 79–100, 109–123, expresses a view of English meter in general and of Hopkins which we take to be substantially in accord with our own.

[11] Alexander J. Ellis, "Remarks on Professor Mayor's Two Papers on Rhythm," *Transactions of the Philological Society 1875–1876* (Strasburg, 1877), p. 442, distinguished "nine degrees" of "force" or stress in English and likewise nine degrees of "length," "pitch," "weight," and "silence." Cf. R. M. Alden, *English Verse* (New York, 1904), p. 4 n.

To take another kind of example: let us suppose that Pope had written:

A little advice is a dangerous thing.

Persons who say that the line is one of Pope's four-beat lines will be hard put to explain why it isn't a good line; it still has its four strong beats. Yet nobody can actually say that the revised line is a good Popean line and goes well with the other lines of the *Essay on Criticism*. And all we have changed is the position of one relative accent, which makes it impossible that the syllable "is" should receive a stronger accent than the preceding syllable, and hence impossible that there should be five iambs in the line.

A líttle advíce is a dángerous thíng.

That one shift of accent throws us immediately into the anapestic gallop, and we have a line that belongs in Anstey's *Bath Guide*.

Another kind of example:

Ah, Sunflower, weary of time.

Hardly the Goldsmith or Anstey anapestic gallop. Yet unmistakably an anapestic line. The strong syllables "Ah," and "flow-," coming where they do, create a heavy drag. Nevertheless, "sun" is even stronger, at least stronger than "flow-," a fact which is crucial. A reader can take the two opening syllables as he likes, as iamb, trochee, or spondee (if there is such a thing), and still not defeat the subsequent anapests. The very weak syllables "er" and "y" in two key iambic stress positions make it unthinkable that the line should be read as iambic.

Again: the beginning of the line is a characteristic place, in both iambic and anapestic lines, for the full inversion.

Ruin hath taught me thus to ruminate.

Whether 'tis nobler in the mind to suffer . . .

Softly, in the dusk, a woman is singing to me;
Taking me back down the vista of years, till I see . . .

But:

Hail to thee, blithe spirit!

This is something different. The unquestionably iambic movement following the very strong first syllable [12] might, if we were desperate, be accounted for

12 The problem of "rising" and "falling" meters is one which we are content to touch lightly. Temporal theorists, working on the analogy of the musical downbeat, tend of course to make all meters falling. George R. Stewart, Jr., a moderate timer, makes the following revelatory statement: "If a person comes upon a road and walks a few rods before arriving at the first milestone, he will have to pass five milestones, counting the first, before he has walked four measured miles; in other words, since the start and the finish must be shown, five markers are necessary to establish four units. In verse the stresses are the markers, and the feet are the units. Five stresses can mark off only four

by saying that the word "Hail" breaks into two syllables, "Hay-ul," with a resultant needed extra weak syllable and the familiar opening pattern of iambic inversion. But a much more energetic and irrefutable assertion of the iamb appears in the progressive rise or stress increase of the three syllables "theé, b̋lithe, s̋́pirit." (Note well: the slack of a given foot can be stronger than the stress of the preceding foot.) For a trochaic reading of this line, you would have to have "thee̋, b́lithe," a rhetorical impossibility, making a nonsensically hopping line.

The notion of an accentual spondee (or "level" foot) in English would seem to be illusory, for the reason that it is impossible to pronounce any two successive syllables in English without some rise or fall of stress — and *some* rise or fall of stress is all that is needed for a metrical ictus. This fact produces in English iambic meter two kinds of ambiguous situations or metrical choices, that of two weak syllables coming together, and that of two strong syllables coming together. In each of these situations, the iambic principle is saved merely by the fact that certain unhappy choices are impossible.

> Rocks, caves, lakes, fens, bogs, dens, and shades of death.

Certainly it is impossible to pronounce the first two, the first three, the first six syllables of this line with a perfectly even stress. On the other hand, no determinate pattern of stresses seems dictated. No doubt several are possible and are actually employed or experienced by various readers of this Miltonic passage. To us the most plausible seems as follows:

> R̋ocks, cáves, lákes, fe̋ns, bógs, d̋ens . . .

The more regularly iambic reading, "Rócks, ca̋ves, lákes, fe̋ns," etc. seems forced. The only reading which will clearly defeat the iambic movement is absurd: "Rőcks, cáves, la̋kes, féns, etc."

Two weak syllables together present perhaps the more difficult problem. But all cases will not be equally difficult.

> In profuse strains of unpremeditated art.

intervals, so that what we ordinarily call a five-foot line might be more properly described as a four-foot line with a little left over at beginning and end" (*The Technique of English Verse*, p. 42). (For Mr. Stewart "rising" and "falling" are qualities of phrasing, not of meter, p. 37.) Suppose, however, that we are counting not "measured miles" but precisely milestones — not equal times but precisely stresses. And suppose that a man walks not a "few rods" but a full mile before reaching the first milestone. The first slack syllable of the iambic line is as much a mile as any other slack syllable. The line begins at the beginning of that syllable. The iambic line which starts with a strong and then *one* weak syllable is a more difficult matter. But many such lines, like the one from Shelley's "Skylark" which we discuss above, can be shown in one way or another to be in fact iambic. The shape of the phrases is likely to have much to do with it. Other lines of this sort, such as some in Tennyson's "The Lady of Shalott," may in fact be ambiguous — that is, they may be susceptible of being satisfactorily read either as iambic or as trochaic.

Here certainly the crucial fact is that "strains" is *more* stressed than "-fuse." Only observe that much — come out on the fourth syllable with an ictus, and the first two syllables can be stressed any way anybody wants. There are only two possible ways: "Ín pro-" or "In pró-." The second way, invoking a kind of Miltonic indult for the disyllable beginning with "pro-," makes the line more regularly iambic, but it is not necessary.

Upon the supreme theme of Art and Song . . .

This is the same thing, only pushed ahead to the second and third feet of the line. The situation of the four syllables here, two weak and two strong, has been described as a kind of compensation, a "hovering" of the accent, or as a "double or ionic foot" (Ransom, *Kenyon*, XVIII, p. 471). And doubtless some such notion does something to help our rationalizations. But we may observe also that only the coming together of the two strong accents makes possible the coming together of the two weak. "The" and "su-" are so weak only because "-preme" is so strong; and because "-preme" is so strong, "theme" has to be yet stronger. (Imagine a group of persons arguing about themes. One says theme X is good. Another says theme Y is good. Another says, "Yes, but the supré́me théme is Zeta." Just the reverse of the stress required in the Yeats line.) In a system where the only absolute value, the ictus, consists only in a relationship, we needlessly pursue a too close inquiry into the precise strength of the stronger point in the relationship. A somewhat more difficult, double, example of the two-weak, two-strong pattern is provided by Marvell.

To a green thought in a green shade.

One may begin by observing that whatever we do with the two pairs of weak syllables, it remains absolutely certain that "thought" is stronger than "green," and that "shade" is stronger than "green." (The relative strength of the two "greens" produces of course the peculiarity of the logico-rhythmic character of the line — the interaction of its sense with its meter. But here we speak precisely of the meter.) "To a," because of its introductory position, presents no difficulty. "In a" is more curious just because of its medial position. Probably a rather marked caesura, in spite of the continuing syntax and the shortness of the line, is created by the head to back juxtaposition of the two ictuses "thought" and "in." This again is part of the peculiar gravity of the line. The most plausible reading seems to us:

Tó a gré́en thó́́ught ín a gré́en shá́́de.

If anybody wants to read:

To a grén thó́ught in a grén shá́de,

arguing for two anapests compensated for by two single-syllable strong feet, there is probably no triumphant way to refute the reading. Still the lack of pause between "green" and the nouns which follow it is against the single-syllable foot. The single-syllable foot occurs in lines that sound like this: "Weave, weave, the sunlight in your hair."

Some of the most perplexing problems confronting the theorist of English meter — no matter to what school he belongs — are those arising in connection with the "dipody" or double-jump single foot (x′x″). This foot was much used by narrative poets of the late Victorian and Edwardian eras and also, because of its accentual difficulties and ambiguities, has been a favorite ground for exercise in several kinds of temporal scansion. Regular or nearly regular instances of the dipody are perhaps easy enough.

I wo″uld I we′re in Sho″reham a′t the se″tting o′f the su″n.

A recent handbook remarks very sanely: "Although the meter is duple insofar as there is an alternation between unaccented and accented syllables, there is also an alternation in the degree of stress on the accented syllables . . . the result is that the two-syllable feet tend to group themselves into larger units" (Laurence Perrine, *Sound and Sense* [New York, 1956], p. 160). "You will probably find yourself reading it as a four-beat line." It is a kind of strong-accent meter, with number of syllables and minor stresses tightened up into a secondary pattern. An easy enough substitute for the dipody will be of course the anapest (xx′). The iamb also (x′) is available, and also the single strong-stress syllable, either at the start of the line, or just after a medial pause.

B″rooding o′'er the glo″om, spi′ns the bro″wn e′ve-ja″r.

Thus dipodic meters can occur where no single line has more than two dipodies, and many lines have only one, and in these latter the reader may well have a choice just where to place the dipody. Meters of this sort are very slippery, elusive. One's first feeling on reading them may be that a strong lilt or swing is present, though it is hard to say just how it ought to be defined. A recurrent feature may be that the line seems to start on a strong stress, with falling meter, but then, with the aid of the agile dipody swings up midway into a rising meter to the finish. The number of syllables in the line will vary greatly, and the principle of relative stress operates with a vengeance — the weaker syllable of the dipody showing all sorts of relations to the stresses of the other feet. It is a tricky, virtuoso meter, very apt in nursery rhymes and in the rakish, barrack-room, mad-hatter, pirate-galleon narratives of the era to which we have alluded above. Meredith's pleasant little monstrosity "Love in the Valley" is a striking instance of the difficulties. It seems safe to say that no *great* English poems have been accomplished in any variant of this meter. The theory of meter which we are defending is, we believe, better fitted to explain — and reveal the ambiguities of — the dipodic meter than any other theory. But the illustration and arguing of the point are perhaps beyond present requirements.

IV

It is one of the hazards of an argument such as this that it is often on the verge of slipping from questions about something that seems to be merely and safely a matter of "fact" to questions about value. It is quite possible that some prosodists of the linguistic and musical schools would grant that meter, as we have described it, is a fact, but in the same breath would put it aside as of little consequence, at least when compared to the strong-stress pattern or some principle of equal timing. This was, for instance, the spirit of D. W. Prall's attack on the traditional metric in his *Aesthetic Analysis* (New York, 1936, esp. pp. 117, 130). Such a metric was trivial, "artificial," misleading. Our own difference from some recent writers may partly be reduced to a difference in emphasis, which reflects a different estimate of significance. We maintain not only that meter, in our sense, does occur, but that it is an important feature of verse.

To make out a broad-scale case for this claim might require much space and effort. Fortunately, we can do perhaps all that is necessary at the moment if we work upon an assumption that is now quite widely entertained, or indeed is a commonplace with students of poetry today: that there are tensions between various poetic elements, among them meter and various aspects of sense, and that these tensions are valuable.

One of the good features of Mr. Chatman's *Kenyon* essay is his constant appeal to an idea of "tension" between the full spoken poem and some kind of metrical pattern. "I believe that the beauty of verse often inheres in the tensions developed between the absolute, abstract metrical pattern and the oral actualization of sequences of English sounds" (p. 436). A student in a seminar presided over by one of the present writers was stumped, however, in scanning a line at the blackboard and refused to put the next stress mark anywhere at all. "I don't see how to show the interaction between the meter and the sense." As if by scanning he *could* show the interaction. As if anybody expected him to. As if the meter itself could be the interaction between itself and something else. This interest in tension, or interaction, is excellent. But how can there be a tension without two things to be in tension?

> Ẃondring upón this wórd, quáking for dréde.
> (*Clerk's Tale*, l. 358)

Here is a very special relation of phrase to meter. The double inversion, at the start of the line and again after the caesura, gives the two participial verbs a special quiver. But this depends on the fact that there *is* a meter; the inversions otherwise would not be inversions.

You can write a grammar of the meter. And if you cannot, there is no meter. But you cannot write a grammar of the meter's interaction with the sense, any more than you can write a grammar of the arrangement of metaphors. The interactions and the metaphors are the free and individual and unpredictable (though not irrational) parts of the poetry. You can perceive them, and study them, and talk about them, but not write rules for them. The meter, like the grammar and the vocabulary, is subject to rules. It is just as important to observe what meter a poem is written in (especially if it is written in one of the precise meters of the syllable-stress tradition) as it is to observe what language the poem is written in. Before you recognize the meter, you have only a vague apprehension of the much-prized tensions.

Perhaps it needs to be said that there is a difference between deviations from a meter (or "exceptions," as Mr. Ransom calls them) and the constant strain or tension of a meter (as an abstract norm or expectancy) against the concrete or full reality of the poetic utterance. The deviations are a part of the tension, but only an occasional part. The deviations occur only here and there — though some of them, the inverted first foot, the dropping of the first slack syllable, the extra slack syllable internal to the line (elided, or not elided in the anapest) — occur so often as to assume the character of an accepted complication of the norm. But the tension in the wider sense is always there. Here one might discourse on the "promotion" and "suppression" of syllables to which both the linguists and Arnold Stein refer. These are useful terms. There is no line so regular (so *evenly* alternating weak and strong) that it does not show some tension. It is practically impossible to write an English line that will not in some way buck against the meter. Insofar as the line does approximate the condition of complete submission, it is most likely a tame line, a weak line.

And thus: "scanning" a line is not a dramatic, or poetic, reading of a line. Scanning a line is reading it in a special, more or less forced, way, to bring out the meter *and* any definite deviations or substitutions. Scanning will not bring out the other parts of the tension; it will tend to iron them out. On the other hand, a good dramatic, or poetic, reading will tend to bring out the tensions — but note well that in order to do this it must be careful not to override completely and kill the meter. When that is done, the tensions vanish. (Another reason why the meter must be observed is, of course, that if a line is truly metrical, a reading which actually destroys the meter can only be an incorrect reading — by dictionary and rhetorical standards.) A good dramatic reading is a much more delicate, difficult, and rewarding performance than a mere scanning. Yet the scanning has its justification, its use. We would argue that a good dramatic reading is possible only by a person who *can* also perform a scansion.

"The trouble with conventional metrics," complains Mr. Chatman, "is that because it cannot distinguish between levels of stress and intonation, it often cannot distinguish meaningful from trivial performances" (p. 436). The answer is that metric is not required to do this, though it is needed for it. Mr. Chatman or another reader will have to make his own reading as meaningful as possible, but he will be in a better position to do this if he recognizes the meter. We are speaking all along, if not about a sufficient, yet about a necessary, rule for poetic reading.

If we may insert a brief pedagogic excursus: Schoolteachers nowadays, beginning in grade school and going right up into graduate school, probably try much too hard to prevent their students from a "mechanical" or thumped-out scansion, telling them rather to observe the variations, the tensions — telling them in effect to promote all tensions as much as possible. But the fact is that the tensions and the variations will pretty much take care of themselves if the student lives long enough and provided he is equipped with just one principle (of no precise application) that the variations and tensions are there and ought somehow to be recognized. The variations and tensions tend to assert themselves. The meter, because it is artificial, precisely measured, frail if meticulous, tends to be overridden and, if not actually destroyed (as it cannot be in any correct reading), at least obscured. This you can see if you ask college Freshmen to scan a passage of Milton or to write fifteen lines in imitation. The probability is that the student of average gifts, if he has never at any stage of his schoolroom education been required or allowed to whang out the meter, is not aware that it is there and hence has very little notion of what the teacher means by the tensions.

For the word "tension," let us substitute at this point, in a concluding suggestion, the word "interplay" — meaning the interplay of syllable-stress meter with various other features of linguistic organization, but especially with those which are likely to set up other quasi-metric or rhythmic patterns. One of the disadvantages of the old strong-stress meter is doubtless its limited capacity for interplay. The stress pattern of the meter is so nearly the same as the stress pattern of the syntax and logic that there is nothing much for the meter to interplay with. The same must be true for all meters depending on patterns of repeated or parallel syntax — such as the meter of the Hebrew Psalms and the free verse of Walt Whitman. Where such meters gain in freedom and direct speech-feeling, they lose in opportunity for precise interplay. Conversely, where syllable-stress meters lose in freedom and naturalness of speech-feeling, they gain in the possibility of precise interplay. Perhaps this suggests a reason why the greatest English poetry (Chaucer, Shakespeare, Milton, Pope, Wordsworth) has after all been written in the more artful syllable-stress meter — not in the older, simpler, more directly natural strong-stress meter.

It is no doubt possible to think of many kinds of interplay, with many resulting kinds of total poetic feel. Maybe some of the languor and soft drag of Tennyson's verse, for instance, comes sometimes from the interplay between the rising iambic motion of the line and the falling trochaic character of a series of important words.

> It little profits that an idle king . . .
> To follow knowledge, like a sinking star . . .

Again, and very frequently in English verse of the tradition, the special rhythmic effects arise from the fact that the stress pattern of the iambics either more or less coincides with or more or less fails to coincide with the pattern of the stronger logical stresses, thus producing a movement either slow or fast, heavy or light.

> That, like a wounded snake, drags its slow length along . . .
>
> Flies o'er th'unbending corn, and skims along the main.

The same kind of thing combines further with the number and length of the words involved in a line to produce contours of tension so special as perhaps better not translated into any other kind of meaning but simply regarded as shapes of energy. The 10,565 lines of Milton's *Paradise Lost,* all but two or three of them iambic pentameter lines, abound in illustrations of Milton's virtuosity. To show two extremes in one respect, recall a line we have already quoted and set beside it another.

> Rocks, caves, lakes, fens, bogs, dens, and shades of death . . .
> Immutable, immortal, infinite . . .

Eight strong stresses in one line; three in the other. But five *metric* stresses in either. And if that were not so, there would be nothing at all remarkable about the difference between eight and five.

It is, finally, possible, as we have already observed, that a given line in a given poet may invite scanning in either the older strong-stress way or in the Chaucer-Tennyson syllable-stress way — four beats by the old, five beats by the new. If a poem written on the whole in syllable-counting pentameters happens to show here and there lines which have one somewhat lighter stress and hence four stronger stresses, this is not very remarkable. For in the nature of things, as we have already observed, five stresses will always include one weakest. We have already sufficiently illustrated this phenomenon. But if a poem written on the whole in a meter of four strong stresses, with indeterminate number of syllables, at some point tightens up, counts syllables, and tilts minor accents into an iambic pentameter, this is something else. A wise and shifty modern poet, always in search of rhythmical invention, writes a stanza containing in the middle such a line as:

> Her hair over her arms and her arms full of flowers,

and at the end:

> Sometimes these cogitations still amaze
> The troubled midnight and the noon's repose.

This is playing in and out of the metrical inheritance. Part V of *The Waste Land* begins:

> After the torchlight red on sweaty faces
> After the frosty silence in the gardens
> After the agony in stony places . . .

Coming after four parts of a poem written largely in strong-stress meter, these lines, with their marked swinging parallel of construction, will most likely be read at a fast walk as strong-stress meter, four stresses to the first, three each to the second and the third. But each is also a perfectly accurate pentameter line, each complicated in the same two traditional ways, the inverted beginning and the hypermetric ending. ("Whether 'tis nobler in the mind to suffer . . .")

It is probably not until about the time of Mr. Eliot and his friends that the free and subtle moving in and out and coalescing of strong-stress and syllable-stress meters in the same poem, the same stanza, begins to appear with any frequency. This is something remarkable in the history of metrics. But the understanding of it depends precisely upon the recognition of the few homely and sound, traditional and objective, principles of prosody upon which we have been insisting throughout this essay. Without recognition of the two distinct principles of strong-stress and of syllable-stress meter, it seems doubtful if anything at all precise or technical can be said about Mr. Eliot's peculiar rhythms and tensions.

John Hollander

THE METRICAL EMBLEM

In some remarks entitled "Literature and Language," R. A. Sayce, an English critic, voiced a complaint which I expect has recently diminished, and will continue to diminish, in force and frequency. Objecting to what he feels has become a dominant trend in poetic analysis, "This, then," he insists, "is the first great problem of literary language — to discover the relation between technical studies of prosody or prose rhythm and the music of words." I think that we may take Mr. Sayce's implied request as demanding not philosophical clarification (e.g. of the general problem, "What is the connection between our knowledge about a process or thing and our normal uses of that process or thing?"), but instead, a justification of prosodic analysis in terms of its success in confirming and accounting for the almost magical effects upon a reader of the "musical" or non-semantic patterns of poetic structure.

One of the ways in which structural linguistics has been extremely helpful to literary criticism, I think, has been in helping to answer this kind of demand for a grounding of metrical studies in empirical knowledge. A structural grammar of a language does indeed segment the flow of speech and, temporarily at least, seems to hypostatize those segments, to treat them as *things,* and discuss the structure of more complicated things, utterances composed of them. But utterances are speech acts; it is only for the purposes of understanding their structure and function that they are treated as things at all. As far as linguistic theory is concerned, there is no chasm requiring bridging between the study of utterances and knowledge of their effects, meanings, significances, or specific ways of mediating the behavior of other people. The first leads to the second; and it may not be misleading even to say that the second can be defined in terms of the first.

Mr. Sayce, in attempting to show "the difficulties underlying the identification of literature with its linguistic substance," did not make the most fortunate case for his point. Aside from the question whether any such diffi-

This paper was presented at the Social Science Research Council's Conference on Style, held in Bloomington, Indiana, April 17–19, 1958. Reprinted from *The Kenyon Review,* XXI (1959) by permission.

culties exist, his discussion harps on outmoded and obscure musical analogies and betrays no knowledge of linguistic methods much beyond the scope of the school grammar. But beneath his confusions stirs the germ of what may be a legitimate caveat, not against the treatment of literary events as linguistic ones, but against the ways in which this treatment is to be managed. In the following discussion I shall try to illuminate one aspect of this problem of the literary utility of linguistic methods. In the course of it, I shall temporarily revive a distinction that has fallen into recent disrepute, not so much because of what may seem its arbitrariness, but because of the way it has come to abuse standard usage. The distinction between "meter" and "rhythm" that has been used in the past to divide schema from particular, a norm from an actual instance, has come to be disregarded in good part because "meter," "prosody" and "rhythm" are so often used interchangeably by all but the most fastidious. Aside from this, however, there seemed to be no reason for distinguishing, as mutually exclusive but parallel concepts, a particular event and a generalization about many such similar events. A line of verse, for example, and the class of all lines like it (e.g. "*the* iambic pentameter line") were clearly different in type; and the important and interesting cases of those lines which were not exactly like the others, but tempted us to remark that they *purported* to be like them, were afforded no clarification by the meter-rhythm distinction. I should nevertheless like to re-draw it below, but in a slightly different way; and having drawn it, I shall attempt to suggest what it is that the notion of a poem as literature seems to demand of linguistic analysis that recent applications of structural linguistics to poetry have yet to fulfill.

II

"Meaning," "significance," "function," "relevance," on the one hand; on the other, "meter," "prosody," "music," "form." To connect the terms of the first group with those of the second; to distinguish between the terms in each group and to account for and prevent their frequent confusion; and finally, to justify the lines along which these distinctions are drawn, have come more and more in recent years to engage the fullest concerns of poetics. The more specifically instrumental roles played by structural linguistics in this engagement have been considerable; many of its basic principles were brought to bear by I. A. Richards 30 years ago upon the clichés and mystiques that, accumulating over two centuries of poetic theory, had blurred the boundaries and overlappings of these analytic concepts. Working from Richards' foundations, at once impelled and guided by John Crowe Ransom's rigorous demands, poetic theory has accomplished a good deal of useful demolition work. And if it has not been able to erect either the impressive façades of neoclassic aesthetics, nor the epistemological ruins and sensuous visions of romanticism, recent poetic theory has at least managed to stake out its domains, search its title and ground its claim. A modest sort of accomplishment for a mid-20th-Century, English-speaking, speculative discourse, perhaps, but an undeniably useful one.

In addressing itself to the problem of sound and sense, recent inquiry has been particularly successful in clearing away a compost heap of conflicting, often self-inconsistent traditional prosodical theory, increased in the past hundred years by ritually sustained errors and, even more, by an inability to confront what it actually was that contemporary poets were doing. Thomas Hardy was possibly the last major poet to write in a long tradition of English versifying whose founding we might assign to Ben Jonson on the grounds that he confessed to writing all his verses "first in prose." And yet one of Hardy's chief difficulties as a poet resided in his latent uneasiness with a tradition for which he invokes the authority of Wordsworth: "It is supposed that by the act of writing in verse an author makes a formal engagement that he will gratify certain known habits of association." It is possible, that is, to speak of Hardy's *choice of meter* in a way that we would be reluctant to do in the case of Hopkins, Eliot, Pound or Yeats, and, even more, to pass judgment on that choice by designating it an arbitrary one. For it is the poet's own sense of the function of the verse itself which changes from one literary epoch to another, and recent critical methods which treat poems like objects, like artifacts such as vases or sculptures, or even like organisms with souls, all derive in some measure from answers to the requests of modern poems to be treated as just that.

Traditional prosodical analysis, whether carried on for polemical or avowedly speculative reasons, was still a little too much like catalogues of styles in clothing to be able to deal effectively with a body of new poetry that was taking the form of cloth puppets or sea animals whose very garments were their bodies or shells themselves. In such a world of organistic, post-symbolist poetry and criticism it has been the particular utility of structural linguistics to take us back to taxonomy, to encourage us in the use of biological categories that help us to classify, sort, dissect and anatomize the natural history of verse. English poetry since Hardy has cried out for such murder, if murder it be; and the study of literary history itself may be seen to have profited from it, if only because it revealed the long record of prosodical inquiry itself as a history of ideology and of taste in analytic methods.

The uses of structural linguistics as a tool have actually extended beyond the clearing away of traditional confusions, and the resolving of questions like that of quantitative verse in English by undermining the bases of traditional arguments about them. A general program of making more public, of verifying, the private insights of the ear of a sensitive reader, for example, has proved a hopeful one. Particularly in the case of those poets, such as Wyatt, Shakespeare, the Jacobean tragedians, Donne, Yeats and Frost, whose formal diction is always informed by the syntactic and emphatic stress patterns of colloquial speech, have the suppositions, if not the methods, of modern linguistics been helpful.

Today, by an examination of contemporary poetry in which a purely graphic scheme of line arrangement can operate in open conflict with equally prominent phonemic ones, almost any reader can come to understand how aural and visual entities merge in status when they operate as metrical segments. And here a more general application of linguistic theory to poetics presents itself. For just as the conceptual distinction between the phonetic and the phonemic is crucial if one is to talk about the elements of a particular language, so is a clear distinction between the phonetic and the metric basic to a consideration of the role of sound in the game of poetic sense. In short, it is as a heuristic model that phonemics might be most useful to poetic theory, rather than merely as an implement for the treatment of a poem as a spoken utterance.

There is good reason, I think, in the light of recent work and old warnings both, for drawing this distinction. In the first place, although poems are neither purely spoken utterances nor inscriptions, their peculiar status, straddling the two, seems to lose itself under certain kinds of analysis that start out with putting the poem into phonemic transcription. The poem becomes the phonetic parts of its texture, really, while metrical conventions, the whole substance of traditional prosodic theory, are ignored or treated at best as an unexamined donnée, a given condition rather like the fact that the poem is in English, but in no way as binding on the interpretation of discrete signals. It may be that the influence of recent statistical approaches has generated the view that signals with a low probability of occurrence must necessarily have an increased *importance*. Within the framework of information theory, it is certainly true that the more surprising event is the more significant one, for the only kind of significance is defined as a function of the reciprocal of the probability of occurrence. But to equate "information" with "significance" in a non-rigorous sense may not be possible. In many cases, something like the opposite would appear to be true. The extremely high redundancy of capital letters at the beginning of lines of printed verse, for example, renders their informative value, in the above sense, trivial. But their actual role is of considerable importance, being one of definition, or of labelling the utterance in question as a poem. Its significance for the statistical analyst lies in the fact that it sets up prior expectation that will itself affect the relationship between the "surprise value" (for the reader) and the probability of occurrence (for the post-mortem analyst). Information theory must necessarily take the highly probable event more or less for granted. But in the analysis of a poem as a work of literature, these conventional events are of major importance.

It has been rather to the structure of self-contained poetic texts, than to the metrical conventions governing many such texts, that linguistic analysis has been devoted. But the literary critic, or even the well-informed reader, tends to think in terms of both what he is reading and how what he is reading resembles other things that he has read, of the poem as a thing in itself, and as an example of a literary form. The reader of any subtlety at all will often talk about a poem as if he felt that there were two sequences of events going on at once. The literary critic (who may have helped train the reader to talk in this way) will distinguish "meter" from "rhythm," assumed norm from actual instance, and perhaps resort to Gerard Manley Hopkins' notion of "counterpoint" to describe their relation. The greatest temptation to employ this notion arises when one occurrence in a poem seems to be part of two different schemes simultaneously. The process of enjambment will serve as an excellent case in point.

In the most general sense, an enjambment is any lack of alignment between syntax and line structure, but it is usually considered in the cases where a normal correspondence between the two is violated. Textural analysis treats enjambments not only in terms of their effects upon the poem's "flow of movement," but for their direct semantic operation. The most obvious cases of this occur when a compound is broken up between two lines, suddenly revealing, in a startling way, that the whole, rather than the separable part, is to be employed:

> And one can have a savory or a sweet
> Potato after dinner, if he chooses.

Another example might be that of the covert allusion for which only a line division seems to provide optimum syntactic ambiguity:

> Under a soupy tree
> Mopes Daphnis, joined by all
> The brown, surrounding landscape:
>
> Even in Arcady
> Ego must needs spoil
> Such a beautiful friendship!

Here the rhymes and the sense (depending on a modern colloquial use of "ego" as *amour propre*), as well as the line structure, force a separation of the two words which, when juxtaposed, recall the famous *memento mori* in the paintings of Guercino and Poussin, *Et in Arcadia Ego,* with the exception here that vanity, rather than death as the speaker, is made the ubiquitous subject. T. S. Eliot's notorious

> Princess Volupine extends
> A meagre, blue-nailed, phthisic hand
> To climb the waterstair. Lights, lights,
> She entertains Sir Ferdinand
>
> Klein. Who clipped the lion's wings
> And flea'd his rump and pared his paws?

makes the name straddle two stanzas as well as two lines, but the abruptly turned-to question nevertheless claims, by its alliterating "clipped," a line-kinship with what is treated as the offending patronymic syllable.

It is to a case which may have actually influenced Eliot in this poem that I should like now to turn. Ben Jonson's ode *To the Memory and Friendship of that Noble Pair, Sir Lucius Cary and Sir H. Morison* is, from the point of view of metrical conventions, not only an extremely programmatic poem, but possibly a didactic one as well. Throughout, successive stanzas are headed "The Turne," "The Counter-turne" and "The Stand" by which are translated the names of the Greek choral triad, *strophe, antistrophe* and *epode*. Jonson's stanzaic form keeps to the pattern of the Pindaric ode, AAB, with two stanzas identical in structure, the third slightly different in its pattern of line-length and rhyme. Although the stanza headings serve more as glosses than as discrete titles, the stanzas are self-contained and end-stopped. When an occasional enjambment does occur, it is of the common type that realigns itself in the very next line, in rhymed poems usually closing a couplet, as in Andrew Marvell's

Thy beauty shall no more be found
Nor in thy marble Vault shall sound
My ecchoing Song: then Worms shall try
That long preserv'd Virginity.

But in Jonson's eighth stanza an enjambment even more startling in some ways than Eliot's occurs:

THE COUNTER-TURNE

Call, noble *Lucius,* then for wine,
And let thy lookes with gladnesse shine:
Accept this garland, plant it on thy head,
And thinke, now know, thy Morison's not dead.
Hee leap'd the present age,
Possesst with holy rage,
To see that bright eternall Day:
Of which we *Priests* and *Poets* say
Such truths, as we expect for happy men,
And there he lives with memories; and *Ben*

THE STAND

Jonson, who sung this of him, e're he went
Himselfe to rest.

This is again a kind of pun-by-discovery. Just as "Sir Ferdinand" is a perfectly proper appellation, abruptly qualified by the enjambed remainder (what French prosody calls the *rejet*), so the line

And there he lives with memories; and *Ben*

is complete in itself, ending its stanza like the others on a full stop (the 17th-Century punctuation often uses colons and semicolons where we would employ commas). Just "Ben" may appear over-familiar; but for the living Cary and the late Morison, as well as the close-knit coterie of friends who called themselves "The Tribe of Ben," "Ben" alone was as frequently employed in dedicatory poems as in conversation. The line ending *"Ben,"* then, is for a coterie reader; with the addition of the *rejet,* it becomes more properly public. But Jonson continues his ninth stanza through an even more grotesque example:

Or taste a part of that full joy he meant
To have exprest,
In this bright *Asterisme:*
Where it were friendships schisme,
(Were not his *Lucius* long with us to tarry)
To separate these twi-
Lights, the *Dioscuri;*
And keepe the one halfe from his *Harry.*

Even more grotesque, perhaps, although some readers might rush through the hyphenation unperturbed, and with some reason to which I shall turn in a moment. But those readers who do dwell over the hyphenation will be following Jonson's conceit of the Greek twins Castor and Pollux being separated by death (this grows into the splitting of the constellation Gemini); they will read the "twi-" of "twi- / lights" as both root and prefix. "To separate these two (or twin) lights" is itself "separated" quite literally; the name, in an almost schematic logical trick, is treated *qua* object in the same way that its metaphorical bearer (the pair of Cary and Morison) is thereby reported to be treated. An effective device, this is not an unusual sort of thing in the Renaissance, being commonly used in polyphonic songs (*cf.* John Wilbye's madrigal "Sweet Honey-Sucking Bees": "For if one flaming dart coming from her eye, / Was never dart so sharp, ah, then you die!," where on the last line, the upper soprano part moves to an *f*♯ on the word "sharp").

But the impulse of many readers to carry along through break, to treat this as the common kind of flowing, non-ironic enjambment, is also of interest. The hyphenated enjambment is rare, but not in the least capricious, in the poetry of Jonson's age; it was used in English verse that was consciously attempting to model itself on certain Greek meters. Thomas Campion's polemical *Observations in the Arte of English Poesie* (1602), a metrical study that urges the abandonment of all rhyme and stressed scansion by English verse in favor of an adopted quantitative system making even less phonemic sense than it may have for Latin, contains an example of hyphenation in one of the model poems therein set forth:

Like cleare springs renu'd by flowing,
Ever perfet, ever in themselves eternall.

The *locus classicus* for this is in Greek choric meters, in Pindar, and in Sappho; Catullus and Horace (I think only once) so hyphenate in their Latin

Sapphics. Its justification in Jonson's ode must be ascribed to a purpose akin in some ways to Campion's, and although he eschewed the latter's prosodic theories, his commitment to classical models was very strong. Any reader in any way aware of the models, either through direct knowledge or through other adaptations, will to some degree recognize the device. Like Campion's and others' quantitative experiments it is a purely graphic convention (it was on the basis of letters, rather than phonemes, that syllables were assigned their weight); but in the case of both of Jonson's enjambments the separation engages the phonemic junctures of English.

One finds extremely queer treatments, incidentally, of enjambments far less surprising than these in so much literary criticism that I should like to make it quite clear that I am not recommending the sort of analysis that F. R. Leavis gives to two lines from Keats's ode *To Autumn:*

> And sometimes like a gleaner thou dost keep
> Steady thy laden head across a brook.

Dr. Leavis remarks that "As we pass the line-division from 'keep' to 'steady' we are made to enact, analogically, the upright steadying carriage from one stone to the next. And such an enactment seems to me properly brought under the head of 'image.' " This notion of analogical enactment is here used in a kind of magical way (like common methods of pointing out onomatopoeic effects that simply assert the already given connection between the sound and its context: "The pig is rightly so called," etc.) to show the peculiar "aptness" of Keats's image, and also, perhaps, to assert that the enjambment itself constitutes a metaphor of some kind. Within this method a circular argument is generally lurking; at best, Dr. Leavis' comments can be taken as a little poem in its own right on the subject of the text before him. There seems to be no real problem about these lines, however; the rather rich effect of the enjambment can be described, without much difficulty, by an appeal to speech. The line arrangement breaks up the verbal compound ['kiyp 'stediy] in much the same way that the name ['ben 'jansn] is separated in the earlier example. The difference is provided by the fact that the latter case takes advantage of an already given juncture, while the "keep/Steady" overhang enforces a new one, thus setting up a kind of sub-line:

> /   / ˘   ˘   / ˘   /
> keep steady thy laden head

(*not* "keep steady thy laden head", scanned ˘ / ˘ ˘ / ˘ /). Operative in this "sub-line" are the rhymes and assonances that associate "laden" and "head" with "steady"; but most important of all is the fact that the indicative is changed by the enforced stress addition into the cozening imperative ['kiyp 'stediy] of the kind colloquially uttered by the bystander who advises, and tries to assist with verbal magic, an actual balancer. No mysterious kind of enactment is necessary to account for a reader's *feeling* of appropriateness here. It is simply necessary to show that the reader is being reminded of the spoken language and forced, as by stress and pitch notation or by a Shavian stage direction, into a particular vernacular utterance. At the most extreme, it might be said that the reader is being put in the role of the steadier, perhaps, of the well-intentioned onlooker full of suggestions and a kind of verbal body-english.

But it is to Ben Jonson's enjambments, and particularly to his second one, that I should like to return. There seem to be two different *sorts* of significance at work here. The first is semantic; the second, more purely formal, in this case, graphic or what we might call *literal.* We have already observed that Jonson's intention throughout the ode seems to be referential (this is the second purported, but first actually imitative "Pindarick Ode" in English); it might be suggested that the overhangs, and particularly the hyphenated one, were consonant, if not actually cooperative, with the strophic titles. It is the fact of their appearance, however, and their role once they have appeared in the texture of the poem, that I wish to contrast here. The significance of the elements of neo-classic "form" in Jonson's ode is quite simply a historical significance; while the ironic and quasi-self-descriptive effects of the two might more properly be considered as showing up under the application of some poetic analogue of a synchronic analysis. (Of course, our knowledge about the "tribe of Ben," the frequent use of the Christian name alone in verse, etc., are historical facts themselves. But in invoking them, one is simply giving the meaning of the word "Ben" in Jacobean and Caroline poems.)

Now even if we want to reject the notion that either or both of these effects of the enjambments are, properly speaking, significances; and especially if we wish to follow a by now proverbial philosopher's guide, "Don't look for the meaning; look for the use," we may observe that their *functions* are clearly different, the uses to which they are put are as divergent as any verbal acts, such as admonishing, deceiving or requesting, can be. The workings of the formal, *metrical* effect are somehow prior to those of *rhythmic* (and since English has phonemic stress, hence *semantic*) processes; the former set up contingencies affecting the latter. The problem of accounting for and charting these contingencies actually underlies some of the most dubious enterprises of traditional prosody, placing much weight on graphic conventions or choices of form, perhaps (as if there were several possible outfits for the same poem, albeit one proper one) without really knowing why they might be important.

Behind so much Western aesthetics since classical antiquity lies a nostalgia for what was believed quite naively to have been a perfect, mystical marriage, in Attic times, of musical mode and ethos, of form and the effect upon human behavior proper to that form; a nostalgia for what was thought to have been a perfect music-poetry that made of human sense an instrument whose own sound was human feeling. The myth of such a golden age in which communication was immediate, and guided only by the channel of suitable form, became in the Renaissance a myth of Literature itself. Like the musical modality that many Greek writers themselves appear to us to misunderstand, meters and verse schemes have seemed to widely differing ages to possess inherent, psychologically affective qualities, and seemed to be measurable by decorum, in that any breach of this in their use would reveal itself upon comparing the nature and function of a mode, form or style. This is a little like the way we *feel,* and have been rightly chastized for thinking, about onomatopoeia, sound symbolism and the like. (It may be worth noting here that the important classic parables of decorum for neo-classic ages included that of Terpander, who was punished for adding an extra string to his lyre, and of Marsyas, who was flayed for playing the wild, passionate *aulos* which the goddess of reason had disgustedly cast aside — in both cases, the breach consisted in strengthening or widening the effectiveness of the music.)

This musical metaphor that underlies the history of literary notions about literary form was such a convenient one for poetic theory, and for so long, precisely because it could accommodate both the notions of formal significance under consideration here. In the whole classical doctrine of form and ethos there lay resolved what later ages came to feel as a dialectic of conventional and instant form, revealed in the struggle for authority of schematic and pathetic accounts of the workings of music and poetry. In antiquity, the only "formal" elements were of the first type, the *metrical* type (although *meter* and *rhythm* had clearly-opposed and also several confused sets of meanings in Greek times); any particular work was distinguishable only cognitively ("rationally") from other works in the same convention. The rationalistic treatment of music by Greek theorists made this possible by ignoring all textless music for theoretical purposes; *song* was always the subject under discussion. A conceptual distinction between "music" and "poetry" of the kind that has been made since the Renaissance was impossible; and there was no need to create musical metaphors to aid in describing the ethos of any particular poetic utterance.

This whole paradise of communication was originally a quasi-mythical account of the power of literature (as opposed to persuasive speech: it was only the later Renaissance that sought metaphorically to identify music and rhetoric). But its power as an ideal account of the less obvious workings of carefully planned utterances held poetic theory in subjection for ages. For an empirical world view that demands much more of its accounts of things, such a myth is hardly even heuristically useful. The ethos of a passage of poetry or of a segment of that passage is to be understood as operating linguistically, that is, in that domain of shared experience of sound that connects a speaker and his hearer. And if there were no such thing as *literature,* but only *poetry;* that is, if all poems were utterances whose structure was as significant as their assertions, making no attempt to share or imitate structures, but only to generate novel ones, then the whole problem of the two kinds of significance would vanish. There would remain only the "rhythm" of poems; there would be no such thing as "meter," for there would be no common scheme, no redundant elements, nothing "given."

But this is not the case. Poets continue to believe in modal myths long after they abandon other creeds. They continue to think in terms of "choosing" a meter even though, in stylistically eclectic ages like our own, they may resurrect, adapt or newly forge their stylistic patterns. And poems continue to be literary events, which is also to say that it may be misleading to consider them as existing in any but a rather peculiar dialect of the language in which they are written. Their literary status in no way obliterates their linguistic status; it qualifies it only. Neither does the classification of a shouted "Go to the devil!" as a curse prevent it from remaining an utterance nevertheless; it merely specifies a rhetorical context. Now "meter" traditionally considered as arising from the literary classification and analysis of poems, jumps into prominence as a result of the historical mapping of several kinds of utterances in their historical contexts. The "rhythm," the flow of the poem in passage (aural or visual), the stream of effect upon the reader, are all just as much the special concern, it is true, of the linguistically oriented poetic analyst as is the "meter" the concern of the historian or of the apologist for a style. To analyse the meter of a poem is not so much to scan it as to show with what other poems its less significant (linguistically speaking) formal elements associate it; to chart out its mode; to trace its family tree by appeal to those resemblances which connect it, in some ways with one, in some ways with another kind of poem that may, historically, precede or follow it.

But we have seen how in one case metrical qualities may coincide, coexist in the same element, with rhythmical ones. This may occur with respect to rhymes, stress patterns, syllabic arrangements, or even larger forms. The sonnet form functions, apparently, in two ways at once. By setting up certain canons of line length, rhyme scheme, etc., and by tending to limit larger syntactical patterns (in the case of a Shakespearean sonnet, by tending to set up an arrangement of a clause with two dependent clauses and a final sentence) the sonnet is spoken of often as demanding a certain kind of logical form. On the other hand, the sonnet form itself is like a title, in that it serves to set up a literary context around the utterance, directing the reader to give to it a certain kind of attention just as the frame around a picture can urge a viewer to look at the picture in a particular way. Thus, to talk about the sonnet form of any poem may be to comment on either its "rhythm" or "meter" or both; about the particular role that it announces for itself, on the one hand, or about its actual movements on stage, so to speak, on the other.

Now this titling, framing (or, as I shall call it, *emblematic* or *badge-like*) function of meter is no less a linguistic operation than are those of smaller elements of the poem. To qualify the study of that function as macro-linguistic, or to confine it to a diachronic domain, may be a strategy necessary to the organization of a whole empirical pursuit. But there seems to be no reason for trying to separate the literary from the overall linguistic in any metaphysical way (perhaps by insisting that there is "something more" to works of literature than the language they are composed of — as Mr. Sayce puts it, their "music" for instance).

Whatever may have been accomplished by traditional metrical studies in the way of dissecting out and displaying this emblematic function of meter may have to be done over again without recourse to beliefs that poems were somehow beyond language, or to methods of analysis that barely hid their function of stylistic prescription. It has always been literary critics per se, arbiters, stylistic apologists and makers of judgments who have directed most attention to the metrical emblem and its framing, self-titling function. In connection with this, it should also be observed that the metrical emblem operates differently under different stylistic climates: an epoch like the Augustan age in England, for example, marked by a canonical style like that of the heroic couplet; or a "pre-literary" or "folk" period in which there may be single authoritative styles, not strictly canonical in the sense that they are ruled into usage so as to exclude certain others, but retaining status because there is little or no contact with foreign or past forms and styles; and finally, an eclectic, history-ridden age like the present one in which such stylistic anarchy prevails that one almost feels that a poem need be defined as any utterance that purports to be one. In the first two cases, the badge of meter has the fundamental work of *defining* the utterance as a literary event (Dr. Johnson could hardly consider Christopher Smart's rich, mad *Jubilate Agno* as a poem; but an age that includes *The Cantos* among its monuments must surely value highly the fragments that Smart in the 18th Century "shored against his ruin"). But in the last case, that of the eclectic age in which competing styles war for a lost authority, the meter becomes more than Wordsworth's "formal engagement"; it becomes almost a stipulation of what a poem ought to be. The frame begins to recommend, so to speak. And the emblem starts to take on a moral.

But the urging of a work of literature, perhaps accomplished by its formal frame, is no less an act of urging than any other kind of exhortation. The analysis of urging and exhorting can no longer be properly linguistic. And, finally, it is *as such* that it lies outside the realm of poetics.

Rulon Wells

COMMENTS ON METER

In basic agreement with the view of Messrs. Wimsatt and Beardsley that meter is an abstraction, I hope to add to its support by a more precise account of this abstraction than they have undertaken to give. This precision is gained by clarifying the relationships between the metrical abstraction and three others: (1) the conventional orthography in which a language is written; (2) a language *tout court,* as contrasted with different periods, different dialects, and different speech varieties (e.g. fast and slow, calm and impassioned) of the language; and (3) the phonemic system of any one dialect of that language at any one time. My account prepares for a rigorous "logical construction" of these four abstractions using the techniques developed by Bertrand Russell.

1. The recorded poem. "*The* poem" is never a datum for an interpreter; what is given to him is rather some record of the poem. There is a *first* (*the original*) *record* of the poem, and there is the class of all *exact copies* of the first record. The rules stating the conditions for exactness will vary with the standard. For example, if conventional orthography is the standard, handwriting may be exactly copied by letterpress type and underscored words may be printed in italic type, but the paragraphing, use of capital letters, etc., of the first record must be preserved. Three standards will concern us here: the standard of conventional orthography, the phonemic standard, and the phonetic standard. The first standard applies primarily to written records; the second and third primarily to spoken records.

In modern Europe the first record of a poem is usually a handwritten or typewritten document written by the poet himself. (The case of Milton dictating to his daughters is unusual in these times.) We may switch mediums in the course of making copies: the switch from spoken to written language is commonly called "transcription" and that from written to spoken language "recitation" or "reading aloud." The varieties of transcription that concern us here are conventional orthographic, phonemic, and phonetic.

Relative to a given standard, copies may be exact or inexact, and two kinds of inexactness are worth distinguishing. A copy that *abstracts* in a given respect leaves out a feature falling under that respect; for example, both phonemic and conventional orthographic transcriptions of spoken language abstract in respect to voice timbre (soprano versus tenor, etc.) and so are phonetically inexact. A copy that *embellishes* in a given respect puts in something; for example, relative to both the phonetic and the phonemic standards, the distinction drawn by conventional orthography between "principal" and "principle," or between "higher" and "hire," is an embellishment.

We may now define *the recorded poem* (a more accurate but rather more cumbersome name would be *the record of the poem*) as the class consisting of the first record of the poem and all exact copies of it, and anyone who has the first record or any exact copy of it may be said to "have" the recorded poem. The relation between the recorded poem and its members is that which Charles Peirce calls the relation between Type and Token.[1]

2. From the recorded poem to the poem. Can we identify the recorded poem with the poem? Or does it at least *define* (determine, identify) the poem? If it does not, we may say that it is an *inadequate* record of the poem. This could only be true if there are two or more possible poems of which, under the recording rules in use, the recorded poem can equally well be a record. Thus the inadequacy of any inadequate record lies in its being ambiguous.

The position that I would myself take is this: the only adequate record of a poem is a class whose members are (*a*) some one phonemic transcription of a spoken recitation of the poem, and (*b*) all exact copies (spoken or written) of this phonemic transcription. (When linguists disagree about how to phonemicize a given language, their different systems are at least intertranslatable: this justifies the simplification of speaking of *the* phonemicization of the language and dialect in which the poem is composed.) I understand phonemicization to include treatment of prosodic (suprasegmental) features, namely, intonation, stress, and juncture, as well as of the segmental features called vowels and consonants.

No record of a poem written in conventional orthography is an adequate record if judged by the phonemic standard, for, at the very least, its recording of the prosody will be inadequate. It may happen, nevertheless, that from this inadequate record an adequate record may be inferred, owing to the fact that the ambiguities that make the record inadequate are resolved by appeal to the general principles of the language. Or again, it may happen that some inadequacies in the record of the poem can be surmounted with the help of external (i.e., other than orthographic) evidence in the poem. The hypothesis

[1] C. S. Peirce, *Collected Papers,* Vol. L (Cambridge, Mass.), pp. 280–281.

that successive lines rhyme may tell us that the inadequate record *read* represents /rijd/ (because it is rhymed with "deed") rather than /red/ (which it would represent if it rhymed with "bread" or with "said"). Or considerations of meaning may show us which of two phoneme sequences "read" represents by telling us whether it is a nonpast or a past-tense verb.

There remain cases in which the inadequacies of a conventional orthographic record cannot be put to rights by assumptions drawn from generalizations about the language and dialect in which the poem is composed or from hypotheses about the meaning or the meter of the poem. Sometimes the inadequacies are insignificant, other times they are serious.

The upshot of all these distinctions is this. Conventional orthography permits *fairly* adequate records; poems or lines whose conventional recording is seriously inadequate are few. But just those relatively few instances are the ones that provoke so many pages of earnest scholarly discussion. What a needless waste of energy!

3. The poem and its meter. I move on now to the stage where the epistemological problem has been solved. The interpreter, I now assume, has inferred an adequate record of the poem; or, at the worst, he has before him a limited set of possibilities, one or another of which must be the true one, and between which the inadequate record available to him does not enable him to choose. What he must do then is work out the meter of each of his possibilities. It may happen, as Messrs. Wimsatt and Beardsley seem to suggest, that all these different possibilities will have the same meter. When that is the case, it can fairly be said that a conventional orthographic record of the poem is adequate to the meter of the poem, even if it is not adequate to the poem. This is one of the ways in which meter is abstract.

The main way, however, in which meter is abstract is this: the meter of a poem can be determined from an adequate record of the poem by (*a*) disregarding all vowels and consonants in the record but retaining the syllable count in each line; (*b*) disregarding intonations and junctures (except that the division between lines is marked by a juncture); and finally (*c*) converting the stress phoneme of each syllable into a metrical accent according to a set of rules.

The rules used are too complicated to be described briefly, but the following crude sketch will make a beginning. These rules are stated in terms of the Trager-Smith system,[2] with primary, secondary, tertiary, and weak stress denoted by the numbers 1, 2, 3, and 4 respectively.

Rule I. Stress 1 always counts as accented, 4 as unaccented; 2 and 3 are indeterminate.

Rule II. Stresses 2 and 3 are to be taken as accented or as unaccented, in any particular occurrence, whichever way will make the meter of the whole poem most uniform.

[2] G. L. Trager and H. L. Smith, Jr., *An Outline of English Structure* (Norman, 1951).

These rules only enable us to determine the meter which sets the norm for the poem. They may seem, and in fact are, insufficient to enable a reader to read a poem that is presented to him in conventional orthography. But this is because he has the additional problem, which I am here supposing solved, of inferring an adequate record. And what he does in practice is to cope with two problems simultaneously, the problem of inferring an adequate record and the problem of determining meter. He may use a tentative solution of one problem to help toward the solution of the other. This is what he does when he supposes a "poetic license." Poetic license is the replacement of the usual prosaic lexical form of a word by a different but similar form, for metrical purposes (meter, rhyme, etc.). Thus in the third line of "Westminster Bridge" the final syllable of "majesty" is subject to two replacements: the diphthong /ij/ is replaced by the diphthong /aj/, and (as an automatic consequence of this, since /aj/ with stress 4 does not occur) stress 4 is replaced by 3. Since stress 3 can be construed as accented (Rule II), "-esty" thus altered is fit to be an iamb and to rhyme with "pass by."

The question whether to suppose a poetic license would never confront an interpreter who had an adequate record. The question is only thrust upon him because he has to solve two problems simultaneously. He does it by using a maximization principle: among the possible interpretations of the ambiguous written record that is given him, he picks that one (if there is just one) with the most regular meter (in other words, one that maximizes the regularity of the meter). But it not seldom happens that he can find *two* interpretations, more regular than all the other interpretations but equal to each other, that deviate from perfect regularity in different ways: one by containing a poetic license, the other by containing an exception. This is the case with Milton's line "Immutable, immortal, infinite." In normal stress the syllable "in" has stress 1, "mut-" and "mort-" have stress 2, and all the others have stress 4. The result is a line whose feet are iambic, pyrrhic, iambic, iambic, and pyrrhic respectively — in other words an iambic pentameter line with exceptions in the second and fifth feet. But the conventional orthography equally represents another phonemic possibility: poetic license replacing the stress 4 of the syllables "-ble" and "-ite" by stresses 2 or 3. An adequate (phonemic) record of the poem would not confront the interpreter with the problem of inferring which phonemic interpretation is the intended one (and therefore the true one).

4. Recitation and style. The set topic of this conference has been style, but these comments have been about meter. What have meter and style to do with each other?

If style is individual, as opposed to what is common and general, the choice of one meter rather than of another may be a point of style on the part of the poet. But once a poem is composed and published, it is ready to be recited; and the differences between one person's recitation and another's *may* be matters of style. Thus recitational style and the metrical abstraction are complementary to each other. Different recitations of the same poem are allowable. What is common to them all includes the metrical abstractions of the poem (its meters, rhymes, alliterations, assonances, etc.); the features in which they differ include the stylistic individualities of the reciters.

But not every individual difference would usually be called stylistic; for example, the differences between a man's and a woman's voice would not, nor would the differences between different dialects. But the differences between a rapid and a slow tempo would be; so also those between a calm and an impassioned recitation, and between one that emphasized the meter and one that played it down. And then style too is an abstraction, like the poem's metrics and phonemics; for just as the poem is common to all its (admissible) recitations, so the style of a given reciter is what is common to all his recitations of different poems. The two abstractions mesh with each other like warp and woof to form the concrete fabric of recitations.

Seymour Chatman

COMPARING METRICAL STYLES

I

Meter is a systematic literary convention whereby certain aspects of phonology are organized for aesthetic purposes.[1] Like any convention, it is susceptible of individual variation which can be called stylistic, taking "style" in the common meaning of "idiosyncratic way of doing something." The goal of metrical stylistics, like that of the stylistics of other features, is to analyze these variations and their role in the design of the whole work of art. Since variations imply norms it is difficult to analyze styles without establishing some outside reference point. A convenient way of doing this is to compare the styles of two authors.

A convenient pair are John Donne and Alexander Pope. Donne wrote a group of satires in the 1590's, two of which Pope imitated: Satire II, "Sir; though (I thank God for it) I do hate" (on lawyers writing poetry), and Satire IV, "Well; I may now receive, and die" (on courtiers). Pope "versified" (his own word) Donne's satires because he felt, like Warton, that Donne had "degraded and deformed a vast fund of sterling wit and strong sense" by harsh diction and faulty meter. Thus we have an instance of a poet consciously attempting to revise another poet's work into his own style, or at least a style acceptable to his period's taste.

My primary intention is to describe the difference between the metrical styles of these poems. However, conclusions of a purely descriptive sort must seem trivial to the literary critic; to gain relevance they need to be "placed" in the whole effect of the poem. The last section of the paper considers broader aesthetic implications of metrical usages.

Before the comparison it is necessary to make some observations concerning the use of phonemics in metrical analysis. In the oral transmission of

Reprinted from *Style in Language*, edited by Thomas A. Sebeok, by permission of The M.I.T. Press, Cambridge, Massachusetts.

[1] I am very grateful to James Sledd for his thoughtful and searching criticism of this paper.

literature it is plain that a reader's vocal representation of segmental features (the individual sounds in sequence, like /p/, /t/, /k/) is more narrowly controlled by the text than his representation of suprasegmental features ("covering" patterns of stress, pitch, and juncture) and metalinguistic features (voice qualification, vocalization, etc.).[2] The reader must follow the author's sequence of segmental phonemes (if not individual phonemic actualizations and distributions) if he is to read correctly; and if he introduces dialectal variations, these are largely irrelevant to the text (e.g., Hamlet speaking with a North Georgia accent is still basically Hamlet). But since suprasegmentals are signaled much less adequately than the sequence of segmental phonemes, and metalinguistic features less adequately still, much is left to the reader's judgment in these matters. Presumably he chooses the suprasegmentals and metalinguistic features which in his opinion fit the whole context; the result is usually called his "vocal interpretation." He does not giggle or shout when reading Hamlet's "To be or not to be" soliloquy but uses metalinguistic features which signal the quiet and complex desperation of the moment. But differing insights into a passage and consequently differing interpretations are bound to arise (and these may admit semantic indeterminacies between the performer and his audience). Besides, there are the differing linguistic and metalinguistic styles of the readers themselves which will add to the complexity (e.g., two readers may agree that a line suggests a specific metalinguistic feature, but they may have different ways of signaling it; this also may prompt indeterminacy). So it seems necessary to distinguish the style of the poem from the performer's interpretation (his selections of appropriate suprasegmentals and metalinguistic features) and the performance style (the way in which he presents these).

It may be objected that we can never adduce the poet's style without introducing our own interpretation and performance style. This may be true, but it does not invalidate the distinction. It seems clear that personal style can be excluded from many sorts of considerations; for example, although two readers may disagree on how to interpret Shakespeare's sonnets, they may still agree that certain stylistic features are typically Shakespearean. Similarly, a critic analyzing Shakespearean and Spenserian sonnets can discount, so to speak, his own performance style while comparing the purely poetic styles.

[2] For "juncture" see fn. 6. The metalanguage is the system of vocal features, not included in the linguistic system, which operates concurrently with it and signals meanings about the speaker rather than about the lexical message he is presenting. The term "style," however, is not equivalent to "metalanguage"; it is taken to mean *individual variation.* Thus we may speak of "linguistic style" (e.g., the unique way an individual makes his /k/'s or the range in cycles between his highest and lowest pitch levels) or of his "metalinguistic style" (the particular way in which he drawls when indecisive or uses overhigh pitch when excited). See R. E. Pittenger and H. L. Smith, Jr., "Basis for Some Contributions of Linguistics to Psychiatry," *Psychiatry,* XX (1957), 71–74, and H. L. Smith, Jr., "The Communication Situation" (multilithed; Washington, 1955).

II

As for segmental phonological effects, it is important first to decide what the subject of inquiry is. I have argued elsewhere [3] that sound symbolism as such — the assumption that individual phonemes have expressive functions over and above their signaling functions in morphemes — is either without objective foundation or is too subliminal to be very useful in linguistics or stylistics. I do not think that the *quality* of individual sounds is productive as a meaningful feature, except insofar as certain conventional associations have grown up around them — that is, by their occurrences in words which they partially evoke when they are uttered alone: for example, /s/ may call up "snake," "smooth," or "soft" (depending on the train of thought in which the subject finds himself); or by suggesting nonlinguistic activity performed by the same parts of the vocal apparatus which produce the phoneme: for example, Burke's association of /p/ and /pf/ with spitting.

So we are basically concerned with the *quantities* of segmental sounds. Most of the conventional sound figures, like rhyme and alliteration, are quantitative contrivances. But what sorts of qualification are useful? Raw computation, like counting the total number of phonemes a poet uses in a poem and comparing *that* profile with norms for the language and for other poets, seems like a fruitless venture. The reader can hardly become aware of the total effect of "normal curve disruption" when it is diffused over the entire poem, and the capacity of eliciting *awareness* of distributional peculiarity seems essential for a feature to emerge as a literary convention. Quantitative effects work only at close range, over two or three words, or in certain conventionally fixed positions, for example, at the end of the line in the rhyming position. So most style analyses of segmental phonemes have been limited to close-range distributions, and there seems to be no reason for changing this procedure.[4]

Here is a representation of the more usual schemes in their ordinary definitions.[5]

A. Repetition Schemes

WORD-INITIAL

1. *Consonant alliteration.* Repetition of the same initial consonant in several adjacent syllables, usually coinciding with word stress: "furrow followed free."

[3] In "Linguistics, Poetics, and Interpretation: The Phonemic Dimension," *Quarterly Journal of Speech,* XLIII (1957), 248–256.

[4] For an important discussion of what constitutes relevancy in style analysis, see C. F. P. Stutterheim, "Modern Stylistics," *Lingua,* III (1952), 52–68: ". . . this is certain, that some formal element, which *is* brought to light through statistical investigation, but cannot be grasped by the consideration of the total experience of this totality, cannot be a stylisticum."

[5] See "Sound-Repetition Terms" by David I. Masson in *Poetics* (Warsaw, 1960) for a more elaborate breakdown of the schemes.

2. *Vowel alliteration.* Repetition of the same initial vowel or diphthong in several adjacent syllables, usually coinciding with word stress: "empty effort." (In some systems *any* vowels may alliterate.)

WORD-FINAL

1. *Rhyme.* Repetition of final stressed vowels and final consonants and consonant clusters, if any, but *not* of initial consonants in the syllable: "be:agree."
2. *Feminine rhyme.* The above, plus any additional unstressed identical syllables: "taker:maker" (but not "taker:sicker," for which see 5 below).
3. *Assonance.* Like vowels, different consonants: "fame:late."
4. *Consonance.* Like consonants, different vowels: "pressed:past."
5. *Homeoteleuton.* Repetition of whole final unstressed syllables where the stressed syllables preceding are consonant: "fission:motion." (Hence, a kind of "defective" feminine rhyme.)
6. *Eye rhyme.* A kind of assonance in which the letters are identical, although they represent different vowels: "blood:mood."

B. JUXTAPOSITION SCHEMES (from "On Musicality in Verse") [6]

1. *Chiasmus.* Reversal of phoneme sequence: /u/:/i/::/i/:/u/— "dupes of a deep delusion."
2. *Augmentation.* CC—CVC: "That slid into my soul."
3. *Diminution.* CVC—CC: "But silently, by slow degrees."

C. SYLLABLE CONTROLLING SCHEMES (for definitions, see p. 144)

1. *Apocope.*
2. *Aphaeresis.*
3. *Vowel and consonant syncope.*
4. *Synaeresis.*
5. *Monosyllabification* (synizesis, synechphonesis).
6. *Pseudo-elision.*

It is important to distinguish between *structural* uses of schemes, that is, between regular recurrences which form the basic structure of the verse (alliteration in Old Germanic poetry, assonance in Old French) and *occasional* uses. Whether a scheme is structural or not is arbitrary and conventional within the individual verse tradition. In English verse, line-end rhyme and near-rhyme are usually structural. Intralinear or word-adjacent rhyme is occasional, as is alliteration. All the syllable-controlling schemes are structural insofar as they assist in metrical arrangements.

The function of rhyme in English verse is primarily metrical, that is, to help mark line endings. Sometimes it has an additional, deeper semantic function. Professor Wimsatt has shown this very clearly in his paper on

[6] In Kenneth Burke, *The Philosophy of Literary Form* (New York, 1957).

rhyme.[7] He describes the "counter-logical" properties of rhyme, the surprise that we feel in observing the curious cooperation in sound that two disparate words have in common. One function of this surprise is to fix or cement the meaning in a more unified and aesthetically satisfying way than could occur by mere juxtaposition. In its lexical function, rhyme, like metaphor or epithet, limits meaning by asking us to consider suddenly the connection of two things whose sound shapes happen to be resemblant. In Professor Wimsatt's example, from "The Rape of the Lock,"

Whether the nymph shall break Diana's law
Or some frail China jar receive a flaw

the rhyme requires us to ask in what respects breaking Diana's law and marring a Chinese vase are similar. The implied answer is that in the rarefied society of which Belinda is a member, losing one's virginity resembles being so clumsy as to scratch a precious vase — both are simply marks of bad taste. In this way, the rhyme actually may provide information by limiting the possibilities of interpretation, just as the vehicle of a metaphor forces us to limit the possible interpretations of the tenor ("not *all* x's, or the whole of *x* but only those *x*'s or parts of *x* which resemble the vehicle *y* in some important respects"). In other words, the structural property of rhyme is to disturb the normal phonemic distribution expectancies by a superimposed pattern which may itself have lexical implications.

It is interesting to observe in detail the differences between Donne's and Pope's rhyming practice. As expected, Pope is very uniform: in the majority of instances, his end rhymes occur in metrically accented ("ictic") syllables. The only exceptions are occasional rhyming feminine syllables, for example,

as a Still, with Simples in it,
Between each Drop it gives, stays half a Minute (126–7).[8]

Donne has approximately the same number of feminine rhymes; his practice differs chiefly in rhyming stressed and unstressed syllables (the final syllables of polysyllabic words, or unstressed function words like prepositions and articles); for example,

O Sir,
'Tis sweet to talke of Kings. At Westminster (73–4).

Similar pairs in Donne's version are "alone:fashion," "one:prison," "yet:merit." It is interesting to see Pope avoid this sort of rhyme, even where he sticks fairly closely to the original. Thus, Donne's

[7] "One Relation of Rhyme to Reason," in *The Verbal Icon* (Lexington, 1954).

[8] All passages from Donne are taken from *The Poems of John Donne,* ed. H. J. C. Grierson (Oxford, 1912), pp. 149–154 and 154–158. The passages from Pope are taken from *The Twickenham Edition of the Poems of Alexander Pope,* ed. J. Butt (London, 1939); iv, pp. 27–49 and 132–145. Parenthetic numerals refer to line numbers. All examples are from Satire IV, unless otherwise indicated.

Now; Aretine's pictures have made few chast;
No more can Princes courts, though there be few
Better pictures of vice, teach me vertue; (70–72) [9]

becomes, in Pope's version,

Tho' in his Pictures Lust be full display'd,
Few are the Converts *Aretine* has made; (94–5).

Donne's

Ran from thence with such, or more haste than one
Who fears more actions, doth haste from prison, (153–4)

becomes in Pope's version

Ran out as fast, as one that pays his bail
And dreads more actions, hurries from a jail. (182–3).

Pope is more likely to keep those lines in Donne which end in full masculine rhymes. For example,

With his tongue . . .
In which he can win widdowes, and pay scores,
Make men speake treason, cosen subtlest whores, (45–6).

[9] The question has been raised whether "virtue" and other words of the sort might not have been pronounced with the accent on the second syllable, as undoubtedly they had been in the Middle Ages. R. Jordan, *Handbuch der Mittelenglischen Grammatik* (Heidelberg, 1934), p. 192, indicates that the stress had already shifted to the first syllable by the thirteenth or fourteenth century in the colloquial language, but in poetry the alternation between the two stress patterns continued, "until the fifteenth century and even later"; in fact even Byron could rhyme *virtué:pursue* in imitation of the older practice (English Bards 1218). It is thus difficult to be certain about the pronunciation in verse of French loan words of this sort, but the following points might be made in defense of assuming the colloquial pronunciation. (1) Donne uses the word "virtue" 65 times in his poetry. There are as many as ten instances in which the syllable is represented in Grierson's text as eliding into the next word (e.g., "Like Vertue' and truth, art best in nakednesse," in "Epithalamion at Lincoln's Inn," l. 128), something which could hardly happen if it carried word stress. (2) In 41 instances there seems to be little question that the stress pattern is "vírtue," since any other pronunciation would introduce a metrical inversion where there is otherwise no reason to assume one; typically the "vir-" falls on an even-numbered syllable in an even-syllabled line: "Then vertue or the minde to admire" in "Negative Love," line 4. (3) In ten instances the word appears as the first word in the line, where it seems easier to assume a simple case of metrical inversion than the pronunciation "virtúe." (4) In only four cases, then, outside of the present one, does the question of the pronunciation "virtúe" arise. In one, the balanced syntax and caesura seem to suggest the normal stress on the first syllable: "Falsehood is denizen'd. Vertue is barbarous" in "To Sir Henry Wotton," line 34. Two other instances occur in the poem "A Letter to the Lady Carey . . ." (ll. 30 and 39): "Have through this zeale, Vertue but in their Gall" and "For, your soul was as good Virtue, as she"; the word occurs eight other times in this poem with an indicated pronunciation of "vírtue," so it would seem probable that these are metrical inversions. The last occurrence of "virtue" where there is doubt occurs, interestingly enough, in a line from Satire I (41) which otherwise contains obvious metrical inversions of the extreme sort which typifies Donne's satirical meter: "Hate vertue, though shee be naked and bare?" which has stresses either on syllables 1,2,5,7,10 or on 2,4,5,7,10 if we assume "vírtue." All in all, these statistics, plus the fact that we know that it was part of Donne's style to sound colloquial, strongly suggest the pronunciation "vírtue" in the present instance.

The poets also differ in the way they use rhymes to construct their couplets. Pope, of course, emphasizes the couplet; the second rhyme coincides with punctuation marks, suggesting end-stoppage, whereas the first line runs on. In Donne, on the other hand, the majority of the lines are couplets only in the sense that the final syllables rhyme; that is, the couplet structure is not regularly confirmed by strong punctuation at the end of second lines. In actual count 77 per cent of Pope's lines are junctural as well as rhymic couplets, in comparison to less than half that number (36 per cent) in Donne. Furthermore, 15 per cent of Donne's couplets contain stronger punctuation at the end of the first line than at the end of the second. The differences can be appreciated after examining Pope's revisions. Of nineteen sets of rhymes that Pope keeps, more than half are changed to closed couplets. Consider, for example,

Donne:

to have been Interpreter
To Babells bricklayers, sure the Tower had stood.
He adds, If of court life you knew the good,
You would leave lonenesse. (64–7)

Pope:

"For had they found a Linguist half so good,
"I make no question but the Tow'r had stood." (84–5)

and
Donne:

Like a bigge wife, at sight of loathed meat,
Readie to travaile: So I sigh, and sweat
To heare this Makeron talke: (115–17)

Pope:

Like a big Wife at sight of Loathsome Meat,
Ready to cast, I yawn, I sigh, and sweat:
Then as a licens'd Spy . . . (156–8).

There is a semantic consideration, too. Pope's rhymes are more likely than Donne's to relate to lexical meanings, either redundantly or ironically. These examples could be added to Mr. Wimsatt's:

who got his pension Rug ("safe")
Or quicken'd a Reversion by a *Drug?* (134–5)
Who in the *Secret,* deals in Stocks secure,
And cheats th' unknowing Widow, and the Poor? (140–1)
Why *Turnpikes* rise, and now no Cit, nor Clown
Can *gratis* see the *Country* or the *Town?* (144–5).

Ironic juxtapositions like "Rug" and "Drug," "secure" and "Poor," and "clown" and "Town" are to be found only in Pope. They are not a part of Donne's satirical style.

When we turn to occasional effects, the picture is less clear, but there are indications of similar differences. The stylistic impetus that makes Pope prefer accurate, full rhymes as a structural feature seems to require him to make equally sure that no chance collocation of sound run afoul of his meaning. This is the negative job of rejecting fortuitous repetitions: purposeless internal rhymes, alliterations, and other sound similarities. For example, Donne has (proportionately) twice as many occurrences of alliteration of two syllables in immediate sequence as Pope, whereas Pope has almost four times as many occurrences of an intervening unstress. This means that Pope wants alliteration to cooperate with the meter, not to oppose it. He usually prefers to add alliteration where an unstressed syllable will fall in between: he revises Donne's "low fear becomes" to read "base fear becomes," "painted things" to "painted puppets," "fresh and sweet" to "fresh and fragrant," "weak ships fraught" to "frigates fraught," etc. Further, he avoids immediately contiguous ("ametrical") alliteration, for example, "win widdowes" becomes "cheat widows."

Pope's alliterations tend to have a syntactic basis. His alliteration of epithet-noun combinations, for example, is carefully done. Its effect is to strengthen through sound repetitions a favorite pattern of Neo-classical poets, bisyllabic modifier plus monosyllabic head: "whited wall," "bawling bar," "popish plot," "Gracious God," "Herod's hangdogs," "courtiers' clothes," "liveried Lords," "body's buff," "frigates fraught," "Dante dreaming," "wits so weak," etc. The alliteration gives these phrases a rounded or finished appearance much favored in the Neo-classical period.[10] Donne, on the other hand, frequently alliterates words that have little structural connection (giving the illusion of mere chance disposition): "dare drown," "leave loneness," "win widdowes," "hearing him," "saith, Sir," "though there," "bear but," etc.

The same is true of occasional rhyme. Donne has such internal rhymes as "land, and," "I sigh," "those hose," "lords, rewards," and such near-rhymes as "Guinea's rarities," "massacre had sure," "treason couzen," "Jovius or Surius," "courtier and wiser," "either my humor," "waxen garden," etc. Donne's propensity for "jingling" is well known; his imitator avoids such effects studiously.

All in all, we get the impression that segmental sound effects are more rigidly controlled by Pope than by Donne and that they are more likely to correspond to lexical meanings. In Donne there is little such correspondence; indeed, it is often difficult to remember that we are reading rhymed verse because of the tendency for his sound effects not to coincide with syntactic and semantic structures.

III

Let us turn to metrical structure per se. It is important to recognize the distinction between the style of the poem and the style of the performer. As far as the style of the poem itself is concerned, the suprasegmental patterns as they are actualized are only relevant insofar as they are possible articula-

[10] See G. Tillotson, *On the Poetry of Pope* (Oxford, second edition, 1950).

tions of the potential that the poet is offering us and *its* style. To keep this clear in my notation, I indicate what I think is the metrical pattern by simply underlining metrical points, while I offer one possible rendition of the lines in phonemic symbols above the line.[11] (When I speak of "meter," then, I always mean *potential* meter.) I make no claims for the adequacy or aesthetic quality of the rendition; other readers will prefer other actualizations. For example, I read the first line of Donne's version

^{2}Wéll$^{3\uparrow 2}$I mày nôw re^{3}céive$^{\uparrow 2}$and ^{3}díe$^{1\downarrow}$,

some might read

^{3}Wéll$^{2\downarrow}$ ^{2}I mày nôw re^{3}céive$^{2\rightarrow 2}$and ^{3}díe$^{1\downarrow}$,

or

^{3}Wéll!$^{2\rightarrow 2}$I mày nôw re^{3}céive$^{1\downarrow}$ ^{1}and ^{3}díe$^{1\downarrow}$,

or other versions. These vary in performance style only, and they all develop from the potential

Well! I may now receive and die.

English meter is generally considered to be bidimensional: I refer to one of these dimensions as the metrical point, and to the other as metrical zero, to avoid confusion with the phonemic terms "stress" and "accent." Although some suprasegmental features like stress are organized as potential elements, meter exists as a system outside the language. It is a rhythmic impulse or set or pattern of impulses in the poet's and his reader's mind. According to some poets, its genesis precedes the actual composition of the poem; for others, it only becomes accountable in terms of the actual selection of words. But whenever it emerges, it is apart from the language system. Many people, I am sure, have had the experience of putting down a poem but hearing the "tune" continue. This "tune" is the meter insofar as it may be abstracted from linguistic content. Similarly, we may approximate the meter by supplying nonlinguistic counters — *te's* and *tum's* — to fill the slots.

What complicates the picture is that English has its own patterns and offers some resistance to filling another set of slots. According to one analysis,

[11] I use a modified version of the Trager-Smith transcription of junctures (*An Outline of English Structure* [Norman, 1951], pp. 47–50), in which / ↑ / stands for / ‖ /, / ↓ / for / # /, and /→/ for /|/. Junctures may be briefly defined as the boundary phenomena which signal important structural splits in utterances. Thus the two utterances "He came quickly, dispersing gifts" and "He came, quickly dispersing gifts" are distinguished by having the juncture in different positions — i.e., "quickly" goes with "came" in the first example and with "dispersing" in the second. These junctures may be of four sorts; a downward movement of the voice / ↓ /, an upward movement / ↑ /, an even movement with sustention or delay of some sort /→/, and an even movement without delay /+/ (the difference between "a name" and "an aim," "that stuff" and "that's tough"). Absence of juncture is called "smooth transition." The four stress marks are the same; /ʹ/ for primary, /^/ for secondary, /ˋ/ for tertiary, and no mark for weak. [*Author's note:* since the appearance of this article I have developed a theory of metrical analysis on another phonological basis, namely that of Dwight Bolinger. See *A Theory of Meter* (The Hague, 1965).]

it has four levels of stress, and these must be adjusted to the two-leveled pattern of meter. It is also assumed to have a four-way junctural system, and one of these junctures must be selected to represent each line ending. Thus, "variation" is a more complex matter than has usually been assumed.

It seems necessary, for example, to distinguish between two kinds of variation. First there is purely metrical or intrasystemic variation. This is of two sorts: (1) the occasional displacement of metrical points from the predominating sequence, for example a trochee amid iambs; and (2) occasional change in syllable count as the indication of line length (from some traditional norm). These variations occur within the poem itself, regardless of the reader's interpretation or style. To take an example from Pope's imitation:

Thus much I've said, I trust without offence (II, 125).

In the context this must be

Thus much I've said . . .

and not

Thus much I've said . . . ,

fixing the metrical point at "thus" to insure a correct lexical and grammatical assignment; that is, "thus" modifies "much" (it answers the question "How much?") and is not a sentence adverb like "as a result."

Another instance is the line

There sober thought pursued th' amusing theme

which, if read aloud as

There sober thought pursued th' amusing theme

would suggest a confusion of "there" with "their."

Secondly, there is what we might call countermetrical variation resulting from the superimposition of suprasegmental on metrical system, whenever the poem is performed. This also takes two major forms, involving (1) the choice of the degree of actual phonemic stress used to fill either metrical point or metrical zero, and (2) the selection of actual phonemic junctures to fill the potential juncture points indicated by the punctuation, context, etc., and the correlation of these with line endings. In the second group, what concerns the style of the poem, again, is only what is potential, not what is actualized, for the reasons advanced. For example, consider the line just quoted:

Thus much I've said, I trust without offence.

This line could be performed as

^{3}Thús mûch$^{2\rightarrow}$ ^{2}Ì've ^{3}sáid$^{1\downarrow}$ ^{2}I ^{3}trúst$^{3\rightarrow}$ ^{2}withòut of^{3}fénce$^{1\downarrow}$

or

^{2}Thûs mùch Ì've ^{3}sáid$^{1\downarrow 2}$I ^{3}trúst$^{2\rightarrow 2}$withòut offénce$^{1\downarrow}$

or

^{2}Thûs mùch Ì've ^{3}sáid$^{2\rightarrow 2}$I ^{3}trúst$^{3\rightarrow 2}$withòut of^{3}fénce$^{2\rightarrow}$

or in a number of other ways. These are all stylistically different performances, but each fulfills the same potential, namely -UU-U-U-U-.[12]

Thus traditional views of variation have been a little too simple and may have given rise to certain inconsistencies, particularly where aesthetic impressions are involved. For example, the impression of *speed* — insofar as it is not merely a lexically induced illusion — may develop from either pure or contrapuntal variation; in the first case, the effect may be produced by adding a few syllables, as in Pope's

Flies o'er th'unbending corn, and skims along the main.

In the second, the effect is produced by using light phonemic stresses to fill the metrical points, as in

Not sò, when swìft Camillia scours the plain.

The reverse effect is achieved by filling metrical zeroes with syllables capable of secondary stresses:

When Ajâx strives sòme rock's vâst weight to throw

The line tôo labours, and the words môve slow.

(although another factor here is the heavy consonant clustering). But there is nothing *intrinsically* "fast" about extra syllables or light actualizations of metrical points or intrinsically "slow" about secondary stresses at metrical zeroes. It is the lexical meaning which induces the perception of speed and gives this feature, like all stylistic features, its "meaning."

For the purpose of the stylistic analysis of metrics, therefore, there are three kinds of variation that may be considered; the configuration of these peculiar to a poem can be seen as constituting an important part of its metrical style. These variations are in (1) syllable count, (2) the arrangement of metrical points in a line, and (3) the potentials for phonemic phrasing signaled by punctuation marks, context, syntax, etc.[13]

[12] In general, I work on the principle that a metrical point can be filled by anything from tertiary to primary stress — that what it takes to fix a syllable as a metrical point is not any specific level of stress but a stress that is stronger than that carried by adjacent syllables. James Sledd has suggested that adjacency to a terminal juncture may sometimes be sufficient to permit a minimally stressed syllable to fill a metrical point.

[13] It will be seen that I do not use the concept of "foot" in my description. I avoid the foot because I do not think that it contributes any more information about the meter than is available without it. Since length has not been distinctive in many dialects in English since the Middle Ages, it is questionable whether feet ever marked temporal quantities in English verse

The stylistic questions arise: "To what extent does the poem preserve a fixed syllable count; what is the nature of its linguistic adjustments to obtain a fixed count; and what are the consequent effects?"

In analyzing older verse we are not always sure how many syllables a given line actually contains. Our knowledge of syllabification in earlier ages is not particularly good, since it often depends on the same sort of evidence which is under question in prosodic analysis. Consistency of graphic representation of elision (apostrophes, special spelling, and marks) started comparatively late, and often modern prosodists, like Bridges [14] have felt obliged to work out systems of interpretation that would explain how to read a given poet's verse without making it sound ametrical. This is done with certain tacit assumptions about how regular meter is. And frequently the regularity is precisely what is in dispute. Therefore, comparisons of stylistic variations

---

as they had in Latin and Greek. Podic segmentation seems applicable in English for only one purpose — to explain the sequential norm and variations of points and zeroes. But I have never been able to discover a good reason for assuming that a metrical accent point has any closer connection with the zero that it follows than with the one that it precedes.

That is, the normal decasyllabic line is

$$1\ \underline{2}\ 3\ \underline{4}\ 5\ \underline{6}\ 7\ \underline{8}\ 9\ \underline{10}$$

It does not matter whether we take this as

$$1\underline{2}\quad 3\underline{4}\quad 5\underline{6}\quad 7\underline{8}\quad 9\underline{10}$$

or

$$1\underline{2}3\quad \underline{4}5\underline{6}\quad 7\underline{8}9\quad \underline{10}$$

or

$$1\underline{2}3\underline{4}5\quad \underline{6}7\underline{8}9\underline{10}$$

or

$$1\quad \underline{2}3\quad \underline{4}5\quad \underline{6}7\quad \underline{8}9\quad \underline{10}$$

except as a matter of convenience of arithmetic. The advantage of the first is only that the "units" turn out to be more uniform among themselves — but only for mathematical reasons, not for linguistic or metrical reasons. The trouble begins when readers think that there actually is some kind of equality among these units; the units are equal only because we *take* them to be equal on a false analogy with the classical languages. That is to say, when we learn to scan (and the effort that it requires suggests that this is not in any sense a language-tied system), we learn to take as broadly "the same" quite different phenomena, solely on the basis of the relative positions in which these phenomena occur. In the "iambic pentameter" line, for example, the important positions are the second, fourth, sixth, eighth, and tenth syllables. That is, these positions "promote" the syllables falling within their precincts. What I mean by "promote" is this: whatever the actual stress, the syllable is interpreted as a metrical point by the reader. Whether it causes an *actual* increase in vocal amplitude or not is a matter of the style of the performance rather than the style of the poem. If the reader wishes to make much of the meter he may increase the syllable's actual stress beyond the norm. If he adopts a more "prosaic" style he may show the metrical point by giving the weakly stressed syllable a slower or clearer articulation. The same difference in rendition may occur in metrical suppression of stress in metrically zero positions, again according to the effect that the interpreter intends. [*Author's note:* in *A Theory of Meter*, pp. 114–119, I accept the notion of feets, for reasons of mathematical simplicity.]

[14] Robert Bridges, *Milton's Prosody* (Oxford, 1921), pp. 4–36.

in syllable count seem to suffer from an innate (perhaps unavoidable) circularity of method.

The general assumption seems to be that lines should be called regular wherever possible — that if a decasyllabic line has more than ten syllables, and it is not intentionally or permissively hypermetrical by some approved variation (as, for example, ending with feminine rhyme), its excess may be seen as resolved in elision. (I take "elision" to mean metrical adjustment by omission and to be a cover term for certain processes which are not always clearly discriminated.)[15] One can describe some of these processes as follows:

(1) *apocope:* the loss of a word-final vowel such that the consonant which *precedes* it clusters with the initial vowel or consonant of the following word (for example, "the army" becomes "th'army" and "to write" becomes "t'write"); (2) *aphaeresis:* the loss of an initial vowel such that the consonant which *follows* it clusters with a following vowel or consonant (for example, "it is" becomes "'tis" and "it were" becomes "'twere"); (3) *vowel syncope:* the loss of a vowel such that a syllable is lost without the syllables on either side being affected (for example, "medicine" becomes "med'cine" and "fluctuate" becomes "fluct'ate"); (4) *consonant syncope:* the loss of a consonant such that the syllables on either side are fused, often by the loss of the second vowel (for example, "seven" becomes "se'en," "devil" becomes "de'l," "by his" becomes "by's" /bayz/); (5) *synaeresis:* the consonantizing of a vowel (usually into /y-/ or /w-/), or the loss of syllabicity of a syllabic consonant, such that it clusters with a following vowel rather than standing alone as a syllable (for example, "many a" becomes /menyə/, "jollier" becomes /jalyər/, "title of" becomes /taytləv/); (6) *monosyllabification* (or *synizesis* or *synechphonesis*): the reduction of contiguous syllabics to a single nucleus (for example, "idea" becomes /aydiy/, "being" becomes /biŋ/); (7) *pseudo-elision:* the assumption of elision between two consonants that cannot be clustered without one of them becoming syllabic (for example, words ending in "-ism," "rhythm," etc.), or consonant clusters that go against English clustering habits (for example, "th'sea" and "th'loss").

To what extent are or were these elisions actualized? Some prosodists have taken them to be mere orthographic fictions, apostrophes being marked solely to suit the numerical decorum of the eighteenth century and having little reference to actual pronunciation. Bridges, for example, writes that sounds are not really lost; they remain and are "heard in the glide, though prosodically asyllabic." According to the researches of Paul Fussell,[16] however, this suggests a misunderstanding about the nature of verse performance in the eighteenth century, and Pope's line was probably pronounced as written:

/wandriŋ in menyə šeyd bičekəhd grɔt/.

It is necessary to recognize that elisions are real things, that they have been observed in some styles of verse performance, and that they can be em-

[15] Cf. J. T. Shipley, *Dictionary of World Literature* (New York, 1943), under the entry "hyphaeresis."
[16] *Theory of Prosody in Eighteenth Century England* (New London, 1955).

ployed by poets in stylistically characteristic ways. Whether they are to be observed in modern performances or not is another matter.[17]

My count shows that twenty lines in Donne's Satires II and IV are ametrical, that is, do not allow of an explanation by elision; this is about 6 per cent. It is interesting to note that in the text of Donne's poems which was printed in the 1735 edition on the pages opposite Pope's versifications eleven lines were regularized by the editor. A nine-syllable line like 176, for example, "Baloun, Tennis, Dyet, or the stewes," became "Baloun or Tennis, Diet, or the Stews"; and an eleven-syllable line (taking "saying" as monosyllabic) "For saying of our Ladies Psalter. But 'tis fit" (217) was adjusted to "For saying our Ladies Psalter. But 'tis fit." In addition, the 1735 edition added a few apostrophes to show elisions not indicated in the original: "so't" for "so it," "so'are" for "so are," "th'loss" for "the loss," etc.[18]

With the exception of aphaeresis, of which Pope has seven occurrences to Donne's one, the relative proportions of *kinds* of elision are quite similar. There is, however, a difference in the number of elisions permitted in a line. Donne regularly allows of multiple elisions, such as:

> Toughly and stubbornly I beare this crosse; But th'houre (140)
> Nay sir, can you spare me a Crown? Thankfully I (144).

The latter is characteristic in that alternatives are possible: we may read the line ". . . my'a Crown? Thankf'lly I" or "me a crown? Thankf'lly'I" (although the latter may not be a permissible cluster in English). Another example is line 214:

> Ten Cardinalls into the Inquisition.

Does one read "Card'nalls" and "the Inquisition" or "Cardinalls" and "th'Inquisition"? Or, as Professor Fred Householder suggests, does *-ion* get two syllables, hence: "Ten Card'nals into th'Inquisition"?

As one would expect, Pope's elisions are more conventional than Donne's. This is demonstrated in two ways: (1) Pope's commoner elisions are more likely to be repeated several times, as if they were well-known and approved methods of controlling the meter (Donne has fewer repetitions); and (2) Donne more frequently employs novel elisions or elisions which seem almost to do violence to the convention, for example, "tufftaffaty," "going," "your Apostles," "Makeron," "perpetuities," "torturing I," "Maccabbees,"

[17] It is not known whether Donne and his contemporaries observed elision in their own verse performances. But in his study of Donne's metrical practice, M. F. Moloney has pointed out that Ben Jonson, although very critical about Donne's treatment of stress placement — ". . . for not keeping of accent, he deserved hanging . . ." — does not object in any way to Donne's "numbers," presumably because he considered them to be adequately adjusted by elision. Moloney goes on to give a detailed account of the importance of elision to Donne, arguing that his verse is no less regular in this respect than Milton's, and placing him in the main stream of the English poetic tradition; "Donne's Metrical Practice," *PMLA,* LXV (1950), 232–239.

[18] As quoted in Volume Five of W. Roscoe's edition of *The Works of Alexander Pope* (London, 1824).

"Heraclitus," etc. Besides, some of Donne's elisions may be taken as unwitting puns: /tum/ for "to whom," /tɔl/ for "to all," /ðerperəlz/ for "their apparels," and so forth. Pope avoids all these except one — he keeps Donne's monosyllabification of "Noah," to the horror of his editor Warton (". . . perhaps the greatest violation of harmony Pope has ever been guilty of").

The second metrical variable, the relative placement of metrical points in the line, constitutes a great difference in the poets' styles. Pope, of course, usually places the point at the second, fourth, sixth, eighth, and tenth syllables. Less than one-quarter of his lines have any metrical displacement, and of these two-thirds are simple transfers of the point from the second syllable to the first, giving 1,4,6,8,10:

Talkers, I've learn'd to bear; Motteaux I knew (50)

while 17 per cent simply transfer the point from the second to the third (thus 3,4,6,8,10):

And the free Soul looks down to pity Kings (187).

There are fewer transfers to later syllables, only four to the fifth, eight to the seventh, and three to the ninth. Pope rarely has more than one such displacement in a line. Only 4 lines in 403 have two displacements; such lines as the following are rare:

	Then as a licens'd Spy, whom nothing can
(1,4,6,9,10)	Silence, or hurt, he libels the Great Man (159)
(1,5,6,8,10)	Those write because all write, and so have still (II, 27).

In Donne's verse on the other hand, a majority of lines, 68 per cent, contain displacement, and many lines have two, three, and even four displacements. Unusual combinations like the following are common:

(2,5,7,9,10)	Now; Aretine's pictures have made few chast (70)
(1,3,6,7,9)	Better pictures of vice, teach me vertue (72)
(1,3,5,8,10)	Velvet, but 'twas now (so much ground was seene) (32)
(3,5,7,8,10)	I bid kill some beasts, but no Hecatombs (II, 108).[19]

Regular lines occur only frequently enough to serve as bare reminders of the norm.

The few lines that Pope keeps intact are either regular to begin with:

As Men from Jayls to execution go (273)
Jests like a licens'd fool, commands like Law (271)
He says our *Wars thrive ill*, because delay'd (163)

[19] Or, as Fred Householder suggests 3,4,7,8,10.

or are easily adjusted to a more regular pattern; thus Donne's 1,4,6,7,10 becomes Pope's 2,4,6,8,10:

> A thing, which would have pos'd Adam to name (20)

becomes:

> A Thing which *Adam* had been pos'd to name (25);

and again,

> Which dwell at Court, for once going that way (16)

becomes:

> Who *live* at *Court*, for going once that Way! (23)

The final variable to be considered is the potential relationship between line structure and phonemic phrasing. In a phonemically oriented prosody this involves two things: the occurrence of terminal junctures *intra*linearly — caesura — and the presence or absence of *inter*linear terminal junctures — traditionally end-stoppage versus run-on or enjambment. It is useful to see these as related concepts. In the first instance, suprasegmental features break metrical continuities; in the second, they smooth over metrical discontinuities.

These adjustments of metrical continuity within and between lines are not orthographic facts; they only exist in performances. As such they reflect the reader's interpretation, which is based not only on the meter but also on the punctuation, the grammar, and the lexical content. Punctuation, grammar, and message are the *causes* of caesura and enjambment, not their manifestation or mode of existence; caesura and enjambment are phonological, not grammatical or lexical entities. In this sense it might be more proper to speak of a line as "suggesting" or "signaling" caesura and enjambment than "having" it.

The strength of the signal is not always uniform. Some situations — say the coincidence of sentence-end with line-end — virtually require a strong juncture, /↓/, and hence end-stoppage. On other occasions, however, the signals are not conclusive, and there is range for personal interpretation. Then it becomes difficult to distinguish the poetic style from the performance style, unless we are prepared, again, to deal in potentials rather than actualizations. But potentials may be all that really exist "in" the poem as text. If different articulations are possible it seems prudent to recognize that fact; indeed, that a poet frequently allows such choices may itself be a style feature of interest (or it may mean nothing). In this matter, as in all others concerning prosody, it seems futile to fight for a single performance, as if it were the only conceivable one. This is what causes the confusing proliferation of scansions and systems of scansions and the unfortunate motion toward prescriptivism in many metrical exercises.

Caesura has been defined by Amos R. Morris as "a perceptible break in the metrical line, properly described as an expressional pause."[20] In a phonemic metrics the term "expressional pause" should read "terminal juncture." This change is necessary because not all junctures contain pauses, and there seem to be several other kinds of phonetic phenomena, like pitch change, change in intensity (fade), and lengthening of final syllables, which operate in differing combinations to signal terminal junctures. The fact that different idiolects use different combinations of these to express what is structurally the same feature may explain some of the disputes that prosodists raise about caesura. So we might revise the definition to read "a perceptible break in the performance of a line, properly described as an intralinear terminal juncture."

The run-on line is defined in Shipley's *Dictionary* as "The carrying of the sense (grammatical form) in a poem past the end of a line. . . ." I am not sure what the parentheses mean: The author cannot have intended to give the impression that the "sense" and the "grammatical form" are the same thing. If we interpret the parentheses to mean "and" — "The carrying of the sense *and* the grammatical form . . ." — the definition is still difficult to accept. The "sense" of a line, I presume, is its meaning. But surely the meaning is carried on past the end of end-stopped lines too, for example in Pope's

> I bought no *Benefice,* I begg'd no *Place;*
> Had no new Verse, or new Suit to show (12–13).

Similarly, as this example demonstrates, the grammar may be carried on beyond the end of an end-stopped line as well; here the subject of the verb "begg'd" is also subject of "Had."

What seems actually "carried on" in a run-on line is the pitch contour, or to use the Trager-Smith term, the *phonemic clause.*[21] This suggests to the ear a carryover of meaning and grammar; however, if our metrics is to be phonemically sound, we must see this as a suggestion only, not as what really occurs. A possible definition of run-on or enjambment is "the occurrence in performance of a phonemic clause (or negatively, the absence of a terminal juncture) across what is represented in the text as line-end." And conversely, end-stoppage is the occurrence of terminal juncture at line-end. This would account for such remarks as the following: "Alec Guinness reads Shakespeare's blank verse as if most of the lines were end-stopped." The point is that in Alec Guinness' performance these lines *are* end-stopped, regardless of the meaning or the grammar or what somebody else's interpretation may be. Caesura, end-stoppage, and enjambment only exist in actual performance, since they are phonological, not orthographic, phenomena.

Thus we may distinguish three kinds of situations at line-end, using quota-

[20] In Shipley, pp. 82–83.

[21] A phonemic clause has its existence purely in phonology. It is defined as "a minimal complete utterance" consisting of only one terminal juncture, "one or more pitch phonemes, one — *and only one* — primary stress, and may have one or more other stresses and one or more plus junctures." (Trager and Smith, p. 49.)

tion marks to emphasize that what is characterized is the line as performed, not as printed.

1. **"Run-on" lines,** where a phonemic clause does not coincide with the line-end, so that nothing greater than plus-juncture (i.e. minimally interrupted transition) intervenes between the two lines. A punctuation mark rarely occurs at the end of such a line.

> but I have been in__
> A purgatorie, such as fear'd Hell is__
> A recreation to, and scarse map of this. (2–4).

The pressure for run-on seems to increase greatly when there is a metrical zero at syllable 10, as in line 2 above, or a caesura after a very late syllable:

> As fresh, and sweet their Apparrells be, as bee__
> The fields they sold to buy them; (180–81)

2. **"Alternative" lines,** where either run-on or end-stopped interpretations are possible, and there is substantial variety among performances. There is either no punctuation mark or a comma; for example, Donne's

> My sin
> Indeed is great, (1–2)

may be interpreted as either

> ^{2}My ^{3}sín$^{2\rightarrow}$
> ^{2}Indéed$^{\uparrow}$ ^{2}is ^{3}gréat^{1}
> or
> ^{2}My ^{3}sîn
> Indêed is ^{3}gréat^{1}

or in other ways.

3. **"End-stopped" lines,** where a terminal juncture is almost obligatory (although *which* terminal juncture is up to the reader's style). The punctuation is usually stronger than a comma:

> as false as they
> Which dwell at Court for once going that way.
> Therefore I suffered this; towards me did run (15–17).

It is often suggested that enjambment is essentially a linguistic impingement on the meter, and that its extensive use gives such verse the appearance of being closer to everyday speech than verse in which the meter exerts more control on the syntax. As Morris puts it (referring to caesura, but certainly the same could be said of enjambment): "It is essentially an instrument not of metrics but of prose, persisting in the artificial pattern of verse, cutting across the metrical flow with a secondary rhythmic movement of normal speech."[22] The poet's control lies chiefly in his skill in so adjusting the natural speech movement that it does not cloud but enhances or enriches the verse movement.

The end-stopped style has a very different effect. Here the metrical structure more heavily restricts the natural speech patterns, thereby controlling the reader's choice of phrasing to a finer degree. Every other line suggests that it is itself a full phonemic clause or that it is to be divided in such a way that a phonemic clause occurs at its end.

Compare Donne's first lines with Pope's version:

Donne

Well; I may now receive, and die; My Sinne
Indeed is great, but I have beene in
A Purgatorie, such as fear'd Hell is
A recreation to, and scarse map of this.

Pope

Well, if it be my time to quit the stage,
Adieu to all the Follies of the Age!
I die in Charity with Fool and Knave,
Secure of Peace at least beyond the grave.
I've had my Purgatory here betimes,
And paid for all my Satires, all my Rhymes:
The Poet's Hell, its Tortures, Fiends and Flames,
To this were Trifles, Toys, and empty Names.

The meaning is roughly the same: the poet has atoned for his sins before dying by visiting the court, a purgatory in comparison to which even Hell loses its terror. But the style differs considerably, and one of the important aspects of that difference seems to be the influence that meter is allowed to exert on the rhetoric and the syntax. Donne's lines suggest phonemic clauses running over line-end and terminating at varying points within the line — between the eighth and ninth syllables in the first line, between the fourth and fifth in the second, between the fifth and sixth in the third, and between the sixth and seventh in the fourth. The binding power of the rhymes is reduced to a minimum. In Pope's version metrical exigencies have altered the syntactic structures of the original in several ways. In the first two lines Pope revises Donne's abrupt juncture after the eighth syllable and run-on into a full-line modifying clause balancing the following main clause in a perfect end-stopped couplet. Similarly, the run-on

I have been in
A Purgatorie

becomes a full-line main clause followed by a somewhat redundant coordinate clause in line six:

I've had my *Purgatory* here betimes,
And paid for all my Satires, all my Rhymes.

[22] Shipley, p. 82.

The end-stopped couplet frequently employs parallelism to satisfy its metrical requirements. Indeed, one very good justification for its heavy use in the Neoclassical couplet is that it makes a virtue of a necessity; the necessity to fill out the line and control phonemic phrasing is turned into a source of poetic virtuosity (or is this a chicken-and-egg matter?).

Not only parallel clauses but also parallel phrases have a tendency to appear as full lines. For example:

> My minde, neither with prides itch, nor yet hath been
> Poyson'd with love to see, or to be seene. (5–6)

becomes:

> With foolish *Pride* my heart was never fir'd
> Nor the vain Itch *t'admire,* or be *admir'd;* (9–10).

Notice how the rhetorical parallelism implicit in Donne's lines, which runs counter to their metrical structure, finds metrical confirmation in Pope's revision.

Pope's lines 7 and 8 are excellent examples of the mechanism of converting run-on lines into end-stopped lines. Run-on is suggested most strongly where elementary structure points confront each other across the line break without phrasal buffering, for example, in Donne's lines ending "Hell is" and beginning "A recreation" (subject, copula, and predicate noun). Pope obviates this bare juxtaposition by inserting the appositive phrase "its Tortures, Fiends and Flames" and by inverting the verb phrase and the modifying prepositional phrase "To this."

Not only are Donne's run-on lines more numerous than Pope's, but he sometimes directly contradicts the rhyme pattern with them; for example:

> The men board them; and praise, as they thinke, well,
> Their beauties; they the mens wits; Both are bought.
> Why good wits ne'r weare scarlet gownes, I thought
> This cause . . . (190–93)

Pope revises these couplets as follows:

> Such wits and Beauties are not prais'd for nought.
> For both the Beauty and the Wit are *bought.* (234–35)

The syntactic frame in which Donne runs-on and Pope end-stops is also worth considering. Compare, for example, the first twenty-six lines of the original Satire IV with the matching thirty-seven lines of Pope's version: in this passage, Donne employs roughly as many run-on lines as end-stopped lines, whereas the only pure example in Pope is ll. 34–35

> One whom the mob, when next we find or make
> A popish plot, shall for a Jesuit take.

Donne's run-on lines break at the following syntactic joints (roughly in order of their strength or "compulsion"):

at word boundary

> As prone to all ill, and of good as forget-
> ful, as proud, as lustful, and as much in debt (13–14);

between auxiliary and main verb

> My mind, neither with pride's itch, nor yet hath been
> Poisoned with love to see, or to be seen (5–6);

between preposition and object

> but I have been in
> A Purgatorie, such as fear'd Hell is
> A recreation to (2–3);

between direct object and its modifier after a factitive verb

> so it pleas'd my destiny
> (Guilty of my sin of going) to think me
> As prone to all ill . . . (11–12);

between verb and prepositional object

> as blaze which did go
> To a mass in jest, (8–9);

between verb and direct-object

> [Glaze] . . . was fain to disburse
> The hundred marks, which is the Statute's curse (9–10);

and between copula and predicate-noun

> Such as fear'd Hell is
> A recreation to, and scarce may of this (3–4).

Pope avoids all of these ways of breaking the line, and in most cases his end-stopping conversions are on straight syntactic grounds. For example, the verb-prepositional object division

> (Glaze) . . . which did go
> To a Mass in jest. . . .

is made conformable by simply shifting the verb to the next line and filling out the previous line with a time adverbial (and the second line with a parenthesis):

> But, as the Fool that in reforming days
> Would go to Mass in Jest (as story says) (15–16).

The preposition-object confrontation

> I have beene in
> A Purgatorie

is replaced by "smoothly" compounding the predicate

> I've had my Purgatory here betimes,
> And paid for all my satires, all my rhymes (5–6).

And the same tactic is used with the auxiliary-main verb split:

> My mind, neither with pride's itch, nor yet hath been
> Poisoned with love to see, or to be seen

becomes

> With Foolish pride my heart was never fir'd,
> Nor the vain itch t'admire, or be admir'd (9–10).

It is interesting to see how even the same division at line end — between subject and predicate — sounds different in the hands of the two poets. Donne's

> Therefore I suffered this; towards me did run
> A thing more strange than on Nile's slime the Sun
> E'er bred . . .

becomes

> Scarce was I enter'd, when, behold! there came
> A thing which Adam had been pos'd to name (24–25).

Pope's *came* is not completely end-stopped, but it does suggest more of a pause than Donne's. The reason, apparently deliberately planned, is the break demanded by the immediately preceding exclamation, coming parenthetically in the dependent clause. The effect is nothing at all like the jumping-off-the-cliff of *towards me did run.*

IV

It is apparent that Pope's verse displays a different sort of control than Donne's. His rhymes are full and equal, his occasional segmental effects are rigidly controlled to coincide with meter, the meter itself tends to be more regular in terms of syllable count and metrical point placement, and, finally, his lines and couplets are usually end-stopped, with a consequent impact on rhetoric and syntax. Since both poets were writing in the same genre, apparently their notions of what the genre required differed considerably. Critics have called Donne's tone and stylistic practices "rough" or "dark," attributing their cultivation to an imperfect knowledge of classical satire. For one thing, the satires of Persius, which had been couched in equivocal language for purely nonliterary reasons, were taken by Renaissance poets as models. More important, there seems to have been some confusion about the etymology of "satire." Renaissance scholarship derived the word from *satyra* ("a rude mixture of cyclic chorus and primitive drama performed by men dressed in animal skins and tails"), rather than from *satura* (the stuffing of a roast, also *lanx satura* "a full dish or tray," whence "a poetic medley," particularly in respect to variety of versification). This led most of the early English satirists to think crudeness and obscurity characteristic of the genre. Thus the "violent and apparently motiveless" style features of Donne's verse [23] and its "harshness" [24] had the very straightforward dramatic purpose of establishing the poet's tone within the tradition as he saw it. J. B. Leishman writes

> [Donne] was . . . imitating . . . the 'harshness' of the Roman satirical hexameter. The fact that many of his lines can only with great difficulty be scanned as five-foot lines is precisely what he intended: he intended the reader to find as much difficulty in reading them as he himself found in reading [classical satires] (*The Monarch of Wit* [London, 1951], ch. 3).

And Clay Hunt writes

> Donne certainly made some attempts in the satires to follow the conventions of the genre of formal verse satire — conventions which were fairly congenial to his temperament . . .

and goes on to refer to the "blunt, crusty, chip-on-the-shoulder moralist . . . snorting his indignation . . . the stock persona of Juvenalian verse satire . . ." [25]

Pope's style in these satires is less smooth than in his other works. According to Ian Jack, Pope also thought that the genre required a "low" style, although "low" had far different connotations in the eighteenth century than it had at the turn of the seventeenth. The permissible variations were more restricted; the "lowest" that Pope could go was to write some "easy Horatian talk." Saintsbury sums up the change in taste when he writes of Donne:

> When they [Elizabeth satirists] assumed this greater license, the normal structure of English verse was anything but fixed. Horace had in his contemporaries, Persius and Juvenal had still more in their forerunners, examples of versification than which Mr. Pope himself could do nothing more 'correct.' . . . In Donne's time the very precisians took a good deal of license. If therefore you meant to show that you were *sans gêne,* you had to make demonstrations of the most unequivocal character . . .[26]

By Pope's time one could be *sans gêne* by means of subtler adjustments. That, apparently, is the interesting thing about restrictive traditions.

The general critical impression is that Donne's "carelessness" establishes a certain tone and a certain feeling, and his control lies precisely in his seeming lack of it. In Ben Jonson's phrase, Donne's negligence is to be interpreted as a "diligent kind of negligence," a self-assured indifference toward externals and even a positive contempt for such superficialities as exact meter.[27] With meter as with rhyme, it was ". . . matter over manner, and the ornamental

[23] Ian Jack, "Pope and 'The Weighty Bullion or Dr. Donne's Satires'," *PMLA,* LXVI (1951), 1009–1022.

[24] Arnold Stein, "Donne's Harshness and the Elizabethan Tradition," *Studies in Philology,* XLI (1944), 390–409.

[25] *Donne's Poetry* (New Haven, 1954), p. 207.

[26] As quoted in *The Poems of John Donne,* ed. by E. K. Chambers (London, 1896).

[27] Arnold Stein, "Donne and the Couplet," *PMLA,* LVII (1942), 695.

qualities of rhyme must be made less important; not be allowed to ring and re-echo in full melodious tones and overtones but made to serve a practical function in a new technique of the couplet" (Stein, p. 677).

Donne's tone, in short, seems to say "Look, I have no time to be bothered with carefully measuring words and sounds. I take them as they come to me in my divine and angry inspiration. My anger is righteous and sincere, and if I stop to tamper with it, to dissect and to analyze it and to put it into *bons mots,* it will cool into ineffectuality."

Pope, on the other hand, presents a tone which is calculated to demonstrate a merciless competence, a cold ability to demolish neatly what he hates. This style strives to give the impression that disposing of the object of one's distaste is analogous and not much more difficult than disposing of the exigencies of one's meter. Pope prefers a stiletto to Donne's blunderbuss.

Roger Fowler

STRUCTURAL METRICS

Over the past fifteen years we have witnessed a good deal of activity in one compartment of applied linguistics, the application of "suprasegmental" phonemics to the analysis of English metre. Starting with a suggestion by Harold Whitehall in 1951 that this was a possible use of Trager-Smith phonology,[1] it has culminated (perhaps) in a full-scale discussion by another of the pioneers, Seymour Chatman. The publication of this book provides an occasion for an appraisal of the assumptions and achievements of the approach.

Structural metrics could be said to be concerned with the reconciliation (through phonemics) of two extremes of analysis. On the one hand is the old belief in two fixed degrees of stress alternating with perfect regularity and uniformly disposed in time. At the other extreme is the instrumental revelation that each of the syllables in a line is realised differently by various complexes of intensity, pitch and length; that there is no identity of weight among the stresses; that there is no clear binary distinction between "stress" and "unstress"; and that there is no equality of time-interval.

Both of these extremes are rejected by modern linguists: the first, "graphic" analysis, derived from classical, quantitative metrics, because it does not fit the facts of English, even if one substitutes "stress" for "length"; the second, because acoustic display gives too much information and is thus meaningless unless a phonemic or other categorizing selection is made.[2] And yet both these modes of analysis do convey sorts of reality: the first is a reflection of a demonstrable perception by readers of verse, even though rationalised unrealistically; the second, the physical reality of actual performance. Neither, by itself, tells us much about the structure of a line; but both are genuine dimensions for

Reprinted from *Linguistics* by permission of Mouton & Company, Publishers, The Hague, The Netherlands. A review-article prompted by Seymour Chatman, *A Theory of Meter*, *Janua Linguarum* 36 (The Hague, 1965).

1 Harold Whitehall, "From Linguistics to Criticism," *The Kenyon Review*, XIII (1951), 710–14.

2 S. Chatman, "Robert Frost's 'Mowing': an Inquiry into Prosodic Structure," *The Kenyon Review*, XVIII (1956), 421, 422 (hereafter referred to as Chatman 1956); R. Wellek and A. Warren, *Theory of Literature*, 3rd ed. (Harmondsworth, 1963), pp. 166, 168.

study. The aim of reconciliation, often unexpressed, is to discover a means of fusing these dimensions, of bringing the notion of "abstract" or "perceived" metre into line with the facts of language.

Structural metrics has always operated with a multi-dimensional or complexly stratified model of verse structure in mind. Whitehall views English metre as a product of two dimensions:

> the traditional "ideal" metrical patterns of much English verse — patterns based on the two-level contrast of stressed versus unstressed syllables — have been "orchestrated" since Marlowe by a poetic adaptation of the actual four-level contrast of speech.[3]

"Orchestration" appears to be the modification of the "ideal" metre by natural suprasegmental phonology to give a "real" and phonemically valid metre: the two-stress metrical system is actualised by four degrees of stress, and the artificial isochronism of feet is modified by superimposition of an isochronism of phrase-stresses. Whitehall's analyses look just like analyses of any sort of English, with no concessions in notation to metre: that "ideal" has been submerged:

Thĕ cúrfèw | tôlls thĕ knéll | ̀of pârtĭng dáy |

But Hawkes, giving a later exposition of Trager-Smith metrics, makes explicit note of the ideal metre and so hints at its survival (in what is presumably a non-phonological state):

Thĕ hôl | y̆ tîme | îs quî | ĕt às | ă Nún |[4]
⏑ – ⏑ – ⏑ – ⏑ – ⏑ –

His strategy is to sophisticate the idea of the foot. Under the influence of the natural stresses of speech, the metrical matrix ⏑ – will be capable of actual (i.e., phonemic) realisation as ⏑ ʹ, ⏑ ^, ⏑ ̀, etc.[5]

Those linguists who have retained the idea that the metre still somehow "exists," despite the phonemic actuality of four stresses, have toyed with such notions as "tension," "counterpoint," "interplay" between what a verse-line is and what it is thought to be. Chatman speaks of "a tension between TWO systems: the abstract metrical pattern, as historical product of the English verse tradition, and the ordinary stress-pitch-juncture system of spoken English, determined as it is by requirements of meaning and emphasis" (1956, p. 422). He goes on to describe the results of tension as " 'promotions' or 'suppressions' of the stress levels of normal non-verse speech under the pressures of the abstract metrical pattern" (p. 424). His analyses here and in the article of 1960 [6] show metre and suprasegmental phonology, with a full display of stress, pitch and juncture.

[3] *The Kenyon Review*, XVIII (1956), p. 418.

[4] T. Hawkes, "The Problems of Prosody," *A Review of English Literature*, III (April 1962), 45.

[5] *Ibid.*, p. 39.

[6] "Comparing Metrical Styles," in T. A. Sebeok, *Style in Language* (New York, 1960), pp. 149–72 (hereafter referred to as Chatman 1960). [*Reprinted here pp. 132–155.*]

Wellek and Warren posit three dimensions: SPECIFIC PERFORMANCE which is "irrelevant to an analysis of the prosodic situation, which consists precisely in the tension, the 'counterpoint,' between the METRICAL PATTERN and the PROSE RHYTHM." [7] This interplay between metrical pattern and prose rhythm, with a product describable in terms of English suprasegmental phonology and yet different from English non-verse, is a theory of metre which I find attractive. And yet it is a theory full of snags and dangerous assumptions, not least of which is the feeling that metre is easily and relevantly described according to the practices of linguistics. As Wimsatt and Beardsley point out, "you cannot write a grammar of the meter's interaction with the sense." [8] The linguist can talk only about the CAUSES of tension (prose rhythm and metre) and recognise them both; the PRODUCT of the tension (performance reduced to phonemic form), as shown by Whitehall, or the upper lines of Chatman's and Hawkes' analyses, has the status of a symptom only.

Since I am going to conduct my essay on *A Theory of Meter* by means of annotated summary and quotation, I pass over Chapter I, which is itself a presummary. Insofar as this is also a statement of intentions and presumed achievements, I shall refer to it piecemeal in the course of my account.

The approach of Chapter II, "The nature of rhythm," is basically psychological, for it presents rhythm (and hence metre) as a product of a natural human perceptual tendency. There is "primary" or "cardiac" rhythm, "the simple repetition of single events between equal time intervals" (p. 22). Although this may exist, it is unlikely to be perceived. We perceive "secondary" rhythm: events will appear to be grouped, perhaps into pairs, and we will believe that there is an alternation of relative prominences:

> When a series of sounds precisely equal in loudness, pitch, and length, and occurring at precisely equal intervals is presented to a subject, the chances are that he will not hear the series as the cardiac rhythm it really is, but as grouped rhythm, that is, he will overestimate every other interval, thus creating a purely subjective distinction between external and internal intervals. He may also begin to perceive a regular difference in prominence (either loudness or pitch or length) among alternating events. (p. 25)

Chatman concludes that

> meter is basically *linguistically determined "secondary rhythm"* — linguistic events grouped regularly in time, such that each group has unity in its internal composition and in its external relations. A "foot" can be defined as one of these groups of events. (p. 29)

This chapter establishes clearly that metre is in the ear of the beholder, in his ability to group and equate sequentially random and physically disparate sound-stimuli. Obviously, there is here a great advance over such unexplained locu-

[7] *Theory of Literature*, p. 169 (my italics).

[8] W. K. Wimsatt, Jr., and Monroe C. Beardsley, "The Concept of Meter: an Exercise in Abstraction," *PMLA*, LXXIV (1959), 596. [*Reprinted here pp. 91–114.*]

tions as "abstract metre" or "ideal metre," which were hardly sufficient to encourage the non-linguist to believe that linguists were positively interested in anything but sheer sound. Much antagonism has sprung from a belief that physical and phonemic investigations must destroy the notion of metrical pattern. Chatman himself, while paying homage to the idea, has consistently denied its linguistic existence. I would like to think of the phonetic variation revealed by the spectrograph as corroboration of the psychological or abstract "existence" of metre. An analogy is the principle of the phoneme. Phonemes are abstractions that, for the sake of communication, we agree to believe in. Phonetics reveals that no sound is ever repeated, but there is not phonetic anarchy: physical "cues" exist: plosion, voice, etc. Similarly, metre is our own simplification and categorization of phonetic variety on the basis of cues: lexical stress, syllable-count, etc.[9]

Chatman examines these cues in Chapter III, "Phonological backgrounds to metrical analysis," which is a treatment of suprasegmental matters arranged in an order to be of use in metrical analysis, and (with the Appendix, "The stress systems of Pike and Trager-Smith" [pp. 225–29]) a survey of phonemicizing approaches to these matters.

As Chatman is concerned with isosyllabic or syllable-counting verse (p. 113), he first discusses the nature of the syllable, which is "the event" in metre, "the essential rhythmic integer" (p. 30). Theories of chest-pulse and sonority are surveyed, but Chatman favours the phonological definition as formulated by O'Connor and Trim: [10] a syllable is a segmental sequence (C)V(C), the exponents of the pattern being selected according to the order- and clustering-rules of the language. He concludes:

> Although there are differences of opinion about the constitution of the syllable, the problem does not seem serious from the point of view of metrics. Metrics is concerned mostly with the number of syllables-as-events; syllables are easily recognized, and the problem of identifying their boundaries rarely matters. . . . The only important question for metrics is "How many syllables are there?" (p. 39)

All we need to know is how many syllables a line has — this is the first of the "configurational" features which start the "metrical set," the pattern-in-our-minds superimposed on the phonological pattern.

Among syllables, some are more prominent than others. When metre occurs, there appears to be a regular relation between prominent syllables: a metrically prominent syllable, recurring at regular intervals and of the same "weight," is an ictus — Chatman keeps the old term. Prominence, he says, cannot be attributed to one phonetic or phonemic feature alone; a syllable may be felt to be prominent, and so signal ictus, because of characteristics of pitch, stress, vowel-quality, or length, or all four. His particular (and deserving) butt here

[9] This is not to say, of course, that metrical units are part of the phoneme-system of a language; they are "produced" by the same mental process, the equation and classification of different physical phenomena.

[10] J. D. O'Connor and J. L. M. Trim, "Vowel, Consonant, and Syllable — A Phonological Definition," *Word*, IX (1963).

is the view that it is "loudness" (stress defined as a correlate of articulatory energy or amplitude) which is the only or chief producer of prominence. This was the belief of traditional metrists after the quantitative model had been buried, and is reflected today in the practices of those who rely exclusively on the Trager-Smith stress-levels. Instrumental analysis reported later in the book reveals that prominence is a matter of high redundancy, achieved by a selection from the four "suprasegmental" features, with the human ear incapable of isolating any ONE feature as significant (p. 49).

Chatman no longer espouses the Trager-Smith formulation of suprasegmental phonology, and it seems that any notion of "degrees" of prominence must be foreign to him.[11] He confesses elsewhere [12] to using "a binary phonemic model" (a cryptic phrase) in his recent work. "Stress" and "non-stress" correspond simply with ictus and non-ictus. But I suspect that much is to be gained by preserving a multi-level view of prominence in order to keep what might be called "allophones" of ictus — different degrees actualizing metrical points as a result of the so-called "tension" between metre as a mental categorization and the variety of cues which signal the categories.

The last section (pp. 52–76) of the phonological chapter is devoted to the linguistic qualities which produce prominence. He follows Bolinger's restatement of a familiar distinction:

> Stress is a fundamental property of full vowel monosyllabic words, and of one syllable in polysyllabic words, which in any environment, accented or not, can serve to distinguish them from what are otherwise homonyms. The actualization of stress is not uniform; its phonetic cues will vary according to the phonological context in which the word finds itself. Nevertheless, it is real; speakers will not ordinarily differ in their sense of where it occurs, and can always make it more prominent on demand. Accent, on the other hand, is the prominence which one syllable in an uttered phrase receives when it is the center of the pitch contour; it is not fixed to the word but to the phrase. (p. 58)[13]

A third concept is introduced, "pitch obtrusion" (p. 62), which is the use of accents involving relatively large pitch-contrasts for "emphasis" and similar functions.

He has outlined those indispensable features of all utterance which produce prominence. All words have (through lexical stress) the potential at fixed points. When words are put together, some syllables will have this potential realized through accent and/or pitch obtrusion. All stretches of utterance

[11] Intermediate degrees are challenged, pp. 68–71, in terms which recall some of the critics' attacks on the Trager-Smith system (e.g., Wimsatt and Beardsley, p. 593): "If *disestablish* is said to have, say, four levels of stress (*dîsêstáblìsh*), what is to prevent us from saying that *antidisestablishmentarianism* has eight?" (p. 71). On p. 68 he comes out into the open: "stress in the limited view we have adopted operates in an 'on-off' fashion; either it is there, or it is not. . . ." Ictus, indeed, is an "on-off" concept; but the "ons" and "offs" can, paradoxically, be distinguished, even if the differences are not phonemically significant.

[12] Sebeok, p. 207.

[13] See Dwight Bolinger, "A Theory of Pitch Accent in English," *Word*, XIV (1958), 112. For the older account, see Daniel Jones, *An Outline of English Phonetics*, 9th ed. (Cambridge, 1960), pp. 248–73.

have this composite stress-pattern, which I would like to call PROSE RHYTHM.[14] Manipulation of word-order, and rigorous control of number of syllables, together with the presence of other configurational features such as rhyme, can encourage a reader to transform the prose rhythm into a metre of binary, alternating contrasts of prominence. For Chatman, the transformation appears to be complete, for the prose rhythm succumbs to the "on-off" contrast of metre. I would prefer to think that the variousness of prominence of prose rhythm survives, in some degree, WITHIN the binary categorization. To use the analogy of the phoneme again: we agree that we use substantially the same phonemes as the speakers of other dialects of our language, but we recognise the allophonic variety which sets them off from us; so every iambic foot is ⏑ –, but we remain conscious of — and derive pleasure from — the variety of its realization.

Chapter IV, "Objective analyses of metrical properties: a survey," has two parts: one on mechanical analysis of actual performance, and the second on "The structuralist approach to meter": respectively, phonetics and phonemics. Kymograph, oscilloscope and spectrograph are described, and some research surveyed. Chatman has said before, of the limitations of acoustic metrics, that "one cannot get more structure out of a machine than one puts in" (1966, p. 422).[15] Now the phonemic value of suprasegmental distinctions is denied (1965, p. 69), and it is somewhat of a puzzle what use is to be made of acoustic data now he has removed that "structure."

In the disappointingly brief second section of this chapter, he comments (pp. 95–96) on some statements by Roman Jakobson. Jakobson makes what I take to be a three-level differentiation which depends on type-token relationships. VERSE DESIGN is the abstract metre; VERSE INSTANCE is a line written in that metre, and it has "invariant features" determined by the design; DELIVERY INSTANCE is an actual performance of that line. Chatman re-words this position, which I among others [16] accept:

> Three ideas now seem clearly established; 1) it is the linguistically relevant, not the unanalyzed speech sounds which signal metrical features; 2) meter itself is a system, parallel to and actualized by, but not to be confused with, the linguistic system; and 3) there is an essential difference between performance (recitation, realization) and abstract metre. (p. 96)

The author makes a further — and less clear — use of Jakobson's proposition, which can be quoted as a way of getting into Chapters V and VI:

> It is but one logical step from this position to recognize the verse instance as a sum or common denominator of all meaningful delivery instances, a hypothesis which underlies much of my own theory of meter. The sum or common denominator is part of the poem itself, the "enduring object" in contradistinction to the many performances of it, which are merely "events." (p. 96)

[14] Wellek and Warren's phrase. See my "'Prose Rhythm' and Metre" in *Essays on Style and Language* (London, 1965), 82–99.

[15] Quoted with approval by Wimsatt and Beardsley, p. 586.

[16] Jakobson, in Sebeok, pp. 365–66; R. S. Wells, in Sebeok, pp. 197–200; Wimsatt and Beardsley, pp. 596–97.

The difficulty is to understand what procedures he has in mind. "Metrical analysis" is the discovery of the verse instance, and here it is said to be deducible from delivery instance, performance. In fact, in Chapter VI it is deduced from PERCEPTION OF performance — the testimony of himself and the "21 professors of English literature" (p. 159). The acoustic analysis (surely, in the true sense analysis of performance?) is used only as secondary evidence. Chatman's words in *Style in Language* (p. 208) show that he is conscious of the essential irrelevance of performance *qua* physical event, and in fact proceed more logically from the position of Jakobson:

> I am not attempting to analyze English meter on the basis of performances; to the contrary (and it is apparently a point I cannot repeat often enough) the phonemic notation of a reading is *not* a metrical analysis. It is simply a way of accounting for the differences in readings, all of which may satisfy the same metrical pattern.

But they by no means resolve the difficulties stumbled over in the present book: difficulties not clarified by the procedurally imprecise "sum or common denominator."

In Chapter V, "The components of English meter," the first component considered is the syllable. The author has already argued (p. 39) that syllable-count is not problematical, despite the indeterminacy of syllable-boundaries; he now minimises the difficulties of elision, reducing it to rule and category. "The poet may select his words in part by considering the number of syllables they contain, and ordinarily he can be sure that this feature will be conveyed to his reader" (p. 112). And "since syllable-count is the most relatively constant feature of meter . . . we may give it priority of application in the analysis of isosyllabic verse" (p. 113).

The grouping of syllables is into lines and feet. The line is numerically determined, and the foot also: for analytic convenience at least, it is "the smallest *submultiple* of the normal line" (p. 117). The foot Chatman presumes to be "a pure metrical convention with no relation to English or to the sense of the poem" (p. 14). Like all other components of metre, it is a concept; but less based on a percept, one supposes, than the others (for the distinction, see p. 105). I would agree that the foot has only a tenuous relation to linguistic reality (ictus is "cued" by prominence, and is an additional foot-defining quality, although the concept is chiefly numerical); but once it has been proposed as an analytic or descriptive category, further use of it can be made. Although boundaries between feet have no linguistic basis, to say that a foot-boundary falls within a word is to say something significant.

We come now to the treatment of ictus, a discussion for which most of the earlier linguistic theory has been a preparation. The author again gives attention to the linguistic conditions — lexical stress and phrase-accent — which determine the siting of ictus and hence the metrical pattern. He believes (p. 126) that it is the lexical stress of polysyllabic words which is most useful in creating the metre. When this has been established, it can be carried on in the absence of an explicitly metre-fixing prose rhythm:

> If ictus is not totally discoverable in the linguistic structure itself it must partly be the product of some extralinguistic phenomenon, like the metrical "set" (in the psychological sense), the running disposition of ictus and non-ictus established by preceding sequences, particularly where these were linguistically unequivocal. (p. 121)

After a disposition to iambs has been created, it will be sufficient for the poet to distribute points open to the imposition of ictus. Certain types of syllable are especially receptive:

> Syllables with full vowels are likely to be more prominent than those with reduced vowels in length, loudness, and pitch-obtrusion, but the prominence is not significant. (p. 125)

Chatman distinguishes

> four different sorts of syllables, or more accurately, syllabic *weights:* **a**) full-vowel monosyllabic words, **b**) stressed syllables of polysyllabic words, **c**) unstressed full-vowel syllables of polysyllabic words, and **d**) unstressed reduced (degraded) syllables of polysyllabic words.

Then, under the heading "Foot-types," [17] he lists the various combinations of types of syllable (**ā + b̆, ă + b̄,** etc.) with illustrations of each. His purpose here is to distinguish between "metre-fixing" and "metre-fixed" types. A metre-fixing foot can be exemplified by **d̆ + b̄** | ălōft | where the stress-pattern is invariable: such a foot will be of first importance in establishing metrical set.

The classification is not offered for its own sake; the author has, in the Introduction, disclaimed an interest in the classification of feet:

> I take the position that the metrist's function is not to find out how many kinds of feet there are, but rather to insure that there aren't any more kinds than necessary. (p. 14)

But he gives the game away by admitting that his distinctions are based on "syllable-weight" (pp. 15 and 123) and this confirms one's suspicion that, with the substitution of other parameters, the classification could have some very positive value. Of course, the provision of as minutely (and immensely) discriminated a categorization as possible is not a viable or useful project.[18] But one must account somehow for differences of "feel" between lines. And the most useful hypothesis that structural metrics can lead us to adopt is that this variety arises from the realization of ictus and non-ictus by syllables of varying weight or prominence.

Chatman's picture of English metre includes level feet, reversal, ambiguity and stress-shift. Some passages, he says, make best sense if equally-stressed feet are allowed into the metrical pattern, despite the impossibility of equal stress in linguistic reality. (And despite Wimsatt and Beardsley [p. 594]; in

[17] The phrase has a more traditional meaning, pp. 118–19.

[18] Epstein and Hawkes (*Linguistics and English Prosody*, Buffalo, 1959) are noticed by Chatman (1965, p. 99) as having attempted classifications.

this matter Chatman is more traditional than his conservative opponents.) Reversal can obviously be caused by dominating lexical and/or accentual pressure, and often by pitch obtrusion. He is more cautious about ambiguous feet. His footnote on p. 149 reveals him as still tender from the exchange with Arnold Stein on "hovering" feet.[19] An ambiguous foot is one "which can be scanned with either the normal disposition of ictus and non-ictus or a reversal." Several examples are to be found in his analysis of Shakespeare's Sonnet 18. Where semantic criteria justify either of two (or more) readings, and formal features select neither unequivocally, he marks both:

Shăll Ī |

Stress-shift is the opposite of reversal. Here metrical demands override lexical stress:

The rich proud cost | ŏf ōut | worn buried age
(Sonnet 64)

After a brief skirmish with Substitutions, Chatman ends his survey of the components of English metre with a dismissal of caesura and enjambment as "pure performance features" (p. 156; cf. Chatman, 1960, pp. 165–170). I cannot allow this judgement to pass unchallenged. His unwillingness to consider metrical stretches more than two syllables long (here and p. 10) is culpable enough, and I shall return to this later. I have written elsewhere on caesura and enjambment,[20] and will at this time say only that semantically and grammatically signalled terminal junctures, both within and between lines, are an essential part of verse-structure. They cannot be ignored without violence to language and meaning. Of course, they may be realized in a variety of ways, as Chatman says; but this does not make them optional, nor alter the fact that they can have a profound effect on the shape of line and line-sequence.

The climax of *A Theory of Meter* is the treatment of Shakespeare's 18th Sonnet. Chatman took eleven commercially available performances of the poem (chiefly by professional actors) and subjected them to spectrographic analysis. He then (presumably, the exact procedure is not well described) applied the linguistically unrevolutionary techniques of syllable-count and foot-division, and marked ictus where it was clearly suggested by stress and accent. His own perceptions were then checked against those of an academic panel in an attempt to find scansions which would eliminate all indeterminacy except in cases of genuinely ambiguous feet. At each stage, the panel's assignments of ictus were compared with the acoustic evidence, demonstrating only (as far as I can see) the acknowledged uselessness of physical data, and the more positive fact that stress, accent, and metrical set can and do compensate for lack of phonetic signal. It is important to realise that performance *qua* physical data forms no part of the analysis itself: just as Chatman has claimed (e.g., p. 142).

[19] "Mr. Stein on Donne," *The Kenyon Review*, XVIII (1956), 443–51, a note which provides important background for the part of *A Theory of Meter* currently under examination.
[20] " 'Prose Rhythm' and Metre," pp. 85–92.

It turns out that the apparently dubious relation between "scansion" and "metrical analysis" is a quite simple one. A scansion is an informed assignment of foot-division, ictus and non-ictus to one performance; a metrical analysis is a CONFLATION [21] of semantically and linguistically justified scansions of several performances, showing agreements and REASONABLE difference of opinion. This is what the analysis looks like:

1. Shăll Ī | cŏmpāre | thēe tŏ | ă sūm | mĕr's dāy?
2. Thŏu ărt | mŏre lŏve | lȳ ănd | mŏre tĕm | pĕrāte:
3. Rŏugh wīnds | dŏ shāke | thĕ dār | lĭng būds | ŏf Māy,
4. Ănd sūm | mĕr's lēase | hăth āll | tŏo shŏrt | ă dāte: (p. 182)

His experience with the Sonnet allows him to state his hypotheses as conclusions:

> 1. Lexical stress unambiguously marks ictus, regardless of the phonetic actuality, unless overridden by accent.
>
> 2. Pitch change is most effective in marking ictus if lexical stress is not a definitive criterion. It functions most powerfully if it is accentual, but pitch obtrusions which are allophonic may also signal ictus in a clear-cut fashion. Length is less effective, although it does operate where pitch is not sufficiently obtruded. Loudness seems least effective; it occasionally operates in the absence of other cues, but most of the time it has little impact. Indeed, it often actually conflicts with concurrent features without upsetting the perception of ictus.
>
> 3. Foot-reversal may be effected where lexical stress is not definitive, but ictus then requires a comparatively greater degree of prominence than it does in the normal foot. The metrical set operates so strongly that a pitch change usually needs to be accentual to reverse the foot.
>
> 4. Vowel reduction generally shows that reducible monosyllabic words are unstressed and hence non-ictic. In very rare cases, accentual features may promote a syllable containing a reduced vowel to ictus.
>
> 5. The difference between the pyrrhic foot and spondee is largely one of the relative length of the syllables. The clearest instances of spondee occur where both syllables are accented in the same way, preferably with an intervening terminal. (pp. 182–83)

Such a set of statements calls for a judgement, and I think this must be "excellent as far as it goes." He has tested a good many basic assumptions in experimentally valid ways; he has established some useful techniques. Above all, he is enlightening on the linguistic cues to ictus: lexical stress, accent, fullness of

[21] Chatman's confusing expressions of this relationship are found on pp. 14 'token/type'; 96 'sum or common denominator'; 105 'process of summing'; 121 'consensus or common denominator'; 167 'consensus.'

syllable, syllable-count and the various other minor signals.[22] He convinces one of the psychological reality of "metrical set." But if the book teaches us only to produce ictic analyses by committee, its ultimate message is too limited. It does not take structural linguistics to allow us to carry out that sort of operation (but Mr. Chatman has used linguistics brilliantly to show us by what mechanisms we do it so confidently). What structural metrics is well fitted to do is explain the differences between, say,

Pinn'd, beaten, cold, pinch'd, threaten'd and abus'd

and

Immutable, immortal, infinite . . .

A generalization to

˘ – | ˘ – | ˘ – | ˘ – | ˘ – |

is not adequate, and if Chatman had pursued the implications of his earlier theory (1956, pp. 422–25), he could have shown how both are iambic pentameters and yet both quite individual.

I accept his account of how metrical stress and its arrangements are perceived—the perception of the verse line as a sequence of groups of ictus and non-ictus comes about through the stimulation by the disposition of certain linguistic features of an innate human tendency to hear secondary rhythm. Once the metre has been established, the stimulation need not be so explicit. An established metre does not, of course, turn the prose rhythm into a system of two-level prominence contrast: an approximation to this state may occur in some excessively 'metred' performances

(Thĕ bóy | stŏod ón | thĕ búr | nĭng déck
Whĕnce áll | bŭt hé | hăd fléd . . .
Cf. Chatman, p. 105)

but ordinarily a metrical line retains multi-level prominence characteristics. To account for differences BETWEEN iambic pentameters, one must record not only the position of ictus, but this full surviving suprasegmental pattern. One must recognise ictus AND SIMULTANEOUSLY the varying prominences which realise it: I differ from Chatman in believing that these are metrically significant.

If we substitute composite prominence for stress, we may find the germ of the idea in the earliest writings on Trager-Smith metrics:

> The two extreme stresses, primary or weak, are poetically fixed, the first being necessarily always a poetic strong, the second always a poetic weak. The two

[22] By abandoning multi-level prominence, he has missed one useful principle, the tendency of adjacent syllables to have different weights. For example, (*tem*) *perate* is rendered | pèrăte |, "pyrrhic as far as *perception* goes, but . . . metrical set suggests of the possibility of iambus" (p. 181). But if the lexical stress is written out for the whole word, we see that the final syllable will in any case tend to be heavier than the second, granted that primary stress goes on *tem*—(surely the trochaic reading | more tem | offered as one possibility, goes too much against lexical stress?). And he seems to be talking about TENSION, here, not AMBIGUITY.

> middle stresses, secondary or tertiary, may be poetic strongs, or poetic weaks. The principle of poetic stress is that a syllable is strong if it is stronger than those which surround it; so that as indicated above, a tertiary stress followed by a weak may count as a poetic strong, while if followed by a secondary or primary stress, it may count as a poetic weak. Those English poets who are generally admired as metrists make use of these differences to produce variety . . .[23]

There is no need to believe that a line- or foot-analysis in these terms is phonemic, however. All we need is a means of symbolizing finer-than-binary prominence. I propose that the Trager-Smith notation (ˊ, ˆ, ˋ, ˘) be adapted to this task on the assumption that four degrees will provide enough contrasts. As has been said many times,[24] once we "dephonemicize" the system, there may be more than four; but four relative degrees may be enough. And the degrees are of prominence, not stress. Interpreted in this way, the phonemic notations of the pioneers make a good deal of sense.

The notion of "tension" also makes sense if we can accept the simultaneous existence of metre as a concept and of the physical reality of multi-level prominence. But the term is undoubtedly misleading, as is "counterpoint." [25] I have argued elsewhere for "syncopation." [26] Syncopation is an effect produced when, holding the metrical set in our minds, we read a line which is not composed entirely of "metre-fixing" syllabic patterns. Obviously such an effect is not open to adequate linguistic notation; but the factors which produce it are, and the "prosodic product," which is composed neither of ictic contrast nor of lexical and accentual prominence patterns, could be said to be a reflex of it.

An understanding of the operation of syncopation depends on the analysis of prose rhythm IN CONTINUITY. Chatman merely picks out a lexical stress from a polysyllabic word and uses it as a cue to ictus within one foot: if the rest of the word falls in another foot, that is quite another matter. So we have

$\breve{\mathbf{a}} + \bar{\mathbf{b}}$ | Swĕet īm |

in one foot, with the rest of the word making up a different foot under a different rule:

$\breve{\mathbf{d}} + \bar{\mathbf{d}}$ | ăgēs |

The formula **a + d + d + d,** broken up into two parts, conceals the continuity of prose rhythm in "images": under the influence of metrical set, ímàgĕs, perhaps. Similarly, Whitehall and Hill's principle that ictus and non-ictus are variously realized as ˊˆˋ˘ and ˆˋ is not fully expressed in a translation of ˘ – into ˘ˊ, ˘ˆ etc.: the continuity of prose rhythm is essential. Although the

[23] H. Whitehall and A. A. Hill, "A Report on the Language-literature Seminar" [of the Linguistic Institute at Indiana, 1953]; H. B. Allen, *Readings in Applied English Linguistics* (New York, 1958), p. 395. R. S. Wells has the same idea in Sebeok, p. 199.

[24] E.g., Wimsatt and Beardsley, pp. 596–97.

[25] Wimsatt and Beardsley suggest "interplay" as an alternative; John Hollander, Sebeok, p. 202, adeptly reveals the inappropriateness of the melodic analogy implied in "counterpoint."

[26] "'Prose Rhythm' and Metre," p. 95.

foot is an abstraction, it need not be thought to have internal structure only: it has boundaries and external relations.

So syncopation is an accentual effect produced by the fit or non-fit of GROUPS of metrical stresses and GROUPS of prose prominences. I will demonstrate the results of this interplay in several pentameter lines.

Hĕr éyes, hĕr háire, hĕr chéeke, hĕr gáte, hĕr vóice.

Chatman would comment that phrase-accent coincides entirely with ictus: this is a perfect "metre-fixing" line. I would add that foot- and phrase-boundaries coincide, and that the junctural separation and grammatical identity of the phrases lead easily to a prosodic interpretation close to simply two-way contrast.

In the next example, the boundary between the fourth and fifth feet does not coincide with a terminal juncture:

Ĭ búrne, Ĭ búrne, Ĭ búrne, thĕn lóud | hè crýde

and hence we must make a different "bridge" between *loud* and *he* from that between *burne* and *I* and *burne* and *then*. I suggest that *he* is slightly more prominent than *I* or *then* — ˋ instead of ˘ perhaps — but it is still non-ictic. In

Sò lóng às mén càn bréathe ŏr éyes càn sée

non-ictus is relatively close to ictus throughout, except that a minor "caesura" is marked by an extra contrast between *breathe* and *or*.

Rôcks, cáves, lâkes, féns, bôgs, déns, ănd shádes òf déath

has syntactic boundaries within the foot, strong phrase-accents coinciding with non-ictus. Here non-ictus is signalled by the highest level of prominence available for the function, ˆ.

Ìmmút | ăblê, | ĭmmór | tàl, ín | fĭnîte |

requires foot-boundaries within words; but the words must be retained as wholes by allowing only one ˊ on each (therefore two ictuses are realized as ˆ) and "promoting" certain non-ictic syllables to ˋ so that they will not be detached from the words they belong to.

The most common form of syncopation is found where a two-syllabled word maintains its prominence-pattern across a foot-boundary. Lexical stress is perfectly adjusted to the position of ictus, but the "light" second syllable of the word, often necessarily in the next foot, cannot be reduced to ˘, or it will detach from the word.

Whĕn yél | lòw léaves,

Bare rú | ìn'd choirs

the twí | lìght of

In iambic metre, no word with initial stress can be realised as ́˘; but words with stress on their second syllable can utilise the contrast between the lowest and highest degrees of prominence:

in me | bĕhóld

ăgáinst | the cold

The prose rhythms of English are in fact the phonology of its grammar, and are quite open to analysis, whether by the Trager-Smith or any other sophisticated method. They need not be deduced from performance. Metrical analysis should see how they are fitted to metre by the manipulation of lexical stress, accent, and full vowels, as Chatman has demonstrated. But they cannot be TOTALLY manipulated, or, if they were, English verse would be a very dull thing, with no grammatical units longer than two syllables, and only two degrees of prominence; no syncopation. I believe that metrical analysis should go further than the documentation of ictus, to consider the patterns formed by its implementation throughout the line. Metrical analysis based on grammatical signals of prose rhythm might then be grammetric [27] prediction rather than phonological description, but it would at least attempt to show how verse in such an inflexible matrix can remain interesting.

[27] For the term, see P. J. Wexler, "On the Grammetrics of the Classical Alexandrine," *Cahiers de Lexicologie*, IV (1964), 61–72, and the same author's "Distich and Sentence in Corneille and Racine" in Fowler, *Essays on Style and Language*, 100–17.

Part Three

GRAMMAR

Like other types of discourse, literary works can be analyzed grammatically. And such analysis has indeed attracted critics who wish to be "precise" about literature. But the fact is that precision of the grammatical kind is limited in scope, often even trivial in relation to larger critical concerns. That which is essential to the literary work of art is not so lightly disposed upon its linguistic surface. The analysis of even "deep" grammatical structure yields linguistic, not aesthetic, results. Grammatical analysis can only be ancillary to the more significant goals of literary criticism. In saying this, however, one is not thereby discounting its importance. Such analysis needs little defense as an implicit or explicit first step towards the kind of elucidations that the modern literary critic is interested in achieving.

Not only literary critics, but linguists as well, have been concerned with literary language. And while it may be true that the latter are not so much interested in literary values as they are in the light that the study of literary works can throw on the structure of language, their methods and findings are not without significance for the literary critic. In any case, the respective aims of critic and linguist in the grammatical analysis of literature should be clearly distinguished. For the one, parsing is a mere preliminary to literary criticism; for the other, it is relevant to a general description of the language itself.

Nor should "grammatical analysis" be conceived in monolithic terms. Available to the scholar today, whether critic or linguist, are a number of different theories of language and grammar. To a significant extent, the adoption of a particular approach will modify or color the kinds of results to be expected. We have therefore included in this section essays which reflect not only the differing aims of literary critic and linguist, but also the consequences of adopting one grammatical schema rather than another.

The first two selections, by Miss Miles and Miss Brooke-Rose, apply to certain literary problems the grammatical categories and relations developed by the classical rhetoricians and traditional grammarians. The emphasis in these two selections is not, however, on the grammatical features themselves (they are understood as given), but rather on certain literary attributes of the poems and devices in which the grammatical features appear. Thus, Miss Miles finds that English poetry written between the sixteenth and the nineteenth centuries oscillates between a clausal and a phrasal syntax, the former characterized by a preponderance of verbs and the latter by a preponderance of adjectives, and she goes on to relate these different syntactic modes to differences of thematic and stanzaic progression.

Miss Brooke-Rose, in her study, uses traditional grammatical analysis to describe the structure of various kinds of metaphor. She shows how different parts of speech and different syntactic constructions underlie the various metaphors and (elsewhere in her book) describes the preferences of several poets for one or another type of metaphoric formation.

Francis' essay is essentially a close reading of a difficult poem, a reading, however, in which certain refinements of structural linguistics such as immediate constituent analysis, suprasegmental analysis, and the notion of lexical compatibility inform the discussion. Consonant with the linguistic emphasis, the poem is given over at the end of the analysis to practitioners of literary criticism.

Halliday's article introduces the notion of a theory of language structure as a background for the study of literary texts. The ranks and categories of the theory may be used as such in investigating a literary text, or they may be realigned to bring together those units which are deemed particularly appropriate to register characteristic literary features. One such realignment is that calculated to register the property "cohesion," presumably a property which literary texts will display in a characteristic mode. The theory without realignment suffices to explain the pattern of consistent departure from regularity observable in Yeats' "Leda and the Swan."

Levin's article treats literary language primarily in terms of its bearing on grammar construction. Comparing specimens of poetic language with the grammar leads, however, to certain conclusions about different types of poetic sequence.

The difference, articulated in transformational grammar, between the surface structure of a sentence and its deep, or underlying, structure (which may comprise a number of sentences) lies at the base of Ohmann's discussion. Since all but the most simple sentences have a deep structure which is quite different from the surface structure and since, moreover, it is in the sentences of the deep structure that the fundamental syntactic and semantic relations obtain, it follows that much of a sentence's meaning can be understood only in the light of its deep structure. On this basis Ohmann suggests that the content of a sentence resides in its deep structure and that its form is the product of this deep structure and whatever grammatical transformations have been applied to yield the resultant sentence. Since the same set of underlying sentences can undergo a variety of transformations and preserve content, Ohmann indicates that style may be a function of the different transformations applied to this underlying sentence-set. In the second part of the article, Ohmann again has recourse to the relations found in the deep structure, this time to explain deviant sentences.

Josephine Miles

ERAS IN ENGLISH POETRY

This is a proposal to consider the periods of English poetic history on the basis of characteristic modes of sentence structure and on the pattern of their sequence.

Conventionally, we have distinguished century-lines as significant to the history of poetry and of literature in general. We speak with a sense of unities when we speak of sixteenth-, seventeenth-, eighteenth-, nineteenth-century poetry. Then also we have tended to divide each century in two, speaking of pre-Elizabethan and Elizabethan, divided at 1557 with Tottel's Miscellany; of metaphysical and neo-classical, divided at the Restoration; of neo-classical and pre-romantic, divided by the death of Pope in 1744; of romantic and Victorian, divided by Scott's death in 1832 or the crowning of Queen Victoria. Often the divisions waver all across the mid-century: from 1640 to 1660, for example, or from 1744 to 1770, as if we had a sense of a middle period, as well as of a beginning and end to each century. I have used such vague words as "sense" and "tend" for our divisions, because I do not think we have an actual philosophy for them, any taxonomical principle of temporal classification. We feel that a literary period begins and ends when a certain kind of writing, or spirit of writing, begins and ends; we set and reset these boundary lines as we redistinguish kinds; yet all the while the century marks seem to preserve their significance, as if writers really were apt to end one kind and begin another with the changing of the numerals. Perhaps these divisions are merely "arbitrary," merely "convenient"? Then would they be convenient if they seemed to run counter to the facts as we felt them to be?

Wondering whether a closer technical look at poetic practice might not discover some descriptive principle of period sequence, I have found that neither diction nor metrics alone seems to provide a pattern regular enough to mark change, but that, on the other hand, both are closely involved with sentence structure which does reveal a sequential pattern. Both serve by certain emphases to support the pattern of basic sentence form.

The distinction which I have found pertinent in kinds of sentence structure

Reprinted by permission of the Modern Language Association from *PMLA*, Vol. LXX (September 1955, Part I) 853–875.

is between the sort which emphasizes substantival elements — the phrasal and coordinative modifications of subject and object — and the sort which emphasizes clausal coordination and complication of the predicate. The first or phrasal type employs an abundance of adjectives and nouns, in heavy modifications and compounding of subjects, in a variety of phrasal constructions, including verbs turned to participles; it is a presentative way of speaking. The second or clausal type emphasizes compound or serial predicates, subordinate verbs in relative and abverbial clauses, action, and rational subordination; it is a discursive way of speaking. The first might say, "Rising and soaring, the golden bird flies into the stormy night of the east"; the second if given the same terms would say, "The golden bird rises and soars; it flies into the night which storms in the east." The motion and concept both differ; and, indeed, the discursive type is less apt to be speaking of "golden birds" at all than to be dealing with abstractions or complex events.

Theoretically, there might be a third type between these two: not merely a scale of degrees between extremes, but a mode of statement characterized by a balance between clausal and phrasal elements. And actually, just as we do in fact find kinds of poetry which are dominantly phrasal or dominantly clausal, so we find a kind of poetry in which sentence structure is balanced between the two. We have, then, three modes technically describable in terms of dominant sentence structure, and emphasized by usage in metre and vocabulary; these I call provisionally the clausal, the phrasal, and the balanced modes of poetic statement.

Classifying the poetry written from 1500 to 1900 in accordance with this distinction, we discover a sequence which runs as follows: clausal — clausal — balanced, clausal — clausal — balanced, phrasal — phrasal — balanced, clausal — clausal — balanced. In other words, there are four groups, one in each century, each begun by an extreme and terminated by a balance. No periods of extreme come immediately together, because each is followed by moderation in a balanced form.

These four groupings appear to coincide closely with the four centuries. The Skeltonic satiric poets of 1500 wrote an extremely clausal poetry, as did Wyatt and Surrey and their followers in mid-century; then the final thirty years were the golden Elizabethan years of a relatively balanced mode. The seventeenth century began with the clausal verse of Jonson, Donne, and Herbert, and continued with that of Cowley and Vaughan; after 1670 came again the balance of the neo-classicists. The eighteenth century began with Prior and Thomson, and continued with Collins and the Wartons, the opposite extreme of phrasal emphasis, countered slightly by the classicism of Pope and Johnson, until finally in 1770 the new balance began to be achieved with Goldsmith, Crabbe, Rogers, even finally Wordsworth. The nineteenth century then began with the active clausal balladry of Coleridge, Byron, Moore, Landor, proceeded with that of the Brownings and the Pre-Raphaelites, and ended again, after 1870, with the balanced modes of Swinburne, Bridges,

Thompson, Phillips, Hopkins — to begin again in the twentieth century the clausal revival of the Donne tradition, in Housman, Hardy, Cummings, Frost, Auden.

That there can be felt some poetic sense of century seems undeniable. Over and over the pattern recurs, of a new mode for a new era, and then of a balanced moderation at the end. Unless the structure of sentence, sound, and reference is utterly impertinent to poetry, which does not seem possible, the slightest suggestion of developing pattern is significant for poetic history; and a pattern as regularly recurrent as this one must be especially so, since it coincides with many commonly accepted patterns. We may learn technically not only how structural patterns coincide with centuries, but also why internal divisions have conventionally suggested a span of middle years: the modes at beginning and end are clear, but the middle years represent modification and transition from one to the other.

One may ask the Why of this discoverable pattern, but I have no idea of the Why, and am indeed still much concerned with the details of the How. It may be simply that artists like others are intensely aware of living and working in a beginning or ending century, and so suit their tones and structures. It may be some repetition we have been caught up in, as many cyclical theorists suggest. Curt Sachs in *The Commonwealth of Art,* François Mentré in *Les Générations sociales,* and Max Förster in "The Psychological Basis for Literary Periods" (*Studies for Wm. A. Read*) are three, for example, who suggest pendular swings. Agnes Young in *Recurring Cycles of Fashion* finds three eras of dress-fashion in each sequence. Dialectics, whether idealist or materialist, suggest a clash of opposites and then a resolution. But the poetic pattern seems rather a matter of mediation between opposites, a pendular swing but not a smooth one, in stages, not in a continuous arc. Perhaps the stages are a matter of generations, as Mentré suggests, with epochs of rebellion, transition, and reconciliation; but we have still to learn why these fit so neatly into each century; consciousness of era seems part of the problem.

At any rate, much more needs to be known before we can decently speculate. The pattern is present in the language of poetry. Could we find it in prosaic language also, in which case it would seem to be a part of social history? Or could we find it analogically in the material structures of other arts, in which case it would seem more specifically aesthetic? Or could we find it in both, as part of a more sweeping human pattern? We do not know, because we have not looked. At least we do know that it is close enough to conventional divisions in English literary history that it may, by confirming most of them, serve to offer alternative suggestions for a few.

We have long accepted, for example, the fact that the last thirty years of the sixteenth century brought a new richness and smoothness to English poetry. Now we may note that technically this meant, among other things, an increased balancing of typically English clausal structures by Latin participial constructions, accompanied by, as cause or consequence, a fuller and smoother pentameter line and a more aesthetic and appreciative vocabulary. Shakespeare's sonnets are representative of the new possibilities. Since it moves toward Latin and away from Saxon structure, this poetry of balance may justly be called classical, just as its kind will be a century later, from 1670 to 1700, when Waller and Dryden even more effectively succeeded in drawing away from the roughly intellectual and clausal poetry of the metaphysicals toward Rome again. Granting these two familiar end-century stages of poise, we may then recognize that they also recur in the eighteenth and nineteenth centuries, in the group of Goldsmith and Crabbe, and then again in the "decadence" of Swinburne and Bridges — a levelling, composing, classicizing of what had gone before, an enriching by sensuous and presentative vocabulary, a filling in and loading of metrical line, a stabilizing of action for the sake of reception. In each of these four end-century periods we find a strong express interest in Latin and Greek poetical style, as a necessary model perhaps for the counterbalancing of preceding native or Biblical extremes. The interests are relative, not wholly repetitive; Crabbe does not necessarily echo Dryden; nor Bridges, Crabbe; but each acts as the same sort of modifier for his immediate predecessors. In the pattern of the whole, their relative positions become clear.

So also in relation to the early and mid-century extreme of the native English clausal structure which we have conventionally recognized in Skelton and Wyatt, in Donne and Cowley, in Byron and Browning, and in their respective eras, we may more clearly recognize the opposite extreme extending through most of the eighteenth century, the phrasal structure of the poetry from Blackmore through the Wartons, too excessive to be "classical" as it is often called, too vigorously opposite to the active romantic mode meaningfully to be called "pre-romantic" as it often is. While classical poetic usage is characterized by regularity of metre and richness of reference along with its structural balance, and while metaphysical and romantic clausal usages are characterized by conceptual vocabulary and stanzaic verse forms, the eighteenth-century phrasal extreme (for which we may supply the label "Sublime," because it combines qualities of the Gothic, the Greek Pindaric, and the Biblical) is characterized by blank verse or irregular ode forms and a vocabulary of lofty ceremony and enthusiasm.

The forward motion of usages never allows a mode exactly to recur, but progressively alters materials even while it is recalling structures. Therefore historians have tended to name the periods of poetic practice seriatim, without labels of significant renewal which would indicate the pattern of tradition as well as of development. Actually our Tudor and metaphysical, our romantic and modern, all share along with a dominantly clausal structure a language of sound and reference which keeps them in close bond. They are early and mid-century forms, in strongest contrast to the early and mid-eighteenth-century form of the Sublime, which swung to an opposite extreme of language. Late century forms, on the other hand, are persistently balanced, in grammatical structure as well as in sound and sense, and may as well be called classical for all four centuries as for the first two.

We could read the pattern of recurrence then as follows, generation by generation: sixteenth-century English clausal — English clausal — classical balanced; seventeenth-century metaphysical clausal — metaphysical clausal — classical balanced; eighteenth-century sublime phrasal — sublime phrasal — classical balanced; nineteenth-century romantic clausal — romantic clausal — classical balanced. This is too heavy a terminology, but it may merely indicate the close relation between what we have felt and what we may learn technically about periods of poetic development. For while subject matter and sound pattern move progressively and selectively forward in one direction, with a few significant renewals, structure moves rather periodically back and forth, in stages from extreme through balance to extreme, conditioning and altering always, as it is altered by, the developing materials of sound and sense it works with. The simple line of motion is something as follows:

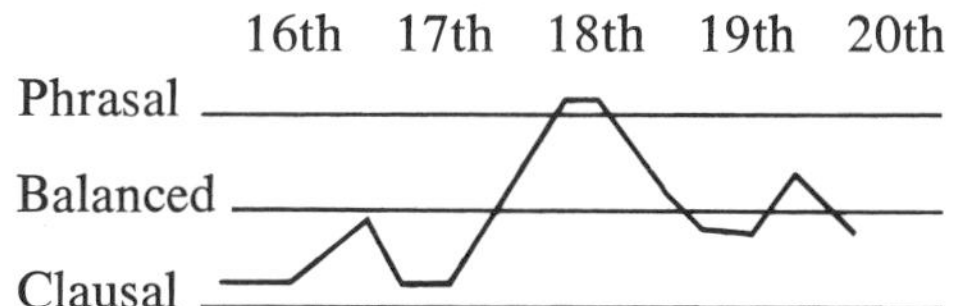

The apparent symmetry of the pattern is interesting and troubling. Does our language so regularly move, even in poetry? Are periods meaningfully marked by the sentence structures of poets?

If the reader is interested in this proposal and its problems, he may wish to consider in more detail how its working-base was arrived at, in order to check the validity of the argument; and he may wish to learn the degree of simplification I have presented.

First, as I have said, I had found that poets seem to use one sentence structure — clausal, phrasal, or balanced — predominantly through their work. A number of studies, by Rostrevor-Hamilton, L. A. Sherman, Gordon Allport, Sapir, Whorf, Spitzer, Sayce, and others, even the editorial comments in concordances, have noted the general consistency in an author's style. Structure is one particular in that consistency. I have determined sentence structure in poetry by relating it to the poetic line: one adjective and one verb per line indicate a balanced structure; more adjectives than verbs per line indicate a dominantly phrasal structure; more verbs than adjectives, a dominantly clausal structure. So, for example, such shorthand as Barclay 8A-21N-12V, or Wyatt 7A-12N-11V, or Jonson 6A-14N-12V, or Cowley 7A-14N-11V, represents the number of adjectives-nouns-verbs for each in an average ten lines; for each, the verbs outweigh the adjectives, and the structure is clausal. Collins 12A-17N-9V, on the other hand, represents adjectival and phrasal dominance; and Pope 11A-20N-11V, a balanced one.

Secondly, such notation for each author is based upon a full count of one thousand lines of his work, which is often most of it, and at least representative of the whole. Statistically, such a selection is larger than necessary, but I have worked descriptively. At any rate one must use common sense as to the adequacy of the selection, and not extend implications without evidence. Gray wrote just about 1,000 lines. Wordsworth wrote 53,000, of which most were balanced, a few thousand were experimentally phrasal, and a few were clausal like Coleridge's *Ancient Mariner*. Always I specify the lines observed, so that the poet's name stands provisionally for these alone. The characteristically classical poet would use in these 1,000 lines about 1,000 adjectives and 1,000 verbs, or 10A-20N-10V in 10 lines. The model classical line of Ovid or Virgil is somewhat fuller because of the hexameter length, but is in the same characteristically balanced proportion: 12A-21N-12V. Note that the nouns, proportionally most stable, are least useful as distinguishing characteristic. Nouns used as adjectives, as in *summer night,* are counted as nouns; all descriptive, numerical, and participial forms are counted as adjectives; and infinitives as verbs, with auxiliaries as part of the single verbal unit. Adjectival dominance is representative of phrasal structure, as predicative is of clausal.

Thirdly, for how many poets have I this 1,000 lines of evidence? For each of the generations up to mid-nineteenth century there are just about 10 poets who come to mind as first or second rate; indeed we have the works of no more than 10 or so for most of the early generations; so I determined upon 10 for each of the 13 eras to 1940, or 130 in all, omitting some out of too great abundance, but none who would alter the picture or change the emphasis. Every reader will prefer other inclusions; but I think as a whole the proportion is faithful. There are not many more than 200 poets in all of Ghosh's *Annals,* to name one fairly objective handbook.

Fourth, we list chronologically the works observed. Each generation is represented by ten works of its maturity, written by poets between ages thirty and fifty. As the first generation of the sixteenth century is so scant as to be exceptional, some significant earlier writers are included there; but the last generation of the Elizabethans is clearer: Chapman, Daniel, Drayton, Hall, Marlowe, Sidney, Shakespeare, Spenser, with Donne and Jonson not quite yet thirty but active especially early; and the next era then, in reaction to the Elizabethan, Carew, Herbert, Herrick, Harvey, Fletcher, Quarles, Sandys, Shirley, Sylvester, Wither. In no single era do all ten poets agree in emphasis; but in almost every era at least four of these agree; and it is upon this relative degree and direction of change in agreement that the distinctions between eras are based. A complete listing of present materials therefore looks as follows, in a filling out of lines already traced with the addition of the poets' names. The order of columns left to right is chronological; as far as I have discovered there is no need to divide more precisely than by decades. The order from bottom to top is from the extreme of clausal structure in the sixteenth century, with verbs twice adjectives, through balance (10A-10V, or 10A-9V, or

ERAS IN ENGLISH POETRY

	1500–40	1540–70	1570–00	1600–40	1640–70	1670–00	1700–40	1740–70	1770–00	1800–40	1840–70	1870–00	1900–40
PHRASAL							Thomson	T. Warton					
							Somerville	Armstrong					
							Dyer	J. Warton		Hemans			
					Milton		Philips	Collins	Bowles	Keats	Tennyson		
				Fletcher			Prior	Lyttleton	Blake		Whitman		
						Wesley		Mason				Wilde	Moore
				Sylvester	More	Blackmore	Blair	Gray					Pound
								Akenside					
BALANCED			Spenser		Waller			Shenstone	Southey	Shelley	Poe	Swinburne	E. Sitwell
	Hawes		Shakespeare			Dryden	Pope		Goldsmith		Arnold	Bridges	Yeats
	Dunbar		Hall			Marvell	Parnell		Crabbe	Bryant		Hopkins	Stevens
	Douglas	Sackville				Addison	Young	Johnson	Wordsworth	Campbell		Phillips	Eliot
				Sandys	Crashaw	Pomfret			Rogers	Macaulay		Thompson	
									Burns	Scott	Longfellow	Dickinson	
									Chatterton		Emerson		
CLAUSAL	Barclay	Lindsay		Quarles		Roscommon	Gay		Coleridge	Byron	Meredith		Cummings
	Lydgate	Gascoigne	Sidney	Carew	Lovelace	Creech				Moore	E. Browning		Frost
	Chaucer	Baldwin	Drayton	Herrick	Denham	Walsh					R. Browning		Auden
	Sternhold	Heywood	Chapman	Shirley	Vaughan	Oldham						Hardy	
	Skelton	Wyatt	Marlowe	Harvey	Cleveland					Landor	Rossetti	Housman	Millay
	Ballad	Surrey	Daniel	Wither	Suckling								
	Langland	Breton	Donne	Herbert	Cowley								
		Googe	Jonson										
		Turberville											

7A-8V), to the phrasal extreme of adjectives twice verbs in mid-eighteenth century. In the first column, for lack of strong poets about 1500, I have placed some interesting predecessors who corroborate the general evidence. The last column, for the early twentieth century, presents at least plausibly representative names. And at least the main pattern is vivid: the sweep from clausal to phrasal structure and back again, through the recurrent stages of balance.

Many interesting details may be noted. Chaucer and his colloquial tradition, for example; and the early participation of the aureate poets in the classical tradition which reaches to Yeats and Stevens. Or the ascending line from Spenser and Waller to Milton and Thomson; and it is interesting that Denham, often grouped with Waller by his contemporaries, here seems far apart. He and Cowley are true transitional figures: most of their work was traditionally clausal, but they were interested in trying a few new forms. Marvell is listed late, for his classically formed satire; note that the more colloquial satire of Creech and Oldham, and then of Gay, with whom Swift could be grouped, is the last of the English clausal mode to fade, until it is revived again at 1800 by Coleridge's and Byron's narrative techniques. Blake's Songs should be linked with Coleridge; but it is rather his phrasal prophetic poetry which predominates, and which is here listed. By mid-nineteenth century, poets as important as Morris, Clough, and Lowell have to be omitted for lack of space, but do not affect the pattern, as their works are respectively clausal, balanced, and phrasal. Inclusion of Phillips in the late nineteenth-century list is based on Jerome Buckley's stress on his importance in *The Victorian Temper*. Kipling, E. A. Robinson, Jeffers would further enforce the clausal side; Hart Crane, Stephen Spender, Dylan Thomas, the phrasal. At least I think the main outlines of the pattern will remain clear through the many changes that are possible. Most readily acceptable to the reader will probably be that part of the pattern which represents the early clausal emphases of Wyatt and the metaphysicals, along with the clearly opposing mode of the eighteenth century. Least acceptable will seem the partially romantic emphasis on balance. I think we may learn a good deal more, however, about the specific nature of nineteenth-century classicism. The discrimination of modes simply fails to make many pertinent distinctions, as between the styles of Hopkins, Bridges, and Swinburne for example; on the other hand, it indicates underlying likenesses which may be worth further study.

The tendency of one sort of sentence structure to predominate in the poetry of a generation, and the tendency in the past four hundred years to move from one extreme of structure, the native clausal, through classical balance, to an extreme of elaborated phrasal structure, and then back again, is borne out by other characteristics of language like sound-structure and vocabulary. Clausal poems, we find, tend to be stanzaic and active poems, working out an argument or narrative in clearly defined stages and formal external order. Phrasal poems, and phrasal eras, on the other hand, emphasize line-by-line progression, and cumulative participial modification, in description and invocation without stress on external rhyming or grouping. So the strongly stanzaic verse of the sixteenth century became moderated in the more skillful blank verse and couplet of its last generation, just as in the next century the metaphysical stanza narrowed to the neo-classical couplet, carrying its linear organization partly inward by caesural balances. Then the eighteenth century aimed for the other extreme, not only a blank verse freer of end-stop emphasis, but even the irregular lines and motions of the ode-forms, settling again into such couplet moderations as Goldsmith's and Crabbe's, before turning back in the nineteenth century to the clausal ballad stanza and in the twentieth to the more metaphysical involutions of Cummings, Frost, and Auden.

In the same way, the major vocabulary, the nouns, adjectives, and verbs most used and most agreed upon in each generation, follow the periodic pattern, though their main line of development is in one direction. Certain primary words thus drop out of poetic usage not to return; others persist through all four centuries; but some come and go in periodic fashion. The persisting ones are the basic human concerns we should expect: God, heart, life, love, and man, modified by value in *good,* by magnitude in *great,* by time in *old,* active in coming, going, taking, making, seeing. The lost words, on the other hand, are those most closely reflecting the limitations of interest in a period: the early cruel fortune, pain, king, lady, and lord, for example; the blood and fire of the metaphysicals; or, at the extreme opposite to these socially analytic and conceptual terms of clausal poetry, the equally limited ceremonious ones of the phrasal eighteenth century: soft, breast, maid, muse, scene, song, youth, virtue, rising and falling.

Most significantly, the terms which neither persist nor vanish but recur do so along with recurring sentence and verse forms. So, for example, the early Tudor vocabulary of concept, in words like mind and thought, word and thing, time and world, recurred strongly again in the clausal poetry of the nineteenth century. So also each century in its last generation — in its classical mode, contributed a special sort of recurring term, sensory and observational, like sweet, heaven, night, sun for the Elizabethans, with their corresponding verbs of lie, love, look; then the neo-classicists' happy, mighty, art, fate, nature, grow; the late eighteenth century's little, sad, tear, woe, weep; and the late nineteenth's young, child, dream, foot, summer, woman: always a vocabulary of human dimension and feeling in the natural world.

As of structural continuity, we may say of this referential continuity that it begins in the sixteenth and seventeenth centuries with emphasis on social and relational terms, moves through the descriptive vocabulary of the classical generations to the sublime and ceremonious world of the eighteenth, and then back to more abstract relational terms again, though never in conceptual vocabulary so strong as at first, and with a late classicism in which direct natural and human image seems partially to have turned to symbol.

One is not surprised to learn that reference and sound work closely with sentence; that the language of poetry is integral in its characteristics. Which moves first: which new sound makes for new sense, or new structure for new sound, is a question needing more than the evidence available. At least, in generational stages, we can see that the three phases move together, though not with equal force; vocabulary is the least likely, structure the most, to return to old stages. All work as one poetic unit: the relational pattern of clausal sentence with stanzaic sound, and with conceptual vocabulary; or the cumulative pattern of phrasal sentence with internal and onomatopoetic sound and with sublime vocabulary; or the distinct, not merely transitional, balanced pattern of structure, line, and human nature in nature which we call classical. Here, in this nucleus of language-properties, we may find some of the basis for a definition of modes; and in modes, of styles; and in styles, of eras.

Perhaps it would be useful to see each mode at work in a single poem, not as widely different as possible, but as close together in one century. Here is first the clausal, Wyatt's sonnet "Against His Tongue":

Because I still kept thee fro' lies and blame,
And to my power always thee honoured,
Unkind tongue! to all hast thou me rend'red,
For such desert to do me wreke and shame.
In need of succour most when that I am,
To ask reward, thou stand'st like one afraid:
Always most cold, and if one word be said,
As in a dream, unperfect is the same.
And ye salt tears, against my will each night
That are with me, when I would be alone;
Then are ye gone when I should make my moan:
And ye so ready sighs to make me shright,
Then are ye slack when that ye should outstart;
And only doth my look declare my heart.

The conceptual terms are typical; the difficulty of speech, thematic. The sonnet structure is tightly woven and enclosed. The sentences are active and clausally constructed; there are 17 verbs to 10 adjectives in the 14 lines. In general, the proportioning in the poetry of Chaucer, Wyatt, Donne, Herrick, Cowley, and later Byron, Browning, Frost, and others, is about 7 adjectives to 14 nouns to 11 verbs in an average 10 lines; and this single poem by Wyatt is fairly representative of it, using just that sort of colloquial language with its *becauses, ifs, whichs,* and *whens.*

What are the simple signs of that classically balanced poetry for which the late Elizabethans then strove? A thoroughly symmetrical proportioning, an inner onomatopoeia and harmony of sound along with the tight outward rhyme, a sensory and emotional vocabulary. This was the less active, more responsive world of the Shakespearean sonnet, clauses balanced by modifying phrases, and some of the need for connectives smoothed away, in a proportioning of ten adjectives to twenty nouns to ten verbs in ten lines. For example, Shakespeare's first sonnet is near the pattern:

From fairest creatures we desire increase,
That thereby beauty's rose might never die,
But as the riper should by time decrease,
His tender heir might bear his memory;
But thou, contracted to thine own bright eyes,
Feed'st thy light's flame with self-substantial fuel,
Making a famine where abundance lies,
Thyself thy foe, to thy sweet self too cruèl.
Thou that art now the world's fresh ornament
And only herald to the gaudy spring,
Within thine own bud buriest thy content
And, tender churl, mak'st waste in niggarding.
Pity the world, or else this glutton be,
To eat the world's due, by the grave and thee.

Adjectives and verbs are nearly balanced here, because many clausal constructions have been made phrasal, in the classical fashion. "But thou, contracted," and "self-substantial," and "making a famine," and "And tender churl," all, by participial, appositional, or compounding construction, turn verbs to adjectives, smooth the transitions, integrate the sound.

Each late-century generation called itself classical, and strove consciously for what it thought to be a Roman mode of language. Sidney's age and Dryden's, and later Wordsworth's and Bridges', wrote of their pleasure in what they called classical proportions. Wordsworth withdrew to the simplicities of classicism under the influence of Goldsmith, away from the eighteenth-century "gaudy and inane"; and Bridges and Hopkins in turn tried to win back some of that gaudiness, to make a balance against the stringencies of the ballad tradition. Furthermore, the great Latin poets themselves wrote the sort of syntax in the sort of line which we, following Dryden, have been calling classical. That is, the proportioning of language by Ovid, Virgil, and Horace was just that balanced one-adjective to two-nouns to one-verb which Dryden together with his poetic colleagues achieved and which he praised in his preface "On Translation" as the "golden" line of classical literature. It suited the rhymed pentameter as it had suited unrhymed hexameter, and it dealt explicitly with emotion and sense of the natural world for Shakespeare and Marvell and Dryden as for Virgil. *Laetus, magnus, amicus, caelum, nox, video* were among the major terms for Roman classicism as for English. The mode was one literally worked for and achieved in England, and was renewed again and again as extremes of English experiment outwore themselves.

The outstanding classical poets to offer the model of a different mode were Pindar and Lucretius. Their cosmic and ceremonious overload of sublime epithets and phrasal constructions indicated a kind of extreme which English poetry did not reach until the eighteenth century. But Biblical richness and the Platonic tradition early offered to such poets as Spenser and Sylvester, and then Milton, the idea of a poetic language as free as possible from clausal complication, as resilient as possible in richly descriptive participial suspension. The signs of such a mode are more adjectives than verbs, some free variation in line length as in the ode, much inner harmony and less rhyme, and a vocabulary of physical presence, ceremony and pleasure. The proportioning of statement ranges from about 12 adjectives — 16 nouns — 10 verbs — in 10 lines for Milton and Collins and Keats to 15 adjectives — 18 nouns — 8 verbs for Thomson and the Wartons in the height of the mode. Even so early as Spenser, the mode of speech is visible; in Spenser's first sonnet:

Happy ye leaves when as those lilly hands,
which hold my life in their dead doing might,
shall handle you and hold in love's soft bands,
lyke captives trembling at the victors sight.
And happy lines, on which with starry light,
those lamping eyes will deigne sometimes to look
and reade the sorrowes of my dying spright,
written with teares in harts close bleeding book.
And happy rhymes bath'd in the sacred brooke,
of *Helicon* whence she derived is,
when ye behold that Angels blessed looke,
my soules long lacked foode, my heavens blis.
Leaves, lines, and rymes, seeke her to please alone,
whom if ye please, I care for other none.

The poem is an exclamation, not an argument. It rests in its adjectives, *happy, trembling, starry, lamping, bleeding, blessed,* in the physical sense of bodily images which are also symbols. *Handle, look, behold,* and *please* are the few significant actions, and they are subordinate to the substance. Connections are provided by participles, and these together with the descriptive adjectives are half again as many as the verbs.

This is the mode which would give us the heavens and earth of *Paradise Lost,* the cosmological reaches of Akenside, the rich details of Thomson, the personifications of Collins, the great aesthetic and social divine wars of Blake, the figure of Keats's Autumn, the vigor of symbol and celebration in Whitman and Henley. In our own day, such poets as Dylan Thomas may lead us back to it. The style of which this mode is an enduring part has been given no name by the literary historians, although the eighteenth-century poets themselves often called it Sublime. It is an extreme which has not appeared strongly in our language for almost two centuries, but an extreme that some of the imagists, under Pound's guidance, may have been aiming at, and may aim at again.

The examples of the three modes, representing as they do the range within one century and within one genre, do not represent the full reach of variation from century to century, particularly in sound-patterning. The Elizabethan classicism did manage to free itself somewhat from the tight stanzaic forms of the clausal mode, into more straightaway couplets and blank verse, but the height of the couplet form for classicism did not come until the next century, and the height of blank verse and freer odal forms not until Milton and his eighteenth-century followers. What I have tried to illustrate in the quotation of the three sonnets is, first, the power of the three modes to work within one genre; and, second, the temporal concurrence of modes, the latent potentiality of all, while one may dominate.

Neither genre nor era seems to control mode, though of the two era seems the stronger. Individual aptitude may be the controlling force, though it might be strongly conditioned by era or by genre-models. At any rate, we find sonnets, epics, pastorals, satires written in any of the modes, apparently depending largely upon period; and we find some versions of each mode, however scant, in every period. The sense of language-complex, the core of fitting together structure, sound, and reference seems to be the basic force for choice and emphasis. Some poets experiment with one and another, as Blake for example tried the clausal mode in his *Songs of Innocence and Experience,* and then turned back to elaborate in his prophetic poems the phrasal pattern with which he had begun. But many poets, Donne, Dryden, Thomson, Keats, Eliot, for example, stay by one identifying mode for their work, sometimes even when they are translating others of a different sort. Sometimes, within an era, the idea of a certain suitability of mode to genre or topic does occur, perhaps even is debated; then we see, for example, Pope modifying his structure somewhat to suit what he considers the satiric tradition. As a whole, we may surmise from present evidence first, that a poet has an aptitude for a mode as basis for development of his individual style; second, that his own and his era's general concept of the importance of distinct genres may condition his adaptation of modes; and third, that much agreement of usage in any one era seems to suggest some temporal conditioning force in the language itself, or at least in the poet's attitude toward it.

At any rate we may testify to the persisting use of all the modes in English poetry, with some correlation in Latin and Greek backgrounds, and we may even surmise that the traditional high, middle, and low styles had some basis in language structure. At least in English we may see a simple correspondence. The phrasal mode of Sylvester, Milton, and the eighteenth century, with its lofty phrases and cadences, and its figures larger than life, and its high passions, was a clear part of what the century itself called the high or sublime style, not so much heroic as cosmic, not so much active as receptive and "passionate," in Pindar's richly ceremonious sense. The balanced and medial mode has been traditionally recognized as classical, the golden mean in the golden line of an adjective, two nouns, and a verb, as Dryden described it, and the sharing of ethos with pathos in human heroism in moderated language. The relation of clausal mode to low style is somewhat less clear in tradition, perhaps because the mode was not so strong in Latin as in English, and the English put it, like the iambic, to uses not all simple, common, and low. Nevertheless, there was some recognition. Elizabethans were troubled that clausal English was low, as Richard Foster Jones has shown us; the long critical argument against monosyllables in poetry was also an argument against English clausal construction and connection; Donne's rough "masculine" style was recognized as low and English, not classical enough; and Wordsworth, when the style was renewed two centuries later in the balladry of Coleridge, had come around to praising the low and common, as Emerson did and as Frost did, not only for the ethos of social tradition, but for the pathos which nature had drawn down to man from the Bible and the sublime. In other words, though there was a shift in meanings by the nineteenth century, a new notion of the low as natural, and a new use of natural vocabulary and colloquialism in clausal construction, the structure itself had persisted and seemed steadily to be recognized as part of the tradition of common or lowly style. The scholarly work of Ernst Robert Curtius, of J. V. Cunningham, Klaus Dockhorn, Sister Miriam Joseph, Erich Auerbach, and Samuel Monk has an interesting bearing on the problems of spirit and intention behind the modes we have here distinguished.

The study of modes should lead to the study of the styles of which they are a part. The question of complexes of usage in language should lead to questions of the ideas and attitudes being conveyed through these complexes, and of the power of stylistic indirections like figurative speech, like metaphor, symbol, hyperbole, and irony, to alter the quality and effect of the medium. But my present concern is the modes themselves, to try to distinguish them clearly so that they may be recognizable, to suggest their usefulness as characteristic of poets and of eras in poetic history. How strong was the Chaucerian tradition of speech in English, how close were Donne and Jonson as opposed to Spenser, how different was Jonson's classicism from Dryden's, how different was Keats's romanticism from Byron's, how much closer was Marvell to Dryden than to Donne, how vividly new was the renewal of an old mode by the ballad-makers of the nineteenth century — these are the sorts of questions which discrimination of modes may help to answer.

For consolidation's sake, let us return from speculation to evidence, and present at the end the full materials from which the evidence was arrived at. In his recent book on pastoral poetry, J. E. Congleton expressed a caution about the symmetry he seemed to find in the main documents of pastoral theory, one for each third of the eighteenth century; he felt that such appropriate pattern might seem to represent his own "tinkering." How much more caution should I feel in the proposing of a four-century pattern to be discerned in English poetic history! There follows therefore a chronological listing, by birthdates and very closely by publication dates, of the poets and the works studied, their basic syntactical proportions and measures, and the nouns, adjectives, verbs most used by four or more of them in each era.

From what the reader may at first think to be a patternless array of data, a simple pattern may begin to emerge: most clearly the tendency toward agreement within groupings, then the force of each third grouping toward balance in structure and innovation in vocabulary, and finally progression as well as recurrence in emphases.

All the evident patterns of agreement and development seem to me to show that as poets have worked through language to construct their world, so historians may work through language to reconstruct it.

TEXTS *

Chronology of Proportions, Measures, and Vocabulary

Birth	*Poet*	*Work — first 1,000 ll.*	*Measure*	*Proportions Adj-Nn-Verb in 10 ll.*
		1500–40		
c. 1330	Langland	Piers Plowman, thr. III.1550 (ed. Skeat).	4′ lines	5–21–18
c. 1340	Chaucer	Prologue, Knight's Tale, 500 ll. each (Works, ed. Robinson).	5′ couplets	7–15–11
c. 1370	Lydgate	Fall of Princes, Temple of Glass, 1554, 500 ll. each (eds. resp. Schick, Bergen).	5′ couplets	6–16– 9
c. 1400	Ballads	Ed. W. M. Hart, first 18 Ballads.	4′–3′ stanzas	5–12–10
c. 1460	Skelton	Colin Cloute, 1545 (ed. Hughes).	2′ couplets	4–10– 7
c. 1460	Dunbar	Thrissil, Terge, Synnes, Makaris, 1508, 700 ll. (EETS).	5′–4′ stanzas	8–11– 7
c. 1460	Hawes	Pastime of Pleasure, 1517, 900 ll.	5′ stanzas	9–13– 8
1474	Douglas	Palice of Honour, Eneados, 1553, 500 ll. each (Works, 1874).	5′ stanzas	8–17– 9
1475	Barclay	Eclogue v, 1521 (EETS).	5′ couplets	8–21–12
c. 1480	Sternhold	Psalms of David, 1547 ff., first 25 (Huntington Lib.).	4′ stanzas	4–11– 8

Main words (most used by four or more; first appearance in lists is italicized).

5 adjectives — *fair*, *good*, *great*, *old*, *poor*.

16 nouns — *day*, *god*, *gold*, *hand*, *heart*, *king*, *lady*, *life*, *lord*, *love*, *man*, *mind*, *thing*, *time*, *word*, *world*.

8 verbs — *come*, *give*, *go*, *know*, *make*, *see*, *take*, *tell*.

		1540–70		
1490	Lindsay	Squire Meldrum, 1548 (Works, ed. Laing).	4′ couplets	6–13– 9
1497	Heywood	Proverbs and Epigrams, 1546, 500 ll. each (ed. resp. J. Sherman and Spenser Soc.).	5′ couplets	9–17–15
1503	Wyatt	Songs, Rondeaus, Odes. 1557 (Works, Boston, 1854).	5′ stanzas	7–12–11

* Choice of texts based partly on convenience for marking and analysis.

Birth	Poet	Work — first 1,000 ll.	Measure	Proportions Adj–Nn–Verb in 10 ll.
1517	Surrey	Sonnets, etc., 1557 (Poems, ed. Padelford).	5′ stanzas	7–17–13
1529	Baldwin	1st 400 ll. and Cambridge, York, Clarence in Mirror for Magistrates (ed. Campbell).	5′ stanzas	7–20–12
1536	Sackville	Induc. and Buckingham in Mirror for Magistrates, 1563.	5′ stanzas	9–18–10
1540	Googe	Eclogs, Epitaphes, Sonettes, 1563 (ed. Arber).	4′ stanzas	5–12– 9
1540	Turberville	Epitaphes, Epigrams, etc., 1567 (ed. J. P. Collier).	4′ stanzas	5–13–10
1542	Gascoigne	The Steele Glas, 1576 (Works, ed. Cunliffe).	5′ blank verse	8–18–12
1545	Breton	School and Fort of Fancie, 1557 (Works, ed. Grosart).	3′ stanzas	5–11– 8

4 adjectives — *cruel*, good, great, old.

16 nouns — day, *death*, *eye*, *fortune*, god, hand, heart, king, life, lord, love, man, mind, *pain*, thing, time.

13 verbs — *bring*, come, *die*, *find*, give, go, know, make, see, *seek*, take, tell, *think*.

1570–1600

Birth	Poet	Work — first 1,000 ll.	Measure	Proportions Adj–Nn–Verb in 10 ll.
1552	Spenser	Faerie Q., Amoretti, 1582, 1594, 500 ll. each.	5′ stanzas	12–16–11
1554	Sidney	Eclogs, 1593, and Astrophel, 500 ll. each.	5′ stanzas	10–20–12
1559	Chapman	Homeric Odes, 830 ll., Juvenal, 300 ll.	5′ lines	8–18–10
1562	Daniel	Delia, 700 ll., and Rosamund, 1592.	5′ stanzas	8–17–13
1563	Drayton	Idea, and Pastorals, 1593, 500 ll. each.	5′ stanzas	9–16–11
1564	Marlowe	Hero and Leander, 800 ll., Ovid Eleg., 200 ll.	5′ couplets	9–16–13
1564	Shakespeare	Sonnets, 1590's (Cambridge ed.).	5′ stanzas	10–17–10
1573	Jonson	Underwood (Oxford ed.).	5′–4′ stanzas	6–14–12
1574	Jos. Hall	Virgidemiae, 1597.	5′ couplets	10–18–10
1576	Donne	Songs and Sonets, 1590's (Random House).	5′–4′ stanzas	7–11–12

7 adjectives — fair, good, great, *high*, poor, *sweet*, *true*.

20 nouns — *beauty*, day, eye, god, hand, heart, *heaven*, life, love, man, *name*, *night*, *son*, *sun*, tear, *thought*, thing, time, word, world.

13 verbs — come, find, give, go, know, *lie*, *look*, *love*, make, see, take, tell, think.

1600–40

Birth	Poet	Work — first 1,000 ll.	Measure	Proportions Adj–Nn–Verb in 10 ll.
1563	Sylvester	Divine Weeks, 1603 (ed. Grosart, 1880).	5′ couplets	11–19–19

Birth	Poet	Work — *first 1,000 ll.*	Measure	*Proportions Adj–Nn–Verb in 10 ll.*
1578	Sandys	Song of Solomon, Jeremiah, 1641	5′–4′ couplets	8–17– 9
1582	P. Fletcher	Purple Island, 1633.	5′ stanzas	14–18–10
1588	Wither	Vox Pacifica, 1645 (Works, Spenser Soc.).	5′ stanzas	6–14–11
1591	Herrick	Hesperides, 1648 (Poems, ed. Grosart).	5′–4′ stanzas	7–14–11
1592	Quarles	Shepherds Oracles, 1644 (Works, ed. Grosart).	5′ couplets	10–17–13
1593	Herbert	The Church, 1633 (Oxford ed.).	5′3′ stanzas	6–15–11
1595	Carew	Poems, 1640 (Roxburghe Library).	5′–4′ couplets	8–15–11
1596	Shirley	Poems, 1646 (ed. R. L. Armstrong, 1941).	4′ cp., st.	7–14–11
1597	C. Harvey	The Synagogue, 1640 (Poems, ed. Grosart).	5′–3′ stanzas	6–12–10

6 adjectives — fair, good, great, high, old, sweet.

16 nouns — *blood*, day, *earth*, eye, *fire*, god, heart, heaven, king, lord, love, man, *power*, *soul*, time, world.

12 verbs — bring, come, find, give, *hear*, know, look, make, see, *show*, take, tell.

1640–70

Birth	Poet	Work	Measure	Proportions
1606	Waller	Poems, 1645 (Works, ed. C. Clarke, 1862).	5′ couplets	11–19–10
1608	Milton	Nativity, L'Al., Il P., Lyc., Comus, 1645 (Minor Poems, ed. M. Y. Hughes, 1939).	5′–4′ stanzas	12–16– 8
1609	Suckling	Fragmenta Aurea, 1646 (ed. A. H. Thompson, 1910).	5′–3′ cp., st.	6–13–12
1613	Crashaw	Steps to the Temple, 1646 (Poems, ed. A. R. Waller).	5′–4′ stanzas	10–18–11
1613	Cleveland	Character . . . , 1647, Works, 1687.	5′–4′ stanzas	7–17–10
1614	More	Psychozoia Platonica, 1642 (Poems, ed. Grosart).	5′ stanzas	12–18–10
1615	Denham	Cooper's Hill ff. 1642, 1668 text (Works, ed. Banks).	5′ couplets	7–15– 9
1618	Lovelace	Lucasta, 1649 (Poems, ed. C. Wilkinson).	5′–4′ stanzas	8–13–10
1618	Cowley	Mistress, 1647.	5′–4′ stanzas	7–14–11
1622	Vaughan	Silex Scintillans, 1650, and Poems (ed. Grosart).	5′–2′ stanzas	7–13– 9

7 adjectives — *bright*, *dark*, fair, great, high, old, sweet.

14 nouns — day, earth, eye, fire, god, heart, heaven, love, man, might, soul, thing, time, world.

15 verbs — bring, come, find, give, go, *keep*, know, live, love, make, see, *stand*, take, tell, think.

Birth	Poet	Work — first 1,000 ll.	Measure	Proportions Adj–Nn–Verb in 10 ll.
		1670–1700		
1621	Marvell	State Poems, London, 1670.	5′ couplets	10–19–10
1631	Dryden	Absalom and Achitophel, 1683 (ed. Noyes, 1950).	5′ couplets	10–19–10
1633	Dillon, Roscommon	Poems, London, 1717, thr. "Prospect," and Horace "Art of Poetry."	5′ couplets	9–17–11
1653	Oldham	tr. Horace and Juvenal, 1683, 1300 ll. (Works, 1854).	5′ couplets	7–17–11
1655	Blackmore	Wit, 1700, 350 ll., Nature, 1711, 500 ll. (Collected Poems, 1718).	5′ couplets	11–19– 9
1659	Creech	Odes, etc. of Horace, tr. 1684 (Tonson, 1737).	5′ cp., st.	8–18–13
1662	Wesley	Poems on Several Occasions, London, 1685.	5′ couplets	11–20– 9
1663	Walsh	Poems, 1692 (British Poets, ed. Chalmers).	5′–4′ stanzas	8–15–13
1667	Pomfret	Poems on Several Occasions, London, 1669, Choice, 100 ll., Death, 220 ll., Love Triumphant, 500 ll.	5′ couplets	11–15–12
1672	Addison	Poems, 1695, 4th Georgic, Ovid Met., and Horace Ode III. (Works, London, 1811).	5′ couplets	10–19–10

8 adjectives — bright, good, great, *happy*, high, *mighty*, *new*, old.

17 nouns — *arms*, *art*, day, eye, *fate*, *fear*, *friend*, god, heaven, life, love, man, *nature*, pain, power, soul, *way*.

11 verbs — bring, come, find, *fly*, give, *grow*, know, make, see, take, think.

Birth	Poet	Work — first 1,000 ll.	Measure	Proportions Adj–Nn–Verb in 10 ll.
		1700–40		
1664	Prior	Poems on Several Occasions, 1688 ff., Solomon, 1720, 800 ll.	5′ couplets	12–15– 9
1675	Somerville	Hobbinol, London, 1740.	5′ blank verse	16–19– 8
1676	Philips	Cyder, London, 1708.	5′ blank verse	12–18– 7
1679	Parnell	Nightpiece and poems ff., Hymn, Hermit, Anne, Piety, Swift (Works, 1721).	5′–4′ couplets	10–18–10
1683	Young	Complaint, London, 1742 (New York, 1868).	5′ blank verse	10–20–10
1685	Gay	Fables, London, 1720	5′ couplets	7–16– 9
1688	Pope	Rape of the Lock, 1712, and Eloisa, 200 ll. (Vol. v of Poems, ed. J. Sutherland, London, 1943).	5′ couplets	11–20–11
1699	Blair	Grave, 1743, 800 ll. (Engl. Poets, ed. Chalmers, xv).	5′ blank verse	11–17– 9
1700	Dyer	Ruins of Rome, 1740, and Fleece, 1757, 500 ll. each (London, 1859).	5′ couplets	13–20– 8

Birth	Poet	Work — first 1,000 ll.	Measure	Proportions Adj–Nn–Verb in 10 ll.
1700	Thomson	Winter, 1726, rev. 1748 (Works, Oxford ed.).	5′ blank verse	15–18– 7

5 adjectives — *dear*, fair, good, great, *soft*.

19 nouns — *air*, day, eye, friend, hand, heart, heaven, *joy*, life, love, man, mind, nature, night, power, *sky*, soul, sun, world.

9 verbs — come, *fall*, fly, give, hear, know, make, *rise*, see.

1740–70

Birth	Poet	Work — first 1,000 ll.	Measure	Proportions Adj–Nn–Verb in 10 ll.
1709	Armstrong	Art of Preserving Health, 1745 (London, 1804).	5′ couplets	14–18– 9
1709	Lyttelton	Eclogues, 1747 (Works, Dodsley, 1774).	5′ cp., st.	12–19–10
1709	Johnson	London, Vanity, and Misc., 1738 ff. (Works, ed. Osgood, 1909).	5′ couplets	10–21–11
1714	Shenstone	Hercules, Schoolmistress, 175 ll., Prog. of Taste (Works, 2 vols., London, 1764).	5′ stanzas	12–19–11
1716	Gray	Poems, 1747 ff. (Oxford ed., 1937).	5′ stanzas	10–17– 8
1721	Akenside	Odes, 1745 (Works, 1808).	5′ blank verse	10–18– 8
1721	Collins	Poems, 1742 ff. (Oxford ed., 1937).	5′ stanzas	12–17– 9
1722	J. Warton	Enthusiast, Odes, 1746 (Engl. Poets, ed. Chalmers, XVIII, 1810).	5′ blank verse cp.	13–19– 8
1725	Mason	Musaeus, 1747, etc. (Poems, London, 1762).	5′ stanzas	12–18–10
1728	T. Warton	Odes, Isis, 1747 (ed. Chalmers, XVIII).	5′ cp., st.	15–19– 8

4 adjectives — fair, great, soft, sweet.

25 nouns — air, art, *breast*, day, eye, friend, god, hand, *head*, heart, heaven, joy, life, love, *maid*, man, mind, *muse*, nature, power, *scene*, *song*, soul, *virtue*, *youth*.

8 verbs — come, find, fly, give, hear, know, rise, see.

1770–1800

Birth	Poet	Work — first 1,000 ll.	Measure	Proportions Adj–Nn–Verb in 10 ll.
1730	Goldsmith	Village, 1770, Traveller, Hermit, (Crowell, 1890).	5′ couplets	11–18–10
1752	Chatterton	Clifton, Bristowe, Hastings, Eclogues (ed. Skeat, 2 vols., London, 1891).	5′–3′ cp., st.	9–18–10
1754	Crabbe	Village, 1783, 500 ll., Eustace Gray, Parish Register, 200 ll. each (Poems, ed. Carlyle, 1908).	5′ couplets	11–18–11
1757	Blake	America, 1794, etc. (ed. Keynes).	5′ lines	12–24–10
1759	Burns	Poems, 1786–94 (2nd ed., Edinburgh, 1793).	4′ stanzas	9–15– 9
1762	Bowles	Sonnets, 1789 (8th ed., London, 1802).	5′ stanzas	13–19–10

Birth	Poet	Work — first 1,000 ll.	Measure	Proportions Adj–Nn–Verb in 10 ll.
1763	Rogers	Pleasures of Memory, 1792 (Oxford ed.).	5′ couplets	11–20–11
1770	Wordsworth	Lyrical Ballads, 1798 (Cambridge ed.).	5′–4′ stanzas	10–16–10
1772	Coleridge	Ancient Mariner, 1798; Christabel (Rinehart ed.).	4′ stanzas	6–13– 9
1774	Southey	Poems, 1795 (Oxford ed.).	5′ stanzas	10–17– 9

11 adjectives — bright, good, great, *little*, old, poor, *sad*, *silent*, soft, sweet, *wild.*

21 nouns — air, *cloud*, day, eye, friend, hand, head, heart, heaven, *hope*, *hour*, joy, life, love, man, sun, thought, time, *woe*, *year*, youth.

11 verbs — come, fly, give, go, hear, know, love, make, see, think, *weep.*

1800–40

Birth	Poet	Work — first 1,000 ll.	Measure	Proportions Adj–Nn–Verb in 10 ll.
1771	Scott	Last Minstrel, 1805 (Oxford ed.).	4′ stanzas	8–17– 8
1775	Landor	Hellenics, 1st 9, 1847 (Oxford ed.).	5′ blank verse	7–15–12
1777	Campbell	Theodoric and Pilgrim (Oxford ed. of Works).	5′ couplets	10–20–11
1779	Moore	Irish Melodies, 1807, 900 ll. (Oxford ed.).	4′ stanzas	7–17– 9
1788	Byron	Hebrew Melodies, 1805, 500 ll., Childe Harold, Manfred, Don Juan, 200 ll. each (Oxford ed.).	4′ stanzas	7–16–10
1792	Shelley	Poems of 1820, thr. Arethusa (Random House).	5′ stanzas	9–19– 8
1793	Hemans	Works, 1839.	4′ stanzas	13–20– 8
1794	Bryant	Later Poems, 1842 (Poems, 1851).	5′ st., bl. v.	9–18– 9
1795	Keats	St. Agnes, Odes, Hyperion I, 1280 ll. (Random House).	5′ st., bl. v.	12–17– 8
1800	Macaulay	Lays of Ancient Rome, 1842, revised 1848.	4′–3′ stanzas	7–15– 7

8 adjectives — bright, *deep*, fair, *long*, old, sad, sweet, wild.

22 nouns — air, day, earth, eye, *father*, *flower*, god, hand, head, heart, heaven, hour, life, *light*, love, man, night, soul, *spirit*, *star*, thought, world.

16 verbs — come, die, fall, give, go, hear, know, lie, look, love, make, rise, see, *seem*, tell, think.

1840–70

Birth	Poet	Work — first 1,000 ll.	Measure	Proportions Adj–Nn–Verb in 10 ll.
1803	Emerson	Poems, 1847 (Boston, 1899).	5′ blank verse	7–15– 8
1806	E. Browning	Rom. of Page, Sonnets, Rosary, III, 8, 1844 (Works, Macmillan, 1903).	4′ stanzas	8–16–10
1807	Longfellow	Ballads and Other Poems (4th ed., 1842).	4′ stanzas	9–19–10
1809	Tennyson	Poems, 1842, v. 1, 1st 21 poems (Oxford ed.).	4′ stanzas	10–14– 6
1809	Poe	Poems, 1845; Raven thr. Israfel (Crowell, 1892).	5′ stanzas	9–16– 8

Birth	*Poet*	*Work — first 1,000 ll.*	*Measure*	*Proportions Adj–Nn–Verb in 10 ll.*
1812	R. Browning	Pippa, Dramatic Lyrics, 500 ll. each (Works, 1887).	5′ stanzas	8–16–12
1819	Whitman	Song of Myself, Exposition, India, 1855 ff. (Dutton).	6′ lines	13–28–10
1822	Arnold	Strayed Reveller, 1849 (Oxford ed., 1922).	5′ stanzas	9–14– 8
1828	Rossetti	Poems, 1850 ff., Damozel thr. Ave, 900 ll. (Dutton).	4′–3′ stanzas	5–16– 8
1828	Meredith	Jerry, 1859, Modern Love, 1862, 500 ll., and Westermain, 1883, 300 ll. (Scribner, 1912).	5′–3′ stanzas	7–14– 9

6 adjectives — *golden*, good, great, old, sweet, *white*.

22 nouns — day, death, earth, eye, god, hand, heart, heaven, life, light, love, man, *mother*, nature, night, *sea*, soul, sun, thing, time, word, world.

15 verbs — come, fall, *feel*, give, go, hear, know, lie, look, love, make, see, *sing*, *speak*, stand.

1870–1900

Birth	*Poet*	*Work — first 1,000 ll.*	*Measure*	*Proportions Adj–Nn–Verb in 10 ll.*
1830	Dickinson	Single Hound, 510 ll., Further Poems, 430 ll., 1889 (Poems, Little Brown, 1939).	4′ stanzas	5–11– 6
1837	Swinburne	Poems and Ballads II, thr. Ave, 1878, 1230 ll. (McKay ed.).	5′ stanzas	10–20– 9
1840	Hardy	Poems of Past and Present, 1898, Misc., 1000 ll. (Macmillan, 1925).	5′ stanzas	6–12– 8
1844	Hopkins	Poems, Pool thr. R. B. (Oxford, 1936).	5′ stanzas	10–19–10
1844	Bridges	Growth of Love, 1876–89, 500 ll., Poems, 1890, 200 ll., Classical Metres, 200 ll. (Oxford, 1936).	5′ st. ll.	10–19– 9
1849	Henley	In Hospital, 460 ll., London Vol., 360 ll. (Macmillan).	5′–4′ lines	13–17– 7
1856	Wilde	Poems, 1882 (Eleutheria, G of E, Impressions), 870 ll.	5′ stanzas	10–17– 7
1859	Thompson	Misc. Poems thr. "Hound" and New, 1893–97, 260 ll., (Oxford ed.).	5′ stanzas	8–15– 8
1859	Housman	Shropshire Lad, Last Poems, 1896 ff., 500 ll. each.	4′ stanzas	5–15–10
1864	Phillips	Marpessa, Wife, Christ, 1890 ff. (Dodd Mead, 1922).	5′ lines	10–14– 9

6 adjectives — dear, fair, little, old, sweet, *young*.

29 nouns — air, *child*, day, death, *dream*, earth, eye, *face*, *foot*, god, hand, heart, heaven, life, light, love, man, mind, nature, night, soul, spirit, *summer*, sun, thing, time, *wind*, *woman*, world.

16 verbs — come, die, fall, find, go, grow, hear, know, lie, live, look, love, make, see, stand, take.

Birth	*Poet*	*Work — first 1,000 ll.*	*Measure*	*Proportions Adj–Nn–Verb in 10 ll.*
		1900–40		
1865	Yeats	Tower, 1928 (Collected Poems, Macmillan, 1940).	5′ stanzas	9–16– 9
1875	Frost	A Further Range (Collected Poems, 1939).	5′–4′ cp., st.	9–15–11
1879	Stevens	Transport to Summer (Knopf, 1947).	5′ stanzas	9–18– 9
1885	Pound	First Cantos (New Directions, 1948).	5′–3′ lines	8–19– 6
1887	Moore	Selected Poems, 1935 (1st 8), Nevertheless (Macmillan, 1944).	4′–3′ lines	9–17– 6
1887	Sitwell	Green Song, 1946, and Street Songs, 1st 350 ll.	6′ lines	10–23– 9
1888	Eliot	Waste Land, 1922 (Harcourt, 1943).	5′–3′ lines	7–17– 8
1892	Millay	Collected Lyrics, 1943.	4′ lines	7–12–11
1894	Cummings	1 × 1 (Holt, 1944).	3′ stanzas	5–11– 7
1907	Auden	In Time of War, and 1st 620 ll. Collected Poems (Random House, 1945).	5′ stanzas	7–16–10

5 adjectives — great, *green*, little, old, white.

21 nouns — air, day, death, earth, eye, face, god, hand, heart, life, light, love, man, mind, night, *nothing*, sun, thing, time, *water*, world.

14 verbs — come, fall, find, give, go, hear, know, lie, look, make, see, seem, take, think.

Christine Brooke-Rose

A GRAMMAR OF METAPHOR

Metaphor, in this study, is any replacement of one word by another, or any identification of one thing, concept, or person with any other. My concern is with how this replacement or identification is made through words. There are considerable differences, both in intention and effect, between one type of grammatical link and another. These will, I hope, emerge as I proceed, and I shall therefore merely list the order of procedure here. I shall deal first with nouns, which are the most complex, then with verbs, then with other parts of speech. I have found five main types of noun metaphor:

(1) *Simple Replacement:* the proper term is replaced altogether by the metaphor, without being mentioned at all. The metaphor is assumed to be clear from the context or from the reader's intelligence. Because of this assumption of recognition, the particle introducing the metaphor becomes much more important than in any other type (articles, no article, indefinite adjective, possessive adjective, descriptive adjective or demonstrative).

(2) *The Pointing Formulae:* the proper term A is mentioned, then replaced by the metaphor B with some demonstrative expression pointing back to the proper term (A . . . that B). This can be a very subtle formula, rather like a syllogism. Other methods of pointing are by parallel construction, by apposition, or with the vocative.

(3) *The Copula:* a direct statement that A is B, which is authoritative in tone and even didactic. It is so direct that it can be used for highly original metaphors or paradoxical equations, and seems wasted on the trivial. It can be varied in many ways, and includes more timid or cautious forms such as *to seem, to call* or *be called, to signify, to be worth, to become.*

(4) *The link with "To Make"*: a direct statement involving a third party: C makes A into B. This is even more explicit than the copula, since the process of change as well as the cause, is given. The metaphor is not allowed to stand on its merits, but the formula allows for unusual changes.

Reprinted from *A Grammar of Metaphor* by Christine Brooke-Rose, by permission of Martin Secker & Warburg Limited, Publishers. [The six sections reproduced here are, respectively, pp. 23–25, 26–29, 68–70, 105–107, 146–149 and 225–227.]

(5) *The Genitive* (in the very wide sense of provenance from): this is the most complex type of all, for the noun metaphor is linked sometimes to its proper term, and sometimes to a third term which gives the provenance of the metaphoric term: B *is part of,* or *derives from,* or *belongs to* or *is attributed to* or *is found in* C, from which relationship we can guess A, the proper term (*e.g.* the *hostel* of my heart = body). The complexity of the type is partly due to the fact that the same grammatical links (chiefly *of,* but also the possessive, the genitive, other prepositions such as *in, with, from, out of,* the verb + preposition, or a verb of provenance, producing, possession) are used to express many different relationships, even the identity of two linked terms: *e.g.* in the *fire* of love, love is the fire, there is no replacement, no proper term to guess; the genitive is purely appositive.

I am giving these main noun types here because I shall occasionally have to refer forward to what I call the Genitive Link (Gp. 5) when discussing other types, since it can often be combined with them. On the other hand I cannot deal with it first, owing to its complexity. It is, also, the most "verbal" of noun metaphors, and makes a useful transition into verb metaphors. The latter I am dividing into intransitive and transitive, not so much as an aesthetic criterion but because of formal differences, the transitive verb being more complex. Lastly I shall deal with adjectives, adverbs, prepositions and pronouns, none of which presents such problems as the noun does. . . .

* * *

The proper term of the Simple Replacement metaphor is not mentioned and so must be guessed: we either have to know the code or the code must be broken. I am dealing with this question of recognising the proper term from a purely syntactic point of view: there is seldom any real obscurity, and I do not for a moment maintain that *the flower* for "lady" is difficult to guess. But we do depend on outside knowledge. Most metaphors are clear in the general context (as opposed to the particular sentence). My point is that Simple Replacement is on the whole restricted to the banal, the over-familiar, or to metaphors which are so close in meaning to the proper term that the guessing is hardly conscious; or that they depend much more on the general context than do other types of noun metaphors.

For this reason the degree of particularisation given to the metaphor is much more important in Simple Replacement than in other types, where particularisation is important for effectiveness rather than for clarity. English here is richer in nuances of particularisation than languages which have no articles, and possibly richer than a language like French, where the article has become a mere mark of the substantive, a mark of quiddity without which the noun remains a pure idea unactualised.[1]

[1] See G. Guillaume, *Le problème de l'article et sa solution dans la langue française,* Paris 1919. Guillaume distinguishes between "le nom en puissance" and "le nom en effet" (the Saussurean distinction between language and speech), and shows that the article bridges this gap. Unfortunately his actualisation theory applies to both the defi-

Mr. Paul Christophersen, in an admirable study [2] examines these degrees of particularisation in English: the definite article, by its association with previous experience, adds special traits to the general meaning of the word. By unambiguous reference to outside knowledge not contained in the idea of the word itself, it gives the sense that the word stands for one definite individual thing, even if our familiarity with it is slight: just as our knowledge of an individual denoted by a proper name may be slight, though we know that only one person is meant. In other words, *the* assumes familiarity or previous knowledge, not necessarily of the thing itself: in talking of a book one can say "the author," without mentioning him or even knowing his name. Mr. Christophersen also makes the tentative suggestion that the much higher frequency of the definite article in French may show that the element of substance (in the sense that the article is a mark of the substantive) is stronger in *le,* while the element of familiarity felt in *the* may not be so pronounced.[3]

All this of course refers to the noun in general, but it is particularly applicable to metaphor by Simple Replacement. When Spenser indulges in the epic habit of not naming his hero, calling him *"the* valiant *Elfe"* or *"the Champioun,"* or when he calls a wood *"the labyrinth,"* we automatically know what he means, because of the article's association with previous experience, that is to say, the context. Similarly Milton calls Satan *"the Foe," "the Enimie," "the Tempter."* Antony can say of Cleopatra *"The Witch* shall die." The article refers us to the general context, almost like a demonstrative.

On the other hand, if we say "the author" when talking of a book, we are in fact using an implied prepositional link [of the book], which, in metaphor, becomes a different type altogether (what I have called the Genitive Link).[4] When Milton says *"the Enimie* of Mankind," he is narrowing the possibilities by giving us an extra link with a third term, mankind, though *Enimie* still "replaces" Satan. Some Simple Replacement metaphors are in fact Genitive Link metaphors with the third term left out: Milton uses *the Foe* as well as *"the Enimie* of Mankind." Similarly the preposition *of,* when expressing identity of the two linked terms, can be merely implied: Chaucer can say *the fir, the snare, the game* (*Tr.* III/484, I/507, II/38 and III/1494), when love is in question, without having to add "of love." So Hopkins: Or is it she cried for *the crown* then (WD. 25, *crown* [of martyrdom]). Again the article refers us

---

nite and the indefinite article, leaving the opposition between them out of account. Nor does it explain why some nouns, such as plurals and continuates, have the article in French and not in English. Guillaume's solution to this difficulty is simply that the French are capable of distinguishing between idea and actualisation everywhere while the English are not. This is only true in the sense that the noun in English often seems to have more "quiddity" of its own without help from the article (*e.g.* "sheer plod makes plough down sillion shine"). In metaphoric use such independence is both valuable and dangerous.

[2] *The Articles — A Study of Their Theory and Use in English* (London 1939).

[3] If this is so it may be due to the more recent development of *the* from the demonstrative *that,* as compared with the development of *le* from *ille.*

[4] See ch. VII for *of* as a link.

to the general context, not only in a quasi-demonstrative role, but by an implied familiarity with outside or previous knowledge, "the *fir* of love" being, already in Chaucer's time, such a cliché that he could drop the words "of love" and assume automatic association.

Automatic association is in fact the keynote in Simple Replacement. Even when the metaphor is not quite so self-evident or banal, we depend very much on the general context, that is to say, on an implied *of*-link with the unstated proper term, or with an unstated third term which would help us to guess the proper term:

> Yet no more [i.e. love] can be due to mee,
> Then at *the bargaine* made was ment . . . *Donne* 10

> I will o'ertake thee, Cleopatra, and
> Weep for my pardon. So it must be, for now
> All length is torture: since *the torch* is out,
> Lie down and stray no farther . . . AC. IV/xiv/44

Donne's *the bargaine,* in a love context "replaces" a more literal idea such as an exchange of vows, or a practical arrangement between lovers, or the process of courtship or seduction. In a religious context it might "replace" something quite different, such as the experience of conversion or the taking of holy orders, and in a commercial context it might be quite literal. More ambiguously, Antony's *the torch,* in the particular scene where he thinks Cleopatra is dead, may "replace" Cleopatra herself, or her life, or their love. Yet alone and out of this context *the torch* might well be equivalent to Chaucer's more general *the fir* [of love], *i.e.* love itself.

Ambiguity is, of course, the great strength of metaphor by Simple Replacement, and I am not suggesting that we have to decode into one specific proper term and one only. In other noun categories, the metaphor is more or less clearly equated with a stated proper term: this does give the poet a much wider scope for more unusual metaphors, but it is also a restriction. Part of the charm of Simple Replacement lies precisely in the fact that the noun not only can "replace" more than one unstated idea, but in the fact that it can also be taken quite literally, even in the general context:

> Stop playing, poet! May a brother speak? . . .
> But why such long prolusion and display,
> Such turning and adjustment of *the harp,*
> And taking it upon your breast, at length,
> Only to speak dry words across its strings? *Browning* 1

Here we have a much more modern type of Simple Replacement. The poet's harp is in one sense merely his technique, his language as an instrument of expression. But since there was a time when poets really did play the harp, we can also take the passage as an imagined but literally described scene. . . .

* * *

The linking methods I have called Pointing Formulae are not only clearer than Simple Replacement, but also more subtle than other types of link, since they replace the proper term A by the metaphoric term B without direct statement. This lack of direct statement can also be a disadvantage: what is subtle when well done can be obscure when the linking is loose or the proper term too far away. Another disadvantage is that some of the formulae lend themselves to abuse in mere repetition.

I have found four main methods of pointing, either directly or suggestively: a demonstrative expression, parallelism, apposition, and the vocative.

The sublety of the demonstrative formula consists in speaking of one thing, and later pointing to it with a replacing name, as if it had become something else in the meantime, rather like a syllogism with the middle premise left out. The change is assumed, yet it is quite clear what is meant, especially with one of the stronger demonstrative expressions:

> And with that word, he gan right inwardly
> Byholden hire, and loken on hire face,
> And seyde: "on *swiche a mirour* goode grace!" *Tr.* II/264

> AGR: A rarer spirit never
> Did steer humanity: but you gods will give us
> Some faults to make us men. Caesar is touch'd.
> MAEC: When *such a spacious mirror*'s set before him,
> He needs must see himself. AC. V/i/31

The metaphor linked so strongly with a proper term can be combined with a Simple Replacement, which is then quite clear:

> Caesar, 'tis his schoolmaster,
> An argument that he is pluck'd when hither
> He sends *so poor a pinion* of *his wing* . . . AC. III/xii/2

The linking can even be at two removes:

> And sweare
> No where
> Lives a woman true, and faire.
>
> If thou findst one, let mee know,
> *Such a Pilgrimage* were sweet . . . *Donne* 2

It is not the woman who is the pilgrimage but the journey to her, strictly speaking unmentioned, though clearly understood: but the woman is, by means of the demonstrative, indirectly changed into an enshrined saint.

Even stronger than *such* or *so/such + adjective* is *the same,* obviously not possible in Simple Replacement, since it must refer to a stated antecedent:

> The force that through the green fuse drives the flower
> Drives my green age; that blasts the roots of trees
> Is my destroyer.
> And I am dumb to tell the crooked rose
> My youth is bent by *the same wintry fever.* *Thomas* 1

But the pure demonstrative in this role can be strong too, providing it points clearly to a fairly close antecedent, not separated by too much other matter:

> How much unlike art thou Mark Antony!
> Yet coming from him, *that* great *med'cine* hath
> With his tinct gilded thee. AC. I/v/35

> The children walking two & two, in red & blue & green,
> Grey headed beadles walk'd before, with wands as white as snow,
> Till into the high dome of Paul's they like Thames' waters flow.
>
> O what a multitude they seem'd, *these flowers* of London town!
> *Blake* SI.7

* * *

The verb *to be* is the most direct way of linking a metaphor to its proper term or terms, and perhaps for this reason, rather less frequently used than other methods, except for the verb *to make,* which is the rarest link. Yet the copula is more varied than would appear possible with such a simple formula as "A is B."

The disadvantage is obviousness. It cannot be repeated too often in one poem or passage, except intentionally as part of a rhetorical effect (*e.g.* in a litany). On the other hand, the very directness is authoritative in tone, a categoric statement by the poet, which we do not feel inclined to question, however odd the metaphor. It allows for originality and paradox, and sounds gratuitous with banal metaphors.

The simplest formula, with the proper term coming first and the copula in the present tense (A is B) is the most direct and on the whole the most frequent. Spenser, Shakespeare and Donne are the most fond of it, but the latter two, especially Donne, make a much fuller use of its simple strength for original metaphors than does Spenser. Chaucer, and most poets after Donne, tend to waste it.

For example, Chaucer, Spenser, Milton, Dryden, Blake, Wordsworth and Browning use it for mere banalities. Luckily, all except Spenser use it little:

> As love for love is skilful *guerdonynge*
> [barely metaphoric even then] *Tr.* II/392

> Rest is their *feast* . . .
> Will was his *guide*. . . . FQ. I/i/35, ii/12

> For loe my loue doth in her selfe containe
> all this worlds riches that may farre be found,
> if Saphyres, loe her eies be *Saphyres* plaine,
> if Rubies, loe hir lips be *Rubies* sound:
> If Pearles, hir teeth be *pearles* . . . *etc.* *Am.* 15

Flours were the *Couch* . . .[5] PL. ix.1039

Take them my tears . . .
'Tis all the *Aid* my present pow'r supplies AA. I/717

God was their *King*, and God they durst Depose. AA. I/418

Folly is an endless *maze* *Blake* SE. 11

A corresponding mild creative breeze . . .
. . . 'Tis a power
That does not come unrecogniz'd, a *storm* . . . *Prel.* I/47

You are a *poem*, though your poem's naught *Browning* 1

. . . then back he sinks at once
To ashes, who was very *fire* before. *Browning* 4

Through Milton, Dryden and Pope, the equations are hardly metaphoric — just calling one thing by another name which could be literal. The Romantics tend merely to personify: [that beauteous River] . . . He was a *Playmate*; those fits of vulgar joy / Which . . . Are prompt *attendants* (*Prel.* I/290, 609); Pleasure is oft a *visitant* (*End.* I/906).[6]

Similarly Thomas uses this simple formula for verbal ideas which could be literally possible: The force that through the green fuse drives the flower . . . / Is my *destroyer* (1). A force in a stem or in roots could literally destroy a man, *e.g.* if it were poison; the parallelism of "drives my green age" is much more effective. And Yeats uses the simple copula merely to create a symbol by direct statement — instead of with his usual implicitness — and to call a stair an ancestral stair:

I declare this tower is my *symbol;* I declare
This winding, gyring, spiring treadmill of a stair
is my ancestral stair. *Yeats* 6

The only real metaphor there is *treadmill* (with *of*). Nevertheless, we can see how authoritative the copula can be. Yeats wastes it here, and seems to feel the gratuitousness, so that he emphasises, not so much the equation as the authoritative tone, by adding "I declare." "This tower is my symbol" would not be half so effective.

But then here are Shakespeare and Donne with the formula at its best, direct, authoritative, equating unusual terms:

Octavia is
A blessed *lottery* to him. AC. II/ii/242

As when mine empire was your *fellow* too AC. IV/ii/22

[5] This is Milton's only example of the simple equation in Book ix, except for an equation of abstractions: our Reason is our Law (654). Cf. Pope: When love is liberty, and nature, law (EA. 92).

[6] But Keats can use it more originally: deepest shades / Were deepest dungeons (*End.* I/692).

She'is *all States,* and *all Princes,* I,
[copula understood in second apposition] *Donne* 5

This bed thy *center* is, these walls, thy *spheare* 5

And her who is dry *corke,* and never cries; 6

Call her one, mee another flye,
We'are *Tapers* too 8

He [love] is the tyran *Pike,* our hearts the *Frye.* 34

For thou thy selfe art thine owne *bait;* 32

Our bodies why doe wee forbeare?
They are ours, though they are not wee, Wee are
The *intelligences,* they the *spheare* . . . 36

* * *

I have called this type of link *The Genitive,* although other grammatical tools besides the genitive case are used. The definition of *genitive* is "a grammatical form of substantives or other declinable parts of speech, chiefly used to denote that the person or thing signified by the word is related to another as source, possessor or the like." In practice, as far as metaphor is concerned, this part-relationship between two nouns, which is essentially one of provenance from or attribution to, can be expressed with prepositional forms which are grammatically datives or ablatives, but, as I hope to show, the above definition of *genitive* can be stretched to include all these, even a verb of possession, which normally takes an accusative in most inflected languages.

The chief difference between this last type of metaphor and the preceding types, is that the metaphor is not necessarily linked to its proper term, but rather to a third term: "A = the *B* of C." The link tells us that the metaphoric term belongs to, or comes from or out of, or is to be found in, or is attributed to, some person or thing or abstraction.

From this relationship of attribution or provenance we can guess (as in Simple Replacement, but with additional help) what the unmentioned proper term A is: *e.g.* "the *hostel* of my heart" means "body."

When this relationship between B and C is not strong enough or self-evident enough for us to guess A, we can be told the proper term with the verb *to be,* or a vocative, or any of the links previously described, from the Pointing Formulae onwards: *e.g.* in "she is the *fountain* of mercy," "the *fountain* of mercy" might be anyone or anything, so we are given the proper term "she."

The Genitive Link metaphor can thus combine two metaphoric relationships in the same word: on the one hand to the proper term, stated or unstated (body, she), and on the other, to the third term with which the metaphor is linked (heart, mercy). The first relationship has already been dealt with in previous chapters. Here we are concerned with the second, which is extremely complex and often ambiguous. The Genitive Link forms the largest group among noun metaphors, larger even than Simple Replacement.

This genitival or provenance relationship between the two nouns is essentially a verbal one, that is, the preposition *of,* or whatever other link is used, stands for a verbal idea which can also be expressed verbally, and the non-metaphoric noun is indirectly changed into something else by the metaphoric noun, just as the verb metaphor changes a noun into something else: *e.g.* in "*roses* grow in her cheeks," *roses* "replaces" an idea of pinkness, fragrance and texture, and "cheeks" becomes a garden. The indirectness of the change is an advantage, since we are less aware of it than in "her cheeks are a garden," which is slightly ridiculous. Yet the metaphoric element is distinctly a noun: the verb, when expressed, is not necessarily a metaphor (roses do grow, and something could grow in cheeks, such as hair); but it is added on as an extra link, which may or may not be metaphoric (*e.g.* in "*roses blossom* in her cheeks," *blossom* is metaphoric in relation to "cheeks"). The metaphoric relationship, however, is between *roses* and "cheeks," and can do without a verb altogether (the *roses* in her cheeks, the *roses* of her cheeks).

The noun metaphor, then, has a proper term A, which can either be mentioned (linked with a copula or other means, A is the B of C), or unmentioned (in which case it has to be guessed, the B of C).

This "replacing" relationship between B and C, however, represents only one kind of Genitive Link. There is a second type which has no proper term to be equated or guessed, and in which B is actually identified with C by means of the genitive: *e.g.* in "the *fire* of love," love is the fire. The genitive is here used appositively, and sometimes it is not clear which is meant: for instance, in "the *roses* of her cheeks," above, the roses could mean the cheeks themselves. And, as a complex and ambiguous variation of this Identity relationship, we have Pure Attribution, which is a split of one idea into two, a thing or person or personification, and an object attributed to it: "the *eyes* of the heart," "the *hand* of God," "the *cloak* of Death." This attribution is not, strictly speaking, identical with the term to which it is linked, but represents it in one aspect (the heart in its seeing capacity, *etc.*). With personified abstractions like love or death, however, we do border on an Identity relationship such as "the *fire* of love" (the *cloak* of Death is death).

The chief weakness of the Genitive Link is that the same grammatical tools can be used to express most of these different relationships. It is their flexibility rather than their precision which makes the relationship clear, but this flexibility can of course be abused. The formal grammatical tools are:

1. *The preposition "of"* (or an equivalent genitive, or a compound): the *roses* of her cheeks, her cheeks' *roses;* the *cloak* of Death, Death's *cloak,* death-*cloak.*

This link is to be the subject of this chapter.

2. *Other prepositions, and a verb + preposition:* the *roses* in her cheeks; the *cloak* flung by Death.

3. *The possessive adjective:* cheeks . . . their *roses;* Death . . . his *cloak.*

4. *A verb of owning, giving, producing:* your cheeks grow *roses;* Death has a *cloak.*

At the same time, there are two basically different metaphoric relationships between the two linked terms, and each relationship can be divided into two main types:

(*a*) *The three-term formula,* in which "B of C = A." A can either be unmentioned (the *hostel* of my heart, the *roses* of her cheeks); or it can be mentioned and equated (she is the *fountain* of mercy, the cuckoo is the *messenger* of Spring).

(*b*) *The two-term formula,* "the B of C," in which B = C. C is itself the proper term, either with an appositive genitive expressing the Identity of B and C (the *fire* of love), or with a Pure Attribution, in which the basic identity is less apparent (*the cloak* of Death).

Unfortunately, these four different types, or two versions of two main types, by no means correspond to the four grammatical tools, any one of which can be used for most relationships.

The preposition *of* is the most frequent of all the grammatical tools. It is also the only one which is used indiscriminately for all four relationships, and it can be varied with the genitive and sometimes the compound. These will be considered in this chapter. Other grammatical links, which will be dealt with in the next chapter, are on the whole more suitable for one relationship than another. . . .

* * *

Naturally, when combing texts for metaphors, one will find *more* transitive verbs than intransitive, in any language which differentiates them, for the simple reason that there are many more possible relationships inherent in the transitive verb, all of which are bound to occur. This, as I have said, seems to me the chief difference between the two, rather than any aesthetic criterion. With the Intransitive verb, there are three possible metaphoric relationships: to the subject, to the indirect object, to both. With the Transitive verb, there are seven.[7]

To the subject: as he that sorwe *drifth* to write (*Tr.* V/1332); till the flies and gnats of Nile / Have *buried* them for prey (AC. III/xiii/166); And very, very deadliness did *nip* / Her motherly cheeks (*End.* I/342); Great hatred, little room, / *Maimed* us at the start (*Yeats* 22).

To the indirect object: Yet in my hart I then both *speake* and *write* / the wonder (*Am.* 3); and with her owne goodwill hir fyrmely *tyde* (*Am.* 67); other men . . . Which . . . can in teares, / In sighs, in oathes, and letters

[7] Because of sheer quantity, I am giving only a few examples of each, and sticking to things animated or the change from thing to thing, rather than human actions attributed to personified abstractions or persons human and divine, which are to me less interesting. I shall give a summary of poets' individual preferences and tendencies at the end of the chapter.

outbid mee (*Donne* 10); How long wilt thou . . . / *Starve,* and *defraud* the People of thy Reign? (AA. I/244); to the open fields I *told* / A prophecy (*Prel.* I/59); And God-*appointed* Berkeley (*Yeats* 6).

To both: nature wants stuff / To *vie* strange forms with fancy (AC. V/ii/97); Whom David's love with Honours did *adorn* (AA. I/880); faith . . . *wrap* me in eternal rest (EA. 302); I fellowed sleep who *kissed* me in the brain (*Thomas* 4).

To the direct object: To *fisshen* hire; Som of his wo to *slen* (*Tr.* V/777, II/1358); The hand could *pluck* her back (AC. I/ii/124); Thy oaths I *quit,* thy memory *resign* (EA. 293); So, I *swallow* my rage (*Browning* 7); There was single eye! / *Read* the unshapeable shock night (WD. 29); That corpse you *planted* last year in your garden (WL. 71); The force . . . *Drives* my green age (*Thomas* 1); I *fled* the earth and, naked, *climbed* the weather (*Thomas* 4).

To the subject and direct object: my cares colde, / That *sleth* my wit (*Tr.* V/1342); and lust did now *inflame* / His corage more (FQ. I/iii/41); a grief that *smites* / My very heart at root (AC. V/ii/104); Till age *snow* white haires on thee (*Donne* 2); Her whom abundance *melts* (*Donne* 6);[8] My teares . . . thy face *coines* them (*Donne* 25); when raging Fevers *boil* the Blood (AA. I/136); Those smiling eyes, *attemp'ring* ev'ry ray (EA. 63), that love doth *scathe,* / The gentle heart (*End.* I/733); And frightful a night-fall *folded* rueful a day (WD. 15); [odours] . . . these ascended / In *fattening* the prolonged candle-flames (WL. 90); My busy heart . . . *drains* her words (*Thomas* 2).

To the direct and indirect objects: Til I my soule out of my breste *unshethe* (*Tr.* IV/776); to *kindle* new desire, / in gentle brest (*Am.* 6); To *grace* it [the heavy day] with your sorrows (AC. IV/xiv/136); Griefe . . . For, he tames it, that *fetters* it in verse (*Donne* 9); to *shape* out / Some Tale from my own heart (*Prel.* I/220); I kiss my hand / To the stars, lovely-asunder / Starlight, *wafting* him out of it (WD. 5); I *spelt* my vision with a hand and hair (*Thomas* 4).

To all three: the peyne, / That *halt* youre herte and myn in hevynesse, / Fully to *slen* (*Tr.* III/1006, presumably *slen* applies to objects of *halt*); the charming smiles, that *rob* sence from the hart (*Am.* 17); Alex: . . . His speech sticks in my heart. / C: Mine ear must *pluck* it thence (AC. I/v/41); the lesser Sunne / At this time to the Goat is runne / To *fetch* new lust (*Donne* 30); Devotion's self shall *steal* a thought from heav'n (EA. 357); a more subtle selfishness, that now / Doth *lock* my functions up in blank reserve (*Prel.* I/247); Thou hast *bound* bones and veins in me, *fastened* me flesh (WD. 1); synthetic perfumes . . . *drowned* the sense in odours (WL. 87); How time has *ticked* a heaven round the stars (*Thomas* 1); a numberless tongue / *Wound* their room with a male moan (*Thomas* 8).

[8] The direct object is changed from person to thing — a human being cannot really melt.

Naturally enough each type of relationship lends itself more readily to different kinds of metaphor. A subject is more often personified or animated, while objects are more often changed from thing to thing. It is rather difficult, for instance, to change the indirect object of an active transitive verb from person of any kind into anything: gods and personifications are more usually conceived as acting upon rather than being acted upon, while human persons cannot be indirect objects in *metaphoric* relationship to a verb unless they are changed into things (since most actions can literally be committed on human beings). A hypothetical example would be "to *intoxicate* him with her" (she becomes drink).

Similarly a direct object is more usually changed from thing to thing than humanised or changed from god or personification to thing. But this relationship is the most suitable, as we can see, for the rare change from person to thing, which is difficult to achieve except by this most direct relationship (he *plough'd* her, to *fish* her, *pluck* her).

The last, three-way relationship is naturally the rarest, and tends on the whole to be restricted to the idea of an emotion or word or idea or apprehension taking another idea into or out of the heart, soul or mind, or body. Donne, Pope and Dylan Thomas are unusual in applying the three-way relationship to outside matters. . . .

W. Nelson Francis

SYNTAX AND LITERARY INTERPRETATION

I take my text from I. A. Richards — appropriately enough, since he has an impressive stature in both disciplines which are here meeting in tentative amity. In his book *Practical Criticism,* after describing four kinds of meaning involved in poetry, he suggests that readers of poetry may be trained by exercise in two kinds of paraphrase, "the one to exhibit the sense of the poem, the other to portray its feeling." The first of these, he goes on to say, "requires only an intelligent use of the dictionary, logical acumen, a command of syntax, and pertinacity." [1] I have observed that even those explicators and critics who stop to perform this more humble and pedestrian analysis before plunging ahead to the headier realms of paradox, tension, and symbolism, however gifted they may be in lexical intelligence, logical perreption, and doggedness, are likely to disregard syntax almost wholly. Anything approaching "command," even of the traditional Latinate kind of parsing, is rare enough. The newer syntax of suprasegmental morphemes, tagmemes, and immediate constituents and the newest syntax of kernels and transforms seem to be totally unknown.

This neglect of one of the principal keys to plain sense can be perilous. I cite only one example. It is from Kenneth Burke — ironically enough from his collection entitled *A Grammar of Motives.* In the essay entitled "Symbolic Action in a Poem by Keats" he develops an interpretation of the "Ode on a Grecian Urn" which depends rather heavily upon a reading of the last six lines of the third stanza of that poem which seems to me to do violence to syntax in a particularly wrong-headed way.

The lines in question are these:

More happy love! more happy, happy love!
For ever warm and still to be enjoy'd,
For ever panting, and for ever young;

Reprinted from Monograph Series, No. 13, *Report of the Eleventh Annual Round Table Meeting on Linguistics and Language Studies,* Institute of Languages and Linguistics, Georgetown University. Used by permission.

[1] I. A. Richards, *Practical Criticism* (Harvest Books, New York: Harcourt Brace, n.d.), 213.

All breathing human passion far above;
That leaves a heart high-sorrowful and cloy'd,
A burning forehead, and a parching tongue.

Mr. Burke comments as follows:

> The poem as a whole makes permanent, or fixes in a state of arrest, a peculiar agitation. But within this fixity, by the nature of poetry as a progressive medium, there must be development. Hence, the agitation that is maintained throughout . . . will at the same time undergo internal transformations. In the third stanza, these are manifested as a clear division into two distinct and contrasted realms. There is a transcendental fever, which is felicitous, divinely above "all breathing human passion." And this "leaves" the other level, the level of earthly fever, "a burning forehead and a parching tongue." From the bodily fever, which is a passion, and malign, there has split off a spiritual activity, a wholly benign aspect of the total agitation.[2]

It is clear from this that Burke takes the clause contained in the last two lines as a modifier of the "happy love" apostrophised in the first line quoted. This, in turn, forces him to read *leaves* with the meaning "departs from, leaves behind." This seems to me — and to several others upon whom I have tried it out — a violent wrench to the syntax of the sentence. Surely in placing the clause where he did and introducing it with the close relative *that,* Keats meant this clause to modify *passion* and intended *leaves* to mean "results in, leaves as residue." He balances three lines about "happy love" against three lines about "human passion"; the unmoving, marmoreal, unsatiated, eternally suspended love memorialized on the urn is far superior to transitory fleshly passion, which, caught in the flux of time, inevitably passes into melancholy and feverish satiation. By wilfully disregarding the syntax, Mr. Burke has also upset the rhetorical balance of the lines, which Keats had emphasized by the triplicate rime structure, the indentation, and the semicolon at the end of the third line quoted.

Howlers of this sort are admittedly not very frequent. I am more concerned about the fact that an explicator faced with a difficult poem or passage almost never uses close syntactic analysis to match the scrupulous attention he gives to lexical matters. The assumptions seem to be that syntax can usually be taken for granted, and that when a favored lexical interpretation collides head-on with syntax, it is the syntax that must give. This second assumption, I suspect, was the cause of Mr. Burke's error about Keats. He wanted *leaves* to mean "transcends," which in turn required the clause of which it is the verb to reach back, across one very eligible antecedent and five adjective phrases in appositional position, to find its head four lines — rather than three words — earlier.

The native speaker can, of course, usually take syntax for granted as long as all goes well. For him, only syntactically ambiguous utterances are of even

[2] Kenneth Burke, "Symbolic Action in a Poem by Keats," in *The Critical Performance,* ed. Stanley Edgar Hyman (New York: Vintage Books, 1956), 266.

passing concern, and these he usually resolves on the basis of lexical, rather than grammatical, clues. So common is this habit — which is perfectly legitimate in easy poetry — that most people aren't really aware of how many syntactic ambiguities there are, especially in written English, where punctuation only partially makes up for the absence of prosodic features. But when the lexical clues fail, when the poet is purposely, almost, one sometimes feels, maliciously, avoiding the texture of lexical compatibilities and mutual reinforcements which characterizes most discourse, then the syntactic ambiguities come out from behind the mask of words to add to the reader's discomfort. No amount of dictionary grubbing seems to help; logical acumen is of no service in deciphering a writer who has abandoned logic; pertinacity leads only to frustration. The remaining avenue — close syntactic analysis — remains unexplored. I do not intend to suggest that it will prove the universal skeleton key to all difficult passages. But if it does nothing else, it will at least put the words in their places, and supply some kind of calculus of probability for appraising the validity of competing readings. I would like to emphasize the idea that syntactic analysis operates largely in the realm of probability; it seldom deals with either clear-cut decisions or heads-or-tails dilemmas. Mr. Burke's reading of Keats which I have criticized above, is not an impossible one; it is simply highly improbable. Keats' passage, in other words, is syntactically ambiguous — not, however, with a 50:50 kind of ambiguity, but something on the order of 95:5. Mr. Burke's error was to pick the 5 side without sufficient justification from the total fabric of the poem, the exigencies of the diction, and the rhetorical structure of the stanza in hand, and without assaying, or at any rate clearly stating, what the syntactic probabilities are.

I should like to spend the remainder of my time with an example, chosen expressly for its difficulty. It is the first sonnet from the sequence "Altarwise by Owl-light" by Dylan Thomas.[3]

Altarwise by owl-light in the half-way house
The gentleman lay graveward with his furies;
Abaddon in the hangnail cracked from Adam,
And, from his fork, a dog among the fairies,
The atlas-eater with a jaw for news,
Bit out the mandrake with to-morrow's scream.
Then, penny-eyed, that gentleman of wounds,
Old cock from nowheres and the heaven's egg,
With bones unbuttoned to the half-way winds,
Hatched from the windy salvage on one leg,
Scraped at my cradle in a walking word
That night of time under the Christward shelter:

[3] Dylan Thomas: *The Collected Poems of Dylan Thomas.* Copyright 1953 by Dylan Thomas, © 1957 by New Directions. Reprinted by permission of the publisher, New Directions Publishing Corporation. Reprinted also by permission of J. M. Dent & Sons Ltd., Publishers, and of the Literary Executors of the Dylan Thomas Estate.

I am the long world's gentleman, he said,
And share my bed with Capricorn and Cancer.[4]

I should like to locate the syntactic ambiguities in this baffling poem, and see how (or if) they can be resolved. This will not, I hasten to add, lead us to a lucid explication of the poem. But it will supply the framework which such an explication, if one is possible, must follow, and set the bounds beyond which it must not venture.

The poem is punctuated as four sentences, the first two separated by the semicolon at the end of line 2, the second and third by the period at the end of line 6, and the last two by the colon at the end of line 12. All the lines are end-stopped; that is, they would be read aloud with some sort of terminal juncture at the end, though in each case the choice of which one of the three terminals might vary with the dialect and individual style of the reader, even if all readers could agree on a single interpretation. Each line is thus treated as a syntactic unit.

The first sentence, lines 1–2, is unambiguous. Trouble begins in line 3, which is syntactically ambiguous because of the morphological ambiguity of *cracked,* which can be either a preterit or a past participle. The line is either a predication, with subject *Abaddon in the hangnail* and predicate *cracked from Adam,* or a modification, with head *Abaddon* and modifier *in the hangnail cracked from Adam,* in which case *cracked from Adam* modifies *hangnail.* In other words, the problem is which IC cut comes first, that after *hangnail* or that after *Abaddon?* In the first case, the line is an independent predication coordinated with that in lines 4–6; in the second case, the whole line must be considered in loose apposition with *gentleman* in line 2, and the *And* at the beginning of line 4 coordinates the predication of lines 1–3 with that of lines 4–6.

The general syntactic structure of lines 4–6 is clear (introductory phrase followed by a predication), but they contain two ambiguities. The first concerns the function of *a dog among the fairies:* is it the subject of the predication, or is it in apposition with *fork?* That is, which IC cut has priority, that after *fork* or that after *fairies?* If the former, the noun-headed phrase in line 5 is in apposition with *a dog among the fairies;* if the latter, it is the subject. The second ambiguity is in the predicate which fills line 6, and concerns the function of the phrase *with tomorrow's scream.* Does it modify only the direct object, *mandrake,* or does it modify the whole complementation, *Bit*

[4] This poem is by way of being a classic challenge to explicators. See, for instance, Elder Olson, *The Poetry of Dylan Thomas* (Chicago, 1954), 63–69; Ralph N. Maud, *Explicator* XIV (1955), 16; Bernard Knieger, *Explicator* XV (1956), 18; Erhardt H. Essig, *Explicator* XVI (1958), 53; Monroe C. Beardsley and Sam Hynes, "Misunderstanding Poetry: Notes on Some Readings of Dylan Thomas," *College English,* XXI (1960), 315–22. Only Olson devotes more than a passing comment to Thomas's syntax, to which he gives up about a page of a ten-page chapter on "Techniques of Language" (60–61). It is, he rightly says, "full of pitfalls for the unwary." His discussion, in purely traditional terms, perhaps increases wariness but gives no clue to how the pitfalls are to be skirted.

out the mandrake? That is, do we cut first after *out* or after *mandrake?* Notice that this determines what screams, the mandrake or the atlas-eater-dog complex.

The broad syntactic pattern of lines 7–12 is also apparent. It is a single long predication, with a subject whose head is *gentleman* built up by a series of appositive and participial modifiers, a predicate which may be single and may be coordinate, and a concluding sentence-modifier filling line 12 and balancing the *then* with which the sentence begins. Apart from some minor uncertainties about the hierarchy of the constituents of the subject, there are three syntactic cruxes of some importance. The first concerns the function of *the heaven's egg:* is it coordinate with *nowheres* or with *Old cock?* That is, do we cut first after *cock,* making *nowheres* and *the heaven's egg* coordinate objects of *from,* or after *nowheres, making Old cock from nowheres* and *the heaven's egg* coordinate appositives, modifying *that gentleman of wounds?* From the point of view of meaning, is the gentleman of wounds also a heaven's egg, or did he just come from one?

Secondly, is *Hatched* a participle, in which case line 10 is one more of the loosely coordinated or pyramided string of modifiers of *that gentleman of wounds;* or is *Hatched* a finite verb, so that line 10 is the first of two predicates in asyndetic coordination, the second being line 11? In IC terms, do we cut first after *leg* or after *winds?* In terms of meaning, was the gentleman already hatched or did he hatch during the course of the poem, before he scraped and spoke?

The third ambiguity in this sentence is relatively minor, in that its effect on meaning is unimportant. Does the phrase *on one leg* modify the phrase *Hatched from the windy salvage* or only *the windy salvage?* Is the first IC cut after *salvage* or after *Hatched?* Does the line say that the hatching took place on one leg, or that the salvage was on one leg?

The final sentence, filling lines 13–14, is syntactically as perspicuous and unambiguous as the first. So far as syntax is concerned, therefore, the difficulties of the poem lie in the middle two sentences, occupying the middle ten lines. We have located six principal ambiguities, which may be thought of either as problems of syntactic relationship or problems of IC division, depending on how you like to approach your syntactic analysis. In either case, how, if at all, are these problems to be resolved? Can we arrive at some sort of estimate of the probabilities of the competing readings?

Assuming that in locating the ambiguities we have exhausted the information conveyed by morphology, concord, word order, and the unambiguous marking of parts of speech, there remain three sorts of clues. These differ in relative significance from one poet or one poem to another; I shall present them in order of decreasing linguistic validity. The first is punctuation, whose primary function is to suggest syntax. Compared with musical or mathematical notation, it is very sketchy and imperfect, but it occasionally affords clues of primary importance to what the poet intended. It may also, of course, only indicate an editor's opinion — as in the usual editions of Emily Dickinson. The second clue is the verse. This may direct us to the stress and juncture structure, which in turn supplies some indications of the syntax. Verse is thus a secondary indicator of syntax; that is why I rank it below punctuation, which is a primary, however imperfect. The third and least reliable clue to the syntax — however important and valuable it may be on the semantic, metaphorical, and symbolic levels of analysis — is the meaning already perceived. This is primarily a matter of the relative lexical compatibility of the words, and using it consists basically of bringing to bear on syntactic problems two of Mr. Richards's other tools, intelligent use of the dictionary and logical acumen. It should be a last resort, for two reasons: it is circular, since we want the syntax to tell us what words go together, rather than vice versa; and it is risky, since the metaphorical mode of poetry often attains its most striking effects by violating lexical compatibility altogether.

Assuming (perhaps a large assumption) that the punctuation of the poem is the poet's own and is in accordance with orthodox conventions, let us see what it can do to help us with our six ambiguities. In the first of them, the interpretation of line 3, the semicolon at the end of line 2 is of paramount importance. It is the strongest mark before the period at the end of line 6, and forces us to divide the first six lines 2:4 rather than 3:3. This in turn eliminates the reading of line 3 as an appositive to *gentleman,* and leaves us no alternative but to interpret the line as a predication, with *cracked* as a finite verb and the first IC cut after *hangnail.*[5]

Punctuation also virtually decides the assignment of *a dog among the fairies* as subject of *Bit out . . .* rather than as appositive to *fork.* The significant mark here is the comma at the end of line 5, which sets off that line as an appositive to *a dog among the fairies,* and would be definitely superfluous if this line alone were the subject. Note that lexical compatibility corroborates this judgment; *dog* goes much more consistently with *atlas-eater, jaw,* and *Bit* than it does with *fork.*

The third crux, the assignment of the phrase at the end of line 6, receives no help from punctuation. Whichever way it is to be read, this punctuation would be conventional. (But note that a comma after *mandrake* would resolve the ambiguity by locating the first IC cut at that point.)

Our fourth problem is the exact nature of the coordination in line 8, and once again punctuation is of no help. The line as punctuated can be read either way: as a coordination of *cock* and *egg* or of *nowheres* and *egg.* A comma at the intended primary cut, either after *cock* or after *nowheres,* while not called for by the usual handbook rules, would have been very helpful.

In case five, the interpretation of line 10, we get a faint suggestion from the absence of a comma at the end of line 11 that our first solution — to take

[5] Knieger (*Explicator* XV) recognizes the significance of the semicolon only to disregard it: "Line 3: 'Abaddon,' in spite of the semi-colon after 'furies,' seems in apposition with 'gentleman.' "

Hatched as a participle — is more probable, since if *hatched* and *scraped* were coordinate verbs, the adverbial material in line 12 would presumably go with both and not be more closely associated with the second. But orthodox punctuation has no clear-cut way to indicate this. The comma at the end of line 10 is ambiguous, since according to one reading it ends the long modifier complex of lines 8–10, and according to the other it replaces the missing coordinator between the two predicates. We could presumably get some help here from studying the incidence of this kind of asyndeton in Thomas's early poetry; how does his usage compare, for example, with that of *Time* magazine?

In our last case, the assignment of the phrase *on one leg* to its proper head, neither interpretation is ruled out by the existing punctuation. In this case, furthermore, placing a comma at the primary cut, either after *Hatched* or after *salvage,* would not have solved the problem but would only have created a new one.

Turning to our second clue, the verse, we can take two of our four unresolved cruxes together. In lines 6 and 8 the problem syntactically and prosodically is the same: whether the primary cut, presumably marked by a single-bar juncture, comes after the second or after the fifth syllable. Metrically speaking, does the caesura come after the first foot or in the middle of the third? Either is possible. But a caesura as early in a decasyllabic line as the second syllable is a rather shocking device, and on the assumption that the poet has an ear (certainly not an unwarranted assumption in the light of the evidence still available in recordings of his readings), we do not expect him to use it twice in one poem. Nor is there any metrical reason to expect it in one of these lines and not the other, since they are metrically virtually identical, even to the initial spondee and the grammatically weak or at best tertiary syllable under the third metrical stress:

Bìt ôut thĕ mándràke wĭth tŏ-môrrŏw's scréam
Òld côck frŏm nówhères ănd thĕ hêavĕn's égg

It seems clear to me that in both cases the verse calls for a feminine caesura — grammatically a single-bar juncture — at the midpoint of the line, with the consequent retardation compensated quantitatively by the following short, weak syllable in stressed position. This in turn leads us to interpret *with to-morrow's scream,* rather surprisingly, as a modifier of the whole phrase *Bit out the mandrake;* and, somewhat more satisfying metaphorically, to take *cock* and *egg* as coordinate.

The same line of analysis settles the disposition of *on one leg* in line 10. Here the caesura after *salvage* is a feminine one, followed once again by an unstressed morpheme *on* in metrically stressed position. To put a single-bar and hence a caesura after *Hatched* — the ictus of the inverted first foot — does metrical violence to the line. Note, by the way, that the pattern of feminine caesura followed by grammatical weak occurs in three other lines that are not ambiguous: after *owl-light* in line 1, *eater* in line 5, and *cradle* in line 11.

Our remaining crux, the interpretation of line 10, receives no help from the verse, since the question concerns the assignment of the whole line *en bloc* to either the preceding string of modifiers or the following predicate, and since all the lines are end-stopped, there is no evidence as to whether line 10 is to be read with a final double-bar, which would make it one more in the string that began with line 7, or whether it has a /232#/ contour like line 11.

It remains to apply the final test, lexical compatibility, to this one remaining syntactical ambiguity. Certainly the key-word *Hatched* belongs with *Old cock* and *heaven's egg,* and *windy salvage* with *half-way winds;* whereas a new set of images begins with *scraped.* This joins with our sense of the relative infrequency of this kind of asyndeton to incline us toward interpreting line 10 as one more in the string of appositive and postpositive modifiers of *that gentleman of wounds.*

We are at last ready for a syntactic reading of the poem:

^{2}Âltarwìse by ^{3}ówl-^{2}lìght^{2} | ^{2}in the hâlf-wày hóuse^{2} |
^{2}The gêntleman lày ^{3}gráveward^{2} | ^{2}with his ^{3}fúries^{1} #
^{2}Abâddon in the ^{3}hángnaìl^{2} | ^{2}crâcked from ^{3}Ádam^{2} #
^{3}Ánd^{2} | ^{2}from his ^{3}fórk^{2} | ^{2}a dôg amòng the fáiries^{2} ||
^{2}The ^{3}átlas-êater^{2} | ^{2}with a jâw for ^{3}néws^{2} |
^{2}Bìt oût the ^{3}mándràke^{2} | ^{2}with tomòrrow's ^{3}scréam^{1} #
^{2}Then^{2} | ^{3}pénny-êyed^{2} || ^{2}that gêntleman of ^{3}wóunds^{2} ||
^{2}Òld côck from ^{3}nówhères^{2} | ^{2}and the hêaven's égg^{2} ||
^{2}With^{3} bónes unbûttoned^{2} | ^{2}to the hâlf-wày wínds^{2} ||
^{2}Hâtched from the wîndy sâlvage on ône ^{3}lég^{2} ||
^{3}Scráped at my crâdle^{2} | ^{2}in a ^{3}wálking wôrd^{2} #
^{2}That nîght of tíme^{2} || ^{2}ùnder the Chrîstward shélter^{1} #
^{2}Ì am the ^{3}lông wórld's^{2} gêntleman^{1} | ^{1}he said^{1} ||
^{2}And shâre my béd^{2} | ^{2}with Câpricòrn and ^{3}Cáncer^{1} #

This is as far as syntactic analysis will take us; the more familiar modes of critical interpretation must go ahead from here. But it seems to me that they can do so now with a firmer ground under their feet than if the syntax had been taken for granted or left to intuition as it commonly is by the ingenious explicators of modern criticism.

Michael A. K. Halliday

THE LINGUISTIC STUDY OF LITERARY TEXTS

The starting-point could be Jakobson's observation: "Insistence on keeping poetics apart from linguistics is warranted only when the field of linguistics appears to be illicitly restricted." [1] It is part of the task of linguistics to describe texts; and all texts, including those, prose and verse, which fall within any definition of literature, are accessible to linguistic analysis. In talking therefore of the linguistic study of literary text we mean not merely the study of the language, but rather the study of such texts by the methods of linguistics. There is a difference between *ad hoc,* personal and arbitrarily selective statements such as are sometimes offered, perhaps in support of a preformulated literary thesis, as textual or linguistic statements about literature, and a description of a text based on general linguistic theory. It is the latter that contributes to what has sometimes been called "linguistic stylistics."

One major significance of this distinction is that a linguistic analysis will relate the text to the language as a whole. Linguistic stylistics is an application rather than an extension of linguistics, and it is this that can ensure the theoretical validity of the statements made. The justification for the use of linguistic methods in literary analysis is that grammatical, lexical, phonological and phonetic theory is already relevant as it stands, and that descriptive statements made about a literary text are meaningful only in relation to the total description of the language concerned. If the linguist hopes to be able to contribute to the understanding of English literature, this is because and to the extent that he can work within the framework of a comprehensive description of the English of the period in question. The categories with which he is operating can be explicitly formulated (and, it is to be hoped, not restricted

Reprinted from *Proceedings of the Ninth International Congress of Linguists,* edited by H. Lunt, by permission of Mouton & Company, Publishers, The Hague, The Netherlands. Newly revised by the author.

[1] See Roman Jakobson, "Linguistics and Poetics," in Thomas A. Sebeok (ed.), *Style in Language,* The M.I.T. Press, Cambridge, Massachusetts, 1960, p. 352. [*Reprinted here pp. 296–322.*]

to below the rank of the sentence), making clear what sometimes seems to be overlooked, that a work of English literature is written in the English language. If all clauses in a poem are shown to have the same structure, it is pertinent to ask whether or not this is the only permitted clause structure in the language; and if not, what its relative frequency is in other texts in samples drawn from "the language in general."

A text is meaningful not only in virtue of what it is but also in virtue of what it might have been. One, perhaps the most relevant, exponent of the "might have been" of a work of literature is another work of literature. Linguistic stylistics is thus essentially a comparative study. To pursue the example above, we should like to know the relative frequency of this clause structure in other works of the same period and the same genre. The more texts are studied, the more what is said about any one text becomes interesting and relevant.

Linguistic stylistics might thus be defined as the description of literary texts, by methods derived from general linguistic theory and within the framework of a description of the language in question, and the comparison of such texts with others, by the same and by different authors, in the same and in different genres.

While insisting that stylistic studies involve the same methods and the same categories as other, non-literary descriptions, we must make the proviso that such studies may require new alignments or groupings of descriptive categories, through which the special properties of a text may be recognized. This may include the bringing together of categories and items described at different levels as well as those only indirectly related in the description of any one level. An example of such a grouping, in which various grammatical and lexical features are brought together, is provided by the concept of "cohesion." [2]

The principal categories subsumed under the heading of cohesion are:

A. Grammatical
  1. Structural (relation of clauses in sentence structure)
    (a) Dependence
    (b) Co-ordination
  2. Non-structural
    (a) Anaphora
      (i) deictics and submodifiers
      (ii) pronouns
    (b) Substitution
      (i) verbal
      (ii) nominal

[2] Another example is "involvement"; see Angus McIntosh, "'As You Like It': a grammatical clue to character," *A Review of English Literature,* 4, April 1963, reprinted in Angus McIntosh and M. A. K. Halliday, *Patterns of Language,* London: Longmans, 1966.

B. Lexical
   1. Repetition of item
   2. Occurrence of item from same lexical set

Cohesion is a syntagmatic relation and, insofar as it is grammatical, it is partly accounted for by structure. Structure is here regarded as a configuration of syntagmatic functions such that a set of items assuming the functions embodied in a given structure can be said to cohere to form a single item of higher rank; thus, in English, clauses cohere by virtue of their function in sentence structure, likewise groups in clause structure. All structure is in this sense cohesive. But the internal structure of the lower units is largely independent of the structure of the text as a whole, so that the structural aspect of cohesion within a text involves only the higher order structures. A more detailed treatment of cohesion would probably include reference to some relations in clause and even group structure, for example those of apposition and of "theme" (the structure of the clause considered as a unit of message); but in the first instance structural cohesion can be limited to the relations between clauses in sentence structure. These are of course very varied, but certain major distinctions are likely to be particularly relevant to the study of literary texts: principally that between co-ordination and dependence, the latter being taken here to include non-defining relative clauses (in contrast to defining relative clauses, which are accounted for in the structure of the nominal group).

Structure, however, is not the only cohesive factor even among grammatical relations. There are certain grammatical categories whose exponents cohere with other items in the text, items to which they do not stand in a fixed structural relation or indeed necessarily in any structural relation at all. Principal among these are the anaphoric items in the nominal and adverbial group: deictics, such as *the, this, that* and the personal possessives; submodifiers like *such* and *so;* adverbs such as *there* and *then;* and the personal pronouns. These items are regarded as cohesive only in their anaphoric use, which however accounts for the majority of instances of all those mentioned except *the,* which is most frequently cataphoric. That is to say, in an example such as *the weeks before Christmas* the function of *the* is to specify that *before Christmas* identifies the sub-set of *weeks* concerned; the reference is thus cataphoric, with no implication of previous mention. Thus deictics and submodifiers used cataphorically, pointing forward to a modifier or qualifier as in *the tallest man, the man who came to dinner, he who hesitates,* are not textually cohesive in this sense; nor is the "homophoric" *the,* signalling that the noun is self-defining, as in *the moon.* Secondary in importance to anaphora, though more frequent in spoken than in written English, is substitution: the use of *do* as substitute lexical item in the verbal group, and of *one* as head in the nominal group, as in *he no longer resisted . . . he might have done if . . . ; these were his arguments . . . a stronger one might have been. . . .*

Lexical cohesion in its clearest form is provided by two or more occurrences, in close proximity, of the same lexical item; less strongly by the co-occurrence of items paradigmatically related in the sense that they may belong to the same lexical set. For example, in a passage by Leslie Stephen in *The Playground of Europe* one paragraph ends *I took leave, and turned to the ascent of the peak;* the next paragraph begins *The climb is perfectly easy.* Thus in the new paragraph the first lexical item, *climb,* coheres with *ascent;* later occur *mountain* and *summit* cohering with *peak.* The lexical set is identified by privilege of occurrence in collocation, just as the grammatical class is identified by privilege of occurrence in structure; the set, in other words, is a grouping of items with similar tendencies of collocation. In this way *climb* and *ascent* cohere with each other because both regularly appear in the environment of *mountain, steep,* etc. The mere occurrence in a text of a high frequency collocation, like *ascent . . . peak,* across the boundary of sentence or paragraph, may itself be a cohesive factor of a rather weaker kind, although its significance would depend on other variables such as the relative frequency of the items themselves. In any case a valid assessment of lexical cohesion requires a study of collocations in very large samples of text, this being necessary to the recognition of lexical sets; little work has yet been done in this field.

The features outlined in the last three paragraphs are perhaps among the main features contributing to the internal cohesion of texts in modern written English. Any given instance of a cohesive relation may combine a number of such features; in *the climb,* cited above, the cohesion is both lexical and grammatical, involving the relation of *climb* to *ascent* and the marking of this relation by the anaphoric *the.* There are clearly other important factors to be recognized: for example grammatical regularity in the form of structural parallelism is under certain circumstances cohesive, when it is reinforced by lexical cohesion or, in verse, by the metric pattern. No reference has been made here to phonological features, but in spoken texts phonology is relevant in at least two ways: first, metric form in verse is itself a cohesive factor, and secondly features of intonation and rhythm operate as exponents of anaphoric relations (for example the rise-fall-rise contour in British English).

The discussion of cohesion as a factor particularly relevant to the study of literary texts is not meant to suggest that all statements in linguistic stylistics require such special alignments of categories. Many of the considerations suggested here are relevant to texts of all kinds; and if the analysis of a literary text proceeds in a manner no different from that employed in textual studies in general this already reveals much that is relevant to the text as a work of literature, and thus to the study of literary language as a whole. To quote Jakobson again: "The set (*Einstellung*) toward the MESSAGE as such, focus on the message for its own sake, is the POETIC function of language."[3] It is

[3] *Op. cit.,* p. 356.

this "set toward the message" that determines the particular type of linguistic patterning that is characteristic of literature.

If we keep the word "pattern" as a general, non-technical name for all the organization, at all levels, that is, a crucial property of language as such, then the special property of literary language is the patterning of the variability of these patterns. In other words, the creative writer finds and exploits the *irregularity* that the patterns allow, and in doing so superimposes a further *regularity*. It is this latter "regularity," as we may reasonably call it provided we avoid giving the term a purely quantitative interpretation, that marks the "focus on the message." This regularity is clearly displayed by the analysis of a text within the framework of a description of the language.

It is difficult to cite examples briefly, since only an account of a number of interacting features in a text is really illuminating, quite apart from the need to contrast these with features of other texts. Two points must suffice: the relation between lexical items and grammatical functions in the verbs, and the structure of the nominal groups, in W. B. Yeats' *Leda and the Swan.*

There are 15 verbal groups in this poem; in addition a further four words of the class "verb" function outside verbal groups, operating directly (that is, without rankshift) in the structure of nominal groups. Table I shows the items involved,[4] classified according to their value in structure. Appended to it, for purposes of comparison, is a similar table for fifteen lines of Tennyson's *Morte d'Arthur,* lines beginning "Then quickly rose Sir Bedivere, and ran." The columns represent the different structural functions of the lexical verbs, ordered so that what might be called the "most verbal" function (finite verb in independent clause) appears on the left, the "least verbal" (within nominal group) on the right. *Leda and the Swan* shows a high proportion of lexical verbs in the "less verbal" structural positions. Moreover, the more lexically "powerful" items, in the sense of those restricted in their collocational range, tend to have the less verbal functions: the main verbal load is carried by very general items such as *hold, push, feel, put on, lie,* while those such as *stagger, loosen, caress* are reduced to the status of noun modifiers. In both these features, this poem stands in sharp contrast to the passage of Tennyson, in which most of the verbs appear in finite verbal groups (nearly all in simple past tense) and the majority also carry more specific expectations as regards their likely collocates.

There are 25 nominal groups in the poem, of which 17 contain modifying (pre-head non-deictic) or qualifying (post-head) items, or both: for example, *the staggering girl, a shudder in the loins, the brute blood of the air.* In English, when a potentially cataphoric deictic occurs in such nominal groups

[4] The table shows the lexical item, which is not necessarily coextensive, either paradigmatically or syntagmatically, with either the verb (item of word rank assigned to the class "verb") or the verbal group (item of group rank assigned to the class "verbal group"). Thus in *did she put on, being caught up,* the verbal groups are *did put on, being caught up,* the verbs (verb words) are *did, put, being, caught,* the lexical items are *put on, catch up.*

it normally is cataphoric: that is to say, in a nominal group such as *the roses in my garden,* containing both *the* and an element which could be defining, the normal function of *the* is to show that *in my garden* does identify the

TABLE I

	Items in verbal group (i.e. functioning as "predicator") in clause structure					Items in nominal group (i.e. not functioning as predicator)
Clause class	Independent	Dependent		Qualifying (rankshifted)		}inapplicable
Group class	Finite	Finite	Non-finite	Finite	Non-finite	
Leda and the Swan	hold push feel engender put on 5	lie let 2	drop catch up master 3	—	beat (2) caress catch lay 5	stagger loosen burn break 4
Morte d'Arthur	rise (2) run plunge clutch wheel throw make shoot flash fall catch brandish draw go 15	shock dip 2	leap flash whirl 3	—	see clothe 2	—

roses in question. In *Leda* 15 out of the 17 nominal groups which have such a (potentially) defining element have also a (potentially) cataphoric deictic, ten of them having in fact *the;* yet only one instance, *the brute blood of the air,* has the expected configuration of cataphoric and defining elements. In all other instances the modifiers are non-defining and the deictic is not cataphoric. What then is the function of the deictic? The personal possessives, presumably, are anaphoric to the title of the poem, not only in *her nape* but also in *her loosening thigh:* the modifier, when present, is descriptive. The various instances of *the* and *that* are also best regarded as anaphoric, but in the non-textual sense: they do not refer back to anything in the text, but rather to some extralinguistic feature which they themselves require to be presupposed.

These two factors, the distribution of verbal items and the structure of the nominal groups, together explain what seems to me to be one of the most striking features of the poem. The preponderance of nominal groups, which contain 46 out of the 56 lexical items in the poem; the constant use, in a "defining" structure, of non-defining, descriptive modifiers, with deictics demanding reference outside the text; the interplay, in the verbs, of "strong" items in "weak" functions with "weak" items in "strong" functions; all these build up a kind of backcloth or tapestry effect, so that the picture is "fixed" and what might otherwise be the narrative of an event becomes an interpretation of it. The reference to a familiar passage of Tennyson here serves a comparative purpose: it shows that a straightforward narrative of action is characterized by very different linguistic properties.[5]

[5] For the general linguistic concepts referred to here see M. A. K. Halliday, "Categories of the theory of grammar," *Word* 17, December 1961; Angus McIntosh, * "Patterns and ranges," *Language* 37, 1961; J. McH. Sinclair, "Beginning the study of lexis," in C. E. Bazell et al. (ed.), *In memory of J. R. Firth,* London: Longmans, 1966. For work in linguistics and literary studies related to the theme of this paper see David Abercrombie, "A Phonetician's view of verse structure," *Linguistics* 6, 1964, reprinted in the same author's *Studies in Phonetics and Linguistics,* London: Oxford University Press (Language and Language Learning 10), 1965; J. R. Firth, "Modes of Meaning," *Essays and Studies* (*The English Association*), 1951, reprinted in the same author's *Papers in Linguistics 1934–1951,* London: Oxford University Press, 1957; Angus McIntosh, * "Linguistics and English studies," in *Patterns of Language* (cf. n.2). M. A. K. Halliday, * "Descriptive linguistics in literary studies," in A. Duthie (ed.), *English Studies Today, Third Series,* Edinburgh: University Press, 1964; John Spencer and Michael J. Gregory, "An Approach to the study of style," in Nils Erik Enkvist, John Spencer and Michael J. Gregory, *Linguistics and style,* London: Oxford University Press (Language and Language Learning 6), 1964; Rulon Wells, "Nominal and verbal style," in *Style in Language* (cf. n.1); and articles in *A Review of English Literature* 6, April 1965. Papers marked * are (re)printed in *Patterns of Language* (cf. n.2).

Samuel R. Levin

POETRY AND GRAMMATICALNESS

In order that a grammar be adequate to a language, it must generate all and only the grammatical sentences of that language. It follows that a grammar may fail to be adequate for one of two reasons: it may generate some sentences which are not grammatical, or it may fail to generate some that are. We may call these two types of inadequacy *overgeneration* and *undergeneration* — compositely, *dysgeneration*. Since the question of grammaticalness is closely bound up with the question of dysgeneration, we shall discuss grammaticalness from the point of view, first, of overgeneration, then from the point of view of undergeneration. The latter discussion will lead us into the question of poetry.

Although in theory a generative grammar should enumerate all and only the grammatical sentences of a language, in actual practice the results can never be so clear-cut. The requirement that the grammar project, from the corpus of observed sentences underlying its construction, an infinite number of sentences beyond the corpus, implies that the rules, aside from being iterative, must have a certain measure of generality. This same generality entails the enumeration — by the same set of grammatical rules — of a large number of sentences whose grammaticalness is sometimes open to question. We are not talking here of anarchic outputs like * *if go ninth John as*. Outputs of this kind would clearly invalidate the grammar. The problem lies rather with outputs that lie more along the margin of grammatical sentences, sequences like * *argumentative windows cook with their destinies*, for example. Outputs of the latter type can be precluded by imposing restrictions on the grammatical rules, but a very large number of such restrictions would have to be imposed if all sentences of the above type were to be precluded, and the greater the number of restrictions so imposed, the less general would the grammatical rules become. The problem thus seems to resolve itself into the question of whether greater generality is desired of the grammar, or whether greater grammaticalness is required of it. But there does not seem to be any obvious way to decide what the optimum decision might be.

Reprinted from *Proceedings of the Ninth International Congress of Linguists*, edited by H. Lunt, by permission of Mouton & Company, Publishers, The Hague, The Netherlands.

Of course, one can say that everything and only what the grammar generates is grammatical by definition. According to this view, if the grammar succeeds in generating a large body of clearly grammatical sentences and if, inversely, it does not generate any clearly ungrammatical sentences, then we accept as being also grammatical whatever sentences of a marginal nature the grammar additionally generates, and no marginal sentences which it does not. Some such solution must, no doubt, be adopted if the question of adequacy is to be coped with at all. But it does not follow from this view, even though all the sentences which the grammar generates are grammatical, that they are all *equally* grammatical. Such an argument would obliterate by fiat a difference that is interesting in a fundamental way, and would leave us with no motivation for investigating the differences between those sentences of which, presystematically, some are grammatical, some are only semi-grammatical, and some are ungrammatical.

As a matter of fact, most of the literature on the subject holds the question of degrees of grammaticalness to be important; it is held to be highly desirable to investigate the relative structures of grammatical, semi-grammatical, and ungrammatical sentences so as to ascertain, if possible, in what relation such sentences stand to the grammatical rules. A priori we might expect those sentences that are semi-grammatical to stand in some different relation to those rules than do those sentences that are grammatical and ungrammatical. We might even expect to find different relations to those rules among sentences that seem semi-grammatical in different ways. These different relations might then serve to explicate the reactions of native speakers, those reactions, that is, on the basis of which we make the distinctions in the first place.

The complementary side to the problem of a grammar's fit to the language arises when it generates not too many sentences, but too few, i.e., when it undergenerates.[1] This situation may result if, either there are no general rules [2] for generating a particular sequence, or if there is a general rule, but it has been so constrained as to prevent it from generating a particular sequence. There are no general rules in the grammar, for example, that would enable us to generate * *if go ninth John as;* obviously, we do not want any such rules. On the other hand, while there is a set of general rules that will generate a string of the form A N V P T N, these rules are presumably constrained so as to prevent the generation of the sequence . . . *seven oceans answer from their dream*. Now, prima facie, it might seem that we would not want the grammar to generate the preceding sentence any more than we would want it to generate * *argumentative windows cook with their destinies*. But it is precisely sentences of the former kind that we encounter in poetry (this one is from Hart Crane's "The Bridge"). Sentences like that of Crane's, of course, raise the question of what part or parts of the language the grammar is supposed to be adequate to.

[1] On the question of fit, see F. W. Harwood, "Axiomatic syntax: the construction and evaluation of a syntactic calculus," *Language* 31.409–413 (1955).

[2] By general rules we mean rules whose constituents (aside from possible constants) are highest-order, that is, have no constraints on them; e.g., $S \rightarrow NP + VP$ or $NP \rightarrow T + N$.

This is not the place to go into that question.[3] What interests us here is that, just as not all the sentences which the grammar generates are equally grammatical, so not all the sentences which it does not generate are equally ungrammatical. Indeed, it is not obvious that they all are ungrammatical.

Chomsky has recently discussed the question of assigning degrees of grammaticalness to sentences.[4] His method, admittedly adumbrative, consists essentially of setting up a hierarchy of categories, as a supplement to the grammar, constructed in such a way that any sequence of words can be represented on each level of the hierarchy. Chomsky's account describes only three such levels and, depending on the depth in the hierarchy at which a given sequence is still grammatically well-formed, it is labeled (1) grammatical (if it is well-formed down through level three), (2) semi-grammatical (if it is well-formed down through level two, but not three), and (3) ungrammatical (if it is well-formed at level one only, on which level there is only one category, the class of all words). An interesting feature of this method is that it assigns degrees of grammaticalness to sequences which the grammar does not generate. Similarly, in this paper we shall deal with sequences which, presumably, a grammar of English would not generate, sequences, thus, that are either ungrammatical or semi-grammatical. As we have pointed out, however, the sequences will come from poetry. In what follows then, we shall discuss the grammaticalness of such sequences, and we shall introduce a procedure which, though different in operation, yields results which are consistent with the results given by Chomsky's formulation.

In judging the degree of grammaticalness of such sentences, we proceed in the following manner: we assume, first of all, that the grammar will not generate them. (If it turns out that a grammar devised for English will, in fact, generate them, that fact is of no consequence to the procedure; other examples are available.) We then ask how the grammatical rules can be fixed so as to generate the sentence in question and, finally, we ask what the consequences of such fixing are to the grammar — in terms of what sentences other than the sentence in question would additionally be generated by the revised rule(s). The degree of grammaticalness of each of the tested sentences is then a function of the number of unwanted consequences (i.e., those sentences beyond the one

[3] It may be mentioned, however, that selecting for examination sequences that have occurred in poetry undercuts the question of what "could" occur given certain circumstances. These sentences *have* occurred; what is more, their occurrence in poetry might legitimately be held to evidence what kinds of constructions the grammar of the language will tolerate when a strain is put on it. It is, in any case, more desirable to deal with actual than with putative sentences. Of course, as we have said, the fact that these actual sentences come from poetry raises the question of what part or parts of the language the grammar is supposed to be adequate to. But we are not directly concerned with that question here. One could perhaps obtain similar examples from the casual language, in which case the question would not arise. But if one cannot obtain such examples from the casual language, then it remains desirable to consider actual sentences — from whatever part of the language they may come. We should notice that putative sentences do not become actual just because a linguist uses them. Such sentences do not belong to the corpus of the language, but rather to the linguist's metalanguage.

[4] Noam Chomsky, "Some methodological remarks on generative grammar," *Word* 17.235ff.

in question) that the revised rule generates: the greater the number of such unwanted consequences entrained, the less grammatical is the sentence in question; the fewer such unwanted consequences the revised rule generates, the more grammatical is the sentence in question.

As examples to work with, we take the two lines *he danced his did*, from Cummings' "Anyone lived in a pretty how town" and *a grief ago*, from Thomas' poem of that name.[5] We assume that these are deviant sentences, in the sense that the grammar will not generate them. Presystematically, it appears, further, that though both are deviant, they are deviant in different ways — which suggests that they should have different degrees of grammaticalness. We then ask how the grammar can be fixed so as to generate them. Now as a general rule, a grammar may be fixed to generate a new sentence in one of two ways: a new rule may be introduced; or items may be shifted from class to class.[6] Both our deviant constructions could be handled by either of these two procedures. Thus, to generate *he danced his did*, we could introduce a new rule, NP ⟶ T + V (we may ignore the morphophonemic question raised by *did*). The sentence could then be generated by the rules:

(1)	S	⟶	NP_1 + VP
(2)	NP_1	⟶	(T) + N
(3)	N	⟶	*he*
(4)	VP	⟶	V + NP_2
(5)	V	⟶	*danced, did*
(6)	NP_2	⟶	T + V
(7)	T	⟶	*his*

Alternatively, we could shift *did* from the class V to the class N; viz., N ⟶ *did*. Then the sentence could be generated in due course from the rule S ⟶ NP + VP, where the NP of the predicate is rewritten T + N, a rule already in the grammar. Whichever alternative we select to generate this sentence, the consequences in terms of unwanted sentences are great. If we select the first alternative, the new rule NP ⟶ T + V, will generate, in addition to *his did*, all kinds of things like *my had, the went*, etc. If we select the second alternative, the shift of *did* to N will entrain as values of A + N, to take just one construction, things like *tall did, enthusiastic did*, etc. Since, on the one hand, the members of V are in the thousands and, on the other hand, the members of A are similarly numerous, thousands of unwanted sentences would be generated by the grammar if it were fixed so as to generate *he danced his did*.

We could of course reduce the number of unwanted consequences if we introduced into the new rule, instead of the general class V, some subclass of V.

[5] The fact that the latter sequence is not a sentence is of little consequence; it is part of one. Dealing with the phrase alone merely simplifies the discussion.

[6] In generative grammar, of course, class assignments are also represented by rules, viz., N → *man*, so that a shift from one class to another is also an instance of a new rule. These are rules for lexical selection, however, and it seems desirable to keep them separate in our discussion from the grammatical rules. We therefore speak of shifting items from class to class.

It is not clear, however, just how we would go about selecting such a subclass. Subclasses are set up on the basis of restricted co-occurrence privileges in many clear instances of grammatical sentences; such would be the division of the class V into V transitive and V intransitive, for one example. In the case of *he danced his did*, however, we obviously have no clearly grammatical instances on the basis of which we could decide to what subclass of V *did* should be assigned. Nor would it do to use the subclass to which *do* belongs in the regular grammatical rules, since the clear cases on the basis of which *do* is assigned to that subclass have no obvious relation to the sentence under consideration here.[7] For reasons similar to those discussed above, there is no obvious way to select a subclass of N if we adopt the alternative procedure of shifting *did* from V to N.

Now let us consider our second sequence, *a grief ago*. There is a rule, or series of rules, which enables us to generate such sequences as *some time ago*, *a while back*, *a year ago*, etc., i.e. T_x N_y D_z. Presumably, the N of this construction is a subclass containing only temporal nouns. To generate *a grief ago*, we lift the restriction from the rule in question so as to include in this N subclass also nouns indicating, say, states of mind, a subclass including *grief*. The revised rule will now generate *a grief ago*, and, in addition, sequences like *a happiness ago*, *some sorrow back*, *a disappointment ago*, etc. Alternatively, we shift *grief* from the subclass N comprising nouns indicating states of mind to the temporal subclass (retaining it of course in the original subclass). The grammar will now generate *a grief ago* and, additionally, such sequences as *a grief back*, *some grief ago*, etc. Now the consequences of fixing the grammar — either way — so as to generate *a grief ago*, seem not nearly as serious as the consequences of fixing it so as to generate *he danced his did*. But since any additional sentences that we might obtain from fixing the grammar so as to generate our two sentences are bound to be of the same grammatical form as the original sentences, our reactions to the new sentences merely duplicate — they do not explain — our reactions to the original sentences.

There is, however, an underlying structural reason for our different reactions, for thinking, that is, that the two sentences and their congeners have different degrees of grammaticalness. The underlying structural difference lies in the fact that there is a much higher functional yield when the grammar is fixed to generate *he danced his did* than there is when it is fixed to generate *a grief ago*. This different yield results from the fact that the constituents involved in the adjustments for *he danced his did* comprise many more members than do the constituents involved in the adjustments for *a grief ago*. To generate *he danced his did* we introduced as part of a new rule a general class, namely V: NP $\longrightarrow$ T + V. Alternatively, we shifted *did* from one general class to another — V to N. To generate *a grief ago*, on the other hand, the new rule amounted to lifting a restriction on an already existing rule. Even though the new class —

[7] That the selection of a subclass of V for *did* is not feasible is borne out by the occurrence in the same poem of the two sentences: *they sowed their isn't* and (*they*) *went their came*, where the two verbs *be* and *come* belong to different subclasses of verbs than does *do*.

comprising temporal and state of mind nouns — is more general than it was previously, it is still much less general than N or V, for example. Alternatively, the shift of *grief* was from one subclass, not general class, to another.

The preceding discussion explains how the degree of grammaticalness of any deviant sentence can be interpreted as a function of the number of unwanted consequences that the revised rule generates: the rules will generate any and all combinations of the members of the constituents constituting the rule; the more members in the constituents, the greater the number of unwanted consequences from the revised rule. The degree of grammaticalness of any sentence not directly generated by the grammar is thus in inverse proportion to the number of unwanted sentences which the revised rule generates.[8]

A sequence like *he danced his did* is not very common in poetry, whereas a sequence like *a grief ago* is quite common: in fact, the latter may be said to be typical of a good deal of diction that is characteristic of poetry. Now, as Chomsky has pointed out, "Given a grammatically deviant utterance, we attempt to impose an interpretation on it, exploiting whatever features of grammatical structure it preserves and whatever analogies we can construct with perfectly well-formed utterances." [9] In performing these operations on *he danced his did*, however, it is quite difficult to know what the proper analogies with well-formed utterances might be, since there are no utterances of this form generated anywhere in the grammar. When we attempt to adjust the grammar (i.e., make analogies) so as to generate utterances of the form *he danced his did*, a very great number of new constructions is entrained, comprising elements that are only remotely, if at all, connected with the sequence in question. The effect of this line is therefore one of diffusion, and not that fusion which we ordinarily associate with poetic language.

It is quite different with *a grief ago*. There the attempt to impose a structure on the sequence is met with success. In analogizing to well-formed utterances of its form, we entertain such sequences as *a while back*, *some time ago*, *a grief back*, etc. If we certify *a grief ago* by lifting the restrictions on the rules that yield the string T_x N_y D_z, then *grief* is associated, by the analogizing process, with the subclass of temporal nouns (*time*, *while*, *year*, etc.).[10] The process of fitting *grief* into this construction thus induces us to regard *grief* as implying time. Since it already implies state of mind (as being a member of that subclass of nouns), there is a fusion here of those two meanings. It is the act of analogizing then that produces the effect of richness which such poetic sequences produce. If we adopt the alternative procedure of shifting *grief* to the subclass N comprising temporal nouns, the same result is produced.

[8] This suggests that the degree of grammaticalness of those sentences that *are* generated by the grammar is in *direct* proportion to the number of sentences which the rule(s) in question generate. We shall not go into this question here. For a discussion of some aspects of the general problem, see Sol Saporta, "The application of linguistics to the study of poetic language," in *Style in language*, ed. Thomas A. Sebeok (The M.I.T. Press, 1960), esp. pp. 84, 91f.

[9] Chomsky, *op. cit.*, p. 234.

[10] In this procedure, *grief* also brings in its train all the other nouns of its subclass, the state of mind nouns like *sorrow*, *happiness*, *disappointment*, etc.

It is not merely paradigmatically, however, that *grief* is associated with temporal meaning. Adjusting the grammar either way so as to generate *a grief ago* causes *grief* to be associated with not only temporal nouns, but also with the temporal adverbs that occur in construction with such nouns. *Grief* thus becomes associated with notions of time syntagmatically as well as paradigmatically.

The important fact about sequences like *a grief ago* is that the grammar limits the framework within which the attempts to render the sequence grammatical must take place. This fact has two important effects: it makes feasible the grammaticalizing of the sequence, and it brings into association with the element(s) in the sequence a group of forms with narrow, well-defined meanings. This latter type of confrontation probably lies behind all metaphor.

Richard Ohmann

LITERATURE AS SENTENCES

Critics permit themselves, for this or that purpose, to identify literature with great books, with imaginative writing, with expressiveness in writing, with the non-referential and non-pragmatic, with beauty in language, with order, with myth, with structured and formed discourse — the list of definitions is nearly endless — with verbal play, with uses of language that stress the medium itself, with the expression of an age, with dogma, with the *cri de coeur*, with neurosis. Now of course literature is itself and not another thing, to paraphrase Bishop Butler; yet analogies and classifications have merit. For a short space let us think of literature as sentences.

To do so will not tax the imagination, because the work of literature indubitably *is* composed of sentences, most of them well-ordered, many of them deviant (no pejorative meant), some of them incomplete. But since much the same holds for dust-jacket copy, the Congressional Record, and transcripts of board meetings, the small effort required to think of literature as sentences may be repaid by a correspondingly small insight into literature as such. Although I do not believe this to be so, for the moment I shall hold the question in abeyance, and stay mainly within the territory held in common by all forms of discourse. In other words, I am not asking what is special about the sentences *of literature*, but what is special about *sentences* that they should interest the student of literature. Although I employ the framework of generative grammar and scraps of its terminology,[1] what I have to say should not ring in the traditionally educated grammatical ear with outlandish discord.

First, then, the sentence is the primary unit of understanding. Linguists have so trenchantly discredited the old definition — "a sentence is a complete thought" — that the truth therein has fallen into neglect. To be sure, we delimit the class of sentences by formal criteria, but each of the structures that

"Literature as Sentences" by Richard Ohmann, from *College English*, January, 1966. Reprinted with the permission of the National Council of Teachers of English and Richard Ohmann.

[1] I draw especially on Noam Chomsky, *Aspects of the Theory of Syntax* (Cambridge, Mass., 1965) and Jerrold J. Katz and Paul Postal, *An Integrated Theory of Linguistic Descriptions* (Cambridge, Mass., 1964).

qualifies will express a semantic unity not characteristic of greater or lesser structures. The meanings borne by morphemes, phrases, and clauses hook together to express a meaning that can stand more or less by itself. This point, far from denying the structuralist's definition of a sentence as a single free utterance, or *form*, seems the inevitable corollary of such definitions: forms carry meanings, and it is natural that an independent form should carry an independent meaning. Or, to come at the thing another way, consider that one task of a grammar is to supply structural descriptions, and that the sentence is the unit so described. A structural description specifies the way each part of a sentence is tied to each other part, and the semantic rules of a grammar use the structural description as starting point in interpreting the whole. A reader or hearer does something analogous when he resolves the structures and meanings of sentences, and thereby understands them. Still another way to approach the primacy of the sentence is to notice that the initial symbol for all derivations in a generative grammar is "S" for sentence: the sentence is the domain of grammatical structure — rather like the equation in algebra — and hence the domain of meaning.

These remarks, which will seem truisms to some and heresy to others, cannot be elaborated here. Instead, I want to register an obvious comment on their relevance to literary theory and literary criticism. Criticism, whatever else it does, must interpret works of literature. Theory concerns itself in part with the question, "what things legitimately bear on critical interpretation?" But beyond a doubt, interpretation begins with sentences. Whatever complex apprehension the critic develops of the whole work, that understanding arrives mundanely, sentence by sentence. For this reason, and because the form of a sentence dictates a rudimentary mode of understanding, sentences have a good deal to do with the subliminal meaning (and form) of a literary work. They prepare and direct the reader's attention in particular ways.

My second point about sentences should dispel some of the abstractness of the first. Most sentences directly and obliquely put more linguistic apparatus into operation than is readily apparent, and call on more of the reader's linguistic competence. Typically, a surface structure overlays a deep structure which it may resemble but little, and which determines the "content" of the sentence. For concreteness, take this rather ordinary example, an independent clause from Joyce's "Araby": "Gazing up into the darkness I saw myself as a creature driven and derided by vanity." The surface structure may be represented as follows, using the convention of labeled brackets:[2] ${}^{S}[{}^{Adv}[V + \mathrm{Part}\ {}^{PP}[P\ {}^{NP}[D + N]]]\ {}^{Nuc}[N\ {}^{VP}[V + N\ {}^{PP}[P\ {}^{NP}[D + N\ {}^{Adj}[V + \mathrm{and} + V\ {}^{PP}[P + N]]]]]]]$
The nucleus has a transitive verb with a direct object. In the deep structure, by contrast, the matrix sentence is of the form ${}^{S}[NP\ {}^{VP}[V + \mathrm{Complement} + NP]]$: "I + saw + as a creature + me." It has embedded in it one sentence with an

[2] Each set of brackets encloses the constituent indicated by its superscript label. The notation is equivalent to a tree diagram. Symbols: S = Sentence, Adv = Adverbial, V = Verb, Part = Particle, PP = Prepositional Phrase, P = Preposition, NP = Noun Phrase, D = Determiner, N = Noun, Nuc = Nucleus, VP = Verb Phrase, Adj = Adjectival.

intransitive verb and an adverb of location — "I gazed up into the darkness" — and two additional sentences with transitive verbs and direct objects — "Vanity drove the creature," and "Vanity derided the creature." Since "darkness" and "vanity" are derived nouns, the embedded sentences must in turn contain embeddings, of, say "(Something) is dark" and "(Someone) is vain." Thus the word "vanity," object of a preposition in the surface structure, is subject of two verbs in the deep, and its root is a predicate adjective. The word "creature," object of a preposition in the surface structure, also has a triple function in the deep structure: verbal complement, direct object of "drive," and direct object of "deride." Several transformations (including the passive) deform the six basic sentences, and several others relate them to each other. The complexity goes much farther, but this is enough to suggest that a number of grammatical processes are required to generate the initial sentence and that its structure is moderately involved. Moreover, a reader will not understand the sentence unless he grasps the relations marked in the deep structure. As it draws on a variety of syntactic resources, the sentence also activates a variety of semantic processes and modes of comprehension, yet in brief compass and in a surface *form* that radically permutes *content*.

I choose these terms wilfully: that there are interesting grounds here for a form-content division seems to me quite certain. Joyce might have written, "I gazed up into the darkness. I saw myself as a creature. The creature was driven by vanity. The creature was derided by vanity." Or, "Vanity drove and derided the creature I saw myself as, gazer up, gazer into the darkness." Content remains roughly the same, for the basic sentences are unchanged. But the style is different. And each revision structures and screens the content differently. The original sentence acquires part of its meaning and part of its unique character by resonating against these unwritten alternatives. It is at the level of sentences, I would argue, that the distinction between form and content comes clear, and that the intuition of style has its formal equivalent.[3]

Sentences play on structure in still another way, more shadowy, but of considerable interest for criticism. It is a commonplace that not every noun can serve as object of every verb, that a given noun can be modified only by adjectives of certain classes, and so on. For instance, a well-defined group of verbs, including "exasperate," "delight," "please," and "astound," require animate objects; another group including "exert," "behave," and "pride," need reflexive objects. Such interdependencies abound in a grammar, which must account for them by subcategorizing nouns, adjectives, and the other major classes.[4] The importance of categorical restrictions is clearest in sentences that disregard them — deviant sentences. It happens that the example from Joyce is slightly deviant in this way: in one of the underlying sentences — "Vanity derided the creature" — a verb that requires a human subject in fact has as its subject the abstract noun "vanity." The dislocation forces the reader to use a supple-

[3] I have argued the point at length in "Generative Grammars and the Concept of Literary Style," *Word*, 20 (Dec. 1964), 423–439.

[4] Chomsky discusses ways of doing this in *Aspects of the Theory of Syntax*, Chapter 2.

mentary method of interpretation: here, presumably he aligns "vanity" (the word) with the class of human nouns and sees vanity (the thing) as a distinct, active power in the narrator's psyche. Such deviance is so common in metaphor and elsewhere that one scarcely notices it, yet it helps to specify the way things happen in the writer's special world, and the modes of thought appropriate to that world.

I have meant to suggest that sentences normally comprise intricacies of form and meaning whose effects are not the less substantial for their subtlety. From this point, what sorts of critical description follow? Perhaps I can direct attention toward a few tentative answers, out of the many that warrant study, and come finally to a word on critical theory. Two samples must carry the discussion; one is the final sentence of "The Secret Sharer":

> Walking to the taffrail, I was in time to make out, on the very edge of a darkness thrown by a towering black mass like the very gateway of Erebus — yes, I was in time to catch an evanescent glimpse of my white hat left behind to mark the spot where the secret sharer of my cabin and of my thoughts, as though he were my second self, had lowered himself into the water to take his punishment: a free man, a proud swimmer striking out for a new destiny.

I hope others will agree that the sentence justly represents its author: that it portrays a mind energetically stretching to subdue a dazzling experience *outside* the self, in a way that has innumerable counterparts elsewhere in Conrad. How does scrutiny of the deep structure support this intuition? First, notice a matter of emphasis, of rhetoric. The matrix sentence, which lends a surface form to the whole, is "# S # I was in time # S #" (repeated twice). The embedded sentences that complete it are "I walked to the taffrail," "I made out + NP," and "I caught + NP." The point of departure, then, is the narrator himself: where he was, what he did, what he saw. But a glance at the deep structure will explain why one feels a quite different emphasis in the sentence as a whole: seven of the embedded sentences have "sharer" as grammatical subject; in another three the subject is a noun linked to "sharer" by the copula; in two "sharer" is direct object; and in two more "share" is the verb. Thus thirteen sentences go to the semantic development of "sharer," as follows:

1) The secret sharer had lowered the secret sharer into the water.
2) The secret sharer took his punishment.
3) The secret sharer swam.
4) The secret sharer was a swimmer.
5) The swimmer was proud.
6) The swimmer struck out for a new destiny.
7) The secret sharer was a man.
8) The man was free.
9) The secret sharer was my second self.
10) The secret sharer had (it).
11) (Someone) punished the secret sharer.

12) (Someone) shared my cabin.
13) (Someone) shared my thoughts.

In a fundamental way, the sentence is mainly *about* Leggatt, although the surface structure indicates otherwise.

Yet the surface structure does not simply throw a false scent, and the way the sentence comes to focus on the secret sharer is also instructive. It begins with the narrator, as we have seen, and "I" is the subject of five basic sentences early on. Then "hat" takes over as the syntactic focus, receiving development in seven base sentences. Finally, the sentence arrives at "sharer." This progression in the deep structure rather precisely mirrors both the rhetorical movement of the sentence from the narrator to Leggatt via the hat that links them, and the thematic effect of the sentence, which is to transfer Leggatt's experience to the narrator via the narrator's vicarious and actual participation in it. Here I shall leave this abbreviated rhetorical analysis, with a cautionary word: I do not mean to suggest that only an examination of deep structure reveals Conrad's skillful emphasis — on the contrary, such an examination supports and in a sense explains what any careful reader of the story notices.

A second critical point adjoins the first. The morpheme "share" appears once in the sentence, but it performs at least twelve separate functions, as the deep structure shows. "I," "hat," and "mass" also play complex roles. Thus at certain points the sentence has extraordinary "density," as I shall call it. Since a reader must register these multiple functions in order to understand the sentence, it is reasonable to suppose that the very process of understanding concentrates his attention on centers of density. Syntactic density, I am suggesting, exercises an important influence on literary comprehension.

Third, by tuning in on deep structures, the critic may often apprehend more fully the build of a literary work. I have already mentioned how the syntax of Conrad's final sentence develops his theme. Consider two related points. First, "The Secret Sharer" is an initiation story in which the hero, through moral and mental effort, locates himself vis à vis society and the natural world, and thus passes into full manhood. The syntax of the last sentence schematizes the relationships he has achieved, in identifying with Leggatt's heroic defection, and in fixing on a point of reference — the hat — that connects him to the darker powers of nature. Second, the syntax and meaning of the last sentence bring to completion the pattern initiated by the syntax and meaning of the first few sentences, which present human beings and natural objects in thought-bewildering disarray. I can do no more than mention these structural connections here, but I am convinced that they supplement and help explain an ordinary critical reading of the story.

Another kind of critical point concerns habits of meaning revealed by sentence structure. One example must suffice. We have already marked how the sentence shifts its focus from "I" to "hat" to "sharer." A similar process goes on in the first part of the sentence: "I" is the initial subject, with "hat" as object. "Hat" is subject of another base sentence that ends with "edge," the object of a preposition in a locative phrase. "Edge" in turn becomes object of a sentence that has "darkness" as subject. "Darkness" is object in one with "mass" as subject, and in much the same way the emphasis passes to "gateway" and "Erebus." The syntax executes a chaining effect here which cuts across various kinds of construction. Chaining is far from the only type of syntactic expansion, but it is one Conrad favors. I would suggest this hypothesis: that syntactically and in other ways Conrad draws heavily on operations that link one thing with another associatively. This may be untrue, or if true it may be unrevealing; certainly it needs clearer expression. But I think it comes close to something that we all notice in Conrad, and in any case the general critical point exemplified here deserves exploration: that each writer tends to exploit deep linguistic resources in characteristic ways — that his style, in other words, rests on syntactic options within sentences (see fn. 3) — and that these syntactic preferences correlate with habits of meaning that tell us something about his mode of conceiving experience.

My other sample passage is the first sentence of Dylan Thomas' "A Winter's Tale":

> It is a winter's tale
> That the snow blind twilight ferries over the lakes
> And floating fields from the farm in the cup of the vales,
> Gliding windless through the hand folded flakes,
> The pale breath of cattle at the stealthy sail,
>
> And the stars falling cold,
> And the smell of hay in the snow, and the far owl
> Warning among the folds, and the frozen hold
> Flocked with the sheep white smoke of the farm house cowl
> In the river wended vales where the tale was told.

Some of the language here raises a large and familiar critical question, that of unorthodox grammar in modern poetry, which has traditionally received a somewhat facile answer. We say that loss of confidence in order and reason leads to dislocation of syntax, as if errant grammar were an appeal to the irrational. A cursory examination of deep structure in verse like Thomas', or even in wildly deviant verse like some of Cummings', will show the matter to be more complex than that.

How can deviance be most penetratingly analyzed? Normally, I think, in terms of the base sentences that lie beneath ungrammatical constructions. Surface structure alone does not show "the river wended vales" (line 10) to be deviant, since we have many well-formed constructions of the same word-class sequence: "machine made toys," "sun dried earth," and so on. The particular deviance of "the river wended vales" becomes apparent when we try to refer it to an appropriate underlying structure. A natural one to consider is "the river wends the vales" (cf. "the sun dries the earth"), but of course this makes "wend" a transitive verb, which it is not, except in the idiomatic "wend its way." So does another possibility, "NP + wends the vales with rivers" (cf. "NP +

makes the toys by machine"). This reading adds still other kinds of deviance, in that the Noun Phrase will have to be animate, and in that rivers are too cumbersome to be used instrumentally in the way implied. Let us assume that the reader rejects the more flagrant deviance in favor of the less, and we are back to "the river wends the vales." Suppose now that "the vales" is not after all a direct object, but a locative construction, as in "the wolf prowls the forest"; this preserves the intransitivity of "wend," and thereby avoids a serious form of deviance. But notice that there is *no* transformation in English that converts "the wolf prowls the forest" into "the wolf prowled forest," and so this path is blocked as well. Assume, finally, that given a choice between shifting a word like "wend" from one subclass to another and adding a transformational rule to the grammar, a reader will choose the former course; hence he selects the first interpretation mentioned: "the river wends the vales."

If so, how does he understand the anomalous transitive use of "wend"? Perhaps by assimilating the verb to a certain class that may be either transitive or intransitive: "paint," "rub," and the like. Then he will take "wend" to mean something like "make a mark on the surface of, by traversing"; in fact, this is roughly how I read Thomas' phrase. But I may be wrong, and in any case my goal is not to solve the riddle. Rather, I have been leading up to the point that every syntactically deviant construction has more than one possible interpretation, and that readers resolve the conflict by a process that involves deep and intricately motivated decisions and thus puts to work considerable linguistic knowledge, syntactic as well as semantic.[5] The decisions nearly always go on implicitly, but aside from that I see no reason to think that deviance of this sort is an appeal to, or an expression of, irrationality.

Moreover, when a poet deviates from normal syntax he is not doing what comes most habitually, but is making a special sort of choice. And since there are innumerable kinds of deviance, we should expect that the ones elected by a poem or poet spring from particular semantic impulses, particular ways of looking at experience. For instance, I think such a tendency displays itself in Thomas' lines. The construction just noted conceives the passing of rivers through vales as an agent acting upon an object. Likewise, "flocked" in line 9 becomes a transitive verb, and the spatial connection Thomas refers to — flocks in a hold — is reshaped into an action — flocking — performed by an unnamed agent upon the hold. There are many other examples in the poem of deviance that projects unaccustomed activity and process upon nature. Next, notice that beneath line 2 is the sentence "the twilight is blind," in which an inanimate noun takes an animate adjective, and that in line 5 "sail" takes the animate adjective "stealthy." This type of deviance also runs throughout the poem: Thomas sees nature as personal. Again, "twilight" is subject of "ferries,"

[5] See Jerrold J. Katz, "Semi-sentences," in Jerry A. Fodor and Jerrold J. Katz, eds., *The Structure of Language* (1964), pp. 400–416. The same volume includes two other relevant papers, Chomsky, "Degrees of Grammaticalness," pp. 384–389, and Paul Ziff, "On Understanding 'Understanding Utterances,' " pp. 390–399. Samuel R. Levin has briefly discussed ungrammatical poetry within a similar framework in *Linguistic Structures in Poetry* (The Hague, 1962), Chapters 2 and 3.

and should thus be a concrete noun, as should the object, "tale." Here and elsewhere in the poem the division between substance and abstraction tends to disappear. Again and again syntactic deviance breaks down categorical boundaries and converts juxtaposition into action, inanimate into human, abstract into physical, static into active. Now, much of Thomas' poetry displays the world as process, as interacting forces and repeating cycles, in which human beings and human thought are indifferently caught up.[6] I suggest that Thomas' syntactical irregularities often serve this vision of things. To say so, of course, is only to extend the natural critical premise that a good poet sets linguistic forms to work for him in the cause of artistic and thematic form. And if he strays from grammatical patterns he does not thereby leave language or reason behind: if anything, he draws the more deeply on linguistic structure and on the processes of human understanding that are implicit in our use of well-formed sentences.

Most of what I have said falls short of adequate precision, and much of the detail rests on conjecture about English grammar, which at this point is by no means fully understood. But I hope that in loosely stringing together several hypotheses about the fundamental role of the sentence I have indicated some areas where a rich exchange between linguistics and critical theory might eventually take place. To wit, the elusive intuition we have of *form* and *content* may turn out to be anchored in a distinction between the surface structures and the deep structures of sentences. If so, syntactic theory will also feed into the theory of *style*. Still more evidently, the proper *analysis* of styles waits on a satisfactory analysis of sentences. Matters of *rhetoric*, such as emphasis and order, also promise to come clearer as we better understand internal relations in sentences. More generally, we may be able to enlarge and deepen our concept of literary *structure* as we are increasingly able to make it subsume linguistic structure — including especially the structure of deviant sentences. And most important, since critical understanding follows and builds on understanding of sentences, generative grammar should eventually be a reliable assistant in the effort of seeing just how a given literary work sifts through a reader's mind, what cognitive and emotional processes it sets in motion, and what organization of experience it encourages. In so far as critical theory concerns itself with meaning, it cannot afford to bypass the complex and elegant structures that lie at the inception of all verbal meaning.

[6] Ralph Maud's fine study, *Entrances to Dylan Thomas' Poetry* (Pittsburgh, 1963), describes the phenomenon well in a chapter called "Process Poems."

Part Four

LITERARY FORM AND MEANING

This section concerns a more fundamental question than any other in this book, namely, what constitutes *literary,* as opposed to other, uses of language? What is literary form? How do works of literature mean?

Three essays — by Wheelwright, Miles, and Richards — consider the old problem of whether literature "means" in a way different from other kinds of discourse. Wheelwright concludes that poetic meaning is indeed of another order because its terms are "plurisigns" — i.e., they tend to operate in several different senses at once. This added connotative freight, this "polyvalence," is welcomed as a peculiar poetic virtue, although Wheelwright does not apparently mean by it what Empson means by "ambiguity." Miss Miles takes issue, urging the bad consequences of equating denotation with monosignificance as criterial for non-poetic discourse and connotation with plurisignificance as criterial for poetry. But we might also ask whether the terms of natural language (as opposed to the languages of mathematics or logic) are in fact pure monosigns. I. A. Richards' demonstration of how excessive commitment to polysemantic interpretation befuddles neophyte readers is a neat illustration of some of the dangers of the theory. Earlier in his essay, Mr. Richards takes up the delicate relations between literary construction and reconstruction, citing verbal associations that *are* legitimate, at least in the creative process. Not the least of these is phonological.

Ransom's explanation of the difference between poetry and other kinds of discourse is that versification inevitably introduces "obstructive, foreign matter" which becomes in the poetic crucible a vital though logically irrelevant local texture. The odd means by which meter and meaning reconcile themselves to each other is the central fact of poetry and what makes it the particular "embodied" thing it is. Ransom searches for an ontological base in the act of creating poetry, in the poetic process. His tone is that of the patient craftsman, reconciled to the inevitable compromise (the best he can make) that this difficult art forces upon its practitioners.

Mukařovský's concern is more directly linguistic. What manner of object is poetry? He finds it to be marked by a distortion of the standard language. ("Distortion," "violation," and "deviation" are similar terms — one should not assume that pejorative implications are intended.) Distortion is necessary to "foreground" ("highlight," "actualize," "deautomatize") aspects of the vernacular which have been stereotyped by the constant utilitarian uses to which it is put.

The idea is explicated in the semological diagram of Jakobson on page 299. Literary language focuses upon the message *per se,* whereby signs become "palpable" and "the fundamental dichotomy of signs and objects" is deepened (p. 302). This central tenet of Russian and Czech Formalist literary theory strikingly parallels Ransom's conception of the *iconic* nature of the literary sign, the dense "bodying forth" that distinguishes literary discourse from other kinds. The rest of Jakobson's essay discusses the means by which the focusing on the message takes place: by sound figures like meter and sound texture, and sense figures like parallelism, ambiguity, metaphor, and metonymy. Jakobson argues strongly for treating poetics as a subdivision of linguistics, in opposition to the arguments of Juilland (for which see below, pp. 374–384).

The section from Beardsley's book *Aesthetics* also seeks a semantic definition of literary language, but on different grounds. The criterion for him is the poet's special interest in and control of implicit (secondary, suggested, connotative) meaning. Admitting the vagueness of any final abstraction, "literature," he moves towards a specification of *kinds* of literature, in three main types: poems, essays, and prose fiction. The strength and orderliness of his argument can best be appreciated by reading later sections of his book on literary definition.

Jan Mukařovský

STANDARD LANGUAGE AND POETIC LANGUAGE

The problem of the relationship between the standard language and poetic language can be considered from two standpoints. The theorist of poetic language poses it about as follows: is the poet bound by the norms of the standard? Or perhaps: how does this norm assert itself in poetry? The theorist of the standard language, on the other hand, wants to know above all to what extent a work of poetry can be used as data for ascertaining the norm of the standard. In other words: the theory of poetic language is primarily interested in the differences between the standard and poetic language, whereas the theory of the standard language is mainly interested in the similarities between them. It is clear that with a good procedure no conflict can arise between the two directions of research; there is only a difference in the point of view and in the illumination of the problem. Our study approaches the problem of the relationship between poetic language and the standard from the vantage point of poetic language. Our procedure will be to subdivide the general problem into a number of special problems.

The first problem, by way of introduction, concerns the following: what is the *relationship* between the extension of *poetic language* and that of the *standard*, between the places of each in the total system of the whole language? Is poetic language a special brand of the standard, or is it an independent formation? — Poetic language cannot be called a brand of the standard, if for no other reason, then because poetic language has at its disposal, from the standpoint of lexicon, syntax, etc., all the forms of the given language, often of different developmental phases thereof. There are such works in which the lexical material is taken over completely from another form of language than the standard (thus, Villon's or Rictus' slang poetry in French literature). Different

Reprinted from the *Prague School Reader on Esthetics, Literary Structure, and Style*, by Paul L. Garvin, Institute of Languages and Linguistics, Georgetown University. Used with the permission of Paul L. Garvin and Georgetown University. Translation and interpolations are by Paul Garvin.

forms of the language may exist side by side in a work of poetry (for instance, in the dialogues of a novel dialect or slang, in the narrative passages the standard). Poetic language finally also has some of its own lexicon and phraseology, as well as some grammatical forms, the so-called poetisms, such as *zor* [gaze], *oř* [steed], *pláti* [be aflame], 3rd p. sg. *můž* [can; cf. Eng. *-th*, plg.] (a rich selection of examples can be found in the ironic description of "moon language" in [Svatopluk] Čech's *Výlet pana Broučka do měsíce* ["Mr. Brouček's Trip to the Moon"]). Only some schools of poetry, of course, have a positive attitude towards poetisms (among them the Lumír Group including Sv. Čech), others reject them.

Poetic language is thus not a brand of the standard. This is not to deny the close connection between the two, which consists in the fact that the standard language is for poetry the background against which is reflected the esthetically intentional distortion of the linguistic components of the work, in other words, the intentional violation of the norm of the standard. Let us, for instance, visualize a work in which this distortion is carried out by the interpenetration of dialect speech with the standard; it is clear then that it is not the standard which is perceived as a distortion of the dialect, but the dialect as a distortion of the standard, even then, if the dialect is quantitatively preponderant. The violation of the norm of the standard, its systematic violation, is what makes possible the poetic utilization of language; without this possibility there would be no poetry. The more the norm of the standard is stabilized in a given language, the more varied can be its violation, and therefore the more possibilities for poetry in that language. And on the other hand, the weaker the awareness of this norm, the fewer possibilities of violation, and hence the fewer possibilities for poetry. Thus, in the beginnings of Modern Czech poetry, when the awareness of the norm of the standard was weak, poetic neologisms with the purpose of violating the norm of the standard were little different from neologisms designed to gain general acceptance and become a part of the norm of the standard, so that they could be confused with them.

* * *

This relationship between poetic language and the standard, one which we could call negative, also has its positive side which is, however, more important for the theory of the standard language than for poetic language and its theory. Many of the linguistic components of a work of poetry do not deviate from the norm of the standard because they constitute the background against which the distortion of the other components is reflected. The theoretician of the standard language can therefore include works of poetry in his data, with the reservation that he will differentiate the distorted components from those that are not distorted. An assumption that all components have to agree with the norm of the standard would of course be erroneous.

The second special question which we shall attempt to answer concerns the different *function* of the two forms of language. This is the core of the problem. The function of poetic language consists in the maximum of foregrounding [aktualisace] of the utterance. Foregrounding is the opposite of automatization, that is, the deautomatization of an act; the more an act is automatized, the less it is consciously executed; the more it is foregrounded, the more completely conscious does it become. Objectively speaking: automatization schematizes an event, foregrounding means the violation of the scheme. The standard language in its purest form, as the language of science with formulation as its objective, avoids foregrounding: thus, a new expression, foregrounded because of its newness, is immediately automatized in a scientific treatise by an exact definition of its meaning. Foregrounding is, of course, common in the standard language, for instance, in journalistic style, even more in essays. But it is here always subordinate to communication: its purpose is to attract the reader's (listener's) attention more closely to the *subject matter* expressed by the foregrounded means of expression. All that has here been said about foregrounding and automatization in the standard language has been treated in detail in Havránek's paper in this cycle; we are here concerned with poetic language. In poetic language foregrounding achieves maximum intensity to the extent of pushing communication into the background as the objective of expression, and of being used for its own sake; it is not used in the services of communication, but in order to place in the foreground the act of expression, the act of speech itself. The question is then one of how this maximum of foregrounding is achieved in poetic language. The idea might arise that this is a quantitive effect, a matter of the foregrounding of the largest number of components, perhaps of all of them together. This would be a mistake, although only a theoretical one, since in practice such a complete foregrounding of all the components is impossible. The foregrounding of any one of the components is necessarily accompanied by the automatization of one or more of the other components; thus, for instance, the foregrounded intonation in [Jaroslav] Vrchlický and [Svatopluk] Čech has necessarily pushed to the lowest level of automatization the meaning of the word as a unit, because the foregrounding of its meaning would give the word phonetic independence as well and lead to a disturbance of the uninterrupted flow of the intonational (melodic) line; an example of the degree to which the semantic independence of the word in context manifests itself also as intonational independence can be found in [Karel] Toman's verse. The foregrounding of intonation as an uninterrupted melodic line is thus linked to the semantic "emptiness" for which the Lumír Group has been criticized by the younger generation as being "verbalistic." — In addition to the practical impossibility of the foregrounding of all components, it can also be pointed out that the simultaneous foregrounding of all the components of a work of poetry is unthinkable. This is because the foregrounding of a component implies precisely its being placed in the foreground; the unit in the foreground, however, occupies this position by comparison with another unit or units that remain in the background. A simultaneous general foregrounding would thus bring all the components into the same plane and thus become a new automatization.

The devices by which poetic language achieves its maximum of foregrounding must therefore be sought somewhere else than in the quantity of foregrounded components. They consist in the consistency and systematic character of foregrounding. The consistency manifests itself in the fact that the reshaping of the foregrounded component within a given work occurs in a stable direction; thus, the deautomatization of meanings in a certain work is consistently carried out by lexical selection (the mutual interlarding of contrasting areas of the lexicon), in another equally consistently by the uncommon semantic relationship of words close together in the context. Both procedures result in a foregrounding of meaning, but differently for each. The systematic foregrounding of components in a work of poetry consists in the graduation of the interrelationships of these components, that is, in their mutual subordination and superordination. The component highest in the hierarchy becomes the dominant. All other components, foregrounded or not, as well as their interrelationships, are evaluated from the standpoint of the dominant. The dominant is that component of the work which sets in motion, and gives direction to, the relationships of all other components. The material of a work of poetry is intertwined with the interrelationships of the components even if it is in a completely unforegrounded state. There is thus always present, in communicative speech as well, the potential relationship between intonation and meaning, syntax, word order, or the relationship of the word as a meaningful unit to the phonetic structure of the text, to the lexical selection found in the text, to other words as units of meaning in the context of the same sentence. It can be said that each linguistic component is by means of these multiple interrelationships in some way, directly or indirectly, linked to every other component. In communicative speech these relationships are for the most part merely potential, because attention is not called to their presence and to their mutual relationship. It is, however, enough to disturb the equilibrium of this system at some point and the entire network of relationships is slanted in a certain direction and follows it in its internal organization: tension arises in one portion of this network (by consistent unidirectional foregrounding), while the remaining portions of the network are relaxed (by automatization perceived as an intentionally arranged background). This internal organization of relationships will be different in terms of the point affected, that is, in terms of the dominant. More concretely: sometimes intonation will be governed by meaning (by various procedures), sometimes, on the other hand, the meaning structure will be determined by intonation; sometimes again, the relationship of a word to the lexicon may be foregrounded, then again its relationship to the phonetic structure of the text. Which of the possible relationships will be foregrounded, which will remain automatized, and what will be the direction of foregrounding — whether from component A to component B or vice versa, all this depends on the dominant.

The dominant thus creates the unity of the work of poetry. It is, of course, a unity of its own kind, the nature of which in esthetics is usually designated as "unity in variety," a dynamic unity in which we at the same time perceive harmony and disharmony, convergence and divergence. The convergence is given by the trend towards the dominant, the divergence by the resistance of the unmoving background of unforegrounded components against this trend. Components may appear unforegrounded from the standpoint of the standard language, or from the standpoint of the poetic canon, that is, the set of firm and stable norms into which the structure of a preceding school of poetry has dissolved by automatization, when it is no longer perceived as an indivisible and undissociable whole. In other words, it is possible in some cases for a component which is foregrounded in terms of the norms of the standard, not to be foregrounded in a certain work because it is in accord with the automatized poetic canon. Every work of poetry is perceived against the background of a certain tradition, that is, of some automatized canon, with regard to which it constitutes a distortion. The outward manifestation of this automatization is the ease with which creation is possible in terms of this canon, the proliferation of epigones, the liking for obsolescent poetry in circles not close to literature. Proof of the intensity with which a new trend in poetry is perceived as a distortion of the traditional canon is the negative attitude of conservative criticism, which considers deliberate deviations from the canon errors against the very essence of poetry.

The background which we perceive behind the work of poetry as consisting of the unforegrounded components resisting foregrounding, is thus dual: the norm of the standard language, and the traditional esthetic canon. Both backgrounds are always potentially present, though one of them will predominate in the concrete case. In periods of powerful foregrounding of linguistic elements, the background of the norm of the standard predominates, in periods of moderate foregrounding that of the traditional canon. If the latter has strongly distorted the norm of the standard, then its moderate distortion may in turn constitute a renewal of the norm of the standard, and this precisely because of its moderation. The mutual relationships of the components of the work of poetry, both foregrounded and unforegrounded, constitute its *structure*, a dynamic structure including both convergence and divergence, and one that constitutes an undissociable artistic whole, since each of its components has its value precisely in terms of its relation to the totality.

It is thus obvious that the possibility of distorting the norm of the standard, if we henceforth limit ourselves to this particular background of foregrounding, is indispensable to poetry. Without it, there would be no poetry. To criticize as faults the deviations from the norm of the standard, especially in a period which, like the present, tends towards a powerful foregrounding of linguistic components, means to reject poetry. It could be countered that in some works of poetry, or rather in some genres, only the "content" (subject matter) is foregrounded, so that the above remarks do not concern them. To this it must be noted that in a work of poetry of any genre there is no fixed border, nor, in a certain sense, any essential difference, between the language and the subject matter. The subject matter of a work of poetry cannot be judged by its relationship to the extralinguistic reality entering into the work; it is rather a component of the semantic side of the work (we do not want to assert, of course, that its relationship to reality can not become a factor of its structure, as for instance in realism). The proof of this statement could be given rather extensively; let us, however, limit ourselves to the most important point: the question of truthfulness does not apply in regard to the subject matter of a work of poetry, nor does it even make sense. Even if we posed the question and answered it positively or negatively as the case may be, the question has no bearing on the artistic value of the work; it can only serve to determine the extent to which the work has documentary value. If in some work of poetry there is emphasis on the question of truthfulness (as in [Vladislav] Vančura's short story *Dobrá míra* ["The Good Measure"]), this emphasis only serves the purpose of giving the subject matter a certain semantic coloration. The status of subject matter is entirely different in case of communicative speech. There a certain relationship of the subject matter to reality is an important value, a necessary prerequisite. Thus, in the case of a newspaper report the question whether a certain event has occurred or not is obviously of basic significance.

The subject matter of a work of poetry is thus its largest semantic unit. In terms of being meaning, it has certain properties which are not directly based on the linguistic sign, but are linked to it insofar as the latter is a general semiological unit (especially the independence of any specific signs, or sets of signs, so that the same subject matter may without basic changes be rendered by different linguistic devices, or even transposed into a different set of signs altogether, as in the transposition of subject matter from one art form to another), but this difference in properties does not affect the semantic character of the subject matter. It thus holds even for works and genres of poetry in which the subject matter is the dominant that the latter is not the "equivalent" of a reality to be expressed by the work as effectively (for instance, as truthfully) as possible, but that it is a part of the structure, is governed by its laws, and is evaluated in terms of its relationship to it. If this is the case, then it holds for the novel as well as for the lyrical poem that to deny a work of poetry the right to violate the norm of the standard is equivalent to the negation of poetry. It cannot be said of the novel that here the linguistic elements are the esthetically indifferent expression of content, not even if they appear to be completely devoid of foregrounding: the structure is the total of all the components, and its dynamics arise precisely from the tension between the foregrounded and unforegrounded components. There are, incidentally, many novels and short stories in which the linguistic components are clearly foregrounded. Changes effected in the interest of correct language would thus even in the case of prose often interfere with the very essence of the work; this would, for instance, happen if the author or even translator decided, as was asked in *Naše Řeč*, to eliminate "superfluous" relative clauses.

* * *

Let us now return to the main topic of our study and attempt to draw some conclusions from what was said above of the relationship between the standard and poetic language.

Poetic language is a different form of language with a different function from that of the standard. It is therefore equally unjustified to call all poets without exception creators of the standard language, as it is to make them responsible for its present state. This is not to deny the possibility of utilizing poetry as data for the scientific description of the norm of the standard, nor the fact that the development of the norm of the standard does not occur uninfluenced by poetry. The distortion of the norm of the standard is, however, of the very essence of poetry, and it is therefore improper to ask poetic language to abide by this norm. This was clearly formulated as early as 1913 by Ferdinand Brunot ("L'autorité en matière de langage," *Die neueren Sprachen*, vol. XX): "Modern art, individualistic in essence, can not always and everywhere be satisfied with the standard language alone. The laws governing the usual communication of thought must not, lest it be unbearable tyranny, be categorically imposed upon the poet who beyond the bounds of the accepted forms of language may find personalized forms of intuitive expression. It is up to him to use them in accord with his creative intuition and without other limits than those imposed by his own inspiration. Public opinion will give the final verdict." It is interesting to compare Brunot's statement to one of Haller's of 1931 (*Problém jazykové správnosti*, op. cit. 3): "Our writers and poets in their creative effort attempt to replace the thorough knowledge of the material of the language by some sort of imaginary ability of which they themselves are not too sincerely convinced. They lay claim to a right which can but be an unjust privilege. Such an ability, instinct, inspiration, or what have you, cannot exist in and of itself; just as the famous feel for the language, it can only be the final result of previous cognition, and without consciously leaning on the finished material of the language, it is no more certain than any other arbitrary act." If we compare Brunot's statement to Haller's, the basic difference is clear without further comment. Let us also mention Jungmann's critique of Polák's *Vznešenost přírody* [*The Nobility of Nature*] cited elsewhere in this study . . . Jungmann has there quite accurately pointed out as a characteristic feature of poetic language its "uncommonness," that is, its distortedness. — In spite of all that has been said here, the condition of the norm of the standard language is not without its significance to poetry, since the norm of the standard is precisely the background against which the structure of the work of poetry is projected, and in regard to which it is perceived as a distortion; the structure of a work of poetry can change completely if it is after a certain time from its origin projected against the background of a norm of the standard which has since changed.

In addition to the relationship of the norm of the standard to poetry, there is also the opposite relationship, that of poetry to the norm of the standard. We have already spoken of the influence of poetic language on the development of the standard; some remarks remain to be added. First of all, it is worth mentioning that the poetic foregrounding of linguistic phenomena, since it is its own purpose, can not have the purpose of creating new means of communication (as Vossler and his school think). If anything passes from poetic language into the standard, it becomes a loan in the same way as anything taken over by the standard from any other linguistic milieu; even the motivation of the borrowing may be the same: a loan from poetic language may likewise be taken over for extraesthetic, that is, communicative reasons, and conversely the motivation for borrowings from other functional dialects, such as slang, may be esthetic. Borrowings from poetic language are beyond the scope of the poet's intent. Thus, poetic neologisms arise as intentionally esthetic new formations, and their basic features are unexpectedness, unusualness, and uniqueness. Neologisms created for communicative purposes, on the other hand, tend towards common derivation patterns and easy classifiability in a certain lexical category; these are the properties allowing for their general usability. If, however, *poetic* neologisms were formed in view of their general usability, their esthetic function would be thereby endangered; they are therefore formed in an unusual manner, with considerable violence to the language, as regards both form and meaning.

* * *

The relationship between poetic language and the standard, their mutual approximation or increasing distance, changes from period to period. But even within the same period, and with the same norm of the standard, this relationship need not be the same for all poets. There are, generally speaking, three possibilities: the writer, say a novelist, may either not distort the linguistic components of his work at all (but this non-distortion is, as was shown above, in itself a fact of the total structure of his work), or he may distort it, but subordinate the linguistic distortion to the subject matter, by giving substandard color to his lexicon in order to characterize personages and situations, for instance, or finally, he may distort the linguistic components in and of themselves, by either subordinating the subject matter to the linguistic deformation, or emphasizing the contrast between the subject matter and its linguistic expression. An example of the first possibility might be [Jakub] Arbes, of the second, some realistic novelists such as T. Nováková or Z. Winter, of the third, [Vladislav] Vančura. It is obvious that as one goes from the first possibility to the third, the divergence between poetic language and the standard increases. This classification has of course been highly schematized for purposes of simplicity; the real situation is much more complex.

The problem of the relationship between the standard and poetic language does not, however, exhaust the significance of poetry as the art form which uses language as its material, for the standard language, or for the language of a nation in general. The very existence of poetry in a certain language has fundamental importance for this language. . . . By the very fact of foregrounding, poetry increases and refines the ability to handle language in general, it gives the language the ability to adjust more flexibly to new requirements, and it gives it a richer differentiation of its means of expression. Foregrounding brings to the surface and before the eyes of the observer even such linguistic phenomena as remain quite covert in communicative speech, although they are important factors in language. Thus, for instance, Czech symbolism, especially O. Březina's poetry, has brought to the fore of linguistic consciousness the essence of sentence meaning and the dynamic nature of sentence construction. From the standpoint of communicative speech, the meaning of a sentence appears as the total of the gradually accumulated meanings of the individual words, that is, without having independent existence. The real nature of the phenomenon is covered up by the automatization of the semantic design of the sentence. Words and sentences appear to follow each other with obvious necessity, as determined only by the nature of the message. Then there appears a work of poetry in which the relationship between the meanings of the individual words and the subject matter of the sentence has been foregrounded. The words here do not succeed each other naturally and inconspicuously, but within the sentence there occur semantic jumps, breaks, not conditioned by the requirements of communication, but given in the language itself. The device for achieving these sudden breaks is the constant intersection of the plane of basic meaning with the plane of figurative and metaphorical meaning; some words are for a certain part of the context to be understood in their figurative meaning, in other parts in their basic meaning, and such words, carrying a dual meaning, are precisely the points at which there are semantic breaks. There is also foregrounding of the relationship between the subject matter of the sentence and the words, as well as of the semantic interrelationships of the words in the sentence. The subject matter of the sentence then appears as the center of attraction given from the beginning of the sentence, the effect of the subject matter on the words and of the words on the subject matter is revealed, and the determining force can be felt with which every word affects every other. The sentence comes alive before the eyes of the speech community: the structure is revealed as a concert of forces. (What was here formulated discursively, must of course be imagined as an unformulated intuitive cognition stored away for the future in the consciousness of the speech community.) Examples can be multiplied at will, but we shall cite no more. We wanted to give evidence for the statement that the main importance of poetry for language lies in the fact that it is an art.

Philip Wheelwright

ON THE SEMANTICS OF POETRY

Discussions about poetry incur a double danger. There is the danger of spoiling the poem under discussion by over-analysis, or by inopportune or inappropriate analysis; and there is the danger of losing sight of the poem in an effort to settle something about the poet's life, about the philosophy espoused, about implicit sociological tendencies, or about clinical effects upon the reader. The first danger can be avoided only by the good sense and good taste of the critic. So long as he keeps his undistracted attention upon the poem itself the delicacy and depth of his appreciation will be the main determinants of critical success, and the achievement of these qualities is a matter of gradual, associative education.

The second danger, that of sliding imperceptibly from a discussion of the poem into a discussion of something with which the poem has historical or conceptual or functional connections, is more definite and therefore more remediable. While a good deal of such divagation can probably be explained by the critic's obtuseness to, and consequent lack of interest in, the *poetry* of a poem, or by his attribution of this negative condition to his readers, or by his better familiarity with adjacent fields, or by his reasoned belief that serious interest in poetry is a contemporary anachronism, I suspect that a more direct obstacle to interpretative relevance in discussing a poem is *semantic*. We desire clarity, and our temptation therefore is to steer away from direct consideration of the poem, where clarity is incalculably difficult, into fields such as psychology, sociology, biography, ethics, or textual criticism, where clarity of a sort is already established. Of course the clarities found within these fields are not the clarities of poetry, they do not include the specific clarity that is sought in the appreciation of some particular poem; nevertheless they have the advantage of being utterable in a way that can be rather widely understood. They have achieved, in each case, their almost proper language.

It is important to understand what these several fields peripheral to poetry have in common. All of them, whatever their incidental differences of empha-

Reprinted from *The Kenyon Review* by permission of the author. This material appears in revised form in a book entitled *The Burning Fountain,* by Philip Wheelwright, copyright and published by Indiana University Press.

sis and idiom, share an aim, an instrument, and a presupposition. Their aim, a *marketable* type of clarity; their instrument, conceptual language, guided implicitly by the canons of formal logic; their presupposition (as a rear line of defense to their instrument), the identification of meaning with conceptual meaning, of truth with propositional truth. That this aim, this instrument, and perhaps even this presupposition have a large utilitarian value, is evident enough. What I want to show is that since poetry reveals a different aim and employs a different instrument, we must build any critical discussion of it upon a different presupposition.

A poem does convey something — a mood, a hint, sometimes a clue, though never, I suspect, a completely expounded answer. Poetry is never entirely sober; its acquaintance with the logic of sobriety is casual and varying. But it has its own deep seriousness (which is not the same as sobriety), its own modes of expression and laws of movement. The problem of the interpretative critic who fixes his eye upon the object (the poem) is semantic in this sense: it concerns the finding of a language adequate to state how poetry, as distinguished from logic and history and science, goes about its business.

What I am proposing in this essay is a sort of Copernican Revolution in semantics. Or perhaps non-Euclidean, or trans-Euclidean, would express the analogy more exactly. For whereas Euclidean geometry was once regarded as the be-all and end-all of geometrical truth, modern mathematicians are able to regard a world in which the postulate of parallels holds true, as merely a *limiting case* (perhaps also an actual case) in the universe of possibilities. Analogously, we may regard the logical positivists, whether scholars like Dr. Carnap or crusaders like Mr. Stuart Chase, as residing a little too doggedly in a Euclidean-like world. The aim, the instrument, and the presuppositions of logical discourse, as developed by the formal and experimental sciences, they accept without serious question. And my belief is that they are wrong, dead wrong, — not of course in the contributions they have made to logical clarity in fields where it is applicable, but in their refusal to admit the possibility of meanings other than those which logical language can express. Not only in poetry are such *metalogical* meanings found: they are of dominant importance in religion, in all the arts that "say" anything, and in moral wisdom as distinguished from moral rules; they are present helter-skelter in the vagaries of daily experience; and they even, I suspect, play a bigger rôle than is usually admitted in science, particularly when it comes to the discovery of fresh hypotheses. Accordingly, what any adequate theory of semantics should include, and what most contemporary theories omit, is an exposition, so far as the nebulous nature of the material allows, of the basic principles of metalogical signification. No such general exposition will be attempted in the present essay however, which is limited to a study of the semantics of poetry alone, — of *how* poetry means, of the sense in which poetry can assert and thus be judged true or false, and of the difference and relations between poetic meanings and the meanings of science and logic.

I

Starting at the *atomic* level of meaning, where we consider the smallest ingredients of meaning distinguishable in logical (or "literal") and poetic language respectively, we may declare: *the atomic ingredient of literal language is the monosign* (called in logic the "term"); *the atomic ingredient of poetic language tends to be the plurisign.* An understanding of what the plurisign is, and how related to and distinguished from the monosign which it approaches as an unreached limit, is prerequisite to clear discussion about poetry. Mr. William Empson in *Seven Types of Ambiguity* has made a survey of prominent types of plurisignation; unfortunately he has confused the matter by his misconception of ambiguity, which differs from plurisignation as "either-or" differs from "both-and." The one is a looseness and duplicity of reference in would-be literal language, the other is a controlled variation and plurality of reference in language that deliberately transcends the literal. The positive nature of plurisignation may be observed in the following aspects.

(1) *The meaning of the monosign is invariant, the meaning of the plurisign is partly contextual.* The law of the monosign is what logicians call the Law of Identity, "A is A": wherever the symbol A is used in a given science or a given discussion, let its meaning be identical in all instances. The safeguard of a monosign's meaning is its definition. I am not inquiring whether the ideal of monosignation is ever perfectly realized; at all events it is what logical discourse aims at, and the first cardinal sin from the logician's standpoint is equivocation. Thus Hobbes has declared that "in all discourses wherein one man pretends to instruct or convince another, he should use the same word constantly in the same sense," — a requirement which, he adds, "nobody can refuse without great disingenuity." Hobbes's view is incontestable when language is used for the purposes which he indicates. But the aim of poetic language is not to "instruct or convince." It is to adumbrate a living insight, and in order not to kill the insight thus adumbrated the language too must be alive. Hart Crane expresses this opposite standpoint when he declares: "As a poet I may very possibly be more interested in the so-called illogical impingements of the connotations of words on the consciousness (and their combinations and interplay in metaphor on this basis) than I am interested in the preservation of their logically rigid significations at the cost of limiting my subject matter and perceptions involved in the poem." The antinomy constituted by these two quotations is easily resolved. Both Hobbes and Crane are individually right: the one speaks as a logician and social scientist, the other as a poet; the one, therefore, requires monosignative clarity, the other achieves what clarity he can amid the manifold impingements of connotative discourse.

A monosign is but the corpse of a once living idea; it may still have fertilizing powers in minds which know how to use it, but in itself it is dead. A plurisign, on the other hand, is alive because it draws fresh life and meaning from each new context. As no two experiences are ever exactly identical, so in poetic language, which keeps as close as possible to the experiential flow, the meaning of a word is in each instance determined partly by the specific context of words, rhythms, images, mythological allusions, etc., in which it occurs. Sometimes the variation of meaning thus produced is more marked than at others. Mr. Empson, on pp. 45–50 of the book just cited, analyzes an excellent example of controlled variation of meaning quoted from Sidney. Shakespeare is a gold mine of examples: his ability to control meanings contextually is unsurpassed. Sometimes, in the comedies and in comic interludes in the tragedies, this degenerates into punning. But in serious passages the effect can become profoundly dramatic: e.g., in the play upon the word "time" in King Richard's final soliloquy (*Richard II:* V. v.).

(2) Not only may the plurisign alter its meanings from instance to instance; it tends also to carry a plurality of meanings in any given instance. This is only to say that the poet uses charged language, associative language, language that stirs both thought and feeling, and perhaps several thoughts and several feelings at once. This fullness of connotation is not always decipherable into a definite multiplicity of reference, but sometimes it is. In fact, from the standpoint of denotative definiteness we may distinguish three types of simultaneous plurisignation.

(i) Sometimes in poetic language two or more simultaneous meanings of a plurisign are clearly distinguishable: i.e., there are two or more denotations joined together in one symbol. A pun is the simplest example of such explicit multiple reference; most puns, however, combine two monosigns mechanically, with a virtual absence of emotional connotation, and so are not poetic. But when the Nurse promises Juliet "To fetch a ladder, by the which your love Must climb a bird's nest soon when it is dark," the uninhibited reader will attach two quite distinct pictures to "climb a bird's nest," which, as their combination is apt and delightful in itself and suitable to the movement of the drama, constitute a genuinely poetic bit of plurisignation. Examples abound. Not only words and phrases but images, statements, and even whole narratives may be plurisignative in this first sense. Numerous images in Dante's *Commedia* are familiar examples: e.g., Virgil, Beatrice, the three beasts, the darkness of Hell, etc. Allegory is simply an extended plurisignation of this kind, carried out systematically as a relation between a set of primary denotations ("literal meaning") and a set of secondary denotations ("allegorical meaning").

(ii) More often only one meaning of a plurisign is denotative, i.e., such as could be adequately represented by some monosign; while the remaining meanings are purely connotative — felt rather than thought — and, although controlled to a high degree by the context, do not have the kind of precision that would enable them to be expressed satisfactorily by monosigns. Probably the greater part of poetry is of this type. "Pray you, undo this button": the request is plain, the denotation single, but the connotative meanings, determined by the context of King Lear's final tragic situation, are tremendous.

And perhaps the immediately preceding line, with its one word repeated five times with shattering effect, is a still better example. It may be added that even in allegorical poetry, where two or more denotative meanings are simultaneously present, there are irreducible emotional overtones, i.e., connotative meanings, as well. It is this transcendent, unanalyzable quality of beauty and mystery that distinguishes a poetic allegory such as the *Divine Comedy* from the allegorical bathos of many a Sunday School tract.

(iii) Finally, a poetic plurisign may carry no denotative meaning, i.e., no conceptually definite meaning at all; it is almost purely evocative, and its referential function approaches zero. The word "expressionism" may be employed, somewhat more broadly than has been customary, to designate poetry of this type. Poetry here approximates to the condition of music: it no longer means, but simply *is*. I doubt that poetry ever quite reaches this pure state, or that it could be recognized as poetry if it did. Nevertheless, lyric songs, choral chants, occasional passages of Swinburne, Lewis Carroll, Rimbaud, Cummings, Hart Crane, Gertrude Stein and others move distinctively far in this direction. We may regard the strictly logical use of language as one pole, the purely evocative, unreferential use as its opposite pole, and poetic language as swinging airily between them, never quite reaching either, on pain of losing either its poetic or its linguistic character.

(3) The recognition of an evocative quality as co-present everywhere in genuine poetry along with whatever specific denotations the poem may carry, suggests a further distinction between the literal and poetic uses of language, i.e., between monosign and plurisign. It may be stated thus: *the monosign is purely referential, the plurisign is to some degree reflexive and evocative*. The monosign is referential in the sense that what it means, what it refers to, its referend, is something distinct from itself. This is proved and illustrated by the familiar fact that a monosign is exactly translatable: the words Hund, chien, and dog "mean the same thing," which proves that the meaning of these words is independent of the particular word chosen to express it. The plurisign, on the other hand, while never entirely lacking in referential function, is at the same time semantically reflexive in the sense that it *is* a part of what it means. That is to say, the plurisign, the poetic symbol, is not merely employed but enjoyed; its value is not entirely instrumental but largely aesthetic, intrinsic.

II

We pass next to the *molecular* level of meaning, investigating the simpler semantic combinations into which monosigns and plurisigns are arranged. At this level the difference between the two uses of language may be stated thus: *the molecular constituent of literal language is the proposition; the molecular constituent of poetic language is the poetic statement*.

A proposition may be defined as *an assertible relation between monosigns.*

By an assertible relation I mean a relation to which the terms true and false can be significantly applied. Thus "Bread is edible" is a proposition, while "Give us this day our daily bread" and "Cast your bread upon the waters" are not. Prayers and commands, questions and ejaculations, since they cannot properly be judged true or false, are not propositions; although they may imply concealed propositions, as when we ask "Have you recovered?" of a man who may not have been ill. A proposition, then, is that species of relation between monosigns that can be asserted as true or false, or as partly the one and partly the other, or as probably or possibly one or the other. The antithesis true vs. false is assumed in all literal language to be, in the last analysis, absolute.

A poetic statement, by contrast, is a *quasi-assertible relation between plurisigns*. I say "quasi-assertible" because it is clear to a reflective lover of poetry that poetic statements involve no such sharp antithesis between true and false as is involved in logical propositions. Do they then involve any sort of truth and falsity at all? I think they do, and it is important to see in what sense this is possible; in what sense there can be such a thing as poetic truth, distinguishable from and unexchangeable with any strictly logical truth.

The possibility, in the sense here intended, has been denied by so generally intelligent a critic as Dr. I. A. Richards, whose views in this respect it is valuable to consider. In *Science and Poetry* (1926) Dr. Richards attacked the following problem. Poetry has persistently the air of making statements, and important ones; yet many such statements, judged by ordinary standards, are false. How then can we accept — that is, in what sense can we accept — a poem that appears to be composed of false statements?

Dr. Richards solves the difficulty by his well-known distinction between statements and pseudo-statements. Briefly: Science consists of statements, poetry consists essentially of pseudo-statements. "A statement . . . is justified by its truth, i.e., its correspondence . . . with the fact to which it points." A pseudo-statement has nothing to do with truth in this sense. It is "a form of words which is justified entirely by its effect in releasing or organizing our impulses and attitudes." Considered as a statement it may be true, or false, or doubtful, or a confused mixture of true, false and doubtful elements. A false or doubtful statement, no less than a true one, may touch off attitudes and actions, as religious chants and political propaganda will bear witness. But considered as a pseudo-statement it is true in a special sense of the word "true" — i.e., poetically, not scientifically true — "if it suits and serves some attitude or links together attitudes which on other grounds are desirable." Here, then, the dualism is seen in all its sharpness: a statement is scientifically true if it corresponds with an outwardly verifiable fact; poetically true — i.e., true as a pseudo-statement — if, regardless of whether or not it corresponds with any outward fact, it successfully organizes some phase of our impulsive and emotional life.

In an article "Between Truth and Truth" (1931) Dr. Richards elaborated his dualism. Two years earlier, in *Practical Criticism,* he had pursued more fully the question of communication in literature. From that standpoint he now reformulated his position. A poem, he now declared, describes and communicates something, but what? "Two alternatives, and not more I think, are before us, two main senses of 'describe' and 'communicate' . . . The first sense is that in which a form of words describes or communicates the state of mind or experience of the speaker; the second is that in which it describes or communicates some state of affairs or fact which the speaker is thinking of or knowing (something in all but one case, that of introspection, *other than* the experience which is his thinking of it or knowing it) . . . To take an extreme instance, when a man says 'I'm damned!' he may be saying that eternal judgment has gone against him or showing that he is surprised or annoyed."

Dr. Richards then turns to John Clare's description of the primrose —

With its crimp and curdled leaf
And its little brimming eye,

about which, in a previous article, Mr. J. Middleton Murry had remarked that it "is surely an accurate description, but accurate with an accuracy unknown to and unachievable by science." Richards complains: Mr. Murry "does not say explicitly whether he takes it as a description of an object (the primrose) or of the experience of seeing one." And he adds: "It seems to me not likely that there will be widespread disagreement with the view that the description applies to the experience of seeing or imagining a primrose rather than to actual primroses."

Clearly Dr. Richards has fallen without realizing it into the trap of metaphysics. This is particularly evident in a footnote to the article just mentioned, where he distinguishes the "sensed or imagined primrose" from the "inferred or constructed common or gardener's primrose" on the ground that the former lacks such scientifically determinable characteristics as weight! Now take this in connection with his distinction in *Coleridge on Imagination* (1934) between "utterances as facts of mind" and "the supposed states of affairs which we take them to be utterances about," and Dr. Richards' general presupposition becomes clear. It is the assumption of scientific positivism, in line with Comte and Carnap, that scientifically determinable objects, like the gardener's primrose which can be weighed, are the only objects there are, and the only objects which can significantly be talked about: that when a poet appears to be talking about anything else he is really not talking about anything objective at all; he is merely representing the history of his mind, "his feelings and attitudes in the moment of speaking, and conditions of their governance in the future" (*op. cit.*). To be sure, Dr. Richards regards the poet's total poetic speech act as "a larger and more complex whole" which besides expressing the poet's subjective experiences does also refer to a supposed state of affairs in the actual world; that is to say, the poetry has a referential and denotative as well as an expressive and connotative function. But it is just in this way of stating the double function of poetry that I think Dr. Richards goes astray. For connotations too may be outwardly referential. Naturally I do not deny that poetry does and should express in some sense the poet's feelings, nor that it may and should have for a reader the beneficent and equilibrating effects described in *Principles of Literary Criticism.* All this is important, but it is not, strictly speaking, the business of the literary critic. Every science has its proper object, and this is as true of literary criticism as of any other science. The object of literary criticism is the poem under consideration, and not either the poet's supposed feelings or the reader's expected benefits. The task of a semantics of poetry, then, is to find a language whereby the nature and reference of the poetic statement (which I take to be a more suitable and less misleading term than 'pseudo-statement') can be articulated without evasion into a field of discourse peripheral and alien to poetry.

The answer, it seems to me, is this. A poetic statement differs from a literal statement not, as Dr. Richards thinks, in that the one has a merely subjective, the other an objective reference, — at least this is an unnecessary and generally irrelevant difference — but in their manner of asserting. There are differences of what may be called *assertive weight.* A literal statement asserts heavily: it can do so because its terms are solid. A poetic statement, on the other hand, consisting as it does in a conjunction or association of plurisigns, has no such solid foundation, and affirms with varying degrees of lightness.

A stanza from Carl Rakosi's *A Journey Far Away* will at once illustrate and confirm this distinction:

An ideal
like a canary
singing in the dark
for appleseed and barley.

While I am not privy to Mr. Rakosi's intentions I take it to be evident that what he is talking about is an ideal and a canary, and not — not directly at least — about his feelings toward them. His feelings are "expressed," to be sure, and roughly similar feelings are stirred in the reader; but that is the psychologist's business. The business of the semanticist is to discover what is being talked about, what is being referred to; he is not concerned with causes and effects. The question then is, what Rakosi is saying and how he is saying it; which becomes pretty clear when we experiment with the sacrilege of translating the stanza into a literal proposition. A single word effects the translation: the copula "is." But how destructive of the original quality of affirmation that word turns out to be! "An ideal is like a canary singing in the dark for appleseed and barley." Note what has been done. Not only has the reader-response been altered through a lessening of the pleasure with which the utterance is received: more than that, the very nature of the affirmation has been changed. This prose version, we feel, overstates its case, it affirms too heavily: no ideal is as much like a canary as that! Rakosi's original utterance did not belabor the point; it suggested only that between an ideal and a canary singing in the dark for appleseed and barley there could be a slight and lovely connection, too tenuous to be expressed by the harsh word "is." So delicate an affirmation does not seriously jostle our other beliefs; we can accept it as true without mental inconvenience. But the literal statement, by reason of its assertive heaviness, falsifies.

Assertive weight should be distinguished from the strength or force of a poetic statement. As an indication of the difference:

> "My heart is like a singing bird
>   Whose nest is in a water-shoot;
> My heart is like an apple-tree
>   Whose boughs are bent with thick-set fruit . . ."
>
> "Come, Miss Rossetti, hearts aren't in the least like apple-trees,
>   you know!"

From this scrap of badinage it is clear that the lighter assertion can be the more forceful, the heavier assertion ridiculously weak. Indeed the combination of poetic delicacy and poetic strength is one of the prime distinguishing marks of authentic poetry.

A poetic statement, then, does not assert its claims so heavily as a proposition; its truth is more fragile. A poem is a complex tension among variously related plurisigns. Some phases of the poetic tension have more of an assertive character than others; and as the assertive character becomes more pronounced a phase of the poetic tension may approximate the character of a literal statement, without ceasing however to be much more. A phase of the poetic tension may contain a literal statement as one of its aspects. When Macbeth cries

> If it were done when 'tis done, then 'twere well
>   It were done quickly —

his words contain an unmistakable literal meaning. This literal meaning could be expressed equally well, from a literal standpoint, in another arrangement of words, as: "If the effects of the deed could but terminate with the performance, it would be well to finish the matter off as quickly as possible." But this literal meaning is only one aspect of the full poetic meaning, and to restate it in the second phraseology is to wrench it away from the associated poetic meanings of the original. The principal poetic meaning in the passage is expressed in the thematic use of the word "done," repeated three times like the tolling of a dirge. Directly and literally the passage asserts the logical proposition which I have just formulated; this is its meaning to the reader's intellect. But if the reader reads with his sensibilities as well as his intellect, he will hear in that insistent repetition of the word "done" a tragic reminder of the irrevocability of a deed once performed. The reminder is expressed obliquely, but in some mysterious way it gains in power by its very obliquity. Now in much the same way that Bach so often passes from a theme in a minor to a final chord in the major key, Shakespeare again and again in his plays marks the close of an emotional sequence by passing from an oblique to a correspondingly literal statement. Thus after a number of variations have been played upon the "done" theme, Lady Macbeth concludes the matter by declaring explicitly (III. ii) "What's done is done," and again in the sleep-walking scene (V. i) "What's done cannot be undone." In the word "done" as used suggestively throughout the play we have a plurisign, which in these two quasi-literal remarks of Lady Macbeth approximates but does not quite reach the character of a monosign. Correspondingly, Lady Macbeth's two statements approximate but do not quite reach the character of propositions.

Take another illustration from the same play: the transition from Scene i to Scene ii of the first act. The continuity of this transition, although evident to anyone conscious of the imagistic pattern, has been overlooked by those interpreters who challenge the authenticity of Scene ii, and is concealed from a modern theater audience by the exigencies of scene-changing. The Weird Sisters end their unholy conclave with the chant:

> Fair is foul, and foul is fair.
> Hover through the *fog* and filthy air.
> . . . .
> What *bloody* man is that?

King Duncan cries, as he meets a bleeding sergeant entering his camp near Forres. There should be a minimum of pause between the Weird Sisters' chant and the King's abrupt query. A cinematic technique would be needed for the proper staging of this sequence. These lines are poetic — which is to say plurisignative — to a high degree. Let us note first two of the simpler plurisigns, the words "fog" and "bloody." Their literal meaning requires no comment: the air at the desert place is dense with actual fog and the sergeant actually bleeds. Their imagistic significance is farther-reaching: fog-gray and blood-red supply the basis of the color-scheme that extends through the play. The words *blood, bleed,* and *bloody* occur more than forty times during the play's course; the contrasting color-image — *fog, murk, darkness* — is alternated and sometimes directly combined with it. Thus Ross (II. iv), remarking on the unnatural *darkness* brought on by the storm, suggests that "the heavens, as troubled with man's act, Threatens his *bloody* stage." Again, in the sleep-walking scene (V. i) Lady Macbeth after exclaiming "Hell is *murky!*" adds a moment later, "Yet who would have thought the old man to have had so much *blood* in him?" Returning to our original passage we may discover yet a third level of meaning in the words "fog" and "bloody." They must be taken not only literally and imagistically, but also symbolically. Fog-gray connotes doubt, bewilderment, the impasse of reason; it is associated throughout the play with weird supernatural forces that hover in the background; it supplies an atmosphere to Macbeth's waverings and loss of direction; it is the color of

Hell, toward which the two protagonists are headed, — indeed Hell, as described obliquely through the play's imagery and other devices (such as the *double entendre* of the Porter scene), is neither more nor less than that atmosphere of foggy bewilderment itself. It is the dusty death that ensues when the brief candle has been finally extinguished. Sheol, not Gehenna, is the sinner's ultimate destination; the *poena damni,* not the *poena sensus,* is his dole. Blood-red, on the other hand, connotes violence, murder, guilt — positive action as contrasted with paralyzing doubts. These connotations effect a curious and powerful counterpoint with the literal, grammatical meaning of the passage in question. Grammatically the Weird Sisters' last couplet is a statement. King Duncan's first utterance is a question. But the Weird Sisters' apparent statement, with its paradoxical identification of opposites, foul and fair, its use of the negative color-symbol "fog," the halting indecisive rhythm of the last line — "Hover through the fog and filthy air" — turns out to be, on a symbolic level, a kind of vague and vast interrogation; while Duncan's question, fired like a pistol shot, with its positive color-symbol "bloody," is on the symbolic level a positive and incisive poetic affirmation.

III

The third level of semantic complexity, as distinguished from the atomic and the molecular, may be called the organic. The distinction, although a little inaccurate, since the organic character of poetic language carries right down into its atomic constituents, is nevertheless broadly useful. The problem here is to discover the semantic function of poetic form: i.e., how the poem can affirm as a whole, how it can make not only the *component statements* previously considered but a *total statement.*

Literal language is built into a variety of distinguishable structures: the argument (where the propositions become premises and a conclusion, connected by "therefore"), explanation ("because"), exemplification ("e.g."), simple enumeration ("and"), balanced enumeration ("but"), and others. They do not concern us here. The patterning of poetic language is more subtle, and its possibilities are as unlimited as the genius of the poet. An intelligent attempt to discriminate the main species of such patterning can be found in Yvor Winters' *Primitivism and Decadence,* pp. 15–63. The problem of semantics, however, refers not to the techniques of patterning but to what and how the patterns connote, and thus in what sense a total statement is possible.

In authentic poetry the total statement is identical with the poem itself. As it can find expression only through the component statements that constitute the poem, it cannot be summarized without essential loss. The "scenario content" of the poem can be summarized, as in Lamb's *Tales* and in many a college syllabus, but the poetic statement is destroyed in translation. Such being the case, it may be wondered how any useful remarks can be made on this subject, and whether a semantics of poetry at this third level of organization is not a delusion. My answer is that while no poetic statement can ever be translated or summarized into literal language adequately, there are cases in which a literal restatement can approximate the poetic original more nearly than in other cases, and that light can be thrown upon the nature of the poetic statement by comparing such approximations.

In 1536 William Tyndale suffered a martyr's death. His writings did not die, and in Shakespeare's time they were widely known and influential. In *Obedience of the Christian Man* Tyndale states:

> God hath made the King in every realm judge over all, and over him is there no judge. He that judgeth the King judgeth God, and he that layeth hands on the King layeth hands on God, and he that resisteth the King resisteth God . . . The King is in this world without law, and he may at his lust do right or wrong and shall give accounts but to God only.

But now comes a counter-theme. Tyndale continues:

> Yea, and it is better to have a tyrant unto thy King than a shadow, a passive King that doth nought himself but suffereth others to do him what they will, and to lead him whither they list . . . A king that is soft as silk and effeminate, that is to say, turned into the nature of a woman, shall be much more grievous unto the realm than a right tyrant.

Here is a royal antinomy, which in another writing Tyndale applies explicitly to the case of King Richard II. Richard is a weak and unjust king, a shadow, "soft as silk and effeminate." Nevertheless his insufficiencies did not, to the Tudor mind, justify deposition. Richard has gathered about him worthless parasites, robbed the exchequer, borrowed money from a faithful subject and then banished him, put his uncle the Duke of Gloucester to death. Ignoring the venerable John of Gaunt's sage and patriotic counsel he unlawfully confiscates his estates. These are wrong acts, but they are not for the king's subjects to avenge. As Shakespeare's Gaunt declares on his deathbed:

> God's is the quarrel . . .
> Let heaven revenge, for I may never lift
> An angry arm against his minister.

Shakespeare's play *Richard II* embodies a total statement which is a poetic translation of the compound literal statement quoted from Tyndale. "Divine sanction of the King *but* human frailty of this earthly king" would express approximately, in literal terms, the theme which Shakespeare has reformulated in the language of dramatic poetry. The first phase of the theme receives poetic formulation in the abundant religious imagery and scriptural allusion in which King Richard's character is embedded. Richard denounces his supposedly false friends as *Judases* damned without redemption; those who show an outward pity are *Pilates* who have delivered him to his sour *Cross;* the Bishop of Carlisle sees England as "the field of *Golgotha* and dead men's skulls"; Bolingbroke tells Exton to wander with *Cain* through shades of night;

there are references to the camel and the needle's eye, to "Come, little ones," to baptismal usurpation, and so on. Besides the allusions to Scripture there are numerous poetic statements combining the king with God, with the sun, and with the firm sanctity of the earth: "Down, down I come, like glist'ring Phaethon" (III. ii. 178); "This earth shall have a feeling . . ." (III. ii. 24); "Not all the water in the rough rude sea Can wash the balm off from an anointed king" (III. ii. 54); and the like. But kings are not only divine, they are human too. The human frailty of Richard is indicated in a variety of ways, chiefly through the symbols (i.e., the plurisigns) *earth, time,* and *unweeded garden.* In earlier passages the earth is mentioned as a royal possession, as a symbol of the sanctity, the power, and the stability of kingship. Later, after Scroop has announced the disastrous rebellion of most of Richard's followers, and the execution of three of his favorites, the earth-tune changes. The talk is now "of graves, of worms, and epitaphs," leading to the pathetic loveliness of

> For God's sake, let us sit upon the ground
> And tell sad stories of the death of kings.

Here is the second symbolic phase of the plurisign *earth-ground,* associated this time with the man-king, not with the king-god. The earth, or ground, is now simply the place where the man-king's bones and hollow skull are to be buried; it is a symbol of the later, descending movement of the play. The poetic statements built around *time,* especially during Richard's final soliloquy in the dungeon of Pomfret Castle, are even more complexly plurisignative.

I hope no reader will so far misunderstand this analysis as to accuse me of saddling Shakespeare with a "philosophy." A philosophy in the sense of explicit and logically related propositions about the nature of things is certainly not found in Shakespeare; he is first and last a dramatic poet, and as such he expresses his moral and metaphysical insights not in the prosy platitudes of Polonius, nor in the wit-fantasies of Mercutio, nor even, so far as one can tell, in the speculative philosophizings of Hamlet; but always in and through his chosen medium, which is the plurisignative language of dramatic poetry. For Shakespeare does say something, he does make "total statements," and whether or not these are to be called his "philosophy" depends on how adaptably one chooses to apply the word.

In any case it will not be disputed, I imagine, that Shakespeare's "philosophy," like the philosophies of Aeschylus and Dante and Keats, is expressed with less assertive weight (which does not mean with less seriousness!) than the philosophies of Aristotle and Aquinas and Professor Whitehead. As I have already argued, poetic language *must* assert less heavily than literal language because of the more delicate and unresolved plurisigns of which it consists, and it *should* assert less heavily because of the kind of effect aimed at. The assertion in a poetic statement, whether component or total, may even be so light as to be scarcely an assertion at all, but simply a kind of equipoise among plurisigns. The total statement of *Measure for Measure* is asserted more lightly, though I suspect with a more deadly seriousness, than the total statement of *Richard II*. The total statement of Mr. Pound's *Cantos* has scarcely any heaviness at all — pure Ariel, no Caliban, although filled with grotesque shadowgraphs of Caliban, which is quite another matter. The general possibilities may be indicated summarily as follows: (1) The poetic statement, with respect to what I shall call *horizontal dimension,* falls between the two poles of full assertion, which is found only in logical discourse, and pure non-assertive tension between plurisigns. A poetic statement may approach indefinitely near to, but never quite reach, either of these poles. Narrative, epic, and didactic poems ordinarily stand closer to the fully assertive pole; lyrical, mystical, and (more pointedly) surrealist and dadaist poems stand closer to the pure non-assertive. (2) With respect to *degree of organization,* which may be called the vertical dimension, a poetic statement may be anything from the simplest component statement up to the total statement which is the poem itself. (3) There is also a third important dimension, which may be called the dimension of *plurisignative fullness,* or *poetic richness,* interdependent but not identical with the first: that is to say, the number of quasi-assertions, of varying weight, which a single poetic statement is simultaneously making. Lady Macbeth's "And when goes hence?" is a small but brilliant exploitation of this dimension. In Dante's *Commedia* the technique of poetic fullness, of asserting on several levels of significance at once, is developed into a magnificent formal pattern, announced by Dante himself in the *Convivio* and more explicitly in the dedicatory letter to Lord Can Grande della Scala.

The foregoing exposition has been intended to define the exact sense in which poetry, in its proper rôle, can *say* anything. This is the first task for a semantics of poetry. Important problems have been left untouched: notably, the relation of poetic expressibility to current ways of living, to religious faith, and to the availability of articulate cultural traditions. My attempted contribution, reduced to its lowest terms, has been one of vocabulary — a set of definitive monosigns by which plurisigns and plurisign-communities might be more clearly talked about. There is a danger here as in any other analytic approach, of spoiling the poetry by talking about it too much or too glibly, of imposing alien patterns upon holy things. But the danger is minimized if, after the necessary theorizing has been done, we are wise enough to become silent and turn back with reverent attention to the poetry.

Josephine Miles

MORE SEMANTICS OF POETRY

Mr. Wheelwright bases his contribution to the "Semantics of Poetry," in a recent *Kenyon Review,* on a terminology by which poetic language can be factually discussed, — "a set of definitive monosigns by which plurisigns and plurisign communities might be more clearly talked about." These are the basic terms of his discussion, *monosign* and *plurisign,* the former used by science, history, logic, denotatively, definitionally, with invariant meaning; the latter used by poetry for evocation, enjoyment, richness and depth of association and connotation. Having set poetic language strikingly apart from logical, scientific and historical language, Mr. Wheelwright then goes on to develop the significances of the distinction and to apply the terms to specific poetic passages to good effect. The whole job is consistent, thorough, and illuminating, but I venture to make some objections to the basic distinction.

The linking of monosignificance, denotation, and scientific truth opposes these three to plurisignificance, connotation, and poetic truth. The opposition has been a favorite one of the critics in recent years. It has been made in one form or another not only by I. A. Richards, whose excess Mr. Wheelwright wisely tempers, but also by Eastman, Empson, Lowes, Leavis, Ransom, Tate, Cleanth Brooks, and many others. It seems to me time to question this opposition, whether dualistic in absolute terms or polar in relative terms. Poetic language seems to me neither one of two major kinds or use, nor more close to one language pole than another. It seems to me a specialization of language by intensities through the forms and patterns of the verse line. Given what people have chosen to call poetry over the centuries, the only way to discover what language is characteristic of it is, it seems to me, to look at that language in all the poetry available; to discover what words for what things are used over what periods of time most often and fully to bear the stresses which poetry puts upon them. In other words, statements about poetic language must come from a more continuous observation of actual poetic content than we have yet condescended to.

Reprinted from *The Kenyon Review,* II (1940) by permission.

When Mr. Wheelwright makes such observation of the actual functioning of Shakespeare's words, for example, he is pointing out verifiable fact, and so making the true statements he desires. But consider the assumptions which he treats as fundamental to these observations. First: the connection of monosignificance, definition, denotation, and scientific truth. *Monosignificance* Mr. Wheelwright uses, and I think confuses, in two ways, as formal logical abstraction ("the ghost of a once living idea"), and as a useful temporarily consistent selection (Hobbes's recommendation to those who seek to instruct or convince). It is thus hard to tell whether he deals on his "atomic level" with words in context or out. In any event, he treats words as if they were single meanings, which definition defines and which denotation denotes and which factual statement makes statements about.

But consider that a word, like its object, appears in innumerable contexts, in every context with a different emphasis and a different selection from its qualities. A word, that is, is a single unit on one level of discrimination, but covers many other units on other levels, all of which are part of the definition, are equally denotable and equally "true." The total of these units as they are grouped in the labelled unit concerned comes into play only in that distinguishing exercise of logic which draws the line between the thing-concerned and the non-thing-concerned, and so takes pains to include every distinguishing feature. Otherwise, usage naturally emphasizes some phases of the word while ignoring others, and thus the play of words is plurisignative, whether in science, which carefully excludes one set of factors while dealing with another; whether in history which subordinates some referents of a word such as *Rome,* by emphasizing others; whether in general conversational talk which plays one phase of a word against another to the constant result of resilience, humor, and misunderstanding.

It seems to me then that while definition gathers together the salient features of the thing which is labelled, denotation can note the thing and some or all of its features separately, and statement using the label is verifiable not in terms of the whole definitional set-up necessarily, but simply in terms of selection made from this.

Take for example the object *primrose,* to which Mr. Wheelwright refers. Its word denotes it as unit, or some of its observable features. Its definition, "A well known plant bearing pale yellowish flowers in early spring, growing wild in woods and hedges and on banks, especially in clayey soil, and cultivated in many varieties as a garden plant" (Oxford Dictionary), establishes its distinguishing factors and builds up many denotations into one. True or verifiable statements about it *select from* these factors; they may say for example, The primrose is yellow: or, It grows wild in woods: or, The girl is picking primroses: or, The primrose and the daisy are growing side by side: requiring for truth just as much of the definition as the context demands, the full definition, denotation, and true statement of all primrose factors being drawn upon only by logic in its primrose and non-primrose distinctions. The terms monosignificance, denotation, definition, and science, do not therefore enforce each other in the way Mr. Wheelwright would have them.

If then, secondly, words are not statically and isolatedly monosignificant in the prose of science and instruction, what better sense can be made of that other of Mr. Wheelwright's realms, the realm of poetry-connotation-plurisignification? There is the minor problem to be ignored that we have here, as in most current literary criticism, to speak in logically unorthodox terms when we consider denotation to be the object's central facts or character, and connotation to be peripheral or associational material. Accepting these meanings, however, we see that connotative language is more personal than denotative, in that there may be less agreement as to the qualities noted, and that verification involves more psychological foundation. Thus the yellowness of a primrose may be part of its denotation, while its likeness to a star or the fact that it reminds one of evenings in a certain garden, or its service as emblem of British conservatism, may be part of its connotation.

It should be noted immediately that such likenesses and associations are not non-scientific or non-verifiable, but are perfectly true so long as the limits of their statement are recognized, and that is of course a requirement for every truth. *Is* and *is like* can both be used in statement of fact. It is not necessary to distinguish between their verities by the metaphor of "assertive weight" which Mr. Wheelwright uses. Thus the troubled analysis of some poetic lines quoted by Mr. Wheelwright as quoted by I. A. Richards, troubles me still further. The lines are John Clare's on the primrose,

With its crimp and curdled leaf
And its little brimming eye.

Evidently Richards gave these as examples of "pseudo-statement," emotional rather than factual statement, since he felt them to be not verifiably true. Mr. Wheelwright corrects this feeling partially — he says these lines are to be distinguished from informational prose not because their statement is less true, but because it is made with less "assertive weight." This is a pretty problem in metaphor to add to "plurisignificance" as a distinguishing factor of poetry; and it is not even necessary.

Clare was simply choosing from among the plurisignificances of *primrose* what he felt was most important to draw out: not, in this case, its definitional elements of color or location or blooming time, but simply here its definitional elements of texture and shape. Well then, he had a word *curdled* for its texture, and a word *eye* for its central shape. This was the reduction which his notion of formality and stress demanded. It was shorthand and intensification of: the texture of its leaf looks like the texture of something curdled, and it has a center like an eye, which brims like an eye too. These statements aren't essentially *pseudo* or of *lighter* assertive weight (one could make a case, in fact, for the heavier weight of poetry). These statements are simply reduced to the point of emphasis which Clare wanted to make. To discuss them semantically, then, I think, would be to discuss their place in the current of their time's meanings: how new and rare was this very emphasis on texture, especially the texture of a flower, and especially in poetry; and how Clare spoke in terms, in these lines, of a whole new way of thought. The lines provide as good an example as I know of the way poetry chooses among the plurisignificances, both denotative and connotative, of a word, taking for statement just those factors it wants to stress, and controlling by context the distance and contribution of other factors in suspension. Science, history, argument, jokes, propaganda, exhortation, equally make their own choices and stresses according to their needs.

Given Mr. Wheelwright's terms *monosignificance, denotation, prose* and *science,* versus *plurisignificance, connotation,* and *poetry,* with his chalk lines making two camps of the lot, I can only wish to rub out the chalk and start over. I should take as basic assumption that, as monosignificance is an abstraction for logic, all language is plurisignificant as all objects and words appear in context. Denotation and connotation are kinds of plurisignificance. Science and poetry are kinds of selection from plurisignificance, the kinds to be distinguished by purpose, use, ingredients of material, plain outward form, and so on, just as the primrose was distinguished.

If, then, Mr. Wheelwright would say that such distinction was still just what he wished to make, that he wished simply to characterize poetry's use of language, not absolutely but in relation to other uses, and that he would do so by saying, *the more plurisignative, the more poetic,* and *the more poetic, the more plurisignative,* I should still have to doubt. For such distinction, though focused firmly enough on the language-material of poetry, would emphasize its punning and ambiguous and suggesting and analogical and symbolizing qualities at the expense of its continuities and stabilities, the decisive lines of choice which Hobbes recommended for prose and which Mr. Wheelwright might be willing to call relative monosignificance (though I should rather omit the term altogether, since Mr. Wheelwright wouldn't like it applied to poetry anyway). These stabilities, which Hobbes said instructors and convincers should employ, are vital to poetry, though Mr. Wheelwright ignores them for poetry altogether. Poetry, as formalizing of thought and consolidating of values, works firmly in the material of the common language of the time, limited by its own conventions of the time. This general language it works in, being tentative, fluid, formal, unfixed, is the most plurisignative. Every word in ordinary conversation for example carries a wealth of possibilities close to the surface; tone of voice and gesture and repetition and emphasis of context, and many external aids such as pointing, have to limit these plurisignificances. Ordinary misunderstanding, explanation, humor are results of failure so to limit. But the more formal ways of thought, narrowing the field of subject matter and the forms for expressing it, limit much of the plurisignificance, the vagaries of denotation and connotation, at the outset. Different sciences have different focuses and ignore vast sections of significance in every word. Mineral contents of *water* exclude temperatures of oceans of water, atomic analyses of water exclude its effects on fevers, and so forth. Exhortation chooses the qualities conducive to the action it exhorts for. History weighs, discards, and subordinates for the sake of an interpretation. Poetry, being the most restricted by structure and device, is deep and full through the force of those restrictions, and selects most intently, controlling strongly the significance of every word by tone, rhythm, and pattern, and by the significance of every other included word. The devices of poetry are more than devices of decoration, they are devices of pressure.

What poetry wishes to press, I think, are those meanings richest and fullest in the thought of its own time, the "prime" meanings which thought has achieved in certain terms, as for example the *soul* and *clay* of the 17th Century, the *nature* and *passions* of the 18th, the *sweetness* and *light* of the 19th, the *blood* and *bone* of the 20th. The poet doesn't select from an infinite number of plurisignificances in language, and he doesn't necessarily select two or three or a dozen plurisignificances to play together for richness of thought, unless his time finds that to be a rewarding way of thought. Rather, the poet thinks somewhat as his time thinks, has selections and stresses of significance already made for him, and in turn makes these deeper and fuller of enforcement by the artful and controlling pattern in which he tells them.

Therefore I should like to trade Mr. Wheelwright's terminology and the equivalent terminology of his contemporaries, along with this complaint, for ten pages of solid fact about the language of poetry not as it might be but as it has been writ. If the teachers of the history of literature had eyes as sharp to see as the current critics have terms to apply, then the conflict between the two with which *The Kenyon Review* is currently concerned would become a simple necessary interchange of materials, and a known history of poetic language would help to define the nature of poetic language.

John Crowe Ransom

WANTED: AN ONTOLOGICAL CRITIC

. . . I assume that there is hardly necessity for an extended argument to the effect that a perfect metrical construction, of which the components were words selected from the range of all actual words, and exclusively for phonetic effects, would not be likely to make sense. It would be nonsense. Nor for another argument to show that a pure logical construction would not be likely to make meter. The latter case we have with us always, in our science, in the prose of our newspapers and business correspondence, in our talk. Even so, there might be some instruction in considering for a moment such a little piece of mathematical discourse as this:

$$(a + b)^2 = a^2 + 2\,ab + b^2.$$

Here the mathematician is saying exactly what he means, and his language is not metrical, and we can discover if we try that he does not want any poet to meter it, on the matter-of-fact ground that the poet would have to take liberties with his logical values. At once a question or two should present themselves very vexingly to the nebulous aesthetician: What sort of liberties does the poet take with a discourse when he sets it to meter? And what sort of discourse is prepared to permit those liberties?

An argument which admits of alteration in order that it may receive a meter must be partly indeterminate. The argument cannot be maintained exactly as determined by its own laws, for it is going to be un-determined by the meter.

Conversely, a metrical form must be partly indeterminate if it proposes to embody an argument. It is useless to try to determine it closely in advance, for the argument will un-determine it.

The second principle, of the two just stated, may seem the less ominous. To most poets, and most readers, the meaning is more important than the meter.

I offer a graph, which will be of course an oversimplification, to show the parts which meaning and meter play in the act of composition.

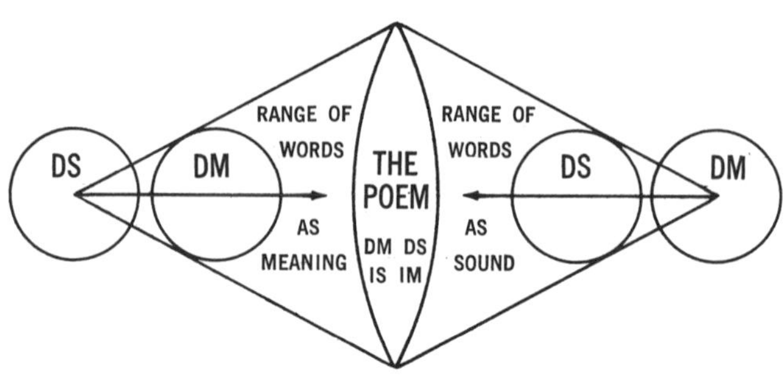

D M stands for determinate meaning, or such of the intended meaning as succeeds in being adhered to; it may be fairly represented by the logical paraphrase of the poem. I M stands for indeterminate meaning, or that part of the final meaning which took shape not according to its own logical necessity but under metrical compulsion; it may be represented by the poem's residue of meaning which does not go into the logical paraphrase. D S stands for the determinate sound-structure, or the meter; and I S stands for whatever phonetic character the sounds have assumed which is in no relation to the meter.

In theory, the poem is the resultant of two processes which come from opposite directions. Starting from the left of the graph, the poet is especially intent upon his meter, D S, which may be blocked out as a succession of unaccented and accented syllables arranged in lines, perhaps with rhyme-endings; but there is D M, a prose discourse, which must be reduced into the phonetic pattern of the meter; his inclination is to replace its words with others from the general field of words which suit the meter, and without much regard for their logical propriety. But he is checked by the converse process, in which the poet starts from the right of the graph with firm possession of D M, a prose meaning, but has to assimilate to it D S, the metrical pattern that he has chosen; his inclination is to replace the required metrical sounds with others that suit his logic and are not quite so good for the meter.

Actually, a skillful piece of composition will have many stages of development, with strokes too subtle and rapid to record, and operations in some sort of alternation from the one direction and the other. The poet makes adaptations both of meter to meaning (introducing I S) and of meaning to meter (introducing I M). For the sake of the pictorial image, I assume the final poem to be the body of language lying between the intersecting arcs at the center; the one arc (on the left) representing the extreme liberties which meaning has taken with meter, and the other arc (on the right) representing the extreme liberties which meter has taken with meaning. Both arcs are required for the bounding of the poem.

6

The most interesting observation for the critic, perhaps, is that the poem is an object comprising not two elements but four; not merely a meaning M, but D M, that part of a meaning which forms a logical structure, and I M, a part which does not belong to the structure and may be definitely illogical, though more probably it is only additive and a-logical; and not merely D S, a meter, but I S, a part of the total sound-effect which may be in exception to the law of the meter but at any rate does not belong to it. These elements are familiar enough to the poet himself, who has manipulated them. Frequently they are evident to the critic too. They should be, very substantially; they are capable of being distinguished to the extent that he is capable of distinguishing them. Logically they are distinct elements, now, in the finished poem, though it may not be possible to trace back the precise history of their development under the tension of composition.

I cannot but think that the distinction of these elements, and especially of D M and I M, is the vocation *par excellence* of criticism. It is more technical than some other exercises which go as criticism, but more informed. It brings the criticism of poetry to somewhat the same level of professional competence as that of the discussions which painters sometimes accord to paintings, and that which musicians sometimes accord to music; and that means, I think, an elevation of our normal critical standard.

If a poet is a philosopher, explicitly or implicitly, treating matters of ethical or at least human importance — and it is likely that he is that — the discussion of his "ideology" may be critical in every sense in which one may be said to criticize systematic ideas; but the ideas of the poet, struggling but not quite managing to receive their really determinate expression, are only his D M, and a better version is almost certain to be found elsewhere in prose, so that their discussion under the poem is likely to be a tame affair. Few poets serve, as Wordsworth and Shelley may be thought to do, as texts for the really authoritative study of ideas; mostly they serve amateur ideologists for that purpose, or serve distinguished critics who fall back upon this sort of thing because nothing is quite prescriptive in their vocation. The more interesting thing to study is the coexistence and connection of D M and I M — the ideas and the indeterminate material in which they are enveloped. This kind of study is much severer, but its interest is profounder and more elemental than the merely ethical; it is an ontological interest.

Possibly an examination of poetry along these lines might finally disclose the secret of its strange yet stubborn existence as a kind of discourse unlike any other. It is a discourse which does not bother too much about the perfection of its logic; and does bother a great deal, as if it were life and death, about the positive quality of that indeterminate thing which creeps in by the back door of metrical necessity. I suggest the closest possible study of I M, the indeterminate meaning.

But there are two kinds of indeterminacy in I M, and I wish to show how the poet in metering his argument yields reluctantly to the first, as to an indeterminacy that means only inaccuracy and confusion, and then gladly to the second, as to an indeterminacy that opens to him a new world of discourse.

First, he tries to shift the language within the range of a rough verbal equivalence, and to alter D M no more substantively than necessary. A given word will probably have synonyms. The order of words in a phrase may be varied. A transitive predication may be changed to a passive; a relative clause to a participial phrase. In the little words denoting logical connections and transitions a good deal of liberty may be taken without being fatal; they may be expanded into something almost excessively explicit, or they may be even omitted, with the idea that the reader can supply the correct relations. A single noun may become a series of nouns, or nearly any other element may be compounded, without introducing much real novelty. Epithetical adjectives and adverbs may be interpolated, if they will qualify their nouns and verbs very obviously. Archaic locutions may be introduced for contemporary ones. A poet is necessarily an accomplished verbalist, and capable of an almost endless succession of periphrases that come nearer and nearer to metered language until finally he achieves what he wants; a language that is metrical enough, and close enough to his intended meaning. . . .

Wordsworth would probably be cited by the historian as one who metered his language with more method than inspiration, especially in his longer work. Here is a passage from the *Prelude,* where he is talking about the power of poetry, and its habitation in a place called "the mystery of words":

. . . there,
As in a mansion like their proper home,
Even forms and substances are circumfused
By that transparent veil with light divine,
And through the turnings intricate of verse
Present themselves as objects recognized
In flashes, and with glory not their own.

It is easy to find specific disagreeable lapses of logic here. There are the painful inversions of order, clearly in the interest of metric: *light divine* and *turnings intricate.* The line *As in a mansion like their proper home* is certainly a curious involution for *As in a mansion which is their proper home.* The third and fourth lines are not transparent for us like the veil talked about: does the veil possess and give off the divine light; and if not, how does it circumfuse the forms and substances with it? The brevity of statement is either pure laziness on Wordsworth's part, or it is a recourse to elliptical expression invited by metrical exigencies. But at this point all our little objections pass into a big and overwhelming one: there is really in this passage scarcely any specific discourse of respectable logical grade. We do not know what any of these pretty things is, or does. No prose would be cynical enough to offer so elusive a content. The mansion, the forms and substances, the magic veil, the divine light, the movement of the turnings, the flashes and the borrowed glory, —

these look like responsible and promising objects, but none of them establishes a sufficient identity when they all assemble together. The poet became a little paralyzed, we may imagine, when he took pen in hand to write a poem; or got that way after going a certain distance in the writing of a long one. I go beyond the direct evidence here, but I assume that making distinguished metrical discourse was such a job, and consisted in his own mind with so much corruption of the sense at best, that he fell into the habit of choosing the most resounding words, and stringing them together as the meter dictated. This is not unusual in Romantic poetry. The point to make about Romantic poetry now is not the one about its noble words, but a negative and nasty one: the noble words are almost absurdly incoherent.

But Pope was not a Romantic, and I suppose the language has known no poet more nice in his expression. I quote:

> Close by those meads, forever crowned with flowers,
> Where Thames with pride surveys his rising towers,
> There stands a structure of majestic frame,
> Which from the neighboring Hampton takes its name.
> Here Britain's statesmen oft the fall foredoom
> Of foreign tyrants and of nymphs at home;
> Here thou, great Anna! whom three realms obey,
> Dost sometimes counsel take — and sometimes tea.

With so great a master of language, it is a little dangerous to insist on the exact place where the meter coming in drove some of the logic out. But the superiority of his logic over Wordsworth's is not so overwhelming as it seems; for the most part it is merely that his improvisations are made to look nearly natural, as if he thoroughly intended them all the time, and meter had nothing to do with them. The *flowers* is arrived at gracefully, but the chief source of any "inevitability" claimed for it is the fact that it rhymes with *towers,* which is more important to the discourse. In four lines we come to Hampton Court, where will presently appear Belinda, whom we have left traveling in her boat on the Thames. Hampton Court has a location with respect to the Thames which we need to know, under the principles of a logical narrative argument; and at Hampton Court assemble the royalty and the fashionable gentry, which we must know too; these are the necessary facts. Hampton Court is close by those "rising towers" which are London-on-Thames, and that is enough as to its location; it is a matter of course that it will be close by the meads too, since the towers will rise out of the meads by the river rather than rise out of the river. If we should invert the two lines, as follows,

> Near where proud Thames surveys his rising towers,
> And where are meads forever crowned with flowers,

something would happen not only to the euphony of the language but to the respectability of its logic, for then it would be plain that the meads-and-flowers line is chiefly useful for filling up a couplet. But the next couplet lacks honest logical economy too. The *structure of majestic frame* is nothing but a majestic structure, with a rhyme-tag added, and the account of the naming of Hampton Court is a metrical but logically a gratuitous expansion of the simple recital of its name. The other two couplets both employ rhyme-words, and contexts to assimilate them, which are so incongruous that they have to be employed in discourse as the occasions of wit. As logicians we need not take much stock in wit as forwarding argument, even when it is free from suspicion as a device to look after difficult rhyme-pairings; it supposes such a lack of an obvious logical relation between two things that any technical bridge of connection must be accepted; but our approval goes to the architect, not to his work; and as for that, the poet's appearance in his own argument is a major irrelevance. No honest "argument" prefaced to a poem would cover the poet's witticisms. We condemn Romantic poets for injecting their burning sentiments into an objective argument, but other poets are given to wit which is likewise at the expense of argument and logic.[1] A final remark will sound a little captious. Hampton Court is in mind, but the word "Court" is not used and possibly its absence troubles the poet; at any rate if he does not have a court he supplies the short passage with three royalties. There is the lady of the meads, a figurative queen, with a crown of flowers; Thames, a figurative patriarch, and at least a prince with all his rising towers (though a little while earlier there was a feminine character of the same name upon whose "silver bosom" Belinda rode in her boat); and actual Queen Anne. It seems an excessive profusion of royalties.

There are certainly readers of the Binomial Theorem who are prohibited by conscience from the reading of poetry; we have just been looking at some of the reasons. On these terms meter may be costing more than it is worth. Milton thought of the possibility, and went so far as to renounce its most binding device, the rhyme; it is employed by

> some famous modern Poets, carried away by Custom, but much to their own vexation, hindrance, and constraint to express many things otherwise, and for the most part worse, than else they would have expressed them.

But greater purists might apply this logic to all the rest of the metrical devices. We turn to Milton's own unrhymed verse, and find:

> Thus while he spake, each passion dimm'd his face
> Thrice chang'd with pale, ire, envy and despair,
> Which marr'd his borrow'd visage, and betray'd
> Him counterfeit, if any eye beheld.

[1] Mr. Cleanth Brooks reproves the sentimentality of simple poets, but puts himself rather off guard by his blanket counter-endorsement of the wit of university or sophisticated poets. If we had an aesthetician's version of Horace's fable of the town mouse and the country mouse, we should be sure to find the latter uttering countrified sentimental discourse, and scorned by the other; but the discourse of the town mouse not only would be smart, it would presently become over-smart, and silly; so that in the long run we should smile at her as at the country cousin, and for much the same reason: naiveté, as plain in personal vanity as in simplicity. Elizabethan comedy finds its butt in the smart town character as readily as in the country simpleton.

The argument of this narrative passage would explain how Uriel, deceived once by Satan in his "stripling cherub's" disguise, perceives now his identity through the satanic passions registered in his appearance, and initiates the next cycle of action by informing the angels guarding Paradise. But the language, as is common enough with Milton, from the point of view of logic is almost like a telegraphic code in its condensation, and omission of connectives; it is expansible to two or three times its length in prose, and readable only with difficulty by unaccustomed readers. Yet it also lapses from strict logic in precisely the opposite direction, by the importation of superfluous detail. The three successive increments of pallor and their respective causes would seem beyond the observation of Uriel, in the sun, and in fact we learn presently that what Uriel actually marked was Satan's "gestures fierce" and "mad demeanor." Milton is aware of this, and gives himself a technical alibi in our passage by being careful to say that the pallor stages betrayed the fraud not necessarily to Uriel but to any good eye that might be close enough to see them. Still, if Uriel did not see them they do not matter.

It would have been hard to persuade Milton out of this passage, with its deficiencies and superfluities; but suppose we might have proposed an alternative version, which would seem safely eclectic and within the standard traditional proficiencies of poetry; and I shall not mind appearing ridiculous for the sake of the argument:

> Speaking, rank passion swelled within his breast
> Till all the organism felt its power,
> And such a pallor in his face was wrought
> That it belied the angelic visage fair
> He had assumed. Uriel, unsleeping guard,
> With supernatural vision saw it plain.

But Milton in his turn would instantly have gibed at it, and on our terms; at the dangling participle and the poetic inversion, as violations of good syntax; and then at the constant tendency, perhaps proceeding from our nervous desire to come with some spirit out of an embarrassing situation, to exceed the proper logical content, as shown in all four first lines by the verbs *swelled, felt, was wrought,* and *belied.* They are ambitious, and start our minds upon little actions that would take us out of the plane of the argument.

Returning to rhymed verse, there is this passage from a poem which deserves its great fame, but whose fabulous "perfections" consist with indeterminacies that would be condemned in the prose of scientists, and also of college Freshmen; though I think in the prose of college Seniors they might have a different consideration:

> Had we but world enough, and time,
> This coyness, lady, were no crime.
> We would sit down, and think which way
> To walk, and pass our long love's day.

Thou by the Indian Ganges' side
Should'st rubies find: I by the tide
Of Humber would complain. I would
Love you ten years before the flood,
And you should, if you please, refuse
Till the conversion of the Jews;
My vegetable love should grow
Vaster than empires and more slow.

I will use the pedagogical red pencil, though I am loath. World, as distinguished from time, is not space, for the lovers already have all the space in the world, and long tenure would not increase it. It is a violent condensation meaning, I think, "the whole history of the world before us," and combining with the supposal of their having the time to live through it; it supports the historical references which follow. *We would, thou should'st, my love should:* the use of the auxiliaries is precise, varying according to rule from person to person, and uniformly denoting determination or command; "we would arrange it so." But it is remarkable that in so firm a set of locutions, which attests the poet's logical delicacy, the *thou should'st* is interchangeable with *you should;* the meter is responsible for the latter version, since otherwise we should have the line, *And thou should'st, if thou pleased'st, refuse,* or, taking the same liberty with tenses which we find actually taken (again for metrical reasons), *And thou should'st, if thou pleas'st, refuse;* but either line clogs the meter. *Which way* is one phrase, but language is an ambiguous thing, and it has two meanings: *in which direction* as applied to *walk,* and *in what manner* as applied to *pass our day.* The parallel series in lines 5–7 is in three respects not uniform: *Ganges* has little need of a defining adjective, except the metrical one, but when once it has become *Indian Ganges* there is every right on the part of its analogue to be styled *English Humber;* and *Ganges' side* calls for *Humber's side,* or for merely *Humber's,* with *side* understood, but rhyme produces for Humber a *tide;* and the possessive case in the first member would call for the same in the second member, but is replaced there actually by an *of*-phrase. *Refuse* brings out of the rhyming dictionary the *Jews,* which it will tax the poet's invention to supply with a context; but for our present purposes the poet has too much invention, for it gives him the historical period from the Flood to the conversion of the Jews, which is a useless way of saying ten thousand years, or some other length of time, and which seems disproportionate to the mere ten years of the same context, the only other period mentioned. *Vegetable* is a grotesque qualification of love, and on the whole decidedly more unsuitable than suitable, though there are features in which it is suitable. *Vaster* would correlate with *slower,* not with *more slow,* but they would not be correlatives at all after *grow,* for *vaster* is its factitive complement and *slower* can only be for *more slowly,* its adverb. Finally, there is the question of how the vastness of the poet's love can resemble the vastness of empires; the elegance of the terms seems to go along with the logic of a child.

7

But the important stage of indeterminacy comes, in the experiment of composition, when the imagination of the poet, and not only his verbal mechanics, is engaged. An "irrelevance" may feel forced at first, and its overplus of meaning unwanted, because it means the importation of a little foreign or extraneous content into what should be determinate, and limited; but soon the poet comes upon a kind of irrelevance that seems desirable, and he begins to indulge it voluntarily, as a new and positive asset to the meaning. And this is the principle: the importations which the imagination introduces into discourse have the value of developing the "particularity" which lurks in the "body," and under the surface, of apparently determinate situations. When Marvell is persuaded by the rhyme-consideration to invest the Humber with a tide, or to furnish his abstract calendar with specifications about the Flood, and the conversion of the Jews, he does not make these additions reluctantly. On the contrary, he knows that the brilliance of the poetry depends on the shock, accompanied at once by the realism or the naturalness, of its powerful particularity. But the mere syllabic measure, and not only the rhyme, can induce this effect. When the poet investigates the suitability of a rhyme-word for his discourse, he tries the imaginative contexts in which it could figure; but the process is the same when he tries many new phrases, proposed in the interest of the rhythm, for their suitability, though his imagination has to do without the sharp stimuli of the rhyme-words. And by suitability I mean the propriety which consists in their denoting the particularity which really belongs to the logical object. In this way what is irrelevant for one kind of discourse becomes the content for another kind, and presently the new kind stands up firmly if we have the courage to stand by it.

The passages cited above were in support of the negative and corrupt I M, but they illustrate also the positive I M, which is poetic texture, for the critic, and ontological particularity, for the philosopher. Wordsworth has the most abstract argument, but instead of pursuing it closely and producing a distinguished logical structure — it might have come to a really superior version of the argument we are here trying to build up, something about the meaning of poetry — he wavers towards some interesting concrete objects, producing a mansion, a veil, a light, and a set of intricate turnings; but here too he is stopped, as if by some puritan inhibition, from looking steadily at his objects to obtain a clear image; so that his discourse is not distinguished either for its argument or for its texture. Pope unquestionably has the narrative gift, which means that he has access to the actual stream of events covered by the abstract argument; he is one of many poets prefiguring our modern prose fiction, and knows that he may suspend his argument whenever he pleases, provided he may substitute another equally positive content, namely, a sub-narrative account of the independent character and history of its items. Milton looks principally like a man out of a more heroic age than Pope, in the casualness and roughness of his indeterminacy, but he is bolder also in the positive detail:

nothing in Pope's passage compares with his stopping to name the three specific passions in the mind of Satan, and to imagine each one as turning Satan's visage paler than the one before had left it. As for Marvell, we are unwilling to praise or to condemn the peccadilloes of his logic, and here is a case where we take no account of the indeterminacy of the bad sort that results from the metering process, and that distresses so many hard-headed readers. This is all overshadowed, and we are absorbed, by the power of his positive particulars, so unprepared for by his commonplace argument.

Indeterminacy of this positive or valuable sort is introduced when the images make their entry. It looks as if there might be something very wise in the social, anonymous, and universal provision of metrical technique for poetry. The meter seems only to harm the discourse, till presently it works a radical innovation: it induces the provision of icons among the symbols. This launches poetry upon its career.

8

The development of metrical content parallels that of meaning. As the meter un-determines the meaning and introduces I M, so the meaning undetermines the meter and introduces "variations," or I S.

The usual minimum of a meter, in English practice, is a succession of lines having a determinate number of determinate feet, and a foot is some syllabic combination having one accented syllable. The most general consequence is that a unit of phonetic structure — a few lines of blank verse, a stanza unit of rhymed verse, a sonnet or whole poem sometimes — is superimposed upon a unit of meaning-structure; within it the foot may not coincide with the word or small logical unit, but the two structures use precisely the same constituent language in the long run, and come out at the end together; and this is a summary feat of remarkable coördination, when we approach it with the prejudice of a person used to working in pure structures, that is, in one structure at a time. In reading the poem we have our ear all the time immediately upon the progress of the meter, just as we have our discursive mind all the time on the course of the argument; so that the two structures advance simultaneously if not by the same steps, and every moment or so two steps finish together, and two new steps start together. And what we call a "phrase" is at once a period in the argument and a definable element in the metrical structure, and "phrasing" means to the poet the act of grouping the words to serve the two purposes simultaneously.

We may suppose that the phonetic effect and the meaning-effect are, in theory, perfectly equal and coördinate. But probably we all have greater actual interest in the meaning than in the sound. Therefore it is convenient to say that the phonetic effect serves as a sort of texture to the meaning. This is to assign to the meaning an ontological addition.

But within the phonetic effect considered for itself alone we find the poet developing for his meter, which is the regular phonetic structure, its own texture, which consists in the metrical variations. He is driven into this course by considerations exactly the same, except in reverse, as those we have seen compelling him to develop within the meaning a texture of meaning. The latter was forced upon him by the necessity of adapting his meaning to the meter; and this is forced upon him by the necessity of adapting his meter to the meaning. When he cannot further reduce his meaning to language more accurately metrical, he accepts a "last version" and allows the variations to stand. These variations of course present the contingency and unpredictability, or in one word the "actuality," of the world of sound. Many phonetic effects are possible really; and here a foot or a phrase holds stubbornly to its alien character and is not assimilated to the poet's purpose. In our habit of reading much into the poem, it seems to me fatal not to read the ontological consideration.

But the texture that is realized within a meter is under conventional restrictions, the like of which have not been formulated for the texture within the meaning. Variations from the meter are permissive but they must be of certain kinds. I suppose experience has shown, or else there is a strange consent of feeling, that the phrasing of the determinate meaning can always be roughly accomplished if allowed a few permissive variations; that the metrical effects, plus the effects allowed in the variations, make language sufficiently flexible to carry any meaning. Take iambic verse, for example, which is the staple for English. Elizabethan dramatic verse became very much loosened up or "Websterized" before it finished, and later Coleridge very nearly got the anapaestic foot adopted as a legitimate variation for the iambic within short rhymed lines. But with these two great exceptions the poets have confined their metrical departures from iambic verse to the permissive variations with remarkable unanimity. So at least until our own period. There have been many poets recently, including the lettered as well as the unlettered, who have cast off the "bondage" of the meters, and employ them only as they find it convenient, or else make it their rule on principle not to cultivate anything approaching metrical determinateness. But I am talking here about the traditional practice. The critic must take it into account if he cares to discuss the traditional poets; there can be no dispute about that.

Shakespeare wrote,

> Whén to | the sés | sions of | swéet sí | lent thóught
>
> I súm | mon úp | remém | brance of | thíngs pást,

but we may safely suppose that he was aware of the possibility of many other versions, as for example,

> When síts | my pár | liamént | of sí | lent thóught
>
> To trý | afrésh | the swéet | remém | bered pást.

The assumption that this version entered his mind is of course without specific evidence, and may be improbable for more reasons than one, but at least it represents a common situation: the option between a fairly determinate meaning consisting with a variant or indeterminate meter, and a revised and less determinate meaning leading to a more determinate meter. Decision is in favor of the former alternative, but it is in the light of the fact that the metrical variations are all permissive and conventional. Here they consist in the following substitutions: a trochaic for the first iambic of the first line; a double foot or ionic for the third and fourth iambics of that line; and a double foot or ionic for the fourth and fifth iambics of the second line. But the meaning is slightly more severe than the alternative meaning, and Shakespeare does not care to tinker with it. In the alternative version the particularity of the figure may be too odd; and even in that version the third foot of the first line would have in "párliamént" an extra syllable, unless we take advantage again of the permissions and say it is "accounted for by elision." [2] To avoid the necessity of elision the poet might consider the possibility of a locution employing "senate"; but he probably does not like just that particularity; and in fact "sessions" may be as far as he wishes to go, not particularizing the legislative or judicial body that results when the members are seated.

In Donne, unless it is in Wyatt, whose meters are very difficult to construe, we have the feeling that we should find indeterminacy of metric carried furthest, sometimes almost to the point of unseating the iambic principle:

> Twó graves | must híde | thíne and | my córse;
> If óne | might, déath | were nó | divórce.

The difficulty of the first line is that every one of the monosyllables, except possibly *and,* is capable of taking a strong logical accent. We do not in fact know how to read it; we do know that the line from which it is in variation is iambic tetrameter; see the following line, completing the couplet, which is dutifully regular. We assign therefore some reading, almost arbitrary, which perhaps metrifies the line sufficiently and respects its structural logic, and we think of that perverseness in Donne which led him so often to mock the law without technically breaking it. Perverseness, that is, as Ben Jonson construed it; and by any account an insubordinacy, or an individualism, which was reluctant to conform, and seemed to offer the pretense that a meaning was involved which was too urgent to tamper with in the interest of meter. But we can defend the substantive orthodoxy of this poet's metrical technique if we should hear complaint against the following line; it has ten syllables, and is shown by its context to be intended for an iambic pentameter:

> Blásted | with síghs, | and súr | róunded | with téars.

The parallelism of *with sighs* and *with tears* suggests that the participles on which they depend are also closely coupled; if we are blasted by the sighs, as by

[2] The three permissive variations in iambic verse have now all been named: trochaic for iambic, ionic for two iambics, and extra syllable accounted for by elision.

winds, we ought to be fairly drowned by the tears, as by floods. But this last is precisely what *surrounded* means. It is the French *surronder* (<Lat. *superundare*), to overflow. The verb in its weak modern sense could hardly find room for two logical accents, and the iambic structure would be close to collapse; but then the logical structure would be impaired too, because it would come in this word to a foolish anticlimax. The only proper reader of the line is the one who trusts the integrity of Donne's metrical intention and looks to see how it can propose to conform here. To this reader the metric is informative. It is strictly the meaning of the line which has determined the variations in the meter, but we have found a meaning which does not destroy the meter, and it is decisive.

Milton is bold in his metric, but his conscience is exacting, and his irregularities come under the conventions. He writes:

Weep nó | more, wóe | ful Shép | herds, wéep | no móre.

The brilliance of this line consists in its falling eventually, and after we have tried other readings in vain, into the entire regularity which was the last thing we expected of it. We are used to receiving the impression, which he likes to give, and which represents a part of the truth, that his determinate meaning produces an indeterminateness in the local meters of nearly every line, even if we understand that this indeterminateness stops at the limits of the permissive convention. Under that impression we were inclined to scan the line this way:

Wéep no | móre, woe | ful Shép | herds, wéep | no móre,

which is a metrical line found many times in Milton; but we were troubled over what happened to the logic of the accentless *woeful.* We said to ourselves, however, that the first *weep no more* had precisely the same logical values as the second one. All the same, the accentless *woeful* is really not up to Milton's level as a workman, and we are not content with it. We finally try the normal meter, and we see that Milton intended us to come to it, and thought we must come to it if we believed in his technical competence. In the phrase *weep no more* it is difficult to say that one word has a heavier logical accent than another; yet we cannot accent them all, as we should like to do, and would do in prose. Or can we? The fact is that, reading the line as we finally do, we not only accent all three words but are obliged to: first *no,* then *weep,* then *more;* for the phrase occurs twice. Again the meter is informative. It could not be if there were not the most minute give-and-take between the meaning and the meter as principles trying to determine each other, and arriving every moment or so at peace with honor, which means careful adjustments by means of reciprocal concessions.

And now I must make an admission that my readers will surely have anticipated. It is not telling the whole truth to say that Shakespeare and other accomplished poets resort to their variations, which are metrical imperfections, because a determinate meaning has forced them into it. The poet likes the variations regardless of the meanings, finding them essential in the capacity of a sound-texture to go with the sound-structure. It is in no very late stage of a poet's advancement that his taste rejects a sustained phonetic regularity as something restricted and barren, perhaps ontologically defective. Accordingly he is capable of writing smooth meters and then roughening them on purpose. And it must be added, while we are about it, that he is capable of writing a clean logical argument, and then of roughening that too, by introducing logical violence into it, and perhaps willful obscurity. We have therefore this unusual degree of complexity in the total structure: the indeterminate sound or the indeterminate meaning, I S or I M, may have been really come to independently, by a poet who senses the aesthetic value of indeterminateness and is veteran enough to go straight after it. But nothing can be introduced into the meaning without affecting the meter, and vice versa; so that I M, and not only D M as was represented in the beginning, un-determines the meter again and produces I S; and, conversely, I S, and not only D S, may un-determine the meaning again and produce I M. It will sound very complicated, but good poets will attest it all if we ask them, and I think they will also offer the objective evidences in their poetry if we are skillful enough to read them. . . .

Monroe Beardsley

THE LANGUAGE OF LITERATURE

Since a literary work is a discourse, its parts are segments of language: a sentence is a part of a paragraph, a word of a sentence. Not that the relation of sentence to paragraph is the same as the relation of word to sentence, but *being a part of* is common to both relations.

When we ask what the ultimate parts, or elements, of literature are, we can give a variety of defensible answers, and must choose between them with reference to the purpose we have now in mind, that is, the purpose of the critical analysis. We could say that it is the sentence that is the smallest complete unit of discourse, and parts smaller than sentences are to be defined and understood in relation to actual or possible sentences. Or, we could say that the elements are the minimal particles of meaningful language, the roots and affixes that make up words: "un-law-ful" contains three of these particles. It is more convenient, however, to count as our elements something between sentences and particles, namely *words*. A word is, roughly, a unit of language such that any division of it will produce some part that cannot stand alone, at least not without a change of meaning: "law" can stand alone, but "un" and "ful" cannot.[1] This definition is imperfect, but fortunately it need not be refined here. A more pressing task confronts us.

Since they are meaningful sounds, words present two aspects for study. Later on, in Chapter V, §14,* we shall discuss the sound-aspect of words; it is their meaning-aspect that we must consider now. Though a good deal of interesting and helpful work has been done on the problem of meaning in recent years, there are still many unanswered questions. To review in detail the present state of the problem would involve us in issues from which we could extricate ourselves only with considerable difficulty. We shall have to

[1] See Edward Sapir, *Language*, New York: Harcourt, Brace, 1921 (reprinted New York: Harvest, 1956), chs. 1, 2.

* *Editors' Note:* not reprinted in present work.

be contented with a general framework of distinctions that are well established and important to the literary critic.[2]

Import and Purport

Under certain conditions, a piece of voluntary human behavior — a gesture, grunt, or cry — acquires the tendency to affect perceivers in some fairly definite way, and this capacity may be called the *import* of that behavior. Since we shall be concerned only with linguistic behavior — spoken sounds, or written marks that stand for such sounds — we can limit the scope of our definitions. A linguistic expression has import *for* a certain group of people, namely those who have been prepared by previous experience to respond to the utterance, spoken or written, of that linguistic expression.

Two basic types of import are to be distinguished. On one hand the linguistic expression may have a tendency to cause certain beliefs about the speaker; it may be so connected with particular mental states that its utterance permits the hearer to make an inference about what is going on in the speaker's mind. This capacity I shall call the *cognitive import* of the linguistic expression — or, for short, its *purport.* For example, when an English-speaking person says "Ouch!" we infer that he has felt a sharp pain. Of course the inference is sometimes not correct: the speaker may be only pretending. But in general the inference will be made and will be correct. The speaker doesn't necessarily intend to communicate information about himself when he says "Ouch!" He is merely giving vent to his feelings. But his exclamation does convey information, and therefore has a purport.

On the other hand, the linguistic expression may have a tendency to evoke certain feelings or emotions in the hearer. This capacity I shall call its *emotive import.* For example, among a certain group of people, an Anglo-Saxon four-letter word may tend to arouse a feeling of horrified shock or disgust; certain sentences about Home, Mother, or Alma Mater may tend to arouse a warm glow of affection.

Since the purport of a linguistic expression is its capacity to evoke a certain belief in the hearer, we can make a further distinction. The utterance of that linguistic expression may lead the hearer to believe something about the *beliefs* of the speaker; or it may lead the hearer to believe something about the *feelings,* or emotions, of the speaker. Thus, when *A* says "Alas!" this has a tendency to make *B* think that *A* feels sad. But when *A* says, "It's growing dark," this has a tendency to make *B* think that *A* believes it is growing dark. When a linguistic expression affects the hearer's beliefs about the beliefs of the speaker, I shall say that it has *cognitive purport,* which I take to be the same as *meaning.* A sentence's meaning is thus part of its purport, but it does not exhaust it. For, in the first place, it may also affect the hearer's beliefs about the speaker's *feelings* — "Oh, dear, what can the matter be?

[2] In this account of meaning I draw heavily, despite some differences in terminology, upon Charles L. Stevenson's *Ethics and Language.*

Johnny's so long at the fair" — and this I shall call its *emotive purport*. And, in the second place, it may affect the hearer's beliefs about other characteristics of the speaker, his nationality, social class, religious affiliations, state, status, or condition, and this I shall call its *general purport*. For example, if you use a technical term of sailing, speleology, herpetology, polo, witch-doctoring, or electronics, your mere use of this term, apart from what you say, will give information about you. And under the same heading we may place the informativeness of upper and lower class speech habits, colloquialisms native to one or another section of the country, and even the clichés that get to be the stereotyped responses of people with certain social or political attitudes — "Operation Rathole" — though most of these are also heavily charged with emotive purport.

Now, of course, when someone says, "It's raining," we do not take this to mean merely that he *believes* it is raining. It means that it *is* raining; it refers, truly or falsely, to something going on in the world outside the speaker's mind. This referential capacity of sentences — their semantical aspect — is by no means completely understood. I think we can say, however, that it is based upon, and in the last analysis explainable in terms of, the capacity of a sentence to formulate beliefs. When we hear the sentence spoken, we may not think of the speaker at all, but only of the rain, and of course we can understand the sentence perfectly well even if we happen to know that the speaker does not believe what he is saying. But to understand the sentence is to know what beliefs it *could* formulate. And this is the same as knowing what it would be like to believe it ourselves: what we would expect to see if we looked out the window, or feel if we went out without a hat. Hence, after we learn the meaning of a sentence, we can speak of its meaning as independent of what any particular speaker does with it.

It will, I think, be helpful at this point to draw up a table of these distinctions, so their relations will be perspicuous:

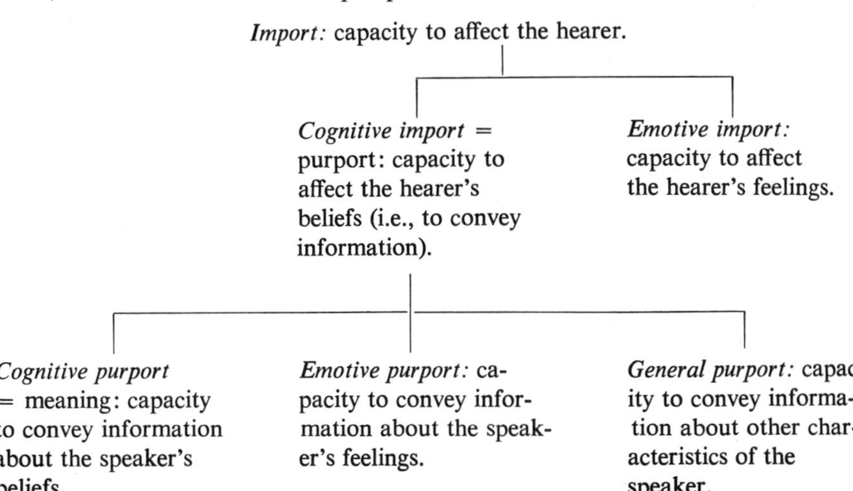
Import: capacity to affect the hearer.
Cognitive import = purport: capacity to affect the hearer's beliefs (i.e., to convey information).
Emotive import: capacity to affect the hearer's feelings.
Cognitive purport = meaning: capacity to convey information about the speaker's beliefs.
Emotive purport: capacity to convey information about the speaker's feelings.
General purport: capacity to convey information about other characteristics of the speaker.

The meaning of a linguistic expression, then, is its capacity to formulate, to give evidence of, beliefs. But we must make still another distinction for this scheme to serve our needs. Normally it is declarative sentences that formulate beliefs; this is their primary role, as when someone says, with earnestness, "The stock market is basically sound." Other kinds of sentence, whose primary role is different, can also be informative; when the broker says, "Hold off before buying stocks," although this is an imperative, it lets us know something about his probable beliefs.

But both of these examples are sentences, and it is not only sentences that have meaning, but words and phrases. Perhaps not *all* words; for example, "is" and "the" do not have meaning by themselves, but they are indispensable parts of linguistic expressions — "God is" and "the man in the moon" — that do have meaning. Now, if I suddenly say "moon," just by itself, I cannot ordinarily affect people's beliefs about my beliefs, though I might affect their beliefs about my sanity. In what sense, then, can we say that "moon" has a meaning? Only in a derivative sense; to say that "moon" has a meaning is to say that it can appear as a functional part of linguistic expressions — e.g., "Jupiter has nine moons" — that do have a meaning. To say that "lorph" has no meaning in English is to say that there is no sentence in English that contains it. In more familiar terms, "moon" has meaning in that it tends to call up an "idea" in the mind of one who knows the language. But this idea is not necessarily an image. You can understand the word "moon" even when it does not occur in a sentence, but you don't understand it unless your beliefs can be affected by some sentence in which it occurs.

Bearing in mind these general remarks about meaning, we can now inquire, more specifically, into the nature of literature. It would be convenient if we could find criteria to distinguish literary discourses from all other discourses — criteria which would then afford us a definition of "literature." The central question of this section is whether literature can be identified by its language, by the way language is used in literature as opposed to nonliterary discourses.

It is not universally conceded that this attempt can be carried through; perhaps we cannot even define "poetry." Literary theorists do often speak of the "language of poetry," implying that "poetry" can be defined as discourse written in a certain kind of language. In some periods of English poetry this was not very difficult; a poem could be recognized by its poetic diction: it said "finny tribes" or "scaly breed" instead of "fish," and "fleecy flocks" instead of "sheep." But we are used to poems with fish in them, alive and dead, plain and fancy, sensuous and symbolic — such poems as Yeats' "Sailing to Byzantium," in which

> The salmon-falls, the mackerel-crowded seas,
> Fish, flesh, or fowl, commend all summer long
> Whatever is begotten, born, and dies.

The old criterion no longer suffices. Nevertheless, we ordinarily speak as though we can distinguish poems from other things.

Even if there is a good definition of "poetry," there may be no good definition of "literature": perhaps when we call a poem a literary work we have a different sense in mind from that required for calling a novel a literary work, because different distinctions are involved. Even so, it would be clarifying to see how close we could come to ordinary uses of the term "literary work" by a definition, and for some purposes it might be worthwhile to abandon the ordinary uses in favor of a better one.

Literature and Emotive Language

The attempts to define "literature" by its language are of two types: those that hinge on the emotive aspect of language, and those that are stated entirely in terms of meaning.

The first type of definition is very neat — in fact, too neat to be acceptable. But it raises some fundamental questions, and calls for careful discussion. It would usually, I think, be offered as a definition of "poetry," rather than "literature" in general, so we shall consider it in this narrower form. Even in this form it is not very plausible, but it has to be considered, for it represents a point of view familiar and frequent enough among those who have thought a little, but not a great deal, about poetry.

The general formula for an emotive definition of "poetry" is: "Poetry is emotive language." And emotive language is further explained as language that has *independent emotive meaning*. The term "emotive meaning" is one that I plan to do without in this discussion; it is precisely when we search about among the distinctions just made for suitable substitutes for this term that we become aware of the confusions it sometimes fosters and hides. Making a vertical cut in our table of tendencies, above, we can distinguish the cognitive force of words, including cognitive import and cognitive purport, and the emotive force of words, including emotive import and emotive purport. Now a very fundamental and far-reaching question arises about the relation between the emotive force of words and their cognitive force, and especially about the extent to which the former is dependent upon the latter. The Independence Theory of this relation is that there is emotive force that is not causally dependent upon cognitive force.

But stated in this broad form, of course, the Independence Theory is hardly discussible; it needs to be broken down in terms of the relevant cross-relations that can be found in a table of imports and purports. There are two Independence Theories, completely distinct from each other; and the questions to which they lead should certainly be dealt with separately. But before we tackle these questions, the notion of Independence is itself in need of clarification. For present purposes, there are two points to be noted. Given any two things, X and Y, we may say that X is independent of Y if

(a) *X* can occur without *Y*, or (b) *X* can change without *Y's* changing. Thus the Bulgarian representatives at the United Nations are independent of the Soviet representatives whenever (a) they vote but the Soviets don't, or vice versa, or (b) they vote differently from the way the Soviets do.

The Independent Emotive Import Theory, as it may be called, is the broader of the two, and the less interesting to us here, but it requires some consideration. According to this theory there is emotive import that is independent of cognitive import — that is, purport. Two questions arise. (a) Are there words or sentences that have emotive import — that is, arouse the hearer's feelings — without having any purport at all — that is, without conveying any information at all about the speaker's beliefs or feelings or other characteristics? This seems in the highest degree improbable. You may use shocking words, which have strong emotive import, but their effect certainly depends to some extent upon their meanings, however vague. The same may be said of words of endearment like "Darling" and "Beloved" at the other end of the emotive spectrum. (b) Then does emotive import vary independently of purport? To test this part of the thesis we would look for a pair of terms that have exactly the same purport but differ in emotive import — that is, convey the same information but arouse different feelings, say, one arouses negative feelings and the other positive ones or none at all. It is safe to say, I think, that no such pair of terms has been produced. This is not merely because in a living language any two words have their different histories and therefore differ to some extent in their total purport. For we do not even find two words very close to each other in their purport and yet markedly different in emotive import. The usual examples, like "house" and "home," "liberty" and "license," "politician" and "statesman," won't do at all. The nearest you can come is probably a pair like "sister" and "female sibling," for they are fairly close in purport, though the first one has some positive emotive import that the second one lacks. But their purport is not the same, for we can think of poetic contexts that would lose purport if "female sibling" were substituted for "sister": for example, "Ye learned sisters" in the first line of Spenser's "Epithalamion."

But even if no unquestionable examples can be produced, this does not, of course, refute the Independent Emotive Import Theory. There are theoretical reasons in favor of it. Suppose Southerners and Northerners react in different ways emotionally to the same word. A plausible case can always be made out for the view that the word has some range of import that is at least a little different for the two groups. Yet it does not follow that the difference in emotional response can be completely explained in terms of the difference in purport. After all, two people can feel very differently about the same thing, and even if the word purports exactly the same thing to both, they might feel differently about that sort of thing, so the word would have a different emotive import. Moreover, suppose the word "foreigner" has a negative emotive import for a person afflicted with xenophobia; he could come to feel differently about foreigners, and consequently respond differently to the word, even if his understanding of its purport did not change.

We are entitled to conclude, I think, that the purport of a discourse, though not the only factor on which its emotive import depends, is the predominant one. I do not say it is impossible to dissociate them, for a particular person, under special circumstances, may be conditioned to respond in a certain way to the sound of a word, but not to its approximate synonym. But this response is idiosyncratic; it does not count as part of the emotive import of the word, which is a settled and fairly regular tendency to produce a particular feeling among a certain group of people. As far as public responses are concerned, the way the word "mother" becomes a bad word in Aldous Huxley's *Brave New World* shows that words can change their emotive import — but that change is not independent of certain changes in belief.

The Independent Emotive Purport Theory holds that there is emotive purport that is independent of cognitive purport, that is, meaning. Again we have two questions. (1) Are there words or sentences that have emotive purport — that is, reveal the speaker's feelings — without having any meaning at all — that is, without revealing the speaker's beliefs? There is a small class of such expressions, simple expletives like "Hell!" and "Ouch!" that probably can qualify for this description, though even their situation is not wholly clear. When you say, "Ouch!" you do show how you feel, and perhaps you don't show what you believe, though it is hard to draw an exact line, of course. (2) Are there pairs of words or sentences that are identical in meaning but different in emotive purport? Similar considerations arise here as in the problem of the independent variability of emotive import, and, oddly enough, the same examples are often quoted, though if they are relevant here, they are not relevant to the former question. But if "sister" and "female sibling" have a different emotive purport, it is partly because of a subtle difference in their meaning. The same is true of "Southern Democrat" and "Dixiecrat," and of "Northerner" and "Yankee."

Even this rather hasty discussion of independent emotive force is enough to show, I think, that anyone who seeks the defining characteristic of poetic language in this region will have a variety of subtly different versions to choose from, and it would be tedious to distinguish and discuss them all here. At one extreme would be a conception of poetry as pure emotive language, that is, of language with emotive purport but no cognitive purport. Such a poem would consist entirely of exclamations — "Damn!" "Oh dear!" "Ah!" and "Mmmmm!" Presumably no one would maintain such a conception, for as soon as these vague exclamations are filled out so that they can show precise and definite feelings, as a poem does — "I am aweary, aweary, I would that I were dead!" — they are no longer merely emotive, and the emotive purport they have seems to be determined and controlled by their meaning. At the other extreme would be the conception of poetry as simply language with a good deal of emotive purport, and perhaps a good deal of emotive import. This is innocuous, but also insufficiently defining, for of course a great many discourses that are not poems at all — cries of help or of alarm, announcements of births and deaths — have greater emotive purport or import than poems are likely to have. It may be that between these two extremes there is an emotive conception of poetry that is both applicable and distinctive, but I do not think so.

An alternative to the Emotive Definitions, then, is to seek for the defining characteristics of literature in the meaning of its language. And the most promising line of thought is that which distinguishes between two levels of meaning, sometimes called *explicit* and *implicit* meaning. There are really two distinctions here, which we must now state as succinctly as possible.

Primary and Secondary Meaning

Consider sentences first. With some exceptions . . . every declarative sentence has a *primary meaning* by virtue of its grammatical form: it presents a complex of meanings of such a sort that it can be said to be true or false. In short, it is a statement. Declarative sentences normally give utterance to beliefs; if one says, "Napoleon was a great general," we usually take him to be saying something he believes to be true. An imperative sentence is not a statement, and therefore does not give utterance to a belief, on its primary level of meaning, but indirectly it may show that the speaker has a belief even though he does not state it. Thus, if one says, "Please shut the window," we may infer that he believes the window should be shut, or perhaps that he believes it is chilly. These beliefs are not *stated,* but they are, in a technical sense of the term, *suggested.* What a sentence suggests I shall call its *secondary sentence meaning.*

A declarative sentence can state one thing and suggest another, and what it states may be true or false, and what it suggests may be true or false. Consider the following sentence: "Napoleon, who recognized the danger to his right flank, himself led his guards against the enemy position." [3] This complex sentence states (1) that Napoleon recognized the danger to his right flank, and (2) that Napoleon led his guards against the enemy position. If either of these statements is false, the sentence is false. But the sentence says more than it states, for it suggests (1) that Napoleon's maneuver occurred *after* the recognition of danger, and (2) that it occurred *because* of the recognition of danger, or in other words that the recognition of danger was the reason he led his guards against the enemy position. Now suppose we should discover that his decision to use his guards had already been made before he recognized the danger to his flank; we might still say that the original sentence was true, "strictly speaking," but we would also want to add that it was misleading, since it suggested something that is false.

[3] This example is from Gottlob Frege, "Sense and Reference," trans. by Max Black, *Phil R.* LVII (1948): 227–28; I also borrow Frege's analysis. (Another translation of this paper, called "On Sense and Nomination," is in H. Feigl and W. Sellars, *Readings in Philosophical Analysis,* New York: Appleton-Century-Crofts, 1949, pp. 85–102.)

What a sentence suggests, then, is what we can infer that the speaker probably believes, beyond what it states. One test for suggestion is that of misleadingness. Suppose there is something meant by the sentence that, if we should discover it to be false, would not lead us to call the sentence false, but only misleading, then that something is suggested, but not stated. The suggestion is part of the full meaning of the sentence, but its presence is not felt to be as central or as basic as the primary meaning, on which it nevertheless depends. That is why I call it secondary meaning. It is usually less emphatic, less obtrusive, less definitely and precisely fixed than the primary meaning, but it may be no less important, even from a practical point of view. What a sentence suggests it says implicitly, rather than explicitly, in the form of insinuation, innuendo, hint, or implication. The difference between "Mrs. Smith is prettier than Mrs. Jones" and "Mrs. Jones is uglier than Mrs. Smith" is a difference of suggestion. If either is precisely correct, the other is misleading. But, "On a scale of beauty, Mrs. Smith would rank somewhat higher than Mrs. Jones, and both would rank very high," approaches scientific language. It may be false, but it cannot be misleading, and therefore suggests nothing.

We shall not stop to consider here the varieties and uses of secondary sentence-meaning. The important point for our purposes is that a great number of rhetorical and compositional devices used in literature can be subsumed under this general heading. Any deviation from what is felt to be the normal grammatical order is a case of secondary sentence-meaning. So is any juxtaposition of ideas that, as in the Napoleon example, implicitly claims a connection between them, but leaves it to the reader to supply the connection himself. When we cannot supply such a connection, we have either obscurity or one kind of nonsense: "Napoleon, who was short in stature, was born in the eighteenth century."

Whatever part of the meaning of a poem depends on syntax, then, or upon the order of lines and sentences and stanzas, is suggestion. And this may constitute an important part of its meaning. If there is bourgeois propaganda in Gray's *Elegy,* it is because it is suggested by comparing the rural genius, frustrated by lack of opportunity, to a desert flower, which after all does not really want to be picked. If there is implicit paganism in *Paradise Lost,*[4] it is because the lines

In shadier Bower,
More sacred and sequestered, though but feigned,
Pan or Sylvanus never slept, nor Nymph
Nor Faunus hunted,

suggest that the pagan bowers had *some* degree of sacredness, just as the sentence, "Jack never had more money than Joe" suggests that Jack had *some* money. Or consider the first stanza of Housman's poem:

[4] These two examples are from William Empson, *Some Versions of Pastoral,* London: Chatto and Windus, 1930, pp. 4, 190.

Cross alone the nighted ferry
With the one coin for fee
Whom on the wharf of Lethe waiting
Count you to find? Not me.[5]

The answer to the question asked is "Me," not "Not me"; the question that "Not me" answers ("Whom *will* you find?") is not asked, but it is nevertheless implicitly there, as the second stanza shows.

When we turn from sentences to parts of sentences, we can make a corresponding distinction between the standard, or central, meaning of a word and its marginal or accompanying meanings. The word "sea" *designates* certain characteristics, such as being a large body of salt water; this is its primary word-meaning. It also *connotes* certain other characteristics, such as being sometimes dangerous, being changeable in mood but endless in motion, being a thoroughfare, being a barrier, and so on. These are its secondary word-meanings. "Sister" and "female sibling" have the same designation, but they differ in connotation, for two women who are not literally siblings may be "sisters under the skin."

The distinction between these two levels of term-meaning is not sharp, but it is operative in all our ordinary speech. Some of the commonest and most important feats of language, especially those carried to a high degree of subtlety and power in literature, depend upon our feeling that the total meaning of a word divides in this fashion. The word "wolf," for example, designates certain characteristics that define a class of animals; it also *denotes* the animals that have those defining characteristics in common. But besides having the characteristics that make them wolves, many wolves have certain other characteristics, or are widely believed to have them: fierceness, persistence, and predatory clannishness. And these characteristics have been ascribed to wolves in contexts that contain the word "wolf," whereas the contexts that contain its technical synonym, *Canis lupus,* have not so commonly ascribed such characteristics to them. Hence, when a person now uses the word "wolf" in certain contexts, we can infer that he probably believes that the entities referred to have some of the characteristics connoted by the term. And these characteristics, unless ruled out by the context, are part of what I call the full meaning of the word, though not of its strict, or dictionary, meaning — that is, its designation.

What a word connotes, then, are the characteristics that it does not designate but that belong, or are widely thought or said to belong, to many of the things it denotes. This is the word's range of connotation. But what it connotes in a particular context — its contextual connotation — is always a selection from its total range; indeed, the range may include incompatible connotations — "sea" connotes both being a barrier and being a highroad. In some contexts, all, or nearly all, its connotations may be kept out by the other words; these

[5] From "Crossing Alone the Nighted Ferry," *The Collected Poems of A. E. Housman.* Copyright, 1940, by Henry Holt and Company, Inc.

are contexts whose meaning is fully explicit, not likely to mislead, as in the best technical and scientific writing. In other contexts, its connotations are liberated; these are most notably the contexts in which language becomes figurative, and especially metaphorical, but this kind of language we shall consider more fully in the following section. It goes almost without saying that it is the language of poetry in which secondary word-meaning is most fully actualized. For example, in the first stanza of Thomas Carew's "Song,"

> Ask me no more where Jove bestows
> When June is past, the fading rose;
> For in your beauties' orient deep
> These flowers as in their causes sleep.

the word "causes" is freighted with a large chunk of Aristotle's metaphysics.

A discourse that has both primary and secondary levels of meaning may be said to have *multiple meaning:* for example, if it contains puns, *double-entendre,* metaphor, ironic suggestion. Multiple meaning is often called "ambiguity," and ambiguity is said to be a special characteristic of the language of poetry. I reserve the term "ambiguity" for linguistic expressions that are doubtful in meaning because they could have either, but not both, of two possible meanings and provide no ground for a decision between them. Where there is suggestion or connotation, no choice is called for; several things are meant at once.

The Semantic Definition of "Literature"

From the foregoing discussion we can now draw some general conclusions. Discourses may be arranged, roughly, in an order with respect to their reliance upon secondary meaning, that is, the proportion of meaning presented *implicitly,* by suggestion and connotation. Toward one end we put discourse that is highly charged with meaning, that condenses, so to speak, a great deal of meaning into a small space. Of course this spectrum is fairly continuous, but we can choose some standard discourses to mark off certain points along it, if we want to take the trouble. Moreover, we can draw a line, even if a somewhat vague one, between discourse that has a good deal of secondary meaning and discourse that has not. We may now try out a definition: a literary work is a discourse in which an important part of the meaning is implicit. This is a Semantic Definition of "literature," since it defines "literature" in terms of meaning.

All literary works fall into three main classes: poems, essays, and prose fiction. The *Spectator* papers and the sermons of Donne are in the second class. Play-scripts and motion-picture scenarios may be counted as fiction. A play as produced consists of a series of human, or humanlike, movements on a stage; it may involve the speaking of words, but it is not a literary work, but something more complicated that is related to literature. In this book we shall not have room to discuss the drama as such. But a play as read, that is, the script of the play, is a literary work, and falls within our classification; it is either a poem, like *Hamlet,* or a prose fiction, like *Ghosts.*

Each of the three classes of literary works presents us with its own problems of definition, that is, of distinction, and we cannot clear them up until we have investigated several other matters that await us in Chapters V and IX. But let us see what can be said at this stage. With respect to the *essay,* to take that first, the problem is to distinguish essays, in the literary sense, from technical writing, articles in the *Journal of Philosophy,* news stories, and so forth. This is certainly a matter of degree, but the question is, Along what scale is the degree to be measured? I think it is the proportion of the total meaning that occurs on the second level, that is, in suggestion and connotation. The literary essay is higher in stylistic reliance upon secondary meaning, and in such qualities as wit, humor, and irony that depend upon it. The line will be rather arbitrary, and of course even after it is drawn we may still look for, and find, what may be called "literary qualities" in nonliterary discourses. But at least we know what we are about.

The distinguishing mark of *fiction* — what marks it off from narrative that is nonfictional — is basically its lack of a claim to literal truth on the first level of meaning; but this definition will have to be amplified and defended in Chapter IX, §22. It might be convenient to include all fiction, so defined, in the class of literature, though some critics, I think, would want to reserve the term "literature" for something a little more substantial than mere statements that are not expected to be believed. In any case, in comparison with history and psychological case studies, fiction tends not merely to describe character abstractly but to leave it partly to be inferred from action, and its judgment upon the significance of events is suggested rather than overtly stated. And this is secondary meaning.

Poetry presents a more complicated problem. First, no doubt, there is a distinction in *sound,* and this we shall explore with some care in Chapter V, §14. Poetry is, at least, organized sound, and one problem is to analyze that organization which defines "verse." But not all verse is poetry. Now suppose that "verse" has been defined; which verses are, in the stricter sense, to be called "poems"? A poem is a verse that carries a large part of its meaning on the second level. It is almost possible to define "poem" in terms of figurative language — metaphor, simile, symbol. But though this will include nearly all poems, it will not include quite all. Consider, for example, the well-known anonymous ballad, "Edward": it has no figures of speech, unless we count "the curse of hell" in the last stanza, but what makes it a poem is all it suggests about motives and consequences of murder, about hate and guilt.

Tentatively, therefore, we may say that "literature" is well defined as "discourse with important implicit meaning." This definition not only draws a useful distinction by calling attention to noteworthy characteristics of the language of literary works, but it corresponds reasonably well with the reflective use of the term "literature" by critics.

It may, nevertheless, be felt that the Semantic Definition of "literature" is too formal, or, in one sense, merely nominal, like the definition of "man" as "featherless biped." And there is indeed another way of defining "literature," which we perhaps ought to consider briefly to round out the present topic; I argue that in the end it practically coincides with the linguistic definition.

Suppose we seek the defining characteristics of literature not in its language but in the world it projects. To put the view first in intentionalistic terms, which can easily be translated into objective ones, the essential thing that the literary creator does is to invent or discover an object — it can be a material object or a person, or a thought, or a state of affairs, or an event — around which he collects a set of relations that can be perceived as connected through their intersection in that object. For example, he might see, or imagine, a young boy's cast-off winter coat on the grass one sunny day in early spring. He creates the substance of literature if he can invest that coat with what I shall call, in a special and somewhat guarded sense, *multiple relatedness*. He sees it as, or makes it into, an indication of the eternal boyish struggle to be free of confinement and out running around unencumbered, or of the end of winter, or of the conflict between parents and children over chills and colds; he makes it function in a plot, as a symptom of motives and character, or as a cause of tragic events; or he may ruminate upon the exquisite carelessness of a crumpled, red-lined snowsuit on the feeble grass, one arm perhaps hanging over into a damp gutter.

I do not mean, of course, that he merely draws *inferences*. If he is interested in only one or two of these things, and is turned aside by curiosity about correlations and explanations — What proportion of American children get colds in March? — he moves toward abstraction, generalization, and science. But if he can hold the individual object in view as a focus of some pattern of human behavior, reflecting a quality of human nature, he has a contemplatable literary object.

My somewhat loose speculation touches already upon some matters that we shall have to deal with more systematically in Chapters V and IX; I venture it here only with reservations. But see what follows from it. We can conceive of the writer going off in different directions toward a lyric poem, a work of fiction, or a light literary essay. But all of them have in common the concern with multiple relatedness, the concrescence of patterns, different from the manner in which the trained botanist sees swampy ground as a likely habitat of certain mushrooms, or the trained political scientist sees the deliberations of the Senate Foreign Relations Committee as a symptom of incipient conflict with the State Department.

But the key words in this account are words like "invest" and "make"; *how* does a discourse — switching back now to objective language — invest the objects it refers to with these characteristics? Only, I should suppose, by means of the secondary levels of meaning; only through connotation and suggestion. So that, even if we start with the world of the literary work, we come back in the end to its language, and that is the reason the Semantic Definition was put foremost.

Roman Jakobson

LINGUISTICS AND POETICS

Fortunately, scholarly and political conferences have nothing in common. The success of a political convention depends on the general agreement of the majority or totality of its participants. The use of votes and vetoes, however, is alien to scholarly discussion where disagreement generally proves to be more productive than agreement. Disagreement discloses antinomies and tensions within the field discussed and calls for novel exploration. Not political conferences but rather exploratory activities in Antarctica present an analogy to scholarly meetings: international experts in various disciplines attempt to map an unknown region and find out where the greatest obstacles for the explorer are, the insurmountable peaks and precipices. Such a mapping seems to have been the chief task of our conference, and in this respect its work has been quite successful. Have we not realized what problems are the most crucial and the most controversial? Have we not also learned how to switch our codes, what terms to expound or even to avoid in order to prevent misunderstandings with people using different departmental jargon? Such questions, I believe, for most of the members of this conference, if not for all of them, are somewhat clearer today than they were three days ago.

I have been asked for summary remarks about poetics in its relation to linguistics. Poetics deals primarily with the question, *What makes a verbal message a work of art?* Because the main subject of poetics is the *differentia specifica* of verbal art in relation to other arts and in relation to other kinds of verbal behavior, poetics is entitled to the leading place in literary studies.

Poetics deals with problems of verbal structure, just as the analysis of painting is concerned with pictorial structure. Since linguistics is the global science of verbal structure, poetics may be regarded as an integral part of linguistics.

Arguments against such a claim must be thoroughly discussed. It is evident that many devices studied by poetics are not confined to verbal art. We can refer to the possibility of transposing *Wuthering Heights* into a motion picture, medieval legends into frescoes and miniatures, or *L'après-midi d'un faune* into music, ballet, and graphic art. However ludicrous may appear the idea of the *Iliad* and *Odyssey* in comics, certain structural features of their plot are preserved despite the disappearance of their verbal shape. The question whether Blake's illustrations to the *Divina Commedia* are or are not adequate is a proof that different arts are comparable. The problems of baroque or any other historical style transgress the frame of a single art. When handling the surrealistic metaphor, we could hardly pass by Max Ernst's pictures or Luis Buñuel's films, *The Andalusian Dog* and *The Golden Age*. In short, many poetic features belong not only to the science of language but to the whole theory of signs, that is, to general semiotics. This statement, however, is valid not only for verbal art but also for all varieties of language since language shares many properties with some other systems of signs or even with all of them (pansemiotic features).

Likewise a second objection contains nothing that would be specific for literature: the question of relations between the word and the world concerns not only verbal art but actually all kinds of discourse. Linguistics is likely to explore all possible problems of relation between discourse and the "universe of discourse": what of this universe is verbalized by a given discourse and how is it verbalized. The truth values, however, as far as they are — to say with the logicians — "extralinguistic entities," obviously exceed the bounds of poetics and of linguistics in general.

Sometimes we hear that poetics, in contradistinction to linguistics, is concerned with evaluation. This separation of the two fields from each other is based on a current but erroneous interpretation of the contrast between the structure of poetry and other types of verbal structure: the latter are said to be opposed by their "casual," designless nature to the "noncasual," purposeful character of poetic language. In point of fact, any verbal behavior is goal-directed, but the aims are different and the conformity of the means used to the effect aimed at is a problem that evermore preoccupies inquirers into the diverse kinds of verbal communication. There is a close correspondence, much closer than critics believe, between the question of linguistic phenomena expanding in space and time and the spatial and temporal spread of literary models. Even such discontinuous expansion as the resurrection of neglected or forgotten poets — for instance, the posthumous discovery and subsequent canonization of Gerard Manley Hopkins (d. 1889), the tardy fame of Lautréamont (d. 1870) among surrealist poets, and the salient influence of the hitherto ignored Cyprian Norwid (d. 1883) on Polish modern poetry — find a parallel in the history of standard languages which are prone to revive outdated models, sometimes long forgotten, as was the case in literary Czech which toward the beginning of the nineteenth century leaned to sixteenth-century models.

Unfortunately the terminological confusion of "literary studies" with "criticism" tempts the student of literature to replace the description of the intrinsic values of a literary work by a subjective, censorious verdict. The label "literary critic" applied to an investigator of literature is as erroneous as "grammatical (or lexical) critic" would be applied to a linguist. Syntactic and morphologic research cannot be supplanted by a normative grammar, and likewise no manifesto, foisting a critic's own tastes and opinions on creative literature, may act as substitute for an objective scholarly analysis of verbal art. This statement is not to be mistaken for the quietist principle of *laissez faire;* any verbal culture involves programmatic, planning, normative endeavors. Yet why is a clear-cut discrimination made between pure and applied linguistics or between phonetics and orthoëpy but not between literary studies and criticism?

Literary studies, with poetics as their focal portion, consist like linguistics of two sets of problems: synchrony and diachrony. The synchronic description envisages not only the literary production of any given stage but also that part of the literary tradition which for the stage in question has remained vital or has been revived. Thus, for instance, Shakespeare on the one hand and Donne, Marvell, Keats, and Emily Dickinson on the other are experienced by the present English poetic world, whereas the works of James Thomson and Longfellow, for the time being, do not belong to viable artistic values. The selection of classics and their reinterpretation by a novel trend is a substantial problem of synchronic literary studies. Synchronic poetics, like synchronic linguistics, is not to be confused with statics; any stage discriminates between more conservative and more innovatory forms. Any contemporary stage is experienced in its temporal dynamics, and, on the other hand, the historical approach both in poetics and in linguistics is concerned not only with changes but also with continuous, enduring, static factors. A thoroughly comprehensive historical poetics or history of language is a superstructure to be built on a series of successive synchronic descriptions.

Insistence on keeping poetics apart from linguistics is warranted only when the field of linguistics appears to be illicitly restricted, for example, when the sentence is viewed by some linguists as the highest analyzable construction or when the scope of linguistics is confined to grammar alone or uniquely to nonsemantic questions of external form or to the inventory of denotative devices with no reference to free variations. Voegelin has clearly pointed out the two most important and related problems which face structural linguistics, namely, a revision of "the monolithic hypothesis of language" and a concern with "the interdependence of diverse structures within one language." No doubt, for any speech community, for any speaker, there exists a unity of language, but this over-all code represents a system of interconnected subcodes; each language encompasses several concurrent patterns which are each characterized by a different function.

Obviously we must agree with Sapir that, on the whole, "ideation reigns supreme in language . . . ," [1] but this supremacy does not authorize linguistics

[1] E. Sapir, *Language* (New York, 1921).

to disregard the "secondary factors." The emotive elements of speech which, as Joos is prone to believe, cannot be described "with a finite number of absolute categories," are classified by him "as nonlinguistic elements of the real world." Hence, "for us they remain vague, protean, fluctuating phenomena," he concludes, "which we refuse to tolerate in our science." [2] Joos is indeed a brilliant expert in reduction experiments, and his emphatic requirement for an "expulsion" of the emotive elements "from linguistic science" is a radical experiment in reduction — *reductio ad absurdum.*

Language must be investigated in all the variety of its functions. Before discussing the poetic function we must define its place among the other functions of language. An outline of these functions demands a concise survey of the constitutive factors in any speech event, in any act of verbal communication. The ADDRESSER sends a MESSAGE to the ADDRESSEE. To be operative the message requires a CONTEXT referred to ("referent" in another, somewhat ambiguous, nomenclature), seizable by the addressee, and either verbal or capable of being verbalized; a CODE fully, or at least partially, common to the addresser and addressee (or in other words, to the encoder and decoder of the message); and, finally, a CONTACT, a physical channel and psychological connection between the addresser and the addressee, enabling both of them to enter and stay in communication. All these factors inalienably involved in verbal communication may be schematized as follows:

CONTEXT

ADDRESSER MESSAGE ADDRESSEE

CONTACT

CODE

Each of these six factors determines a different function of language. Although we distinguish six basic aspects of language, we could, however, hardly find verbal messages that would fulfill only one function. The diversity lies not in a monopoly of some one of these several functions but in a different hierarchical order of functions. The verbal structure of a message depends primarily on the predominant function. But even though a set (*Einstellung*) toward the referent, an orientation toward the CONTEXT — briefly the so-called REFERENTIAL, "denotative," "cognitive" function — is the leading task of numerous messages, the accessory participation of the other functions in such messages must be taken into account by the observant linguist.

The so-called EMOTIVE or "expressive" function, focused on the ADDRESSER, aims a direct expression of the speaker's attitude toward what he is speaking about. It tends to produce an impression of a certain emotion whether true or feigned; therefore, the term "emotive," launched and advocated by Marty [3]

[2] M. Joos, "Description of Language Design," *Journal of the Acoustical Society of America*, XXII (1950), 701–708.

[3] A. Marty, *Untersuchungen zur Grundlegung der Allegemeinen Grammatik und Sprachphilosophie*, Vol. 1 (Halle, 1908).

has proved to be preferable to "emotional." The purely emotive stratum in language is presented by the interjections. They differ from the means of referential language both by their sound pattern (peculiar sound sequences or even sounds elsewhere unusual) and by their syntactic role (they are not components but equivalents of sentences). *"Tut! Tut!* said McGinty": the complete utterance of Conan Doyle's character consists of two suction clicks. The emotive function, laid bare in the interjections, flavors to some extent all our utterances, on their phonic, grammatical, and lexical level. If we analyze language from the standpoint of the information it carries, we cannot restrict the notion of information to the cognitive aspect of language. A man, using expressive features to indicate his angry or ironic attitude, conveys ostensible information, and evidently this verbal behavior cannot be likened to such nonsemiotic, nutritive activities as "eating grapefruit" (despite Chatman's bold simile). The difference between [big] and the emphatic prolongation of the vowel [bi:g] is a conventional, coded linguistic feature like the difference between the short and long vowel in such Czech pairs as [vi] 'you' and [vi:] 'knows,' but in the latter pair the differential information is phonemic and in the former emotive. As long as we are interested in phonemic invariants, the English /i/ and /i:/ appear to be mere variants of one and the same phoneme, but if we are concerned with emotive units, the relation between the invariant and variants is reversed: length and shortness are invariants implemented by variable phonemes. Saporta's surmise that emotive difference is a nonlinguistic feature, "attributable to the delivery of the message and not to the message," arbitrarily reduces the informational capacity of messages.

A former actor of Stanislavskij's Moscow Theater told me how at his audition he was asked by the famous director to make forty different messages from the phrase *Segodnja večerom* 'This evening,' by diversifying its expressive tint. He made a list of some forty emotional situations, then emitted the given phrase in accordance with each of these situations, which his audience had to recognize only from the changes in the sound shape of the same two words. For our research work in the description and analysis of contemporary Standard Russian (under the auspices of the Rockefeller Foundation) this actor was asked to repeat Stanislavskij's test. He wrote down some fifty situations framing the same elliptic sentence and made of it fifty corresponding messages for a tape record. Most of the messages were correctly and circumstantially decoded by Moscovite listeners. May I add that all such emotive cues easily undergo linguistic analysis.

Orientation toward the ADDRESSEE, the CONATIVE function, finds its purest grammatical expression in the vocative and imperative, which syntactically, morphologically, and often even phonemically deviate from other nominal and verbal categories. The imperative sentences cardinally differ from declarative sentences: the latter are and the former are not liable to a truth test. When in O'Neill's play *The Fountain,* Nano, "(in a fierce tone of command)," says "Drink!" — the imperative cannot be challenged by the question "is it true or not?" which may be, however, perfectly well asked after such sentences as "one drank," "one will drink," "one would drink." In contradistinction to the imperative sentences, the declarative sentences are convertible into interrogative sentences: "did one drink?" "will one drink?" "would one drink?"

The traditional model of language as elucidated particularly by Bühler [4] was confined to these three functions — emotive, conative, and referential — and the three apexes of this model — the first person of the addresser, the second person of the addressee, and the "third person," properly — someone or something spoken of. Certain additional verbal functions can be easily inferred from this triadic model. Thus the magic, incantatory function is chiefly some kind of conversion of an absent or inanimate "third person" into an addressee of a conative message. "May this sty dry up, *tfu, tfu, tfu, tfu*" (Lithuanian spell [5]). "Water, queen river, daybreak! Send grief beyond the blue sea, to the sea-bottom, like a grey stone never to rise from the sea-bottom, may grief never come to burden the light heart of God's servant, may grief be removed and sink away." (North Russian incantation.[6]) "Sun, stand thou still upon Gibeon; and thou, Moon, in the valley of Aj-a-lon. And the sun stood still, and the moon stayed . . ." (Josh. 10.12). We observe, however, three further constitutive factors of verbal communication and three corresponding functions of language.

There are messages primarily serving to establish, to prolong, or to discontinue communication, to check whether the channel works ("Hello, do you hear me?"), to attract the attention of the interlocutor or to confirm his continued attention ("Are you listening?" or in Shakespearean diction, "Lend me your ears!" — and on the other end of the wire "Um-hum!"). This set for CONTACT, or in Malinowski's terms PHATIC function,[7] may be displayed by a profuse exchange of ritualized formulas, by entire dialogues with the mere purport of prolonging communication. Dorothy Parker caught eloquent examples: " 'Well!' the young man said. 'Well!' she said. 'Well, here we are,' he said. 'Here we are,' she said, 'Aren't we?' 'I should say we were,' he said, 'Eeyop! Here we are.' 'Well!' she said. 'Well!' he said, 'well.' " The endeavor to start and sustain communication is typical of talking birds; thus the phatic function of language is the only one they share with human beings. It is also the first verbal function acquired by infants; they are prone to communicate before being able to send or receive informative communication.

A distinction has been made in modern logic between two levels of language, "object language" speaking of objects and "metalanguage" speaking of lan-

[4] K. Bühler, "Die Axiomatik der Sprachwissenschaft," *Kant-Studien*, XXXVIII (Berlin, 1933), 19–90.

[5] V. T. Mansikka, *Litauische Zaubersprüche*, *Folklore Fellows Communications 87* (1929), p. 69.

[6] P. N. Rybnikov, *Pensi*, Vol. 3 (Moscow, 1910), p. 217 f.

[7] B. Malinowski, "The Problem of Meaning in Primitive Languages," in C. K. Ogden and I. A. Richards, *The Meaning of Meaning* (New York and London, ninth edition, 1953), pp. 296–336.

guage. But metalanguage is not only a necessary scientific tool utilized by logicians and linguists; it plays also an important role in our everyday language. Like Molière's Jourdain who used prose without knowing it, we practice metalanguage without realizing the metalingual character of our operations. Whenever the addresser and/or the addressee need to check up whether they use the same code, speech is focused on the CODE: it performs a METALINGUAL (i.e., glossing) function. "I don't follow you — what do you mean?" asks the addressee, or in Shakespearean diction, "What is't thou say'st?" And the addresser in anticipation of such recapturing questions inquires: "Do you know what I mean?" Imagine such an exasperating dialogue: "The sophomore was plucked." "But what is *plucked?*" "*Plucked* means the same as *flunked.*" "And *flunked?*" "*To be flunked* is *to fail in an exam.*" "And what is *sophomore?*" persists the interrogator innocent of school vocabulary. "*A sophomore* is (or means) a *second-year student.*" All these equational sentences convey information merely about the lexical code of English; their function is strictly metalingual. Any process of language learning, in particular child acquisition of the mother tongue, makes wide use of such metalingual operations; and aphasia may often be defined as a loss of ability for metalingual operations.

We have brought up all the six factors involved in verbal communication except the message itself. The set (*Einstellung*) toward the MESSAGE as such, focus on the message for its own sake, is the POETIC function of language. This function cannot be productively studied out of touch with the general problems of language, and, on the other hand, the scrutiny of language requires a thorough consideration of its poetic function. Any attempt to reduce the sphere of poetic function to poetry or to confine poetry to poetic function would be a delusive oversimplification. Poetic function is not the sole function of verbal art but only its dominant, determining function, whereas in all other verbal activities it acts as a subsidiary, accessory constituent. This function, by promoting the palpability of signs, deepens the fundamental dichotomy of signs and objects. Hence, when dealing with poetic function, linguistics cannot limit itself to the field of poetry.

"Why do you always say *Joan and Margery,* yet never *Margery and Joan?* Do you prefer Joan to her twin sister?" "Not at all, it just sounds smoother." In a sequence of two coordinate names, as far as no rank problems interfere, the precedence of the shorter name suits the speaker, unaccountably for him, as a well-ordered shape of the message.

A girl used to talk about "the horrible Harry." "Why horrible?" "Because I hate him." "But why not *dreadful, terrible, frightful, disgusting?*" "I don't know why, but *horrible* fits him better." Without realizing it, she clung to the poetic device of paronomasia.

The political slogan "I like Ike" /ay layk ayk/, succinctly structured, consists of three monosyllables and counts three diphthongs /ay/, each of them symmetrically followed by one consonantal phoneme, / . . l . . k . . k/. The make-up of the three words presents a variation: no consonantal phonemes in the first word, two around the diphthong in the second, and one final consonant in the third. A similar dominant nucleus /ay/ was noticed by Hymes in some of the sonnets of Keats. Both cola of the trisyllabic formula "I like / Ike" rhyme with each other, and the second of the two rhyming words is fully included in the first one (echo rhyme), /layk/ — /ayk/, a paronomastic image of a feeling which totally envelops its object. Both cola alliterate with each other, and the first of the two alliterating words is included in the second: /ay/ — /ayk/, a paronomastic image of the loving subject enveloped by the beloved object. The secondary, poetic function of this electional catch phrase reinforces its impressiveness and efficacy.

As we said, the linguistic study of the poetic function must overstep the limits of poetry, and, on the other hand, the linguistic scrutiny of poetry cannot limit itself to the poetic function. The particularities of diverse poetic genres imply a differently ranked participation of the other verbal functions along with the dominant poetic function. Epic poetry, focused on the third person, strongly involves the referential function of language; the lyric, oriented toward the first person, is intimately linked with the emotive function; poetry of the second person is imbued with the conative function and is either supplicatory or exhortative, depending on whether the first person is subordinated to the second one or the second to the first.

Now that our cursory description of the six basic functions of verbal communication is more or less complete, we may complement our scheme of the fundamental factors by a corresponding scheme of the functions:

	REFERENTIAL	
EMOTIVE	POETIC	CONATIVE
	PHATIC	
	METALINGUAL	

What is the empirical linguistic criterion of the poetic function? In particular, what is the indispensable feature inherent in any piece of poetry? To answer this question we must recall the two basic modes of arrangement used in verbal behavior, *selection* and *combination*. If "child" is the topic of the message, the speaker selects one among the extant, more or less similar, nouns like child, kid, youngster, tot, all of them equivalent in a certain respect, and then, to comment on this topic, he may select one of the semantically cognate verbs — sleeps, dozes, nods, naps. Both chosen words combine in the speech chain. The selection is produced on the base of equivalence, similarity and dissimilarity, synonymity and antonymity, while the combination, the build up of the sequence, is based on contiguity. *The poetic function projects the principle of equivalence from the axis of selection into the axis of combination.* Equivalence is promoted to the constitutive device of the sequence. In poetry one syllable is equalized with any other syllable of the same sequence; word stress is assumed to equal word stress, as unstress equals unstress; prosodic long is matched with long, and short with short; word boundary equals word boundary, no boundary equals no boundary; syntactic pause equals syntactic pause, no pause equals no pause. Syllables are converted into units of measure, and so are morae or stresses.

It may be objected that metalanguage also makes a sequential use of equivalent units when combining synonymic expressions into an equational sentence: $A = A$ ("*Mare* is *the female of the horse*"). Poetry and metalanguage, however, are in diametrical opposition to each other: in metalanguage the sequence is used to build an equation, whereas in poetry the equation is used to build a sequence.

In poetry, and to a certain extent in latent manifestations of poetic function, sequences delimited by word boundaries become commensurable whether they are sensed as isochronic or graded. "Joan and Margery" showed us the poetic principle of syllable gradation, the same principle which in the closes of Serbian folk epics has been raised to a compulsory law.[8] Without its two dactylic words the combination "i*nnocent* by*stand*er" would hardly have become a hackneyed phrase. The symmetry of three disyllabic verbs with an identical initial consonant and identical final vowel added splendor to the laconic victory message of Caesar: "*Veni, vidi, vici.*"

Measure of sequences is a device which, outside of poetic function, finds no application in language. Only in poetry with its regular reiteration of equivalent units is the time of the speech flow experienced, as it is — to cite another semiotic pattern — with musical time. Gerard Manley Hopkins, an outstanding searcher in the science of poetic language, defined verse as "speech wholly or partially repeating the same figure of sound." [9] Hopkins' subsequent question, "but is all verse poetry?" can be definitely answered as soon as poetic function ceases to be arbitrarily confined to the domain of poetry. Mnemonic lines cited by Hopkins (like "Thirty days hath September"), modern advertising jingles, and versified medieval laws, mentioned by Lotz, or finally Sanscrit scientific treatises in verse which in Indic tradition are strictly distinguished from true poetry (*kāvya*) — all these metrical texts make use of poetic function without, however, assigning to this function the coercing, determining role it carries in poetry. Thus verse actually exceeds the limits of poetry, but at the same time verse always implies poetic function. And apparently no human culture ignores versemaking, whereas there are many cultural patterns without "applied" verse; and even in such cultures which possess both pure and applied verses, the latter appear to be a secondary, unquestionably derived phenomenon. The adaptation of poetic means for some heterogeneous purpose does not conceal their primary essence, just as elements of emotive language, when utilized in poetry, still maintain their emotive tinge. A filibusterer may recite *Hiawatha* because

[8] T. Maretić, "Metrika Narodnih Naših Pjesama," *Rad Yugoslavenske Akademije* (Zagreb, 1907), 168, 170.

[9] G. M. Hopkins, *The Journals and Papers*, H. House, ed. (London, 1959).

it is long, yet poeticalness still remains the primary intent of this text itself. Self-evidently, the existence of versified, musical, and pictorial commercials does not separate the questions of verse or of musical and pictorial form from the study of poetry, music, and fine arts.

To sum up, the analysis of verse is entirely within the competence of poetics, and the latter may be defined as that part of linguistics which treats the poetic function in its relationship to the other functions of language. Poetics in the wider sense of the word deals with the poetic function not only in poetry, where this function is superimposed upon the other functions of language, but also outside of poetry, when some other function is superimposed upon the poetic function.

The reiterative "figure of sound," which Hopkins saw to be the constitutive principle of verse, can be further specified. Such a figure always utilizes at least one (or more than one) binary contrast of a relatively high and relatively low prominence effected by the different sections of the phonemic sequence.

Within a syllable the more prominent, nuclear, syllabic part, constituting the peak of the syllable, is opposed to the less prominent, marginal, nonsyllabic phonemes. Any syllable contains a syllabic phoneme, and the interval between two successive syllabics is in some languages always and in others overwhelmingly carried out by marginal, nonsyllabic phonemes. In the so-called syllabic versification the number of syllabics in a metrically delimited chain (time series) is a constant, whereas the presence of a nonsyllabic phoneme or cluster between every two syllabics of a metrical chain is a constant only in languages with an indispensable occurrence of nonsyllabics between syllabics and, furthermore, in those verse systems where hiatus is prohibited. Another manifestation of a tendency toward a uniform syllabic model is the avoidance of closed syllables at the end of the line, observable, for instance, in Serbian epic songs. The Italian syllabic verse shows a tendency to treat a sequence of vowels unseparated by consonantal phonemes as one single metrical syllable.[10]

In some patterns of versification the syllable is the only constant unit of verse measure, and a grammatical limit is the only constant line of demarcation between measured sequences, whereas in other patterns syllables in turn are dichotomized into more and less prominent, and/or two levels of grammatical limits are distinguished in their metrical function, word boundaries and syntactic pauses.

Except the varieties of the so-called vers libre that are based on conjugate intonations and pauses only, any meter uses the syllable as a unit of measure at least in certain sections of the verse. Thus in the purely accentual verse ("sprung rhythm" in Hopkins' vocabulary), the number of syllables in the upbeat (called "slack" by Hopkins) may vary, but the downbeat (ictus) constantly contains one single syllable.

In any accentual verse the contrast between higher and lower prominence

[10] A. Levi, "Della Versificazione Italiana," *Archivum Romanicum*, XIV (1930), secs. VIII–IX.

is achieved by syllables under stress versus unstressed syllables. Most accentual patterns operate primarily with the contrast of syllables with and without word stress, but some varieties of accentual verse deal with syntactic, phrasal stresses, those which Wimsatt and Beardsley cite as "the major stresses of the major words" and which are opposed as prominent to syllables without such major, syntactic stress.

In the quantitative ("chronemic") verse, long and short syllables are mutually opposed as more and less prominent. This contrast is usually carried out by syllable nuclei, phonemically long and short. But in metrical patterns like Ancient Greek and Arabic, which equalize length "by position" with length "by nature," the minimal syllables consisting of a consonantal phoneme and one mora vowel are opposed to syllables with a surplus (a second mora or a closing consonant) as simpler and less prominent syllables opposed to those that are more complex and prominent.

The question still remains open whether, besides the accentual and the chronemic verse, there exists a "tonemic" type of versification in languages where differences of syllabic intonations are used to distinguish word meanings.[11] In classical Chinese poetry,[12] syllables with modulations (in Chinese *tsê*, 'deflected tones') are opposed to the nonmodulated syllables (*p'ing*, 'level tones'), but apparently a chronemic principle underlies this opposition, as was suspected by Polivanov [13] and keenly interpreted by Wang Li; [14] in the Chinese metrical tradition the level tones prove to be opposed to the deflected tones as long tonal peaks of syllables to short ones, so that verse is based on the opposition of length and shortness.

Joseph Greenberg brought to my attention another variety of tonemic versification — the verse of Efik riddles based on the level feature. In the sample cited by Simmons,[15] the query and the response form two octosyllables with an alike distribution of *h*(igh)- and *l*(ow)-tone syllabics; in each hemistich, moreover, the last three of the four syllables present an identical tonemic pattern: *lhhl/hhhl//lhhl/hhhl//*. Whereas Chinese versification appears as a peculiar variety of the quantitative verse, the verse of the Efik riddles is linked with the usual accentual verse by an opposition of two degrees of prominence (strength or height) of the vocal tone. Thus a metrical system of versification can be based only on the opposition of syllabic peaks and slopes (syllabic verse), on the relative level of the peaks (accentual verse), and on the relative length of the syllabic peaks or entire syllables (quantitative verse).

In textbooks of literature we sometimes encounter a superstitious contraposition of syllabism as a mere mechanical count of syllables to the lively

[11] R. Jakobson, *O Češskom Stixe Preimuščestvenno V Sopostavlenii S Russkim* (= Sborniki Po Teorii Poèticeskogo Jazyka, 5) (Berlin and Moscow, 1923).

[12] J. L. Bishop, "Prosodic Elements in T'ang Poetry," *Indiana University Conference on Oriental-Western Literary Relations* (Chapel Hill, 1955).

[13] E. D. Polivanov, "O Metričeskom Xarahtere Kitajskogo Stixosloženija," *Doklady Rossijskoj Akademii Nauk*, serija V (1924), 156–158.

[14] Wang Li, *Han-yü Shih-lü-hsüeh* (= Versification in Chinese) (Shanghai, 1958).

[15] D. C. Simmons, "Specimens of Efik Folklore," *Folk-lore* (1955), p. 228.

pulsation of accentual verse. If we examine, however, the binary meters of the strictly syllabic and at the same time, accentual versification, we observe two homogeneous successions of wavelike peaks and valleys. Of these two undulatory curves, the syllabic one carries nuclear phonemes in the crest and usually marginal phonemes in the bottom. As a rule the accentual curve superposed upon the syllabic curve alternates stressed and unstressed syllables in the crests and bottoms respectively.

For comparison with the English meters which we have lengthily discussed, I bring to your attention the similar Russian binary verse forms which for the last fifty years have verily undergone an exhaustive investigation.[16] The structure of the verse can be very thoroughly described and interpreted in terms of enchained probabilities. Besides the compulsory word boundary between the lines, which is an invariant throughout all Russian meters, in the classic pattern of Russian syllabic accentual verse ("syllabo-tonic" in native nomenclature) we observe the following constants: (1) the number of syllables in the line from its beginning to the last downbeat is stable; (2) this very last downbeat always carries a word stress; (3) a stressed syllable cannot fall on the upbeat if a downbeat is fulfilled by an unstressed syllable of the same word unit (so that a word stress can coincide with an upbeat only as far as it belongs to a monosyllabic word unit).

Along with these characteristics compulsory for any line composed in a given meter, there are features that show a high probability of occurrence without being constantly present. Besides signals certain to occur ("probability one"), signals likely to occur ("probabilities less than one") enter into the notion of meter. Using Cherry's description of human communication,[17] we could say that the reader of poetry obviously "may be unable to attach numerical frequencies" to the constituents of the meter, but as far as he conceives the verse shape, he unwittingly gets an inkling of their "rank order."

In the Russian binary meters all odd syllables counting back from the last downbeat — briefly, all the upbeats — are usually fulfilled by unstressed syllables, except some very low percentage of stressed monosyllables. All even syllables, again counting back from the last downbeat, show a sizable preference for syllables under word stress, but the probabilities of their occurrence are unequally distributed among the successive downbeats of the line. The higher the relative frequency of word stresses in a given downbeat, the lower the ratio shown by the preceding downbeat. Since the last downbeat is constantly stressed, the next to last gives the lowest percentage of word stresses; in the preceding downbeat their amount is again higher, without attaining the maximum, displayed by the final downbeat; one downbeat further toward the beginning of the line, the amount of the stresses sinks once more, without reaching the minimum of the next-to-last downbeat; and so on. Thus the distribution of word stresses among the downbeats within the line, the split

[16] K. Taranovski, *Ruski Dvodelni Ritmovi* (Belgrade, 1955).
[17] C. Cherry, *On Human Communication* (New York, 1957).

into strong and weak downbeats, creates a *regressive undulatory curve* superposed upon the wavy alternation of downbeats and upbeats. Incidentally, there is a captivating question of the relationship between the strong downbeats and phrasal stresses.

The Russian binary meters reveal a stratified arrangement of three undulatory curves: (I) alternation of syllabic nuclei and margins; (II) division of syllabic nuclei into alternating downbeats and upbeats; and (III) alternation of strong and weak downbeats. For example, Russian masculine iambic tetrameter of the nineteenth and present centuries may be represented by Figure 1, and a similar triadic pattern appears in the corresponding English forms.

Three of five downbeats are deprived of word stress in Shelley's iambic line "Laugh with an inextinguishable laughter." Seven of sixteen downbeats are stressless in the following quatrain from Pasternak's recent iambic tetrameter *Zemlja* ("Earth"):

I úlica za panibráta
S okónnicej podslepovátoj,
I béloj nóči i zakátu
Ne razminút'sja u rekí.

Since the overwhelming majority of downbeats concur with word stresses, the listener or reader of Russian verses is prepared with a high degree of probability to meet a word stress in any even syllable of iambic lines, but at the very beginning of Pasternak's quatrain the fourth and, one foot further, the sixth syllable, both in the first and in the following line, present him with a *frustrated expectation*. The degree of such a "frustration" is higher when the stress is lacking in a strong downbeat and becomes particularly outstanding when two successive downbeats are carrying unstressed syllables. The stress-

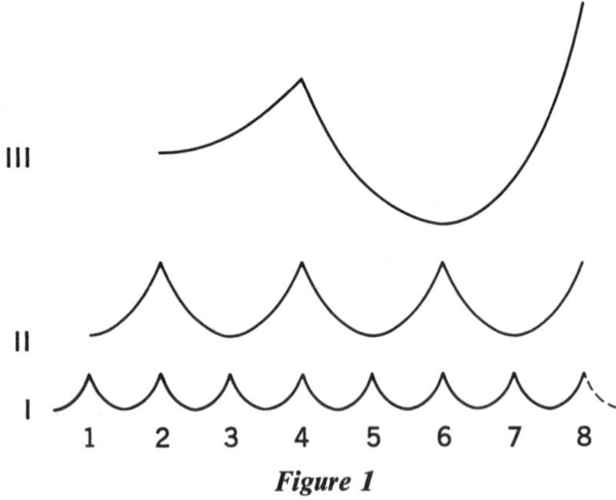

Figure 1

lessness of two adjacent downbeats is the less probable and the most striking when it embraces a whole hemistich as in a later line of the same poem: "Čtoby za gorodskjóu grán' ju" [stəbyzəgərackóju grán'ju]. The expectation depends on the treatment of a given downbeat in the poem and more generally in the whole extant metrical tradition. In the last downbeat but one, unstress may, however, outweigh the stress. Thus in this poem only 17 of 41 lines have a word stress on their sixth syllable. Yet in such a case the inertia of the stressed even syllables alternating with the unstressed odd syllables prompts some expectancy of stress also for the sixth syllable of the iambic tetrameter.

Quite naturally it was Edgar Allan Poe, the poet and theoretician of defeated anticipation, who metrically and psychologically appraised the human sense of gratification for the unexpected arising from expectedness, both of them unthinkable without the opposite, "as evil cannot exist without good." [18] Here we could easily apply Robert Frost's formula from "The Figure a Poem Makes": "The figure is the same as for love." [19]

The so-called shifts of word stress in polysyllabic words from the downbeat to the upbeat ("reversed feet"), which are unknown to the standard forms of Russian verse, appear quite usually in English poetry after a metrical and/or syntactic pause. A noticeable example is the rhythmical variation of the same adjective in Milton's "Infinite wrath and infinite despair." In the line "Nearer, my God, to Thee, nearer to Thee," the stressed syllable of one and the same word occurs twice in the upbeat, first at the beginning of the line and a second time at the beginning of a phrase. This license, discussed by Jespersen [20] and current in many languages, is entirely explainable by the particular import of the relation between an upbeat and the immediately preceding downbeat. Where such an immediate precedence is impeded by an inserted pause, the upbeat becomes a kind of *syllaba anceps*.

Besides the rules which underlie the compulsory features of verse, the rules governing its optional traits also pertain to meter. We are inclined to designate such phenomena as unstress in the downbeats and stress in upbeats as deviations, but it must be remembered that these are allowed oscillations, departures within the limits of the law. In British parliamentary terms, it is not an opposition to its majesty the meter but an opposition of its majesty. As to the actual infringements of metrical laws, the discussion of such violations recalls Osip Brik, perhaps the keenest of Russian formalists, who used to say that political conspirators are tried and condemned only for unsuccessful attempts at a forcible upheaval, because in the case of a successful coup it is the conspirators who assume the role of judges and prosecutors. If the violences against the meter take root, they themselves become metrical rules.

Far from being an abstract, theoretical scheme, meter — or in more explicit terms, *verse design* — underlies the structure of any single line — or, in logical terminology, any single *verse instance*. Design and instance are correlative concepts. The verse design determines the invariant features of the verse instances and sets up the limits of variations. A Serbian peasant reciter of epic poetry memorizes, performs, and, to a high extent, improvises thousands, some-

[18] E. A. Poe, "Marginalia," *The Works*, Vol. 3 (New York, 1857).

[19] R. Frost, *Collected Poems* (New York, 1939).

[20] O. Jespersen, "Cause Psychologique de Quelques Phénomènes de Métrique Germanique," *Psychologie du Langage* (Paris, 1933).

times tens of thousands of lines, and their meter is alive in his mind. Unable to abstract its rules, he nonetheless notices and repudiates even the slightest infringement of these rules. Any line of Serbian epics contains precisely ten syllables and is followed by a syntactic pause. There is furthermore a compulsory word boundary before the fifth syllable and a compulsory absence of word boundary before the fourth and tenth syllable. The verse has, moreover, significant quantitative and accentual characteristics.[21]

This Serbian epic break, along with many similar examples presented by comparative metrics, is a persuasive warning against the erroneous identification of a break with a syntactic pause. The obligatory word boundary must not be combined with pause and is not even meant to be perceptible by the ear. The analysis of Serbian epic songs phonographically recorded proves that there are no compulsory audible clues to the break, and yet any attempt to abolish the word boundary before the fifth syllable by a mere insignificant change in word order is immediately condemned by the narrator. The grammatical fact that the fourth and fifth syllables pertain to two different word units is sufficient for the appraisal of the break. Thus verse design goes far beyond the questions of sheer sound shape; it is a much wider linguistic phenomenon, and it yields to no isolating phonetic treatment.

I say "linguistic phenomenon" even though Chatman states that "the meter exists as a system outside the language." Yes, meter appears also in other arts dealing with time sequence. There are many linguistic problems — for instance, syntax — which likewise overstep the limit of language and are common to different semiotic systems. We may speak even about the grammar of traffic signals. There exists a signal code, where a yellow light when combined with green warns that free passage is close to being stopped and when combined with red announces the approaching cessation of the stoppage; such a yellow signal offers a close analogue to the verbal completive aspect. Poetic meter, however, has so many intrinsically linguistic particularities that it is most convenient to describe it from a purely linguistic point of view.

Let us add that no linguistic property of the verse design should be disregarded. Thus, for example, it would be an unfortunate mistake to deny the constitutive value of intonation in English meters. Not even speaking about its fundamental role in the meters of such a master of English free verse as Whitman, it is impossible to ignore the metrical significance of pausal intonation ("final juncture"), whether "cadence" or "anticadence," [22] in poems like "The Rape of the Lock" with its intentional avoidance of enjambments. Yet even a vehement accumulation of enjambments never hides their digressive, variational status; they always set off the normal coincidence of syntactic pause and pausal intonation with the metrical limit. Whatever is the reciter's way of

[21] R. Jakobson, "Studies in Comparative Slavic Metrics," *Oxford Slavonic Papers*, III (1952), 21–66. Cf. also R. Jakobson, "Über den Versbau der Serbokroatischen Volksepen," Archives Néerlandaises de Phonétique Expérimentale, VII–IX (1933), 44–53.

[22] S. Karcevskij, "Sur la Phonologie de la Phrase," *Travaux du Cercle Linguistique de Prague*, IV (1931), 188–223.

reading, the intonational constraint of the poem remains valid. The intonational contour inherent to a poem, to a poet, to a poetic school is one of the most notable topics brought to discussion by the Russian formalists.[23]

The verse design is embodied in verse instances. Usually the free variation of these instances is denoted by the somewhat equivocal label "rhythm." A variation of *verse instances* within a given poem must be strictly distinguished from the variable *delivery instances*. The intention "to describe the verse line as it is actually performed" is of lesser use for the synchronic and historical analysis of poetry than it is for the study of its recitation in the present and the past. Meanwhile the truth is simple and clear: "There are many performances of the same poem — differing among themselves in many ways. A performance is an event, but the poem itself, if there *is* any poem, must be some kind of enduring object." This sage memento of Wimsatt and Beardsley belongs indeed to the essentials of modern metrics.

In Shakespeare's verses the second, stressed syllable of the word "absurd" usually falls on the downbeat, but once in the third act of *Hamlet* it falls on the upbeat: "No, let the candied tongue lick absurd pomp." The reciter may scan the word "absurd" in this line with an initial stress on the first syllable or observe the final word stress in accordance with the standard accentuation. He may also subordinate the word stress of the adjective in favor of the strong syntactic stress of the following head word, as suggested by Hill: "Nó, lèt thĕ cândĭed tóngue lîck ăbsùrd pómp," [24] as in Hopkins' conception of English antispasts — "regrét névér." [25] There is finally a possibility of emphatic modifications either through a "fluctuating accentuation" (*schwebende Betonung*) embracing both syllables or through an exclamational reinforcement of the first syllable [àb-súrd]. But whatever solution the reciter chooses, the shift of the word stress from the downbeat to the upbeat with no antecedent pause is still arresting, and the moment of frustrated expectation stays viable. Wherever the reciter put the accent, the discrepancy between the English word stress on the second syllable of "absurd" and the downbeat attached to the first syllable persists as a constitutive feature of the verse instance. The tension between the ictus and the usual word stress is inherent in this line independently of its different implementations by various actors and readers. As Gerard Manley Hopkins observes, in the preface to his poems, "two rhythms are in some manner running at once." [26] His description of such a contrapuntal run can be reinterpreted. The superinducing of an equivalence principle upon the word sequence or, in other terms, the *mounting* of the metrical form upon the usual speech form, necessarily gives the experience of a double, ambiguous shape to anyone

[23] B. Èjxenbaum, *Melodika Stixa* (Leningrad, 1922), and V. Žirmunskij, *Voprosy Teorii Literatury* (Leningrad, 1928).

[24] A. A. Hill, Review in *Language*, XXIX (1953), 549–561.

[25] G. M. Hopkins, *The Journals and Papers*.

[26] G. M. Hopkins, *Poems*, W. H. Gardner, ed. (New York and London, third edition, 1948).

who is familiar with the given language and with verse. Both the convergences and the divergences between the two forms, both the warranted and the frustrated expectations, supply this experience.

How the given verse-instance is implemented in the given delivery instance depends on the *delivery design* of the reciter; he may cling to a scanning style or tend toward prose-like prosody or freely oscillate between these two poles. We must be on guard against simplistic binarism which reduces two couples into one single opposition either by suppressing the cardinal distinction between verse design and verse instance (as well as between delivery design and delivery instance) or by an erroneous identification of delivery instance and delivery design with the verse instance and verse design.

> "But tell me, child, your choice; what shall I buy
> You?" — "Father, what you buy me I like best."

These two lines from "The Handsome Heart" by Hopkins contain a heavy enjambment which puts a verse boundary before the concluding monosyllable of a phrase, of a sentence, of an utterance. The recitation of these pentameters may be strictly metrical with a manifest pause between "buy" and "you" and a suppressed pause after the pronoun. Or, on the contrary, there may be displayed a prose-oriented manner without any separation of the words "buy you" and with a marked pausal intonation at the end of the question. None of these ways of recitation may, however, hide the intentional discrepancy between the metrical and syntactic division. The verse shape of a poem remains completely independent of its variable delivery, whereby I do not intend to nullify the alluring question of *Autorenleser* and *Selbstleser* launched by Sievers.[27]

No doubt, verse is primarily a recurrent "figure of sound." Primarily, always, but never uniquely. Any attempts to confine such poetic conventions as meter, alliteration, or rhyme to the sound level are speculative reasonings without any empirical justification. The projection of the equational principle into the sequence has a much deeper and wider significance. Valéry's view of poetry as "hesitation between the sound and the sense" [28] is much more realistic and scientific than any bias of phonetic isolationism.

Although rhyme by definition is based on a regular recurrence of equivalent phonemes or phonemic groups, it would be an unsound oversimplification to treat rhyme merely from the standpoint of sound. Rhyme necessarily involves the semantic relationship between rhyming units ("rhyme-fellows" in Hopkins' nomenclature). In the scrutiny of a rhyme we are faced with the question of whether or not it is a homoeoteleuton, which confronts similar derivational and/or inflexional suffixes (congratulations-decorations), or whether the rhyming words belong to the same or to different grammatical categories. Thus, for example, Hopkins' fourfold rhyme is an agreement of two nouns — "kind" and "mind" — both contrasting with the adjective "blind" and with the verb "find." Is there a semantic propinquity, a sort of simile between rhyming lexical

[27] E. Sievers, *Ziele und Wege der Schallanalyse* (Heidelberg, 1924).

[28] P. Valéry, *The Art of Poetry*. Bollingen series 45 (New York, 1958).

units, as in dove-love, light-bright, place-space, name-fame? Do the rhyming members carry the same syntactic function? The difference between the morphological class and the syntactic application may be pointed out in rhyme. Thus in Poe's lines, "While I nodded, nearly *napping*, suddenly there came a *tapping*. As of someone gently *rapping*," the three rhyming words, morphologically alike, are all three syntactically different. Are totally or partly homonymic rhymes prohibited, tolerated, or favored? Such full homonyms as son-sun, I-eye, eve-eave, and on the other hand, echo rhymes like December-ember, infinite-night, swarm-warm, smiles-miles? What about compound rhymes (such as Hopkins' "enjoyment–toy meant" or "began some–ransom"), where a word unit accords with a word group?

A poet or poetic school may be oriented toward or against grammatical rhyme; rhymes must be either grammatical or antigrammatical; an agrammatical rhyme, indifferent to the relation between sound and grammatical structure, would, like any agrammatism, belong to verbal pathology. If a poet tends to avoid grammatical rhymes, for him, as Hopkins said, "There are two elements in the beauty rhyme has to the mind, the likeness or sameness of sound and the unlikeness or difference of meaning." [29] Whatever the relation between sound and meaning in different rhyme techniques, both spheres are necessarily involved. After Wimsatt's illuminating observations about the meaningfulness of rhyme [30] and the shrewd modern studies of Slavic rhyme patterns, a student in poetics can hardly maintain that rhymes signify merely in a very vague way.

Rhyme is only a particular, condensed case of a much more general, we may even say the fundamental, problem of poetry, namely *parallelism*. Here again Hopkins, in his student papers of 1865, displayed a prodigious insight into the structure of poetry:

> The artificial part of poetry, perhaps we shall be right to say all artifice, reduces itself to the principle of parallelism. The structure of poetry is that of continuous parallelism, ranging from the technical so-called Parallelisms of Hebrew poetry and the antiphons of Church music up to the intricacy of Greek or Italian or English verse. But parallelism is of two kinds necessarily — where the opposition is clearly marked, and where it is transitional rather or chromatic. Only the first kind, that of marked parallelism, is concerned with the structure of verse — in rhythm, the recurrence of a certain sequence of syllables, in metre, the recurrence of a certain sequence of rhythm, in alliteration, in assonance and in rhyme. Now the force of this recurrence is to beget a recurrence or parallelism answering to it in the words or thought and, speaking roughly and rather for the tendency than the invariable result, the more marked parallelism in structure whether of elaboration or of emphasis begets more marked parallelism in the words and sense. . . . To the marked or abrupt kind of parallelism belong metaphor, simile, parable, and so on, where the effect is sought in likeness of things, and antithesis, contrast, and so on, where it is sought in unlikeness.[31]

[29] G. M. Hopkins, *The Journals and Papers.*
[30] W. K. Wimsatt, Jr., *The Verbal Icon* (Lexington, 1954).
[31] G. M. Hopkins, *The Journals and Papers.*

Briefly, equivalence in sound, projected into the sequence as its constitutive principle, inevitably involves semantic equivalence, and on any linguistic level any constituent of such a sequence prompts one of the two correlative experiences which Hopkins neatly defines as "comparison for likeness' sake" and "comparison for unlikeness' sake."

Folklore offers the most clear-cut and stereotyped forms of poetry, particularly suitable for structural scrutiny (as Sebeok illustrated with Cheremis samples). Those oral traditions that use grammatical parallelism to connect consecutive lines, for example, Finno-Ugric patterns of verse [32] and to a high degree also Russian folk poetry, can be fruitfully analyzed on all linguistic levels — phonological, morphological, syntactic, and lexical: we learn what elements are conceived as equivalent and how likeness on certain levels is tempered with conspicuous difference on other ones. Such forms enable us to verify Ransom's wise suggestion that "the meter-and-meaning process is the organic act of poetry, and involves all its important characters." [33] These clear-cut traditional structures may dispel Wimsatt's doubts about the possibility of writing a grammar of the meter's interaction with the sense, as well as a grammar of the arrangement of metaphors. As soon as parallelism is promoted to canon, the interaction between meter and meaning and the arrangement of tropes cease to be "the free and individual and unpredictable parts of the poetry."

Let us translate a few typical lines from Russian wedding songs about the apparition of the bridegroom:

A brave fellow was going to the porch,
Vasilij was walking to the manor.

The translation is literal; the verbs, however, take the final position in both Russian clauses (Dobroj mólodec k séničkam privoráčival, // Vasílij k téremu prixážival). The lines wholly correspond to each other syntactically and morphologically. Both predicative verbs have the same prefixes and suffixes and the same vocalic alternant in the stem; they are alike in aspect, tense, number, and gender; and, moreover, they are synonymic. Both subjects, the common noun and the proper name, refer to the same person and form an appositional group. The two modifiers of place are expressed by identical prepositional constructions, and the first one stands to the second in synecdochic relation.

These verses may occur preceded by another line of similar grammatical (syntactic and morphologic) make-up: "Not a bright falcon was flying beyond the hills" or "Not a fierce horse was coming at gallop to the court." The "bright falcon" and the "fierce horse" of these variants are put in metaphorical relation with "brave fellow." This is traditional Slavic negative parallelism — the refutation of the metaphorical state in favor of the factual state. The negation *ne* may, however, be omitted: "Jasjón sokol zá gory zaljótyval" (A bright

[32] R. Austerlitz, *Ob-Ugric Metrics. Folklore Fellows Communications*, CLXXIV (1958), and W. Steinitz, *Der Parallelismus in der Finnisch-Karelischen Volksdichtung. Folklore Fellows Communications*, CXV (1934).

[33] J. C. Ransom, *The New Criticism* (Norfolk, Conn., 1941).

falcon was flying beyond the hills) or "Retív kon' kó dvoru priskákival" (A fierce horse was coming at a gallop to the court). In the first of the two examples the *metaphorical* relation is maintained: a brave fellow appeared at the porch, like a bright falcon from behind the hills. In the other instance, however, the semantic connection becomes ambiguous. A comparison between the appearing bridegroom and the galloping horse suggests itself, but at the same time the halt of the horse at the court actually anticipates the approach of the hero to the house. Thus before introducing the rider and the manor of his fiancee, the song evokes the contiguous, *metonymical* images of the horse and of the courtyard: possession instead of possessor, and outdoors instead of inside. The exposition of the groom may be broken up into two consecutive moments even without substituting the horse for the horseman: "A brave fellow was coming at a gallop to the court, // Vasilij was walking to the porch." Thus the "fierce horse," emerging in the preceding line at a similar metrical and syntactic place as the "brave fellow," figures simultaneously as a likeness to and as a representative possession of this fellow, properly speaking — *pars pro toto* for the horseman. The horse image is on a border line between metonymy and synecdoche. From these suggestive connotations of the "fierce horse" there ensues a metaphorical synecdoche: in the wedding songs and other varieties of Russian erotic lore, the masculine *retiv kon* becomes a latent or even patent phallic symbol.

As early as the 1880's, Potebnja, a remarkable inquirer into Slavic poetics, pointed out that in folk poetry a symbol appears to be materialized (*oveščestvlen*), converted into an accessory of the ambiance. "Still a symbol, it is put, however, in a connection with the action. Thus a simile is presented under the shape of a temporal sequence." [34] In Potebnja's examples from Slavic folklore, the willow, under which a girl passes, serves at the same time as her image; the tree and the girl are both copresent in the same verbal simulacrum of the willow. Quite similarly the horse of the love songs remains a virility symbol not only when the maid is asked by the lad to feed his steed but even when being saddled or put into the stable or attached to a tree.

In poetry not only the phonological sequence but in the same way any sequence of semantic units strives to build an equation. Similarity superimposed on contiguity imparts to poetry its thoroughgoing symbolic, multiplex, polysemantic essence which is beautifully suggested by Goethe's "Alles Vergängliche ist nur ein Gleichnis" (Anything transient is but a likeness). Said more technically, anything sequent is a simile. In poetry where similarity is superinduced upon contiguity, any metonymy is slightly metaphorical and any metaphor has a metonymical tint.

Ambiguity is an intrinsic, inalienable character of any self-focused message, briefly a corollary feature of poetry. Let us repeat with Empson: "The machinations of ambiguity are among the very roots of poetry." [35] Not only the

[34] A. Potebnja, *Ob"jasnenija Malorusskix i Srodnyx Narodnyx Pesen* (Warsaw, I, 1883; II, 1887).

[35] W. Empson, *Seven Types of Ambiguity* (New York, third edition, 1955).

message itself but also its addresser and addressee become ambiguous. Besides the author and the reader, there is the "I" of the lyrical hero or of the fictitious storyteller and the "you" or "thou" of the alleged addressee of dramatic monologues, supplications, and epistles. For instance the poem "Wrestling Jacob" is addressed by its title hero to the Saviour and simultaneously acts as a subjective message of the poet Charles Wesley to his readers. Virtually any poetic message is a quasi-quoted discourse with all those peculiar, intricate problems which "speech within speech" offers to the linguist.

The supremacy of poetic function over referential function does not obliterate the reference but makes it ambiguous. The double-sensed message finds correspondence in a split addresser, in a split addressee, and besides in a split reference, as it is cogently exposed in the preambles to fairy tales of various peoples, for instance, in the usual exordium of the Majorca storytellers: "Aixo era y no era" (It was and it was not).[36] The repetitiveness effected by imparting the equivalence principle to the sequence makes reiterable not only the constituent sequences of the poetic message but the whole message as well. This capacity for reiteration whether immediate or delayed, this reification of a poetic message and its constituents, this conversion of a message into an enduring thing, indeed all this represents an inherent and effective property of poetry.

In a sequence, where similarity is superimposed on contiguity, two similar phonemic sequences near to each other are prone to assume a paronomastic function. Words similar in sound are drawn together in meaning. It is true that the first line of the final stanza in Poe's "Raven" makes wide use of repetitive alliterations, as noted by Valéry,[37] but "the overwhelming effect" of this line and of the whole stanza is due primarily to the sway of poetic etymology.

> And the Raven, never flitting, still is sitting, *still* is sitting
> On the pallid bust of Pallas just above my chamber door;
> And his eyes have all the seeming of a demon's that is dreaming,
> And the lamp-light o'er him streaming throws his shadow on the floor;
> And my soul from out that shadow that lies floating on the floor
> Shall be lifted — nevermore.

The perch of the raven, "the pallid bust of Pallas," is merged through the "sonorous" paronomasia /pǽləd/ — /pǽləs/ into one organic whole (similar to Shelley's molded line "Sculptured on alabaster obelisk" /sk.lp/ — /l.b.st/ — /b.l.sk/). Both confronted words were blended earlier in another epithet of the same bust — *placid*/plǽsId/ — a poetic portmanteau, and the bond between the sitter and the seat was in turn fastened by a paronomasia: "*b*ird or *b*ea*st* upon the . . . *b*u*st*." The bird "is sitting // On the pallid bust of Pallas just above my chamber door," and the raven on his perch, despite the lover's imperative "take thy form from off my door," is nailed to the place by the words /ǯʌ́st əbʌ́v/, both of them blended in /bʌ́st/.

The never-ending stay of the grim guest is expressed by a chain of ingenious

[36] W. Giese, "Sind Märchen Lügen?" *Cahiers S. Puşcariu* I (1952), 137 ff.

[37] P. Valéry, *The Art of Poetry.*

paronomasias, partly inversive, as we would expect from such a deliberate experimenter in anticipatory, regressive *modus operandi*, such a master in "writing backwards" as Edgar Allan Poe. In the introductory line of this concluding stanza, "raven," contiguous to the bleak refrain word "never," appears once more as an embodied mirror image of this "never": /n.v.r/ — /r.v.n/. Salient paronomasias interconnect both emblems of the everlasting despair, first "the Raven, never flitting," at the beginning of the very last stanza, and second, in its very last lines the "shadow that lies floating on the floor" and "shall be lifted — nevermore": /nέvər flítíŋ/ — /flótíŋ/ . . . /flór/ . . . /líftəd nέvər/. The alliterations which struck Valéry build a paronomastic string: /stí . . . / — /sít . . . / — /stí . . . / — /sít . . . /. The invariance of the group is particularly stressed by the variation in its order. The two luminous effects in the chiaroscuro — the "fiery eyes" of the black fowl and the lamplight throwing "his shadow on the floor" — are evoked to add to the gloom of the whole picture and are again bound by the "vivid effect" of paronomasias: /ɔ́lðə símɪŋ/ . . . /dímənz/ . . . /Iz drímɪŋ/ — /ɔrɪm strímɪŋ/. "That shadow that lies /láyz/" pairs with the Raven's "eyes" /áyz/ in an impressively misplaced echo rhyme.

In poetry, any conspicuous similarity in sound is evaluated in respect to similarity and/or dissimilarity in meaning. But Pope's alliterative precept to poets — "the sound must seem an Echo of the sense" — has a wider application. In referential language the connection between *signans* and *signatum* is overwhelmingly based on their codified contiguity, which is often confusingly labeled "arbitrariness of the verbal sign." The relevance of the sound-meaning nexus is a simple corollary of the superposition of similarity upon contiguity. Sound symbolism is an undeniably objective relation founded on a phenomenal connection between different sensory modes, in particular between the visual and auditory experience. If the results of research in this area have sometimes been vague or controversial, it is primarily due to an insufficient care for the methods of psychological and/or linguistic inquiry. Particularly from the linguistic point of view the picture has often been distorted by lack of attention to the phonological aspect of speech sounds or by inevitably vain operations with complex phonemic units instead of with their ultimate components. But when, on testing, for example, such phonemic oppositions as grave versus acute we ask whether /i/ or /u/ is darker, some of the subjects may respond that this question makes no sense to them, but hardly one will state that /i/ is the darker of the two.

Poetry is not the only area where sound symbolism makes itself felt, but it is a province where the internal nexus between sound and meaning changes from latent into patent and manifests itself most palpably and intensely, as it has been noted in Hymes's stimulating paper. The super-average accumulation of a certain class of phonemes or a contrastive assemblage of two opposite classes in the sound texture of a line, of a stanza, of a poem acts like an "undercurrent of meaning," to use Poe's picturesque expression. In two polar words phonemic relationship may be in agreement with semantic opposition, as in Russian /d,en,/ 'day' and /noč/ 'night' with the acute vowel and sharped consonants in the diurnal name and the corresponding grave vowel in the nocturnal name. A reinforcement of this contrast by surrounding the first word with acute and sharped phonemes, in contradistinction to a grave phonemic neighborhood as the second word, makes the sound into a thorough echo of the sense. But in the French *jour* 'day' and *nuit* 'night' the distribution of grave and acute vowels is inverted, so that Mallarmé's *Divagations* accuse his mother tongue of a deceiving perversity for assigning to day a dark timbre and to night a light one.[38] Whorf states that when in its sound shape "a word has an acoustic similarity to its own meaning, we can notice it. . . . But, when the opposite occurs, nobody notices it." Poetic language, however, and particularly French poetry in the collision between sound and meaning detected by Mallarmé, either seeks a phonological alternation of such a discrepancy and drowns the "converse" distribution of vocalic features by surrounding *nuit* with grave and *jour* with acute phonemes, or it resorts to a semantic shift and its imagery of day and night replaces the imagery of light and dark by other synesthetic correlates of the phonemic opposition grave/acute and, for instance, puts the heavy, warm day in contrast to the airy, cool night; because "human subjects seem to associate the experiences of bright, sharp, hard, high, light (in weight), quick, high-pitched, narrow, and so on in a long series, with each other; and conversely the experiences of dark, warm, yielding, soft, blunt, low, heavy, slow, low-pitched, wide, etc., in another long series." [39]

However effective is the emphasis on repetition in poetry, the sound texture is still far from being confined to numerical contrivances, and a phoneme that appears only once, but in a key word, in a pertinent position, against a contrastive background, may acquire a striking significance. As painters used to say, "Un kilo de vert n'est pas plus vert qu'un demi kilo."

Any analysis of poetic sound texture must consistently take into account the phonological structure of the given language and, beside the over-all code, also the hierarchy of phonological distinctions in the given poetic convention. Thus the approximate rhymes used by Slavic peoples in oral and in some stages of written tradition admit unlike consonants in the rhyming members (e.g., Czech *boty*, *boky*, *stopy*, *kosy*, *sochy*) but, as Nitch noticed, no mutual correspondence between voiced and voiceless consonants is allowed,[40] so that the quoted Czech words cannot rhyme with *body*, *doby*, *kozy*, *rohy*. In the songs of some American Indian peoples such as Pima-Papago and Tepecano, according to Herzog's observations — only partly communicated in print [41] — the phonemic distinction between voiced and voiceless plosives and between them and nasals is re-

[38] S. Mallarmé, *Divagations* (Paris, 1899).

[39] B. L. Whorf, *Language, Thought, and Reality*, J. B. Carroll, ed. (New York, 1956), p. 267f.

[40] K. Nitch, "Z Historii Polskich Rymów," *Wybór Pism Polonistycznych* I (Wrocław, 1954), 33–77.

[41] G. Herzog, "Some Linguistic Aspects of American Indian Poetry," *Word* II (1946), 82.

placed by a free variation, whereas the distinction between labials, dentals, velars, and palatals is rigorously maintained. Thus in the poetry of these languages consonants lose two of the four distinctive features, voiced/voiceless and nasal/oral, and preserve the other two, grave/acute and compact/diffuse. The selection and hierarchic stratification of valid categories is a factor of primary importance for poetics both on the phonological and on the grammatical level.

Old Indic and Medieval Latin literary theory keenly distinguished two poles of verbal art, labeled in Sanskrit *Pāñcālī* and *Vaidarbhī* and correspondingly in Latin *ornatus difficilis* and *ornatus facilis*,[42] the latter style evidently being much more difficult to analyze linguistically because in such literary forms verbal devices are unostentatious and language seems a nearly transparent garment. But one must say with Charles Sanders Peirce: "This clothing never can be completely stripped off, it is only changed for something more diaphanous." [43] "Verseless composition," as Hopkins calls the prosaic variety of verbal art — where parallelisms are not so strictly marked and strictly regular as "continuous parallelism" and where there is no dominant figure of sound — present more entangled problems for poetics, as does any transitional linguistic area. In this case the transition is between strictly poetic and strictly referential language. But Propp's pioneering monograph on the structure of the fairy tale [44] shows us how a consistently syntactic approach may be of paramount help even in classifying the traditional plots and in tracing the puzzling laws that underlie their composition and selection. The new studies of Lévi-Strauss [45] display a much deeper but essentially similar approach to the same constructional problem.

It is no mere chance that metonymic structures are less explored than the field of metaphor. May I repeat my old observation that the study of poetic tropes has been directed mainly toward metaphor, and the so-called realistic literature, intimately tied with the metonymic principle, still defies interpretation, although the same linguistic methodology, which poetics uses when analyzing the metaphorical style of romantic poetry, is entirely applicable to the metonymical texture of realistic prose.[46]

Textbooks believe in the occurrence of poems devoid of imagery, but actually scarcity in lexical tropes is counterbalanced by gorgeous grammatical tropes and figures. The poetic resources concealed in the morphological and syntactic structure of language, briefly the poetry of grammar, and its literary product, the grammar of poetry, have been seldom known to critics and mostly disregarded by linguists but skillfully mastered by creative writers.

The main dramatic force of Antony's exordium to the funeral oration for

[42] L. Arbusow, *Colores Rhetorici* (Göttingen, 1948).

[43] C. S. Peirce, *Collected Papers*, Vol. 1 (Cambridge, Mass., 1931), p. 171.

[44] V. Propp, *Morphology of the Folktale* (Bloomington, 1958).

[45] C. Lévi-Strauss, "Analyse Morphologique des Contes Russes," *International Journal of Slavic Linguistics and Poetics*, III (1960); *La Geste d'Asdival, École Prâtique des Hautes Études* (Paris, 1958); and "The Structural Study of Myth," in T. A. Sebeok, ed., *Myth: A Symposium* (Philadelphia, 1955), pp. 50–66.

[46] R. Jakobson, "The Metaphoric and Metonymic Poles," in *Fundamentals of Language* ('s Gravenhage, 1956), pp. 76–82.

Caesar is achieved by Shakespeare's playing on grammatical categories and constructions. Mark Antony lampoons Brutus's speech by changing the alleged reasons for Caesar's assassination into plain linguistic fictions. Brutus's accusation of Caesar, "as he was ambitious, I slew him," undergoes successive transformations. First Antony reduces it to a mere quotation which puts the responsibility for the statement on the speaker quoted: "The noble Brutus // Hath told you. . . ." When repeated, this reference to Brutus is put into opposition to Antony's own assertions by an adversative "but" and further degraded by a concessive "yet." The reference to the alleger's honor ceases to justify the allegation, when repeated with a substitution of the merely copulative "and" instead of the previous causal "for," and when finally put into question through the malicious insertion of a modal "sure":

The noble Brutus
Hath told you Cæsar was ambitious;
For Brutus is an honourable man,
But Brutus says he was ambitious,
And Brutus is an honourable man.
Yet Brutus says he was ambitious,
And Brutus is an honourable man.
Yet Brutus says he was ambitious,
And, sure, he is an honourable man.

The following polyptoton — "I speak . . . Brutus spoke . . . I am to speak" — presents the repeated allegation as mere reported speech instead of reported facts. The effect lies, modal logic would say, in the oblique context of the arguments adduced, which makes them into unprovable belief sentences:

I speak not to disprove what Brutus spoke,
But here I am to speak what I do know.

The most effective device of Antony's irony is the *modus obliquus* of Brutus's abstracts changed into a *modus rectus* to disclose that these reified attributes are nothing but linguistic fictions. To Brutus's saying "he was ambitious," Antony first replies by transferring the adjective from the agent to the action ("Did this in Caesar seem ambitious?"), then by eliciting the abstract noun "ambition" and converting it into a subject of a concrete passive construction "Ambition should be made of sterner stuff" and subsequently to a predicate noun of an interrogative sentence, "Was this ambition?" — Brutus's appeal "hear me for my cause" is answered by the same noun *in recto*, the hypostatized subject of an interrogative, active construction: "What cause withholds you . . . ?" While Brutus calls "awake your senses, that you may the better judge," the abstract substantive derived from "judge" becomes an apostrophized agent in Antony's report: "O judgment, thou art fled to brutish beasts . . ." Incidentally, this apostrophe with its murderous paronomasia Brutus-brutish is reminiscent of Caesar's parting exclamation "Et tu, Brute!" Properties and activities are exhibited *in recto*, whereas their carriers appear either *in obliquo* ("withholds you," "to brutish beasts," "back to me") or as subjects of negative actions ("men have lost," "I must pause"):

> You all did love him once, not without cause;
> What cause withholds you then to mourn for him?
> O judgment, thou art fled to brutish beasts,
> And men have lost their reason!

The last two lines of Antony's exordium display the ostensible independence of these grammatical metonymies. The stereotyped "I mourn for so-and-so" and the figurative but still stereotyped "so-and-so is in the coffin and my heart is with him" or "goes out to him" give place in Antony's speech to a daringly realized metonymy; the trope becomes a part of poetic reality:

> My heart is in the coffin there with Cæsar,
> And I must pause till it come back to me.

In poetry the internal form of a name, that is, the semantic load of its constituents, regains its pertinence. The "Cocktails" may resume their obliterated kinship with plumage. Their colors are vivified in Mac Hammond's lines "The ghost of a Bronx pink lady // With orange blossoms afloat in her hair," and the etymological metaphor attains its realization: "O, Bloody Mary, // The cocktails have crowed not the cocks!" ("At an Old Fashion Bar in Manhattan"). Wallace Stevens' poem "An Ordinary Evening in New Haven" revives the head word of the city name first through a discreet allusion to heaven and then through a direct pun-like confrontation similar to Hopkins' "Heaven-Haven."

> The dry eucalyptus *seeks god in the rainy cloud.*
> Professor Eucalyptus of New Haven *seeks him in New Haven* . . .
> The instinct *for heaven* had its counterpart:
> The instinct for earth, *for New Haven*, for his room . . .

The adjective "New" of the city name is laid bare through the concatenation of opposites:

> The oldest-newest day is the newest alone.
> The oldest-newest night does not creak by . . .

When in 1919 the Moscow Linguistic Circle discussed how to define and delimit the range of *epitheta ornantia*, the poet Majakovskij rebuked us by saying that for him any adjective while in poetry was thereby a poetic epithet, even "great" in the *Great Bear* or "big" and "little" in such names of Moscow streets as *Bol'shaja Presnja* and *Malaja Presnja*. In other words, poeticalness is not a supplementation of discourse with rhetorical adornment but a total re-evaluation of the discourse and of all its components whatsoever.

A missionary blamed his African flock for walking undressed. "And what about yourself?" they pointed to his visage, "are not you, too, somewhere naked?" "Well, but that is my face." "Yet in us," retorted the natives, "everywhere it is face." So in poetry any verbal element is converted into a figure of poetic speech.

My attempt to vindicate the right and duty of linguistics to direct the investigation of verbal art in all its compass and extent can come to a conclusion with the same burden which summarized my report to the 1953 conference here at Indiana University: "Linguista sum; linguistici nihil a me alienum puto." [47] If the poet Ransom is right (and he is right) that "poetry is a kind of language," [48] the linguist whose field is any kind of language may and must include poetry in his study. The present conference has clearly shown that the time when both linguists and literary historians eluded questions of poetic structure is now safely behind us. Indeed, as Hollander stated, "there seems to be no reason for trying to separate the literary from the overall linguistic." If there are some critics who still doubt the competence of linguistics to embrace the field of poetics, I privately believe that the poetic incompetence of some bigoted linguists has been mistaken for an inadequacy of the linguistic science itself. All of us here, however, definitely realize that a linguist deaf to the poetic function of language and a literary scholar indifferent to linguistic problems and unconversant with linguistic methods are equally flagrant anachronisms.

[47] C. Levi-Strauss, R. Jakobson, C. F. Voegelin, and T. A. Sebeok, *Results of the Conference of Anthropologists and Linguists* (Baltimore, 1953).

[48] J. C. Ransom, *The World's Body* (New York, 1938).

I. A. Richards

POETIC PROCESS AND LITERARY ANALYSIS

My title, I notice, can seem to break my subject up into two halves. I would therefore like to begin by suggesting that it would be unfortunate if we let any clear-cut division, much less any opposition or contrast, form *too early* in our thought. ?Poetic Process? . . . ?Literary Analysis? : [1] Each phrase can be highly elastic, each serves to name many very different things. And their boundaries can shift very suddenly. What I would wish on this occasion to be concerned with chiefly is the fruitful interactions of the energies so describable (Poetic Process — the activities through which a poem comes into being; Literary Analysis — the attempt to anatomize a poem) with side glances only at the possibilities of mutual frustration. A good deal of Poetic Process consists in, and advances by, Literary Analysis and, on the other hand, Literary Analysis is often Poetic Process attempting to examine and appraise itself.

One other preliminary: there are sayings that truly deserve to be called "ever memorable" in the sense that the more constantly we bear them in mind the more error we shall be spared. Among these, should we not give a high place to Coleridge's "Do not let us introduce an Act of Uniformity against Poets"? [2] There are many ways of passing Acts of Uniformity: one is by framing definitions. Here are four lines in which Wordsworth reminds Coleridge that they are no friends of

that false secondary power, by which
In weakness, we create distinctions, then

[1] The marks ?———? mean 'query.'

[2] Coleridge, letter to Thelwall, December 17, 1796.

> Deem that our puny boundaries are things
> Which we perceive, and not which we have made.[3]

It will be only to some Poetic Processes, occurring in some poets only, and on some occasions only, that what I may contrive to say will apply. Similarly with Literary Analyses: there are more ways than one of exploring our enjoyments.

Among our more obvious sources of information upon Poetic Process, where shall we place the poet's own account of the matter? It is customary at present to play it down — although any scrap of paper carrying any reference, however oblique, to circumstances of composition or any gossip about occasions is hoarded for the record as never before. Poets of standing — whatever their friends and relatives may be doing — remain as sparing of explanations as ever: to be mysterious and unforthcoming about his own work seems a part of the poet's role. Those who have departed from it have often seemed to feel the need of a cloak. Stephen Spender, in his *The Making of a Poem,*[4] is one of the few exceptions. Edgar Allan Poe [5] uses both cloak and mask: in explaining how "The Raven" came into being he begins by dressing the revelation up as a mere "magazine paper." Coming from such a "magaziner" as Poe, this is surely an ambivalent phrase.

> I have often thought how interesting a magazine paper might be written by an author who would — that is to say who could — detail, step by step, the processes by which one of his compositions attained its ultimate point of completion. Why such a paper has never been given to the world, I am much at a loss to say — but perhaps the authorial vanity has had more to do with the omission than any other cause.

We may perhaps linger on this phrase "authorial vanity." We are on ticklish ground here as Poe very well knows. He goes on:

> Most authors — poets in especial — prefer having it understood that they compose by a species of fine frenzy — an ecstatic intuition — and would positively shudder at letting the public take a peep behind the scenes, at the elaborate and vacillating crudities of thought — at the true purposes seized only at the last moment — at the innumerable glimpses of idea that arrived not at the maturity of full view — at the fully matured fancies discarded in despair as unmanageable — at the cautious selections and rejections — at the painful erasures and interpolations — in a word at the wheels and pinions.

Alas, we find nothing of all this in what follows. Instead we are given an ostentatious parade of allegedly perfect adjustment of selected means to fully foreseen ends. Poe, so eager — in Harry Levin's phrase — "to convince the world of his self-mastery," spares no pains to make this clear.

[3] Wordsworth, *The Prelude* (1805–1806), Book II, 221–224.

[4] London, 1955.

[5] "The Philosophy of Composition," in *The Complete Poems and Stories of Edgar Allan Poe* . . . ed. by A. H. Quinn (New York, 1951), pp. 978–987.

> It is my design to render it manifest that no one point in its composition is referable to accident or intuition; that the work proceeded, step by step, to its completion with the precision and rigid consequence of a mathematical problem.

What species of "the authorial vanity" is this? Who shall say? But, however "The Raven" may in fact have been written, we know that most poems are not composed so; the authors' manuscripts, where first drafts are available, at least show us that.

Now to the group of questions with which I am most concerned. It is time to state them, and in somewhat provocative form, so that — whether or not I can do anything toward answering them — the questions themselves may be strikingly posed for your consideration. "What, if anything, have its occasion, origin, motivation, its psychological and compositional history to do with the being of the completed poem?" I am trying to pose this group of questions in such a way that — for readers with the scatter of prepossessions which you, I conjecture, enjoy — a sizable section will reply at once with (*a*) "Why, *everything,* of course!" and another sizable section with (*b*) "Why, *nothing,* of course!" and yet another with (*c*) "Well, it depends, of course!" And I will be happy if those in the last section outnumber those in the first two.

I will try now to bring the problem into better focus in two very different ways: *first,* by sketching some of the reasons that may prompt a thinker to reply with *a* or *b* or *c; secondly,* by taking a short poem [6] for which I have special information — since I wrote it myself — and detailing some of "the elaborate and vacillating crudities of thought . . . the true purposes seized only at the last moment . . . the painful erasures and interpolations," in a word the sort of thing Poe left out of his account of the composition of "The Raven." I am doing this in the hope of making the problem as concrete as possible, so that we may possibly be able to put our fingers on questions about the Poetic Process which concern the Being or Nature of the poem and separate them from questions where "the answer little meaning — little relevancy bore." That is the program.

First, why should anyone answer "Why, *everything* . . . !"? Chiefly — don't you think? — because he takes the questions historically, or psychologically or biologically, as asking "By what steps, through what causal sequences, has the poem come to consist of these words in this order?" If so, the occasion, the motivation, the psychological and compositional history do have *everything* to do with the poem.

Then, why should anyone answer "Why, *nothing* . . . !"? Chiefly — don't you think? — because he takes the question linguistically, or stylistically, as asking: "Given these words in this order, what gives them the powers they have?" Asked so, we can see, I think, that the poet's biography need have nothing to do with the powers of the poem.

Finally, the deliberations and discriminations of those who might answer

[6] "Harvard Yard in April/April in Harvard Yard," which has now appeared [in *Goodbye Earth and Other Poems* (New York, 1958)].

"It depends . . . !" are more complex to describe. Here come in questions about the kind of poetry it may be and its relations to the rest of the known poetry of the author, to his other utterances, to the literature and colloquial of the period, to possible sources, to echoes, and so forth. Perhaps I can best summarize these considerations by remarking that the author in his Poetic Process, in his actual work on the poem, is an imaginary construct — a handsome creation of the imagination — based on our understanding of the poem. Such is the normal case, the type situation. We then use this imaginary construct — the poet at work — to help us in further interpretation, and we often forget meanwhile that he is our theoretical invention.

Let me turn now to the unusual, the abnormal case, the nontypical situation when we *have* access through the author's testimony — made from the best of his knowledge and belief — about what went on in the Poetic Process. After looking at this poem and at the privileged commentary or explanation, we may, I hope, be in a better position to ask certain questions about what Literary Analysis can tell us of *what is* and *is not* in the poem.

A poem may be regarded as a suitcase (I regret that my metaphor is so old-fashioned) which the poet may think he packs and the reader may think he unpacks. If they think so,

> They know not well the subtle ways
> I keep, and pass, and turn again.

So, at least, the poem, I think, is entitled to retort.

Here is the poem:

HARVARD YARD IN APRIL
APRIL IN HARVARD YARD

Or rather, here is not the poem but only its title — otherwise I should not tax your patience long. It was, I believe, said of the library at Yale "This is not the library; the library is inside!" In a moment I will be putting on the page what? . . . not the poem itself but its lines. A "poem itself" is a most elusive thing, I suggest, that can never be put on any screen or page. Can we even put the words of a poem on a page? I wonder. We can put a notation for them there. But there are many linguists and the like about these parts these days, and I know better than to use the word lightly.

When I put a notation for the words of my poem on the screen, I shall avail myself of another of my authorial privileges *and read them.* That is, I shall give you, through the auditory channel, another notation: an acoustic notation ?parallel? (but we must question this word) to the optical notation. This reading, of course, acts as a most powerful persuader as to how the words are to be taken — much more subtle, penetrating, and comprehensive than the glosses and comments which follow. But, I need hardly point out — or need I? — that an author's reading (like any other reader's) has no authority which does not derive from the poem itself. These readings, these renderings, these vocal interpretations are ways of packing, or finding, in the poem what may or may not be there. The author no more than his reader, I submit, can wish things into his poem — or wish them out. Consider the title. It is supposed to have a great deal to do with the poem. But I (as author) cannot settle that. No more can you (as reader). It is something to be settled between the poem and its title. They settle it; we do not. With its duplications and the time-space shift of "in," and the quasi-personification of April and the seesaw of emphasis, the title was added after the poem was finished. It was added partly to summarize, partly to give warning of, certain balancings within the poem.

Words in titles operate in a peculiar suspension and here we have a name within the title. "Harvard Yard," in particular, and "yard" in more general uses, will be charged very differently for different readers: for alumni of different universities and for American and British usage. For the British a yard is a rather humbly useful, limited, outdoor working space, unlike a garden and with no suggestion — with almost an antisuggestion — of groves academic or sacred. Echoes of "prison yard" I would expect to be weak, although certain lines in the poem might invite them.

But it is time now for the poem.

HARVARD YARD IN APRIL
APRIL IN HARVARD YARD

To and fro
Across the fretted snow
Figures, footprints, shadows go.

Their python boughs a-sway
The fountain elms cascade
In swinging lattices of shade
Where this or that or the other thought
Might perch and rest.
And rest they ought
For poise or reach.
Not all is timely. See, the beech,
In frosty elephantine skin
Still winter-sealed, will not begin
Though silt the alleys hour on hour
Débris of the fallen flower,
And other flowery allure
Lounge sunlit on the Steps and there
Degrees of loneliness confer.

Lest, lest . . . away!
You may
Be lost by May.

The poem began, I recall, as a not-at-all wish-fulfilling dream of spring flight from Harvard — in lines in part contained in the *coda:* something like

Happiest they
Who would away
Who may be gone
By May.

These and similar tentatives were nursed awhile in traverses through the Yard to and from my office — the Yard's character as a pre-eminent locus of "to-and-fro-ing" (physical and spiritual) not coming into clear consciousness until the poem was almost finished. Only then, argument and counterargument (often not meeting) came to mind as a ground justifying some comparing of the fretted snow with tracked and retracked sheets of paper, together with a feeling that "figures" (line 3) could be numerals. There was earlier an echo from a lecture remark I had made: "The printed words of a poem are only its footprints on paper."

To and fro
Across the fretted snow
Figures, footprints, shadows go.

"Shadows," on the other hand, in actual composition looked forward from the first to "shade" (line 6). Afterward, as confirmation and support, I thought of de la Mare's

When less than even a shadow came
And stood within the room . . . ,

also of

Coming events cast their shadows before them . . . ,

and of T. S. Eliot's [7]

The lengthened shadow of a man
Is history, said Emerson.

and, beyond all, of F. H. Bradley's [8] "The shades nowhere speak without blood and the ghosts of Metaphysic accept no substitute. They reveal themselves only to that victim whose life they have drained and to converse with shadows he himself must become a shade."

How soon the day-by-day doings of the trees with the coming of spring began to belong to the poem I cannot clearly recall: "fountain" from my very first sight of American elms had seemed the obvious descriptive word; but only after 21 years and through the poem did I learn it is just that, the obvious descriptive word.

Python boughs: in and for the poem the peculiar writhe of boughs, at once sinuous and angular, emphasized itself. Early drafts played with "snakey," but, with "a-sway," "cascade," and "shade" present, another vowel seemed desirable, and since "lithe" and "writhe" were highly active in attempts to describe what was striking me, "python" felt final.

[7] *The Complete Poems and Plays 1909–50* (N.Y., 1952).
[8] *Essays on Truth and Reality* (Oxford, 1944), p. 14.

A-sway: the slighter motions of bare boughs are more visible before leafage comes, and in spring, when the eye is watching for every advance, there is more occasion than in winter to observe them. Winter gales agitate them, but with spring breezes they seem to stir of their own will as an outcome of the mounting sap.

Cascade: the thickening fringes and tassels of budding leaf and flower on outermost pendent sprays were green or golden drops defining the outline of the fountain's fall; their "shade," although thin, softening and cooling the glare of sunlight on the snow.

Perch: comparison of thoughts with birds seems inevitable. Trumbull Stickney's grand lines, for example:

> Sir, say no more. Within me 'tis as if
> The green and climbing eyesight of a cat
> Crawled near my mind's poor birds.

Timely: when thoughts turn to trees, in academic groves at least, Mother Eve and her Tree of Knowledge are not far off. I would like to think that the poem contained originally a suggestion that the Tree (python boughs) was itself the Tempter, but that was an afterthought.

Silt the alleys: "silt" proposed itself as suggesting sand — product of breakup, unlubricative, arid, unfruitful; "alleys," channels for to-and-fro-ing, worn into grooves, out of true, and clogged by the grit of work.

Débris: hourly wastage of new, ungerminated, uncared for ideas, which may choke the channels; the wreckage and waste of "essential omission" — to use Whitehead's phrase — the saving neglect, which strains (and trains) the academic.

Allure: a lure is an apparatus used to recall hawks, a bunch of feathers within which, during its training, the hawk finds its food. Catachrestically, it can be both a snare and a mark to be shot at. The young scholar might be glad to borrow Cupid's bow to use on selected members of Radcliffe who at this season begin to decorate the chapel steps in their spring fabrics.

Degrees of loneliness: very different from the degrees that are conferred on those very steps at commencement. The line consciously echoed Donne's "The Extasie" (l. 44): "Defects of loneliness controls" — "Degrees of loneliness confer."

Lost: in terms not only of the allure but of examination results and the perplexities of study. The coda uses, as I have mentioned, what was the temporal germ of the poem.

Now from such detail, what, if anything, of general import can be extracted? How far can knowledge of what went on in the process of composition, however faithfully or tediously reported, serve as evidence of what is or is not *in the poem?*

You will recognize, I believe, that all this is chiefly a device — somewhat elaborate, I grant — for directing our attention to this tricky phrase "in the poem." If you can bear it, let us look through this little collection of samples of things I must aver *were* in the process of composition and ask of some of them whether and how they may not also be IN THE POEM.

First, this impulse — spring fever, nostalgia for the beyond, itchy-footedness — what I describe as a "not-at-all wish fulfilling dream of spring flight" out of which the poem started and with which, in the coda, it ends: if any of this feeling has got in, it will not be — will it? — simply because it is talked about, mentioned, or even, in any obvious sense, implied — as by

away!
You may
Be lost by May.

We plainly have to, and do, make a distinction between the overt or manifest content — the inventory of items that should not be omitted in a paraphrase — and what is truly operative in a poem. We would all agree that things may be mentioned and even insisted upon in a poem and yet remain perfectly inert, helpless, and noncontributive. (We should not, however — should we? — conclude that because they are inert (mere dead matter) they are therefore *always* unnecessary and better away. They may serve as catalysts or supporting tissue.)

This distinction between what is overt or manifest and what is operative — whether overt or not — is dangerous, of course. It lets us allege things about poems and deny things about them too easily. It opens the doors, typically, to allegations about the Unconscious.

For example, a friend to whom I had shown this poem and who had liked it — which pleased me because he is an admirable and well-recognized poet — was disappointed by and most suspicious, I believe, of the annotations I have been offering you. They did not, for him, contain the right sort of revelations of hidden passions in me. Alas! Is it any good my saying that *although there may be that sort of thing in the poem* there was nothing of the sort anywhere in the process of composing it. There may be murder in a poem without the author himself being either murdered or a murderer. But, no, once certain dealings with the Unconscious are on the tapis, the best-informed denial turns into additional evidence.

To talk of evidence, what sorts of evidence are really available for the presence or absence of X (whatever it may be) in the poem? This, to me, is the central question, as important as it is difficult to answer. And it is my hope that I may find support for the view that the best, if not the only, sorts of evidence are fundamentally linguistic — have to do with relations of words and phrases to one another — and furthermore (to retort with suspicion to suspicion) that evidence from a poet's alleged biography or psychology is seldom competent in any honest court.

To return to my example, if there *is* spring fever in this poem, it is there as outcome of a very complex set of mutual influences among its lines: in their movement as far as that is a derivative from their meaning, and in their meaning, in and through such things as the optative "might" in

> When this or that or the other thought
> *Might* perch and rest

in and through the fatigued flaccidity of "this or that or the other thought," in and through the alliterative pattern of

> perch and rest.
> And rest they ought
> For poise or reach.

in and through the subjunctives following "though"

> silt lounge confer.

Mind you, I am painfully aware that it is easy enough to allege such things: to pick this or that out of the inconceivably complex fabric of an utterance and say that here are more particularly the conveyers of this or that impulse and part of the poem. It is quite another matter to *prove* anything of the sort. We do not, I imagine, even know what the criteria of good proof in such matters would be. We can, of course, consent — agree to find them there — but that falls far short of proof.

On the other hand, the sorts of agreement which I am pointing to with this word "consent" are indispensable. Proof in these matters, if we ever attain it, will be by consent rather than by compulsion. Moreover, it is through such agreement about how words work together — the minute particulars of their cooperations — that discussion, analysis, and criticism must proceed. When two readers *differ,* they can discover and locate and describe their differences of interpretation only thanks to their consent together on other points.

Here let me touch on a misconception which, nowadays, I think — in my experience as a teacher — frustrates more potentially good readers of poetry than any other. To the word "shadow" (and "shade") a few minutes ago I appended a little string of quotations from de la Mare, a proverb, T. S. Eliot, and F. H. Bradley. These were uses of "shadow" that the Poetic Process considered in fixing — although not in forming — its third line "Footprints, figures, shadows go." But, of course, of course — I mean it *should* be of course — no sort of identification of these particular quotes and references is required for the understanding of the line. They belong to the Poetic Process, not to the Literary Analysis. None the less, Literary Analysis, in trying to bring out the force of a word such as "shadow" in such a setting, very often finds it necessary to adduce a number of such other uses. Poetry cannot and does not use such words as though they had never been used before or as though they had only been used in one way. And the teaching of the reading of poetry to students who (somehow or other) have read little poetry anyhow, and very little of it reflectively, does have to play the part of a leisurely dictionary and acquaint students with "this and that and the other" relevant use.

This is a characteristic part nowadays of the technique of Literary Analysis. It is parallel to much that is done for the other arts, a necessary way of helping words to mean more nearly all they should. But, — and here is where the frustrating misconception I spoke of comes in — far too many students somehow suppose that *they,* as readers, ought somehow to have known and thought of just those instances of the use of the word that the analyst has found convenient and illuminating to adduce for his purpose. So Literary Analysis gives rise, by accident as it were, to a set of unreal difficulties and imaginary obstacles quite parallel to those we would have if we supposed that to read aright we must somehow divine all the uses of a word that may have beguiled and guided a poet in the manifold choices of Poetic Process.

This sort of avoidable frustration comes up especially when a Literary Analyst — to bring out the force of a line — sets, say, a passage of Plato beside it. He does not mean necessarily that the poet in the Poetic Process was thinking of the passage, or that the poet need know the passage or even have heard of Plato. All he means is that in the line, in the cooperations among its words, there is active something which can also be exemplified (and often can best be exemplified) in the Plato passage. In brief, he is using a historical reference technique to make what is a linguistic and not a historical point. The "Platonism" he is concerned with is something which is *in the language.*

You remember Emerson's farmer to whom he lent a *Republic.* The farmer returned it saying "That man has a lot of my ideas!" It was true — if we will allow that the farmer's ideas are the ideas offered him, in some way, through the semantic structure of his language. My ideas are, in a deep sense, *in* my language — in the relations between words which guide me in their use. I have to admit, though, that these phrases, "*in* the poem" and "*in* the language," persuade me that I very imperfectly understand this innocent-seeming little word "in."

Let us look now at another example of relevant relations among words, equally active this time in Poetic Process and Literary Analysis. Among the factors operative in choosing "python boughs a-sway" — in place of, say, "snakey boughs a-sway" — in line 4 were the marginal presence, as I mentioned, of the words "lithe" and "writhe." I may well have thought of "withe" and "scythe," too; and there would also be the less perfect rhyme "alive." For "snakey," on the other hand, there was no such morphemic support; on the contrary: "shakey" — no good at all; "break" — no, no; "fake" — oh, horrors! So "python boughs" it had to be.

I take this as my type specimen of mutual influences among words of the order that is most conspicuously exemplified in rhyme: similarities in sound introducing and reinforcing relevancies of meaning. "Python" was not a rhyme word here, but where rhyme is in use other words than rhyme words do often have their susceptibility to influence from their rhyme field increased.

Now all this, with many other mutual influences among words which need never come into clear consciousness, belongs alike to Poetic Process and to Literary Analysis. In choosing his words, the poet is allowing himself to be guided in ways in which (he hopes) his reader may also be guided. The reader, in turn, may be following — in his awareness of the meaning, in his analysis, and in his appraisal — very closely in the footsteps of the Poetic Process. But the important thing, as I see it, is that both are under the control of the language, both are subject to their understanding of it.

Contrast, now, this happy and healthy condition with the sad state of a reader who is trying to guess — he knows not how — about what some poet at some precise, but unidentified, minute of his mortal journey may have been undergoing.

Of course, we all know that much in criticism and commentary which seems to be discussing the poet and reads as if it were about what he was doing as he wrote, *is not* really about that sort of thing at all. No, it is about what the poem has done and is doing to the critic — the critic who is inventing and projecting a poet's mental processes as a convenient way of talking about something else.

Mr. T. S. Eliot remarked — in his BBC talk, "Virgil and the Christian World" — that for a poet "his lines may be only a way of talking about himself without giving himself away." Well, a great deal of criticism which looks like microscopic biography — a minute by minute, line by line, blow by blow account of the poet's battle with his poem — is no more than the *critic's* way of talking about *himself* without giving the critic away either. Thus a reviewer will quote a line: "One wondered whether the loaded earth . . ." and go on to wonder: "Did one (i.e., the poet, who should be *I*, not *one*) really wonder that, or did one think one ought to wonder something?" This looks like an almost insane attempt to nose into another person's private reflections, but it is not. It is merely the reviewer's way of trying to indicate that the line does not seem very good to him.

Sometimes, however, the biographic assumption hardens: "Even when the pioneer work was completed anybody attempting a fresh critical appraisal of Wordsworth's poetry was faced with some dispiriting machete work if he was to establish the biographical detail to which the criticism would have to be referred."

A *fresh critical appraisal* of poetry *having to be referred* to *biographical detail:* doesn't that make you feel a little uncomfortable? Suppose some barrelful of papers were to roll out of some attic in Stratford-on-Avon. Could it really force us to revise our critical appraisal of *King Lear* or could another batch of Dead Sea Rolls or Scrolls demote the poetry in *The Book of Job?* Personally, I would be extremely sorry to learn one more fact about either author. And I confess that, if I were to be granted such opportunities in the next world, I would as lief *not* meet Homer as any man.

To be more serious, if possible: what I am hoping to suggest is that some of the criticism of Literary Analysis which seems so often nowadays to be pegged to the poet's personality would be more profitable if it discussed the linguistic grounds — the powers in the words and movement of the poem — which make the reader invent and project spiritual characteristics and spiritual adventures for the poet. In short, I have a hope that in time this amalgam of the gossip column and the whodunit will become a less dominant ingredient in criticism. Poetry is so much more than a source for low-down on the lives of poets. To let a thing of the seeming scale of *Ulysses* become chiefly a ground for speculations about Joyce's sexual history — is that not rather a sad comedown from more important sorts of concern with literature? I know, of course, that to an individual nothing can seem more important than his own sexual history. But are we not in some danger of forgetting that general communications should be about matters of general interest?

To take as a minute, a tiny, innocuous, example the second line of "Harvard Yard in April":

To and fro
Across the *fretted snow*

fret: eat; eat away; consume; torture by gnawing; gnaw at; wear away by friction; chafe; roughen; cause to ripple, as a breeze frets the surface of water; tease; vex; worry . . . (OED).

Over this "fretted snow" a reader could, if he cared, *either invent* a particularly disgruntled, impatient, spring-fever-beset author who projects his own discomfort even on the very snow, and so on, *or* let the word "fretted" itself — as a highly charged meeting point of various meanings — come to livelier life. The dictionary spreads the meanings out for us. But I am thinking of how the word can strike us before we separate such things — if, indeed, apart from dictionaries, we ever do. The dictionary adds a comment apropos of "gnaw at" which pleased me when I saw it. It says "Now only of small animals." A mouse, I suppose, can fret a bit of cheese (as a fret saw does plywood); but when a grizzly bear chaws up a man, that is not fretting. I liked that; it seems to offer my line "Across the fretted snow" a sort of bonus of meaning I had not been clearly enough aware of. It turned the people who had been leaving all those tracks on the snow into only small animals after all and gave a diminishing-glass sharpness to the scene.

But my point is that "fretted," if it has this power, gets it from its relations to other words — as a node of possibilities of meaning — not from the fact that an author (me in this case) had been pumping petulance into it. No matter how fevered, or how cool, the author may be, he cannot do anything with the word unless the language lets him, unless it is willing to work for him so: "For words it is not poets make up poems."

Perhaps I have overlabored this plea for the emancipation of Literary

Analysis from biographic explorations or conjectures. I realize that it will not be welcome everywhere: it looks like an attempt to put a great many people out of their jobs. I would like before I close, to turn to another aspect of contemporary literary analysis — an increasing tendency to read meanings into poems at random, regardless of linguistic limits. I have a small but choice exhibit of awful warnings to show you — all written by people who were at the time of their writing doomed of their own choice to hard labor for the rest of their natural lives — no, I mean for the rest of their employable lives — teaching helpless children in classrooms how to be discerning readers.

The first two lines of Mr. Eliot's "A Cooking Egg" read:

> Pipit sate upright in her chair
> Some distance from where I was sitting.

There has been, as you know, some discussion among critics about what sort of a person Pipit may best be supposed to be *in the interests of the poem as a whole*. Views have ranged from taking her as a retired nurse or governess to taking her as a Bloomsbury *demi-vierge*. The discussion came to a climax in an appeal from Dr. E. M. W. Tillyard, Master of Jesus, to the poet to explain the poem and set our minds at rest, an appeal to which Mr. Eliot, very wisely I think, has not responded.

However, one of my students, being faced with the problem, bethought her of the dictionary. There she found grounds for this:

> Pipit sate upright in her chair . . .

> According to Webster's New Collegiate Dictionary, "sate" may mean "to satisfy or gratify to the full a desire" or "gratify to the point of weariness or loathing, satiate." Pipit has obviously satisfied the "I" for she sits upright, at a distance; a state of satiation has occurred.

It is an interesting point in *linguistics* to consider why we are sure that words in such an instance do not work like that.

Or consider this. The last verse of Donne's "The Extasie" reads

> And if some lover, such as wee,
>   Have heard this dialogue of one,
> Let him still marke us, he shall see
>   Small change, when we'are to bodies gone.

> *To bodies gone:* there is an ambiguity in the phrase; is it "gone away from our ecstasy to our bodies" or "gone (in respect) to bodies" — gone entirely away from them? I think this ambiguity is operative.

Another comment on these same last three words of the poem:

> *To bodies gone:* "to" may be a play on words: if read aloud and thought of as "two," it signifies the sacrifice of spiritual union necessary for two people to indulge in physical love.

Observe that both these teachers-to-be feel free to ignore the rest of the line:

> he shall see
> Small change, when we'are. . . .

Their prepossessions enable them to find a meaning accurately opposite to "I must not say 'that which Donne put there'— (I don't know anything about that) but 'that which the rest of the poem expressly requires.' "

Compare another commentator who, perhaps, moves toward the point— but by what strange means!

> *Let him still marke us:* the word "still" can mean "without moving" and the sense of the line is changed to "let him notice that we are quiet and motionless."

Are you completely worn out? Or may I show you another double right-angle swivel?

An important movement in Coleridge's "Dejection: An Ode" begins

> Hence, viper thoughts, that coil around my mind
> Reality's dark dream!
> I turn from you, and listen to the wind
> Which long has rav'd unnotic'd.

> The poet retunes himself by *turning* inward to his soul. . . . He is coming through a storm which has made him hear the tune. His horror upon noticing makes him *turn* from the world of the senses and the outside.

Lastly, the last verse of Marvell's "The Garden" opens with the lines:

> How well the skillful Gardner drew
> Of flow'rs and herbes this Dial new

> First, the word "well" draws its meaning from a pun. It seems to mean how carefully constructed the world is. It would seem to me that "well" has the connotation of a source of water, a deep hole in the ground. That is, nature is a well which has great depth and from which deep and eternal meanings and values can be drawn.

All very true, no doubt, but not anything that the semantic texture of the language will allow the two lines to mean or that the rest of the poem will invite us to understand here. Surely a teacher-to-be should have a better sense than this of what is and is not admissible in an interpretation.

What can have been happening to cause this alarming condition, this reckless disregard of all the means by which language defends itself? I have not been exaggerating; such things are far too frequent in the English studies of those who are likely to become teachers. My instances could be duplicated by every teacher of teachers. Some essential control over interpretation seems to have been relaxed.

At an occasion on which so many authorities in linguistics, criticism, and related studies are gathered together, it seemed appropriate to offer evidence that their work may have more immediate, practical relevance to education than is sometimes supposed.

Part Five

STYLE AND STYLISTICS

How integral is style to the literary work of art? Is it something that can be detached and studied in and for itself; or does dealing with it necessarily entail a consideration of the entire work, ultimately even the entire communication situation? Merely to put these questions is to suggest the great complexity attaching to the notion of style. There is no question that there is such a thing, but it is not at all clear what it is.

Let us assume that style is something that confers distinctiveness on a literary work. Is this distinctiveness a function of the subject matter, the author's experience or personality (or the reader's?), the way in which the language is used, a combination of these things? Given the complexity of the problem, it would appear that any definition will be arbitrary to some extent. With style we thus find ourselves in the same case as with fundamental notions in other areas — what is meaning, for instance, or harmony, or the beautiful?

As with these and similar notions, the difficulty with style is not that we cannot define it — the difficulty is simply that it is impossible to define it in a way that would command universal assent. Definitions tend to be either too broad or too narrow. On the one hand are definitions which hold that style is the totality of impressions which a literary work produces (or that it is the author himself), and on the other are those which would restrict it to sundry and ornamental linguistic devices. The first course diffuses the notion of style, the second trivializes it.

In spite of these difficulties, the question of style has figured at the center of many critical discussions. It is clearly something fundamental. In this section are the views of a number of scholars who, representing a range of critical and linguistic orientation, come at the subject from various angles. The different emphases and results observable in these treatments attest to both the interest and the complexity of the subject.

The first essay, by Croll, is concerned with the description of a particular style, that of baroque prose. Croll distinguishes two predominant species, which he refers to as the "curt style" and the "loose style." As he shows, the emphasis in both is on expressiveness, and not on the formal elegance that directed the efforts of earlier, Ciceronian, writers. A good portion of the essay is devoted to a discussion of the formal, syntactic characteristics of the baroque style and how these determine the particular force and movement of its expression.

Wimsatt's essay is more theoretical. For him style is a function of the ultimate selection and combination of words and, since words mean, style and meaning are indissoluble. An experience (feeling, or idea) is committed to writing. The experience, as such, may be common to many, but the expression of it by different writers will vary — as they individually select and combine words to express that experience. The experience therefore means different things to them — and to us. It is such differences of meaning that constitute style. If an author uses characteristic turns of expression, these turns reflect his style of cognition, hence his meaning.

Juilland evaluates the utility of linguistics in stylistic analysis. He argues against the view that the techniques of linguistics would be sufficient for stylistic analysis, since all they can disclose are linguistic facts. If one insists on using such techniques in stylistic analysis, stylistically relevant features will either be assimilated to linguistic facts or escape the analysis altogether. Juilland discusses difficulties in the conception of style as deviation from the norm, and concludes that perhaps one use of linguistic analysis lies in isolating the deviations which will provide the proper subject matter for stylistic analysis.

In Hill's conception style is a function of trans-sentence relations, these relations imparting a distinctive meaning to a discourse. He distinguishes two aspects of the phenomenon. First, since linguistic items occurring across sentence boundaries are partially predictable, such occurrences may either presuppose an antecedent use of a word (Hill instances the use of the definite article in this connection) or point to the subsequent appearance of a word. In both these processes a sense of cohesion is induced. Second, stylistic relations force us out into the area of meaning in a special way: we confront meaning not only in its ordinary linguistic aspect, but in this aspect colored by cultural values. In such a confrontation metalinguistic and metastylistic meanings are combined. Hill then examines three poems in terms of their use of analogy, and shows how the range and function of this device illustrate his views on style.

For Ohmann the polar views — style as manner and style as totality — are equally unsatisfactory. The first view yields superficialities, the second leaves us with no proper subject. After discussing the difficulties in I. A. Richards' notion that style is the way that forms of thought are clothed in words, Ohmann suggests a basis in epistemic choice: style is a reflection of an author's private screening of the universe about him. Such choices can be made, and are thus significant, even within the limits imposed by the grammatical structure of an author's language. Now in order for epistemic choices to be relevant to the question of style, they of course have to be expressed: there must be a series of propositions, and that is the subject of Ohmann's next argument. Since any proposition can be expressed by more than one sentence, the particular selection of the sentence must be an aspect of a writer's style. Finally, Ohmann comments on the role that emotional factors play in style.

Riffaterre, in his first article, describes a behavioristic method for isolating stylistic devices. He discusses the problems that the time dimension raises for stylistic analysis: stylistic relevance is not constant through time. Linguistic norms are examined and are found wanting as explanations of stylistic effect. Therefore, he proposes his own explanation: the context is the norm; a stylistic device produces its effect by contrasting against (being unpredictable in) the context in which it occurs. Riffaterre's second article describes two kinds of context, micro- and macro-, and shows how, by using these notions, various stylistic effects can be rationalized.

In Milic's view style consists in the choices that a writer makes from among the various possibilities that the language makes available. Since the language is continually changing, it offers different forms within which the writer may exercise his options: his reading and general sensibility may incline him to include as options linguistic features that properly belong to a stage of the language antecedent to his time or even such options as his sensitivity to the future development of the language may sanction. Because the choices available to any writer are so extensive (actually infinite), all styles turn out to be individual styles. For this reason, Milic argues, generalizations that group styles under a chronological (or any other kind of) rubric are untenable.

Morris W. Croll

THE BAROQUE STYLE IN PROSE

1. Introduction

In the latter years of the sixteenth century a change declared itself in the purposes and forms of the arts of Western Europe for which it is hard to find a satisfactory name. One would like to describe it, because of some interesting parallels with a later movement, as the first modern manifestation of the Romantic Spirit; and it did, in fact, arise out of a revolt against the classicism of the high Renaissance. But the terms "romantic" and "classical" are both perplexing and unphilosophical; and their use should not be extended. It would be much clearer and more exact to describe the change in question as a radical effort to adapt traditional modes and forms of expression to the uses of a self-conscious modernism; and the style that it produced was actually called in several of the arts — notably in architecture and prose-writing — the "modern" or "new" style. But the term that most conveniently describes it is "baroque." This term, which was at first used only in architecture, has lately been extended to cover the facts that present themselves at the same time in sculpture and in painting; and it may now properly be used to describe, or at least to name, the characteristic modes of expression in all the arts during a certain period — the period, that is, between the high Renaissance and the eighteenth century; a period that begins in the last quarter of the sixteenth century, reaches a culmination at about 1630, and thenceforward gradually modifies its character under new influences.

Expressiveness rather than formal beauty was the pretension of the new movement, as it is of every movement that calls itself modern. It disdained complacency, suavity, copiousness, emptiness, ease, and in avoiding these qualities sometimes obtained effects of contortion or obscurity, which it was not always willing to regard as faults. It preferred the forms that express the energy and labor of minds seeking the truth, not without dust and heat, to

From: *Studies in English Philology* edited by Kemp Malone and Martin B. Ruud. The University of Minnesota Press, Minneapolis.

the forms that express a contented sense of the enjoyment and possession of it. In a single word, the motions of souls, not their states of rest, had become the themes of art.

The meaning of these antitheses may be easily illustrated in the history of Venetian painting, which passes, in a period not longer than one generation, from the self-contained and relatively symmetrical designs of Titian, through the swirls of Tintoretto, to the contorted and aspiring lines that make the paintings of El Greco so restless and exciting. Poetry moves in the same way at about the same time; and we could metaphorically apply the terms by which we distinguish El Greco from Titian to the contrast between the rhythms of Spenser and the Petrarcans, on one hand, and the rhythms of Donne, on the other, between the style of Ariosto and the style of Tasso. In the sculptures of Bernini (in his portrait busts as well as in his more famous and theatrical compositions) we may again observe how ideas of motion take the place of ideas of rest; and the operation of this principle is constantly to be observed also in the school of architecture associated with the same artist's name. "In the façade of a Baroque church," says Geoffrey Scott, "a movement, which in the midst of a Bramantesque design would be destructive and repugnant, is turned to account and made the basis of a more dramatic, but not less satisfying treatment, the motive of which is not peace, but energy." [1]

And finally the change that takes place in the prose style of the same period — the change, that is, from Ciceronian to anti-Ciceronian forms and ideas — is exactly parallel with those that were occurring in the other arts, and is perhaps more useful to the student of the baroque impulse than any of the others, because it was more self-conscious, more definitely theorized by its leaders, and more clearly described by its friends and foes. In some previous studies I have considered the triumph of the anti-Ciceronian movement at considerable length; but I have been concerned chiefly with the theory of the new style; and my critics have complained, justly, that I have been too difficult, or even abstract. In the present study I hope to correct this defect. Its purpose is to describe the *form* of anti-Ciceronian, or baroque, prose.

There are of course several elements of prose technique: diction, or the choice of words; the choice of figures; the principle of balance or rhythm; the form of the period, or sentence; and in a full description of baroque prose all of these elements would have to be considered. The last-mentioned of them — the form of the period — is, however, the most important and the determinant of the others; and this alone is to be the subject of discussion in the following pages.

The anti-Ciceronian period was sometimes described in the seventeenth century as an "exploded" period; and this metaphor is very apt if it is taken as describing solely its outward appearance, the mere fact of its form. For

[1] *The Architecture of Humanism*, p. 225.

example, here is a period from Sir Henry Wotton, a typical expression of the political craft of the age:

> Men must beware of running down steep places with weighty bodies; they once in motion, *suo feruntur pondere;* steps are not then voluntary.

The members of this period stand farther apart one from another than they would in a Ciceronian sentence; there are no syntactic connectives between them whatever; and semicolons or colons are necessary to its proper punctuation. In fact, it has the appearance of having been disrupted by an explosion within.

The metaphor would be false, however, if it should be taken as describing the manner in which this form has been arrived at. For it would mean that the writer first shaped a round and complete oratorical period in his mind and then partly undid his work. And this, of course, does not happen. Wotton gave this passage its form, not by demolishing a Ciceronian period, but by omitting several of the steps by which roundness and smoothness of composition might have been attained. He has deliberately avoided the processes of mental revision in order to express his idea when it is nearer the point of its origin in his mind.

We must stop for a moment on the word *deliberately*. The negligence of the anti-Ciceronian masters, their disdain of revision, their dependence upon casual and emergent devices of construction, might sometimes be mistaken for mere indifference to art or contempt of form; and it is, in fact, true that Montaigne and Burton, even Pascal and Browne, are sometimes led by a dislike of formality into too licentious a freedom. Yet even their extravagances are purposive, and express a creed that is at the same time philosophical and artistic. Their purpose was to portray, not a thought, but a mind thinking, or, in Pascal's words, *la peinture de la pensée*. They knew that an idea separated from the act of experiencing it is not the idea that was experienced. The ardor of its conception in the mind is a necessary part of its truth; and unless it can be conveyed to another mind in something of the form of its occurrence, either it has changed into some other idea or it has ceased to be an idea, to have any existence whatever except a verbal one. It was the latter fate that happened to it, they believed, in the Ciceronian periods of sixteenth-century Latin rhetoricians. The successive processes of revision to which these periods had been submitted had removed them from reality by just so many steps. For themselves, they preferred to present the truth of experience in a less concocted form, and deliberately chose as the moment of expression that in which the idea first clearly objectifies itself in the mind, in which, therefore, each of its parts still preserves its own peculiar emphasis and an independent vigor of its own — in brief, the moment in which truth is still *imagined*.

The form of a prose period conceived in such a theory of style will differ in every feature from that of the conventional period of an oratorical, or

Ciceronian, style; but its most conspicuous difference will appear in the way it connects its members or clauses one with another. In the period quoted above from Wotton the members are syntactically wholly free; there are no ligatures whatever between one and another. But there is another type of anti-Ciceronian period, in which the ordinary marks of logical succession — conjunctions, pronouns, etc. — are usually present, but are of such a kind or are used in such a way as to bind the members together in a characteristically loose and casual manner. The difference between the two types thus described may seem somewhat unimportant; and it is true that they run into each other and cannot always be sharply distinguished. The most representative anti-Ciceronians, like Montaigne and Browne, use them both and intermingle them. But at their extremes they are not only distinguishable: they serve to distinguish different types, or schools, of seventeenth-century style. They derive from different models, belong to different traditions, and sometimes define the philosophical affiliations of the authors who prefer them.

They will be considered here separately; the first we will call, by a well-known seventeenth-century name, the *période coupé,* or, in an English equivalent, the 'curt period' (so also the *stile coupé,* or the 'curt style'); the other by the name of the 'loose period' (and the 'loose style'); though several other appropriate titles suggest themselves in each case.[2]

II. STILE COUPÉ

1

One example of the *période coupé* has already been given. Here are others.[3]

> Pour moy, qui ne demande qu'à devenir plus sage, non plus sçavant ou éloquent, ces ordonnances logiciennes et aristoteliques ne sont pas à propos; je veulx qu'on commence par le dernier poinct: j'entends assez que c'est que Mort et Volupté; qu'on ne s'amuse pas à les anatomizer. — MONTAIGNE, II, 10, "Des Livres."

> 'Tis not worth the reading, I yield it, I desire thee not to lose time in perusing so vain a subject, I should peradventure be loth myself to read him or thee so writing; 'tis not *operae pretium.* — BURTON, *Anatomy of Melancholy,* "To the Reader."

> No armor can defend a fearful heart. It will kill itself within.
> — FELLTHAM, *Resolves,* "Of Fear and Cowardice."

> Mais il faut parier; cela n'est pas volontaire; vous êtes embarqués.
> — PASCAL, *Pensées,* Article II.

[2] For example, the *stile coupé* was sometimes called *stile serré* ('serried style'), and Francis Thompson has used this term in describing a kind of period common in Browne. For synonyms of "loose style" see a succeeding section of this paper (§ III).

[3] The punctuation in all cases is that of editions which profess to follow in this respect good seventeenth-century editions or manuscripts.

L'éloquence continue ennuie.

Les princes et les rois jouent quelquefois. Ils ne sont pas toujours sur leurs trônes; ils s'y ennuient: la grandeur a besoin d'être quittée pour être sentie. — PASCAL, *Pensées,* "Sur l'Éloquence."

The world that I regard is myself; it is the microcosm of my own frame that I cast mine eye on: for the other, I use it but like my globe, and turn it round sometimes for my recreation. — BROWNE, *Religio Medici,* II, 11.

Il y a des hommes qui attendent a être dévots et religieux que tout le monde se déclare impie et libertin: ce sera alors le parti du vulgaire: ils sauront s'en dégager. — LA BRUYÈRE, *Des Esprits Forts.*

In all of these passages, as in the period quoted from Wotton, there are no two main members that are syntactically connected. But it is apparent also that the characteristic style that they have in common contains several other features besides this.

In the first place, each member is as short as the most alert intelligence would have it. The period consists, as some of its admirers were wont to say, of the nerves and muscles of speech alone; it is as hard-bitten, as free of soft or superfluous flesh, as "one of Caesar's soldiers." [4]

Second, there is a characteristic order, or mode of progression, in a curt period that may be regarded either as a necessary consequence of its omission of connectives or as the causes and explanation of this. We may describe it best by observing that the first member is likely to be a self-contained and complete statement of the whole idea of the period. It is so because writers in this style like to avoid prearrangements and preparations; they begin, as Montaigne puts it, at *le dernier poinct,* the point aimed at. The first member therefore exhausts the mere fact of the idea; logically there is nothing more to say. But it does not exhaust its imaginative truth or the energy of its conception. It is followed, therefore, by other members, each with a new tone or emphasis, each expressing a new apprehension of the truth expressed in the first. We may describe the progress of a curt period, therefore, as a series of imaginative moments occurring in a logical pause or suspension. Or — to be less obscure — we may compare it with successive flashes of a jewel or prism as it is turned about on its axis and takes the light in different ways.

It is true, of course, that in a series of propositions there will always be some logical process; the truth stated will undergo some development or change. For example, in the sentence from Montaigne on page 344, the later members add something to the idea; and in the quotation from Pascal's *Pensées sur l'Éloquence,* on the same page, the thought suddenly enlarges in the final member. Yet the method of advance is not logical; the form does not express it. Each member, in its main intention, is a separate act of imaginative realization.

[4] The phrase comes from a midseventeenth-century work on prose style (*Precetti,* repr. Milan, 1822) by Daniello Bartoli, and is there applied to *il dir moderno.*

In the third place, one of the characteristics of the curt style is deliberate asymmetry of the members of a period; and it is this trait that especially betrays the modernistic character of the style. The chief mark of a conventional, or "classical," art, like that of the sixteenth century, is an approximation to evenness in the size and form of the balanced parts of a design; the mark of a modernistic art, like that of the seventeenth, and the nineteenth and twentieth, centuries, is the desire to achieve an effect of balance or rhythm among parts that are obviously not alike — the love of "some strangeness in the proportions."

In a prose style asymmetry may be produced by varying the length of the members within a period. For example, part of the effect of a sentence from Bishop Hall is due to a variation in this respect among members which nevertheless produce the effect of balance or rhythmic design.

> What if they [crosses and adversities] be unpleasant? They are physic; it is enough if they be wholesome.[5] — HALL, *Heaven upon Earth,* XIII.

But the desired effect is more characteristically produced by conspicuous differences of form, either with or without differences of length. For instance, a characteristic method of the seventeenth century was to begin a succession of members with different kinds of subject-words. In the sentence from Wotton (page 343) the first two members have personal subjects, the third the impersonal "steps"; in the following from Pascal the opposite change is made.

> Mais il faut parier; cela n'est pas volontaire; vous êtes embarqués.

In both of these periods, moreover, each of the three members has a distinct and individual turn of phrase, meant to be different from the others. Again, in the period of La Bruyère quoted on page 345 each new member involves a shift of the mind to a new subject. (Observe also the asymmetry of the members in point of length.)

Sometimes, again, asymmetry is produced by a change from literal to metaphoric statement, or by the reverse, or by a change from one metaphor to another, as in the last example quoted from Pascal, where the metaphor of one embarked upon a ship abruptly takes the place of that of a man engaged in a bet. Or there may be a leap from the concrete to the abstract form; and this is an eminently characteristic feature of the *stile coupé* because this style is always tending toward the aphorism, or *pensée,* as its ideal form. The second passage quoted from Pascal on page 345 illustrates this in a striking way. It is evident that in the first three members — all concrete, about kings and princes — the author's mind is turning toward a general truth, which emerges complete and abstract in the last member: *La grandeur a besoin d'être quittée pour être sentie.*

[5] Note how exactly this reproduces a movement characteristic of Seneca: "Quia tua, uter [Caesar or Pompey] vincat? Potest melior vincere: non potest non pejor est qui vicerit."

The curt style, then, is not characterized only by the trait from which it takes its name, its omission of connectives. It has the four marks that have been described: first, studied brevity of members; second, the hovering, imaginative order; third, asymmetry; and fourth, the omission of the ordinary syntactic ligatures. None of these should, of course, be thought of separately from the others. Each of them is related to the rest and more or less involves them; and when they are all taken together they constitute a definite rhetoric, which was employed during the period from 1575 to 1675 with as clear a knowledge of its tradition and its proper models as the sixteenth-century Ciceronians had of the history of the rhetoric that they preferred.

In brief, it is a Senecan style; and, although the imitation of Seneca never quite shook off the imputation of literary heresy that had been put upon it by the Augustan purism of the preceding age, and certain amusing cautions and reservations were therefore felt to be necessary, yet nearly all of the theorists of the new style succeeded in expressing their devotion to their real master in one way or another. Moreover, they were well aware that the characteristic traits of Seneca's style were not his alone, but had been elaborated before him in the Stoic schools of the Hellenistic period; and all the earlier practitioners of the *stile coupé,* Montaigne (in his first phase), Lipsius, Hall, Charron, etc., write not only as literary Senecans, but rather more as philosophical Stoics.

Senecanism and Stoicism are, then, the primary implications of *stile coupé.* It must be observed, however, that a style once established in general use may cast away the associations in which it originated; and this is what happened in the history of the curt style. Montaigne, for instance, confessed that he had so thoroughly learned Seneca's way of writing that he could not wholly change it even when his ideas and tastes had changed and he had come to prefer other masters. And the same thing is to be observed in many writers of the latter part of the century: St. Évremond, Halifax, and La Bruyère, for instance. Though these writers are all definitely anti-Stoic and anti-Senecan, all of them show that they had learned the curt style too well ever to unlearn it or to avoid its characteristic forms; and there was no great exaggeration in Shaftesbury's complaint, at the very end of the century, that no other movement of style than Seneca's — what he calls the "Senecan amble" — had been heard in prose for a hundred years past.

2

The curt or serried style depends for its full effect upon the union of the several formal traits that have been described in the preceding section. We have assumed hitherto that these traits are as rigorous and unalterable as if they were prescribed by a rule; and in the examples cited there have been no significant departures from any of them. But of course slight variations are common even in passages that produce the effect of *stile coupé;* and some searching is necessary to discover examples as pure as those that have been cited. This is so evidently true that it would need no illustration except for the fact that certain kinds of period eminently characteristic of seventeenth-century prose arise from a partial violation of the "rules" laid down. Two of these may be briefly described.

a) In a number of writers (Browne, Felltham, and South, for example) we often find a period of two members connected by *and, or,* or *nor,* which evidently has the character of *stile coupé* because the conjunction has no logical *plus* force whatever. It merely connects two efforts of the imagination to realize the same idea; two as-it-were synchronous statements of it. The following from Browne will be recognized as characteristic of him:

> 'Tis true, there is an edge in all firm belief, and with an easy metaphor we may say the sword of faith. — *Religio Medici,* I, 10.

Again:

> Therefore I perceive a man may be twice a child before the days of dotage; and stand in need of Aeson's bath before threescore. — *Ibid.,* I, 42.

Often, too, in a period consisting of a larger number of members the last two are connected by an *and* or the like. But this case can be illustrated in connection with the one that immediately follows.

b) The rule that the successive members of a *période coupé* are of different and often opposed forms, are asymmetrical instead of symmetrical, is sometimes partly violated inasmuch as these members begin with the same word or form of words, for example, with the same pronoun-subject, symmetry, parallelism, and some regularity of rhythm, thus introducing themselves into a style that is designed primarily and chiefly to express a dislike of these frivolities. It is to be observed, however, that the members that begin with this suggestion of oratorical pattern usually break it in the words that follow. Except for their beginnings they are as asymmetrical as we expect them to be, and reveal that constant novelty and unexpectedness that is so characteristic of the "baroque" in all the arts.

One illustration is to be found in the style of the "character" writings that enjoyed so great a popularity in the seventeenth century. The frequent recurrence of the same subject-word, usually *he* or *they,* is the mannerism of this style, and is sometimes carried over into other kinds of prose in the latter part of the century, as, for instance, in writings of La Bruyère that are not included within the limits of the character genre,[6] and in passages of Dryden. It is indeed so conspicuous a mannerism that it may serve to conceal what is after all the more significant feature of the "character" style, namely, the constant variation and contrast of form in members that begin in this formulistic manner.

[6] For instance, in the famous passage "De l'Homme" describing the beastlike life of the peasants of France.

The style of the "character," however, is that of a highly specialized genre; and the form of the period with reiterated introductory formula can be shown in its more typical character in other kinds of prose, as, for example, in a passage from Browne describing the Christian Stoicism of his age:

> Let not the twelve but the two tables be thy law: let Pythagoras be thy remembrancer, not thy textuary and final instructor: and learn the vanity of the world rather from Solomon than Phocylydes.[7] — *Christian Morals,* p. xxi.

Browne touches lightly on these repetitions, and uses them not too frequently. Balzac uses them characteristically and significantly. A paragraph from his *Entretiens* (No. XVIII, "De Montaigne et de ses Escrits") may be quoted both in illustration of this fact and for the interest of its subject matter:

> Nous demeurasmes d'accord que l'Autheur qui veut imiter Seneque commence par tout et finit par tout. Son Discours n'est pas un corps entier: c'est un corps en pieces; ce sont des membres couppez; et quoy que les parties soient proches les unes des autres, elles ne laissent pas d'estre separées. Non seulement il n'y a point de nerfs qui les joignent; il n'y a pas mesme de cordes ou d'aiguillettes qui les attachent ensemble: tant cet Autheur est ennemy de toutes sortes de liaisons, soit de la Nature, soit de l'Art: tant il s'esloigne de ces bons exemples que vous imitez si parfaitement.

The passage illustrates exactly Balzac's position in the prose development of the seventeenth century. Montaigne is indeed — in spite of his strictures upon him — his master. He aims, like Montaigne, at the philosophic ease and naturalness of the *genus humile;* he has his taste for aphorism, his taste for metaphor; he is full of "points," and loves to make them show; in short, he is "baroque." But by several means, and chiefly by the kinds of repetition illustrated in this passage (*c'est . . . ce sont; il n'a point . . . il n'y a pas mesme; tant . . . tant*), he succeeds in introducing that effect of art, of form, of rhythm, for which Descartes and so many other of his contemporaries admired him. He combines in short the "wit" of the seventeenth century with at least the appearance of being "a regular writer," which came, in the forties and fifties, to be regarded in France as highly desirable. In his political writings, and especially in *Le Prince,* his iterated opening formula becomes too evident a mannerism, and on page after page one reads periods of the same form: two or three members beginning alike and a final member much longer and more elaborate than the preceding that may or may not begin in the same way. The effect is extremely rhetorical.

3

Finally, we have to observe that the typical *période coupé* need not be so short as the examples of it cited at the beginning of the present section. On

[7] The period occurs in the midst of a paragraph in which each main member of each period begins with a verb in the imperative mood.

the contrary, it may continue, without connectives and with all its highly accentuated peculiarities of form, to the length of five or six members. Seneca offered many models for this protracted aphoristic manner, as in the following passage from the *Naturales Quæstiones* (vii. 31):

> There are mysteries that are not unveiled the first day: Eleusis keepeth back something for those who come again to ask her. Nature telleth not all her secrets at once. We think we have been initiated: we are still waiting in her vestibule. Those secret treasures do not lie open promiscuously to every one: they are kept close and reserved in an inner shrine.

Similar in form is this six-member period from Browne's *Religio Medici* (I, 7):

> To see ourselves again we need not look for Plato's year: every man is not only himself; there have been many Diogeneses, and as many Timons, though but few of that name; men are lived over again; the world is now as it was in ages past; there was none then but there hath been some one since that parallels him, and is, as it were, his revived self.[8]

What has been said in a previous section of the characteristic mode of progression in *stile coupé* is strikingly illustrated in such passages as these. Logically they do not move. At the end they are saying exactly what they were at the beginning. Their advance is wholly in the direction of a more vivid imaginative realization: a metaphor revolves, as it were, displaying its different facets; a series of metaphors flash their lights; or a chain of "points" and paradoxes reveals the energy of a single apprehension in the writer's mind. In the latter part of the seventeenth century a number of critics satirize this peculiarity of the Senecan form. Father Bouhours, for instance, observed that with all its pretensions to brevity and significance this style makes less progress in five or six successive statements than a Ciceronian period will often make in one long and comprehensive construction. The criticism is, of course, sound if the only mode of progression is the logical one; but in fact there is a progress of imaginative apprehension, a revolving and upward motion of the mind as it rises in energy, and views the same point from new levels; and this spiral movement is characteristic of baroque prose.

III. THE LOOSE STYLE

1

In the preceding pages we have been illustrating a kind of period in which the members are in most cases syntactically disjunct, and we have seen that in this style the members are characteristically short. It is necessary now to illustrate the other type of anti-Ciceronian style spoken of at the beginning, in

[8] Felltham uses this manner with too much self-consciousness. See, for instance, a passage on the terse style (*Resolves,* I, 20) beginning: "They that speak to Children assume a pretty lisping."

which the members are usually connected by syntactic ligatures, and in which, therefore, both the members and the period as a whole may be, and in fact usually are, as long as in the Ciceronian style, or even longer.

It is more difficult to find an appropriate name for this kind of style than for the other. The "trailing" or "linked" style would describe a relation between the members of the period that is frequent and indeed characteristic, but is perhaps too specific a name. "Libertine" indicates exactly both the form of the style and the philosophical associations that it often implies; but it is wiser to avoid these implications in a purely descriptive treatment. There is but one term that is exact and covers the ground: the term "loose period" or "loose style"; and it is this that we will usually employ. In applying this term, however, the reader must be on his guard against a use of it that slipped into many rhetorical treatises of the nineteenth century. In these works the "loose sentence" was defined as one that has its main clause near the beginning; and an antithetical term "periodic sentence" — an improper one — was devised to name the opposite arrangement. "Loose period" is used here without reference to this confusing distinction.

In order to show its meaning we must proceed by means of examples; and we will take first a sentence — if, indeed, we can call it a sentence — in which Bacon contrasts the "Magistral" method of writing works of learning with the method of "Probation" appropriate to "induced knowledge," "the latter whereof [he says] seemeth to be *via deserta et interclusa.*"

> For as knowledges are now delivered, there is a kind of contract of error between the deliverer and the receiver: for he that delivereth knowledge desireth to deliver it in such form as may be best believed, and not as may be best examined; and he that receiveth knowledge desireth rather present satisfaction than expectant inquiry; and so rather not to doubt than not to err: glory making the author not to lay open his weakness, and sloth making the disciple not to know his strength. — *Advancement of Learning,* Book I.

The passage is fortunate because it states the philosophy in which anti-Ciceronian prose has its origin and motive. But our present business is with its form; and in order to illustrate this we will place beside it another passage from another author.

> Elle [l'Imagination] ne peut rendre sages les fous; mais elle les rend heureux à l'envi de la raison, qui ne peut rendre ses amis que miserables, l'une les couvrant de gloire, l'autre de honte.[9] — PASCAL, *Pensées,* "L'Imagination."

There is a striking similarity in the way these two periods proceed. In each case an antithesis is stated in the opening members; then the member in which the second part of the antithesis is stated puts out a dependent member. The symmetrical development announced at the beginning is thus interrupted and cannot be resumed. The period must find a way out, a syntactic way of carry-

[9] There should, rhetorically speaking, be semicolons, not commas, after *raison* and *miserables.*

ing on and completing the idea it carries. In both cases the situation is met in the same way, by a concluding member having the form of an absolute participle construction, in which the antithetical idea of the whole is sharply, aphoristically resumed.

The two passages, in short, are written as if they were meant to illustrate in style what Bacon calls "the method of induced knowledge"; either they have no predetermined plan or they violate it at will; their progression adapts itself to the movements of a mind discovering truth as it goes, thinking while it writes. At the same time, and for the same reason, they illustrate the character of the style that we call "baroque." See, for instance, how symmetry is first made and then broken, as it is in so many baroque designs in painting and architecture; how there is constant swift adaptation of form to the emergencies that arise in an energetic and unpremeditated forward movement; and observe, further, that these signs of spontaneity and improvisation occur in passages loaded with as heavy a content as rhetoric ever has to carry. That is to say, they combine the effect of great mass with the effect of rapid motion; and there is no better formula than this to describe the ideal of the baroque design in all the arts.

But these generalizations are beyond our present purpose. We are to study the loose period first, as we did the curt period, by observing the character of its syntactic links. In the two sentences quoted there are, with a single exception, but two modes of connection employed. The first is by co-ordinating conjunctions, the conjunctions, that is, that allow the mind to move straight on from the point it has reached. They do not necessarily refer back to any particular point in the preceding member; nor do they commit the following member to a predetermined form. In other words, they are the loose conjunctions, and disjoin the members they join as widely as possible. *And, but* and *for* are the ones employed in the two sentences; and these are of course the necessary and universal ones. Other favorites of the loose style are *whereas, nor* (= *and not*), and the correlatives *though . . . . yet, as . . . . so.* Second, each of the two periods contains a member with an absolute-participle construction. In the loose style many members have this form, and not only (as in the two periods quoted) at the ends of periods, but elsewhere. Sir Thomas Browne often has them early in a period, as some passages to be cited in another connection will show. This is a phenomenon easily explained. For the absolute construction is the one that commits itself least and lends itself best to the solution of difficulties that arise in the course of a spontaneous and unpremeditated progress. It may state either a cause, or a consequence, or a mere attendant circumstance: it may be concessive or justificatory; it may be a summary of the preceding or a supplement to it; it may express an idea related to the whole of the period in which it occurs, or one related only to the last preceding member.

The co-ordinating conjunctions and the absolute-participle construction indicate, then, the character of the loose period. Like the *stile coupé,* it is meant to portray the natural, or thinking, order; and it expresses even better than the curt period the anti-Ciceronian prejudice against formality of procedure and the rhetoric of the schools. For the omission of connectives in the *stile coupé* implies, as we have seen, a very definite kind of rhetorical form, which was practiced in direct imitation of classical models, and usually retained the associations that it had won in the Stoic schools of antiquity. The associations of the loose style, on the other hand, are all with the more skeptical phases of seventeenth-century thought — with what was then usually called "Libertinism"; and it appears characteristically in writers who are professed opponents of determined and rigorous philosophic attitudes. It is the style of Bacon and of Montaigne (after he has found himself), of La Mothe le Vayer, and of Sir Thomas Browne. It appears always in the letters of Donne; it appears in Pascal's *Pensées;* and, in the latter part of the century, when Libertinism had positively won the favor of the world away from Stoicism, it enjoyed a self-conscious revival, under the influence of Montaigne, in the writings of St. Évremond, Halifax, and Temple. Indeed, it is evident that, although the Senecan *stile coupé* attracted more critical attention throughout the century, its greatest achievements in prose were rather in the loose or Libertine manner. But it must also be said that most of the skeptics of the century had undergone a strong Senecan influence; and the styles of Montaigne, Browne, Pascal, and Halifax, for instance, can only be described as displaying in varying ways a mingling of Stoic and Libertine traits.

2

Besides the two syntactic forms that have been mentioned — the co-ordinating conjunctions and the absolute construction — there are no others that lend themselves by their nature to the loose style, except the parenthesis, which we need not illustrate here. But it must not be supposed that it tends to exclude other modes of connection. On the contrary, it obtains its characteristic effects from the syntactic forms that are logically more strict and binding, such as the relative pronouns and the subordinating conjunctions, by using them in a way peculiar to itself. That is to say, it uses them as the necessary logical means of advancing the idea, but relaxes at will the tight construction which they seem to impose; so that they have exactly the same effect as the loose connections previously described and must be punctuated in the same way. In other words, the parts that they connect are no more closely knit together than it chooses they shall be; and the reader of the most characteristic seventeenth-century prose soon learns to give a greater independence and autonomy to subordinate members than he would dare to do in reading any other.

The method may be shown by a single long sentence from Sir Thomas Browne:

> I could never perceive any rational consequence from those many texts which prohibit the children of Israel to pollute themselves with the temples

of the heathens; we being all Christians, and not divided by such detested impieties *as* might profane our prayers, or the place wherein we make them; *or that* a resolved conscience may not adore her Creator anywhere, *especially* in places devoted to his service; *where,* if their devotions offend him, mine may please him; if theirs profane it, mine may hallow it.[10] — *Religio Medici,* I, 3.

The period begins with a statement complete in itself, which does not syntactically imply anything to follow it; an absolute participle carries on, in the second member. Thereafter the connectives are chiefly subordinating conjunctions. Observe particularly the use of *as, or that,* and *where:* how slight these ligatures are in view of the length and mass of the members they must carry. They are frail and small hinges for the weights that turn on them; and the period abounds and expands in nonchalant disregard of their tight, frail logic.

This example displays the principle; but of course a single passage can illustrate only a few grammatical forms. Some of those used with a characteristic looseness in English prose of the seventeenth century are: relative clauses beginning with *which,* or with *whereto, wherein,* etc.; participial constructions of the kind scornfully called "dangling" by the grammarians; words in a merely appositional relation with some noun or pronoun preceding, yet constituting a semi-independent member of a period; and of course such subordinating conjunctions as are illustrated above. It is unnecessary to illustrate these various cases.

3

The connections of a period cannot be considered separately from the order of the connected members; and, in fact, it is the desired order of development that determines the character of the connections rather than the reverse. In the oratorical period the arrangement of the members is "round" or "circular," in the sense that they are all so placed with reference to a central or climactic member that they point forward or back to it and give it its appropriate emphasis. This order is what is meant by the names *periodos, circuitus,* and "round composition," by which the oratorical period has been variously called; and it is the chief object of the many revisions to which its form is submitted.

The loose period does not try for this form, but rather seeks to avoid it. Its purpose is to express, as far as may be, the order in which an idea presents itself when it is first experienced. It begins, therefore, without premeditation, stating its idea in the first form that occurs; the second member is determined by the situation in which the mind finds itself after the first has been spoken; and so on throughout the period, each member being an emergency of the situation. The period — in theory, at least — is not made; it becomes. It completes itself and takes on form in the course of the motion of mind which it expresses. Montaigne, in short, exactly described the theory of the loose style

[10] Italics are mine.

when he said: "J'écris volontiers sans project; le premier trait produit le second."

The figure of a circle, therefore, is not a possible description of the form of a loose period; it requires rather the metaphor of a chain, whose links join end to end. The "linked" or "trailing" period is, in fact, as we have observed, an appropriate name for it. But there is a special case for which this term might better be reserved, unless we should choose to invent a more specific one, such as "end-linking," or "terminal linking," to describe it. It is when a member depends, not upon the general idea, or the main word, of the preceding member, but upon its final word or phrase alone. And this is, in fact, a frequent, even a characteristic, kind of linking in certain authors, notably Sir Thomas Browne and his imitators. The sentence last quoted offers two or three illustrations of it: the connective words *as, especially,* and *where* all refer to the immediately preceding words or phrases; and in another period by the same author there is one very conspicuous and characteristic instance.

> As there were many reformers, so likewise many reformations; every country proceeding in a particular way and method, according as their national interest, together with their constitution and clime, inclined them: some angrily and with extremity; others calmly and with mediocrity, not rending, but easily dividing, the community, and leaving an honest possibility of a reconciliation; — *which* though peaceable spirits do desire, and may conceive that revolution of time and the mercies of God may effect, yet that judgment that shall consider the present antipathies between the two extremes, their contrarities in condition, affection, and opinion, — may with the same hopes expect a union in the poles of heaven. — *Religio Medici,* I, 4.

Here the word *which* introduces a new development of the idea, running to as much as five lines of print; yet syntactically it refers only to the last preceding word *reconciliation.* The whole long passage has been quoted, however, not for this reason alone, but because it illustrates so perfectly all that has been said of the order and connection of the loose period. It begins, characteristically, with a sharply formulated complete statement, implying nothing of what is to follow. Its next move is achieved by means of an absolute-participle construction.[11] This buds off a couple of appositional members; one of these budding again two new members by means of dangling participles. Then a *which* picks up the trail, and at once the sentence becomes involved in the complex, and apparently tight, organization of a *though* . . . . *yet* construction. Nevertheless it still moves freely, digressing as it will, extricates itself from the complex form by a kind of *anacoluthon* (in the *yet* clause), broadening its scope, and gathering new confluents, till it ends, like a river, in an opening view.

The period, that is, moves straight onward everywhere from the point it has reached; and its construction shows ideally what we mean by the linked or trail-

[11] Observe that the period from Browne quoted on pp. 353–54 begins with movements of the same kind.

ing order. It is Browne's peculiar mastery of this construction that gives his writing constantly the effect of being, not the result of a meditation, but an actual meditation in process. He writes like a philosophical scientist making notes of his observation as it occurs. We see his pen move and stop as he thinks. To write thus, and at the same time to create beauty of cadence in the phrases and rhythm in the design — and so Browne constantly does — is to achieve a triumph in what Montaigne called "the art of being natural"; it is the eloquence, described by Pascal, that mocks at formal eloquence.

4

The period just quoted serves to introduce a final point concerning the form of the loose period. We have already observed that the second half of this period, beginning with *which,* has a complex suspended syntax apparently like that of the typical oratorical sentence. The anti-Ciceronian writer usually avoids such forms, it is true; most of his sentences are punctuated by colons and semicolons. But, of course, he will often find himself involved in a suspended construction from which he cannot escape. It remains to show that even in these cases he still proceeds in the anti-Ciceronian manner, and succeeds in following, in spite of the syntactic formalities to which he commits himself, his own emergent and experimental order. Indeed, it is to be observed that the characteristic quality of the loose style may appear more clearly in such difficult forms than in others. For baroque art always displays itself best when it works in heavy masses and resistant materials; and out of the struggle between a fixed pattern and an energetic forward movement often arrives at those strong and expressive disproportions in which it delights.

We shall return to Browne in a moment in illustration of the point, but we shall take up a simpler case first. In a well-known sentence, Pascal, bringing out the force of imagination, draws a picture of a venerable magistrate seated in church, ready to listen to a worthy sermon. *Le voilà prêt à l'ouir avec un respect exemplaire.*

> Que le prédicateur vienne a paraître: si la nature lui a donné une voix enrouée et un tour de visage bizarre, que son barbier l'ait mal rasé, si le hasard l'a encore barbouillé de surcroît, quelques grandes vérités qu'il annonce, je parie la perte de la gravité de notre sénateur.

Unquestionably a faulty sentence by all the school-rules! It begins without foreseeing its end, and has to shift the reader's glance from the preacher to the magistrate in the midst of its progress by whatever means it can. Observe the abruptness of the form of the member *quelques grandes vérités.* Observe the sudden appearance of the first person in the last member. Yet the critic who would condemn its rhetorical form would have also to declare that there is no art in those vivid dramatic narratives that so often appear in the conversation of animated talkers; for this period moves in an order very common in such conversation.[12]

In this passage the free and anti-Ciceronian character of the movement is chiefly due to its dramatic vividness and speed. It follows the order of life. Sometimes, however, we can see plainly that it is the mystical speculation of the seventeenth century that changes the regular form of the period and shapes it to its own ends. Sir Thomas Browne provides many interesting illustrations, as, for instance, in the period quoted in the preceding section, and in the following:

> I would gladly know how Moses, with an actual fire, calcined or burnt the golden calf into powder: for that mystical metal of gold, whose solary and celestial nature I admire, exposed unto the violence of fire, grows only hot, and liquefies, but consumeth not; so when the consumable and volatile pieces of our bodies shall be refined into a more impregnable and fixed temper, like gold, though they suffer from the action of flames, they shall never perish, but lie immortal in the arms of fire. — *Religio Medici,* I, 50.

With the first half of this long construction we are not now concerned. In its second half, however, beginning with *so when,* we see one of those complex movements that have led some critics to speak of Browne as — of all things! — a Ciceronian. It is in fact the opposite of that. A Ciceronian period closes in at the end; it reaches its height of expansion and emphasis at the middle or just beyond, and ends composedly. Browne's sentence, on the contrary, opens constantly outward; its motions become more animated and vigorous as it proceeds; and it ends, as his sentences are likely to do, in a vision of vast space or time, losing itself in an *altitudo,* a hint of infinity. As, in a previously quoted period, everything led up to the phrase, "a union in the poles of heaven," so in this everything leads up to the concluding phrase, "but lie immortal in the arms of fire." And as we study the form of the structure we can even observe where this ending revealed itself, or, at least, how it was prepared. The phrase "like gold" is the key to the form of the whole. After a slow expository member, this phrase, so strikingly wrenched from its logical position, breaks the established and expected rhythm, and is a signal of more agitated movement, of an ascending effort of imaginative realization that continues to the end. In a different medium, the period closely parallels the technique of an El Greco composition, where broken and tortuous lines in the body of the design prepare the eye for curves that leap upward beyond the limits of the canvas.

The forms that the loose period may assume are infinite, and it would be merely pedantic to attempt a classification of them. In one of the passages quoted we have seen the dramatic sense of reality triumphing over rhetorical formalism; in another, the form of a mystical exaltation. For the purpose of

[12] It may be said that Pascal's *Pensées* should not be cited in illustration of prose form because they were written without revision and without thought of publication. But a good deal of characteristic prose of the time was so written; and the effect at which Bacon, Burton, Browne, and many others aimed was of prose written in that way.

description — not classification — it will be convenient to observe still a third way in which a loose period may escape from the formal commitments of elaborate syntax. It is illustrated in a passage in Montaigne's essay "Des Livres" (II, 10), praising the simple and uncritical kind of history that he likes so much. In the course of the period he mentions *le bon Froissard* as an example, and proceeds so far (six lines of print) in a description of his method that he cannot get back to his general idea by means of his original syntactic form, or at least cannot do so without very artificial devices. He completes the sentence where it is; but completes his idea in a pair of curt (*coupés*) sentences separated by a colon from the preceding: "C'est la matière de l'histoire nue et informe; chascun en peult faire son proufit autant qu'il a d'entendement." This is a method often used by anti-Ciceronians to extricate themselves from the coils of a situation in which they have become involved by following the "natural" order. A better example of it is to be seen in a passage from Pascal's essay on "Imagination," from which another passage has already been cited.

> Le plus grand philosophe du monde, sur une planche plus large qu'il ne faut, s'il y a au-dessous un précipice, quoique sa raison le convainque de sa sureté, son imagination prévaudra. Plusieurs n'en sauroient soutenir la pensée sans pâlir et suer. — *Pensées,* "L'Imagination."

Nothing could better illustrate the "order of nature"; writing, that is, in the exact order in which the matter presents itself. It begins by naming the subject, *le plus grand philosophe,* without foreseeing the syntax by which it is to continue. Then it throws in the elements of the situation, using any syntax that suggests itself at the moment, proceeding with perfect dramatic sequence, but wholly without logical sequence, until at last the sentence has lost touch with its stated subject. Accordingly, this subject is merely left hanging, and a new one, *son imagination,* takes its place. It is a violent, or rather a nonchalant, *anacoluthon.* The sentence has then, after a fashion, completed itself. But there is an uneasy feeling in the mind. After all, *le plus grand philosophe* has done nothing; both form and idea are incomplete. Pascal adds another member (for, whatever the punctuation, the *plusieurs* sentence is a member of the period), which completely meets the situation, though a grammatical purist may well object that the antecedent of *plusieurs* was in the singular number.

Pascal is usually spoken of as a "classical" writer; but the term means nothing as applied to him except that he is a writer of tried artistic soundness. He is, in fact, as modernistic, as bold a breaker of the rules and forms of rhetoric, as his master Montaigne, though he is also a much more careful artist. *La vraie éloquence,* he said, *se moque de l'éloquence.*

5

Two kinds of style have been analyzed in the preceding pages: the concise, serried, abrupt *stile coupé,* and the informal, meditative, and "natural" loose style. It is necessary to repeat — once more — that in the best writers these two styles do not appear separately in passages of any length, and that in most of them they intermingle in relations far too complex for description. They represent two sides of the seventeenth-century mind: its sententiousness, its penetrating wit, its Stoic intensity, on the one hand, and its dislike of formalism, its roving and self-exploring curiosity, in brief, its skeptical tendency, on the other. And these two habits of mind are generally not separated one from the other; nor are they even always exactly distinguishable. Indeed, as they begin to separate or to be opposed to each other in the second half of the century we are aware of the approach of a new age and a new spirit. The seventeenth century, as we are here considering it, is equally and at once Stoic and Libertine; and the prose that is most characteristic of it expresses these two sides of its mind in easy and natural relations one with the other.

IV. The Punctuation of the Seventeenth-Century Period

The "long sentence" of the anti-Ciceronian age has received a remarkable amount of attention ever since it began to be corrected and go out of use; and there have been two conflicting views concerning it. The older doctrine — not yet quite extinct — was that the long sentences of Montaigne, Bacon, Browne, and Taylor were sentences of the same kind as those of Cicero and his sixteenth-century imitators; only they were badly and crudely made, monstrosities due to some wave of ignorance that submerged the syntactic area of the seventeenth-century mind. Their true character, it was thought, would be shown by substituting commas for their semicolons and colons; for then we should see that they are quaint failures in the attempt to achieve sentence-unity.

The other view is the opposite of this, namely, that we should put periods in the place of many of its semicolons and colons. We should then see that what look like long sentences are really brief and aphoristic ones. The contemporary punctuation of our authors is again to be corrected, but now in a different sense. This is the view urged by Faguet in writing of Montaigne, and by Sir Edmund Gosse concerning the prose of Browne and Taylor.

This later view is useful in correcting some of the errors of the earlier one. But, in fact, one of them is just as false as the other; and both of them illustrate the difficulties experienced by minds trained solely in the logical and grammatical aspects of language in interpreting the forms of style that prevailed before the eighteenth century. In order to understand the punctuation of the seventeenth century we have to consider the relation between the grammatical term *sentence* and the rhetorical term *period.*

The things named by these terms are identical. *Period* names the rhetorical, or oral, aspect of the same thing that is called in grammar a *sentence;* and in theory the same act of composition that produces a perfectly logical grammatical unit would produce at the same time a perfectly rhythmical pattern of sound. But, in fact, no utterance ever fulfils both of these functions perfectly, and either one or the other of them is always foremost in a writer's mind. One or the other is foremost also in every theory of literary education; and the historian may sometimes distinguish literary periods by the relative emphasis they put upon grammatical and rhetorical considerations. In general we may say, though there may be exceptions, that before the eighteenth century rhetoric occupied much more attention than grammar in the minds of teachers and their pupils. It was so, for instance, in the Middle Ages, as is clear from their manuals of study and the curricula of their schools. It was still true in the sixteenth century; and the most striking characteristic of the literary prose of that century, both in Latin and in the vernacular tongues, was its devotion to the conventional and formal patterns of school-rhetoric.

The laws of grammatical form, it is true, were not at all disturbed or strained at this time by the predominance of rhetorical motives. There was no difficulty whatever in saying what these rhetoricians had to say in perfect accordance with logical syntax because they had, in fact, so little to say that only the most elementary syntax was necessary for its purposes. Furthermore, the rhetorical forms they liked were so symmetrical, so obvious, that they almost imposed a regular syntax by their own form.

But a new situation arose when the leaders of seventeenth-century rationalism — Lipsius, Montaigne, Bacon — became the teachers of style. The ambition of these writers was to conduct an experimental investigation of the moral realities of their time, and to achieve a style appropriate to the expression of their discoveries and of the mental effort by which they were conducted. The content of style became, as it were, suddenly greater and more difficult; and the stylistic formalities of the preceding age were unable to bear the burden. An immense rhetorical complexity and license took the place of the simplicity and purism of the sixteenth century; and, since the age had not yet learned to think much about grammatical propriety, the rules of syntax were made to bear the expenses of the new freedom. In the examples of seventeenth-century prose that have been discussed in the preceding pages some of the results are apparent. The syntactic connections of a sentence become loose and casual; great strains are imposed upon tenuous, frail links; parentheses are abused; digression becomes licentious; *anacoluthon* is frequent and passes unnoticed; even the limits of sentences are not clearly marked, and it is sometimes difficult to say where one begins and another ends.

Evidently the process of disintegration could not go on forever. A stylistic reform was inevitable, and it must take the direction of a new formalism or "correctness." The direction that it actually took was determined by the Cartesian philosophy, or at least by the same time-spirit in which the Cartesian philosophy had its origin. The intellect, that is to say, became the arbiter of form, the dictator of artistic practice as of philosophical inquiry. The sources of error, in the view of the Cartesians, are imagination and dependence upon sense-impressions. Its correctives are found in what they call "reason" (which here means 'intellect'), and an exact distinction of categories.

To this mode of thought we are to trace almost all the features of modern literary education and criticism, or at least of what we should have called modern a generation ago: the study of the precise meaning of words; the reference to dictionaries as literary authorities; the study of the sentence as a logical unit alone; the careful circumscription of its limits and the gradual reduction of its length; the disappearance of semicolons and colons; the attempt to reduce grammar to an exact science; the idea that forms of speech are always either correct or incorrect; the complete subjection of the laws of motion and expression in style to the laws of logic and standardization — in short, the triumph, during two centuries, of grammatical over rhetorical ideas.

This is not the place to consider what we have gained or lost by this literary philosophy, or whether the precision we have aimed at has compensated us for the powers of expression and the flexibility of motion that we have lost; we have only to say that we must not apply the ideas we have learned from it to the explanation of seventeenth-century style. In brief, we must not measure the customs of the age of semicolons and colons by the customs of the age of commas and periods. The only possible punctuation of seventeenth-century prose is that which it used itself. We might sometimes reveal its grammar more clearly by repunctuating it with commas or periods, but we should certainly destroy its rhetoric.

W. K. Wimsatt, Jr.

STYLE AS MEANING

"Betwixt the formation of words and that of thought there is this difference," said Cicero, "that that of the words is destroyed if you change them, that of the thoughts remains, whatever words you think proper to use." [1] This is a clear statement of the view of style and meaning which today may be conveniently called "the ornamental." The ancient rhetoricians all seem to have something like this in mind.[2] They may stress the need of meaning, or may in their metaphysics insist on the interdependence of matter and form, but when they reach the surface of meaning, the plane of most detailed organization, they are not able to speak so as to connect this with meaning. It is as if, when all is said for meaning, there remains an irreducible something that is superficial, a kind of scum — which they call style. One may consult as representative the whole treatment of rhetorical figures in Quintilian's *Institute*.

There is the opposite theory of style, one that has been growing on us since the seventeenth century. "So many *things,* almost in an equal number of *words,*" says Sprat.[3] And Pascal, "La vraie éloquence se moque de l'éloquence." [4] And somewhat later Swift, "Proper words in proper places, make the true definition of a style"; [5] and Buffon, "Style is simply the order and movement one gives to one's thoughts." [6] By the nineteenth century the doc-

Reprinted from *The Prose Style of Samuel Johnson* by W. K. Wimsatt, Jr., by permission of Yale University Press.

[1] *De Oratore,* III, *lii, in Cicero on Oratory and Orators,* ed. J. S. Watson (New York, 1890), p. 252.

[2] Cf. Benedetto Croce, *Aesthetic as Science of Expression and General Linguistic,* trans. Douglas Ainslee (London, 1929), pp. 422–9.

[3] Thomas Sprat, *History of the Royal Society* (London, 1702), p. 113. Cf. Richard F. Jones, "Science and English Prose Style in the Third Quarter of the Seventeenth Century," *PMLA,* XLV (1930), 977–1009.

[4] *Pensées,* VII, 34, ed. Ernest Havet (Paris, 1866), Vol. I, p. 106; cf. VII, 28, *op. cit.,* Vol. I, p. 105.

[5] *A Letter to a Young Clergyman, Lately Entered into Holy Orders,* 1721, *Prose Works,* ed. Temple Scott (London, 1898), III, 200–01.

[6] *An Address Delivered Before the French Academy* [generally known as the *Discours sur le Style*], 1753, in Lane Cooper, *Theories of Style* (New York, 1907), p. 171. This, rather than the too-often-quoted "The style is the man," is Buffon's real definition

trine is proclaimed on every hand — very explicitly, for example, by Cardinal Newman:

> Thought and speech are inseparable from each other. Matter and expression are parts of one: style is a thinking out into language. . . . When we can separate light and illumination, life and motion, the convex and the concave of a curve . . . then will it be conceivable that the . . . intellect should renounce its own double.[7]

In one of the best books on style to appear in our own day, Mr. Middleton Murry has said:

> Style is not an isolable quality of writing; it is writing itself.[8]

It is hardly necessary to adduce proof that the doctrine of identity of style and meaning is today firmly established. This doctrine is, I take it, one from which a modern theorist hardly can escape, or hardly wishes to.

The chief difficulty with the modern doctrine of style lies in its application to rhetorical study. The difficulty appears in two ways: partly in the implicit abandonment of the doctrine when rhetorical study is attempted, but more largely in a wide, silent rejection of the whole system of rhetoric. "We have done with the theory of style," proclaims an eminent critic in Crocean vein, "with metaphor, simile, and all the paraphernalia of Graeco-Roman rhetoric.[9] Now it must be contended that we have not done with "metaphor" — that we still have an important use for the term.[10] But for scarcely any other term of rhetoric have we better than a shrug. We no longer are willing to take seriously a set of terms which once — for centuries — were taken seriously, and which must, no matter how unhappy their use, have stood for something. In throwing away the terms it is even possible we have thrown away all definite concept

---

of style — a point well taken by W. C. Brownell, *The Genius of Style* (New York, 1924), p. 46.

7 "Literature, a Lecture in the School of Philosophy and Letters," 1858, in *The Idea of a University* (London, 1907), pp. 276–7. In Lane Cooper's *Theories of Style* one may conveniently find similar expressions by Coleridge, Wackernagel, De Quincey, Schopenhauer, Lewes, Pater, and Brunetière (esp. pp. 10, 207, 222–3, 252, 320, 391, 399, 401, 422). See also *Pensées de J. Joubert,* ed. Paul Raynal (Paris, 1888), II, 275–8, Titre XXII, paragraphs IX–XXV; August Boeckh, *Encyklopädie und Methodologie der Philologischen Wissenschaften* (Leipzig, 1886), p. 128.

For the opposite way of thinking, see William Minto, *Manual of English Prose Literature* (Edinburgh and London, 1881) (first published in 1872), Introduction, pp. 14–15; George Saintsbury, "Modern English Prose," 1876, in *Miscellaneous Essays* (London, 1892), pp. 83, 84, 99.

8 J. Middleton Murry, *The Problem of Style* (Oxford, 1922), p. 77; cf. pp. 16, 71. Cf. Walter Raleigh, *Style* (London, 1897), esp. p. 62; Herbert Read, *English Prose Style* (London, 1932), *passim.* Mr. Logan Pearsall Smith would probably admit that the rich and poetic prose for which he pleads is as much a matter of expression as the plainest (*S.P.E. Tract No. XLVI, Fine Writing* [Oxford, 1936], esp. pp. 203, 220). For a cross-section of opinion from modern professional writers, see Burges Johnson, *Good Writing* (Syracuse University, 1932).

9 J. E. Spingarn, *Creative Criticism* (New York, 1917), p. 30.

10 Cf. *post* p. 371.

of the things they once stood for. The realities of antithesis and climax, for example, are perhaps less and less a part of our consciousness. But literary history without these old realities and their old terms is impossible; without an evaluation of them it is superficial. The fact is that Cicero used "figures" of this and that sort — moreover, he wrote criticism about them. Hooker and Donne and Johnson used such figures too. And the old terms when used to describe these old writings do mean something. We cannot avoid admitting that we recognize certain things as denoted by the terms, that we know the nominal definitions. Furthermore, we are not ready to call Cicero and the rest simply bad writers. We may insist, and properly, that the accounts they give of their devices, their theories of rhetoric, are insufficient — even baneful as guides to composition; as for the living use they made of what they called "devices," their actual saying of things, in this we see that their intuition was better than their theory.

II

Any discourse about a definition of "style" is fruitless if it concerns itself too simply with protesting: style *is this* or *is that*. Definitions are impervious to the "lie direct," mere "intrenchant air" for the sword of evidence. The only reason a term *should* mean something is the history of its application, the fact that it *has* meant something. We may say that dubious terms have a kind of repertoire of related meanings. But the meaning of a term in a given instance is what any man decides to make it, and if I dislike what he makes it, I may not tell him he is mistaken.

Nevertheless I may dislike it, and justly. This is the problem in facing definitions — that they do often bother us as bad definitions and make us wish vehemently to reject them. The basis for our uneasiness is ultimately one of relevance, relevance of a definition to the principles of the whole science of which the term is accepted as a part. If there is not a fixed real meaning for a term, there is at least an ideal one, a something to which the term *should* refer if it is to be used in its science without producing nonsense. It is the purpose of definition to determine *what* is referred to, and the business of him who formulates a definition to determine what *should be* referred to, as most relevant to the presiding science. The first step toward forming a definition, a theory, of "style" must be taken in the science of literary esthetics, more specifically in a consideration of the nature of words as esthetic medium.

It is the nature of words to mean. To consider words only as sounds, like drum taps, or to consider written letters as patterned objects, as in alphabet soup, is the same as to consider a Stradivarius as material for kindling wood. There is, to be sure, a certain truth in the contention that it is useless to speak of the limits of each art. If a painter of abstractions succeeded in conveying a concept which he described as rhythmic, it would be pointless to contend that such a concept should properly be expressed in music. Insofar as the painting did succeed as an expression, there would simply be *that* expression. On the other hand, even Croce will admit that different artistic intuitions need different media for their "externalization." [11] Even when the various media are considered as forming a continuum, a spectrum, one point in the spectrum is not another point. Red is not green. Stone is not B flat. Stone can be used for a statue; B flat cannot. Words can be used to "mean" in a way that nothing else can. In various senses the other arts may be called expressive or communicative. But it is not in any such senses that words are expressive. When Maritain says that "music *imitates* with sound and rhythms . . . the movements of the soul," [12] and when Dewey says that architecture " 'expresses' . . . enduring values of collective human life," [13] they are speaking of the kind of representation we should speak of if we said that the images of autumn, nightfall, and a dying fire in Shakespeare's sonnet stand for his sense of mortality, or if we said that the whole poem is a symbol of his sense of mortality. While the music and the architecture *are* the symbols of what they represent, the words of a writing must *express* a meaning which *is* a symbol. "A poem should not mean But be," writes Mr. Archibald MacLeish. But a poem cannot *be* in the simple sense that a statue or a piece of Venetian glass *is*. For each thing insofar as it *is*, must *be*, have *being*, according to its nature. The nature of words is to mean, and a poem *is* through its meaning.

There are such things as the Caroline shape poems, the winged or altar shapes of Herbert or Quarles; there are the typographical oddities of E. E. Cummings. There are illuminated manuscripts or illustrated books, Gothic books of Gospels, arabesque texts of the Koran on mosque walls. And people may even have wondered what they ought to think of Cummings. But nobody thinks that the Gospel suffers when not read in the Book of Kells. It is clear that in the case of illuminations and illustrations of a text there is not a single art expression, but two running side by side. Words, music, costume, and stage may make one expression in an opera; the poetry of Vachel Lindsay read aloud and the accompanying dance may have made one expression; it may be possible to conceive a text so referred to and interrelated with a series of pictures that the two make one expression.[14] Yet it remains true that what we call literature, whether prose or poetry, has not been a graphic medium. It has not been possible or worth while to employ words in this way.

[11] Benedetto Croce, *op. cit.*, pp. 114–16. Cf. C. K. Ogden *et al.*, *The Foundations of Aesthetics* (London, 1925), p. 28; David Daiches, *The Place of Meaning in Poetry* (Edinburgh, 1935), esp. pp. 30, 61–3.

[12] Jacques Maritain, *Art and Scholasticism,* trans. J. F. Scanlan (London, 1930), p. 58.

[13] John Dewey, *Art as Experience* (New York, 1934), p. 221. Cf. Gilbert Murray, "An Essay on the Theory of Poetry," *Yale Review,* x (1921), 484; Theodore M. Greene, *The Arts and the Art of Criticism* (Princeton, 1940), esp. p. 108.

[14] Mr. Archibald MacLeish's *Land of the Free* (New York, 1938) is "a book of photographs illustrated by a poem. . . . The original purpose had been to write some sort of text to which these photographs might serve as commentary. But so great was the power and the stubborn inward livingness of these vivid American documents that the result was a reversal of that plan" (p. 89).

But language is spoken before it is written; even after it is written it is implicitly spoken; and language as sound has potentialities far beyond those of language as written or visual.[15] Sound is in some sense the medium of literature, no matter how words are considered as expressive. What is more questionable is how near this medium ever can come to being that of music. Sound in its conventional semantic value is certainly not a musical medium. Further it is not musical in its whole complex of suggestive or directly imitative values, onomatopoeia, and all the more mysteriously felt shades of sound propriety.[16]

A more difficult problem of sound in literature is that of meter and such associates as rhyme and alliteration. But it is usual to insist that these elements of verse are in some way expressive. They express the emotion of poetic experience; or, by inducing in us a pattern of expectancy and playing against that the surprise of variation, they make us realize more intensely both sense and emotion.[17] Or, the verse of a whole poem may be considered as a form, an aspect or way of being known, which gives unity and particularity to the whole — makes it the special poetic symbol that it is.[18] It may be possible to say that this second kind of expressiveness is on the same level as that of music and architecture mentioned above, a direct symbol of experience. But in this case it will be necessary to remember that the expression of the verse coalesces with and is in effect the same as that of the words in their semantic function.

Here we might let the question of language as sound medium rest were it not for the persistent appearance of the mysterious critical term "prose rhythm." From what has been said of verse it is plain that a prose rhythm is conceivable — that is, some alternation of sounds akin to meter, though more variable. If such a succession of sounds could be detected with certainty in any body of prose, and if one had no sense that this was unconnected with the meaning or detracted from it, then it would have to be admitted that in the given case a prose rhythm as an expressive medium did exist. The general question, then, is not whether there *can* be a prose rhythm but whether there *is*. And a particular question, such as that concerning English literature, is but the general question narrowed — whether there *is*. Certain things may be asserted: I. The rhetoricians of antiquity found in Greek and Latin oratory a rhythm which they analyzed almost as definitely as verse meter, particularly in

[15] Cf. Otto Jespersen, *Language, Its Nature, Development and Origin* (London, 1922), *passim;* D. W. Prall, *Aesthetic Judgment* (New York, 1929), pp. 289–90.

[16] Many of these values, as a matter of fact, are not, as has been commonly thought, due to any direct expressiveness of sounds but rather to linguistic analogies as ancient as the roots of language (Leonard Bloomfield, *Language* [New York, 1933] pp. 244–5; I. A. Richards, *The Philosophy of Rhetoric* [New York, 1936], pp. 63–5). For a treatment of word sounds as suggestive of or appropriate to meaning, see Otto Jespersen, *Language* (London, 1922), pp. 396–406.

[17] Cf. I. A. Richards, *Principles of Literary Criticism* (New York, 1934), "Rhythm and Metre," pp. 137–42. It may be too that meter has a hypnotic function. See Edward D. Snyder, *Hypnotic Poetry* (Philadelphia, 1930), pp. 19, 39 ff.

[18] Cf. Lascelles Abercrombie, *Principles of English Prosody* (London, 1923), pp. 15–18, 31; *The Theory of Poetry* (New York, 1926), pp. 70, 95, 138, 140–6.

the sequence of syllables ending clauses, the cursus.[19] II. The cursus was also a part of Medieval Latin prose.[20] III. There are some who hold that variations of the cursus occur in English prose.[21] IV. There is, however, no agreement, but the widest divergence of opinion, among those who have made extended studies of the nature of rhythm in English prose. Their number is not small (and each is at odds in some respect with almost all the others): those who would scan, or make meter; those who are interested in some vaguer kind of periodicity, time measurement; those who rely on the cursus; and those who find rhythm in the movement of phrases.[22]

It would be within the province only of a very special investigation to dare say what English prose rhythm *is*. And I have admitted above that the question is not whether there *can* be a prose rhythm. Yet there are some things that can be said about the possibilities of prose rhythm. If it is a quality of sound, it is either expressive of something or not. If not (if, say, it is like the number of times the letter "t" occurs on a given page), it is not a medium of art and therefore claims no interest; it is not in fact prose rhythm at all. Secondly, if it is expressive, it expresses either the same meaning as the words do otherwise, or it does not. If it expresses the same meaning, it may, like meter, express perhaps from the same level as words do otherwise, perhaps from a level more like that of music. These possibilities are admissible.[23] But thirdly, if it expresses other than the same meaning, then it must express some meaning

[19] See, for example, John W. Sandys, *A Companion to Latin Studies* (Cambridge, 1921), p. 655. François Novotný, *État Actuel des Études sur le Rhythme de la Prose Latine* (Lwów, 1929), sees "un bel avenir dans notre science," but confesses: "Ces essais et leur résultats dépendent bien souvent du sentiment esthétique subjectif de l'observateur" (p. 33).

[20] See, for example, Karl Strecker, *Introduction à l'Étude du Latin Médiéval,* trad. par Paul van der Woestijne (Gand, 1933), pp. 51–3; Edouard Norden, *Die Antike Kunstprosa* (Leipzig, 1898), II, 950–1.

[21] See, for example, Oliver Elton, "English Prose Numbers," *Essays and Studies by Members of the English Association,* IV (Oxford, 1913), 29–54; Morris W. Croll, "The Cadence of English Oratorical Prose," *Studies in Philology,* XVI (1919), 1–55.

[22] Cf. John Hubert Scott, *Rhythmic Prose,* "University of Iowa Humanistic Studies," Vol. III, No. 1 (Iowa City, 1925), p. 11. Norton R. Tempest, a more recent writer, is a scanner and at the same time belongs to the cursus school (*The Rhythm of English Prose* [Cambridge University Press, 1930], p. 134). André Classe is a timer with a kymograph, who proposes "only . . . to investigate the question of rhythm from the phonetic point of view" (*The Rhythm of English Prose* [Oxford, 1939], pp. 1, 4, 135). Such investigation doubtless does discover physical facts, but just as phoneticians distinguish between the gross acoustic quality of words and that part of the acoustic quality which has semantic value, so literary students may distinguish between the gross discoverable physical facts about "rhythm" and that part of the facts which relates to expression. Professor Sapir has distinguished between the phonetic and the esthetic analysis of rhythm ("The Musical Foundations of Verse," *Journal of English and Germanic Philology,* XX [1921], 223–4).

[23] Under this head, rather than under what follows, should be considered meter in prose, in Dickens, for example. Here there is a linguistic expressiveness, just as in poetry, but not a coalescence, as in poetry, with the rest of the meaning of the words. Cf. *post* pp. 370 ff., what I call "bad style." For some flagrant examples of meter in prose, see H. W. and F. G. Fowler, *The King's English* (Oxford, 1906), p. 295.

which is proper to nonverbal sounds — some kind of musical meaning. This is perhaps conceivable, that words should do two separate things, convey their language meaning, and at the same time be a nonlinguistic tune — perhaps even harmonious with the language meaning. This, however, seems improbable in view of the limited musical value of spoken word sounds. It is, like the pictorial value of print in typographical poems, very slight.[24] Music is not written in words, but in tones and time.

The notion of a separate music is further crippled if we consider that it is impossible for any system of sound in prose to be unconnected with its meaning — that is, neither contribute to it nor detract from it. Suppose a man to be writing a double composition, both prose and music; then in the use of any given piece of language he must, consciously or unconsciously, choose for the meaning or for the music. (It is impossible that two such disconnected effects should often coincide.) Or, to change the sense of "must," he must choose for the meaning and sacrifice the music, for the meaning of words is their nature, while the music of words is negligible. "In the vast majority of those words which can be said to have an independent musical value," says Mr. Middleton Murry, "the musical suggestion is at odds with the meaning. When the musical suggestion is allowed to predominate, decadence of style has begun." [25]

Let me close this part of the discussion by indicating my own notion of what ought to be called prose rhythm — if something must be called that. The notion has been well expressed by H. W. Fowler: "A sentence or a passage is rhythmical if, when said aloud, it falls naturally into groups of words each well fitted by its length & intonation for its place in the whole & its relation to its neighbors. Rhythm is not a matter of counting syllables & measuring the distance between accents." [26] Prose rhythm is a matter of emphasis; it is putting the important words where they sound important. It is a matter of coherence; it is putting the right idea in the right place.[27]

"Rhythm" as applied to prose is a metaphor. "Rhythm," when used literally, means "measure" or "regularity," and since the movement of good prose

[24] Cf. D. W. Prall, *Aesthetic Judgment* (New York, 1929), pp. 289, 295; *Aesthetic Analysis* (New York, 1936), pp. 105–6.

[25] J. Middleton Murry, *The Problem of Style* (Oxford, 1922), p. 86. And it seems to me that this is also true of criticism: when the musical suggestion predominates, decadence has begun. The authors of books on prose rhythm are aware of their danger but they cannot save themselves. See, for example, William M. Patterson, *The Rhythm of Prose* (New York, 1916), p. 84; John Hubert Scott, *op. cit.*, pp. 24, 36–7, 127, 133.

[26] *A Dictionary of Modern English Usage* (Oxford, 1927), "Rhythm," p. 504.

[27] Mr. Ezra Pound says: "The attainment of a style consists in so knowing words that one will communicate the various parts of what one says with the various degrees and weights of importance which one wishes" (*Guide to Kulchur,* quoted in *Times Literary Supplement,* XXXVII [1938], p. 489).

For a detailed study of inversion of subject and predicate and position of adverbs in English according to sense, see August Western, *On Sentence-Rhythm and Word-Order in Modern English* (Christiania, 1908), esp. p. 9. P. Fijn van Draat, "The Place of the Adverb, A Study in Rhythm," *Neophilologus,* VI (1921), 56–88, esp. 62, 87, admits Western's general principle but would connect certain variations not with sense but with "rhythmic formulas."

is precisely *not* regular but varied with the sense, the union of the terms "prose" and "rhythm" has been none the happiest.

III

A first step toward a theory of style might be the reflection that one may say different things about the same topic — or different things which are very much alike.[28] A rose and a poppy are different, but both are flowers. Sidney writes, "Come, sleep! O sleep, the certain knot of peace, etc." Shakespeare writes, "O sleep, O gentle sleep, Nature's soft nurse, etc.," and again, "Sleep that knits up the ravell'd sleave of care, etc." It is not that these writers have had the same meaning and have "dressed" it, or expressed it, differently. Rather they have had the same subject, the benefits of sleep, or beneficent sleep, but have had different thoughts, different meanings, which have found expression in different language. They have expressed different, if similar, meanings. Even Betterton, when he recasts one of Shakespeare's passages on sleep, has not merely reëxpressed the same meaning; he has actually changed the meaning. Different words make different meanings.

It is true that meaning is not identical with words.[29] Meaning is the psychic entity, the something in the mind — for which material is not adequate. In the language of the scholastics: *Voces referuntur ad res significandas mediante conceptione intellectus.*[30] Nevertheless, words do determine meanings relentlessly. To come at it another way, meanings vary persistently with variations of words.[31] It may be well to recall one of Newman's figures, "the convex and the concave of a curve." The convex is not the concave, but if we conceive the curve as a line, then every change in the concave produces a corresponding change in the convex. There is that much truth in the contention of Croce: "Language is a perpetual creation. What has been linguistically expressed is not repeated. . . . Language is not an arsenal of arms already made, and it

28 Cf. A. C. Bradley, *Poetry for Poetry's Sake* (Oxford, 1901), pp. 12–13.

29 Cf. Alfred North Whitehead, *Modes of Thought* (New York, 1938), pp. 48–9; Alan H. Gardiner, *The Theory of Speech and Language* (Oxford, 1932), p. 70; Edward Sapir, *Language* (New York, 1921), pp. 14, 238; I. A. Richards, *The Philosophy of Rhetoric* (New York, 1936), p. 13; Louis H. Gray, *Foundations of Language* (New York, 1939), pp. 88, 93–4.

30 St. Thomas Aquinas, *Summa Theologica,* I, q. 13, a. 1, quoted by Désiré Cardinal Mercier, *A Manual of Modern Scholastic Philosophy* (London, 1919), II, 154.

Cf. Alan H. Gardiner, *op. cit.,* pp. 44 ff., 70 ff., 102–3.

31 The term "meaning" as I am using it may be taken to include all that Ogden and Richards have divided into different kinds of language meaning — the really referential, symbolic, intellectual meaning, and the group of emotive meanings (C. K. Ogden and I. A. Richards, *The Meaning of Meaning* [New York, 1936], pp. 11–12, 126, 186–7, 224–30). Obviously if such is the meaning to which we refer, if we are thinking of works of literature, not treatises of mathematics or philosophy, it is much easier to see how meaning depends on the very words in which it is cast. I choose not to emphasize this, however, because, as will be seen shortly, some of the effects of style in which I am interested are very slightly if at all dependent on emotive meaning.

is not a *vocabulary,* a collection of abstractions, or a cemetery of corpses more or less well embalmed." [32]

We may be tempted to believe that we have at length distilled words or style away from meaning when we think of *bad* style. It might be plausible and would probably be useful to formulate some rule like this: Style occurs in isolation only when it is bad, when it fails to coincide with meaning.[33] This might be almost the truth where writing is so bad that it is meaningless — for example, in errors of expression made by one unfamiliar with a language, matters of syntax and elementary vocabulary. But poor expression in the wider sense cannot be reduced to this. The nature of words is against it — their constant tendency to mean. It is not as if we could forget or fail to put meaning in words. They persist in meaning, no matter what we intend or are conscious of. We may fail to say what we intend, but we can scarcely fail to say something.

Bad style is not a deviation of words from meaning, but a deviation of meaning from meaning. Of what meaning from what meaning? Of the actually conveyed meaning (what a reader receives) from the meaning an author intended or ought to have intended. This is true even of those cases where we might be most tempted to say that the fault of style is mere "awkwardness," since the meaning is conveyed completely. In such cases, the awkwardness consists in some absence of meaning (usually but implicit) or in some contrary or irrelevant meaning, which we disregard, inferring the writer's real meaning, at least so far as it would be explicit. We must do this so continually for most writing — seek out the meaning, put the most relevant construction on every word and phrase, disregard what tries to say the wrong thing — that we fail to sense any lack of meaning and dub the cause of our annoyance metaphorically and conveniently "awkwardness."

The question what the author ought to have said is the true difficulty in judging style. *Ut jam nunc dicat,* says Horace, *jam nunc debentia dici.* It is the only difficulty, for it is the only question, and it is one we implicitly answer every time we judge style. We do it by our sense, more or less definite, of what the author intends to say as a whole, of his central and presiding purpose. The only consideration that can determine an author in a given detail is the adequacy of the detail to his whole purpose.[34] It does not follow that when we are sure this or that phrase or passage is bad style we shall always

[32] *Op. cit.,* pp. 150–1; cf. p. 68, on translation. Cf. Leone Vivante, *Intelligence in Expression* (London, 1925), pp. 2–3.

[33] Frederick Schlegel has said: "Although, in strict application and rigid expression, thought and speech always are, and always must be regarded as two things metaphysically distinct, — yet there only can we find these two elements in disunion, where one or both have been employed imperfectly or amiss" (*Lectures on the History of Literature* [New York, 1841], pp. 7–8).

[34] H. B. Lathrop, in arguing that emphasis is an aspect of coherence, and coherence an aspect of unity, has shown admirably how the school-book terms may be squared with this philosophy of style ("Unity, Coherence, and Emphasis," *University of Wisconsin Studies in Language and Literature,* No. 2, *Studies by Members of the Department of English* [Madison, 1918], pp. 77–98).

refer our judgment precisely to our impression of the whole.[35] The steps in subordination are too complicated. Furthermore, a fault in one whole can have something in common with a fault in another whole; whence arises the classification of faults of style and a tendency to refer individual faults only to the class definition.[36] The whole is usually forgotten.

From the foregoing one may begin to infer that a detailed study of style can be fruitful — even in the hands of those who least connect style with meaning. If faults can be classed, so to some extent can merits. That which has for centuries been called style differs from the rest of writing only in that it is one plane or level of the organization of meaning; it would not be happy to call it the outer cover or the last layer; rather it is the furthest elaboration of the one concept that is the center. As such it can be considered. The terms of rhetoric, spurned by Croce and other moderns, did have a value for the ancients, even though they failed to connect all of rhetoric with meaning. To give the terms of rhetoric a value in modern criticism it would be necessary only to determine the expressiveness of the things in language to which the terms refer. This has been done for metaphor, which used to be an ornament, but has now been made "the unique expression of a writer's individual vision" or "the result of the search for a precise epithet." [37] Mr. Empson has spoken ingeniously of that highly "artificial" figure the zeugma.[38] Mr. Bateson has praised a hypallage.[39]

The greatest obstacle to recognizing the expressive value of rhetorical devices is the fact that they recur. One notices that Cicero uses a *litotes* or a *praeteritio* several times in a few pages, or so many hundreds of balances are counted in the *Ramblers* of Johnson. This suggests play with words, disregard of meaning. One is likely to reflect: if these devices express something, then the author must be expressing, or saying, much the same thing over and over — which is useless; therefore the author is really not trying to say anything; he is using words viciously, for an inexpressive purpose.

Such an attitude would not have been possible if the theoretical rhetoricians had not thrust forward the repertory of devices so as to throw them out of focus and conceal their nature as part of language. No one thinks, for example, that sentences because they recur are artificial, that they say the same thing over or say nothing. This is the key to what our attitude toward devices ought to be. Sentences are expressive; so also are declensions, and conjuga-

[35] For small faults of inconsistency and irrelevancy in a composition largely good, one would have to examine only a short section of the surrounding text. At the other extreme might be a composition by a schoolboy, where one could guess the central meaning only from the title or from what the schoolboy said when asked, or where there might not be any at all.

[36] An operation essential to the economy of thinking, but one which can lead to error when the reason for considering the class as faulty is forgotten, and faults of one type of whole are referred to another — for example, when what would be a fault in a poem of heroic couplets is adduced against the verse of *Christabel.*

[37] J. Middleton Murry, *The Problem of Style* (Oxford, 1922), pp. 13, 83.

[38] William Empson, *Seven Types of Ambiguity* (New York, 1931), pp. 89–90.

[39] F. W. Bateson, *English Poetry and the English Language* (Oxford, 1934), p. 22.

tions; they are expressive forms.[40] They express, not ideas like "grass" or "green," but relations. The so-called "devices," really no more devices than a sentence is a device, express more special forms of meaning, not so common to thinking that they cannot be avoided, like the sentence, but common enough to reappear frequently in certain types of thinking and hence to characterize the thinking, or the style. They express a kind of meaning [41] which may be discussed as legitimately as the more obvious kinds such as what a man writes about — the vanity of human wishes or the River Duddon.

It might be better if the term "device" were never used, for its use leads almost immediately to the carelessness of thinking of words as separable practicably from meaning. That is, we think of a given meaning as if it may be weakly expressed in one way but more forcefully in another. The latter is the device — the language applied, like a jack or clamp, or any dead thing, to the meaning, which itself remains static and unchanged, whether or not the device succeeds in expressing it. There is some convenience in this way of thinking, but more philosophy in steadily realizing that each change of words changes the meaning actually expressed. It is better to think of the "weak" expression and the "strong" expression as two quite different expressions, or, elliptically, two different meanings, of which one is farther from, one nearer to, what the author ought to say, or what he intends to say. The whole matter of emphasis, which is the real truth behind Herbert Spencer's wooden theory of economy in words, seems to be best considered in this light. (To keep the mind from being fatigued while receiving ideas — this is Spencer's function for style.[42] One may object that the most important thing about the mind is not that it can be fatigued — but that it can entertain splendid, though often difficult and fatiguing, conceptions.) If a word is to be placed here or there in a sentence in order to be effective, to have due weight, this ought to be thought of not as a juggling of words round a meaning to give the meaning emphatic expression, but as a choice of a more emphatic rather than a less emphatic meaning, or, strictly, the choice of the meaning needed, for meaning exists through emphasis; a change of emphasis is a change of meaning. We must preserve a notion of words, even in their most purely suggestive functions, as something transparently intellectual, not intervening between us and the meaning but luminous and full of their meaning and as if conscious of it.

[40] Cf. Alan H. Gardiner, *The Theory of Speech and Language* (Oxford, 1932), pp. 130–4, 158–61.

[41] The better modern treatments of rhetoric have recognized this. See, for example, Alexander Bain, *English Composition and Rhetoric* (New York, 1886), esp. pp. 20–64, though it is hard to think the doctrine of expressiveness is an abiding principle when he says that one of the functions of metaphor is to "give an agreeable surprise" (pp. 30–1). For a treatment of figures as common elements of speech, see James B. Greenough and George L. Kittredge, *Words and Their Ways in English Speech* (New York, 1901), pp. 14–17.

[42] "The Philosophy of Style," in Lane Cooper's *Theories of Style* (New York, 1907), pp. 273–4. What if a passage were read twice or pondered at length? Would it not lose most of its force — through being relieved of the duty of preventing our misconceptions? Spencer's essay appeared first in the *Westminster Review* of 1852.

The expressiveness of the rhetorical device is not always so easily analyzed as that of the sentence or declension — frequently it is a form of implicit expressiveness, one which is certainly present but not simply in virtue of meanings of words or of syntax or of morphology. For example, one of the most frequent forms of implicit expressiveness, or meaning, is that of equality or likeness — with its opposite, inequality or unlikeness. Any succession of words, phrases, or sentences must in any given degree be either like or unlike, and appropriately or inappropriately so in accordance with whether the successive explicit meanings are like or unlike. The "jingles" collected by H. W. and F. G. Fowler [43] are admirable illustrations of the fault which consists in a likeness of word sounds and hence of implicit meaning where there is no corresponding explicit meaning to be sustained. "To read his tales is a baptism of optimism," they quote from the *Times*. Here there is a nasty jingle of "ptism," "ptimism" — nasty just because the two combinations so nearly alike strive to make these words parallel, whereas they are not; one qualifies the other. The case is even plainer if we take an example of the common "ly" jingle, "He lived practically exclusively on milk," and set beside it something like this: "We are swallowed up, irreparably, irrevocably, irrecoverably, irremediably." [44] In the second we are not conscious of the repeated "ly" as a jingle, any more than of the repeated "irre." The reason is that behind each of these parallel sounds (implicit parallel meanings) there is a parallel explicit meaning. So far as we advert to the sounds as sounds at all it is with a sense of their concordance with the structure of meaning. Such is perhaps the most frequently underlying reason why expressions are approved of or objected to as "euphonious" or "cacophonous," "harmonious" or "inharmonious."

And matters of sound are not the only ones to which the principle of equality and inequality applies. Even so basically wrong a thing as parataxis, the monotony of a schoolboy's writing, consists just in that he is using the same form of meaning in successive clauses and hence fails to relate his meanings, that is, fails to express the really different meanings which lurk dimly in his mind as his real intention or are at least what he should intend. Hypotaxis, the rare-sounding opposite of parataxis, but no other than all modulated writing, consists in the use of different forms of meaning to sustain the sequence of the complex whole meaning. The author whose style is the subject of this study offers on every page emphatic demonstrations of implicit meaning through equality; and it will be one of the purposes of the study to show that what is sometimes called cumbrousness or pompousness in Johnson is but the exaggeration into more rigid lines of an expressive principle that lies in the very warp of all verbal discourse.

[43] *The King's English* (Oxford, 1906), p. 291. Cf. H. W. Fowler, *A Dictionary of Modern English Usage* (Oxford, 1927), "Jingles," pp. 308–9.

[44] The first is from E. F. Benson, quoted in *The King's English*, p. 292; the second, from John Donne, Sermon LXVI, in *Donne's Sermons,* ed. Logan Pearsall Smith (Oxford, 1919), p. 10.

Alphonse G. Juilland

REVIEW OF *L'ÉPOQUE RÉALISTE; PREMIÈRE PARTIE: FIN DU ROMANTISME ET PARNASSE*, BY CHARLES BRUNEAU

* * *

I. Stylistics and Linguistics

1.1. Importance of the work. This work is of double importance: first of all as a contribution to the history of literary French in the 19th century, then — and here perhaps is its principal interest — as an exposition of the stylistic doctrine upon which it is based. As one of the reviewers of the preceding volumes already felt, "under the title of *History of the Language* volume XII, he [Bruneau] may well have given us an illustration of a new 'stylistic' method applied to the study of the literary movement" (Gérald Antoine, "En marge d'un livre récent: Stylistique et histoire de la langue à l'époque romantique," *Revue d'histoire littéraire de la France* 53.175–87 [1953]). That which in volume 12 was only vaguely glimpsed has since become a certainty: in the meanwhile Bruneau has become aware of a doctrine which formerly was only latent, and, in a study-manifesto which has aroused many commentaries and to which I will refer in the following paragraph ("La stylistique," *Romance Philology* 5.1–14 [1941]), he has formulated it explicitly by taking a stand against other stylistic doctrines and principally against the "literary stylistics" (or "neostylistics" or "stylistic criticism") as represented by Leo Spitzer, Damáso Alonso and Helmut Hatzfeld.

It is not my intention to discuss here the stylistic theory outlined by Bruneau in the above-mentioned study, because I prefer at this time to judge it accord-

Translated and reprinted from *Language* 30 (1954) by permission of the editor. Asterisks indicate omitted passages.

ing to the results obtained in practice such as they are recorded in the book which concerns us. But since in the first place it is in the name of scientific rigor that Bruneau rejects "impressionistic stylistics," which in his opinion does not offer the guarantees of certainty of the exact sciences,[1] and since among these, stylistics is called a part of the science of language,[2] there is some interest in comparing, in terms set by himself, stylistics with linguistics, the science of the features of the literary language with the science of the features of language. All the more since, in recent times, more and more numerous voices have been raised to demand the application of the techniques of linguistic investigation to literary material, to aspects of style.[3]

1.2. Pure stylistics. Stylistics, properly speaking, is, according to Bruneau, pure stylistics, which, he says, belongs to the category of social sciences. And

1 Efforts to conceive of the study of literature as a more or less exact science go quite far back into the past. A substantial bibliography of such attempts will be found in Wellek and Warren, *Theory of Literature* (New York, 1949); and also in Hatzfeld, *A Critical Bibliography of the New Stylistics, Applied to the Romance Literatures,* 1900–1952 (Chapel Hill, 1953). A recent effort: Guy Michaud, *Introduction à une science de la littérature* (Istanbul, 1950).

2 "Taking the strictly linguistic point of view, I shall try to define exactly the field of stylistic studies." ("La stylistique," 1).

3 The application of linguistic methods to the analysis of literary material has been attempted more than once by scholars working in the spirit of traditional linguistics. In Europe, Saussurian doctrine has directly engendered Genevan stylistics, whose founder and principal exponent was Charles Bally; finally, see Robert Godel, "La stylistique est-elle une science linguistique?" *Cahiers Ferdinand de Saussure* 11.4–5 (1953). Hjelmslevian glossematics has furnished the basic principles for several outlines of structural theories of literature: for example, A. Stender-Petersen, "Esquisse d'une théorie structurale de la littérature," *TCLC* 5.277–387 (1949); Svend Johansen, "La notion de signe dans la glossématique et dans l'esthétique," *ibid.*, 288–302; Johansen, *Le symbolisme, étude sur le style des symbolistes français* (Copenhagen, 1945); Knud Togeby, *L'oeuvre de Maupassant* (Copenhagen and Paris, 1954).

The structural school whose teachings have proved to be the most fruitful in this area has been, however, the Prague school. Combined with Russian literary formalism, Prague functionalism has given birth to Czech literary structuralism, headed by Roman Jakobson and Jan Mukařovský, which has had a decisive influence on the Polish literary school, called "integralist," founded by Manfred Kridl and Franciszek Siedlecki; for the basic principles of these schools, see William E. Harkins, "Slavic formalist theories in literary scholarship," *Word,* 7.177–85 (1951).

In the United States, linguistics has inspired several attempts at reappraisal of literary material in the behaviorist spirit. Note: M. Joos, "Verbal parallels and recurrent images," in the book by M. L. Hanley, *Word Index to Joyce's Ulysses* (Madison, Wisconsin, 1937 [1944]); A. A. Hill, "Toward a literary analysis," in *English Studies in Honor of James Southall Wilson,* ed. by Fredson Bowers (Charlottesville, 1951); H. Whitehall, "From linguistics to criticism," *Monograph Series on Languages and Linguistics* [Georgetown University] 4.87–93 (1953); W. F. Twadell, "The Kerker lexicon and the Gretchen episode," *Monatshefte,* 45.354–70 (1953); Eugene Dorfman, *The Roland and the Cid: A Comparative Structural Analysis* (Columbia diss. 1950, Microfilm publication No. 1843).

For supplementary bibliographical information, see A. Juilland, *Bibliographie de la linguistique fonctionnelle et structurale* (complementary thesis, Sorbonne, 1951, MS). For a critique of structural methods in literary analysis, see D. Alonso, *Poesia española: Ensayo de métodos y límites estilísticos* (Madrid, 1950), which rejects the functionalism of Troubetskoy as well as other modern linguistic doctrines.

following Matoré, the author "sets it in a framework between sociology, social psychology, and psycho-physiology on the one hand, and on the other hand static linguistics and lexicology (historical, descriptive)." The linguist who knows to what extent the efforts to make of linguistics an autonomous science — "immanent" or "pure" — and to grasp the linguistic act in its proper structure are necessarily combined with efforts to rid this discipline of logical, psychological, sociological, biological and physiological commitments will be left slightly bemused by the assurance with which Bruneau places pure stylistics precisely at an intersection with disciplines which are neighboring or are postulated to be such. If a pure stylistics is possible — and this still remains to be proven — it is not, in any case, in the direction of these heterogeneous disciplines that it will find its points of support and reference. The lesson which linguistics offers us, which guide Bruneau, is on this point strict: it is rather in a reaction, an anti-psychological, anti-sociological, anti-physiological reaction that stylistics may find some day its immanence and its purity.

1.3. Stylistics as an autonomous science. Once the auxiliary disciplines have been ruled out — and in fact Bruneau does rule them out — is it possible that linguistics may offer to stylistics solid foundations for establishing an autonomous science of literature? Bruneau seems to be convinced of this, and he is far from being the only one. For him as well as for other stylisticians, not necessarily linguists, only the science of language appears to be capable of providing stylistics with the rigorous techniques of investigation which in these matters can allow us "to (know) and, up to a certain point, to (foresee)" (ibid. 7). Under these conditions, for stylistics to be able to avoid duplicating the efforts of linguistics and to enjoy an independent status, it must have above all else a proper domain and a specific object: namely, literary-language features (or stylistic features), opposed to the language features *tout court,* which form the proper object of linguistics. But as it happens that the language feature and the style feature coincide materially, it is indeed by different techniques of investigation that we expect the differentiation of the same natural object into two or several objects of science. Now on this terrain stylistics cannot borrow anything essential from linguistics under the threat of finding itself completely assimilated by linguistics: the two objects of science being 'naturally' identical, the role of method becomes decisive, for it is method which in the last analysis ratifies the natural object to confer upon it the dignity of an object of science. By operating with linguistic methods on any object at all, we can do only linguistics: if any object postulated as unknown "responds" and "lends itself" to linguistic methods, it is because the object in question is a language, and that fact renders useless an independent science like pure stylistics. If the feature in question, one that is specifically literary in character, is something else than a linguistic feature, it will escape by this very fact the methods of linguistic investigation: for linguistic methods, the features of the literary language are no more than linguistic features pure and simple. And if the literary feature is a certain kind of language feature, i.e., a language feature having a certain differential character, this character will necessarily escape linguistic methods: the linguistic perspective will reduce to two dimensions an object which is supposed to have at least three.

1.4. Linguistic methods and stylistic analysis. It is easy to furnish proof: those who wish to use strictly linguistic methods in literary investigations forget too often that by submitting the work (or a "text") of Hugo for example, to a rigorous linguistic analysis, the result will be a grammar: very nearly, the grammar of the French language such as it was used in literary milieux during the period in question. Obviously one could hope that this grammar will be a *certain* grammar, the grammar of Hugo specifically, and that it will be opposed to certain other grammars, the grammar of Gautier for example: the oppositions between these "grammars" will take account of certain differences which taken together will be designated as "style." Linguistic methods having thus isolated certain facts, which would be designated as literary, the style of a writer (or his "language") would have to be defined as the totality of the differential characteristics which oppose and distinguish the style of a certain writer from the style of another. This definition would be oppositional and relative, therefore variable: in this conception the definition of the "style" or the "language" of an author (or of a "school," or of a "period") will vary in relation to the language of the opposed author (etc.). For example, the definition of the "language" of Hugo will not be one, invariable thing as it is generally conceived to be by the diverse systems of stylistics: such and such a characteristic of Hugo's prose which is pertinent when it is being opposed to Gautier's would become non-pertinent in relation to Michelet and, vice versa, such and such a characteristic irrelevant in relation to Gautier would become distinctive for the "style" of Hugo compared with that of Michelet.

This conception of "style" would have as a consequence a total reversal of perspective in the analysis of literary material: in place of comparative literature such as it is practiced in our day an "opposed" literature would be substituted. To current kinds of literary investigations — essentially based on the research of "sources," themes, motifs, etc., and aiming above all at the establishment of "relationships" (thus identities), in which the differential elements are envisioned as an amorphous and indifferent mass setting off the common characteristics which are thereby invested with definitional value, there would be opposed a method in which the common elements — of substance (themes, motifs) or of form (procedures, types, figures, expressions) — would shade off, yielding to differential elements which, coming into the foreground, would assume the identificatory function.

Thus, one would reverse the terms of the equations established by comparative literature, in which it is the common elements that are the marked terms as opposed to differential traits conceived as neutral and non-marked: as in functional linguistics, the differential elements would become the marked terms which serve to define.

Theoretically it would be a matter of taking the same road in the opposite direction: instead of departing from the particular in search of the reductive principle which can lead to the general, instead of descending from the multiple ramifications towards the single root, we would proceed from common elements as if from a neutral base in order to go up, step by step, from difference to difference, straight up to the extreme and individual ramifications of the literary typological tree.

1.5. Disadvantages of linguistic methods in stylistics. As attractive as it may appear in theory, this procedure is afflicted in practice with certain limitations that we might bring to light. Indeed, from the differential point of view, phonology and morphology naturally would give nothing; for it would be necessary to oppose languages of writers who are very far apart in time in order to avoid the near-identity of the analyses, which would moreover be stylistically inconclusive. As for differences in syntax and vocabulary ("stylistic figures" should also be introduced) whose decisive verdict is being awaited, these would be considerably reduced, at least in the inventory: for almost each lexical element, syntactic term or stylistic figure characteristic of the "language" of Hugo will be found at least once in Gautier, and vice versa. So that even on these terrains which are supposed to be favorable, we will be reduced to resorting to statistical data: if we are to account for differences of style such and such a construction which is rare in Gautier, would appear with an x frequency in Hugo and x^2 in Michelet. Without denying the great importance of frequencies in stylistic and literary investigations, the fact remains that it is linguistics which teaches us that material of this kind is not analytically decisive. And what is more, it is not on a basis of linguistic statistics that a pure stylistics may be constructed.

Moreover, such a procedure involves certain dangers which prudent handling will nevertheless allow us to avoid up to a certain point. Indeed, a great majority of differences will predictably be in the realm of "innovations" (of vocabulary, syntax, and "style"). Now, "felicitous" innovations, those which have a "value" to the extent to which they correspond to the "spirit" of the language (in other words, to its structural laws), are precisely the ones which have been ratified by the language, that is to say, adopted by other writers to enter the common linguistic and literary heritage. It follows that, from the very fact of their validation, the most significant material is in danger of becoming irrelevant from the definitional point of view, because, being found elsewhere, it has lost its differentiating value. So there will remain, as characteristic and analytically decisive matter, unfortunate "innovations," those which the language (I mean a writer's colleagues and history) has condemned: by such a procedure, we risk being led to judge an author in his exaggerations and abuses, therefore by what is negative in his language, or at least not characteristic.

1.6. Stylistics as a "science of deviation." This leads us directly to the definition of stylistics as a "science of deviations" (ibid. 6). Considering the stylistic feature, according to this concept, as a deviation in respect to usage, as an infringement of the linguistic norm,[4] amounts to giving a negative definition of "stylistics": in a "text," that which is not a linguistic feature pure and simple is stylistic. This indicates to us the ways in which we might eventually use methods which are, properly speaking, linguistic in the analysis of literature: by submitting a literary work to a strictly linguistic analysis, everything which, in the "text," lends itself to criteria of this kind is a pure linguistic feature, and by this very fact cannot constitute a stylistic feature. The stylistician will thus be able, with the aid of linguistic methods, to isolate his field of operations: the application of such a procedure will allow him to ignore for purely literary analysis the features identified in the course of linguistic analysis and to concentrate solely on the residual matter, which has resisted or escaped linguistic criteria. In this preliminary phase, the stylistician will be led to consider stylistic features in a transcendental way — by relating them to linguistic features — and to operate provisionally with negative judgments: the "stylistic" feature will be the non-linguistic feature, and this "metastylistics" will be conceived as a sort of counter-grammar.

Only in a second phase, which would constitute stylistics properly speaking, would the stylistician be freed from obligations to linguistics in order to attack the residual elements by his own method, suited to the specificity of the literary object. Thus he may hope to establish the basis for an immanent discipline and eventually for the kind of pure stylistics foreseen by Bruneau.

1.7. Disadvantages of this concept. Let us note, however, that even in this preliminary phase, linguistic methods must be used with caution, for they involve more than one danger and might compromise stylistic analysis proper. It is possible that the deviation, which is not linguistic material in the sense defined above, is not stylistic material either, but something else — to be defined

[4] This follows from the paradoxical character of the norm (linguistic, literary, esthetic, or other): synchronically conceived, the norm rests on an arbitrary judgment; historically defined, it rests on a circular judgment.

As far as the linguistic norm is concerned, Bernard Bloch has more than once emphasized its arbitrary nature and protested against its abuse. Indeed, the linguistic norm has no absolute value; in purely descriptive terms, the appearance of the "deviation" nullifies the "norm" by the very fact of its appearance. The only descriptive conception of the norm would be the one offered by statistical data; nevertheless, this implies an arbitrary solution: once the criteria of existence and non-existence have been abandoned in favor of criteria of frequency, it is impossible to establish, in quantitative terms, a precise boundary line between the norm and the deviation.

There remains the dynamic solution, which would consist in conceiving of the norm and the derivation in terms of process. This solution, unfortunately, does not help us much, for it rests on a circular judgment: after defining the deviation in relation to the norm (descriptively established), we can define the norm only in regard to the deviation.

later — a mistake, for example. And we will not avoid the dangers by defining the deviation, with Bruneau, after Valéry, as a certain kind of mistake, as a "deliberate mistake" (ibid. 6). Since Valéry is no longer among us, let us invite Bruneau — who seems, moreover, to be opposed to introspection (ibid. 7) — to provide us with the objective criteria capable of distinguishing in these matters the deliberate from the accidental. Let us not forget that what was deliberate — a deviation — yesterday, is involuntary — the norm — today; that even synchronically, what is deliberate, hence conscious, in one individual, is mechanical in another; finally, that in the same individual, a deviation which is deliberate in certain circumstances becomes mechanical in certain others.

There is still more: the conception of stylistics as a "science of deviations" — implying the rejection of "normal" material, which is then abandoned to linguistics — can cloud irremediably one's perspective on the set of literary features. For the same feature, identified by linguistic criteria as a linguistic feature pure and simple, may, when illuminated differently and taken in a different network of relationships, be validated on another level, specifically, on the literary level. By ignoring in literary analysis a piece of evidence which is linguistically "banal" (i.e. corresponding to the linguistic "norm"), we run the risk of omitting a constitutive element of the literary structure (to be determined).

Therefore it appears to me that the use of linguistic methods in the analysis of literature must be carried out with a great deal of prudence: moreover, their scope seems to be limited to preliminary work, to the clearing of the field, and may remain without direct repercussions on stylistic analysis.

1.8. Stylistics as an exact science. Is it possible to have a stylistics such as Bruneau and so many others demand, that is, a discipline of a type analogous to the sciences termed "exact"? At least in the present state of our knowledge and with the methods of stylistic investigation now available to us, it seems to me that we must answer, against Bruneau, in the negative. For those who wish to bring to stylistics the advantages of the surprising conquests of modern linguistics in order to make it an equally rigorous discipline forget only too often the essential difference between stylistics and linguistics, as well as all other exact sciences: namely, that the sciences called "exact" — including linguistics — operate with judgments of existence, while stylistics (or the science of literature) operates essentially with value judgments. The linguist is content to record; he must sometimes interpret; he never has to evaluate. In contrast, the stylistician, having to deal with an object indissolubly linked to the problem of the "beautiful," cannot be content with recording and classifying: he must also take account of the value of the recorded material; this is an aspect which completely changes the perspective. This difficulty does not seem foreign to the preoccupations of Bruneau, for whom "stylistics cannot ignore this question of value" (ibid. 7).

1.9. Stylistics as a science of values. It follows that the possibility of making stylistics a rigorous science, of a more or less "exact" type, depends entirely on the possibility of transforming judgments of (literary) value into judgments of (literary) existence. As long as we have not found an adequate method for bringing about this transformation, the demands of Bruneau are premature: any effort to resort to linguistics will be nullified and stylistics will be in no way able to claim the dignity of a true science.[5] This is not the place to discuss by what means such a transformation could offer, if not a solution, at least a few clarifications of the revolution in perspective by which the structural schools have succeeded in transforming judgments based on the famous "Sprachgefühl" into judgments of linguistic existence. Perhaps, in an analogous manner, stylistics will some day succeed in exploding the notion of "literary taste" — which in a way corresponds to "linguistic feeling" — by making explicit the totality of the latent literary judgments which engender it.[6]

1.10. Linguistics and stylistics. Contrary to the general tendency and to the views expressed by Bruneau, the result of these general considerations is that if linguistics has precious lessons to give stylistics, it is certainly not by lending its methods. What linguistics has to offer — and not only to stylistics — is a certain way of approaching the material, a certain spirit of submission to the specificity of the object, aiming above all at seizing it in its most characteristic aspect. The linguist who knows that he has not succeeded in making his science autonomous except by reacting against the servitudes imposed on it by logic, psychology, sociology, and physiology, will strongly advise the stylistician in search of a "pure" doctrine not to place its object at the intersection of these disciplines. On the contrary, he will encourage him to do his utmost to break the bonds of neighboring disciplines (at least provisionally), and, beginning from a certain point, of linguistics itself. He may re-establish

[5] There is some interest in quoting Helmut Hatzfeld's description of the avant-garde position of one of the pioneers of the "exact science" of literature which, despite its premature, even Utopian aspects, will not fail to captivate, at least in theory, the anti-mentalist researchers who draw their inspiration from the teachings of Bloomfield. Michel Dragomirescu, *La science de la littérature* (3 vols.; Paris, 1928), "has the most radical viewpoint on stylistics, which he calls literary technology. He believes that having selected and analyzed the masterworks of world literature from all angles with an aesthetic, strictly anti-historical approach, one must arrive at an aesthetic-critical synthesis which is self-evident to everybody, so that there will be 'only one opinion as to value and character of a masterwork. Then only will happen in the Science of Literature what occurs quite naturally in the Natural Sciences' (I, 169), namely there would be no history of masterworks, as there is no history of minerals." (Hatzfeld, *A Critical Bibliography of the New Stylistics,* 262.)

[6] It must be recognized that the method of Spitzer, without aiming at rigor in a consistent way, proves to be — when considered from this point of view — efficacious, having a flexibility admirably suited to the complexity of literary material. Even certain "florid" formulations, which Bruneau opposed relentlessly, often conceal valid principles; we must simply make these principles explicit, and reformulate them in objective terms in order to confer operational status on them.

such relationships later, but from a position chosen by himself. In other words, the dialogue will be resumed only later, when stylistics will be able to do so on an equal footing, and in its own terms. And it is perhaps in this temporary movement of liberation that the science of style will find itself.

On this point, then, I am very far from the position of Harold Whitehall, for whom "no criticism can go beyond linguistics" ("From Linguistics to Criticism," 713). For myself, I am tempted rather to believe that literary analysis properly speaking begins just where linguistics stops (exactly as, going in the opposite direction, linguistics begins where literary study stops). It is true that I may be mistaken. But in that case, criticism loses its entire *raison d'être,* being engulfed by linguistics. It goes without saying that linguistics can and must furnish a sure point of departure for literary studies, just as articulatory physiology, for example, serves as a basis for phonematics. Nevertheless, to wish to reduce literary study to linguistics would be equivalent to wishing to reduce phonematics to phonetics, or even to physiology or acoustics, in other words, to renouncing the most decisive conquests of modern linguistics. But it is obvious that on a certain level, the most immediate one, these two categories coincide: materially, the literary act is a language act. What is perhaps less obvious, but nonetheless true, is that the literary act is something more than a language act pure and simple: it is a language act invested with an extra dimension, the literary dimension. Since this "literary dimension" has not yet been defined, or even identified, some might doubt its reality. It will suffice to remind them that, materially, the language act too coincides with the acoustic act (or with the graphic act), and this does not prevent it from being something more than an acoustic act pure and simple: it is an acoustic act with an extra dimension, the linguistic dimension.

This way of conceiving literary material corresponds, at the beginning, to that of Hill and Whitehall, for whom "a work of literature is therefore a language act, like other language acts, but differentiated from them by characteristics of its own" ("A Report on the Language-Literature Seminar," 1).[7] But I would hesitate to follow the authors when they deduce, "As a further assumption, which in part necessarily follows from the first, we believe, that a work of literature can be behavioristically investigated as a language act."

[7] In the same spirit, see the definition of verse given by J. Lotz: "All verse is a glossic phenomenon but all glossic phenomena are not verse; thus verse may be defined by adding to linguistic phenomena, the special marks that make verse; to put it in terms of logics, a glossic phenomenon in general is the *genus proximum* to which, in order to define verse, you have to find a *differentia specifica* — "Notes on Structural Analysis in Metrics," *Helicon,* 4.125 (1940). Once again, the problem is to know whether the differentia specifica lends itself to the same methods of investigation as the genus proximum (the linguistic act properly speaking); this seems excluded, by definition.

See also the recent definition proposed by B. Bloch, "Linguistic Structure and Linguistic Analysis," *Monograph Series on Languages and Linguistics* [Georgetown University] 4.42 (1953): "the STYLE of a discourse is the message carried by the frequency distributions and the transitional probabilities of its linguistic features, especially as they differ from those of the same features in the language as a whole."

For in the proposed definition, the differentiation between the literary and the language act is made by certain "characteristics of its own" (my "extra dimension"), whose nature we do not know. All we can affirm is that they are not of a linguistic nature, for otherwise their incorporation into the definition would become tautological, contained as they would be in the "language act." Now, as long as we have not seized and defined these characteristics, nothing authorizes us to judge their nature beforehand and to affirm that it is such that they may be "behavioristically investigated." Indeed, the material identity of the linguistic act and the literary act does not allow us to bring about this analytical reduction. Once again, it is appropriate to keep in mind that the language act coincides materially with the acoustic act, and that this does not prevent linguistic methods from being essentially different from the techniques of investigation of acoustics or articulatory physiology; we must also remember that linguistics, which collaborates with these disciplines, has acquired an independent status: it has ceased to be a branch of acoustics or physiology. The same holds true for the science of literature: while taking advantage of linguistic data, it cannot, in my opinion, be conceived as a simple branch of linguistics.

What follows is an essential disagreement concerning the most urgent needs of literary studies. Indeed, I disagree just as deeply with Whitehall when he asserts that "the kind of linguistics needed by recent criticism for the solution of its pressing problems . . . is not semantics, either epistemological or communicative, but down-to-the-surface linguistics, microlinguistics and not metalinguistics" ("From Linguistics to Literary Criticism," 713). It is, of course, tempting to apply, in literature, the Russelian principle "Divide and conquer," and to submit this kind of material to the operation of dissociation into line of expression and line of content, which has given such fine results in structural linguistics. One might also effect the analysis of both chains separately, as glossematics recommends, or try to reduce as far as possible the system of content to the chain of expression, as Whitehall advocates in the spirit of Bloomfieldian linguistics. Unfortunately, in one and the other case, the identification of literary analysis with linguistic analysis becomes fatal and inevitable. It is sometimes useful to cut the Gordian knot. But in that case it is necessary to give up the rope, and in our case, it is precisely the rope that must be examined. For the literary act is a much more fragile thing than the simple linguistic act; it might not withstand this dismemberment, insofar as it is precisely in an indissoluble integration of form and content (to use traditional terminology) of expression and content (to use the more rigorous terminology of modern linguistics) that its specific nature resides. Here again, I shall oppose Whitehall in asserting that the impasse in which literary studies are trapped today is the direct consequence of the precarious state of studies of content and of the fact that they have lagged far behind studies of expression. Against Whitehall, then, I should say that the kind of linguistics most urgently needed by literary studies is semantics. The future of literary studies depends most essentially on the establishment of a healthy but flexible semantics, of a rigorous but comprehensive study of content.[8]

* * *

[8] A fairly recent resurgence of interest in semantic research allows us to hope that literary studies will soon be able to move on firmer ground as far as the content is concerned. Several general treatments have appeared in the last few years. See especially: S. Ullmann, *The Principles of Semantics* (Glasgow, 1951); S. Öhmann, *Wortinhalt und Wortbild: Vergleichende und Methodologische Studien zur Bedeutungslehre und Wortfeldtheorie* (Stockholm, 1951); R. Hallig and W. von Wartburg, *Begriffssystem als Grundlage für die Lexikografie* (Berlin, 1952); Heinz Kronasser, *Handbuch der Semasiologie: Kurze Einführung in die Geschichte, Problematik und Terminologie der Bedeutungslehre* (Heidelberg, 1952).

But my particular concern is to call attention to a few recent articles, undertaken at least in part in the structural spirit of modern linguistics: R. S. Wells, *The State and Prospects of Semantics* (mimeographed; 1950); B. V. Lindheim, "Neue Wege der Bedeutungsforschung," *Neuphilologische Zeitschrift* 3.101–15 (1951); S. Öhmann, "Theories of the Linguistic Field," *Word* 9.123–34 (1953); S. Ullmann, "Descriptive Semantics and Linguistic Typology," *Word* 9.225–40; and especially the revealing study of Charles Bazell, "La sémantique structurale," *Dialogues* 3.120–32 (1953).

Archibald A. Hill

POETRY AND STYLISTICS

All the world knows that poetry is to be enjoyed; that enjoyment is its sole reason for being. When no one enjoys a poem, it is promptly forgotten. I have no wish to disagree with such a set of self-evident truisms; I wish instead to point out that, true as such statements may be, they are not the whole truth about poetry, and that to assume that they are the whole truth not only makes us misunderstand the nature and function of poetry, but blinds us to much of the beauty of poetry and dulls us to its enjoyment.

For one thing, if all that matters about poetry is the enjoyment, and enjoyment is its only measure, we are immediately faced with a question — whose enjoyment? We live now in a splintered kind of society, in which each one of us must choose between a myriad competing groups — we can be Republicans or Democrats, Episcopalians, Baptists, Catholics, or Mormons, scientists, business men, soldiers, or technicians. It is less and less possible for any one man to embrace the experience of more than a few of these competing groups. The result is that the broad base of shared experience, the property of the whole community, which was the foundation of truly national poetry like the Homeric epics, is no longer characteristic of our society. Poetry speaks, not to the whole community, but to this or that splinter of it at a time. We have western poets and eastern poets, English poets and American poets, intellectual poets and anti-intellectual poets. We even have groups who are anti-poetic, and believe that all poetry, all enjoyment of poetry, and all poets belong to a splinter group. We have no poets and no poetry who speak clearly, and without necessary interpretation, to all the speakers of English, as Homer spoke to all the Hellenes.

If poetry is thus no longer an art with the wide and unquestioned appeal it had in the days of minstrels and troubadours, the critic and teacher of it finds himself in an uncomfortable position. He can no longer simply say that this poem is great because every one — every speaker of English — en-

 This article was presented as part of the Peters Rushton Seminars in Contemporary Prose and Poetry, the University of Virginia, 21 September 1956. Reprinted by permission of the author.

joys it deeply. And he can not even measure a poem by the permanence of its appeal. The differentiation which has splintered our contemporary society has cut it off from the past as well. We can not now assume that an American teen-ager is automatically equipped to appreciate the poetry of Wyatt and Surrey. To read the poetry of Wyatt and Surrey it is as necessary to study it as it is to study any poetry from a community different from our own — it is always necessary to know the code before we can get the message. Those of us who have faced the task of teaching poetry to students in contemporary America, sooner or later begin to ask ourselves embarrassing questions about who enjoys the various kinds of poetry we teach. Eliot appeals to sophisticates, Kilmer to Babbitts. Perhaps there is an easy answer for those who know which group is the more valuable to our society — and which group should therefore be the arbiter of taste. Yet many teachers will admit that we can not judge between groups in any high-handed and authoritative fashion, and that we can not even take the judgments handed down to us from a time when our society was less complex, and the poetically excellent was simply definable as what an English gentleman would like.

It would seem that if we who study poetry are to be able to talk about it to others than the members of our various tiny groups, we should find some other approach than pure enjoyment. We should find, or create, an approach which takes as its aim a secure and demonstrable increase of understanding. There are those who say that such an approach is impossible without sacrifice of the enjoyment which all agree is the basis of poetry, as it is of all art. To say so, is to give a council of despair. A more hopeful belief is that understanding is a good in itself, and that understanding need not be in conflict with other things which are good. Possibly, even, as understanding increases, it may bring more of enjoyment with it. It is not an unreasonable position to say that all things in the world of man and nature can be studied by the human intelligence. True, we shall never reach complete understanding of anything in the world of nature and of man. If we should say that it is therefore useless to strive for knowledge, we would then abdicate our heritage. Or should we say that poetry belongs in a world which transcends intelligence, and so is something which we can not know, we are confusing the world of man — since poets are men — with the world beyond the world of men, which indeed we can not know.

In this talk I shall try to give something of an approach to poetry which is based on understanding, and which studies the poem itself, and does not study who enjoys it or how much. Do not, I ask, assume that I deprecate enjoyment. I even hope that an indirect approach may increase enjoyment. Also, all that I shall say tonight is tentative, and necessarily delivered with the reservation that when more is known, what we can say now may seem naive, or positively wrong.

The approach with which I am concerned here is to the meaning of poetry. I shall omit any analysis of its externals — repaying as study of rhyme and metre may be. But poetry always says something, indeed it says something more than what is said in ordinary language. An approach to poetry which does not somehow reach the central core of meaning is about as useful as one of Carlyle's wrappages and hulls.

We shall get to specific poems in due time, but unfortunately it is necessary to lay a groundwork in relatively abstract theory first. I shall talk first of all about the nature of language and of meaning, then about the nature of the special kind of language which is poetry, and I hope that by doing so I will be able to describe the central paradox of poetry. Poetry is language, but is somehow something more than language, and different from it.

Ordinary talk — the sum total of ordinary talk — is a sort of island, separated from dry land on each side. On one side is a dry land of sounds, which the physicist, the acoustician, and the phonetician study and map for us. On the other side is a dry land of objects, actions, emotion — all the things we talk about. Nobody can map it for us very well as yet, though anthropologists, sociologists, and psychologists are trying. In the middle is the island of language, the area that linguists have been working to map for centuries. Somehow the ordinary user of language moves easily, and without thinking about it, from dry land to island and dry land again, and when he does so, he has completed an act of communication. We all make the journey every day. But in spite of centuries of study, the linguist only now begins to have some inkling of how it is that the journey is made.

Let us change our figure of the island for one more appropriate to the student who is trying to understand the acts of communication, and the system back of them. To use a formulation from the work of the linguist Trager, there are three levels within the system of communication. The lowest level is the world of sounds, the noises we make with our faces. This is the prelinguistic level. The middle level — our island — is the microlinguistic. This is the world of language as a system and pattern, the world of sentences, clauses, phrases, words, and word-elements. This is the world of the analytical student of language, whether he calls himself grammarian, philologist, or linguist. The upper, and final level, is the metalinguistic. This is the world of the things we talk about, and when we find a correspondence between entities and structures in the microlinguistic world, and entities and structures in the metalinguistic world, this correspondence is the meaning of the microlinguistic items and structures. The metalinguistic world is, then, the world of meaning.

Stated with this figure, the ordinary language user makes his microlinguistic world, in which he knows his way perfectly, a map by which he can guess the structure of the metalinguistic world of things. When the map enables him to move through the metalinguistic world, and come to the desired result, he uses his microlinguistics successfully; when he comes out somewhere else, there is something wrong either with the language or the way it was used. To use a very simple example, when we hear a sentence like "lions, tigers, and house-cats are all felines," the language structure groups for us three nouns as members of a larger class. We expect to be able to identify the nouns, and we expect that when we examine them, they will indeed prove to have certain similarities which justify classing them together. Our microlinguistic structure checks out in the metalinguistic area. But if we hear "centaurs, unicorns, and horses are all equines," we will hunt in vain through the metalinguistic area for confirmation, and as the semanticists are fond of telling us, the sentence is meaningless. At the moment I need emphasize only one point — we arrive at meaning, from this point of view defined as knowledge of the metalinguistic world, by guessing at it from the microlinguistic. The process is one which can be called extrapolation.

We have defined one kind of meaning as correspondence between something microlinguistic, and something metalinguistic. This correspondence meaning is, however, only one kind of meaning, and only one way of defining it. Quite a different way of defining meaning is to say that anything whose occurrence is partially predictable is meaningful, so that meaning can be defined as partial predictability. Let me use a somewhat ludicrous example. Suppose that every time I begin to speak, I pull my ear, and that every time I stop speaking I pull my nose. It would not take long for anyone watching me to be able to predict every ear-pull and every nose-pull. Ear pulls and nose pulls would be totally predictable, so much so that you would know when I was pulling my ear and when I was pulling my nose whether you were watching me or not. Ear pulls and nose pulls could be disregarded. To use the jargon of the communication theorists, they would be redundant, that is, meaningless.

Suppose, on the other hand, I use a form which you have never heard before. The form is *thaltep*. You could not have predicted that this was the form I would use, nor can you now predict how I will use it again. The form is again meaningless, this time not because it is totally predictable, but because it is totally unpredictable. If finally, I use forms which we would agree are meaningful, such as *table, house, dog,* a good many predictions can be made about how they will occur. We can quickly say that "put it on the — " is a sequence after which *table* is likely, *dog* and *house* less likely, so that we can predict which will occur with probability, though not complete accuracy. The forms are partially predictable in the sequence I have chosen, and so meaningful in it.

Now if you have accepted the identification of meaning with partial predictability, we can find more kinds of meaning than correspondence-meaning by using the concept. Items are meaningful in these terms, at all levels of the communication diagram I have drawn up. A sound — something which belongs to the prelinguistic world — can be partially predictable. An English sentence is far more likely to begin with the sound of *th,* for instance, than with the sound of *z,* and an English sentence will never begin with *ng*. These sounds then are partially predictable; they are sounds which make some difference to the English language. And note how we operate with them — we use them in the next higher level. When we hear such a sound as *ng,* we guess that something is ending in the microlinguistic structure — not that something is beginning.

Next, items are predictable on the linguistic level. For instance, suppose we see horses in a field. It is quite likely that we shall employ a sentence or sentences containing the linguistic item *horse,* and we will be able to say a good deal about what linguistic situations will accompany it. It may have a definite article, or a plural ending, but it is less likely to have the ending *-ing.* We observe all these occurrences of *horse,* and assume that there is an understandable relation between the creatures we see, and the occurrences of the word. Now suppose I use the sentence I quoted earlier. "Centaurs, unicorns, and horses are all equines." We assume, because we understand the relation of what we see to the word *horse,* that if we saw more of the metalinguistic world, we would find items in it which have the same relation to the words *centaur* and *unicorn.* We extrapolate, in short, from the items which belong on the microlinguistic level, to the level next higher, the metalinguistic. It is an accident of language that here we would be wrong. The sentence, in spite of the semanticists, is meaningful, because the items are partially predictable in relation to the higher level.

I have labored over the three communication levels, and these three levels of meaning at perhaps wearisome length. They are, however, all necessary to the understanding of the structure of poetry. A next, and equally fundamental statement is that the area which I have called microlinguistics contains no larger units than the sentence. Complete utterances of several sentences fall outside microlinguistics which is the area of activity and study within which the student can analyze and describe sentences and their parts, but not the relationships between sentences. A current definition of style and stylistics, is that structures, sequences, and patterns which extend, or may extend, beyond the boundaries of individual sentences define style, and that the study of them is stylistics. It is almost a commonplace that the special qualities of literature which set it apart from ordinary speech all fall within this area, and that style, if not the man, is at least the literary man. Stylistics always falls, then, between the area of microlinguistic items and structures and the ultimate area of metalinguistic correspondences. In ordinary speech, style is relatively unimportant — though after all, we recognize that if a speaker uses terms like *cranium* and *mandible,* he is talking in a different style from one who uses *head* and *jaw* — the first style is one in which a series of items like *cranium* and *mandible* are likely to occur in a whole series of sentences, and we guess that the man is talking to an anatomist or physical anthropologist.

If style is so peculiarly the domain of literature, we can return to our three-level picture of ordinary communication, and draw a related map for literary communication.

metalinguistic	metaliterary
style	microliterary (stylistics)
microlinguistic	preliterary
prelinguistic	

That is, phonetics and acoustics are irrelevant to the study of literature. Microlinguistics — the language and its structure — is something that we have to know before we can study the literature profitably, just as a user of language, or a student of language, must know the basic sounds before he can use the language or study it. The metaliterary is once more the area of correspondence, the correspondence-meanings of literature. Here I would suggest that correspondence-meaning for literature is somewhat narrower, and at the same time more important to us as human beings, than is correspondence-meaning for ordinary speech. Correspondence-meaning for ordinary speech may be to the world of things as things alone. Correspondence-meaning for literature is always to things as a culture — an organized social community — sees and values them. A physicist's speech may give a model of atoms and molecules. A poet's speech gives a model of the values, the emotions, the judgments of beautiful and ugly, good and bad, by virtue of which we act as members of a community. In this sense, ordinary speech may be said to give a model of the world and all that is in it. Literature gives a model of a culture. It is this fact which makes literature both narrower than ordinary speech, and so much more humanly important.

If the special microliterary area is that of style, we should be able to demonstrate that there is a special type, or types, of stylistic meaning, an area or areas in which items are partially predictable. The task is not difficult. First, linguistic items may be partially predictable in such a way as to enable us to use them in the area of style — to find out more about the whole series of utterances than we would otherwise know. An example of a microlinguistic item, partially predictable on that level, but enabling us to move into the stylistic level, is the definite article. If I use a sentence such as "I met a man, the man was a friend," we can make a linguistic statement here, in that the article was used because *man* indicated an item referred to before. If however, I say "the sun is shining," I use the definite article even if *sun* has not been previously mentioned. We can form a stylistic conclusion by saying that the article is used with an item which would be the most likely to have been referred to by the language entity, had the stylistic corpus been large enough to include other instances. This is an example of stylistic meaning in the sense that it is extrapolation from a partially predictable linguistic item to greater knowledge of the stylistic area.

The other type of stylistic meaning is the occurrence of an item or structure which is partially predictable in terms of stylistics, and which enables us to move into the metalinguistic (and metastylistic) area of correspondences. I shall use an extremely simple example.

"John is a fox, Mary is a cat, William is a *rat*." I call this a stylistic structure, since no matter how punctuated, the way I said it was to give three stylistically parallel sentences. The first two made the occurrence of *rat* in the third at least partially predictable — I could, of course, have called William a goose, or a wolf, or a sheep, but some animal name was almost certain. And notice that I move into the area of correspondence-meaning quite differently from the movement based on a single sentence — "William is a rat," said alone, may mean that William is the name of a pet rat. The stylistic structure is meaningful, and takes precedence over the merely linguistic structure and the linguistic meaning.

I said much earlier that I would hope to throw some light on the central paradox of poetry, that it is a kind of language, yet more than language and different from language. It is just here that we reach the paradox, and explain it. All literature makes stylistic structures, and carries stylistic relations through many sentences. Poetry, more than any other kind of literature, develops and heightens stylistic structures — rhyme and meter are external stylistic devices stretching over all the sentences in the poem — poetic vocabulary defines a special type of stylistic lexicon — the figures and images of poetry are stylistic devices of content, in which we rightly feel that the real heart of the poem often lies. This stylistic heightening makes possible an aim that the poet almost always holds — he tries to transcend the linguistic meanings by giving stylistic structures which change them and add to them, so that the poem as a whole has meaning which would escape us if we considered only its parts.

One of the ways in which modern poetry, that kind where modern might be in quotes, differs from traditional poetry, is that often the poet tries to say something nonsensical on the linguistic level, hoping that it will become meaningful on the stylistic level. Thus e. e. cummings wrote

"anyone lived in a pretty how town."

As ordinary English, the line does not make sense. Yet as we read the poem as a whole, the general stylistic structure enables us to translate it as approximately "an ordinary man lived in an ordinary, pretty kind of town." Cummings has played a sort of game of linguistics against stylistics, yet the game is not so different from the ordinary procedure of the poet; its strangeness consists only in that he adopts the linguistically unpredictable deliberately.

In bringing this fairly extensively developed body of theory to bear on three individual poems, I shall confine myself to discussing the use that three poems make of a single stylistic device. The device is analogy. There is nothing new in saying that poets make use of analogies; the familiar critical terms metaphor and simile describe two main types of them. What I shall try to show is that development of the analogy is the device by which the poet gives stylistic unity to his poem, and makes it meaningful in ways beyond the meaning of sober, everyday sentences. We shall see that the device is characteristic of poetry, and that it may lead to meanings almost as much in conflict with the linguistic as were the stylistic and linguistic meanings in the line from cummings.

Our first poem is this from Sandburg:

LOST *

Desolate and lone
All night long on the lake
Where fog trails and mist creeps,
The whistle of a boat
Calls and cries unendingly
Like some lost child
In tears and trouble
Hunting the harbor's breast
And the harbor's eyes.

The poem obviously offers no very great difficulty in understanding. The whistle of a boat reminds the poet of a lost child crying, and that seems clear enough. The analogy is overt, since the poet tells us flatly "like some lost child." Yet the simple over-all structure is not quite all that is here, since the separate parts of the two halves of the analogy are brought into a more detailed relationship with each other. The whistle is to the boat on the lake, as tears are to the child away from its mother. The phrase "the harbor's breast," compresses a sub-analogy. "Breast is to mother, as X is to harbor." Note that we are left to supply the identity of the missing X — one of two places in the poem where we meet such an implicit analogy. The X is not hard to supply: in this case it is the mooring at which the boat comes to rest. The second X, of course, is in the compressed phrase, "harbor's eyes," where eyes are to mother as X is to harbor — evidently harbor's lights.

Sandburg's little poem is obviously a simple one. If it has interest it must somehow be in the analogies around which it is built. We can point to a number of ways in which these analogies are interesting. The first one is of no literary importance, though of interest to us in this particular kind of study. By throwing together items which belong to the two halves of his analogy — *eyes* which belong with the child-mother half, and *harbor* which belongs with the boat-harbor half, Sandburg gives us a phrase which is compressed — "harbor's eyes" — and leaves one term in his proportional analogy as an unsolved X, which the reader must supply. The reader can be relied on to solve it, since the structure of the analogy forces the solution. This sort of unsolved X is one of the principal ways in which an analogy is made to say something which is there stylistically, but linguistically not present at all.

Second, the poem starts with a simple comparison. Probably none of us

* From *Chicago Poems* by Carl Sandburg. Copyright 1916 by Holt, Rinehart and Winston, Inc. Copyright 1944 by Carl Sandburg. Reprinted by permission of Holt, Rinehart and Winston, Inc.

have failed to respond to the loneliness of a train or boat whistle at night. The ascription of human emotional value to such a sound is a commonplace, and might be considered one of the tritest comparisons a poet could make. It is the points of correspondence, as the single general analogy is worked out in a series of linked subanalogies, that give the poem structure, unity, and some sense of originality. Further, as by now we might expect of a poetic structure, it always suggests correspondences with the metaliterary world of cultural values — we can extrapolate from literary structure to a structure of meanings. For me, at least, the lost boat, compared to a child who has lost the security of its mother's breast, suggests an identification with the society we live in. We, too, are lost, and long to return to a simpler society in the childhood of the world. The Sandburg poem is simple, indeed, but the stylistic structure is certainly more meaningful than would be the linguistic statement — "that boat sounds like a lost child."

From Sandburg, we can turn to a lyric by Emily Dickinson.

The Soul selects her own society,
Then shuts the door;
On her divine majority
Obtrude no more.

Unmoved she notes the chariot's pausing
At her low gate;
Unmoved, an emperor is kneeling
Upon her mat.

I've known her from an ample nation
Choose one;
Then close the valves of her attention
Like stone.

The Sandburg and Dickinson poems are alike in using analogies, and in having easily discoverable surface meanings. The simplest reading of this second poem might be to say that the soul chooses friendships in an arbitrary way. Yet when we leave this first message, we find that Emily Dickinson operates throughout with a series of different but related analogies, all of which leave unsolved X's, and as we shall see, the solution of the X's greatly modifies the surface, linguistic meaning of the several sentences. In the Sandburg poem, we found a single overtly stated general analogy, with subanalogies, and unsolved X's were found only in the sub-analogies.

Let us start with the first two lines. The analogy is complex to state, and would have to be in a form something like this:

The soul selects X^1	as X^2 selects society
The soul shuts X^3	as X^2 shuts a door

In spite of the large number of unsolved X's, it is still not difficult to supply identification:

The soul selects a companion	as a housedweller lets in society
The soul shuts her avenues of emotional communication	as a housedweller shuts the door

The overall comparison is of a soul dwelling in the body, to a human being dwelling in a house.

The next two lines offer another analogy. *Choice* (of society) is to the soul as *majority* is to X. Our question is, then, in what kind of entity can we equate majority with choice? I know of only one such entity, and so only one candidate for the solution of this particular X. It is a parliamentary body. The soul is now various, a world of its own, selfgoverning and democratic. Part of the concept is old — a poet in an older and more aristocratic society said "My mind to me a kingdom is." It seems peculiarly American, however, to compare the soul, even in this indirect fashion, with Congress.

The choice of the soul has been called a divine majority — I think you would agree that the soul is here pictured as a divine body politic, with something of the majesty of government.

Yet note the next verse, simpler in its related analogies. The soul rejects visitors, as X (who has a low gate with a mat) rejects charioteer and emperor. The X is a housedweller again, but the house is surely a cottage. There is again something peculiarly American in identifying an individual soul with the majesty of government, and, in turn, in placing that government in a cottage where it can reject an emperor.

It is in the last verse of the poem that the real surprise lies. The analogy runs something like this.

The soul selects one individual from a nation
(as X^1 selects one X^2 from a host of X^2s)
The soul closes her attention immutably
as X^1 closes its valves like stone

The analogies can not, I think, be solved without remembering the previous ones, which have already established the soul as a living being with an exterior dwelling, having doors that can be closed.

What is this X^1 to which we have several clues — that it selects one item, closes something called valves, and is like a stone afterward? I am quite sure that the analogies force a single answer, and that the answer is therefore a part of the poem, though the answer is nowhere stated in the poem. Only one type of living being has valves which close like hinges — a bivalve mollusc, as probably some of you have already guessed. Further, it is not a clam, but an oyster, since the oyster "selects" — though the term is in quotes — a grain of sand, as the soul selects her "one" from an ample nation.

Notice how the analogies transform the poem. There could scarcely be a more superficially unpromising comparison than to say the soul is like an oyster. Yet the analogies carry us straight to a comparison of the one selected by the soul, of whom she makes a friend, to the grain of sand selected by the oyster, of which it makes a pearl. In this particular poem, I do not see how the final meaning can be reached without solution of the implicit analogies, though of course, we can like the poem without understanding it. Yet I can not believe that the grain of sand and pearl, nowhere mentioned, are not a part, indeed the most important part, of the total design. And as with Sandburg, the analogies carry us far out into cultural correspondences. The recluse Emily Dickinson speaks of love and friendship in terms which imply wounding, then healing and transformation. All of us know these contradictory impulses towards privacy and companionship, of which so much of human relationship consists. Emily Dickinson has given us a model of a conflict in our cultural values, and has presented a solution. Stylistic structure has transcended language, and enabled Emily Dickinson to say to us what can not — or can not easily — be said in sentences of prose.

The last of these poems is different from either of the others, first because it has been so institutionalized that we accept it without thinking about it, or really reading it, merely as a part of our traditions. Second, because it can be read and valued highly, without working out the analogies it contains; it can give, indeed, the impression of being completely understood with none of the analysis we gave to Emily Dickinson. The analogies must therefore, if study of them is to be justified, modify or increase the understanding of the poem enough to make their exposition worth the effort, and must not spoil our appreciation of the poem.

COMPOSED UPON WESTMINSTER BRIDGE, SEPTEMBER 3, 1802

Earth has not anything to show more fair:
Dull would he be of soul who could pass by
A sight so touching in its majesty:
This City now doth, like a garment, wear
The beauty of the morning; silent, bare,
Ships, towers, domes, theatres, and temples lie
Open unto the fields, and to the sky;
All bright and glittering in the smokeless air.
Never did sun more beautifully steep
In his first splendour, valley, rock, or hill;
Ne'er saw I, never felt, a calm so deep!
The river glideth at his own sweet will:
Dear God! the very houses seem asleep;
And all that mighty heart is lying still!

I do not need to comment on the surface meaning of the poem. All of us recognize that Wordsworth saw the city in unwonted beauty, and was moved by it with a religious emotion. All of us can share the emotion. Let us see how study changes this, and whether it enriches it.

We can pass over the first three lines as not relevant to our purpose; they contain no important analogies. The first analogy is in line 4 —

"This City now doth, like a garment, wear
The beauty of the morning."

That is, beauty of the morning is to the city as garment is to X. Only human beings — normally at least — wear garments. The city is then like a human being. The garments are next described — "silent, bare, ships, towers, domes, theatres, and temples lie open unto the fields, and to the sky." The garment is not like a suit of clothes, or an overcoat. It is such as to reveal the city and its structures. We can express all this by an analogy which builds on the first one —

The city wears a garment which reveals its structures, as human being of X type wears a garment which reveals its body.

The garment which thus reveals beauty is not the sort of garment we talk about as worn by men or children. It is like the garment of a beautiful woman, and the city is not like a human being merely, but like a woman.

The woman-city, further, lies in calm and beautiful morning sleep. As well as the city and its parts, there is another set of entities in the poem. They are *fields, sky,* and *river*. These can easily be grouped as belonging to non-man-made nature, opposed in principle to the man-made city. There is no commoner attitude in our literature than the truism that God made the country, but man made the town — true or not, we all know the attitude. Yet the relation of these representatives of nature is not given here as one of conflict with the city. The woman-city

"lies open unto the fields, and to the sky."

And below

"The river glideth at his own sweet will."

The analogy can be constructed thus:

Nature is to the city, as X is to woman.

I submit, therefore, that language and situation in this poem force the conclusion that this final missing X is lover — and that nature and city are compared to man and woman in the sleep of lovers.

I am aware enough that these analogies, thus made overt, might be thought of as shocking. Yet they need not be, and should not be. A further statement in the poem throws light on how we are to view the comparison

"The sun . . . in his first splendour . . ."

One way of reading the line would be to take it as a reference merely to the first light of this particular September 3. But throughout the poem there are hints that the scene is touched by a lost beauty — the air is smokeless, for instance, though presumably Wordsworth's negative statement implies that it was not often so. Wordsworth uses *temples* instead of the more prosaic and realistic *churches,* as if he would suggest a past more beautiful than the usual present. For these reasons, I believe that *first splendour* refers rather to the dawn of the world, than to the dawn of September 3. City and nature are as lovers, but lovers with an innocence and beauty lost since Eden.

I do not think I need to carry the central woman-city analogy much further into the metaliterary realm of value and cultural correspondence. It is enough to say man and nature are reconciled, released, and united, as men and women are in love. Wordsworth did not often talk so of the works of man, and I think we can agree that he is a greater poet for the vision of a reconciliation which he grasped that morning on the bridge. The analogies are, I believe, the central structure of the poem — they are the way in which the larger unity of style is made to transcend the limitations of the microlinguistic. Wordsworth's success could not be achieved, I think, without them. His success, in turn, is a revealing example of the way in which poetry is language, yet more than language, and different from it.

Richard Ohmann

PROLEGOMENA TO THE ANALYSIS OF PROSE STYLE

The considerations of this essay are of a very primitive sort. If they are prolegomena to the study of style, they are preliminary by several stages to the study of style in the novel. What is more, a few decades ago they would have seemed utterly superfluous to most rhetoricians, who were quite content to think of style as the verbal dress of disembodied thought. Yet now comes a school of criticism which aims to discredit the split between form and content, a school which argues that no two different utterances mean the same thing, and, more radically that, "every statement is a unique style of its own."[1] This organicist position, in spite of its stringency, has appealed increasingly to critic and linguist alike.[2] In fact it has nearly attained the status of dogma, of an official motto, voiced in the triumphant tones of reason annihilating error. Appealing as the idea is, commonplace though it has lately become in criticism, semantics, and linguistics, it would seem to render futile most extant stylistic analysis, if not to undercut the whole idea of style. For if style does not have to do with *ways* of saying *something,*[3] just as style in tennis has to do with ways of hitting a ball, is there anything at all which is worth naming "style"? If not,

From *Style in Prose Fiction (English Institute)*, edited by H. C. Martin, Columbia University Press, New York.

[1] Andrews Wanning, "Some Changes in the Prose Style of the Seventeenth Century" (Ph.D. dissertation, University of Cambridge, 1938), p. 20.

[2] An example of the linguist's position: "It is a well-tried hypothesis of linguistics that formally different utterances always differ in meaning. . . ." Leonard Bloomfield, "Linguistic Aspects of Science," *International Encyclopedia of Unified Science,* I (Chicago, 1955), 253.

[3] Here, as with too many pseudo-philosophical problems, ordinary language seems to have been the villain. Our speech makes a separation between saying and thing said: one *says it.* And if expressing is an action that one performs on an idea, just as hitting is an action performed on a tennis ball, why not different *ways* of expressing an idea? The distinction works with vocal speech, for the same words can be spoken with different stress, pitch, tone, and so forth; but a moment's reflection shows that it does not apply to the written word, and that any approach to stylistics empowered by a split between form and content is in serious theoretical trouble.

most critics of style have really given us judgments about what writers mean, masquerading as judgments about manner. The critic can talk about what the writer says, but talk about style he cannot, for his neat identity — one thought, one form — allows no margin for individual variation, which is what we ordinarily mean by style. Style, then, becomes a useless hypothetical construct half way between meaning and the person who means, and the study of style would seem to be the moribund offspring of a prolific reification: the assumption that because there is a word "style," there must be a thing to match.

Confronted with this dilemma, the conscientious critic can only say, with Wittgenstein, "Whereof one cannot speak, thereof one must be silent," and rejoice at the elimination of another pseudo-discipline. The trouble with this ascetic solution is that the critic may still feel it useful to speak of style. If he *is* unwilling to see stylistics tossed into the positivist's scrap-heap, along with ethics and metaphysics, he may work out a compromise: the most common is to say that style is part of what we ordinarily call meaning,[4] that it is peripheral meaning, or subterranean meaning, or connotative meaning. Such a solution is fruitful, I think, but it leads to a new problem. If style exists, by courtesy of this redefinition, where are its boundaries? Which part of meaning is to be called style, and which is really meaning? In short, how can we tell style from not-style?

These difficulties are not, I hope, mere compliant straw men to be handily blown down. They are real, and they are crucial, for on their resolution depend answers to these questions: What is style? What kind of scrutiny will it reward? What can it show about the writer?

1

Let me begin the argument, unabashedly, where so many critical arguments begin — with I. A. Richards.

Socrates is wise.

Wisdom belongs to Socrates.

Mr. Richards offers these two sentences as a capsule demonstration of the way in which we "can put one thought form into many different word patterns." [5] He does not, as he may seem to do, neatly sever form and content; he is arguing a more subtle case, and one which ends by leaving form and content neither quite joined nor totally separated — a happy compromise, seemingly, for the beleaguered would-be critic of style. Let us examine it.

Mr. Richards uses the example concerning the wisdom of Socrates in a discussion calculated to refute J. S. Mill's contention that "the principles and rules of grammar are the means by which the forms of language are made to correspond with the universal forms of thought." [6] On the contrary, argues Mr. Richards, anyone who wishes to predicate wisdom of Socrates may cast his

[4] This is Mr. Wanning's theoretical justification for proceeding with his study.

[5] *Interpretation in Teaching* (New York, 1938), p. 285.

[6] *Inaugural Lecture at St. Andrews,* quoted by Richards, p. 280.

thought in one of several molds. Conversely, in English, thoughts of incompatible forms often take the same syntactical shape: for example, "I see a tiger" and "I kick a tiger." It is obvious that to kick a tiger is to act on it, whereas to see a tiger is to be affected in a complicated way by it. Mr. Richards submits that the tiger would no doubt administer a terminal lesson in logic to the man who confused sentence forms with forms of thought in this disastrous fashion.

His contention that the two sentences about Socrates express *congruent* thoughts is not, however, a contention that they express the *same idea,* or mean the *same thing,* or are *equivalent.* In one statement Socrates is the given quantity; in the other, wisdom. One sentence works by limiting the denotation of "Socrates," by eliminating possible statements such as "Socrates is stupid," and "Socrates is foolish." The other sentence focuses on a set of attributes and ways of behaving called "wisdom," and tells of one point in space-time where we can find it, namely in Socrates. One sentence belongs in a context of curiosity about Socrates; it might come in answer to the question, "What sort of mind had Socrates?" The other might satisfy someone who is looking, not for an honest, but for a wise man. The two sentences differ in the type of information given, in pattern of emphasis, in the sort of expectation they satisfy. In short, they say different things.

Rather than artificially separating idea from expression, Mr. Richards suggests that ideas fall into a finite set of categories, according to logical shape or form. His medial position between a dualism of manner and matter which is currently heretical, and a monism which is orthodox but fatal, allows to style a tenuous existence as the manner of clothing ethereal forms of thought in neatly tailored word patterns.[7] Under the aegis of this theory the study of a writer's style becomes the examination of the formal changes he works on each group of ideas, of the metamorphoses through which he puts each form of thought.

Attractive as this theory may seem to the critic who wishes to talk about style, but is hard put to see what style is, I think it must be rejected, even at the cost, possibly, of a final lesson in logic from Mr. Richards's tiger. For one thing, these shadowy forms of thought are so indistinguishable from each other, so nearly hidden by overlapping word patterns, that, rather than implementing a rigorous criticism, they would make it inhumanly difficult. Mr. Richards's distinction between seeing and kicking a tiger is easy enough to follow; one idea is of the form *"a* receives sense data from *b,"* and the other is of the form *"a* acts on *b."* But what of the sentence "I feel a tiger"? To which form of thought does it belong? A new form of thought must no doubt be established to contain this sentence. But the process is endless; as rapidly as the forms multiply, borderline sentences will rise up to plague the classifier, who may eventually find, as a result of his labors, that the number of forms precisely equals the number of sentences.

[7] This rescue maneuver is my inference from Mr. Richards's position; *his* main aim is to debunk the monism of Mill's grammar.

In raising this objection I have tentatively accepted the notion of "forms of thought," and merely questioned the practicability of their use by a critic. But the disconcerting proliferation of thought forms calls the whole theory into question. If there is a separate form for every thought, then the concept of "form" is identical with that of "thought," and we can dispense with one or the other. To look at the matter from another angle, let me press somewhat further the hypothetical meeting of man and tiger, attending to forms of thought. To an observer the tiger consists of certain sense data — color, texture, odor, shape, motion, sound — data related to each other in extremely complex ways, however simple and primitive an object the tiger may seem to the adult's highly integrated mind. The man is a similar complex. Both tiger and man are capable of receiving sensations from, say, the jungle around them, as well as from each other. And the jungle, like man and tiger, is a welter of surfaces, glints of light, disorderly movements, unmusical noises. In this tangle of sensation the man sees trees, plants, a tiger; but these *Gestalten* are not inherently *there;* they are arbitrary ways of breaking up the flux; arbitrary, that is, except that the man has in the past been rewarded for using them, to the extent that parts of his environment (e.g. the tiger) demand, with special persistence, recognition as separate things.[8] When the man kicks the tiger, an exceedingly intricate shift takes place in the arrangement of sense data, a shift which is indistinguishable *in type* from the shifts which are occurring every millionth of a second. There has been a change; something has happened, but something is always happening, and it is man who separates one phenomenon from another, both by seeing and by naming. Our habits of sorting and classifying are so ingrained that we cannot describe or imagine things as they appear to the tiger, or in the infant's "blooming, buzzing confusion." The world in itself, the infant's world, is barren of form, without order, mere raw material for man's perceptual and verbal manipulation. The forms of thought, then, are not inherent in things as they are. There is no logical or ontological reason why, on some tiger-infested tropical island, a people could not see man and tiger as one entity, and give a single name to this "object." Then "I kick the tiger" might run, "The tigerman coalesces footwise," and "I see the tiger" could read, "The tigerman coalesces eyewise." Surely the two ideas are now of the same form, as are the two sentences.

In another section of *Interpretation in Teaching,*[9] Mr. Richards argues that communication depends on a sameness of experience — a uniformity offered from without and a uniformity as organized from within. His acceptance of "forms of thought" must depend on this "sameness," on a belief that experi-

[8] This view is, to the best of my knowledge, in accord with current perception theory. For instance: "perception is never a sure thing, never an absolute revelation of 'what is.' Rather, what we see is a prediction — our own personal construction designed to give us the best possible bet for carrying out our purposes in action. We make these bets on the basis of our past experience." W. H. Ittelson and F. P. Kilpatrick, "Experiments in Perception," *Scientific American Reader* (New York, 1953), p. 581.

[9] Page 68.

ence affords common elements to all men. But if my analysis is correct, experience is not molded from without, except in so far as nature rewards certain of man's sorting responses to the passing show and punishes others. It is interesting to note that we may be led into a misconception partly by the very word "experience." A logician points out that " 'experience' itself is a relational term masquerading as a thing-name; *x* is an experience if and only if there is some *y* (the experiencer) which stands in the experience relation to *x*." [10] Ordinary language urges us to think of experience as a constant, offered with impartial sameness to all experiencers, rather than as an infinite series of relations of which no two need be alike.

The conception of experience as a series of relations is damaging also to Mr. Richards's claim that experience has "uniformity as organized from within," for it seems extremely improbable that any experiencer should ever stand in exactly the same relation to a field of perception as any other experiencer, or, indeed, that any man should see the same way twice. I do not wish to peddle a crippling subjectivism; communication does take place, and we must act most of the time as if there were uniformity of experience. At the same time it seems more accurate to speak behavioristically and say that men often *respond* similarly to similar fields of perception — respond similarly, that is, either in words or in action.

Neither the external world, then, nor our "experience" of it offers any ready-made forms of thought to the analyst who wishes to see style as the way in which ideas get into words. What nature does offer to experience, however, and experience to language, is a constant *formlessness*. Just as, in the existentialist view, man is confronted in his search for ethical order by the indifference of the universe, man in his search for perceptual order faces a chaotic world-stuff which gives no hints as to the proper method of sorting. But Camus calls the world's moral anarchy benign, in that it allows us to consider man the maker of his own morality, and the chaos pictured by modern psychologists has a parallel advantage: the perceiver, according to this theory, shapes the world by choosing from it whatever perceptual forms are most useful to him — though most often the choice is unconscious and inevitable. The unfriendly behavior of tigers may, to be sure, coerce him in his perceptual sorting, and his choice of perceptual forms largely governs his choice of linguistic categories, but the selections are initially free, in an important sense.

In these multifarious *ur*-choices, these preverbal and verbal pigeon-holings, style has its beginnings. If the critic is able to isolate and examine the most primitive choices which lie behind a work of prose, they can reveal to him the very roots of a writer's epistemology, the way in which he breaks up for manipulation the refractory surge of sensations which challenges all writers and all perceivers. In this Heraclitean flux, and not in the elusive forms of

[10] Charles W. Morris, "Foundations of the Theory of Signs," *International Encyclopedia of Unified Science,* I, 123.

thought, is the common source of all perceptions, all sentences, all prose. The stream of experience is the background against which "choice" is a meaningful concept, in terms of which the phrase *"way* of saying *it"* makes sense, though "it" is no longer a variable. Form and content are truly separate if "content" is not bodiless ideas, but the formless world-stuff. And if such a hypothesis carries forward the analysis of style only a comfortless millimeter or so, at least it offers to that discipline a firm theoretical base, and a justification as well, inasmuch as it establishes an accessible and interesting connection between style and epistemology.

2

Before this hypothesis can be of use, however, it requires major refinement. The most obvious barrier to a fruitful consideration of these fundamental epistemic choices is the fact that most of them are irrevocably made for any given writer by the particular language he writes in. A James Joyce or a Gertrude Stein may reshuffle linguistic forms in an attempt to draw aside the curtain that English places between us and the world of psychic and physical phenomena, but most conventional writers permit English to govern their epistemologies, as do all who merely speak the language. In other words, writers in English deal with bare experience only as it is censored by their language; they manipulate linguistically a world which is already highly organized for them.

Take, for example, the question of grammatical case. In English, a language which, compared to its neighbors, is syntactically rigid and very slightly inflected, most contemporary linguists recognize two cases [11] (as opposed to the four, five, or six of earlier grammarians). Of these two, genitives are relatively uncommon, so that nearly all occurrences of nouns are in one case. This limitation of cases means that a noun standing by itself, say "dog," calls attention merely to the animal of that name, and tells us nothing about it, not even that it is *not* a dog seen in an attitude of possession, since we have many constructions such as "hair of the dog" which express the genitive idea without recourse to the genitive case. The isolated word "dog's" names an animal *seen as owning something;* that is, it conveys a somewhat different idea. It also creates a different set of expectations; to say "dog" is probably to stimulate the question "What about a dog?"; but the word "dog's" leads to the question "Dog's what, and what about it?" Thus English offers the

[11] "Contemporary" in a loose sense: Otto Jespersen, whose semi-notional approach to grammar has made him seem old-fashioned to many later linguists, is one who argues against more than two cases in English; *The Philosophy of Grammar* (London, 1924), pp. 173–86. Writers of the Fries-Trager-Smith era also favor a two-case system, as for example, Paul Roberts in *Understanding Grammar* (New York, 1954), pp. 39–40, and Donald Lloyd and Harry Warfel in *American English in Its Cultural Setting* (New York, 1956), pp. 241–42.

speaker or writer two different notions of a certain four-footed animal; it sees the canine beast in two different ways.

In French, by contrast, there is only one form of *chien.* That word in isolation tells nothing about the dog at all. At the atomic level of meaning English has two things where French has but one. When we turn to Latin, with its six cases, the difference becomes more obvious. To translate *canis* properly, we would have to use a term such as "dog-doing-something-or-having-something-predicated-of-it" (actually, a full translation would be much more complex even than this). *Canem* might be partially rendered "dog-being-acted-upon-or-seen-as-the-goal-of-action." In Latin there is no conceivable way of expressing the English idea of "dog," untrammeled by ideas of position, agency, attitude, possession, mode of being perceived, and so forth. There is in Latin no symbol which is so free to be manipulated syntactically.

The writer in English, therefore, sees the universe through a verbal screen which divides it up less finely; classes are larger in English, because less subtly distinguished. What we conceive of as one thing, the writer of Latin must have conceived of, in some unquestioning, preverbal way, as six different things. These are the epistemic implications of case. The implications for style are equally significant: the importance of word order in English, the many possibilities of achieving emphasis in Latin by placement of a word, the greater dependence of the English writer on "function words." Epistemic differences of this sort run through the whole Indo-European family of languages, but within that family the similarities are more noticeable than the differences, and one must examine languages of other groups to find out how radically verbal environments can differ.

Benjamin Lee Whorf, a pioneer in metalinguistics, studied Western languages in juxtaposition with esoteric languages such as Hopi, and found that we treat the cosmos as much more segmented than do they — often artificially so.[12] We objectify time into a thing with boundaries and divisions instead of seeing it in terms of relations in lateness as Hopi does. We have "distributed nouns," such as "meat," "water," and "butter," whereas Hopi has none; nor does Hopi have abstract nouns. Evidently the Hopi language is in some sense closer to the raw material of perception than English is, with its complex and sophisticated system of categories.

It is notorious that Korzybski, Hayakawa, and other semanticists go further than Whorf, attacking Western languages for making inaccurate distinctions and concealing the functional relationships of nature.[13] Supposedly, Indo-European language structure was responsible for our long slavery to Aristo-

[12] *Language Thought, and Reality* (Cambridge, Mass., and New York, 1956), esp. "The Relation of Habitual Thought and Behavior to Language" and "Languages and Logic."

[13] See, for example, "What Is Meant by Aristotelian Structure of Language?," in *Language, Meaning and Maturity,* ed. by S. I. Hayakawa (New York, 1954).

telian philosophy and Newtonian physics [14] and is to blame for a good share of our present neuroses to boot. This criticism of ordinary language seems to me even more utopian than that leveled against it by the early positivists, and logically faulty as well. The semanticists use the very language which, according to them, hoodwinks us so severely to point out the fallacies of thought which it induces. Certainly a language which permits analysis of its own artificialities — which in effect transcends its own limitations — will suffice for most ordinary thinking.

Thus I find attacks on the cosmological limitations of English beside the point. What *is* relevant to the study of style is the fact that any language persuades its speakers to see the universe in certain set ways, to the exclusion of other ways. It thereby limits the possibilities of choice for any writer, and the student of style must be careful not to ascribe to an individual the epistemic bias of his language. A writer cannot escape the boundaries set by his tongue, except by creating new words, by uprooting normal syntax, or by building metaphors, each of which is a new ontological discovery. Yet, even short of these radical linguistic activities, an infinite number of meaningful choices remain to be made by the writer. A heavy dependence on abstraction, a peculiar use of the present tense, a habitual evocation of similarities through parallel structure, a tendency to place feelings in syntactical positions of agency, a trick of underplaying causal words: any of these patterns of expression, when repeated with unusual frequency, is the sign of a habit of meaning, and thus of a persistent way of sorting out the phenomena of experience. And even single occurrences of linguistic oddities, especially in crucial places, can point to what might be called temporary epistemologies.

Here, then, is one way in which the term "style" is meaningful, one kind of *choice* which really exists for the author. This view does not, of course, represent an entirely new departure from conventional stylistics, even though my formulation has been elicited by the chaos of past criticism. Style as epistemic choice may be what John Middleton Murry has in mind when he says that "a true idiosyncrasy of style [is] the result of an author's success in compelling language to conform to his mode of experience." [15] It probably is what W. K. Wimsatt refers to when he calls style "the last and most detailed elaboration of meaning." [16] New or not, this approach to style has the advantage of being philosophically defensible, as well as the advantage of yielding results that have to do with the literary work as a whole, not merely with its (nonexistent) window dressing. Finally, the method which I suggest saves the study of style from having to rely *only* on those impressionistic, metaphorical judgments which have too often substituted for analysis: dignified, grand,

[14] According to this view it is not surprising that the Hopi have produced no Newton, but it is surprising that no Einstein has risen among the Pueblos.

[15] *The Problem of Style* (London, 1922), p. 23.

[16] *The Prose Style of Samuel Johnson* (New Haven, 1941), p. 63. Mr. Wimsatt is one critic who has fruitfully approached style in this way, both in this book and in *Philosophic Words* (New Haven, 1948).

plain, decorative, placid, exuberant, restrained, hard, and the whole tired assortment of epithets which name without explaining.[17]

Yet this account of style is not complete. The naive, commonsense feeling that style is a *way* of saying *something* demands more than a cursory dismissal. For one thing, a discussion of style as epistemic choice can operate effectively only over wide areas of prose, where habitual kinds of choice become evident. There is little sense in comparing the epistemic decisions of a writer who is discussing a rowing match with those of a writer on Christian ideas of teleology. The very choice of subject matter precludes a large number of stylistic decisions: it can force the writer to be concrete or abstract, for instance. Thus the criticism of style requires a more manageable backdrop than the entire panorama of the world. If, as Wittgenstein says, "the world is the totality of facts, not of things," [18] perhaps individual facts, or combinations of them, will serve the purpose.

This position is the one that I propose to take, and I shall use the term "proposition" to describe what is expressed by sentences. As before, Mr. Richards's remarks will provide a convenient starting place for the argument. During a discussion of logic [19] he lists these three sentences:

Mussolini is mortal.
Voltaire is witty.
Havelock Ellis is old.

A logician, he says, would claim that these sentences "express propositions of the same form," a contention which "is flagrantly not so." The first sentence, Mr. Richards says, means "Mussolini will die sometime"; the second means "Voltaire makes remarks which cause in certain people a peculiar pleasure, and in others a peculiar annoyance"; the third, "Havelock Ellis has lived through many years." These sentences show that "the similar adjectives stand for very different forms." Mr. Richards's analysis is revealing, and the particular logician he has in mind [20] *had* made the error of assuming that syntactical structure is a key to the structure of propositions. But Mr. Richards makes precisely the same error in implying that his *translations* of the first three sentences reveal the structure of the propositions they express, for he takes the translations as showing that the propositions are of different forms. And by what superior right is the sentence "Mussolini will die sometime" a better indication of propositional form than the sentence "Mussolini is mortal"? Or for that matter, why not other sentences, such as "Mussolini's life will end," or "Mussolini will not live forever"? If the first two sentences ex-

[17] Such terms may be legitimately used to name habits of meaning which have been described specifically; see, for instance, Mr. Wimsatt's discussion of "plain" and its opposite, *Prose Style of Johnson,* p. 101. The more usual procedure, however, is to use them as if they had clear a priori meaning.

[18] Ludwig Wittgenstein, *Tractatus Logico-Philosophicus,* trans. by C. K. Ogden (London, 1922), p. 31.

[19] *Interpretation in Teaching,* p. 370.

[20] Susan Stebbing, *A Modern Introduction to Logic* (London, 1930), p. 51.

press the same proposition, then there are many other sentences which do so, and these sentences are of many syntactical forms. I see no way of picking one of such a group of sentences as *the* mirror of the proposition it expresses.[21]

The difficulty, of course, is that a "proposition," as Mr. Richards uses the term and as I wish to use it, has no form at all. The form of a proposition, like the forms of thought, is illusory, if I am right in what I take a proposition to be. It is the class of all sentences which are related to a fact or a cluster of facts in this way: if the fact (or cluster) exists, the sentences are all true; if the fact does not exist, the sentences are all false. In other words, they contain no parts which will not stand or fall with the fact. The process of determining, by observing facts, whether a sentence is true or false, is called "verification." [22] What may have led Mr. Richards to claim that his translations revealed the propositional forms which had been concealed by the original versions, is the fact that the restatements are more nearly descriptions of the facts which would go to *verify* the propositions involved.

Thus, for a sentence to express a proposition is for it to be a member of a group of sentences. But this class membership does not imply that a given sentence is one sub-form of a main propositional form. Rather, all members of the class have a most general form: the form "x is the case," or $f(x)$. And this form they have in common with *all* sentences, and with all propositions, for "the general propositional form is a variable." [23] This form distinguishes propositions from expletives, isolated words, commands, and so forth, none of which state that anything is the case, but it does not distinguish one proposition from another.

[21] The truth is, I think, that most logicians would say that Mr. Richards's *sentences* are of the same form, and not the propositions they express.

[22] See A. J. Ayer, *Language, Truth and Logic,* rev. ed. (New York, 1946), pp. 13, 35, for a positivist's account of the criterion of verifiability. See also Alfred Tarski, "The Semantic Conception of Truth and the Foundations of Semantics," *Semantics and the Philosophy of Language* (Urbana, Ill., 1952), esp. pp. 15–17. According to Tarski, whose article is a classic in the field, the general definition of "truth" is a logical conjunction of all equivalences of the form "x is true, if and only if p," where "p" is any "true" sentence and "x" is the name of that sentence (i.e., that sentence in quotation marks). Tarski's definition seems to bypass propositions altogether by applying the term "true" to sentences only; and in view of the long dispute over propositions among logicians and philosophers, Tarski's move may be a wise application of Occam's razor. But it has the disadvantage of throwing out a term which is in common use by both philosophers and laymen, and the more severe disadvantage of leaving no term at all to describe that which sentences express. For these reasons I follow Ayer, *The Foundations of Empirical Knowledge* (London, 1940), pp. 100–1, in retaining the term. But I am made uncomfortable by an identification of "proposition" and "sentences which are true or false" (as in Wittgenstein, *Tractatus,* pp. 61–103), and more uncomfortable by a gentleman's agreement to use the term "proposition" while confessing ignorance as to its meaning. My own definition (which I have not seen elsewhere) is somewhat odd in that it requires us to think of a *class* of sentences as being true or false. But it jibes reasonably well with most technical usage, and has notable advantages for the study of style, the main one being that it places something between sentences and the facts, thus allowing meaningful talk of what sentences express (propositions) as well as of what they describe (facts).

[23] Wittgenstein, *Tractatus,* p. 103.

Propositions, then, offer a second locus for the analyst of style. Many sentences can express the same proposition; that is, they can be jointly verifiable by reference to the same fact. This is Bloomfield's contention when he states that "formally different utterances," though they always differ in meaning, may be equivalent "as to some partial phase of meaning." Equivalence covers "the phase of meaning which is observable indifferently by all persons," and "it is only the accompanying personal and social adjustments which differ." [24] These "adjustments" in language I would call "style," but it is worth noting again that they, as well as the root idea, are *meanings,* and not merely embellishment. Style is the hidden thoughts which accompany overt propositions; it is the highly general meanings which are implied by a writer's habitual methods of expressing propositions. Thus, as an aid to analyzing a writer's dissection of the entire universe, the critic may examine what the writer does with modest corners of that universe — that is, with particular facts and particular propositions.

Some theory such as the one I have been suggesting must be held by the modern critic who looks to style for insight into meaning, who believes that "the consideration of style is a consideration of complete meanings, and there is little of any importance that can be studied that is not a consideration of meanings." [25]

3

So far I have been outlining a theory of style which describes choices that I have called epistemic. These choices are important, for they are the critic's key to a writer's mode of experience. They show what sort of place the world is for him, what parts of it are significant or trivial. They show how he thinks, how he comes to know, how he imposes order on the ephemeral pandemonium of experience. These insights into a writer's world view are well worth pursuing, to whatever extent style can yield them. But an account of style which focuses on discursive content alone is only partial; style as it appears, for example, in the novel, I have left largely untouched. For the limits of speakable thought are not the boundaries of experience, or even of rational experience, and thoughts not included in the totality of verifiable propositions are nonetheless an integral part of style, as of knowledge. Thus argues Susanne Langer, who finds post-positivist man on "a tiny grammar-bound island" of human thought, in "the midst of a sea of feeling." [26] He wants to talk of good and evil, substance, beauty, and so forth, but whenever he does, he lapses into nonsense (according to the positivists). Mrs. Langer's method of egress from the narrow cage is well known. She calls symbolism of the sort tolerated by radical empiricists "discursive," and claims that even

[24] *International Encyclopedia of Unified Science,* I, 253.
[25] Wanning, "Some Changes," p. 20.
[26] *Philosophy in a New Key* (New York: Mentor edition, 1948), pp. 70–71.

beyond its limits there is a possibility of genuine semantic. This semantic she calls "presentational symbolism," because its symbols "are involved in a simultaneous, integral presentation." [27] Of this sort is the symbolism of single words, or cries, or music and the visual arts. It is a symbolism of emotional configurations, Mrs. Langer contends, for feelings have contours just as do thoughts, though of a different kind. They are static, grasped in sudden gestalts, rather than formed by gradual accretions of meaning. And to presentational symbolism belongs a large part of what we call "style," a part with which I have yet to deal.

Mrs. Langer says elsewhere,[28] "A statement is always a formulation of an idea, and every known fact or hypothesis or fancy takes its emotional value largely from the way it is presented and entertained." For "idea" my term is "proposition," and this substitution brings Mrs. Langer's statement into close parallelism with my analysis of varying descriptions of facts — but with this exception: her point is that one proposition may be expressed in many different *emotional* forms. The claim is incontestable; a large portion of the submerged meaning in prose is presentational, and the constant shaping of emotions is an always audible counterpoint to the melodic line of discursive thought. The presentational part of prose does not, of course, get communicated by a special set of symbols or by a code of emotive punctuation marks. It is buried in an exceedingly complex set of relationships among the same symbols which transmit the discursive meaning. These relationships are what Bloomfield referred to as "accompanying personal and social adjustments."

Many critics see the emotional freight of literature as of primary importance, even in prose that is mainly discursive. Hence epigrams such as "Style is the man himself," or "Style is ingratiation." [29] Certainly the configurations of feeling which accompany any argument are vital in governing its reception by the reader. The writer must observe the amenities common to all human relationships, by "saying the right thing," as Kenneth Burke puts it, by showing himself a particular human being in a certain social relationship with his auditor.[30] Style adds the force of personality to the impersonal forces of logic and evidence, and is thus deeply involved in the business of persuasion. Students of rhetoric since Plato have been largely concerned, at one or another level of sophistication, with analyzing the role of emotion in inducing agreement, and with the methods of embodying it in writing.

But an analysis of tone, distance, dramatic situation, and the rest, solely as ways of persuading, is only a partial analysis, and one which can lead to the damaging distrust of rhetoric as tricky and insidious. Emotion enters prose not only as disguises for slipping into the reader's confidence, but as sheer expression of self. Complete honesty demands that the writer not only state

[27] *Ibid.*, p. 79.

[28] *Feeling and Form* (New York, 1953), p. 258.

[29] Kenneth Burke, *Permanence and Change* (New York, 1935), p. 71.

[30] See Reuben Arthur Brower, *The Fields of Light* (New York, 1951), chap. 1, for this view of tone.

his ideas accurately, but also take an emotional stance. A proposition is never held altogether dispassionately, nor can it be expressed without some indication of feeling (except in the artificial languages of logic and mathematics, where symbols and structural patterns have no connotations, no psychic contexts). This being so, the writer must either recreate in prose the emotional concomitants of his thinking, or be in some degree unfaithful to himself. To acknowledge the expressive value of tone, however, is not to say that it is isolated from the persuasive value. When a writer such as Newman creates a full picture of the frame of mind in which he approaches a problem and reader, he is being honest, certainly, but his self-revelation may have the effect of persuading the reader to follow the same emotional path. With Arnold and many other writers the two uses of tone are even more inextricably fused. Arnold argues for a temper of mind, rather than for a set of specific doctrines. In his prose, therefore, tone *is* the argument, in large measure: ingratiation and personality become one, for the case stands or falls depending on whether Arnold's feelings and attitudes are attractive to his readers.[31] His use of language is presentational in that a full understanding of his prose depends on a grasp of the emotional pattern which it presents.

Feeling enters discursive prose, then, as expression and as persuasion. In addition there is a third way, I think, which is almost beyond the power of language to describe. A sentence, at its inception, raises questions rather than answering them. The first word or two may limit the field of possible things-to-be-said, but they do not really transmit information. They may name something, or set an attitude toward something, or indicate a shift in direction from a previous sentence, but they always give rise to questions such as "What about it?" or "What am I to think of in that way?" These demands for completion of a sequence are of course subverbal; they are the vaguest sort of dissatisfaction with suspended thought, with a rational process not properly concluded. As the sentence progresses some of the demands are satisfied, others deferred, others complicated, and meanwhile new ones are created. But with the end of the sentence comes a kind of balance which results from something having been *said*. There may be a new set of indefinite expectations which remain for future sentences to gratify or disappoint, but one circle is completed, one temporary equilibrium gained. The very act of predication is an emotional act, with rhythms of its own. To state something is first to create imbalance, curiosity, where previously there was nothing, and then to bring about a new balance. So prose builds on the emotional force of coming to know, of pinning down part of what has previously been formless and resolving the tensions which exist between the human organism and unstructured experience. Mrs. Langer speaks of the

> feeling that naturally inheres in studious thinking, the growing intensity of a problem as it becomes more and more complex, and at the same time more

[31] I am indebted for this notion to John Holloway, *The Victorian Sage* (London, 1953), p. 207.

> definite and "thinkable," until the demand for answer is urgent, touched with impatience; the holding back of assent as the explanation is prepared; the cadential feeling of solution, and the expansion of consciousness in new knowledge.[32]

To emotion, then, as well as to epistemic choice, the stylistic critic must turn his attention. This part of the study is and always has been particularly enticing, perhaps because the individual character of a writer emerges with special clarity in the patterns of feeling which are habitual with him. The epistemic part of style, moreover — a writer's method of dissecting the universe, as expressed by the infinite number of choices he makes — is likely to seem indistinguishable from what he overtly *says*. Yet this is all the more reason for pursuing stylistic meaning through the maze of surface meaning. That which is not immediately obvious may be just as central to the spirit of the writer, and therefore just as valuable to know, as that which starts up unbidden from the page. And, finally, it should be said that a dichotomy between thought and emotion, though useful, is artificial. A writer's characteristic way of manipulating experience is organically related to his feelings about coming to know; his attitude toward the reader and toward the process of communicating is also part of the whole.

The view of style which I have been outlining clearly takes prose as a serious literary venture. What Leo Spitzer says of the purely imaginative forms is also true of good discursive prose: "the lifeblood of the poetic creation is everywhere the same, whether we tap the organism at 'language' or 'ideas,' at 'plot' or at 'composition.' "[33] This rather mystical theory makes good sense if "lifeblood" is translatable to "modes of experience and habits of feeling." Spitzer's dictum means only that a work of prose can be self-consistent just as a good poem is, its fabric all of a piece. Such a view is the direct antithesis of the older one, which saw style as sugar-coating; if my hypothesis is legitimate, style is just as useful a key to total meaning as is any other element. For this reason, and for no other, it is worth studying: to say something about style is to contribute fresh insight into the artistic contours of the work as a whole.

[32] *Feeling and Form*, p. 302.
[33] *Linguistics and Literary History* (Princeton, 1948), p. 18.

Michael Riffaterre

CRITERIA FOR STYLE ANALYSIS

Abbreviations: *AR* = 'average reader,' as defined in 2.2.2 (never used in the ordinary sense); *poem* = 'literary work of art' (cf. 0.2); *SD* = 'stylistic device.'

PROGRAM

0.1. Linguistics and stylistics. Subjective impressionism, normative rhetoric and premature aesthetic evaluation have long interfered with the development of stylistics as a science, especially as a science of literary styles. Because of the kinship between language and style, there is hope that linguistic methods can be used for the objective and exact description of the literary use of language. This, the most specialized and complex linguistic function, cannot be neglected by the linguists either.

Linguistic, structural description of style, however, requires a difficult adjustment: on the one hand, *stylistic facts can be apprehended only in language, since that is their vehicle;* on the other hand, *they must have a specific character, since otherwise they could not be distinguished from linguistic facts.* A purely linguistic analysis of a work of literature will yield only linguistic elements; it will describe those elements of a sequence which happen to have a stylistic value along with the neutral ones; it will isolate no more than their linguistic functions without discerning which of their features make them stylistic units as well. Still, the application of linguistic methods to such units would give us an objective knowledge of their double role as elements of both the linguistic and the stylistic systems. But this application requires a preliminary sorting. It is necessary to gather first all those elements which present stylistic features, and secondly, to subject to linguistic analysis only these, to the exclusion of all others (which are stylistically irrelevant). Then and only then will the confusion between style and language be avoided. For this sifting, preliminary to analysis, we must find specific criteria to delineate the distinctive features of style.[1]

Reprinted from *Word,* Vol. 15, no. 1 (April 1959), by permission.

[1] The dangers of applying linguistic methods to literary facts without a specific stylistic viewpoint were emphasized by A. G. Juilland in his review of Ch. Bruneau, *Histoire de la langue française,* vol. 13, in *Language* XXX (1954), 313–338. In this

0.2. Scope. I shall try to outline some distinctive characteristics of the communication process in literature, and to take them into account when I introduce criteria relevant to style only. By *literary style* I mean any *written individual* form of *literary intent,* i.e. the style of an author or, preferably, of a single literary work of art (hereinafter called *poem*), or even of one isolable passage.

Style is understood as an emphasis (expressive, affective or aesthetic) added to the information conveyed by the linguistic structure, without alteration of meaning. Which is to say that language expresses and that style stresses, but the special values thus added to communication are not my concern; the consideration of these will come at the descriptive stage of stylistic research, or rather, at a metastylistic (e.g. aesthetic) stage. This paper limits itself to finding criteria and modes of existence of such values or stresses: its aims are exclusively *heuristic.*

0.3. Meaning of 'individual'. If stylistic phenomena occurred at random, without a code of reference, they would not be perceived. Even if style were only a metalinguistic fringe, there must be constants in its relationship to linguistic facts — without which constants style would collide with these facts: consequently, a general structure of style can probably be constructed.[2] But

review Juilland clears the ground neatly but does not offer a practical solution; he does give useful bibliographical indications for the linguist's side of the question. On the stylistic approach proper, H. Hatzfeld's *Bibliografía critica de la nueva estilística aplicada a las literaturas romanicas* (Madrid, 1955) is more complete than the English edition (1953); it is strongly biased in favor of Spitzer's methods (see *Romanic Review* XLVI [1955], 49–52). P. Guiraud's *La Stylistique* (Paris, 1954) is a survey of the main trends of style studies; so is Hatzfeld's "Methods of Stylistic Investigation," *Literature and Science: Proceedings of the 6th Congress of the International Federation for Modern Languages and Literatures* (Oxford, 1955), 44–51. These various works are primarily concerned with style studies in the Romance field, where they were systematized first. On the important Russian theoretical discussions of style analysis and its practical applications in the Slavic field, see V. Erlich, *Russian Formalism: History — Doctrine* (The Hague, 1955); the "Discussion of Problems of Stylistics" in *Voprosy jazykoznanija* 1954, no. 4, 76–100; A. B. Stepanov, "Problems of the Stylistics of Literary Usage in the *Učenye zapiski* and *Trudy* [of Soviet Universities], 1955–1957" (in Russian), *Voprosy jazykoznanija* 1958, no. 4, 108–115. Various American attempts have been made by A. A. Hill, S. Chatman, and others to adapt linguistic methods or techniques to stylistics. The fundamental difference between their approach and the one proposed here is that they do not introduce specific criteria; I shall devote a full discussion to their efforts in the near future. — In spite of its title, "Language and Style," S. Ullmann's introduction to his *Style in the French Novel* (Cambridge, 1957), 1–39, does not explore the nature of the interrelation of language and style. On the problem seen from the literary point of view, see R. A. Sayce, "Literature and Language," *Essays in Criticism* VII (1957), 119–133. Outside of the structuralist school, linguists side with the stylisticians and do not satisfactorily clarify the position of stylistics inside or outside of linguistics (see J. Marouzeau, "Langue et style," *Conférences de l'Institut de Linguistique de Paris,* 1945). The theoretical consequences to be drawn from the differentiation between language and style, and their methodological implications, remain a field largely unexplored. *Editors' Note:* The major portion of the Juilland review is reprinted here, pp. 374–384.

[2] The possibility of a style structure has been questioned, e.g. by R. L. Wagner, *Supplément bibliographique à l'Introduction à la linguistique française* (Geneva, 1955), pp. 8–11.

then, individual forms are to style what speech is to language. Studying them should give us basic data for a future system. I shall therefore exclude from the present essay all consideration of literary "dialectology": [3] as soon as elements from a literary language are used by an author for a definite effect, they become units of *his* style; and it is this particular realization of their value which is relevant, not their potential value in a standard system. If they are *not* used for a definite effect, all we can say is that they form for an individual style a background context more specialized than common speech would be — but they themselves are not style.

Now spoken individual styles are at best difficult to describe, easily stereotyped and therefore less differentiated from one another and from standard language than are written styles. Literary styles are complex, but for that very reason have features which permit clear differentiation. Hence I have chosen them for this heuristic experiment.

DISTINCTIVENESS OF LINGUISTIC COMMUNICATION IN LITERATURE

1.0. The features I have just mentioned do not characterize every reduction of language to writing; [4] they are those which can be exploited by an author with literary aims (two-dimensionality, for instance, could be included; but it is used mostly in technical languages, and in literature it seems to have remained, so far, extra-linguistic, e.g. poetry with lines printed in the shape of the object described). I shall attempt to describe briefly what seems to me two distinctive features of literary communication, and then to show that these features can serve to elaborate some criteria of existence for the stylistic fact.

1.1. The encoder. The task of the author as encoder of the message is more exacting than that of the speaker. A speaker has to triumph over his addressee's inertia, absent-mindedness, divergent or hostile train of thought; he has to emphasize repeatedly, and this overdoing is concentrated on the most important points of the discourse.[5] But the writer has to do much more to get his message across, for he lacks linguistic or extra-linguistic means of expression (intonation, gestures, etc.), for which he must substitute underscoring devices (hyperbole, metaphor, unusual word order, etc.). Moreover, the

[3] The difference between style and literary language was clearly seen by Yury Šerech, "Toward a Historical Dialectology: Its Delimitation of the History of Literary Language," *Orbis* III (1954), 43–57, but he centers his attention on literary language.

[4] E.g. the features defined by C. F. Hockett, *Course in Modern Linguistics* (New York, 1958), §62.5; for one thing, whenever a literary style aims at reproducing actual speech, it passes the boundaries of Hockett's *writing style.* Examples of literary two-dimensionality are to be seen in Mallarmé, "Un coup de dés," in Apollinaire, *Calligrammes,* in e. e. cummings' poetry, etc.

[5] For instance, wherever personal interest plays a role, as in the negation; good example of stylistic variety in H. Spitzbard, "Negationsverstärkungen im Englischen," *Die neueren Sprachen* II (1957), 73–83. On this "overdoing," see J. Marouzeau, *Traité de stylistique latine* (Paris, 1946), pp. 155ff.

speaker can adjust his speech to meet the addressee's needs and reactions; whereas the writer must anticipate all kinds of potential inattention or disagreement and give his devices a maximum efficiency valid for an unlimited number of addressees. And then there is the complexity of interplay between mere communication and the expressive, affective and aesthetic connotations (these latter exist in speech too, but the combinations cannot be so intricate as when built on paper at leisure; and the aesthetic intent is much less important).[6] The combination of connotations depends, naturally, on both the author's personality and his intentions.[7]

1.2. Control of the decoding. All this may sound self-evident, but I should now like to discuss how the encoder meets the challenge. Because the writer is obliged to be more forceful, has more to handle than the speaker, and has to write it down and later to correct it, he is *more conscious* of his message. The author's greater consciousness is not simply attention given to the encoding operation in order to make possible any prospective decoding: such attention is a necessary minimal condition for a written message anyway (e.g. in informal letters, in military orders: the addressee is expected to read them correctly, in his own interest, whereas the reader of novels may discard them, if not interested, without inconveniencing himself). The author's consciousness is his preoccupation with *the way he wants his message to be decoded,* so that not only its meaning but his attitude towards it is conveyed to the reader, and the reader is forced to understand, naturally, but also to share the author's view of what is or is not important in his message.

This means going counter to the natural behavior of the receiver. We know that most of the time the transmission of a spoken chain is effected elliptically, for "that context and the situation permit us to disregard a high percentage of the features, phonemes and sequences in the incoming message without jeopardizing its comprehension." [8] This is just as true of a written text where the reader infers words from fragmentary spelling features, and reconstructs the whole of a sentence from the few words he actually perceives. Because the probability of occurrence in the written chain varies for different features, "it is possible, from a part of the sequence, to predict with greater or lesser accuracy the succeeding features." Under these circumstances, the decoding

[6] The founder of modern stylistics, Ch. Bally, limited style to "expression des faits de la sensibilité par le langage" (*Traité de stylistique,* 1902; ed. 1951, I, no. 19), but he excluded literary style. Recently, Herbert Seidler tried to limit literary style to the language's emotive potentials (*Gemüthaftigkeit*); see his *Allgemeine Stilistik* (Göttingen, 1953), pp. 62, 70, 76, etc.

[7] This is so obvious that there is no point in separating "two fundamental ways of looking at style," one regarding literary style as an individual form of expression bearing the stamp of personality, the other seeing it as "the means of formulating our thoughts with the maximum of effectiveness," as S. Ullmann still does (*Style in the French Novel,* Cambridge, 1957, pp. 2ff.) following P. Guiraud's *Stylistique* (Paris, 1954).

[8] Roman Jakobson and Morris Halle, *Fundamentals of Language* (The Hague, 1956), §1.5. I use *ellipsis* and *explicitness* in accordance with the description of the *Fundamentals.*

is bound to be erratic, more so than with a spoken chain, since a serious lapse of attention can always be compensated by rereading; the interpretations of the reader will be freer, and the intentions of the author may be foiled. If he wants to be sure they are respected, he will have to control the decoding by encoding, at the points he deems important along the written chain, features that will be inescapable, no matter how perfunctory the reception. And since predictability is what makes elliptic decoding sufficient for the reader, *inescapable elements will have to be unpredictable.*

In spoken transmission, the utterer can resort to the explicit clear-speech form, instead of a blurred form. This substitution is obviously not possible in writing, since conventional spelling and grammatical correctness have already subjected the decoder to explicitness.[9] The only procedure open to the encoder, when he wants to impose his own interpretation of his poem, is thus to prevent the reader from inferring or predicting any important feature. For predictability may result in superficial reading; unpredictability will compel attention: the intensity of reception will correspond to the intensity of the message.[10]

Since such a control of the decoding is what differentiates expressivity from ordinary writing (which is indifferent to the mode of decoding provided decoding takes place), and since this differentiation corresponds to the complex of the author's message, we can see in it the *specific mechanism of individual style.*

It follows that an analysis of style based only on relevant features must concern itself with this fundamental mechanism. At the descriptive stage, it will be an application of information theory with special emphasis on the coding processes.[11] At the heuristic stage, our task is to gather the facts to be analyzed, namely the *elements which limit freedom of perception in the process of decoding*. If linguistic analysis cannot discriminate these elements from the irrelevant ones, it is because their potential is not realized in the physical body of the message, but in the receiver: thus the actual perception of the elements could be the criterion for their identification, and it seems that stylistics could use the reader as the listener is used in speech analysis.

[9] Italics and other typographical devices may be a substitute for explicitness, but this is rare (except in technical writing): e.g. in English, italics representing effective stress are mostly used for *do, have,* possessive and personal pronouns.

[10] The stylistic cancellation of normal predictability creates expressivity by a process similar to what happens when we test speech intelligibility. An announcer utters isolated root words which a listener endeavors to recognize correctly, without any context or situation to aid him in the task of discrimination: the word, "deprived of any prompting context, either verbal or non-verbal, [. . .] can be recognized by the listener only through its sound-shape. Consequently, in this situation the speech sounds convey the maximum amount of information" (Roman Jakobson, C. Gunnar M. Fant, Morris Halle, *Preliminaries to Speech Analysis,* Technical Report no. 13, MIT Acoustics Lab.; 2nd ed., 1955, p. 1).

[11] This may call for modification of Joshua Whatmough's adaptation of the communication diagram to literature in his *Poetic, Scientific and Other Forms of Discourse* (New York, 1956), p. 219.

1.3.0. Permanence of the message. Writing insures the physical survival of the literary message as the author conceived it; the patterns set for the control of decoding remain unchanged. But the decoders' linguistic frame of reference changes with the passing of time; the moment may even come when there is nothing left in common between the code to which the message refers and the code used by its readers. Meanwhile, the decoding of the poem's message reflects the extent to which the patterns of control suffer from the evolution of the code. This phenomenon has been neglected because its two faces (permanence of the code used in encoding and controlling; impermanence of the code used in decoding) have been considered separately; and this destroys its essence. The linguist, for instance, sees the poem as a mine of data for the reconstruction of a past state of the language. The stylistician tries to reconstitute the effects the poem's style had at the time of its creation, and to "correct" accordingly the reactions of modern readers. So much for the synchronic aspect; it is regarded from the viewpoint of the archaeologist. Others (critics and historians) devote themselves to retracing the evolution of readers' responses and how they confer upon the poem a value either ephemeral or eternal or renascent. These changes, however, are accounted for by the evolution of esthetic norms or by the content of the poem. The essential role of form perception is hardly considered.

1.3.1. I submit that the specific viewpoint of stylistics should encompass this simultaneity of permanence and change. It should *combine synchrony and diachrony,* which is made possible by the dichotomy between encoder and decoder. On the one hand, a state of the language, in its structural integrity and its pre-set stylistic patterns of decoding control frozen by writing. On the other hand, actualizations of the poem's potentials, by successive generations of decoders, within the limits of the poem's patterns and the readers' codes, conflicting or not. The study of this combination will provide the history of the prolongation of effects despite the gradual vanishing of the code of reference for which they had been prepared. At the same time it will provide, for all synchronies considered, one after another, a description of the adjustment of two anachronic systems (the encoder's and that of any later decoder) maintained in synchronic contact. From the linguistic viewpoint, the problem is absolutely different from that of the conservatism of writing style in the face of changing speech habits. It has nothing to do with partial resistances to evolution, but with the degree to which and the manner in which an immutable system can continue working in changing sets of reference, with a widening chasm between the author's and the reader's codes (whereas, in the evolution of a normal language system, encoders and decoders continue to have a common code). From the stylistic viewpoint, we can find in the survival of SDs as efficient units an experimental confirmation of the expressivity revealed by other means of investigation.

1.3.2. The combination diachrony–synchrony appears in another form, this time within the poem: in the use of archaisms as SDs. The stylistic specificity of archaisms lies in this: that they suppose a special code (common to encoder and decoder) characterized by the consciousness of past states of the language.[12] When into a context given forms are introduced which belong to a state of the language anterior to the context, they create a contrast which commands the attention of the reader. The archaism does function in the system of the context (and yet a synchronic description of the latter would overlook its archaic nature) but its function is twofold: as a linguistic unit it has its place reserved in the framework of simultaneous relationships; but as a stylistic unit it is decoded in reference to a second system, a past one whence the reader knows it comes (and yet a diachronic inquiry would overlook it as a functional element of the synchrony). The phenomenon of the archaism is certainly not novel — but the above reformulation has the advantage of having been done in stylistic terms.

Such reformulation will bring to light or permit explanation, by a few mechanic principles, of phenomena such as the following. The combination diachrony–synchrony which defines archaisms is contained in the poem's system and, physically, is as immutable as the other components of the system. However, integrated as it is with the exterior combination diachrony–synchrony, which represents the prolongation in time of the poem itself, the interior combination is modified by the exterior. As the unchanging poem grows chronologically older, i.e. is realized by readers further removed from its time of composition, the encoded divergence between the archaism and its context, and the resulting SD, disappear; the archaism and its context become an undifferentiated sequence which is felt to be either normal or archaic throughout.

Here again, during the life of the poem as well as at the time it was created, its actual perception by the reader, and the devices designed to insure it, are the essential characteristics of linguistic communication with literary intent.

[12] See L. Flydal, "Remarques sur certains rapports entre le style et l'état de langue," *Norsk Tidsskrift for Sprogvidenskap* XVI (1952), 241–258, especially pp. 244–248 (against Saussure who denied that the speaker is conscious of the linguistic past, *Cours de linguistique générale,* Paris, $_4$1949, pp. 117, 127; cf. Ch. Bally, *Traité de stylistique* I, no. 24). But Flydal weakens his demonstration when he extends the concept *archaism* to stereotyped phrases used normally in modern French (e.g. *à son corps défendant*), which are neither felt to be archaisms nor used stylistically as such. Furthermore, in order to justify his use of diachrony, Flydal treats archaisms as "incomplete systems" (*systèmes partiels,* p. 244) within the synchrony under investigation. He does this by shifting his definition from "parts of systems" (*partie des systèmes*) to "incomplete systems." This is a serious confusion. There are indeed complete archaic systems, extending to the whole of a poem (e.g. Balzac's *Contes drolatiques,* all written in "reconstituted" Middle French), but they are artificial. Moreover they are not a style but a kind of literary language, forming a background to style, a complete mimetic written standard (cf. 3.1.0 and footnote 24); such systems appear in fragmentary form, in historical novels, in the speech of the characters (e.g. *Kenilworth*).

Perception and Style Analysis

2.0. The stylistic type of communication defined above must now be located among the components of the written chain by means of criteria adapted to the nature of this type.

Since this communication is at the outset the author's response to an exceptional challenge, one would be tempted to start from his intentions and then to observe how they are realized in the text. But if the linguist has the relatively simple task of collecting all the features of speech of his informant without rejecting any, the stylistician must choose only those features which carry out the most conscious intentions of the author (which does not mean that the author's consciousness encompasses all the features). Now, it is often impossible to recognize these intentions except by analyzing the message, which makes the argument circular; or if they have become known by other means (philological enquiry, author's statement, etc.), they usually have a general character and cannot serve for the critique of specific passages. Finally, evaluating the realization of a writer's aims implies value judgments which belong to a metastylistic stage.

2.1. The use of the decoder in analysis. We have a better approach through the reader. For he is the consciously selected target of the author; the SD is so contrived that the reader cannot overlook it or even read without being guided by it to the essentials. Conversely the prolongation of stylistic effects in time as well as the perception of the poem at any given time depends entirely on the reader. This interdependence between the SD and its perception is, in short, so central to the problem that it seems to me we may use this perception to locate stylistic data in the literary discourse. Unfortunately taste changes and each reader has his prejudices. Our problem is to transform a fundamentally subjective reaction to style into an objective analytic tool, to find the constant (encoded potentialities) beneath the variety of judgments, in short to transform value judgments into judgments of existence. The way to do it is, I believe, simply to disregard totally the content of the value judgment and to treat the judgment *as a signal only*.

2.2. Analytic procedure. The procedural principle is the axiom "No smoke without fire." However right or wrong they may be, the value judgments of the reader are caused by some stimulus within the text. In the sender–receiver function which actualizes the poem, the receiver's behavior may be subjective and variable, but it has an objective invariable cause. In the linguistic message, more or less perceived, the passage from potential to actual style effect is a twofold phenomenon: first, the stylistic unit, and then, the aroused attention of the reader. It follows that stylistic investigation will have to use *informants*. These will provide us with reactions to the text: for instance, a native endowed with consciousness of the object language will read the text and the stylistician will draw from him his reactions. The segments of the text which cause his reactions, the informant will call in turn beautiful or unaesthetic, well or poorly written, expressive or flavorless; but the analyst will use these characterizations only as clues to the elements of the relevant structure. The analyst will not consider whether or not they are justified on the level of aesthetics. Furthermore, contrary to Bloomfield's rules for the use of informants in linguistic investigation,[13] it would be better to have cultivated informants who are prone to use the text as a pretext for a show of learning: they will notice more facts in their eagerness to make many comments and exaggerate the difference between what they call style and what they consider more "normal" expression. Such secondary responses, misleading in linguistics,[14] and possibly elicited by ephemeral fashions or prejudiced aesthetic beliefs, will not harm the objectivity of the inquiry because, once again, they will be recorded only as signals of what causes them. So far style analysts have started from their own judgments of value; they have habitually confused them with stylistic facts, a confusion which stems from normative rhetoric; and they have rationalized on the basis of this confusion, supplying motives or labeling it common-sense evidence. Quite to the contrary, I hold that the stimulus referred to and which prompted the reaction is indeed present; but it must be considered independently of the reaction once the reaction has helped delimit it. *Stripped of its formulation in terms of value, the secondary response becomes an objective criterion for the existence of its stylistic stimulus.*[15]

2.2.1. The core of the procedure here proposed lies in separating clearly the psychological processes and cultural conditioning of the perception from its stimulus. This is enough to differentiate the procedure from Spitzer's,[16] or to substitute objectivity for his impressionism. Spitzer draws from one detail an inference as to the psyche of the author, which hypothesis is then controlled by a scrutiny of other striking details occurring in the same text. Thus

[13] *Outline Guide for the Practical Study of Foreign Languages* (Baltimore, 1942), pp. 2–4.

[14] As Bloomfield showed during his controversy with Spitzer: L. Bloomfield, "Secondary and Tertiary Responses to Language," *Language* XX (1944), 45–55.

[15] I applied this criterion, without developing its theory, in my *Style des Pléiades de Gobineau; essai d'application d'une méthode stylistique* (mimeographed version, New York, 1955; printed revised ed., New York and Geneva, 1957). Hatzfeld (*Romanic Review* XLVIII [1957], p. 219) tried to assimilate my informant to Dámaso Alonso's reader-critic. He thus missed the essential point completely, i.e. that I disregard the reader's criticism as criticism. I observe it as a behavior. No matter how subjective the nature of a behavior (cf. G. Gougenheim, *Revue des sciences humaines,* no. 87, p. 344), its relation to a cause is an objective fact.

[16] In fact the present procedure develops and objectively formulates Spitzer's (cf. Juilland, *loc. cit.,* p. 321, footnote 7). See my "Réponse à M. Leo Spitzer: sur la méthode stylistique," *Modern Language Notes* LXXIII (1958), 474–480 (1958), especially, pp. 475–476 and 478. On Spitzer's method, see his *Linguistics and Literary History* (New York, 1948), 11–39, or his summary (with his reply to Wellek and Warren) in "Explication de texte," *Archivum linguisticum* III (1951), p. 1, footnote 1; also J. Hytier, *Romanic Review* XLI (1950), 42–59.

Spitzer builds on the first clue which thrusts itself upon his attention, indeed, on his own interpretation of it. This interpretation in turn rests upon the assumption that there is a relationship between a given feature of the discourse and a state of mind. Thus we have an isolated point of departure for an all-encompassing construction, a strong temptation to be subjective. In the procedure I propose the analyst will scrupulously avoid hypotheses on facts designated and will wait, before building a structure, until all signals collected constrain him by their interplay and convergence to an interpretation taking them all into account. What is more alarming still in Spitzer's method, the purported control by other striking details may cause the analyst unconsciously to exclude clues which might have struck him were it not for his preconceived construction. Not only has the stylistic stimulus been confused with the value judgment, but the control, applied to the judgment instead of its source, is exercised upon the coherence of the analyst's response rather than upon the text as it should be.

2.2.2. Aspects of the informant. The preceding does not imply that Spitzer's reactions cannot be used when reduced to their stimuli. And for that matter, any previous commentary on style can be used with this double proviso: that such critical comments or value judgments or applications of systems must have been formulated about specific textual passages, and that we will disregard their meaning absolutely. This is especially important for poems of the past; for the stylistician will be able to locate possible SDs each time he finds in previous editions or bodies of criticism a footnote to the text: it does not matter that this note was intended to clarify for lay readers what was thought to be a grammatical difficulty, a poetic licence or an obscure meaning. All such responses, regardless of terminology or viewpoint, have stimuli; and these may be stylistic. Error and bias are unimportant: misinterpreting facts still points to facts. Even a denial of stylistic value at any one point may imply stylistic value. (This, contrariwise, cannot apply to linguistic description which, by definition, is total, defines all the discrete elements of the recorded sequences while not separating those which are actually perceived from those which are not.)

The analyst himself may play the role of informant; but obviously he will have more trouble separating his own secondary responses from their stimuli than with other informants, and the more so as he re-reads. One could conceive of an experimental translation into another language as a type of informant: an instance of "free" translation might warn us that there was at that point a SD which defied literal translation. However, structural differences between languages, as well as SDs, may prompt the use of free translation; the problem would be further complicated by the second stylistic analysis on the translation.

These various types of informants will give us clues to the stimulus(i) encoded in the discourse. And for the stimulus(i) encoded in a poem of the past, the operation may be repeated for each generation of readers. The group of informants used for each stimulus or for a whole stylistic sequence will be called *Average Reader* (hereinafter AR).

2.2.3. The AR's metalanguage. Though we reject the AR's own interpretation of his reaction, it is useful to keep his technical terms, which constitute a fragmentary metalanguage borrowed mostly from the categories of rhetoric (metaphor, hyperbole, etc., or their common speech equivalents).[17] Such labels may be erroneous or not, like the value judgment which accompanies them, but they inform us about the linguistic consciousness of the AR's period in history and give us an idea of the effect of the SD's in relation to this Sprachgefühl: for instance, French Symbolist poets used a number of nouns in *-ance,* so many indeed that these nouns became a trademark of their style; for these poets these nouns were archaisms endowed with the quaint charm of things past. One of the most poetic was *assouvissance* and Flaubert made effective use of it; half a century later, when post-Symbolism had popularized this morpheme as a stylistic potential, Flaubert's archaism was reacted to and admired, now as a neologism.[18] The connotation of the word is not affected even if historical linguistics discovers that the element, foreign to the *état de langue* and interpreted as a neologism, is actually an archaism. Error for the linguist, fact for the stylistician. Metalinguistic distortions may serve as evidence of the diachronic extension of style effects (as outlined in 1.3.1).

2.3. Efficiency of the AR. Aside from the AR's ability to perceive the specific character of style, he is especially useful as a heuristic tool since his perception reproduces — indeed, it is the very process of — the phenomenon observed (decoding of the literary message), and it places the analyst in the decoders' own position without the latter's subjective liabilities. Instead of starting with an arbitrary, culture-conditioned, common-sense segmentation of the text or with an irrelevant (e.g. linguistic) one, the analyst is enabled to delimit the elements by which the author curbed the decoder's freedom (shallow reading, etc.) and increased the probability of perception. Thanks to the AR, the analyst can observe how the very efficiency of these SDs keeps them operative despite linguistic evolution. Thus we can fuse into one the study of style in its genesis and original context, and the study of its survival in time, with all that these teach us about successive synchronic time-slices in the language.

For style analysis proper, the AR should permit a directness and a rapidity

[17] An extension of this notion to the use of traditional grammatical terms by the informant would be wrong. The stylistic effect often overlaps linguistic units. A grammatical term such as *adjective* may cover various SDs: metaphor, expressive word-order unit, rhythm, etc. Even when style and grammar units do coincide, to start from grammar would be to run the risk of assigning a permanent stylistic value to a linguistic unit, no matter what the context.

[18] Alex. François, *La Désinence* -ance *dans le vocabulaire français* (Geneva, 1950), p. 36.

impossible with other approaches: this is evident in the case of elusive facts, such as the emotive connotation of gender in Fr. *mer* (f.) or *océan* (m.). But take simpler cases such as the expressivity of a periphrasis, a very common SD, stylistically efficient because the reader feels it as an unusual substitute for a commonplace noun. For the linguist, the structure used for the periphrasis has nothing to distinguish it from the norm; only a complex computation of probabilities of occurrence could reveal anything exceptional there and even so could not guarantee that this something is perceived. Still the AR's reactions will pinpoint it at once.

Stylistic Context

3.0. Shortcomings of the AR criterion. However practical and objective it may be, the AR criterion suffers from a double limitation:

3.0.1. The variety of actual decoders may conceivably result in such a pulverization of the structure of the text that the resulting segmentation into stylistic units would be too complex to be interpreted. (In fact, even superficial observation of readers' opinions on books and a survey of published criticism on given poems indicate that the dangerous dispersion does not occur until the interpretative stage: once the widely conflicting value judgments are weeded out, we find they all sprang from relatively few points in the text.)

3.0.2. The AR's validity is limited to the state of the language he knows: his linguistic consciousness, which conditions his reactions, does not reach beyond a short span of time in the evolution of his language. Hence two categories of error. (1) Errors of addition: normal, hence irrelevant linguistic elements of a past state of the language look like stylistic units (e.g. archaisms), because they have disappeared from the language system used by the readers and therefore strike them as abnormal. (2) Errors of omission (which are, by the way, beyond the reach of linguistic analysis): relevant stylistic elements of the poem are in time assimilated into standard usage; they become and look like normal irrelevant speech units in a later state of the language, ceasing accordingly to be noticeable to the readers; thus they lose their effect.

An example of omission is French *réussite* 'successful achievement,' which does not produce any stylistic effect; no modern informant will be able to feel the effect it had in a 17th-century text on a 17th-century reader because *réussite* (as opposed to *heureux succès,* a synonym void of stylistic value) was a bold novelty: at that time everyone sensed it as a recent borrowing from Italian *riuscita.* An error of addition would occur, in turn, now that *réussite* has lost its pristine vigor and *succès* no longer needs the adjective *heureux* to be a synonym of *réussite.* Consequently, *heureux succès* is felt as an archaism and is used now as an expressive equivalent of *réussite.* Yet the informant who gives it this expressive value in a 17th-century text is wrong, since it was then normal.

Such AR reactions are one of the interesting consequences of the poem's extension in time (see 1.3ff.). The errors of omission (obviously distinguished from the additions which never were style) are errors *only in the synchrony* represented by the poem at its birth: their identification concerns only the literary historian and the stylistician studying the constants of literary language of the time and their use as background style (see 0.3). But in the diachronic prolongation of that recorded synchrony, they are *not* errors, they are stylistic facts; they correspond to the invariable elements of the poem's frozen system, elements whose reference to the code varies with the modifications of this code, i.e. with the successive states of the language which, in turn, correspond to the successive generations of readers.

3.1.0. Irrelevance of the linguistic norm. The limitations outlined above make it imperative to add new criteria to complete and control AR's results. The SDs are, we remember, unpredictable for the decoder, against the background pattern of predictability offered by the frame of the language. Would it then be possible to discover the SD in any deviation from the linguistic norm? Most stylisticians believe so,[19] but it is difficult to see how we can use the deviation as a criterion, or even how we can describe it.

Against its use as a criterion, Juilland (*loc. cit.,* 1.6–1.7) raised strong objections based chiefly on its limitation in scope: if we are to see style in the deviation from the norm, we will have to limit style to what is left of the written chain after eliminating every element which we can describe in its totality through linguistic analysis, and must therefore define as normal. But the answer is that we cannot then account for the fact that this very material we now reject may play a stylistic role when seen in other relationships.[20] And furthermore, the analysis will be warped in any case, because the departure from the norm is an ambiguous factor oscillating between consciousness (style) and automatism (unconscious mistake, mechanical imitation or self-imitation). (It will be noted that, of these weaknesses inherent in the criterion, the first could be obviated by the use of AR reactions, if this did not create a vicious circle.) Thus, if we were to use the linguistic norm at all, these limitations would dictate a complex, hardly practical set of precautions.

Now, to this use of the norm I see an objection which is more fundamental

[19] L. Spitzer, *Linguistics and Literary History,* p. 11; J. Mukařovský, "Standard Language and Poetic Language," in *A Prague School Reader,* P. L. Garvin, ed. (Washington, 1955), 19–35, especially pp. 20, 25, 31, 33; Wellek and Warren, *Theory of Literature* (Harvest Books, ed. 1956), pp. 166, 169, 171; R. A. Sayce, *Style in French Prose* (Oxford, 1953), pp. 1, 88, 131; Ch. Bruneau, "La Stylistique," *Romance Philology* V (1951–1952), 1–14, especially p. 6; P. Guiraud, "Stylistiques," *Neophilologus* XXXVIII (1954), 1–12, especially 7–8.

[20] The sorting out of all stylistic features which I suggested in 0.1 does not have this disadvantage. I select elements only because of their actual value in a definite context; without the context, they are neutral and free to form any or no stylistic associations.

than those just mentioned, namely not so much that the linguistic norm is virtually unobtainable,[21] but that it is irrelevant. It is irrelevant because the readers base their judgments (and the authors their devices) not on an ideal norm, but on their individual concepts of what is the accepted norm (e.g. what the reader "would have said" in the author's place). These multiple norms are given some common traits by normative grammar.[22] Can we at least evaluate them with some approximation to accuracy? An overall norm, even for a short period of history and for a single social class, will not do, because even a relatively stable state of the language is the theater of transformations that style is likely to reflect.[23] Aside from the author's milieu, we have to take into account his readings, his literary affiliations and probably a second standard, the written norm. This again will not suffice: modern literatures offer many instances of a third standard (I should call it the *mimetic written norm*), which is a very fragmentary system the writer uses to suggest substandard speech.[24] All these norms should be taken into account and our task should be done over for each generation of readers. Even

[21] As Juilland points out (*loc. cit.*, p. 318, footnote 5); he seems however to have hesitated before the radical conclusion: total rejection of the norm. To his arguments, of a logical nature, against the possibility of establishing a norm, another argument could be added, based on the importance of perception in matters of style: if the linguistic norm is presented in the form of frequencies and probabilities of occurrence, it must be recognized that a considerable gap exists between a divergence quantitatively expressed and the threshold of its actual perception by the reader; he seldom perceives any but wide divergences. There are deviations with stylistic effect, and others without.

[22] Which in turn is too conservative to be really used as a norm. It is true that some countries respect the grammarians' edicts more than others. In French style it is possible to discern the influence of a grammatical norm artificially imposed (see L. C. Harmer, *The French Language Today,* London, 1954, 11–46). This, however, is exceptional. German literature provides an example of a totally different situation.

[23] Cf. C. F. Hockett, "The Terminology of Historical Linguistics," *Studies in Linguistics* XII (1957), 57–73, especially 63–64.

[24] I do not have in mind consistent efforts towards real imitation but the conventional reproduction of a few typical forms of substandard speech, with spelling changes to indicate a given pronunciation (a good example of both imitation and mimetic written norm is G. B. Shaw's *Pygmalion*, Act I). Since the system is incomplete, the discrepancy between the narrative proper and the characters' speech is smaller; but this incompleteness follows a regular pattern, e.g. modern French conjugation, first person, and second person formal:

Substandard Speech	Mimetic Written Norm	Written Norm
[ʃsɛpɑ] [ʃʃɛpɑ]	*je sais pas*	*je ne sais pas*
[vusavɛpɑ]		*vous ne savez pas*

I am using examples from Bj. Ulvestad, *An Approach to Describing Usage of Language Variants* (Indiana University Publications in Anthropology and Linguistics 12, 1956), p. 43; he does not distinguish a mimetic written norm. I here correct his assumptions concerning French facts, which require the concept of a third norm. There is still another possibility: the creation of a mimetic norm by an author in order to particularize a character rather than a social class. It does not correspond to an accepted usage and could be termed *nonce-standard:* it would be interesting to see how far this can go without making the decoding impossible (a good example of nonce-standard is Shylock's speech: O. Jespersen, *Growth and Structure of the English Language*, London, ₉1938, §231).

if the notion of norm must be retained for the interpretative stage of stylistics, it cannot be used at the heuristic stage.

3.1.1. The context as a norm. At this stage, however, there is a way of avoiding the application to the text of a vague koiné or of a shifting Sprachgefühl: that is, by substituting the context for the norm.[25] Each SD, tentatively identified by the AR, has as its context a concrete, permanent background; one does not exist without the other. The hypothesis that context plays the role of the norm and that style is created by a deviation from it is a fruitful one. If in the style-norm relationship we understood the norm pole to be universal (as it would be in the case of the linguistic norm), we could not understand how a deviation might be a SD on some occasions and on others, not. For, if the variation from the general norm is constant, then the effect must be constant too. To cite an example, an unusual word-order such as, in Modern French, the Verb–Subject order (VS), when it is neither interrogative nor preceded by an adverb, is always abnormal and constitutes a constant deviation: we would expect it to be constantly expressive; yet it is *ceteris paribus* now a device for stressing the verb, now an indifferent sequence. Nor could we understand that a linguistic unit whose role is in certain relationships purely functional can become a SD elsewhere; nor again that a worn-out SD, having become a cliché without effect, can be rejuvenated and can regain expressivity on a background of ordinary speech; nor, finally, that the so-called 'naked styles' like Voltaire's, which seem never to depart from the simplest forms of everyday usage, could have any distinctiveness. The variability of effect of a constant anomaly is on the contrary immediately explained if the pole of opposition varies as well; and this pole varies by definition if it is the context. In the example cited above, the abnormal VS order (1) is linguistically constantly abnormal; (2) is expressive in a context where the preceding clauses present the normal SV order; (3) is no longer expressive if it appears in a context with a high frequency of VS order. Because of this frequency the reader's Sprachgefühl, which normally warns him of the VS anomaly, is dulled; the occurrence of one more VS unit becomes highly probable — in other words, the norm. There is no longer a style-creating contrast. Confirmation of this interpretation may be seen in the stylistic evolution of the last thirty years: the VS order has been so popular a SD that it tends to lose its expressivity in contrasting contexts, and it is now used for the most part as a conventional unit of the written standard.[26]

The application of the context as a criterion and as a corrective to the AR's shortcomings is easy: if there is no contextual contrast at the point where

[25] Used as another criterion, along with the AR method, this mechanical contrast with context should not leave much to the subjective Sprachgefühl (cf. L. Hjelmslev and H. Uldall, *Outline of Glossematics*, part I, Copenhagen, 1957, p. 3).

[26] On this typical example, see R. Le Bidois, *L'Inversion du sujet dans la prose contemporaine* (Paris, 1952), xvii + 448 pp.; the facts are presented from the grammarian's viewpoint; this obscures at times the stylistic reality.

AR's reaction indicates the probable presence of a stylistic stimulus (that is, if the hypothetical SD and its context do not present any discrepancy, such as a difference of social level between words, entailing conflicting connotations, or a different word-order, or a change from parataxis to hypotaxis, etc.), then we can assume that there was on the part of the AR an over-response to the text (cf. 3.0.1) or an error by addition (cf. 3.0.2). In that case we may safely dismiss the initial clue.

3.2.1. Definition of the stylistic context. Since stylistic intensification results from the insertion of an unexpected element into a pattern, it supposes an effect of rupture which modifies the context. This brings out a radical difference between 'context' in its common sense and stylistic context. A stylistic context is not associative, it is not the verbal context which reduces polysemy or adds a connotation to a word.[27] The stylistic context is a linguistic *pattern suddenly broken by an element which was unpredictable,* and the contrast resulting from this interference is the stylistic stimulus. The rupture must not be interpreted as a dissociating principle. The stylistic value of the contrast lies in the relationship it establishes between the two clashing elements; no effect would occur without their association in a sequence. In other words, the stylistic contrasts, like other useful oppositions in language, create a structure.[28] A consequence of the principle of contrast is that it enables us to draw the line easily between a personal style and a literary language: literary language in a poem needs no contrast; it is in fact a predictable pattern, whose linguistic elements receive no stylistic value from merely belonging to the language (e.g., Latin *letum* is the poetic-language equivalent of *mors* 'death' and is nothing more than the predictable substitute of *mors* in the poetic context); should the same elements appear in a context where no such conventional words are expected, they will be SDs (e.g., *letum* in familiar poetry has an ironical effect; Horace, *Sat.* 2,6,95, places it in the mouth of his philosophizing city-mouse).

3.2.2. Let us examine more closely the stylistic context. The patterning which conditions the reader for the "surprise" follows necessarily the progression of the sequences. The context could be represented as a linear segment oriented in the direction of the eye's progress in reading a line. Along this vector, information, forms, and the memory of preceding sequences will accumulate. The more clearly delineated the pattern is, the more effective the contrast will be (e.g., a narrative context with verbs in the past tense leading to the contrast of a single historical present; a series of rhetorical periodic sentences leading to the contrast of a sequence of short asyndetic nominal sentences).

[27] See S. Ullmann, *Principles of Semantics* (Oxford, 2nd ed., 1957), pp. 60–63, 109.
[28] Cf. H. J. Pos, "La Notion d'opposition en linguistique," *Onzième Congrès International de Psychologie* (Paris, 1938), p. 245.

Two corollaries to this definition can be formulated. First, the stylistic context has a narrowly finite extension, limited by the memory of what has just been read and by the perception of what is now being read; the context follows the reader, so to speak, covering all the sequences of the discourse. This explains the *polyvalence* of the SD, that is, the capacity for one device to give rise to many effects (e.g., a given word-order can stylistically affect any group of words where order is variable, regardless of the meaning which is stressed).[29] Second, there can be an overlapping of stylistic units: if we define such units as Context+SD, it may happen that the SD establishes a new pattern and thus becomes the beginning of a context which is the first member of the next stylistic unit. For instance, aside from the type Context→SD→Return to context, we may have the type Context→SD starting new context→SD (e.g., for the first type, normal statement→hyperbole→normal statement; for the second type, normal statement→hyperbole→hyperbolic context→litotes). These occurrences imply that there is no such thing as an instrinsically stylistic device (e.g., an hyperbole in an hyperbolic context will pass unnoticed).

Borderline cases exist where the stylistic effect seems to stem less from contrast than from a cluster of SDs. The presence of such groups may become for the analyst a supplementary criterion.

3.2.3. Context and convergence. By stylistic clusters, I do not mean phenomena like the special case of phonetic expressivity where sounds seem to the reader to echo the meaning of words (*harmonie imitative, Lautmalerei*). The SD's effect supposes a combination of semantic and phonetic values; either one, separated from the other, would remain potential. I mean instead the accumulation at a given point of several independent SDs. Alone, each would be expressive in its own right. Together, each SD adds its expressivity to that of the others. In general, the effects of these SDs converge into one especially striking emphasis. For example, in Melville, *Moby Dick,* Chap. 51:

> And heaved and heaved, still unrestingly heaved the black sea, as if its vast tides were a conscience.

There is here an accumulation of (1) an unusual VS word-order; (2) the repetition of the verb; (3) the rhythm created by this ternary repetition (plus the combination of this phonetic device with the meaning: the rise and fall of the waves is "depicted" by the rhythm); (4) the intensive coordination (*and . . . and . . .*), reinforcing the rhythm; (5) a nonce word (*unrestingly*) which by its very nature will create a surprise in any context; (6) the metaphor emphasized by the unusual relationship of the concrete (*tides*) to

[29] On the mechanism of *polyvalence,* see my *Style des Pléiades,* p. 211 and passim; S. Ullmann, *Style in the French Novel,* pp. 9, 20.

the abstract (*conscience*) instead of the reverse. Such a heaping up of stylistic features working together I should like to call *convergence*.[30]

We have here a good example of the extent to which decoding can be controlled by the author. In the above instance it is difficult for the reader not to give his attention to each meaningful word. The decoding cannot take place on a minimal basis because the initial position of the verb is unpredictable in the normal English sentence, and so is its repetition. The repetition has a double role of its own, independent of its unpredictability: it creates the rhythm, and its total effect is similar to that of explicit speech (cf. 1.2). The postponement of the subject brings unpredictability to its maximum point; the reader must keep in mind the predicate before he is able to identify the subject. The "reversal" of the metaphor is still another example of contrast with the context. The reading speed is reduced by these hurdles, attention lingers on the representation, the stylistic effect is created.

We can find instances where the stylistic effect does not seem to imply any material context; in such instances, the convergence alone supplies the SD: it is the case for compressed poetic forms, such as the Japanese *hai-kai,* the prose poem (here *poem* is used in its common meaning), the monostich or one-line poem, and its corresponding prose form, the aphorism. In another case, the convergence is our only resource: the stylistic investigation of the beginning of any literary utterance. Here there is no patterning preparatory to contrast.

3.2.4. The convergence lowers the threshold of perceptibility of the SD, because of its cumulative nature; it may also function as a semantic context, limiting the polysemy of the word it stresses; thus the intentions of the author are made more clear. On the other hand the convergence is the only SD which we can describe with certainty as a conscious device; even if the convergence is first formed unconsciously or if it is accidental, it cannot escape the author's eye when he re-reads. Whether it be simply maintained or elaborated, it represents a case of extreme awareness in the use of language and may be the most complex stylistic form.

The usefulness of the convergence as a criterion is evident. Suppose a SD noted by the AR, but not presenting a clear-cut contrast with the preceding context; if it presents a convergence, its stylistic reality will be proven. Moreover, the convergence may give us an opportunity to correct the AR's errors of omission: even if there is no longer a common code, shared by author and reader, as is the case for medieval literatures, there is hope that analysis may identify, in the text, converging elements whose presence will reveal the SD which is no longer felt.

Indeed convergences may be the stylistic factor which insures the survival

[30] Convergence as a device was briefly noted by Marouzeau, *Traité de stylistique latine* (1946), 339–340, who saw its heuristic value, but did not suspect its importance in the "prolongation" of the poem's life.

of the system encoded in the poem. If, in a convergence, successive generations of readers cease to perceive some of the component SDs because they no longer create contrasts in the new codes of reference (e.g., when a neologism has been assimilated to ordinary vocabulary; when a metaphor has become a cliché of the standard literary language, etc.), there is a chance that at least one of the components will be preserved as a stimulus of expressivity and will continue to represent the complex of decoding-control devices which had been placed there by the author.

CONCLUSION

To make stylistics a science, or to delimit that area of linguistics which will treat the literary use of language, it is not sufficient to begin from a subjective apprehension of the elements of style. It therefore seemed obvious that a heuristic stage should precede any attempt at description. The criteria presented here should permit objective determination of the facts: as criteria, context and convergence require only the observation of forms without prejudgment of their content or value; with the AR, value judgments are utilized only insofar as they reveal stimuli.

The criteria are specific because they correspond to the distinctive features of the poem. I have attempted to describe these literary features as a special case of linguistic communication, characterized by a modification of the coding processes and by the permanence of the literary message. If this reformulation is found useful, it will be because it tries to account for facts economically, without artificial separation of language and style. Once stylistic facts have been identified, linguistic analysis, applied to them only, will be relevant; prior to their identification, it cannot alone isolate them.

Michael Riffaterre

STYLISTIC CONTEXT

1.1. The definition of literary style as a departure from the linguistic norm raises difficulties of application in style analysis. In a previous paper [1] I therefore proposed to replace the notion of overall norm with that of stylistic context, and to study stylistic devices (hereinafter *SD*) in relation to this context. The context, by definition inseparable from the SD, (1) is automatically relevant (which is not necessarily true of the norm); (2) is immediately accessible because it is encoded, so that we need not rely on an elusive and subjective *Sprachgefühl;* (3) is variable and constitutes a series of contrasts to the successive SDs. Only this variability can explain why a linguistic unit acquires, changes, or loses its stylistic effect according to position, why every departure from the norm is not necessarily a fact of style, and why style effects occur without abnormality.[2]

1.2. The meaning of a message can be received with minimal decoding. More is required if the writer wants to force upon his reader's attention certain formal features to which he attaches special importance (e.g. esthetic intent). But what permits minimal decoding is that it is possible with variable accuracy to predict, from part of a sequence, the features which follow. Control of the decoding, then, is achieved through low predictability.[3] We can therefore define the stylistic context as a pattern broken by an unpredictable element (this contrasting factor being the SD).

Reprinted from *Word,* Volume 16, No. 2 (August, 1960), by permission.

[1] In my "Criteria for Style Analysis" (hereinafter *Criteria*), *Word* XV (1959), 154–174, esp. §§3.0–3.2.4 *; see also my review of S. Ullmann's *Style in the French Novel,* in *Word* XV (1959), 404–413, esp. pp. 407–409.

[2] On this variability of effects, or *polyvalence,* see my review cited footnote 1, page 409. Similarly, L. Spitzer, after comparing — with a very different approach — more styles than any stylistician ever had, concluded that the stylistic sign is "empty" (see, for example, *Modern Language Quarterly,* XIX [1958], 235, footnote 8).

[3] See *Criteria,* §§1.1–1.2.

* *Editors' Note:* Reprinted here pp. 423–430.

Style is not a string of SDs, but of binary oppositions whose poles (context/SD) cannot be separated. Far from concentrating on the SDs just because they are the salient, easily classified features, style analysis (and later, esthetic metanalysis) must devote as much attention to the unmarked elements of the oppositions. This paper, mostly orientational, seeks to give as simple and complete an account as possible of the various aspects of the context.

1.3. Two categories of facts require an expansion of the above definition: *A*. Certain literary pieces are so short that they seem not to have "time" to form the contextual pattern which permits contrasts: e.g., *haiku,* monostich, prose aphorism, motto, epigraph, etc.;[4] other similar cases: the beginning of literary utterances and the clusters of SDs, or *convergences,*[5] where the accumulation of SDs does not seem to allow enough context between them to prevent saturation (and yet saturation does not occur). *B*. The context could be represented by a linear segment, following the decoding process, therefore oriented in the same direction as the sentences. The existence of this orientation is implied by the process of reading, by word order devices, and by rhythms. However, in short texts, like those mentioned above, the SDs can be recorded at a glance, or the end of the passage can be perceived, in advance of actual reading, by peripheral vision.[6] Furthermore, even in texts of ordinary length, the reader can always reread what stopped him in his first casual decoding.[7] In all these cases, we may wonder whether the effect of surprise does not dwindle and whether orientation is not intermittent. These limitations to the scope of the definition can be removed if we introduce a distinction between context inside and outside of SD, that is, between the context which creates the opposition constituting the SD, and the context which modifies this opposition by reinforcing or weakening it. This solution makes

[4] The size limits of this type are very narrow: a poem hardly longer than a monostich, such as the Latin elegiac distich, would not fall in the same category, since the complexity of the metric pattern makes up for its brevity. Quotations from other authors must also be excluded, because they are provided with a new context. Dictionaries of quotations, on the contrary, should be included: they are meta-texts only for the style analysis of a literary work as a whole, but isolated, without consideration of the compiler's reasons for excerpting them, they may be studied to determine to what extent a context can be cut off without destruction of the stylistic effect.

[5] On this phenomenon and its name, see *Criteria* §3.2.3. It is encoded in the written text and must not be confused with the concurrence of several sets of signals, such as can be observed in the *performance* of certain oral literary forms (see T. A. Sebeok, "Folksong Viewed as Code and Message," *Anthropos* LIV [1959], 141–153, esp. 141–42).

[6] On perception in reading (word recognition, peripheral vision, etc.), see the handy summary of M. A. Tinker, "Visual Apprehension and Perception in Reading," *Psychological Bulletin* XXVI (1929), 223–240; the yearly summaries of "Reading Investigation" by Wm. S. Gray in the *Journal of Educational Research.*

[7] It may be an almost unconscious re-reading by peripheral vision; or a conscious search for the solution of some decoding problem: this search entails several simultaneous Markov processes working forward and backward (see a good example in A. A. Hill, "An Analysis of *The Windhover:* An Experiment in Structural Method," *Publications of the Modern Language Association* LXX (1955), 968–978, esp. 975–976).

it unnecessary to assume the existence of two styles of different natures, whose "cohabitation" within the same text would be hard to explain, and enables us to outline a hierarchy of structures without gaps or incompatibilities, wherein higher levels of structure can be stated in terms of the units of the preceding level. I shall call the first type *microcontext* (rather than segmental) and the second *macrocontext.*

2.1. Definition of the microcontext. (The term *context* here is not taken in its common meaning; it is considered independently from any influence of the macrocontext, although such an influence always exists, except under the conditions described in 1.3.*A;* this special use of *context* may be awkward, but does not seem much more objectionable than, say, the coexistence of a linguistic and a common sense *redundancy*). Let there be in a (literary) sequence a group of features bound together on one or more levels of the linguistic system by a structural and semantic relationship. If the group has a stylistic effect, its stimulus consists of less predictable elements encoded in one or more constituents. The microcontext consists of the other constituents which remain unmarked; contrast is created in opposition to these constituents (the reader perceives the degree of unpredictability in relation to them).[8] The group as a whole (context + contrast) forms the SD. The essential characteristics of the microcontext are: (1) it has a structural function as a pole of a binary opposition, and consequently: (2) it has no effect without the other pole; (3) it is spatially limited by its relationship to that pole (in other words, it does not encompass elements irrelevant to the opposition and may be limited to one linguistic unit). Its constituents can be multiple, discontinuous (e.g., the disjunct group in a disjunction), or simultaneous (e.g., the unchanged part of a renewed cliché, the blended words in a portmanteau word).

It should be possible to build a (stylistic) grammar of the conditions under which contrasts occur; some of their aspects are obvious enough to permit the establishment of relative measurements; for example, the effectiveness of the contrast is in direct proportion to its degree of unpredictability, that is, to the degree of predictability allowed by the internal context.[9]

Ex. (1*a*) Corneille, *Cid,* I.1273: *Cette obscure clarté qui tombe des étoiles* (semantic contrast; both *obscure* and *clarté,* as separate units, have a high determinacy, since the topic is the military use of darkness; but as constituents of a single structure, they form the least probable unit; *clarté* stands in contrast with the context *obscure; obscure clarté* is the SD apprehensible as a

[8] It is obvious that I do not start my analysis from this unmarked element (at the present stage, this would amount to falling back upon the concept of norm), but from the contrast immediately perceived by the reader; for a discussion of this approach, see *Criteria,* Chap. 2.

[9] Like this paper, the examples given are orientational: they are introduced as further clarification; but no measurement will be attempted in the present study. Once again, I am trying only to provide a coherent organization of materials, using nothing but relevant features.

unit, which is demonstrated by the frequent quotation since then of *obscure clarté* as an isolated phrase).[10]

(1*b*) Use of certain prepositions for others, different in function, such as French *à* for *en, sur, sous;* or of conjunctions stripped of their function, such as *car* used where no causative construction is in order (both devices were characteristic of the French Symbolist school);[11] such SDs are strong because they affect the very structure of the grammatical system.

(1*c*) Pope, *Rape of the Lock,* II, 105–109: *Whether the Nymph shall* (. . .) *stain her Honour, or her new Brocade,* (. . .) *Or lose her Heart, or Necklace, at a Ball.* (syllepsis:[12] the metaphorical meaning of the verb in the two contexts — *stain her honour, lose her heart* — makes the shift to its ordinary meaning unpredictable; this and the resulting forced parallels *honour / brocade, heart / necklace* impose maximal decoding).

In each case the context compensates for its brevity by narrowly limiting the reader's choice of predictions.

2.2. Microcontexts in short sequences. Thus it is clear that microcontexts make style possible even in a short sequence. It is enough that the sequence contain one or more SDs or a convergence of SDs; these exclude casual decoding. Ex. (2) Emily Dickinson, *Bolts of Melody,* Fragment 635: *Or fame erect her siteless citadel* (a case of self-sufficient style, since this isolated line was found noted on the flap of an envelope, indicating the writer's desire to preserve a form rather than a content. Stylistically, *fame erect* and *siteless citadel* contain each a contrast which in both cases impose metaphorical interpretations; *citadel* is more predictable in the frame *erect X,* but the contrast is immediately reestablished by *siteless;* furthermore *siteless* is expressive because it is a nonce-word in opposition to words of the common code and because it forms a contrast — non-existence versus existence — to both *erect* and *citadel*).

In short sequences, there is no macrocontext to heighten the effect of a SD (§3.2.); on the other hand, none diminishes it either (§3.3.).

2.3. Maximal decoding. There remains the question of the surprise effect, which must be distinguished from the unpredictability which causes it. The latter defines statistically a certain mode of occurrence. The SD presenting this occurrence may well be perceived at a glance or anticipated by peripheral reading: this will undoubtedly lessen the surprise effect. But it cannot dimin-

[10] Note that *clair-obscur* does not appear in French until 40 years later, and then only in its Italian form and in technical parlance: there was no association susceptible of weakening the SD.

[11] See L. Spitzer, *Aufsätze zur romanischen Syntax und Stilistik* (1918), pp. 289ff.

[12] This example is borrowed from Justin O'Brien, "Proust's Use of Syllepsis," *PMLA* LXIX (1954), 741–752; this article can be used as a monograph on syllepsis in general. On zeugma, closely related to syllepsis, see G. O. Rees, *Français Moderne,* XXII (1954), 287–295; R. Le Bidois, *ibid.,* XXIV (1956), 81–89, 259–270.

ish the sense of abnormality (abnormality *hic et nunc,* not in relation to the awareness of the norm) which results in increased attention, i.e. maximal decoding.

Rereading, for example, may resolve a semantic ambiguity, but it does not modify the order of the contextual elements; we do not read backwards, we jump back and then move again in the usual direction. Our memory, now working forward, informs us of what is to follow, and in fact destroys surprise; but, by the same token, we again pass through the forms whose unpredictable arrangement had necessitated rereading, and this process imprints them more deeply than did the initial surprise.[13]

On the other hand, predictability in itself is not an absolute, except within stereotypes. This permanent uncertainty, and the margin which must exist between statistical and perceived unpredictabilities would reduce surprise (although it remains basic in devices such as: syllepsis; anacoluthon — breaking off of the sentence when it has reached the point where readers can guess the end —; adverb where an adjective has a higher probability). Perhaps this is the reason why surprise is frequently supplemented by the effect of the macrocontext (see §3.2.). Within the microcontext, however, the fact that the reader is forced into a more thorough decoding is enough to account for the functioning of the SD, even if surprise is entirely absent. Such maximal decoding is dictated, for instance, by disjunctive word-order: the interruption of the sentence compels the reader to make an effort of retention and attention until the sequence is resumed. Ex. (3) E. M. Forster, *Collected Tales* ("Other Kingdom"), p. 82: *My name is Harcourt Worters — not a well-known name if you go outside the City and my own country, but a name which /, where it is known /, carries /, I flatter myself /, some weight.* (The disjunctions would not suffice to nullify the predictability of the word sequence, especially after *carries* which introduces a stereotype. What brings out the speaker's pompous, self-righteous vanity, what produces the contrast is the suspension of the sentence after *which.*)

Effects of surprise can be combined with those of maximal decoding (e.g. when, after the disjunction, the sentence is not resumed in the expected or most probable fashion, but with a different construction or vocabulary).

3.0. Definition of the macrocontext. The macrocontext is that part of the literary message which precedes the SD and which is exterior to it. (It is this type of context which is closest to *context* in its everyday meaning.) Since

[13] Cf. the related question of the duration of stylistic effects through successive "performances" of the text (see *Criteria* 1.3.0–1.3.1; Wellek and Warren, *Theory of Literature,* 1956, Chap. XII). The conditions of unpredictability are maintained in the "frozen" structure of the message; thus successive performers will be exposed to the same phenomenon. For a reader "performing" repeatedly, memorization will cancel unpredictability, but will preserve the formal characteristics of the text. Whether memorized or unexpected, style remains an active factor. As for literary imitation, it renews the SD by transferring it to a new context (e.g. Vergil using Homeric devices): this last process is no different from the use of a cliché in a new environment.

its decoding supposes a spatial orientation, we see that the phrase *oriented linear segment* in our preliminary definition applies to this context: it could not have applied to the microcontext. This characteristic permits the storing up of information which will ultimately modify the effect of the compound (microcontext/contrast) SD.

The terminus of the context is known by definition; its starting point is not. Insofar as its effect on the SD is known through the reader's reactions, the point of the earliest perception of context might be said to vary in function of the reader's attention and memory, that is, his ability to recognize formal similarities and dissimilarities. On the other hand, if the SD is a rupture effect, it is tempting to conclude that the context reaches back to the last occurrence of an identical or similar SD. Such a solution, however, would not account for cases where the context precedes a hapax phenomenon, and cases where the SD is a *tic* of the author's speech (in this instance, a given form is surprising and easily noticeable because it is characterized by recurrences in semantic or situational contexts, where it has no conditioning other than psychological; a *tic* then is recalled over lengths of text whose extent and variety far exceed what could be reasonably attributed to the context as a functional unit). The starting point cannot be seen in *any* SD preceding the one under study, since, as we shall see (§3.1.), macrocontexts may contain SDs. It cannot be said that any linguistic boundary, such as the limit of a sentence, marks *de facto* the starting point of a context, since stylistic effects may overlap linguistic units (although, in fact, the context often starts with a paragraph or other punctuation).[14]

Probably we should here admit a certain area of indeterminacy, perhaps a permanent one if we consider that any notion of limit in style analysis is only approximate because of the reader's variable threshold of perception. The starting point can then be identified more closely if we use the very definition of the context, that is, the notion of pattern. We should not posit a pattern homologous to the SD: the homology may indeed exist (e.g. in French non-interrogative sentences, a pattern of clauses presenting verb-subject order may prepare a contrast with subject-verb order, which elsewhere would be "normal"); it is not of course a necessary condition, since a pattern can be disrupted by elements foreign to it (e.g. foreign language quotations or nonsense utterance; sometimes zero elements, such as suspension points). But it

[14] *A*. Note that in this respect microcontext can be relatively long: even a repetition, for instance, can be the immediate constituent of a SD; the longer the repetitive pattern lasts before being broken, the stronger the rupture effect — *B*. Of course we must distinguish: (1) the repetition as SD, that is, a contrast-creating structure which consists of the rhythmic or arhythmic recurrence of an element (e.g. a verbal ending); (2) the repetition as microcontext; (3) the repetition of SDs, that is, the recurrence of the same stylistic structures with various contents, this being a case of loose terminology, the normative metalanguage of traditional literary criticism — *C*. I use here (and elsewhere) the verb *prepare*. I mean it to describe a context building toward a SD (e.g. in a period, free rhythms preparing the contrasting clausula, or a long protasis preparing the antithetic climax of a short apodosis); I never mean it as a statement of the writer's intentions.

is safe to substitute continuity for homology and to say that the context begins at the point where the reader perceives the existence of any continuous pattern.[15]

3.1. Types of macrocontexts. Two types seem to me to cover all possibilities: (*A*) *Context* → *SD* → *Context*. This type is characterized by the resumption after the SD of the contextual pattern which prepared it. The most frequent example of this type is the injection into the context of a word foreign to the code used (borrowing, archaism, neologism).[16] Ex. (4) G. B. Shaw, *Getting Married*, Preface (*Selected Plays*, IV, 329): *Poor Mr. Pecksniff* (. . .) *is represented as a criminal instead of as a / very typical English / paterfamilias / keeping a roof over the head of himself and his daughters.* (The borrowing *paterfamilias* is unpredictable and herein lies the effect of the device, whose immediate constituents are *very typical English* and *paterfamilias*. This effect is oriented by contrast with the context, which emphasizes ordinariness and its ridiculous side [proper name, cliché *keeping a roof over*]; the orientation could be different if Shaw, instead of a borrowing already in use and stylistically marked, had used his own nonce-word; the mechanism of the device would still have been based on surprise. Following this device, the sentence continues with its ordinary vocabulary and the resumption of the interrupted line helps make the SD appear *relatively* abnormal.)

(*B*) *Context* → *SD starting new context* → *SD*. The SD generates a series of SDs of the same type (e.g. after an SD by archaism, proliferation of archaisms); the resulting saturation causes these SDs to lose their contrast value, destroys their ability to stress a particular point of the utterance, and reduces them to components of a new context; this context in turn will permit new contrasts. Ex. (5) Tacitus, *Vita Agricolae*, XXXVII, 1–6; too long to be quoted here, this narrative of a Roman victory over the Britons contains the following sequence of tenses: (a) a series in the pluperfect, imperfect and perfect / (b) a series in the infinitive of narration / (c) one historical present / (d) a series similar to (a). This sequence corresponds to dramatic shifts in the action: (a) the confusion of battle / (b) the sudden victory and general slaughter / (c) the last surge of resistance / (d) the mopping-up operation. The sequence, translated in terms of stylistic opposition is: (a) *context* / (b) *SD composed of a group of three infinitives* (supported and unified by a convergence of expressive meanings and asyndeton: *sequi, vulnerare, capere*)

[15] *Continuity* should not be taken as an assumption about the author's psychological processes. Without doubt the pattern corresponds to a certain continuity in the writer's mind (true even of *écriture automatique* in French Surrealistic writings: this device was in deliberate opposition to the continuity produced by reflection, but it aimed nevertheless at recording the continuity of subconscious mental activity), but it does not *depict* it in the form of a sequence of words; to believe so would be a metalinguistic confusion (cf. the "chronological" interpretation of Latin word-order in sentences like *urbem captam hostes diripuerunt*).

[16] See Joshua Whatmough, *Poetic, Scientific and Other Forms of Discourse* (1956), pp. 105–107.

which set off a context made of infinitives (this time without convergence and spaced by long phrases) / (c) *SD* / (d) *resumption of the initial context*.[17]

There might be an extreme case in which the SD, instead of creating a new context, would function as a context for another device following immediately. Instances of this type are by no means clearly defined, because saturation tends to cancel the contrast.

3.2. The emphatic function of macrocontexts. The context reinforces the stylistic effect of the device. It amplifies the contrast established by the microcontext. This is probably the most frequent effect in style, and it is obtained in both types *A* and *B;* indeed it is the only effect possible with type *A*. Without attempting to cover all modes of emphasis, I shall indicate two opposite aspects of its function which may serve to point to fruitful analytic procedures.

The contrast of the SD may be prepared by a stylistically unmarked context: e.g. prevalent use of the favorite sentence-type will constitute a stylistic zero-degree by opposition to which SDs will stand out; "casual" speech may have the same effect. However "casualness" has yet to be defined; linguistic analysis permits us to approach a definition: but a relevant definition should cover only the forms "casualness" assumes in *written* speech; moreover we must still determine to what extent the reader is conscious of or reacts to what linguistic analysis describes (in other words, *stylistic* analysis should be limited to what is accessible to the reader).[18] In any case, the existence of such "blank" contexts can be experimentally confirmed by examining writers' successive drafts: these often show deletions intended to create a vacuum in the midst of which the SD is conspicuous.[19] Such deletions demonstrate that context is as important a part of style as the SD. Another aspect of this fact is the role of context as a mechanism to space out the SDs; aligned in too close succession, they may cancel one another (see 3.3.); their effect may vary in proportion to their proximity (for example, a common artefact of dramatic dialogue, the repeated phrase peculiar to a given character, may be a

[17] We find many similar instances in the interplay of *narrative / direct discourse / indirect discourse / free indirect discourse;* see S. Ullmann, *Style in the French Novel*, pp. 94–120; bibliography of this device, in A. G. Landry, *Represented Discourse in . . . Mauriac* (1953), pp. 76–79.

[18] It could be said that this type of context is close to the linguistic norm. The departure, however, is not from the "consciousness of the norm," but from a written background.

[19] Editors classify these deletions indiscriminately under the head of *concision;* but this involves the introduction of the idea of simplicity, which is an esthetic criterion hard to define and irrelevant in an inquiry as to the *existence* of style; the deletion amounts to an increase, objectively measurable, in the distance between SDs. E.g. Balzac, who is far from aiming at simplicity, deletes many emphatic devices (*tout* modifying adjectives, *c'est . . . qui / que . . .*, etc.). These features, frequent in speech, are dropped significantly from written conversations: without intonation, they would only be padding, and their omission permits a rapid succession of sudden contrasts more suggestive of the vividness of actual speech than a total recording would be. See Mario Roques, "Manuscrit et éditions du *Père Goriot*," *Revue universitaire* XIV (1905), 34–42, 71–76, 178–183.

tool of psychological realism; but if repeated more often, that is, if the contextual spacing between occurrences is shortened, it becomes a comic factor).

A more frequent form of the emphatic function, however, is anticipatory: the context prefigures one of the immediate constituents of the SD. Chiasmus is a case in point. Ex. (6): given the SD (*microcontext*) *sleep eternal* / (*contrast*) *in an eternal night* /, if the macrocontext contains a noun-adjective pattern (a pattern conventionally characteristic of poetic utterances), the parallel structure links macrocontexts and microcontexts; e.g. Swinburne, *The Garden of Proserpine,* 80ff.: *Then star nor sun shall waken / Nor any change of light; / Nor sound of waters shaken, / Nor any sound or sight; / Nor wintry leaves nor vernal, / Nor days nor things diurnal; / Only the sleep eternal / In an eternal night.* (Here there is an immediate contact between the contrasting feature and what precedes it, and the stylistic effect is further heightened by the cumulative sequence of the pattern, which reinforces its homologue within the SD.) [20]

3.3. The leveling function of macrocontexts. By this I mean the destruction of the contrasts, the result of which is that the SDs sink to the level of the context and are no longer distinguished from it (e.g. the loss of effect a neologism suffers when surrounded by too many nonce-words). This leveling function is possible because the macrocontext is a cumulative process. The function has two possible sources: it may be the consequence of shorter spaces between SDs — greater proximity prevents the formation of patterns that would prepare contrasts; or else it may result from a type B context, in which a given SD can expand into a pattern which in turn creates a bipolar opposition to another SD.

The intensity of this phenomenon is in direct proportion to the frequency of occurrence of devices belonging to the same class.[21] We can speak of the SD as a contaminating element which modifies the role of the context as the "unmarked" member of an opposition.

3.4. The general implications of the above may eventually program future style analysis: since devices can be reduced to the level of the context, any

20 Needless to say, this is a very partial analysis. It does not take into account rhyme and rhythm, or concurrent and overlapping SDs such as (*context*) *nor . . . / only . . .* , which in turn contains *nor any . . . / nor. . . .*

21 If the devices were identical in form and content, we would have *one* SD: repetition (cf. footnote 14). The reasons for these high frequencies range from unconscious or conscious self-imitation (on stylistic contagion, see L. Spitzer, *Linguistics and Literary History,* p. 191, n. 46; J. Marouzeau, *Revue des études latines* XIV [1936], 58–64; XXVI [1948], 105–108) to a reaction against normative precepts forbidding repetitions. We shall have to inquire whether there are SDs whose microcontext makes them immune to saturation (e.g. disjunctive word-order, because it suspends decoding altogether) and we shall need statistics, based exclusively on stylistically relevant data. This is in synchrony a problem similar to that of the duration of SDs in diachrony (i.e. resistance to wearing out through repeated performances and "traditionalization"; see, for example, M. Riffaterre, "La durée de la valeur stylistique du néologisme," *Romanic Review* XLIV [1953], 282–89).

concept of an intrinsic stylistic value is void (e.g. the expressivity "inherent to" iterative verbal forms, superlatives, etc.). In its place, the leveling function is distributional in nature and therefore measurable. Consequently it will be possible to define conditions of occurrence. Unlike those already known through the direct application of statistics to the linguistic message (these sets can define the literary utterances but cannot differentiate the linguistic material and the stylistic use thereof), we seek conditions relevant only to what is *perceptible as style.*[22]

As an analytic criterion, the concept of context has varied applications. When literary language (or more specialized systems such as verse) is treated as a restricted norm, that is, with more limitations than the overall linguistic norm, there is the danger of seeing style only as a further restriction and to evaluate it by mere subtraction (e.g. by identifying "unpoetic" [23] words). But if literary language is analyzed as a sequence of contexts, then proper emphasis will fall on the enrichment furnished by new stylistic possibilities: these conventionally structured contexts make SDs out of features which would have no contrasting value in a "casual" context or which would saturate it and thereby alter its nature; a conventional frame permits stronger effects without such disfiguring modifications.[24] The leveling function presents the advantage of accounting for what I have called elsewhere *nonce-standards,* the fragmentary language systems which the author uses to suggest the speech of one of his characters or to parody a style. These can be seen as special contexts developed by saturation from SDs originally borrowed by the author from the subject of his evocation and set against the background of his own style.[25] Study of these particular cases should give a purely linguistic basis

[22] The *mot juste,* for example, may be defined by its fitness, whose measure in language is statistical (J. Whatmough, *Poetic . . . Discourse,* pp. 119–121). But its stylistic relevance does not lie in its fitness, which is defined in relation to the linguistic structure; it lies in the variability of its effects in relation to different contexts (and to different poetic dogmas). The *mot juste* may be a SD, or it may create a context so "fitting" that vague, "unfitting" words will become devices by contrast.

[23] For example, in Latin, see Bertil Axelson, *Unpoetische Wörter,* Lund, 1945.

[24] It is significant that poetic language frequently uses *Umgangssprache* forms: they would have no effect in their usual context; they have an effect in the contrived setting of meter. Pointing in this direction are observations such as Meillet's that "la poésie (latine) n'a pas le purisme de la prose" (*Esquisse d'une histoire de la langue latine,* 1938, p. 220); prose, unprotected by conventional forms, was not able to use "ordinary" words without losing its literary character. (Cf. frequent remarks in poetic glossaries that certain words belong equally to the "poetic and familiar" vocabularies: clearly they are SDs in the former, contextual in the latter). See in French the use of substandard speech forms *l', m', j', n'* (*le, me, je, ne*) in Jules Laforgue's poems. Normative conditioning of the literary message, which linguistic analysis bypasses, should become apparent (see L. Kukenheim "Réflexions non-structuralistes," *Neophilologus,* 1955, 161ff.).

[25] See *Criteria,* p. 169, n. 24 and footnote 12. (These must not be confused with situational norms, predetermined by the topic.) For example: elements suggesting (not transcribing) either foreign pronunciations (e.g. speech of German characters in Balzac, of Jews on the English Victorian stage), or idiolectal features used for psychological characterization (e.g. Mr. Jingle's way of speaking in the *Pickwick Papers*), or social attitudes (e.g. parodic use of stereotypes; see M. Riffaterre "Sur un singulier d'André

to the description of literary realism and of ironic styles, for which external criteria (psychological, normative, etc.) are generally employed. In another direction, we could ask whether the leveling at a given point can become irreversible attrition or whether positional factors suffice to renew stylistic effects; the answers to such questions may ultimately permit the elaboration of a diachronic stylistics.

Gide. Contribution à l'étude des clichés," *Français Moderne* XXIII [1955], 39ff.), or other authors' styles (e.g. Proust's pastiches; imitations of the Bible; for the latter even one feature may suffice, see L. Spitzer, *Linguistics and Literary History,* p. 150; Uriel Weinreich, "On the Cultural History of Yiddish Rime," *Essays in Jewish Life and Thought,* 1959, p. 423ff., esp. 434–435; on a much more complex mimetic standard, see Y. Le Hir, *Lamennais écrivain,* 1948, pp. 241–332). A good example of SDs which create a nonce-standard is the hyphenated neologisms Carlyle employs in *Sartor resartus* to suggest "German-philosophical" style.

Louis T. Milic

AGAINST THE TYPOLOGY OF STYLES

A typology is a classification and a typology of styles is an arrangement of styles into categories, such as periods of time (Elizabethan, Restoration, Victorian or modern), kinds of influence or derivation, such as Euphuistic, Senecan, Ciceronian, or of impression, such as ornate, formal, learned, simple, plain and casual. Such classifications are based on the belief that groups of writers have styles that are alike and that any single member of such a group is typical of it. I am convinced that this model, which has a certain antiquity in literary history, is false and unnecessary. It cannot contribute anything to our understanding of literary style. Moreover, we can explain stylistic phenomena without the aid of such categories.

The assumptions on which I base my disagreement are the following:

1. A writer's style is the expression of his personality.
2. A writer must write in his own style.
3. A writer can be recognized in his style.
4. No writer can truly imitate another's style.
5. The main formative influences on a writer are his education and his reading.
6. A writer's language is governed by the practice of his own time.
7. Language changes gradually with time.

There is nothing very revolutionary here. Much of it is summed up in Buffon's aphorism: "Le style, c'est l'homme même."

I shall illustrate my thesis by reference to Restoration prose. Let me begin by quoting an authority, Professor James Sutherland:

> . . . Can we talk . . . about "Restoration prose," or are the two words merely a convenient way of referring to the prose that was written in England between 1660 and the closing years of the century? For myself, I believe that there *is* a prose style that is characteristic of the Restoration . . . and that this style is the genuine expression of a particular and definite type of culture.[1]

[1] James R. Sutherland, "Restoration Prose," *Restoration and Augustan Prose,* Los Angeles, 1956, pp. 1–2.

Professor Sutherland's studies of English prose need no encomia. I have selected his work because it is quite representative of typological *Stilforschung* in its assumptions and superior to most in originality and scholarship. My intention in singling out his work is to point to some limitations of this tradition.

The problem that I am interested in discussing will come into focus if we ask where this prose is to be found. Here is his answer:

> The prose I have in mind was written to perfection by Dryden and Halifax; with individual variations by such men as Robert South, Bishop Burnet, and Jeremy Collier; by Etherege and Rochester in their letters; with further variations by Roger L'Estrange in his pamphlets and translations; by Walter Pope in his *Life of Seth Ward* and by Robert Wolsey in his Preface to Rochester's *Valentinian;* by Thomas Sprat in his *History of the Royal Society* and by Robert Hooke in his *Micrographia;* and by many other minor writers. I do not think I should seriously confuse the issue if I added Cowley in his Essays and perhaps Stillingfleet in his *Origines Sacrae.* But I have got to admit that if there *is* such a thing as Restoration prose, not all the writers living in that period wrote it. There are a few of the greatest prose writers of the time whom I obviously cannot possibly include: one of these is John Bunyan, and another is Clarendon, and for various reasons I would exclude Isaac Barrow, the Hon. Robert Boyle, John Evelyn, Richard Baxter, Thomas Rymer, and such eccentrics as Thomas Burnet, the author of *The Sacred Theory of the Earth.* And I don't know what to do with Samuel Pepys.[2]

This is a very select list, almost an eccentric one. It says yes to Dryden but no to Bunyan, yes to Burnet and no to Clarendon, yes to Collier and no to Rymer. It mentions Robert Wolseley [sic] and Walter Pope, who are rare birds indeed, and yet talks of minor writers. Moreover, it leaves out altogether John Dennis, Thomas Traherne, Andrew Marvell, William Congreve, Sir William Temple, Samuel Butler and John Locke, all of whom wrote prose of some distinction. Such a process of selection seems to suggest that writers of Restoration prose were not in the majority during the Restoration. In other words only some, perhaps a minority, of the writers of this time wrote Restoration prose. The typological criterion then is not merely chronological; there seems to be something else.

This new quality is sometimes called plain prose or the plain style. This well-known notion — that a change occurred in English prose style during the seventeenth century, in the direction of plainness or simplicity — has been present in the writings of literary historians for some time. A. A. Tilley, for example, in 1911, observed:

> Perhaps the most important literary achievement within this period is the creation of a prose style which, in structure if not in vocabulary, is essentially the same as that of today . . . possessing before all things, the homely virtues of simplicity, correctness, lucidity and precision.[3]

[2] *Ibid.,* p. 2.

[3] "The Essay and the Beginning of Modern English Prose," *The Cambridge History of English Literature,* ed. Sir A. W. Ward and A. R. Waller, Cambridge, 1911, Vol. VIII, p. 368.

The change can be illustrated very simply. The most dramatic way to sense its real force is to read ten pages of Milton's polemical prose and to follow this with ten pages of Dryden's critical prose. To most modern readers, this is like coming out of a tunnel into the sunshine. The typical response is, How did this happen, that is, How did the English come to write so simply, so clearly, so informally after having written so much the other way? The implication of this form of the question is that before 1660 everyone wrote like Milton and after that date like Dryden.

To promote this feeling or impression into a theory, it is necessary only to group a few extreme cases around our two antagonists in order to produce two schools. On Milton's side, we put Browne, Clarendon, Taylor, Lancelot Andrewes . . . ; Dryden is teamed with Swift, Steele, Addison, Shaftesbury, Defoe. . . . Examples are easily come by. The following pair of citations would find few to disagree that the first of the two passages is less plain than the second:

> Not to insist upon the examples of Moses, Daniel, and Paul, who were skilful in all the learning of the Egyptians, Chaldeans, and Greeks, which could not probably be without reading their books of all sorts, in Paul especially, who thought it no defilement to insert into Holy Scripture the sentences of three Greek poets, and one of them a tragedian, the question was notwithstanding sometimes controverted among the primitive doctors, but with great odds on that side which affirmed it both lawful and profitable, as was then evidently perceived, when Julian the Apostate and subtlest enemy to our faith made a decree forbidding Christians the study of heathen learning: for, said he, they wound us with our own weapons, and with our own arts and sciences they overcome us.[4]

> For there is a perpetual dearth of wit; a barrenness of good sense and entertainment. The neglect of the readers will soon put an end to this sort of scribbling. There can be no pleasantry where there is no wit; no impression can be made where there is no truth for the foundation.[5]

The second is in fact three sentences of Dryden, but together they take up less than half the space of Milton's single sentence.

If the case were always so clear, we should have no problem in characterizing plain prose and I would have no argument. Matter, however, does not follow categories. So for example, Isaac Barrow, who is relegated to Professor Sutherland's NO list, is described in the *Cambridge History of English Literature* as noted for "the clearness and simplicity which under his influence began to mark the prose of the later seventeenth century." His general manner "is an anticipation of Addison."[6] To show the practical difficulties of this sort of classification, I shall give a passage from Robert South from the YES list as well as one from Isaac Barrow.

[4] John Milton, "Areopagitica," *Prose Selections,* ed. Merritt Y. Hughes, New York, 1947, pp. 218–219.

[5] John Dryden, "A Discourse Concerning the Original and Progress of Satire," *Essays,* ed. W. P. Ker, Oxford, 1900, Vol. II, p. 81.

[6] Vol. VIII, p. 296.

> We are all naturally endowed with a strong appetite to know, to see, to pursue Truth; and with a bashfull abhorrency from being deceived, and entangled in mistake. And as success in enquiry after Truth affords matter of joy and triumph; so being conscious of error, and miscarriage therein, is attended with shame and sorrow. These desires Wisdom in the most perfect manner satisfies, not by entertaining us with dry, empty, fruitless theories, upon mean and vulgar subjects; but by enriching our minds with excellent and useful knowledge, directed to the noblest objects, and serviceable to the highest ends.[7]

Now for the second passage:

> As nothing can be of more moment; so few things, doubtless, are of more difficulty, than for men to be rationally satisfied about the estate of their souls, with reference to God and the great concerns of eternity. In their judgment about which if they err finally it is like a man's missing his cast when he throws dice for his life; his being his happiness and all that he does or can enjoy in the world is involved in the error of one throw. And therefore it may very well deserve our best skill and care to enquire into those rules by which we may guide our Judgment in so weighty an affair both with safety and success.[8]

I wonder how many readers would be able to pick out the work of the Restoration prose writer from the other. Barrow's does not seem to be distinguishable from South's by means of the criterion of plainness. I am not suggesting that the Cambridge History is correct in placing Barrow in the plain group and Sutherland wrong in excluding him. I do not believe there is much evidence for either side and neither has offered anything like an incontestable or even a workable criterion. Calling it the plain style is not enough.

What is this plain style? According to Sutherland it is an English "simpler, less ornate, more colloquial, more practical."[9] A linguist might describe the syntax of Milton as nested or embedded and that of Dryden as linear. But neither of these descriptions will really help us when we come to average cases, such as those of South and Barrow, rather than extreme ones. The typological procedure is not very enlightening in this kind of problem. It tends to deal in impressionistic generalities, which may be adequate for getting a vague sense of the difference between two modes of expression but not adequate for analyzing the difference between two particular examples.

Whether one examines the claims of one set of theorists who try to account for the emergence of plain prose in terms of the influence of pulpit oratory, or whether one is willing to accept the views of those who attribute it to the influence of the Royal Society and its desire for scientific writing, or accepts the opinion that it derives from the conversation of well-bred aristocratic gentlemen, who prized easy informality, lack of affectation and a stress on the col-

[7] Isaac Barrow, "The Pleasantness of Religion," *Seventeenth-Century Verse and Prose,* ed. Helen C. White, Ruth C. Wallerstein and Ricardo Quintana, New York, 1952, Vol. II, p. 178.

[8] Robert South, "An Account of the Nature and Measures of Conscience," *Seventeenth-Century Verse and Prose,* Vol. II, pp. 186–187.

[9] *On English Prose,* Toronto, 1957, p. 57.

loquial, does not matter very much. All three of these explanations and any others that may arise are attempts to explain with ingenuity what can be explained without it.

I am prepared to concede without any reservation that the English of nearly any writer of the eighteenth century sounds different from that of most writers of the seventeenth. I am also willing to grant that the writing of many writers of the Restoration is easier to read than that of the subjects of the early Stuarts. What I am not willing to grant is that we need a theory of types in order to explain this development. The matter can be explained quite satisfactorily with some of the axioms cited earlier. On the scientific principle that an economical explanation based on opinions generally held is better than one requiring a number of dubious assumptions, I would suggest that the typological explanation of the plain style represented by Professor Sutherland be dismissed. I shall summarize the grounds.

Consider what we need to believe in order to accept a typological explanation of Restoration prose. First, we must believe that there is a hypothetical entity called Restoration prose, whose characteristics can be defined only generally. Second, we must agree that this entity is the common property of a certain number of writers of that period but not of some others, admittedly first-rank writers, and not only the work of a minority but of that minority only in certain works which can be specified. Third, we are invited to agree that the writers who partake of the mystic entity represent a significant subculture within the society, one which presumably is closer to the real work of the society than those outside it, however great the writers excluded may be.

The last of these points, that the writers who are thus isolated represent a significantly dominant aspect of the culture cannot detain us long. Both common sense and statistics tell us that lists of members of an in–group tend to be fallacious. The real members of the group may only be known to the truly *in* people, who keep their identities secret, like the Gray Eminence. Apart from the evident difficulty of at this distance assembling a group of writers who will constitute the spirit of the Restoration, it would seem even more hazardous to prefer the claims of one group over those of others. The courtiers no doubt had influence, but was it literary? The scientists, dissenters, the merchants, all had competing claims, not to mention the dramatists and the pamphleteers.

The constitution of the group representing the spirit of the Restoration raises insistent questions of logic. If Etherege and Rochester were members of the significant minority, why did this fact only make itself known when they wrote letters? Why was L'Estrange only *in* in his pamphlets and Cowley in his essays? More mysterious still, why was Walter Pope only part of the circle in a single *Life* and Wolseley in a preface to someone else's work? The inconsistency of such an argument requires no deep searching to detect.

The most interesting point is the first, the problem of describing the characteristics of Restoration prose. Description proceeds by the accumulation of detail, a sound procedure in dealing with style. But descriptions of style usually proceed by generalization, by abstraction of qualities from masses of detail. Style is difficult to handle simply because it is a mass of detail. To classify a particular set of such details by means of an abstraction is to make a claim that these details are more important than others, that they fall into a configuration and that this abstraction outweighs others that might be constructed out of the same materials. For example, when following the trend of modern comment we call today's prose colloquial or informal, we are constructing a category of informality with certain characteristics and are implicitly claiming that most of today's writing conforms to those characteristics. Both of these steps are more difficult than appears at first. Since we cannot examine all writing, how can we determine that today's prose is indeed informal? We cannot examine more than a fraction of it and that fraction may not be a true random sample. It is based on our preferences. The reader of the *Christian Century,* the *Journal of the History of Ideas* and *Victorian Studies* will get a different idea of the state of modern prose than will the reader of the *New York Times,* the *New Republic* and the *New Yorker* or for that matter the reader of *Playboy, Mad* and the *Evergreen Review.* Unless we take special precautions to be objective and cross-sectional, our evidence will be hopelessly biased and we shall be making generalizations which, however perceptive, will be inapplicable to more than a segment of the population.

The problem of criteria is even more difficult: how do we decide what makes a prose informal? Many critics do this intuitively. Without pointing to anything in the language, they say it sounds informal to them. This kind of impressionism is equivocal: another critic may say it does not sound informal to him. There is no way to settle so metaphysical a dispute. A better procedure is to particularize informality by means of a set of indicia. When they are present, the prose can be called informal; when they are absent, the reverse. Unfortunately, this leaves a great many cases unsettled, when some of the indicia are present and some not, when some sentences are informal and some are not. No consistent classification can emerge from this kind of disorder. Unless a policy on such questions is established in advance, no statements of description can be made with reliability.

In other words, one important objection to the typology of styles is the matter of method or procedure. It is *practically* impossible to make an accurate generalization about an abstraction so remote and inchoate as the dominant feeling or quality of the writings of a group of people expressing themselves on every subject during a period of forty years. The human animal is too various to be so categorized. Group personalities of this kind have no reality, any more than national languages have a character, as once was thought. Only individuals have personalities and therefore only individuals can have a style.

Style has many definitions but most of them are merely casual variations on a theme. On the basis of the uncontroversial axioms I offered at the beginning of this paper, I would now claim that an individual's style is his habitual and consistent selection from the expressive resources available in his language. In other words, his style is the collection of his stylistic options. Options or choices are not always exercised consciously; they are often habitual practices of which the practitioner is as unconscious as he is of the way that he bends his leg in walking or the way that he ties his shoelace. His reading, the way he has been taught to write, the bent of his mind have all influenced him in the direction of a particular uniqueness. To this may be added the ingredient of conscious rhetorical choice. The net effect is an individual style, which be it noted may be as individual among literary hacks as among literary geniuses. Milton and Dryden each write in their unique individual styles because of who and what they are. What divides them is personality; what unites them is chronology.

The language changes all the time, but it changes very slowly, at times so imperceptibly that it gives the illusion of being stable, so that speakers who become aware of changes raise passionate outcries about corruption and decay. All speakers are bound by these changes but not all writers are chronologically at the same point in time. At any given moment, there are writers imbued with the lexical choices and the syntactical options of a previous era. And there are some who are on the frontier of change, coining new words like any teen-ager. Thus the co-existence of several chronological states of the language at one time provides the medium within which the rich variety of individuals can express itself. Between these two poles, the changing language and the individual writer, all the facts of style can be satisfactorily accounted for.

The individual's style is the aggregate of his stylistic selections from the particular state of the language that he construes as the real one of his time. The consistent choices that he makes from it to serve his own expressive requirements constitute his style, his literary personality. It is evident that the writer's choices will be determined by certain fashions in education, in rhetoric and in literature, but the main tendency of writers in a given time is to be unlike rather than alike. The notion of period styles underrates this tendency and implies a uniformity of expression which is wildly at variance with the facts.

The writers of plain prose or what has been called the clear stream — Dryden, Addison, Swift, Fielding &c.[10]— are granted by this typology a uniformity which is quite foreign to their practice. A selection of passages might be made from the works of any single writer to support the claim that he prefers short sentences or long sentences, few adjectives or many and so on. Similarly, the plain style is not the prerogative of a given period; it is a rhetorical tendency which is present in all ages. A history of the plain style might be written showing that it arose in the sixteenth century and was practiced by

[10] James Sutherland, "Some Aspects of Eighteenth-Century Prose," *Essays on the Eighteenth Century Presented to David Nichol Smith,* Oxford, 1945, p. 94.

writers from Bacon to E. B. White. The history of ornate prose would show a similar line, ending let us say with Churchill or Walter Lippmann.

The division of eighteenth-century prose into the clear stream and the ornate one oversimplifies the problems it is striving to solve. Most people in Johnson's time did not regularly write balanced Johnsonian prose, not even Johnson himself. Balanced prose, employing the devices of antithesis and parallelism, has been in some degree a feature of formal writing in all periods, including our own. It is my conviction that such classes as plain style, ornate style, balanced style, may only be useful to describe individual sentences, paragraphs or perhaps even whole compositions, whenever they may have been written. But when such classes are tied to chronology and culture, they imply more than can be justified by a strict examination of the facts.

The dominant modern style, according to some observers, is the plain or casual or informal style. Many teachers and writing advisors recommend the following of this model. Yet we know that many highly admired writers of the present day do not do so. Writers of great reputation practice more elaborate forms, not to mention the esoteric language of the social scientists.[11] Whatever may be the central characteristics of modern prose style, they are not likely to tell us much about modern writing because the average of a very large number tends to iron out interesting peculiarities. That is a great danger of excessive typology.

The typology of styles seems to have descended to us from the practice, standard in literary history, of grouping writers in schools of drama or poetry, such as the Georgic poets, the bourgeois dramatists, the graveyard poets, whose subject matter and formal manner coincided significantly. But types of styles, schools of styles, genres of styles, and periods of styles are not analogous entities. A writer's style emerges from the tension between the state of the language that he uses and the demands of his individuality striving to express itself with the same materials as other individuals and struggling against the restraining powers of fashion, tradition and rhetoric.

Rhetorical training conditions both the writer and the reader and in that way may come to affect the language itself. The rhetorical inversion of one era is the normal word-order of another. But the scope of rhetoric is limited and affects mainly the more visible outward aspects of the repertory of stylistic resources provided by a language. To be sure, some writers have more or less consciously emphasized certain rhetorical features in their writing (Gibbon, Johnson, Macaulay), but these are not by themselves significant. Rhetoric becomes significant when it can be related to the writer's unconscious expressive mechanism, when it represents the controlling power, both limiting and enabling, of outer form upon idea and meaning. In that sense, it becomes one of the contributing factors to the totality we call an author's style. The contribution of conscious rhetorical adornment to the total style of an author is put

[11] A number of critics, including Cyril Connolly and Roland Barthes, have expressed concern about the modern stress on a plain, featureless prose.

into proper perspective when his theoretical pronouncements about style are compared with his actual performance. When Swift tells us about his ideals of style, he is not giving an accurate description of what he actually does. His own practice is some distance away from what he thought he was doing or what he would have liked to do. In fact, in the words of one scholar, Swift was always struggling against a tendency to write in just the way he disliked.[12] If this is true, it surely refutes the arguments of those who would credit a writer with the power to alter his style at will, as if he had a wardrobe — or a stable — of different styles for different occasions.[13] The extent of his ability to adapt his style is probably limited to certain superficial aspects, among which are included rhetorical devices and diction.

In sum, the proper subject of stylistic speculation is the individual writer. To understand the style of the individual, we must concern ourselves first with the individual's writings and second with the linguistic resources from which his peculiar style is a selection. Typologies attract our attention to specious and minor similarities among authors. They are misleading because they take us away from what is really significant, the individual author's own peculiarity, his difference from his contemporaries, which is what is truly his style.

[12] Jonathan Swift, *An Enquiry into the Behavior of the Queen's Last Ministry,* ed. Irvin Ehrenpreis, Bloomington, 1956, p. xxxi.

[13] This is the so-called *persona* theory. See, for example, Paul Fussell, Jr. "Speaker and Style in *A Letter of Advice to a Young Poet* (1721), and the Problem of Attribution," *Review of English Studies,* X (1959), 63–67.